Sport Finance

Third Edition

Gil Fried, JD

University of New Haven

Timothy D. DeSchriver, EdD

University of Delaware

Michael Mondello, PhD

University of South Florida

Human Kinetics

Library of Congress Cataloging-in-Publication Data

Fried, Gil, 1965-
   Sport finance / Gil Fried, Tim DeSchriver, Michael Mondello. -- 3rd ed.
      p. cm.
   Includes bibliographical references and index.
   1. Sports--Finance. 2. Sports administration. I. DeSchriver, Timothy D., 1968- II. Mondello, Michael, 1968- III. Title.
   GV716.F75 2013
   796.0691--dc23

                                        2012032363

ISBN-10: 1-4504-2104-0 (print)
ISBN-13: 978-1-4504-2104-1 (print)

The web addresses cited in this text were current as of August 2012, unless otherwise noted.

Acquisitions Editor: Myles Schrag; **Developmental Editor:** Kevin Matz; **Assistant Editor:** Susan Huls; **Copyeditor:** Bob Replinger; **Indexer:** Andrea Hepner; **Permissions Manager:** Dalene Reeder; **Graphic Designer:** Joe Buck; **Graphic Artist:** Denise Lowry; **Cover Designer:** Keith Blomberg; **Photograph (cover):** © Lilyana Vynogradova/istockphoto.com; **Photographs (interior):** © Human Kinetics; **Photo Asset Manager:** Laura Fitch; **Photo Production Manager:** Jason Allen; **Art Manager:** Kelly Hendren; **Associate Art Manager:** Alan L. Wilborn; **Illustrations:** © Human Kinetics, unless otherwise noted; **Printer:** Sheridan Books

Printed in the United States of America

10 9 8 7 6 5 4 3 2 1

The paper in this book is certified under a sustainable forestry program.

Human Kinetics
Website: www.HumanKinetics.com

United States: Human Kinetics
P.O. Box 5076
Champaign, IL 61825-5076
800-747-4457
e-mail: humank@hkusa.com

Canada: Human Kinetics
475 Devonshire Road Unit 100
Windsor, ON N8Y 2L5
800-465-7301 (in Canada only)
e-mail: info@hkcanada.com

Europe: Human Kinetics
107 Bradford Road
Stanningley
Leeds LS28 6AT, United Kingdom
+44 (0) 113 255 5665
e-mail: hk@hkeurope.com

Australia: Human Kinetics
57A Price Avenue
Lower Mitcham, South Australia 5062
08 8372 0999
e-mail: info@hkaustralia.com

New Zealand: Human Kinetics
P.O. Box 80
Torrens Park, South Australia 5062
0800 222 062
e-mail: info@hknewzealand.com

E5594

Contents

Preface

If you saw the movie *Jerry Maguire*, you might have thought about studying sport law or becoming a players' agent. Similarly, if you have been tracking Tiger Woods' phenomenal success in endorsing various products from Nike to Buick, and then his subsequent demise, you might want to study sport marketing. If you enjoy watching Super Bowl advertisements more than the games themselves, you might want to enter the exciting field of sport advertising. Few students, however, contemplate studying sport management to prepare themselves to work in the area of sport finance. Sport finance can be more exciting than all these disciplines. Marketing, sponsorship, facility construction, sport law, and all the other sport management disciplines cannot be undertaken without knowledge of the financial position of the team, business, or organization. Thus, sport finance is the linchpin for all decisions and actions in sport business.

Students who believe that sport accounting and finance are not as exciting as sport law, marketing, or advertising are wrong. Some of the most interesting jobs in sport focus on finance-related issues. For example, National Football League and National Basketball Association teams normally have "capologists" who are directly responsible for ensuring that the team does not violate the salary cap for its players. Sport marketing has changed from being just a creative pursuit to being a financially driven field. No major sponsorship deal is completed without data and financial analysis leading the creative process. Financial numbers can tell us important facts about a business. So, although sport finance has never been considered an exciting component within any sport and fitness administration curriculum, it might be one of the most important topics that you study. Note also that although the competition for jobs in event management and sport marketing is fierce, the competition for jobs in sport finance areas is less intense. The primary reason for such job availability is the scarcity of trained people who have significant skills in finance and appreciation for how those skills can help a sport business grow.

No business, organization, or government entity can survive without money. The saying "Money makes the world go 'round" accurately reflects the sport industry. Some professional sports organizations are now worth more than a billion dollars, and television networks spend billions to air premier events. Sport finance analyzes where the money comes from, where the money goes, and how to use any remaining money to foster future growth. Thus, sport finance is the key for the decision-making process in any sport business. A thorough knowledge of sport finance is the key to making it into high-level managerial positions where the decisions are made.

The stock market skyrocketed several hundred percent in the 1980s and 1990s. Thereafter, it fell significantly, costing people millions of dollars in paper losses. But if you held on and kept investing in the market when it declined, you would have been rewarded when stocks increased from 2003 through 2007, when the stock markets again hit all-time highs. Investors who did not sell by 2007 might have lost their investment when the stock market again plunged because of the 2007-09 recession. The stock market is one of the best examples of how financial conditions can grow and shrink over time and why a company can be strong one day and file for bankruptcy the next. Sport businesses were not immune to this financial carnage. Some sport companies have had ups and downs during the past 20 years. If you had invested a small amount in 1980 in Nike stocks, you could have made a fortune. You could also have made a significant amount of money if you had invested in Nike shares in early 2006 when the price was as low as $75.52 per share had you sold those shares at the peak later that year when they were selling for $101.20. In 2011 the stock ranged in price from a high of $98 to a low of $69. Thus, depending on the day that a person sold the shares, she could have either made a profit or lost money. This example represents one of the most important issues associated with finance: It is all about timing. If a payment is received one day later, it can significantly change a company's financial position. A balance sheet examines a company's financial position on a specific day. An income statement examines a company over a one-year period. No matter what dates are used, all financial analysis is focused on a specific period so that the evaluation has value and relevance.

Stocks tend to increase and decrease based on multiple factors, from increased profits to the loss of a major account or the retirement of a major endorser. What factors drive the stock price down? Does such a decline represent market conditions alone, or can the company's board of directors develop policies that can reduce the value of the stock? Would any resulting turnaround in the company's performance significantly enhance the company's value? What can the company do to increase its stock value? Would a high stock value indicate corporate financial strength? If the company reduced overall salaries by $100 million per year, would the stock value increase because of the increased savings? If all shoe production was moved from Asia to America, would profits change and why? A thorough financial analysis can help answer these questions. This book is designed to help you understand the numerous financial issues faced by any sport or fitness business or entity.

PURPOSE OF THE TEXT

The need for a strict sport finance text has come to the fore over the past 20 years with the push to build new sports facilities and the financial projections made by the facilities' opponents and proponents. Similarly, fitness facilities have fueled significant career opportunities, and managers in this industry encounter numerous unique financial issues. Sport entrepreneurs have to deal with financial issues such as how to develop a business plan with a pro forma budget, what finance vehicle is most effective for raising start-up capital, and how to control inventory. With professional football teams selling for $800 million, a team owner or general manager will not trust financial decisions to anyone who does not have a strong background in finance. Last, with Title IX affecting many high school and college athletic programs, schools need to know how to work with the dollars that they have in order to comply with the law. These examples are just a few of the issues that you might face in your future career. One aim of this text is to give you a framework to help you deal with those issues.

Sport Finance is designed to walk the reader through the finance process. It provides you with the basic skills needed to help raise, manage, and spend money in sport settings. It covers a number of key financial concepts, such as the following:

- What a business needs to succeed
- What makes businesses operate
- Where businesses obtain necessary start-up capital
- How to determine how much money is available

- How to read newspaper business pages for meaning
- What typical expenses sports organizations incur
- Why sport businesses succeed
- Why sport businesses fail
- How sports organizations can grow

The purpose of this text is to give a broad overview so that the reader can understand what drives the financial success or failure of any entity in the sport industry.

INTENDED AUDIENCE

Our goal is to create an intermediate finance text that is ideal for business school–based sport and fitness administration programs, sport finance classes, and graduate programs in various other disciplines. The point of the designation is to emphasize that the book is comprehensive, but we believe it is also important to develop the text for people who have never previously read a finance or accounting text. With this book you will be able to grasp fundamental finance and accounting concepts regardless of your knowledge level. If you have some finance or accounting skills, this text will expand your knowledge and provide some real-world application of that knowledge. The text also provides a strong framework within which you will be able to apply financial principles in your future career.

If you are already an industry professional, you could rely on the text to help you understand financial markets, develop money-saving strategies, learn how to invest properly for future growth, and develop business finance strategies. With a significant discussion on budgeting, executives can refresh their knowledge and skills on a daily basis.

ORGANIZATION

Sport Finance is organized into seven parts that help the reader understand the influence of sport finance on a business. The chapters are arranged so that the reader can understand the elements that influence the financial world and then apply specific issues to the sport business world.

Part I deals with the importance of finance in the sport industry and includes a thorough analysis of the various issues composing sport finance and various financial skills. Through using several current trends the reader is exposed to examples of how finance transcends sport. One of the primary focuses of any financial analysis is to promote understanding of revenue and expenses, which is covered in this section. Because financial planning is impossible without an understanding of accounting basics, part I gives special attention to fundamental finance and accounting issues. Part I also stresses the key to financial planning, which is how to develop and analyze a budget.

Part II examines various environments that affect finance, ranging from business structures and financial markets to government entities that control taxes and interest rates. This section examines the markets where money is made and invested to help businesses grow. But its primary focus is on government regulations that affect everything from how stocks can be sold and appropriate business structures to tax and bankruptcy regulations that influence the financial success of businesses.

Part III addresses the information needed to answer questions or solve problems associated with the financial health and future direction of a sport business. By analyzing data contained in income statements and balance sheets, students will learn how to analyze a business' strengths and weaknesses. Industry ratios, financial statements, and the time value of money are highlighted in this section of the book.

Part IV examines where the money is located. These chapters look at how businesses find the capital that they need to operate. Discussions focus on funding options for various types of entities, ranging from a government entity that needs to raise more taxes to a business that is searching for venture capital, pursuing a public offering, or selling corporate bonds.

Part V discusses the outflow of money and basic financial management. What are typical expenses, and how do businesses budget for them? This part of the book also highlights short-term planning and ways to document monetary needs. An additional focus is on ways to manage the money that you obtain or owe as a sports manager. Finally, this part of the book provides a comprehensive overview of the inventory management and production control processes, which are critical for concession and sporting goods businesses. The failure to manage inventory and the production process properly can lead to significant financial losses.

Part VI centers on the profit distribution process, including retained earnings, dividends, and company growth through acquisition of additional businesses. The section then covers the tracking of money and details accounting techniques that you can implement to make sure that financial auditing

is successful. The section ends with examining techniques to exit a business whether closing or selling a business.

eBook
available at your campus bookstore or HumanKinetics.com

Part VII covers current issues affecting the sport industry. This section is the newest one in the third edition. It provides a detailed analysis of the current recession and how various sport entities are dealing with these financial conditions. The section then provides an industry analysis to help show how financial issues are affecting various segments of the sport industry. The last part of this new section contains a significant case study for a Division II athletic department to examine the various revenues, expenses, and other financial issues occurring over the course of a year.

Each chapter ends with pertinent class discussion questions. These questions are designed to channel dialogue among students and to give instructors ideas for helping students engage with the material over and above just reading the text. Boldfaced words in the text are found in the glossary at the back of the book. Key points are highlighted throughout each chapter. In addition, an instructor guide is available providing more discussion topics and material.

INSTRUCTOR RESOURCES

As an added benefit to instructors, this new edition features several ancillaries to aid in your teaching of classes using this text. The authors appreciate that some sport finance instructors have training in other disciplines and might need additional assistance. Thus, these updated resources make it easier to develop and teach basic through advanced concepts.

- The instructor guide includes a student syllabus as well as chapter outlines for the instructor. The chapter outlines contain a summary, lecture aides, in- and out-of-class activities, additional readings, and teaching tips.

- The test package includes more than 300 multiple choice questions that the instructor can use to build tests.

- The PowerPoint presentation includes more than 300 slides that present the text information in an easy-to-follow format. Several tables from the book are included in the presentation package to help further student understanding.

Acknowledgments

I could not have asked for two better coauthors. They diligently wrote their chapters and assisted with the instructor guide, making this one of the best texts I have had the pleasure to work on. Tim was helpful throughout the entire process, and Mike, as someone who really understands sport finance, was a significant boost to the project. My two coauthors went beyond the call for this text, and I thank them for their effort. Each coauthor brought significant value and helped shape the text into one of the strongest in the sport management area.

I would like to extend a special thanks to Dr. Allen Sack, Dean Lawrence Flanagan, and the entire College of Business faculty and staff at the University of New Haven for all their assistance. They recognize the value of sport finance and are launching a sport finance based online Masters of Science program in 2013 to help share the value and need of sport finance to the entire world. I would also like to thank my graduate research assistant Kristen Sackett for her help in researching changes for this revised edition.

A special thanks also goes out to my wife and children (Gavriella, Arieh, and Rebecca) for their patience during the writing and revising of this text. It was a long process that took a significant amount of their time and understanding.

The folks at Human Kinetics were wonderful in helping us make this third edition that much stronger. Many subsequent editions contain just minor updates. The gang at HK, however, including Myles Schrag and Kevin Matz, challenged us to make the book fresh and improved.

Gil Fried

I would like to extend a special thanks to my two coauthors. Gil Fried has been the driving force behind this project since its inception. His guidance and persistence were critical for ensuring the successful completion of this book. The new member of our team, Mike Mondello, brought new energy and perspective to the project. His contribution has been invaluable, and he will be a pleasure to work with on future editions. I would be remiss not to mention past coauthor Steve Shapiro. Steve did a great job on the first two editions and his contributions are greatly appreciated. I would also like to thank Myles Schrag and the staff at Human Kinetics. Their efforts on each edition have been greatly appreciated.

I would also like to thank my colleagues in the sport management field whom I have worked with over the past years. Their encouragement and kind words have not gone unnoticed. People such as Dave Stotlar, Bill Sutton, Jay Gladden, Dan Mahony, Dennis Howard, Dan Rascher, Lisa Masteralexis, and Edgar Johnson (just to name a few) make me proud to be an academician in sport management. I would like to thank my parents, Richard and Jean DeSchriver, for loving and supporting me for all these years. They instilled within me a passion for education and teaching that will last forever. Last and most important, I would like to thank my wife, Kerry, for her patience and encouragement during the publication process.

Tim DeSchriver

I would like to thank both Gil Fried and Tim DeSchriver for having the confidence to extend an invitation to collaborate with them. As someone who has admired their work, I had an easy decision to make when they asked me to join them. My initial involvement allowed me to gain a greater appreciation for the significant roles that my colleagues fulfilled and the overall time commitment that a project of this magnitude requires. Gil and Tim both provided timely mentoring with questions and suggestions. Also, the Sport Management Program at Florida State University provided me with the necessary resources and time to complete the project. My colleagues at FSU represent some of the best scholars in our field, and working with them over the years has been a pleasure. In addition, I would like to acknowledge the professional approach that HK's Myles Schrag brought to the team. Finally, a special thanks goes to my family, whose support has always remained unwavering regardless of my limitations.

Mike Mondello

x

Basics of Sport Finance

You cannot fully grasp sport finance without knowing the fundamentals. The information in part I will help you understand and apply financial concepts in later chapters.

Chapter 1, "Financial Issues in Sport," highlights the basics of sport finance by introducing various issues such as how sports teams have increased in value over the years, why sport broadcasting contracts continue to increase in value, whether the high cost of sports sponsorship is appropriate, and whether government funding of sports facilities produces a benefit to the local community or team.

Chapter 2, "Basic Financial Concepts," covers the basic component of financial analysis—revenue and expenses. Where do teams get money to pay huge player salaries? Where do college athletic departments obtain funds compared with high school athletic departments? Every sport organization obtains funds from various sources, such as ticket sales, sponsorship deals, and concession sales. Similarly, every sport organization has expenses, such as salaries, rent, taxes, and utilities. This chapter analyzes the various types of revenues and expenses and then describes how to track them and plan for them in the future. The chapter ends with an analysis of some accounting principles that help you understand how the revenue, expense, and budgetary numbers are calculated.

Chapter 3, "Budgeting 101," introduces students immediately to one of the most important tools for financial analysis—a budget. The authors would love to say that every sport business has a budget, but in reality many do not use this important tool. Some businesses operate from the seat of their pants without knowing where they are going or why they are constantly facing financial hardships. A budget helps guide a business or organization similar to the way that a road map or GPS helps a driver. Thus, a budget is a planning tool that will help the organization reach predetermined goals. This chapter examines the fundamentals of what a budget is, how to gather the data needed to prepare a budget, how the financial planning process works, and how a pro forma budget can set the direction for future growth.

chapter 1

Financial Issues in Sport

Chapter Objectives

After studying this chapter, you should be able to do the following:

♦ Understand how important managing money is for anyone in the sport industry.

♦ Understand how math, strategy, and managerial skills are crucial for financial decision making.

♦ Appreciate that some sport businesses are billion-dollar enterprises.

♦ Critically analyze the value of sport broadcasting contracts.

♦ Appreciate that sport sponsorship represents a strategic financial decision.

♦ Understand major developments in stadium construction trends.

popular song has a line stating, "Money makes the world go 'round." Although many people might disagree with that statement, it is hard to undertake many things in life without money. Imagine if no one had any money. How would we obtain the items we need? How could businesses grow? How could we save for the future? These are typical questions that could arise if our society did not utilize money. More practically, what would happen to us if our checking accounts did not balance? What would happen to us if our cars broke down and we needed to buy new ones? Would we have a favorable credit history for obtaining a loan? Would we need someone to **cosign** a loan, agreeing to pay the balance if we defaulted on the loan? How would we balance our financial obligations with another obligation added to the mix? Would the new car increase our insurance costs to the point that we might not be able to afford the monthly payments? These questions typically arise when we make personal financial decisions.

Similar to all businesses, sport businesses raise similar financial questions with every decision they make. Should a new franchise join a league? Should an athlete be signed at $5 million or $6 million a year? How much should ticket prices rise in any given year? If someone wants to start her own sport business, where can she obtain the funds? Should a college cancel certain sports or add other sports to meet budgetary and legal obligations? These questions are asked and answered every day by means of financial analysis. Sometimes these issues are minor issues. Other times the issues can be complex. The 2011 National Football League (NFL) lockout focused on the best way to split the revenue pie between the owners and the players. Although many might think that wealthy owners and players can handle monetary loss associated with a missed or delayed season, numerous smaller businesses such as sports bars, concessionaires, and parking lots, as well as thousands of employees, could suffer significant financial harm during a lockout or strike. This one example highlights how interconnected the sport business world is and how a change affecting one entity can affect many others. Thus, monetary issues come up throughout a typical business day, and each business needs people who are trained to analyze where the money is or where to obtain additional funds if necessary.

Sport financial issues change on a regular basis. Stocks can shoot up one day and plummet the next in response to various news stories. As an example, in 2012 Jeremy Lin was not resigned by the New York Knicks and the next week the value of Madison Square Garden stocks dropped $93 million. New strategies and techniques can also change how businesses run. For example, in the 1990s gym equipment leasing started gaining in popularity. With equipment sometimes costing $2,000 each, it became expensive to outfit a complete health club. Leasing companies jumped into the fray and set monthly payments based on various factors such as credit rating, financial conditions, business experience, and the total cost of the items leased (Cohen, 1999). Leasing allows a club owner to use other people's money to generate revenue, and the leasing expenses can be deducted as a business expense. This scenario can help highlight a financial strategy that shows how important financial analysis is for a sport executive. Assume that a health club has a gross profit of $5,000 per month (income after expenses) and decides to lease $36,000 of commercial fitness equipment. The club will have to pay monthly payments of $843 for 60 months (five years of payments, which would total $50,580 in payments to lease the equipment). Because most companies pay roughly 30% of their gross income in taxes, $1,500 of their $5,000 profit would go to Uncle Sam. With a lease, however, the $843 paid to the lender could be deducted from the $5,000, leaving a taxable amount of $4,157. This reduces the total gross income and likewise reduces the total tax obligation. Using the same 30% tax rate the taxes owed drop from $1,500 to $1,247. This represents a savings of $253 because the lease payment is expensed. If the club owners multiply the effective payment (the true payment after reducing the tax obligation) by the lease term, the math would be $590 multiplied by 60 months for a total of $35,400. The $35,400 obligation is less than the original $36,000 cost of the equipment. Thus, even though the owner would have to pay $14,580 in interest for leasing the equipment, the end amount after taking into consideration tax savings generates a better deal for the owner.

Because of the attractive terms, leasing became a major enterprise and accounted for 25 to 40% of all fitness equipment sales in 1999 (Cohen, 1999). By 2011 the number of facilities using equipment leasing was significant, and leasing had even trickled down to home fitness equipment. Part of the push for leasing has come from the equipment manufacturers who are trying to drive sales; they would rather have equipment leased than lose a possible sale. The example of leasing fitness equipment highlights how financial issues can affect how

INDUSTRY SPOTLIGHT

As the 2011 National Basketball Association (NBA) season ended, the league was facing a major financial hurdle. The NFL was already in a lockout, and the NBA was facing a similar standoff with its players. The NBA is a $4 billion per year industry. During the 2011 season it notched its seventh consecutive season of achieving greater than 90% capacity at its arenas. It had strong television ratings and merchandise sales (McCarthy, 2011). This rosy picture masked a financial time bomb. The league was estimating losses of close to $300 mil-

lion, and the commissioner, David Stern, predicted that 22 of 30 clubs would lose money in 2011. Part of the financial plea by the owners focused on changing the revenue-sharing model, which under the collective bargaining agreement paid the players 57% of the league's revenue and left the owners with the remaining 43%. With average salaries ranging around $5 million a year, management had little room for error because signing an underperforming player could saddle a team with millions of dollars in losses for years to come.

a sport executive makes decisions. This book was written to highlight the importance of financial decision making to the sport industry. By knowing how to apply appropriate financial decision making, a sport manager can become much more successful.

Sport finance entails numerous unique issues, but these nevertheless mirror the finance issues faced by all other businesses. For example, financial mistakes can be made by anyone, whether poor or wealthy. Numerous successful athletes have done well for themselves only to lose their fortune because of fraud or financial mismanagement. Some people might claim that these athletes did not know how to manage their money, but numerous "smart" people have been defrauded in highly publicized scandals or schemes as well. Two schemes snared a number of successful college and professional coaches who thought that they were investing wisely but lost their investment (Bohn, 2011).

This chapter presents tools that can help anyone more critically examine financial proposals and determine whether a deal is too good to be true or a solid investment. The chapter also focuses on current sport finance issues by first covering the basics of managing money and then turning to the skills needed to be effective as a financial manager. We then examine the valuation of sports teams, which can be valued at over a billion dollars, and consider why sports broadcasting contracts are sometimes worth over a billion dollars. We consider some of the changes that are affecting sports sponsorship and the financing of new stadiums and arenas. The background material in this chapter should

give you a strong foundation in some of the basic concepts that you must understand to appreciate the complexities of sport finance.

MANAGING MONEY

Although **money** is important for making everyday decisions, it is not an end in itself for most people. We strive for personal financial independence, but we also normally realize that money only helps us enjoy our lives to the fullest. What good is a million dollars if we cannot enjoy spending the money? People traditionally work hard to earn money to enjoy the finer things in life (e.g., traveling, retiring, or spoiling family members). Businesses, however, traditionally do not have the same vision about the role that money plays in their existence. Businesses exist solely to make money for their owners and stockholders. If a company has other goals besides earning a profit, it still needs to focus on the bottom line to pay **bills** and meet its payroll. For example, even if a company's primary goal is to make ecologically friendly products to save the rain forest, the company will not be in business if it is unable to sell those products at a price sufficient to cover the costs of running the business. Nonprofit organizations also exist to make money so that they can further their primary goals. Special Olympics needs to sell products, sponsorship, and advertising to raise the funds necessary to offer programs for its athletes.

Besides paying the bills, making and managing money provide the framework for future growth. Finding, managing, tracking, and spending money refer to specific finance-related functions within a company or business. Failure to manage funds properly will cause a business to fail. Successful financial management results in business growth. The best product in the world would not survive if sound financial planning did not support the sales effort. Economic forecasts help determine potential sales patterns or the times when raw goods need to be purchased. If sales are expected to be phenomenal, then the business may need to borrow money from a lending institution or the public to finance new manufacturing facilities.

Sound financial planning is especially critical when the development process for a product is expected to be long. For example, new nutritional supplements typically require several years of development and testing on humans before they are approved by the Food and Drug Administration (FDA) for consumer distribution. Sport nutrition products, such as various muscle builders, are a good example. These products might have to go through the FDA review process (which is cumbersome and involves multiple hurdles that can take years to overcome) and then have to meet government guidelines concerning the health information on the label before they can be sold. A number of supplements have been shut down by the federal government for violating such regulations, and some players have unknowingly ingested supplements that ended up containing banned substances not listed in the ingredients label, which is in violation of FDA regulations. Most pharmaceuticals do not make it through the review process and do not get FDA approval to be sold. Other products might be pulled after being on the market for years because of new research highlighting a concern. During the FDA review process, a company might not have any income but still needs to pay bills, wages, and operating expenses. By managing money wisely and working with potential investors, such as venture capitalists, the company could generate the needed finances without jeopardizing product development. The key to financial success, as highlighted by this simple example, is financial planning.

All managerial decisions require a comprehensive review of internal and external constraints. Environmental factors, such as the cost of borrowing money, involve both types of constraints. **Internal constraints** can include a company's credit history, sales volume, product lines, accounts receivable, inventory balances, and management structure. **External constraints** can include inflationary conditions, significant competition, high interest rates, weak **economic indicators**, shrinking of the money supply by the government,

and the political environment. Although it takes money to make money, you cannot make money unless you understand all the internal and external variables that affect your ability to manage your finances. Thus, a team owner cannot start budgeting for future growth after construction of a new stadium if the voters have not yet approved public funding for the stadium. Internal constraints, such as ticket prices, are moot issues until the external constraints—the votes—are finalized.

Financial principles apply to every business, nonprofit organization, and government entity. In the United States, people are concerned about the financial health of the Social Security system and the possibility that it might go bankrupt in the future. The United States government, as well as governments around the world, is struggling to repay significant financial obligations incurred when expenses far exceeded revenue. Some nonprofit organizations have suffered from scandals involving key executives who abused financial control to live a lavish lifestyle. Countless businesses have filed for bankruptcy protection because they failed to make required payments in a timely manner. All these scenarios are examples of poor financial planning. The sports world is not immune to such problems. From the building of a public stadium that sits nearly dormant for years to the folding of a new league because of the aggressive marketing efforts of a stronger rival league, problems in the sports world often result from the lack of critical financial planning. The common denominator in most professional sports strikes is financial planning. For example, some owners have raised the salary bar for other owners, and after the bar has been raised it becomes almost impossible, without violating antitrust laws, to lower the salaries. The result has been an environment of haves and have-nots. Some teams are able to survive and generate enough revenue to put forth a consistently strong product, but other teams flounder with low salaries. Some teams use strategic financial planning to help their bottom line. A recent example of such financial mismanagement was seen in the 2010 Commonwealth Games held in Delhi, India. The comptroller and auditor general report presented to the Indian government after the games highlighted that the games cost 16 times the original estimate of US$270 million. The report showed that the organizing committee was riddled with favoritism and bias, that the plan was ill conceived and ill planned, and that due diligence was lacking at all levels (Cutler, 2011). The games ended up costing $4.1 billion, and generated only

$38 million (Cutler, 2011).

One of the most famous examples of leveraging a team to reach financial success involves the San Diego Padres. They spent a significant amount of money on top-level talent during the 1998 season to help win the National League championship. They also won a vote to use public funds to help build a new ballpark. The team spent $53 million in 1998 compared with only $32.8 million in 1997 (Truex, 1999). Thereafter, the team was dismantled. Some of the top talent was traded, was not signed, or signed with other clubs as free agents, thus significantly reducing the payroll (Truex, 1999). But the increased spending and the winning record helped garner public support for building a facility. The team's $20 million investment was returned many times over by the increased revenue that the team received from the new stadium.

Teams in various leagues have undertaken similar spending sprees. The Florida Marlins went on a spending spree before the 1997 World Series and then dismantled their high-salaried team. After winning the World Series, the owner cut the team payroll by 70% the next year to $16 million. In the San Diego case, analysts conjectured that the owners spent lavishly to produce a great product and a winning team. Voters would have a harder time voting against a new stadium for a winning team. In contrast, voters would probably not feel remorse about turning down a stadium bond vote for a team that had never won. After the team received the positive vote, the need for an expensive winning team ended, and the Padres could return to a lower payroll level. Team payrolls do not occur by chance. Financial planning sets the stage for team success.

These examples highlight that basic financial planning can help generate revenue or save money. The basic concept of money management is to keep increasing revenue and revenue sources while at the same time reducing expenses, eliminating some expenses, or spreading out expenses over a longer period. None of these steps can be taken without significant financial planning, and such planning requires basic financial skills.

FINANCIAL SKILLS

Executives do not just make decisions. The most successful executives use financial skills to plan their decisions. To document and plan for future financial success, a sports organization needs someone trained in developing, analyzing, projecting, and interpreting financial information. The need for strong financial skills keeps growing as the sport industry evolves and more money is at stake. When budgets were small, a coach was often asked to run the athletic program. But now, with huge budgets and demands for financial accountability, specific training is needed to succeed. For example, in 2006 Ohio State University's (OSU) athletic department, which runs 36 sports, became the first college athletic department in the United States to have a budget surpassing $100 million. By 2011 the OSU athletic budget was up to $126 million (Dosh, 2011). To manage an operation of that size, trained professionals are needed. The job description in the box is typical for a high-level financial job.

TYPICAL JOB DESCRIPTION FOR A HIGH-LEVEL SPORT FINANCE POSITION

XYZ is a sport management company seeking a highly motivated chief financial officer. This person will serve as a strategic partner and internal consultant by providing guidance to all individuals associated with our various financial systems. Responsibilities will include, but are not limited to, company-wide budgeting, financial forecasting, statistical reporting, audits, new business development, payroll preparation, state and federal tax compliance, and information systems. Qualified candidates should hold a certificate such as a CPA or CMA or possess an MBA in conjunction with an accounting bachelor's degree. Five to eight years of senior-level financial experience is necessary to gain a full understanding of projections, techniques, systems, and methodology. The ideal candidate will also possess strong leadership and managerial skills to help lead a group of 20 employees in various areas such as ticket processing, accounts receivable, accounts payable, and outside contracts administration.

As highlighted by this job description, senior executives with solid financial skills can have a significant number of opportunities available to them in the future. Clearly, different jobs and tasks require different financial skills. The terms *finance, accounting,* and *economics* often cause confusion for students. **Accounting** is the process of calculating revenue and expenses through receipts and other facts to determine the numbers for a company or entity. Managerial accounting is more closely aligned with finance because it focuses on identifying the costs required to produce a good or service so that financial planning can be done more effectively. **Finance** is the process of examining the numbers, determining what they mean, and identifying what the past was and future will be for a company or entity. This process often entails identifying current and future revenue and expenses and determining future budgets to help an organization succeed. **Economics**, in contrast, takes the numbers and financial projections from numerous companies or entities to explore future trends. If numerous sporting goods companies are projecting strong returns because of a new fitness craze, for example, economists could take that information and hypothesize about new economic changes or trends that affect the sporting goods segment of the industry. Thus, some careers involving sport finance can be described as accounting, finance, or economics positions rather than all being lumped in the category of sport finance.

The skills needed to succeed in sport finance are diverse. No single kind of training is required to excel in finance, but the key skill that anyone in finance needs to master is basic math. Although calculators and computers can help perform numerous calculations, a person needs to know how the numbers are calculated to make effective use of them. Math is not an end all for sport finance. Numbers are useful only if someone can apply them. For that reason, finance is much more than accounting or economics. Accounting and economics require critical skills, and their results and analysis are important. Sport finance, however, requires the added element of pulling together information from various sources, times, entities, and other areas to gaze into a crystal ball and project and plan for the future. This task requires an appreciation for the assets of an organization and ways in which to use them most effectively. Thus, finance is really applied management focused on financial constraints or opportunities. Without having a strong perspective of an organization and its future direction, a sport financier could not effectively put a story to the numbers.

The analogy of a story associated with finance is appropriate here. Financial numbers tell a story. They can tell whether a business will be profitable or whether it will need financial assistance. By examining numbers from a prior year a manager can determine whether an organization was effective or whether the strategic plan was significantly flawed. To be effective, a manager needs to know what the numbers are and then be able tell a story with the numbers to inspire investors, employees, or other constituents.

BILLION-DOLLAR TEAMS

The 21st century witnessed the first sale of a professional team for more than $1 billion when Malcolm Glazer, owner of the Tampa Bay Buccaneers, purchased a controlling interest in vaunted soccer powerhouse Manchester United. The $1.47 billion takeover bid included Glazer's using $503 million of his own money, taking out loans for $490 million, and issuing preferred securities for $509 million. In essence, only one-third of the money came from Glazer, and the rest came from lenders and other investors. Because he did not put that much of his own money forward, the team was going to be saddled with significant loan obligations. Interest expense was estimated at more than $55 million a year, just to pay for borrowing the money to finance the deal. A $55 million obligation was significant for the team. In the year of the transaction, Manchester United had revenues of only $300 million and $90 million in profits (Cohen & Holmes, 2005). Glazer purchased the club by buying 97.3% of the team's shares that were trading on the London Stock Exchange. Before his takeover attempt, the shares were selling for between 250 and 280 pence per share. Glazer offered 300 pence per share in cash to buy his majority share, which allowed him to take the team private. Mr. Glazer is now the sole owner; previously the team was publicly listed and owned by numerous investors (Sharecast, 2005). In 2010 the team completed a $747 million bond issue to refinance their mounting debt. Although revenue has grown under Mr. Glazer (an increase of 72% to more than $400 million a year), the team was paying over $100 million a year on its debt. The team probably would have had a huge loss had it not sold one of its best players for $120 million (Scott, 2010). Manchester United was not alone in coming under American ownership. Liverpool was sold in 2010 by its primary lender (Royal Bank of Scotland) to New England Sports Ventures (owners of the Boston Red Sox) for $476 million ("Liverpool sale awaits judge's ruling," 2010). These numbers tend to show that top-level soccer teams have been the best investment, but some teams in America have also significantly increased in value over the past couple years, especially NFL teams.

NFL teams have shown more **appreciation** than baseball teams because of the hard salary cap that limits the amount that teams can pay their players, a loyal fan base interested in attending the limited number of games played, and huge television broadcast contracts. The most valuable franchise is often thought to be the Dallas Cowboys, who were worth around $2.1 billion in 2012. At the same time the New York Yankees were considered the most valuable MLB franchise with an estimated worth of $1.3 billion. The most valuable franchises are normally located in the largest markets where they can leverage new stadiums and significant broadcast contracts. Because of the large broadcast contracts for NFL teams, even lower-quality teams (with poor win–loss records) are valuable. One of the interesting team valuations entails the New York Jets and the New York Giants, who share a new stadium. The Jets were worth approximately $1.1 billion in 2011 (based on revenue of $238 million), and the Giants were worth around $1.2 billion (on $241 million in revenue) (Massey, 2011). With NFL franchises valued at around a half-billion dollars, it is hard to believe the teams' values when the original franchises were issued. Curly Lambeau paid $50 in 1922 for the Green Bay franchise. In 1925 Tim Mara paid $500 for the New York Giants franchise. Art Rooney acquired the Pittsburgh Steelers franchise in 1933 through an unconventional method—he won the rights in a card game ("From $50 in 1922," 1999).

Significant financial resources are needed to own these expensive teams, and it is not just United States owners who are buying internationally. International investors are helping to purchase teams based in the United States. One such purchase that garnered significant publicity was the 2009 purchase of a controlling interest in the New Jersey Nets by Russian billionaire Mikhail Prokhotov. The deal included buying 80% of the team, 45% of the team's Brooklyn arena project, and the right to purchase 20% of nonarena real estate projects ("NBA going global with sale of Nets," 2009).

These deals and valuations are often fueled by significant borrowing. One example was Frank McCourt, who lost control of the Los Angeles Dodgers because of overspending. He had purchased the team from Fox in 2004 for $430 million and by 2011 had debt exceeding $600 million (Nightengale, 2011). The team was sold for $2.3 billion in 2011.

Why would a team's **value** fluctuate so much in such a short time? The simple answer could be the team's profit margin or total **assets**, as discussed later in this text. Another reason could be an arbitrary value based on fan and investor speculation rather than true financial value. Some wealthy people are interested in owning an expensive toy and could throw all logic out the window if they are in a bidding war with a rival and want more than anything to own a professional team. As Dallas Mavericks owner Marc Cuban said, "It's every little kid's dream . . . to own their favorite team. I think it's a tremendous opportunity" ("Web billionaire," 2000).

BILLION-DOLLAR BROADCASTING DEALS

The financial growth of sport in North America has been fueled by the phenomenal growth of broadcasting rights deals. Among the jewels in the sports broadcasting empire are the NFL, the NCAA basketball championships, the Olympics, and college football's Bowl Championship Series. Although events such as NASCAR races, golf tournaments, and the Kentucky Derby are popular, the broadcasting rights fees are not in the same stratosphere as the top four broadcasting deals. For example, the NCAA received $2.8 billion from CBS for a seven-year contract. The NFL, while seeing its ratings decline almost 10% since 1998, has seen its rights fees soar. DirecTV is paying $3.5 billion over five years for its exclusive NFL Sunday Ticket package, which is a 75% increase from their prior rights deal (Lowry & Grover, 2004). In total, the previous NFL contract generated $3.735 billion per year for the NFL, which was more than the national rights fees for the NBA, MLB, NASCAR, the PGA, and the NCAA basketball tournament combined (Hiestand, 2004).

ESPN's first broadcast was on September 7, 1979, and the network aired its first NCAA basketball championship in 1980. ESPN started with 1.4 million viewer homes, but by 2004 it reached more than 88.3 million households. An average of 94 million Americans consumed ESPN's diverse array of media (TV, radio, magazine) each week for an average of about one hour each day (Martzke & Cherner, 2004). The growth of aired events has also spawned a growth in competition between broadcasters. ESPN was the first specialized sports broadcaster, but others have emerged on the scene and have helped foster a bidding war. A number of professional teams who used to air their games on

Fox Sports switched in 2004 to Comcast. The battle between the two powerful regional sports networks (RSNs) is fueled in part by their popularity. As they acquired additional sport properties, their ratings increased, and with the increased demand for their programs they were able to increase the price per subscriber. Although a channel such as CNN charges a cable company $0.40 per subscriber, ESPN charged $2.25 per subscriber in 2004, and the RSNs are not far behind at $2 per subscriber (Grover & Lowry, 2004). By 2009 ESPN was charging $3.20 per subscriber. ESPN was charging around $5.15 per subscriber in 2012, which could account for 10% of a typical cable bill.

As highlighted already, broadcast networks are dishing out huge sums to air sports events. Cable providers (from regional networks to sports packages such as "all-access" football, hockey, basketball, and baseball games), ABC, CBS, NBC, and ESPN are all competing to win sports fans. The economic reality is that sports broadcasts draw viewers, which means that they draw advertisers. Advertisers are willing to pay more for advertisements on the top broadcasts, which has fueled the bidding war for the best shows and has led to low bids for less popular broadcasting events.

The biggest moneymaker by far is football. The NFL's contracts are a multibillion-dollar enterprise. Fox extended its National Conference deal by agreeing to a $4.4 billion contract ($550 million per season), which included rights to half the Super Bowl games during that time. Both FOX and CBS have renewed their Sunday-afternoon broadcast packages through 2011, in both cases with modest increases. *Monday Night Football*, on the other hand, moved to ESPN; the Disney-owned network is paying $1.1 billion per year from 2006 to 2014 for the rights to the lucrative broadcasts. In 2011 ESPN extended its contract to cover *Monday Night Football* for nearly $2 billion a year through 2022-2023. Such a sum shows how far the NFL

has progressed from the 1970s when the combined total of all broadcast contracts was $46.25 million (Durand, 2011). Meanwhile, NBC, after losing their AFC package to CBS in 1997, reclaimed its share of the NFL broadcast rights with a deal worth an average of $650 million per year from 2006 to 2012 that gave them the Sunday-night package as well as the Super Bowl and Pro Bowl in 2009 and 2012 (*Univision*, 2005). The growth in broadcast fees can be attributed to multiple variables such as the high cost of attending an NFL game (estimated at an average cost of $413 for a family of four in 2009) and the fact that some fans (35%) preferred watching a football game on high-definition television rather than attending a game in person (Leahy, 2010). Table 1.1 highlights the various NFL media rights holders (minus radio and wireless carriers).

One of the best broadcasting properties after the NFL is NASCAR. According to Nielsen ratings, NASCAR was, for a while, second only to the NFL in sports viewership. In 2005 NASCAR's 5.8 average rating beat the NBA's regular season and playoffs; the NCAA tournament; PGA golf; and the NHL's regular season, playoffs, and Stanley Cup finals (Patsuris, 2003).

NASCAR also follows the NFL in the money race. In 1999 NASCAR entered into a $2.4 billion six-year contract with General Electric–owned NBC and AOL Time Warner's TNT, which together aired half the season. News Corporation's Fox and FX networks aired the rest. NBC and TNT highlight that NASCAR's ratings jumped 59% from 2000 to 2002, and those numbers continued to grow on a yearly basis (Patsuris, 2003) until the economic downturn in 2008. The ratings in 2010 were down from 4 to 6% on Fox, TNT, and SPEED, but down in double digits for some races on ESPN. Younger audiences were still tuning in, but racing saw an overall decline in ratings and attendance. NASCAR was a good investment ten years ago, but is not paying off as well as other broadcasting investments. Some

Table 1.1 Media Rights Holders

Contract period	Rights holder	Estimated annual value (in billions)
2006-2013	ESPN	$1.1 (to increase to $1.8 through 2022-2023)
2006-2013	Fox	$.720
2006-2013	CBS	$.619
2006-2013	NBC	$.603
2011-2014	DirecTV	$1.0 (Durand, 2011)

sports can gain and lose popularity but NFL, college football, and college basketball have been the most stable and valuable broadcasting rights.

A sport that is huge in Europe and on the rise in the United States is soccer. Univision Communications and the ABC and ESPN television networks have paid a record $425 million to air World Cup soccer and other events from 2007 to 2014 (*Univision*, 2005). Univision also paid $325 million for exclusive Spanish-language rights to air the events throughout the United States and Puerto Rico. ABC and ESPN, both owned by the Walt Disney Company, paid $100 million for English-language rights (*Univision*, 2005).

Although the big networks continue to offer big money for broadcasting rights, new networks are popping up and hoping to get a foot in the door. When ESPN offered the NHL less than $60 million to broadcast the league's games, negotiations broke off. Comcast's Outdoor Life Network (OLN), renamed Versus, offered $135 million over two years for the rights to NHL telecasts. If your cable provider did not offer OLN, you could have caught your favorite hockey team on XM Satellite Radio. XM had 4.4 million subscribers and announced a 10-year $100 million agreement to become the exclusive satellite radio network of the NHL in 2007 (NHL Press, 2005). After the NHL rebounded in popularity, its rights were sold in 2011 to NBC and Versus for an estimated $2 billion through 2020-2021. This agreement provided the stability that the NHL needed after being bounced around across various networks and cable providers over a period of several years (Hipes, 2011). Besides new broadcasting entrants, new technology is also changing the way that sports broadcasting attracts fans.

Sporting events are also moving into the digital, wireless age. ESPN started to sell a wireless service for sports fans called Mobile ESPN. Mobile ESPN delivers sports scores, breaking news, and commentary as well as some audio and video clip services to ESPN mobile phones (*Univision*, 2005). After several months, however, ESPN stopped selling the phones because they were not successful. The content is still being provided but to other phone companies as an additional service. High-technology companies are also cashing in on broadcasting rights. BSkyB, or Sky television, features sports, entertainment, and breaking news through mobile phones, personal digital assistants, and portals including Sky.com and Skysports.com (*Sky Media*, 2005). World Championship Sports Network (WCSN) is the first programming network dedicated to capturing athletes and international sports federation competitions from around the world. WCSN showcases a variety of global sports including track and field, gymnastics, skiing, and volleyball (World Championship Sports Network, 2005).

The future of broadcasting rights is significantly affected by the Internet and the way in which people want to watch and participate in sport. With 3-D technology, fantasy sport leagues, and countless hand-held devices (and their numerous apps), the prospect for continued growth in rights fees is sure to continue.

SPORTS SPONSORSHIP

Sports sponsorship has changed significantly over the years from athletes promoting a given product to corporations that are willing to pay large sums to place their product at a sport event or slap their name on the side of a building. In the 1980s almost every player in the NBA had a shoe deal, but by 1998 only about half of the 400 players in the league had shoe contracts, and that number was dwindling rapidly (Fatsis, 1998, May 14). Reebok alone dropped more than 110 NBA players who had previously been under contract. Reebok also slashed its baseball sponsorship lineup from 280 to 140 athletes and its football players from 550 to around 100 (Fatsis, 1998, May 14). Several years later the focus had shifted to sponsoring and having exclusive long-term licensing agreements with leagues such as the NFL, NBA, WNBA, NBDL (National Basketball Development League), and IRL (Indy Racing League) and stars such as Allen Iverson. Other shoe and apparel companies reduced their sponsorship commitments as well. Major stars such as Shaquille O'Neal had their contracts terminated or bought out. Larry Johnson earned around $800,000 per year from Converse in the early 1990s, but in 1998 he received only $7,500 in free merchandise (Fatsis, 1998, May 14). By 2010 the landscape kept changing as many star players received only free shoes from a shoe sponsor. Only the superstars were able to make money, often times by developing their own specialized and endorsed shoes. Shoe sponsorship also grew internationally. Shaquille O'Neal was sponsored at the end of his career by Li-Ning, a Chinese sports apparel company trying to reach a broader international audience.

Nike was founded as a company that made shoes for track and field athletes. At one point it had deals with 20 sports federations worldwide and was outfitting more than 2,000 athletes, not including all the college programs that it sponsored (Walker, 2004). In 2005 Nike signed an apparel and equipment deal with 15-year-old golf sensation Michelle Wie, reportedly worth $5 million per year. Before signing Wie, Nike negotiated a deal worth $40 million over five years with Tiger Woods when he turned pro in 1996. Because Woods had not yet accomplished anything on the Professional Golfers' Association (PGA) Tour, some critics viewed the deal as risky. But Nike got its investment back and much more. Before signing Woods, Nike had negligible golf revenue, but with Woods' success their revenue shot to an estimated $500 million per year. Woods' next deal with Nike paid him $25 million per year (Badenhausen, 2005). Nike's golf business could be attributed in part to Tiger Woods, but the company did not sell golf shoes before Tiger. Therefore, some of the growth is attributable just to developing a new product line. With the decline in Woods' popularity because of an infidelity scandal, the value of the sponsorship opportunity declined, and through fiscal year 2010 Nike's golf business declined 2% to $638 million.

The sports shoe and apparel companies were not alone in changing how they viewed sponsorships. Sponsors sometimes have difficulty placing a value on a sponsorship property, so any sponsorship decision is subject to significant fiscal scrutiny. Coca-Cola had a 12-year relationship with the NFL through 1998. The next deal paid the NFL only $6 million a year as compared with $15 million in prior years ("Coke signs," 1998). The new and greatly reduced sponsorship package allowed teams for the first time in many years to negotiate their own local sponsorship deals.

The reduced value associated with the new contract between Coca-Cola and the NFL (a decline from $15 to $6 million) may have come about because Dallas Cowboys owner Jerry Jones struck his own deals with competing sponsors. Jones sold sponsorship rights for the old Texas Stadium to Pepsi. Because Pepsi was sponsoring the stadium, not the team, Jones was technically not violating the old NFL and Coca-Cola contract. But because the Cowboys were the only team that played in Texas Stadium, the sponsorship agreement implied indirect sponsorship of the Cowboys by Pepsi. The resulting confusion reduced the sponsorship value for Coca-Cola, leading to the subsequently smaller sponsorship agreement. After losing their NFL sponsorship exclusivity, Coca-Cola focused on individual NFL teams, other leagues such as FIFA (4-year, $500 million sponsorship agreement), and

the NBA, which has a "100-year" agreement with the company, signed in 1993 and renewed every 4 years.

The entry of PepsiCo (parent company of Pepsi) into the NFL mix helped the newcomer grow its relationship with the entire NFL, which led to a full-fledged league contract. In 2004 PepsiCo and the NFL extended their partnership agreement through February 2011 in a deal estimated at $560 million. PepsiCo contracted to acquire the rights to all NFL trademarks, including use of the NFL shield logo, Super Bowl, and Pro Bowl as well as collective use of the 32 NFL team marks for the Pepsi, Tropicana, and Frito-Lay brands. This agreement was in addition to PepsiCo's Gatorade division's announcement of a similar partnership extension with the league through 2011. In total, PepsiCo is projected to spend more than $1 billion for both deals (Parry, 2004). In 2011 PepsiCo renewed their sponsorship deal through the 2022 playoff for $1 billion a year.

Sponsorship can come in various forms. For example, a professional league can sponsor a farm team. The NBA had a partnership arrangement with the Continental Basketball Association (CBA) through 2001. The NBA then decided to move away from the CBA and start its own developmental league. The loss of the NBA as a sponsor doomed the CBA, which filed for bankruptcy in 2001 ("CBA ceases operations," 2001). Losing sponsors also hurts smaller events, community events such as run-a-thons, and even larger events such as collegiate football bowl games. But sponsorship is a fickle beast, and trends can change quickly. This was seen in the early part of this century with the phenomenal growth of NASCAR and golf sponsorship. Will corporate interest in sponsoring NASCAR continue? The key is in the numbers. If the broadcast ratings and attendance stay strong, the sponsors will keep coming back. For any sponsorship effort, the key is proving value through strong numbers. For example, NASCAR sponsorship was all the rage through 2007. But after the economy declined, it became harder for NASCAR to sell sponsorships, and when attendance and TV ratings started falling, proving the value of sponsorships became even more difficult.

Stadium naming rights have gone through some ups and downs over the past several years. To protect the name of the facility, some stadium projects did not pursue naming-rights deals. For example, although the team could have earned possibly hundreds of millions of dollars, the New York Yankees refused to sell the naming rights for their new stadium that opened in 2009. The New York Mets, in contrast, sold their naming rights to Citigroup for $20 million a year. Several facilities were also able to land similar attractive naming-rights deals, such as the New Meadowlands Stadium, which sold the naming rights to MetLife, and some facilities were able to land naming-rights deals even before they broke ground on construction, such as Barclays Bank Arena in Brooklyn and Farmers Field in Los Angeles. Such contracts guaranteed these sponsors years of publicity before the facility even opened and might generate significant publicity even if Farmers Field is never built. Some of the largest sponsorship naming-rights deals are found in table 1.2.

Almost anything can be sponsored. People have had company names tattooed on their bodies for the right price. One interesting sport sponsorship property entails football (soccer) jerseys in Europe. The largest of these sponsorship contracts is for FC Barcelona's sponsorship with the Qatar Foundation. The five-year, $204.5 million contract will pay the team $40.9 million a year to promote the research foundation. From there the sponsorship numbers decrease to $35.7 million a year for Deutsche Telekom's sponsorship of FC Bayern Munich, Standard Chartered Bank's $33 million annual payment to sponsor Liverpool FC, and Aon's payment of $32.7 million per year to have its name on Manchester United's jerseys (Bennett, 2011). In the United States, the NBA agreed in 2012 to allow jersey advertising patches starting in 2013-2014. Such advertising placement is estimated to be worth around $100 million.

Although most sponsors are hoping to generate positive publicity or drive increased sales, this result does not always occur. The following list highlights some failed sponsorship naming-rights attempts:

♦ MCI WorldCom had the naming rights for a hockey and basketball arena in Washington, D.C., before filing for bankruptcy in 2002. The arena is now called the Verizon Center.

Table 1.2 Largest Naming-Rights Deals

NFL				
Stadium	**City**	**Sponsor**	**Price (mil)**	**Number of years**
Farmers Field	Los Angeles	Farmers Insurance	$600	30
MetLife Stadium	East Rutherford, NJ	MetLife Insurance	$425-$625	25
Reliant Stadium	Houston	Reliant Energy	$310	31
Gillette Stadium	Foxboro, MA	Gillette	$240	15
MLB				
Stadium	**City**	**Sponsor**	**Price (mil)**	**Number of years**
Citi Field	Queens, NY	Citigroup	$400	20
Minute Maid Park	Houston	Coca-Cola	$178	28
Citizens Bank Park	Philadelphia	Citizens Bank	$95	25
Great American Ball Park	Cincinnati	Great American Insurance	$75	30
ARENA DEALS				
Arena	**City**	**Sponsor**	**Price (mil)**	**Number of years**
Barclay's Center	Brooklyn	Barclays PLC	$200	20
American Airlines Center	Dallas	American Airlines	$195	30
Philips Arena	Atlanta	Royal Philips Electronics	$185	20
Nationwide Arena	Columbus, OH	Nationwide Insurance	$135	Indefinite
TD Garden	Boston	TD Bank	$119.1	20
Staples Center	Los Angeles	Staples	$116	20

Adapted, by permission, from SportsBusiness Journal research, 2011, "Largest naming-rights deals," *Street & Smith's SportsBusiness Journal* 14(21): 22-23.

- CMGI was the name sponsor of the New England Patriots before the company collapsed with the other dot coms. The facility now is sponsored by Gillette.
- Wachovia, before it closed, sponsored the basketball and hockey arena in Philadelphia, which in 2008 was renamed after another bank, Wells Fargo Center.
- Before filing for bankruptcy in 2002, United Airlines had its name plastered on Chicago's basketball and hockey arena. Luckily, the airline is still running, and the facility is still called the United Center.
- The most famous naming flop involved the baseball stadium in Houston named after the disgraced Enron Corporation. The stadium is now named after a wholesome orange juice supplier, Minute Maid (Elstein, 2011).

The key for any sponsorship deal is determining why the deal was made. Some companies sponsor a team, player, event, or stadium to drive sales. Others might attempt to improve their image or reputation. Many professional teams sponsor a variety of charitable causes to show that they are concerned about their community. As an example, Chesapeake Energy has been involved in gas fracking operations in and around Pennsylvania. The controversial practice associated with shale gas has led the company to work hard to educate those where they operate, and one of the best ways to educate others is through sports sponsorship. The company spent more than $10 million in recent years on athletic sponsorship with universities such as Penn State University and Ohio State University (Roberts, 2011).

FINANCING NEW STADIUMS AND ARENAS

The most dynamic sport finance topic in the past 20 years is stadium construction deals. Through 2001, 111 major professional sports franchises were operating in North America, and 91.9% (102) had moved into new or significantly renovated stadiums (Smith, 2001). Several additional teams, such as the Arizona Cardinals, moved to new facilities as the 21st century was starting. The most recent significant year of development was 2010 when six major facilities opened to the public (Target Field, New Meadowlands Stadium, Consol Energy Center, Amway Center, Red Bull Arena, and PPL Park). In 2003, the biggest year on record before 2009, over $2 billion was spent on new stadiums and arenas, not including another approximately $1 billion spent on college stadiums and arenas. In 2009 over $3.2 billion was spent on professional facilities and over $1 billion on college facilities (Muret, 2011). Part of this huge jump can be attributed to the new Yankees Stadium and Citi Field,

ROCKIES' STADIUM DEAL

The Colorado Rockies built their stadium with a six-county-area 1% sales tax. The team contributed $53 million, and Coors Brewing made **scheduled payments** of $1.5 million per year for naming rights. Under the 17-year lease, the city receives 20% of parking revenue on game days and 3% of the revenue from a brew pub. The team receives 100% of net concession revenue (Rogus, 1997). In the old facility, Mile High Stadium, the team averaged 55,350 spectators for each game, and about 4.5 million fans came through the turnstiles in 1993. The Rockies opened Coors Field in 1995 and during their honeymoon years averaged about 48,000 fans per game and 3.8 million fans for the first three seasons. These numbers were lower than Mile High's attendance totals, but Coors Field was built with a smaller seating capacity. By 2006 the team was drawing only about 25,000 fans per game and totaled only 2.1 million over the season (Baseball-almanac.com, n.d.). Even with lower attendance, the team was able to make more money through luxury seating and increased broadcasting revenues. The high attendance average for the first couple of years in a new stadium is commonly called the honeymoon effect because fans want to come out to see what is new at the facility. But similar to what occurs in many marriages, over time the passion decreases, and that is when attendance starts to decline.

along with other expensive stadiums; the billion-dollar Meadowlands and Cowboys Stadiums, two of the most expensive stadiums ever built, were completed in 2010.

Bond issues, economic factors, taxing issues, financial guarantees, legal wrangling, and political shenanigans can all be explored when examining stadium construction deals. Venerable Yankees Stadium was built in 1923 for $2 million. In 1973 New York City refurbished the stadium for $100 million. In 1996 New York City proposed a new stadium on the west side of Manhattan that had an estimated cost of $1.06 billion (Sportsfund, 1996). In 2001 New York recommended two new $800 million stadiums, one for each MLB team, which would require the teams and cities to split $50 million a year in **debt service** (to repay the money borrowed to build the stadiums) ("Double play for New York," 2001).

Although the push for these two new facilities took various forms, the drive to land the 2012 Olympics in New York helped fuel the rapid planning for the stadiums. The Yankees unveiled plans to build an $800 million stadium next door to the existing Yankee Stadium, built with private funds (Smith, 2005). The Mets were also hoping for support and funds for a new stadium that could have been used for the opening ceremonies and other competitions. But when New York lost the bid to host the 2012 Olympic Games, the plans were put on the back burner, even though the Mets still wanted to build a new stadium. Both the Yankees and the Mets pursued building their own facilities, with minimal public funding, next to their existing facilities. The hope of drawing the Olympic Games has spurred numerous construction booms such as the $43 billion spent for buildings and infrastructure for the 2008 Beijing Olympics. The 2014 Sochi Winter Olympics in Russia were initially expected to cost $12 billion, but recent estimates indicate that the cost will soar to around $33 billion.

In addition to building baseball stadiums, New York is currently pursuing various facility options such as moving the New Jersey Nets to a new home in Brooklyn. The total taxpayers' cost for stadiums or arenas built from 1995 through 2000 has been estimated at more than $9 billion (Kraker, 1998). Another estimate capped the building boom at $7 billion from 1998 through 2006, and the number keeps increasing when new stadiums and arenas are approved by voters (Noll & Zimbalist, 1998). The building boom has slowed after the hot run in the 1990s, but facilities are still being built at

both the professional and collegiate level, such as new soccer stadiums for Major League Soccer teams. Although numerous facilities were being built to keep or attract professional sports teams, such investments might not always make economic sense or stand on sound financial analysis.

In a 1990 study the Heartland Institute examined 14 stadiums built from 1954 through 1986; these facilities had a net accumulated value of negative $139.3 million ("Sports stadiums," 1990). The city that lost the least was Buffalo, New York; the War Memorial Stadium lost taxpayers only $836,021. In contrast, the New Orleans Superdome lost Louisiana taxpayers $70,356,950 ("Sports stadiums," 1990). After the construction boom in the 1990s, additional research showed that stadiums and arenas were not a wise financial investment if examined strictly from an economic perspective (Smith, 2001). Although stadium proponents claim significant benefit to building a new stadium, one researcher studied per capita income growth in 48 metropolitan areas. In the 30 cities that had facility changes in the preceding 10 years, 27 showed no significant relationship between income growth and building a facility, and 3 experienced reduced income (Baade, 1994). Another study by researchers from the University of Dayton concluded that public subsidies for constructing MLB stadiums were not necessary because teams recovered all or almost all of their construction costs, typically within 12 years of completing a facility ("Study: No taxes for stadiums," 2004). Public support for Olympic Games has clearly indicated that although some increase in tourism spending occurs, the long-term benefits of a new stadium are minimal if no primary tenant will occupy the facility and a strategic plan to generate revenue after the Olympic Games is not in place.

Municipalities interested in luring a new team or keeping an existing one argue that tax dollars should help finance facility construction because entertainment dollars are brought from outside the community, thus infusing "new" moneys into the local economy (Howard & Crompton, 2004). The municipalities are urging voters to approve the allocation of funds to build the facilities, and the teams are supporting these efforts. But the average level of team contribution to new NFL stadiums built through 2001 was only 29%, or $82 million, of the typical construction cost for a football stadium (*NFL stadium financing*, 2001). This trend changed over the next decade. Since the Los Angeles Rams moved back to Saint Louis (1995), 28 of the 32 franchises in the league have built new stadiums or renovated old stadiums. The total cost for such construction was $10 billion of which $6 billion was covered by taxpayers. Several major stadiums were built primarily with private funds during this period including Carolina (1996), New England (2002), Dallas (2009), and the New Meadowlands for the Giants and Jets (2010) (Broudway & Kuriloff, 2012). Even without any team contributions, some municipalities are willing to foot the entire price of a facility to become a "big-league" city. Besides the increased economic activity and the increased sales, income, and employment tax revenues from those attending games and working at the facilities, proponents argue that the facilities help promote community image (Baim, 1994).

Although significant benefits can be derived from new sports facilities, projections highlighting potential increased tax revenue or other benefits are often significantly inflated to help support the case for building a new facility (Howard & Crompton, 2004). In fact, the combined revenue of the five major professional sports teams in Chicago accounts for only 0.08% of the personal income throughout the city of Chicago (Kraker, 1998). One study concluded that the departure of an NBA team from a city results in no measurable impact on a region's per capita income, and thus building a new arena does not make sense as a cornerstone for economic development ("Football strike?" 2001).

One of the reasons that projected economic impacts may conflict is that the people who determine them may not be reliable sources. Consultants who prepare economic impact reports may use incorrect multipliers, assume that everyone who attends the facility would not have spent money elsewhere in the city, or build in a host of other incorrect assumptions (Baim, 1994). Thus, as is the case for all issues associated with financial analysis, the numbers are only as good as their source and need to be verified in more or less the same way that financial statements should be **audited** by a neutral third party.

Although numerous consulting reports show potential profits attributable to a facility, many studies have shown that few facilities are able to cover their costs (Baim, 1994; Noll & Zimbalist, 1998; Smith, 2001). One major study concluded that older arenas with little debt and numerous scheduled events (NBA, NHL, Ice Capades, family shows, circuses, and so on) tended to make the highest profit, whereas new stadiums for outdoor sports were least profitable (Baim, 1994). The

disparity among economic impact studies is highlighted by two studies conducted in 1992 when the San Francisco Giants were considering a move to San Jose, California. A study conducted in San Francisco estimated economic losses of $3.1 million per year if the team moved. A study conducted for San Jose produced different results. The San Jose study concluded that if the team moved the approximately 45 miles (70 km) from San Francisco to San Jose, the yearly economic impact for San Jose would be between $50 and $150 million annually (Howard & Crompton, 2004).

The potential hypocrisy associated with stating the financial need to build a stadium or arena was highlighted in a suit by former Tampa mayor William Poe, who tried to stop a referendum to build a new stadium for the Tampa Bay Buccaneers. The Buccaneers were claiming significant financial hardship and the need for a new stadium to be economically competitive with other NFL teams. Poe was able to show that at no time did any city official ever ask to see the Buccaneers' financial statements to ensure that the team owner was telling the truth (Henderson, 1996).

Projects such as the Louisiana Superdome, Arrowhead Pond (now Honda Center), United Center, the Rose Garden, Texas Motor Speedway, and Busch Stadium rely on various funding techniques ranging from private contributions to **municipal bonds**. Municipal notes and bonds are publicly traded securities that have the benefit of not having to comply with all the registration requirements that other publicly traded securities do (Greenberg & Gray, 1996). Chapter 10 covers several types of municipal bonds including general obligation, special tax, revenue, and lease-backed financing bonds, as well as certificates of participation. Municipal bonds use public funds to help build new facilities. For example, by negotiating a strong agreement that requires the municipality to pay the bulk of the costs, the team interested in playing in the facility can preserve its capital and increase its revenue stream. Because of the tough economic environment since 2008, voters have not been as willing to subsidize new projects requiring public funds. In 2011 the New York Islanders attempted to persuade voters to approve a $400 million hockey arena and minor league baseball park. Placed in a special election as the only item on the ballot, the election itself cost taxpayers $2 million. Approximately 56% of the voters voted against the referendum, and the team is threatening to leave when its lease expires in 2015 (Tkach, 2011, August 1).

Besides considering municipal bonds, facilities and various government entities can examine other critical financing issues such as the tax status of the bond interest income (taxable or tax exempt), the credit strength of the bond-issuing entity, and the collateral or security that would be used to secure the bonds. All these concerns come into play when the final financing package for the facility is being negotiated. Negotiations are an opportunity to design a creative comprehensive financing package containing any necessary bells and whistles to encourage all parties to commit to the project. The following examples point to the economic and financing backdrop behind several stadium or arena deals.

Louisiana Superdome

In *The Sports Stadium as a Municipal Investment* (1994), Dean Baim highlighted several unique stadium deals, including the Louisiana Superdome deal. In 1966 Louisiana voters approved the state constitutional amendment that formed the Louisiana Superdome Authority and allowed the state to borrow $35 million for the project. The facility was completed at a cost of $125 million. The original bond issue was to be backed by a 4% hotel and motel occupancy tax. The full faith and credit of the state of Louisiana were to be excluded from backing the bond offering. Because the costs far exceeded the initial $35 million price tag, the state agreed to lease the stadium at an annual rent equal to the shortfall experienced by the authority for servicing the facility's debt obligation. Thus, the state's credit was not used to secure the debt obligation (Baim, 1994).

Chase Manhattan Bank led a syndicate prepared to underwrite the Superdome's bonds, but the syndicate collapsed when a gubernatorial candidate threatened to derail the project if he was elected. This pressure led to collaboration between a local banker and an Arkansas bank to sell the $113 million in bonds needed to start construction (Baim, 1994).

To become successful (self-sufficient) economically, the Superdome needed to earn between $26,000 and $35,000 in daily rental income (Baim, 1994). This number was projected even before any tenants were being considered for the facility. Thus, Louisiana was hoping for a dream to come true—"If you build it, they will come." Louisiana is not alone. Stadium and arena projects are routinely passed even if no host tenants exist or the facility cannot cover its own debt obligations after the proj-

ect has been completed (Andelman, 1993). Opponents of a San Diego facility referendum explicitly projected that the stadium could not pay for itself, yet the measure passed with 72% of the votes (Baim, 1994). Such possibly foolish investments in a losing venture are made not strictly for financial reasons but for the prospect of economic growth, urban revitalization, or possibly improved quality of life in the area. The value of the investment in Louisiana was called into question after Hurricane Katrina caused significant damage to the dome. Through hard work and a significant investment of time and money, the Superdome was fixed and was used by the New Orleans Saints for the 2006 football season.

Arrowhead Pond of Anaheim

Located in the heart of southern California, Arrowhead Pond of Anaheim (now the Honda Center) is a 650,000-square-foot (60,000 sq m) arena that serves as home to the NHL Ducks. Arrowhead Pond was constructed through a comprehensive financing package involving several parties. The city of Anaheim issued $103 million in a certificate of participation bond. This bond was guaranteed by a **letter of credit** from Ogden Facility Management. Because the city of Anaheim was not forced to underwrite the bond with its own security, it repaid Ogden by giving the company the exclusive right to manage the arena for 30 years. Ogden also receives a management fee and could have earned between 75% and 85% of all yearly profits from the facility (Greenberg & Gray, 1996), but filed for bankruptcy in 2002.

United Center

The Chicago Bulls and Blackhawks play in the United Center, built in 1994 at a cost of $175 million; 80% of the financing was from private bank loans, and 20% was from the building owners. The entire project was privately funded by the United Center Joint Venture, which is headed by William Wirtz (owner of the Blackhawks) and Jerry Reinsdorf (majority owner and team chairman of the Bulls) (*Building information*, 2001). United Airlines pays $1.8 million each year for naming rights (Rogus, 1997). The original Chicago Stadium, which housed the Bulls and Blackhawks for years, was built for $7 million in 1926. The new center is almost four times the size of the first stadium, and its average electric bill is $155,000 each month (*Building information*, 2001).

Rose Garden

The Rose Garden in Portland is a 785,000-square-foot (73,000 sq m) facility that hosts a range of events from NBA and WNBA games, college basketball, and professional hockey to concerts, rodeos, ice shows, and monster truck rallies. In a complex blend of private and public funding, the Rose Garden was built with the help of Portland Trailblazers owner Paul Allen, who contributed $46 million in cash. Three major banks loaned a total of $16 million to the pot. Last, nine insurance companies purchased $155 million in privately placed bonds, paying 8.99% interest over 27 years (Greenberg & Gray, 1996). The city of Portland paid $34.5 million for street, parking, and other improvements. These city-funded projects will be paid for by a ticket tax of 6.5%, which will pay off the city's contribution in 6 years and thereafter provide Portland with a perpetual return on its investment (Greenberg & Gray, 1996).

Texas Motor Speedway

Stadiums and arenas for professional sports teams are not the only facilities currently being built. Several companies with nationally traded stock are developing and building racetracks throughout the United States. The largest such track to date is the Texas Motor Speedway. The speedway was paid for by Speedway Motorsports but received significant government assistance (e.g., the city of Fort Worth spent $7 million on road improvements and $4 million for water and sewer improvements, and the county threw in $5 million for road improvements). The facility can hold more than 250,000 spectators for a race.

Before the speedway was built, economists pegged the potential economic spending impact at between $11 and $200 million annually for only several events each year (Moffeit, 1999). The potential economic impact to the region was greatly reduced by a sweetheart deal in which the owners would not have to pay any city or county property taxes for 30 years—a benefit valued at over $100 million. Thus, although the city and county would generate some economic benefits from events, the city and county also lost a significant amount of tax revenue from the sweetheart deal. Each year the city captures approximately $700,000 in speedway-related tax revenue. Because the speedway opened in 1997, the figures are fairly new. But the initial numbers indicate that the $700,000 in added tax revenue represented 10% of the city's sales tax revenue in 1998. Furthermore, the speedway helped increase motel and hotel tax revenue by 20% in 1997. A unique aspect of the racetrack is that condominiums and Speedway Club towers have been built on the property, and all the condominiums are already sold. The facilities and track were projected to contribute 400 full-time jobs to the local economy year round and 5,000 part-time jobs during race week (Moffeit, 1999), but these estimates were very high.

Busch Stadium

The St. Louis Cardinals played in the old Busch Stadium through the 2005 season and ended the facility's remarkable history in the playoffs. In January 2004 groundbreaking began for the new Busch Stadium. It was completed in two years and held its first game in April 2006. The Stadium was financed through private bonds, bank loans, a long-term loan from St. Louis County, and money from the team owners. The development, including Ballpark Village, was estimated to cost $646 million, and the stadium alone cost $346 million. In 2006 every game sold out, giving a total attendance of 3,407,104 for the season, the second largest in team history (*New ballpark for Missouri*, 2007). As part of the negotiation process with the city and state, the Cardinals agreed to donate more than 100,000 tickets each season to community groups, and the team capped the price of 6,000 seats to a 2002-adjusted $12 per ticket to make sure that affordable seats would be available.

The new Busch Stadium was designed by HOK Sports and built by Hunt Construction, both internationally known for their work with stadiums and arenas. The facility was constructed in three stages; part of the stadium was built and then the old structure was demolished before the new stadium was completed. Because the facilities were so close to one another, implosion (using explosives to make the building cave in on itself) of the old stadium was not an option; the crew had to spend a month tearing it down with a wrecking ball. Directly north of the stadium, the team plans to build Ballpark Village, which will contain residential space, commercial space, a hall of fame, and an aquarium. It was finally approved in 2012 and the first phase should open in 2014.

Gillette Stadium and Patriot Place

Not all stadium construction projects require a complex funding scheme. Some of the most successful stadium projects involve one primary funding source. Robert Kraft borrowed $452 million to help build Gillette Stadium, which opened in 2002. This loan required annual debt payments of $20 million a year. Kraft at the time was only the third NFL owner to pay for his own facility. The new stadium was slated to generate $40 million per year just from sponsorship and premium seating revenue. Massachusetts taxpayers paid $72 million for infrastructure improvements and road construction around Gillette Stadium (Copeland, 2004).

The key to the success of the stadium, besides having a winning team when it opened, has been Patriot Place, an 800-acre (325 ha) complex surrounding the stadium and also privately owned by Mr. Kraft. The land was next to the old Foxboro Stadium and was already owned by Mr. Kraft when he was exploring options to move the team south of Boston or even to Connecticut. The complex includes large stores, restaurants, theaters, night clubs, and a host of retail opportunities. Patriot Place has become the ultimate destination location where people want to go to see and be seen. Thus, it made sense for Mr. Kraft to build and finance the project so that he could control his ultimate vision, assume the potential risks of the project, and reap the rewards when it paid off.

CONCLUSION

The examples presented in this chapter demonstrate the breadth of financial issues that can affect a sports administrator. Issues not yet touched on include Title IX compliance for high school and college athletic programs, fund-raising for youth sports, ways that a sporting goods company might issue stock to gain critical expansion funds, and countless others. These topics indicate the wide range of issues that intertwine sport and finance.

Financial concerns permeate every decision made in the sport industry. Even a decision that might seem innocuous from a financial standpoint, such as whether to play a given athlete, presents critical financial considerations. Any time a baseball player performs, he may draw additional fans, may foul off a significant number of pitches that can give rise to more commercial break opportunities, or may get a hit that qualifies him for a financial benefit. If the player is injured, the team can lose revenue, face higher workers' compensation premiums, and incur higher rehabilitation-related costs. Thus, every decision in sport can represent a potential financial impact.

Class Discussion Topics

1. How many pairs of sports or athletic shoes do you own? What are the brands? Did you buy the shoes? How much did you pay? What is your most expensive model? Why is this important for sport finance?

2. Did you attend a professional sports event within the last year? Where did you go? Did you buy the tickets? How much did you pay? Did you buy any concession items? What items did you buy? How much did you pay? Is price a factor in your purchase decisions as they relate to sport?

3. Have you ever developed a budget? What have you developed a budget for, and did you follow it? If you were able to follow the budget, did you meet your financial goals? If you did not follow the budget, what influenced you not to stick to your plan?

4. What problems might affect your ability to balance a checkbook?

5. Have you ever set up a bank account? What steps were involved?

6. Have you ever borrowed money? What was that experience like? Were you able to pay everything back that you owed?

(continued)

7. If you had lots of money and wanted to invest in a sport, which sports team or event would you buy or sponsor? Why? If you did not have much money, would you make a sport-related investment or take a more traditional approach, such as banks or the stocks of large corporations?

8. Do you think that building new stadiums or arenas is a wise investment? Back your answer with some analysis of the economic justification as well as the financial justification.

9. Identify 10 reasons why a larger corporation would want to put its name on the outside of a large stadium or arena. What are 10 reasons against such an investment?

10. Do you think that there are too many sports teams or events? Does a large number of teams and events hurt the industry by diluting the market?

chapter 2

Basic Financial Concepts

Chapter Objectives

After studying this chapter, you should be able to do the following:

- Understand where revenue comes from for sport enterprises.
- Appreciate all the various expenses that affect a sport enterprise.
- Distinguish between revenue and expenses.
- Describe the difference between finance and accounting.
- Understand the objectives of an accounting system.
- Understand the basics of T-accounts and general data-entry techniques.
- Understand the difference between cash and accrual accounting systems.
- Explain the need for accuracy in accounting and financial data.
- Explain the importance of audited financial statements.
- Appreciate the difference between sport finance and sport economics.

Chapter 2 deals with the key to financial understanding—revenue and expenses. All businesses revolve around money. Money is needed to pay bills, pay employees, order items, sell items, pay taxes, or borrow money, just as some examples. The question becomes where the money comes from, where it goes, how to track it, and why the economy functions in a given manner. This chapter investigates these issues by first examining revenue and expenses for various sports organizations. The chapter then examines the role that accounting plays in identifying and tracking revenue and expenses. The chapter ends with an analysis of sport economics and the ways in which actions by various stakeholders can affect the financial decisions reached by a sports organization.

DERIVING FULL VALUE OF SPONSORSHIP INCOME PROJECTIONS

Brian Foote, The Wilkinson Group

My name is Brian Foote, and I am the senior vice president of sales and marketing for the Wilkinson Group (TWG). During the last decade, TWG has delivered pro forma budgets and sponsorship planning for stadiums, arenas, and events, such as AT&T Park, Pepsi Save Mart Center, Cisco Field, Wells Fargo Pavilion, Brita Coastal Clean-Up, San Jose Grand Prix, Cisco Net Aid, the Got Milk? Gravity Tour, and the WOWIO College Tour.

During that time, we have had to structure a number of different sponsorship architectures to account for the front-end financial obligations and expected revenue generated by these projects.

Sample Sponsorship Income Pro Forma

I have provided some of the program elements that we consider in order to derive full value of sponsorship income projections over the life of a property or event.

In the sample scenario let's say that we were providing an annual sponsorship forecast plan for an event like Xterra or Tough Mudder, which provided outdoor adventure racing fun in locations across the United States over the course of the 2012 calendar year. The expected sponsorship income was over $1 million.

Sponsorship Categories

- Naming rights and title sponsorship ($500,000)
- Presenting sponsor ($250,000)
- Pouring rights ($150,000)
- Two category sponsorships ($75,000 each)
- Product placement ($50,000)
- Ticket-back sponsorship ($25,000)
- Promotions sponsor ($25,000 plus product)
- Four hospitality packages ($10,000 each)
- Product placement ($10,000)

Sponsorship Pricing

Pricing the expected sponsorship value within a project's pro forma is always challenging and often changes as an event becomes closer to reality. Impressions are a huge part of the calculation for sponsor–buyers to justify their expenditure as well as any pull-through on product sales (ROI) or retail integration that is vital for proving the value of the investment.

Valuation Anchors Your Projections

The process of determining value is often intensive, especially with naming-rights valuations on properties of $1 million or more per year. I have prepared reports at TWG often running upward of 100 pages to defend the rationale of pricing calculations within a pro forma budget. Thus, I have to be able to show the value so that others can make informed decisions based on objective facts rather than subjective opinions.

Calculating Your Valuation

You should consider several fundamental calculation elements in the financial planning of your facilities project or event as it pertains to sponsorship budgets:

- Continents and countries
- Regional or designated market areas
- Media impressions (traditional, digital, social, commercials, live mentions)
- Digital and fixed signage impressions
- Expected audience attendance and ticket sales
- Tickets, hospitality, and client entertainment packages
- On-site transaction opportunities (pouring rights, financial services)
- Meet and greet opportunities (celebrity, athlete, executive)
- Media appearances ("Present the check")
- Public relations value
- Celebrity endorsement
- Community marketing
- Product integration
- Mobile engagement
- Promotions and giveaways

Measuring Return on Investment (ROI)

In general, a good sponsorship program is forecasted in the realities of the measurable return on investment (ROI) that it can drive for its participating corporations and the return on experience that those sponsorships derive for attendees. My advice to both property owner and sponsor clients is that if you give customers personalized value and experience, they will reward you with their business.

Accounting for Activation Costs

Remember that in sports sponsorship (as with trade shows, conferences, and events), the sponsor needs to think through additional costs to make sure that they can activate their sponsorship properly and derive its full value.

For example, if the sponsor is handing out branded, reusable athletic bags and a water bottle to "green your event" rather than using plastic bags and cups, remember that they will need to account for the layout, printing, and production of their branded bags and water bottles, in addition to their sponsorship fees in your pro forma. These costs could increase significantly over the life of a sponsorship and even cost more than the value of the sponsorship. Anyone who sells sponsorships needs to know the potential revenue and expenses associated with the complete sponsorship strategy rather than just one segment of the sponsorship.

REVENUES AND EXPENSES

We all have bills to pay. We also normally have a source of funds, whether from a job, loans, or family. This section highlights how we make and spend money in the sport business. **Revenues** represent money coming into a sport business. Revenue can come from ticket sales, broadcast contracts, concession sales, sponsorship agreements, and a host of other opportunities. The opposite of revenues is expenses. **Expenses** are costs that are incurred. Typical expenses for a professional team include player salaries, equipment, travel, executive salaries, and other expenses ranging from rent to insurance premiums. Each business has different revenues and expenses, and they are constantly changing. A health club might have revenues of $1 million one year, but if 100 members do not renew their memberships, the revenues can plunge. Similarly, if members owe the club money, the club has **credit** in money owed. On the flip side, if the club does not pay its employees then it owes money, which is a debt. If you have ever spent more than you could afford on a credit card, your expenses might spiral out of control and create debt. **Debt** is the owing of money to others. If you pay all your expenses as they arise, you can avoid debt.

The following example presents the revenues and expenses of a typical public high school athletic program:

Revenues	Expenses
Local and city school taxes	Facility repair and maintenance costs
Federal tax subsidies for education	Uniform and equipment costs
State taxes	Travel and lodging costs
Participation fees	Insurance costs
Donations	Umpire costs
Booster clubs	Utility costs
Concession revenue	Salaries and benefits
Attendance revenue	Advertising costs
Broadcasting revenue	Promotional costs
Advertising revenue	Office supplies
Fund-raising efforts	
Licensing revenue	
Sponsorship revenue	

Balancing Revenue and Expenses

Understanding revenue and expenses is critical because a sports organization will constantly work to balance its revenue and expenses to keep operating. If revenues decline an organization will either have to find new revenue sources or have to slash expenditures. For a multitude of reasons, many revenue-generating techniques do not work in a given community. Parents may not want to support a program. Local advertisers may be unwilling to spend their advertising dollars on the school. City regulations may prohibit using certain fund-raising techniques. Although the revenue-generating options may be limited, the expenses normally do not share the same fate. Expenses were outpacing revenues by such a large amount in the 1990s that some schools started charging students for each sport that they played; canceling busing to road games; and eliminating sports such as golf, water polo, and junior varsity sports (Chi, 1992). This trend continued into the next century as more schools charged athletes or eliminated sports altogether. The sport most affected by rising expenses is ice hockey, which can cost high school athletes and their parents thousands of dollars. By 2011 a large number of high school athletic programs had been cut, had their funding significantly curtailed, or required parents to contribute an even greater percentage.

Colleges are also facing budget cuts. Given various concerns such as compliance with Title IX and the Americans with Disabilities Act, numerous collegiate athletic programs are facing difficult financial times. The problems are compounded by the fact that most Division I athletic programs operate at a deficit. At one point in the 1990s, the Illinois state legislature was even considering eliminating all state funds for intercollegiate athletics (Hiestand, 1992). Since the 1990s college sports have changed. Unfortunately, that change has not been in a positive financial direction. In 2009 only 14 of the 106 schools in the National Collegiate Athletic Association's (NCAA's) top division (Football Bowl Series, or FBS) made money, and the median loss was $10 million (Joyner, 2010). In 2010 the number of schools that were self-sufficient increased to 22. In 2010 only 58% of football programs at the highest level and 56% of men's basketball programs were self-sufficient (Phelps, 2011). Men's basketball programs have had more success at generating a profit because their expenses are much lower than those of football programs. The NCAA study showed that revenue had increased nearly 6% from 2008 to 2009, but during the same period expenses increased 11%. The average revenue of FBS schools was $32.3 million, and the average expenses were $45.9 million. The increase in expenses fueled a spate of conference realignments and even a new broadcast network as a means to increase revenue to keep pace with expenses. The revenue and expense problems in intercollegiate and interscholastic sports are not unique—the same concerns can affect any business.

Revenues and expenses are often similar for almost all industries. For example, all businesses, nonprofit organizations, and government entities have salary expenses and need to pay rent in some manner. The following items are typical revenues and expenses of a health club:

Revenues	Expenses
Membership fees	Employee salaries and benefits
Health food sales	Rent
Equipment sales	Equipment (purchases and leases)
Interest from investments	Insurance
	Advertising
	Professionals (accounting, legal)
	Maintenance and repair expenses
	Utility expenses
	General expenses

In professional or collegiate sports, revenues are derived primarily from ticket sales, broadcasting rights, or both, and the primary expenses are salaries and benefits (Howard & Crompton, 2004). Regardless of the team or league, every sports organization has the same basic revenue streams from the sale of goods or services and the same basic expenses of salaries, rent or mortgage, maintenance, advertising, raw goods, and various supplies. Any of these numbers can be large and may appear impressive. But after critically examining such numbers, anyone trained in financial analysis can see that many businesses with substantial revenue streams are not profitable. Many professional sports teams earn significant revenue from attendance and broadcast rights but fail to cover their fixed operating costs (Howard & Crompton, 2004). No business can survive a constant monetary wound that keeps bleeding. For that reason, many Canadian hockey teams have packed their bags or are considering packing their bags to move to greener pastures in the United States (Harper, 1999). By the 1996-1997 National Hockey League (NHL) season, only six clubs remained in Canada after teams left Winnipeg and Quebec City for the United States (Kowall, 2001). Teams were leaving Canada because of such economic hardships as high taxes (expenses), payment of players in American dollars (expenses), and the lower value of the Canadian dollar (revenues) (Harper, 1999). A reversal of fortune for Canadian hockey occurred in 2011 when an American team, the Atlanta Thrashers, moved to Canada to become the "new" Winnipeg Jets.

To have revenue, a team needs to play. With the NHL lockout in 2004-2005, teams were not able to generate revenue from games but could generate revenue from licensed goods. To reduce expenses, many NHL teams laid off most of their staffs, but this cutback does not change other fixed expenses such as interest on loans or accountant and attorney fees. The same situation occurred with the 2011 NFL lockout when many front office positions were not filled, and many league and front office positions were eliminated in anticipation of the 2011 NBA lockout.

Professional sport has changed drastically since the 1930s (see A Costly Rain Delay sidebar). Contractually obligated revenues such as broadcasting contracts and luxury box revenue have made the prospects for significant one-day losses highly unlikely. But sport has a way of producing strange results, and rain delays, freak injuries, and unexpected economic conditions can all affect a team's bottom line. The following paragraph appeared in the same 1936 article shown in A Costly Rain Delay sidebar:

> Last year the New York Yankees sent Ruth to the Boston Braves. It was soon apparent that they had made a big mistake, for their attendance fell off even though the team was leading the league. Ruth, despite the fact that he had slowed to a walk, was still a terrific drawing card in New York. When the Braves made their first 1935 appearance in Tammany Town, 42,000 fans turned out to cheer him. Ruth, with the Braves for less than half the season, made enough money for them in that short space of time to allow them to break even on the season despite the fact that they finished in last place. (Lewis, 1936)

The Babe Ruth case is not an isolated example of a financial blunder involving trading or releasing an athlete. In any given year, a player might be a low-level performer for one team but blossom for another. Conversely, a player can be a star one day and washed up the next. Thus, the business of managing sports teams, organizations, or facilities includes both potential profit centers and traps that can lead to financial ruin. The convergence of numerous variables that can increase or decrease revenue in a moment makes sport management traditionally more complex than financing in other business sectors. But by analyzing a company's financial objectives, sport finance students can often determine that a short-term loss might be beneficial for generating larger profits in the long run. Financial objectives are often found in financial **disclosure** documents required by federal regulators. For example, Nike's financial objectives are included in its **Form 10-K** annual report. The company's annual 10-K and quarterly **Form 10-Q** reports are filed with the Securities and Exchange Commission (SEC) as required by law. The reports can be accessed from numerous financial websites, including the SEC's own website at www.sec.gov.

By seeing how revenues and expenses change over time, students can learn much about an industry. For example, in the 1930s professional sport was not as popular as it is today, and teams had to promote themselves constantly. For that reason, the team income statement shows $38,400 to pay the travel expenses of 12 newspaper

A COSTLY RAIN DELAY

An example of a team's revenue and expenses gives an idea of the potential monetary gains and losses that may be present in professional sport.

Although it does not appear that the team's economic condition is all that bad, the revenue, expenses, and pretax profits can swing sharply at any given moment. The numbers shown are not hypothetical; rather, they are the actual revenue and expense numbers for a professional team in 1935. The numbers appeared in an article by a professional team owner who was highlighting the potential perils associated with a team's bottom line. The writer also recounted how in 1934 another team, the New York Giants, had been within a game of first place and had been scheduled to play a doubleheader against the Philadelphia Phillies. A capacity crowd of 50,000 was expected for the games. But a drizzle began to fall, resulting in postponement. When the games were later replayed, the Giants were already out of the pennant picture, and a crowd of only 2,000 attended the doubleheader. Because of the rain delay, the Giants lost more than $55,000 (Lewis, 1936).

Professional Baseball Team × Income Statement

REVENUES ($)	
Baseball attendance revenue	650,000
Revenue from facility rental	60,000
Revenue from concessions	35,000
Total revenue	$745,000
EXPENSES ($)	
Players' salaries (35 players)	235,000
Price for new players	90,000
Transportation bills	15,000
Hotel bills	15,000
Rental expenses and salaries	85,000
Maintenance costs	20,000
Spring training costs	25,000
Players' supplies	11,000
Insurance costs	12,000
Salaries and expenses for 3 scouts	20,000
Expenses for 12 newspapermen	38,400
Sundries	11,600
Total expenses	$578,000
Profit before taxes	$167,000

Data from Lewis 1936.

reporters (see A Costly Rain Delay). Because the team was paying the way for the reporters, they were less likely to write negative stories. The resulting positive publicity was designed to help sell more tickets. Teams no longer have to pay reporters to travel to cover them, but they still need to include a line item in their budgets (see chapter 3) to pay for food that is given to reporters in the pressroom. The following section is a brief analysis of some of the cutting-edge revenue and expenses that can be found in sports organizations.

Revenue

Revenue can come from numerous sources as highlighted earlier. Some traditional sources include ticket sales, concession sales, broadcast revenue, and sponsorship sales. The 2008 Olympic Games in Beijing received 50% of its revenue from broadcasting rights, 40% from sponsorship, 8% from ticketing, and the remaining 2% primarily from licensing and other revenue sources (Kalwarski, 2008). Thus, although many people might think that the greatest revenue for Olympic

Games comes from ticket sales, the truth is that ticket sales make up less than 10% of Olympic revenue. Some of the less traditionally known sources of revenue include student fees, selling players, high schools' selling of licensed goods, and selling all-you-can-eat opportunities at the ballpark.

Student fees at many colleges, for example, can account for up to 24% of the required annual bill for in-state students. Student fees at 222 Division I public school totaled $795 million for the 2008-2009 academic year (Appenzeller, 2011). Many schools charge student fees that are relatively inexpensive, but at least six schools, all from Virginia, charged their students over $1,000 a year in athletic fees in 2008-2009 (Berkowitz, Upton, McCarthy, & Gillum, 2010). The University of Iowa charged students $1,289 for student fees, but none of those fees went to support athletics. In contrast, Longwood charged its students $4,440 in student fees, including $2,022 in athletic fees (Berkowitz, Upton, McCarthy, & Gillum, 2010). In 2010 Rutgers University used nearly $27 million in university and student fees to balance its athletic budget ($64 million in expenses and revenue of only $37 million), and the budget required over $115 million in assistance from the university from 2006 through 2010 (Berkowitz & Upton, 2011). Rutgers was not alone; subsidies amounted to $1 for every $3 spent on Division I athletics. Other BCS schools that required significant institutional, government, or student support in 2009-2010 included the University of Connecticut ($14.5 million), University of South Florida ($14.1 million), University of Maryland ($13.7 million), and University of California, Berkley ($12 million) (Berkowitz & Upton, 2011). The significant need for student fees and government support encouraged the University of California, Berkley to eliminate certain sports unless they found their own source of funding.

Many administrators of high school programs, which have already tried using fees to help balance their budgets, have used financial planning to focus on where they can generate additional revenue. The Licensing Resource Group (LRG) has signed over 7,000 high schools and was expected to add more than half of the 27,000 high schools in the United States. The program places school-licensed goods in national outlets such as Wal-Mart and Kohl's (Halley, 2010). The program was designed to tap into the 7.5 million high school athletes and their followers who might want to buy athletic-related apparel. Estimates are that schools in the program would generate between $30 and several thousand dollars. The prospect of competing against high school logos for shelf space caused a rash of letters from prominent college programs to high schools demanding that they stop using logos that could impede on the copyrights owned by college programs (Halley, 2010).

Financial planning applies not only to high schools and colleges but to every sports organization. The higher the stakes are, such as those that surround billion-dollar professional teams, the greater the need is for financial planning. Real Madrid increased its net profit a whopping 31.7% in 2010-2011 to €31.6 million on revenue of €480.2 million. This sum is the largest revenue obtained by any sports organization in the world (Cutler, 2011, September 19). This revenue did not take into account the transfer of players. Internationally, soccer players are bought and sold by teams on a regular basis. Real Madrid went on a spending spree in 2009 when they purchased Ronaldo from Manchester United for €93.9 million. They also bought another player, Kaka, from AC Milan for €68.4 million.

Financial planning can address immediate issues that affect the bottom line or the development of long-term strategies. Spurred by a major decline in spring-training attendance (12% decline in 2009), several MLB teams developed innovative strategies to sell more tickets. For example, the Toronto Blue Jays sold tickets for a little over $1 per game when fans bought a $95 pass for 81 games (Nightengale & McCarthy, 2009). Teams developed other innovative strategies such as allowing fans to bring in their own food and offering all-you-can-eat discount programs. The Los Angeles Dodgers developed an all-you-can-eat section for the rarely full right-field seating section. For $35 ($40 on game day) around 3,000 fans can get unlimited Dodger Dogs, nachos, peanuts, popcorn, and soft drinks to enjoy during the game. The profitable beer, ice cream, and candy products were not included in the package. These seats became much more popular than the left-field seats, which sold for $10 without any food.

Expenses

Although numerous revenue sources are available and the opportunity is always present to develop new ones, certain fixed expenses will normally exist regardless of where new revenue might come from. Coaching contracts, electrical bills, travel expenses, equipment costs, and numerous other expenses occur on a regular basis. Because most expenses occur on a monthly or other periodic basis, a sports organization can normally predict future expenses. Because of their predictability, expenses can be monitored and, when feasible, reduced. Numerous sports organizations started doing just that in various harsh economic climates. Actions to reduce expenses included terminating coaches, reducing coaching contracts (from 12 month to 10 months), limiting facility usage hours, reducing travel costs, and eliminating paper usage.

One of the greatest expenses for any sports organization is personnel costs. The cost for employees from coaches to custodians adds a significant amount to the bottom line cost for any sports organization. College coaches at the highest level can earn over $4 million dollars a year. Although many might question such expenditures, some coaches have proven their worth. Nick Saban was paid $4 million a year when he signed on as the coach of Alabama's famed football team in 2007. When Saban arrived, the athletic department posted a

$10.5 million profit, which shot up to $22 million in 2009 (Wieberg, 2010).

Player costs are the primary expense for professional teams. The Green Bay Packers of the NFL are a publicly traded sport company, so their financial information is open for review. The team had a profit of $20.1 million in 2009 and $9.8 million the next year. Part of the decline in profit could be attributed to player costs, which increased from $139 million to $161 million. Player costs had been increasing 11% a year from 2006 through 2010, whereas revenue had increased only 5.5% annually ("Packers say player costs cut into profits," 2010).

Although personnel costs are a critical component of any sports organization's bottom line, all expenses need to be examined. The adage is that it costs money to make money, and this belief can be seen in the cost to raise money through sporting events. Walk-a-thons and other sport-based fund-raising events can raise a lot of money, but they also can cost a lot. Walk-a-thons typically cost 50 cents on the dollar compared with the average fund-raising cost of 15 to 20 cents per dollar for other nonprofit fund-raisers. Thus, for every dollar a walk-a-thon raises, it spends about 50 cents to raise those funds. Expenses include event producers, consultants, trade shows, technology vendors, caterers, printers, and other fund-raising costs. A more precise breakdown for a typical one-day fun run could include runner supplies (19%), furniture (16%, including tents, rental toilets, and signage), security and safety (15%), and fund-raising commissions (2%). The remaining 48% would be the net proceeds to the charity (Kadet, 2011).

college teams spent a huge amount on lodging for players at hotels, for home games, to avoid noise and distractions. North Carolina State University paid over $85,000, the University of North Carolina Chapel Hill spent over $78,000, and Clemson University spent over $110,000 (Appenzeller, 2011).

OVERVIEW OF ACCOUNTING CONCEPTS

Revenue and expenses are numbers. They are not abstract ideas. Thus, a million dollars in a sponsorship deal needs to be documented somewhere. Finance and financial management cannot be understood without knowing basic accounting concepts. Accounting is the art of processing the revenue and expense numbers to develop appropriate reporting procedures upon which financial decisions are made. Accounting issues we touch on in this chapter are basic T-accounts, the way in which cash is received and processed within a business, and methods by which businesses make sure that the numbers that managers rely on are correct. Understanding a balance sheet or income statement is impossible without knowing how the numbers were obtained. This section presents some of the basic accounting concepts that you will need to know after you start analyzing comprehensive financial records.

Accounting requires the identification, measurement, recording, and communication of financial information associated with various critical events. A high school might be required to engage in statistical accounting to track students or supplies and might have to engage in financial accounting to track revenues and expenses (Horine, 1999). This text overviews financial accounting and the methods that a sport business manager might use to track revenues coming into the business and expenses flowing out of the business. Although keeping track of the number of towels used at a health club might seem a simple task, financial accounting can be difficult and complex.

Accountants must track all the money that is owed to countless vendors, employees, or even the government. Overall, accounting is a complex art and science that tracks revenues and expenses from numerous areas to provide an accurate record of a business' financial position. The recent focus on *"Moneyball"* and analytics shows the value of critical numerical analysis in sports. By critically breaking down the numbers, sports executives can more appropriately compare numerous elements such as one type of player versus another player to determine whether the player is a good investment. Mariano Rivera's $15 million contract in 2010 could be looked at as one large expense for the New York Yankees, and the financial analysis for the team would focus on the value of the contract. In contrast, the accounting analysis for his performance could be broken down to $16,164 per pitch, $333,333 per strikeout, and $65,217 per batter faced (Lowenstein, 2011).

The objective of accounting for any organization is to provide information for the following purposes (Freeman, Shoulders, & Lynn, 1988, p. 6):

- Making decisions about the use of limited resources, including the identification of crucial decision areas and determination of objectives and goals
- Effectively directing and controlling an organization's human and material resources
- Maintaining and reporting on the custodianship of resources
- Contributing to the overall effectiveness of the organization

Financial accounting is one side of the accounting process. Financial accounting focuses more on tracking numbers while managerial accounting focuses on planning for the future, similar to finance. In fact, managerial accounting provides financial managers with the tools to help plan for the future. Managerial accounting provides economic and financial information for managers and includes activities such as the following:

- Explaining manufacturing and nonmanufacturing costs and the way in which they should be reported on financial statements
- Computing the cost of providing a good or service
- Determining how costs change based on activity level such as the cost for producing 100 units compared with 1,000 units or a million units
- Understanding and evaluating how well an organization is utilizing its resources
- Creating a means to evaluate actual results compared with projected results (Weygandt, Kieso, & Kimmel, 2005)

CONCEPTS INTO PRACTICE

Suppose that a fitness center has 2,000 members who pay at different times during the month, or possibly not at all. Some members may have the funds electronically removed from their bank accounts. Others may pay with their credit cards, in which case the health club has to process and track all the credit card transactions and then pay the credit card companies a small percentage of the amount charged. Other members may pay with cash or checks, pay late and need to pay a late fee, or demand a refund.

With all the cash, checks, and credit card transactions, money can be easily lost or stolen. To avoid such a problem, the center owners can develop policies and procedures to monitor revenues and minimize losses. They could develop a policy that one person receives the payments, another enters the material into the accounting software system, and a third deposits the payments at the bank. With three people handling the revenue, one cannot easily steal money without the others finding out. But such a system increases overhead because more employees are involved in the process. The flip side is that the cost will likely be offset by the benefit of avoiding significant employee theft. The owner could also hire an accountant to review all the financial records at the end of the year to verify their accuracy.

The primary difference between managerial and financial accounting include the following:

- The primary user of reports produced by the managerial accounting process are internal users (officers and managers), whereas financial accounting reports are used primarily by stockholders, creditors, and regulators.
- Managerial accounting reports are not audited, whereas financial accounting reports are audits by certified public accountants.
- Managerial accounting reports are detailed and often have a focus on business subunits (such as concession sales for a team), whereas financial accounting reports focus on the entire organization, are not as detailed, and follow generally accepted accounting principles for validity (Weygandt, Kieso, & Kimmel, 2005).

Finance emphasizes recording, monitoring, and controlling the financial consequences of various activities and analyzing the need for additional funds to meet current and future demands (Spiro, 1996). These tasks cannot be completed without economic analysis and the data system that has been developed through accounting. Accounting is often performed by a **controller** who is responsible for documenting what happened, not what should have happened. Thus, the focus is on accuracy as dictated by industry-defined rules. **Managerial accounting** is the process used to develop financial forecasts and monitor various budgets and costing models (Spiro, 1996). The output produced by the controller provides the opportunity for a company to open the lines of communication among different divisions or echelons to help achieve the company's goals and objectives. Through managerial accounting, the controller can produce data designed to facilitate internal success, but the same data can be used for external needs, such as shareholder relations.

In contrast to the responsibilities of a controller and the managerial accounting process, a **treasurer** has distinct responsibilities that focus mostly on external factors. Thus, although the controller manages internal financial and accounting-based concerns, the treasurer deals with banks, stockholders, institutional investors, bondholders, and other stakeholders or potential stakeholders. The information developed through the accounting process assists the treasurer in obtaining additional funds to help achieve business goals and objectives.

The accounting objectives just identified are highlighted in detail by Larry Horine of Appalachian State University in his book *Administration of Physical Education and Sport Programs*. Horine (1999) highlights 12 important objectives for a sports organization's accounting system:

1. The data should be collected to help plan for the program's future.
2. The financial records must be kept in an orderly manner.
3. An orderly and professional accounting method must be implemented to track authorized expenditures.
4. Appropriate forms must be prepared to help standardize and create a definite paper trail for receipts and expenditures.
5. A system or process needs to be developed and implemented to coordinate the receipt of goods and services and to ensure that all such goods and services meet required standards before any final payments on the goods or services are made.

6. Transactions need to be documented in such a way that an independent auditor can examine the transactions and determine to whom money was paid and for what purpose.

7. Revenue must be tracked to determine if fiscal obligations can be paid. Tracking should determine what funds were obtained, from whom, and for what purpose.

8. Special funds need to be accounted for in a separate accounting manner to track such items as planned giving and major gifts, which are nontraditional revenue sources.

9. All information documented through the accounting process needs to be prepared in such a way that an external reviewer can adequately audit all accounts.

10. Any accounting system must be adequate to meet the organization's needs, with special consideration for size and complexity.

11. Any accounting system must meet all state, federal, regional, and association standards and guidelines.

12. Any accounting system must provide the opportunity to analyze management decisions and produce appropriate reports to evaluate past managerial decisions and pave the way for future decisions.

When we are analyzing accounting issues, understanding the difference between the concepts of stock and flow is imperative. **Stock** refers to wealth in a variety of forms such as cash, assets, real estate, and accounts receivable that are available at any specific point in time. In contrast, **flow** refers to expenditures or receipts between two specific points in time. These two concepts are associated with two of the most important types of documents produced through the accounting process. Stock is shown on a balance sheet that documents the value of a company at a specific time. An income statement, on the other hand, portrays the flow that has been occurring in a company throughout a specified business year. Every company needs to use both the stock concept and the flow concept to analyze its financial position.

To track revenues and expenses between balance sheet dates, accountants use their own unique systems. Accountants have developed the **T-system** to document monetary transactions. This text includes a brief discussion of T-accounts; students who take a course in accounting can spend several weeks on this topic. The discussion here is intended to overview the process through which the final total numbers used in financial state-ments are determined. For additional information on T-accounts, please refer to a basic accounting textbook.

Accountants refer to entries made on the right side of the T as **credits** and to entries on the left side of the T as **debits** (see figure 2.1a). Whereas people who are not accountants might interpret the terms *debit* and *credit* to mean specific activities, such as paying a bill or buying on credit, for the purpose of accounting these terms just refer to sides of the T where various transactions are recorded (Spiro, 1996). A company's balance sheet may provide the best example of the application of the T-system (see figure 2.1b). Corporate assets are listed on the left side (debits), and liabilities and **owners' equity** are listed on the right side (credits). In conventional usage of the terms, something that is owned by the business would be thought of as a credit to the bottom line, not a debit or reduction in the company's value. But in the T-system, when assets are added to the company's bottom line, the process is referred to as debiting that asset. Similarly, if liabilities are increased, then the specific liability account is credited. The confusion associated with accounting terms can be easily set aside if the terms are not the focal point of analysis; rather, the reader should just know that certain entries are placed on the right and others on the left side of the T.

Although the terminology might be confusing, the process is important and is universally used to document financial transactions.

Because multiple accounts are being changed, the process is often referred to as **double-entry bookkeeping**. Use of this technique, along with other accounting practices, must comply with generally accepted accounting practices to be accepted by the greatest number of potential readers, such as government officials, shareholders, and financial analysts. If troublesome questions arise regarding the documentation of more complex transactions, an accountant might refer to guidelines called **generally accepted accounting principles (GAAP)**, as interpreted by the Financial Accounting Standards Board (FASB) and the American Institute of Certified Public Accountants. FASB is mostly relevant to public companies.

T-account		Balance sheet	
Debits	Credits	Assets	Liabilities
			Owners' equity
a		*b*	

Figure 2.1 *(a)* A T-account and *(b)* the T-system applied to a company's balance sheet.

CONCEPTS INTO PRACTICE

Assume that a fitness center owner has two customers who owe money on their monthly dues. The T-accounts for customer A and customer B would show the monthly $100 fee added to accounts receivable for the business (see figure 2.2).

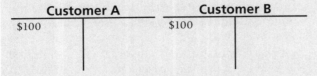

Customer A	Customer B
$100	$100

Figure 2.2 T-accounts for two fitness center customers who owe money on their monthly dues.

If these customers are the only two people who owe money, then the owners would have $200 debited to their accounts receivable account. Assume that the owners also have $10,000 in their cash account. Figure 2.3 shows how these two accounts would look.

Accounts receivable	Cash
$200	$10,000

Figure 2.3 T-accounts showing the fitness center's accounts receivable and cash accounts.

If customer B pays $50 toward his overdue **balance**, the following changes would need to be made to the T-accounts (see figure 2.4). Customer B's prior obligation of $100 has been reduced by the $50; the owners are now owed only $150 through accounts receivable and have gained $50 for their cash account.

Customer B		Accounts receivable		Cash	
$100	$50	$200	$200	$10,050	
				$50	

Customer B	Accounts receivable	Cash
$50	$150	$10,050

Figure 2.4 T-accounts reflecting customer B's $50 payment.

Cash Versus Accrual Basis

The scope of this text does not permit analysis of all accounting-related issues, but a key topic that requires discussion here is the method for reporting income. Although most business owners charged with keeping their own business records would record a cash receipt the day that they receive it and would record a payment the day that the bill is paid, this technique might not be correct. According to GAAP, revenues and expenses can be recorded either on a cash basis or on an **accrual** basis. The accrual basis is the preferred technique, but the cash method is allowed by GAAP under specific limited circumstances, such as when a business conducts all transactions with cash. In **cash basis budgeting**, income and expenses are recorded when cash is received or paid; sales made on credit or bills that are owed are not recorded until they are actually paid. This process is also referred to as the **cash system of accounting**. The accrual method recognizes revenues when they are earned and recognizes expenses when they are incurred. In other words, accrual-based reporting does not consider when money is received or paid, only when the act occurred that resulted in the revenue or expense. Normally GAAP requires the use of accrual accounting regardless of the size of the business. Only in rare circumstances when all transactions are in cash will GAAP allow a company to use the cash system of accounting. Thus, the fitness center owners would have to record income when lessons are given or memberships are due regardless of whether the customer has paid.

Art of Accounting

Many refer to accounting as an art rather than a science (Griffin, 1991). Although financial analysis cannot exist unless accounting systems have developed the appropriate numbers for analyzing past performance, there is never any guarantee that the numbers relied on are correct. Accounting produces financial statements consisting of numbers, but the numbers refer only to those components of a business that are quantifiable. Over the past several decades a new approach to managerial accounting has been the balanced scorecard approach, which examines numerical and subjective criteria to understand how an organization is doing. The balanced scorecard is a performance evaluation tool used to evaluate all aspects of a company's operation in an integrated fashion. Through taking a cause-and-effect approach, the balanced scorecard can help a business understand that every action has an effect and that without proper planning and acting across a company, the company would have a hard time meeting financial and other objectives.

Accounting systems also use professional judgments and estimates when absolute objective evidence does not exist (Griffin, 1991). Although such judgments are typically accurate, anyone reading financial statements has to assume that the information may include inaccuracies. There is never a sure bet in finance, and the best you can hope for from financial statements is an accurate portrait of a business based on data analyzed by an accountant—a human being who can also make errors.

Audited Financial Statements

Accountants can make errors; an auditor is often the last person who can possibly discover any discrepancies. This concern was highlighted in the multiple accounting scandals at companies such as Enron, WorldCom, Tyco, and Adelphia. The ease with which companies, executives, and accountants could manipulate company records encouraged Congress to pass the Sarbanes-Oxley Act of 2002, forcing executives of publicly traded companies to certify that all their financial data were accurate. Violators could face significant fines and even incarceration. Executives still need accountants to audit the numbers to ensure their accuracy. Most companies attempt to obtain an independent audit of the work performed by their accountants. Such an audit is often undertaken even if an external accounting firm was used to prepare the initial financial statements. An auditor uses the Statements on Auditing Standards issued by the Auditing Standards Board of the American Institute of Certified Public Accountants. These standards were developed to help ensure that audits are conducted in a systematic manner. After thoroughly analyzing all the financial statements, the auditor prepares a report that includes the following statements (Griffin, 1991):

- The auditor is independent from the company's management.
- The financial statements were audited.
- The financial statements are management's responsibility, and the auditor's role is to express an opinion on the financial statements.

After the audit is completed, the auditor prepares an opinion that addresses the fairness of the finan-

cial statements, the degree to which the financial statements comply with GAAP guidelines, and any noticeable changes in accounting principles from industry norms (Griffin, 1991). The final opinion reached by the auditor can be

- an unqualified opinion that the statements are accurate,
- a qualified opinion,
- an adverse opinion indicating that the statements do not conform with required principles, or
- a **disclaimer** indicating that the auditor was unable to complete the report because the company failed to provide certain data.

A typical unqualified opinion might include a statement such as the following:

> In our opinion, the financial statements above present fairly, in all material respects, the financial position of the team as of June 31, 2010, and the results of its operations and its cash flows for the year then ended in conformity with generally accepted accounting principles.

Auditing is covered in detail in chapter 15.

The accounting system objectives discussed in this section relate to what has already happened. Accounting statements are reviewed to determine what occurred during the designated period. But accounting does not indicate what should occur in the future. Budgeting is the process that can indicate what steps should be taken in the future. The budget sets the company's road map for the future and is based on the company's goals and objectives. Budgeting, which is covered in chapter 3, is the first step in the financial process after the accountants analyze past performance.

ECONOMIC VERSUS FINANCIAL ANALYSIS

One final note of importance to those starting to analyze the foundation of sport finance is that, as with accounting and finance, there is significant difference between finance and economics. Economics is the study of social, governmental, and numerous other factors that can influence the financial state of the sport industry, but economics is not sport finance. For example, economic analysis can highlight that the economy is in a tailspin or that that the oversupply of tickets will drive down the value of certain tickets. Such analysis would be important to help a sports organization make a decision. If too many outstanding tickets exist the sport organization will need to make a financial decision. For example, in the 2012 Olympics a number of events were poorly attended. The economic analysis might be that the tickets were too expensive for less popular events. The financial decision based on this oversupply would be to let people in for free, drop prices, or play in front of empty seats. Such a decision entails financial planning and examining the overall organizational goals. The British gave away tickets to off-duty soldiers and school children so they could still sell tickets to the general public. Such a strategy allows the organizers to look good, fill seats to make the event more enjoyable, and look better on TV. This shows how an economic issue can be translated into a financial decision.

The convergence of economic and financial analysis could be seen in the 2011 NFL lockout. The financial side of the equation would be the potential loss of revenue and the planning that organizations would do to adjust to the lost revenue. The economic impact was a much bigger issue because the running of a typical NFL season has significant ripple effects throughout the economy. Papa John's pizza chain sold over one million pizzas on the 2010 Super Bowl Sunday. Similarly, Buffalo Wild Wings had a 15% increase in weekly revenue during the NFL season compared with regular weeks (Weise, 2011). The prospect of a cancelled NFL season would mean a significant loss of revenue through numerous other industry segments that would normally not be affected by how a sports team or league acts. In fact, a typical NFL season generates around $12 billion in sales for ancillary activities such as betting, licensed goods, and even fantasy football leagues (Weise, 2011). The total "gross football product" from everything from naming rights and broadcasting rights to sponsorship and ticket sales was estimated in 2011 at $9.3 billion, which was almost as much as the combined financial impact of the other three major professional leagues (MLB $6-7 billion, NBA $3-4 billion, and the NHL $1 billion). The NFL does not publish statistics, but the Green Bay Packers cleared over $60 million in ticket and box revenue and $13 million from concession and parking revenue. When these numbers are spread across the 32-team league, the NFL generated nearly $2 billion in ticketing and box revenue and almost $500 million in concession and parking revenue. These numbers can be analyzed from a different

perspective in that 17 million fans attended NFL games in 2010 and paid from $54 to $117 per ticket (Burke, Hendrickson, & Roberts, 2011). Those numbers help show how powerful the NFL is and how it has the economic clout to dictate what other players in the sport field do. The NFL can dictate what broadcasters might do in the future to avoid losing NFL rights or to help gain such rights. Thus, although financial analysis might indicate whether a football team in the NFL would generate a profit, economic analysis would dictate how businesses and consumers would accept decisions made by NFL teams. Financial analysts might calculate that by raising ticket prices $1 in a given year a team might be able to generate an additional $800,000 in revenue. Economists, on the other hand, might look at the same price increase and explore the cost–benefit impact of such an action and the likelihood that the law of diminishing returns would indicate that the increased ticket prices would deter some buyers from purchasing tickets and in fact reduce future income. Of course, because of the high demand for particular teams or sports, certain economic analysis is of little value when the demand for a product is so great that the owner can keep raising prices because fans will accept those increases to maintain their affiliation with the team.

One example of how economic analysis is critical for financial decision making is the concept of elasticity of demand, which measures the degree to which a change in pricing affects the unit sales of a product. Thus, if ticket prices were increased $10 for a $100 ticket, the demand would be inelastic if such a change would not affect demand. If 1,000 fans purchased this ticket the prior year and 1,000 will purchase the ticket at the new price, the demand is inelastic. But if 500 fans refused to pay the increased price, the demand would be considered elastic.

Economic impact is a key focus of sport economics. Many people disapprove of public funding to build sport facilities. The argument raised by these people is that a private owner is gaining a benefit when public funds are used to build these facilities. Supporters of such projects point to the increased economic activities associated with building a sport facility. This analysis is sometimes focused on financial analysis and the ability of a given public entity to afford to build a facility. This analysis would examine the cost for issuing debt and the source of the money to pay back the debt. Economists can track whether such deals are a value for a community. The public has spent almost $7 billion of the $13.146 billion spent on NFL stadiums since 1990, which averages out to $250 million per stadium. These stadiums have a significant impact on their local communities. The stadiums employ almost 100,000 stadium workers, and local economic activity spurred by NFL games averaged $20 to $21 million per game in local economies, which totals about $160 million per market and a league-wide $5.1 billion impact on local businesses (Burke, Hendrickson, & Roberts, 2011). Thus, significant evidence shows that building an NFL stadium might not be a financially sound decision for a community, but it might make significant economic sense. The same analysis can be applied to college football games. An economic impact study of the University of Arizona football team showed that out-of-state fans spent $606.45 per person, whereas in-state fans spent only around $275 associated with the game. The estimated direct spending impact on Tucson from one game was $8.2 million and $37.5 million for the seven-game home schedule. Using an economic tool called a multiplier (which helps account for how money reverberates through a given community), the visitor spending had an economic impact of $61.6 million, which translated to 638.7 full-time annualized jobs (Witner, 2011).

The convergence of economics and finance can be seen in many examples when economic conditions might change and businesses need to use astute financial planning to remain financially sound. In 2011 the Bronx Parking Development Co. was facing a large $6.8 million interest payment on $237 million in tax-exempt bonds issued to fund construction of three parking facilities near the new Yankee Stadium. If they missed the payment they would default on the bonds, and the bondholders could possibly seize the 21 acres (8 ha) of buildings containing 9,000 parking spaces. The problem was that the $23 charge for parking in the garages scared many fans, and the garages never were more than 60% full on game days. Instead of parking in these garages, an estimated 800 cars a game parked at the local Gateway Shopping Center where parking cost $4 an hour. The Bronx Parking Development Co. was also affected by the increase in fans taking the train to the stadium (Potkewitz, 2011). The parking lot operator had a financial plan under which they would be able to generate a profit, but the economic realities of fans' efforts to save money by taking the train or parking farther away at a cheaper price affected those financial plans.

CONCLUSION

This chapter provided an initial glimpse into the variety of revenues and expenses that sports organizations can encounter. The chapter then examined sport accounting as a means to determine where money is going or coming. By using standardized methods all parties can hope to have accurate information on which to base financial decisions. Sport finance is separate and distinct from sport economics, but the two intersect when planning and evaluating plans to make sure that projections will occur. Sport finance is a numbers game. Numerous revenues and expenses constitute the game pieces. Profits and losses are highlighted in the outcome of the game. Through adherence to basic accounting protocol, the finance game is played with a host of additional rules such as tax considerations and stock regulations that affect a sport entity's movements in the game. By understanding all the necessary moves and the various strategies available to the contestants, a sports organization can win the game.

Although this game metaphor may appear contrived, it represents a reality in sport finance. Sport finance is as much a game as the games played on athletic fields or courts. Sport finance professionals need to play a heads-up game to take advantage of various laws, economic conditions, or other variables to maximize value. Through intelligent financial manipulations, a skilled player can turn a loss into a profit. As Paul Beeston, former president of the Toronto Blue Jays, said, "Under generally accepted accounting principles, I can turn a $4 million profit into a $2 million loss, and I can get every national accounting firm to agree with me" (Howard & Crompton, 2004, p. 12). This text does not analyze the ethical issues associated with such conduct, but it raises the red flag so that you will understand that financial data can be manipulated. Thus, care should be exercised in reviewing all financial statements. Whenever a question arises you have the ultimate responsibility to ask questions and not just assume that others have done the analysis work for you.

The free enterprise system centers on finance. Any business dealings need to entail significant financial analysis. Finance involves three primary areas of analysis: money and the capital markets, investments, and financial management (Brigham & Ehrhardt, 2005). These three skills are critical for anyone interested in working in the sport industry and, more specifically, for anyone responsible for fiscal oversight in a sport-related program. An individual charged with financial-related duties will need to assume the following responsibilities (Brigham & Ehrhardt, 2005):

♦ Forecasting and planning to help lay the foundation for future success

♦ Investing in major assets such as plants and equipment

♦ Coordinating other employees and managers to ensure that people are working in the most effective manner

♦ Managing the business' interaction with financial markets (e.g., determining how much money to raise and in what manner)

This text provides an overview, but it cannot fully prepare any student to assume complete responsibilities in managing a finance department or performing a similar job. Financial managers need to obtain specific knowledge in areas such as which assets a firm should purchase and why, how to finance those assets, how to forecast future revenue streams, and how to manage existing resources effectively. Although the skills discussed in this chapter are important, financial managers are judged primarily on whether they have been successful in maximizing a corporation's stock value. Accomplishing increased stock valuation is an immense task that requires every unit within the business to operate together (Brigham & Ehrhardt, 2005).

Class Discussion Topics

1. What are the primary revenue sources for a nonprofit sports organization?
2. What are the primary expenses faced by a college athletic department?
3. What are the differences between expenses at a Division I program and a Division III program?
4. What is the difference between accounting and finance?
5. Why is accounting important for financial analysis?
6. Why is understanding sport economics important for someone working in sport finance?
7. Develop a list of revenue and expense streams for a professional baseball team.
8. Develop a list of revenue and expense streams for a nonprofit health club.
9. Develop a list of revenue and expense streams for a publicly traded sportswear company.
10. Develop a list of revenue and expense streams for a NASCAR racing team.

chapter 3

Budgeting 101

Chapter Objectives

After studying this chapter, you should be able to do the following:

- ◆ Appreciate the need and value of financial planning.
- ◆ Understand the value and use of budgets.
- ◆ Appreciate the data that needs to be gathered to plan and create budgets.
- ◆ Follow all the steps involved in the financial planning process.
- ◆ Define financial planning.
- ◆ Distinguish between long-term and short-term financial planning and understand how to minimize risk.
- ◆ Understand what a pro forma budget is and why it is important.
- ◆ Know how to develop a comprehensive business plan for a new and existing business.

This chapter starts with examining the importance of financial planning. Every coach goes into a game with a plan. That plan might focus on which players to start, what offense to use, and what defensive strategies to use. Some coaches are known for scripting most of the game and writing down every play that they expect to run during a given period or under certain circumstances. The same basic concept applies to financial planning. Every sport organization needs to determine before a new year or season starts what they want to accomplish and then develop a road map. The map that is used is a budget. The budget focuses on what the business wants to accomplish during a set period for a given product or industry unit. Financial planning entails examining future income and expenses to help steer a company in a given direction. Every business decision requires planning. Strategic planning has gained popularity as a way of critically analyzing given business scenarios to generate appropriate solutions. This same strategic planning perspective applies to financial planning. Every monetary issue needs to be examined for fiscal soundness. Every dollar needs to be planned for to maximize that dollar's impact. Planning for most typical contingencies can help a business operate smoothly and save money.

This chapter highlights the various components necessary to plan effectively. The first step is to obtain the necessary internal and external data on which to base decisions. The next step is to make use of the data for both short-term and long-term planning. The last section of this chapter deals with the final step: how to develop a pro forma budget as a key to writing an effective business plan.

IMPORTANCE OF FINANCIAL PLANNING

Financial planning can help provide appropriate solutions for the types of problems businesses face every day, such as the need to

- develop new products,
- spend more money on research and development,
- retire a given product line,
- borrow funds for future expansion,
- issue commercial paper,
- issue more stock,
- issue more bonds,
- sell existing assets,
- purchase new assets,
- move the business to another location,
- acquire a competing company, or
- file for bankruptcy protection.

As the list suggests, every future action that a business might undertake entails financial planning.

An example of financial planning comes from the Texas Rangers. This example is used because of the dynamic process involved in trying to sign a superstar athlete and the complexity of the process for revenue and expense issues. In December 2000 the Rangers made history by signing free agent Alex Rodriguez to a 10-year, $252 million contract. Considered by many to be the best player in the league, Rodriguez also became the highest paid. Shortly after the Rangers signed Rodriguez, they announced an increase in ticket prices. Individual tickets were going to cost $2 more, making the average ticket price $22.08. Club seats increased in price from $25 to $40, and upper-reserved seats and bleacher seats went from $10 to $12 ("Pay-Rod," 2001). Of all the major league teams, only the New York Yankees and Boston Red Sox had higher average ticket prices.

But why did the Rangers raise their prices? Would the increased revenue cover Rodriguez's contract? Was the team just savvy in thinking that people would pay to see the best ballplayer in baseball? Table 3.1 shows the average attendance at Ameriquest Field before, during, and after Rodriguez played for the Rangers (he was traded to the New York Yankees in February 2004). Attendance did fluctuate throughout his tenure with the team, but his presence did not produce significant attendance growth. The higher ticket prices and the club's inability to win could also have affected attendance totals.

Table 3.1 Average Attendance at Ameriquest Field

Year	Average attendance per game
1999	34,253
2000	31,956
2001	34,592
2002	29,043
2003	25,856
2004	31,818

Data from Baseball-Almanac 2004.

In the same year that the Rangers signed Rodriguez, they signed a 10-year, $250 million broadcast contract with Fox. This deal would cover Rodriguez's contract, leaving other revenue such as ticket sales and souvenir sales to cover other payroll obligations.

A comparison of Alex Rodriguez's contract with those of other well-known superstars at the same time highlights the fact that his deal was about $100 million larger than the next closest long-term contract deal (the 8-year, $160 million contract for Manny Ramirez). But as highlighted in table 3.2, when salaries are examined on a yearly basis rather than a long-term contract, two athletes earned more than A-Rod did in the 2006-2007 season. It should be noted that table 3.2 lists only players from the top four professional league sports in the United States. In contrast table 3.3 lists the total

Table 3.2 Top Salaries for Major Professional Sports, 2006-2007

Athlete	Team	Salary in millions ($)
Jason Giambi	New York Yankees	23,428,571
Michael Vick	Atlanta Falcons	23,102,750
Alex Rodriguez	New York Yankees	22,708,525
Derek Jeter	New York Yankees	21,600,000
Kevin Garnett	Minnesota Timberwolves	21,600,000
Shaquille O'Neal	Miami Heat	20,000,000
Matt Hasselbeck	Seattle Seahawks	19,005,280
Jalen Rose	Phoenix Suns	18,441,500
Jason Kidd	New Jersey Nets	18,084,000
Jermaine O'Neal	Indiana Pacers	18,084,000
Orlando Pace	St. Louis Rams	18,000,000
Walter Jones	Seattle Seahawks	17,701,320
Manny Ramirez	Boston Red Sox	17,016,381
Todd Helton	Colorado Rockies	16,600,000
Tom Brady	New England Patriots	15,654,180

Data from the USA Today Salary 2011.

Table 3.3 Top Salaries Including Winnings and Endorsements for Major Professional Sports, 2010

Name	Sport	Team	Earnings in millions (salary/ winnings, endorsements)
Tiger Woods	Golf	n/a	90.5 million (20.5, 70)
Phil Mickleson	Golf	n/a	61.6 million (9.6, 52)
Floyd Mayweather	Boxing	n/a	60.2 million (60, .2)
LeBron James	Basketball	Miami Heat	45.7 million (15.7, 30)
Roger Federrer	Tennis	n/a	43 million (n/a)
David Beckham	Soccer	LA Galaxy	42 million (n/a)
(t) Fernando Alonso	Motorsports	Ferarri	40 million (n/a)
(t) Manny Pacquiau	Boxing	n/a	40 million (n/a)
Alex Rodriguez	Baseball	New York Yankees	37 million (33, 4)
Shaquille O'Neal	Basketball	Boston Celtics	36 million (21, 15)

Data from Highestpaidatheltes.com.

top earners in all sports and when endorsement and prize money is included, Alex Rodriquez was the highest paid MLB player, and the third highest paid league sports player behind LeBron James and David Beckham. This distinction shows the importance of having the right information for analysis. Even though Alex Rodriquez earned almost $14 million more, his salary was dwarfed by the salaries of Tiger Woods and Phil Mickleson.

The only contract that came close to Rodriguez's was Manny Ramirez's deal with the Boston Red Sox. Before the Sox signed Ramirez, they announced an increase in ticket prices for the 2001 season. Teams often leverage new stars, and their large salaries, by raising ticket prices. An example from the 2010-2011 season was seen with the Miami Heat's signing of Chris Bosh and LeBron James. Their salaries were both set around $16 million for 2011 and $17,545,000 for 2012. Their teammate Dwayne Wade earned only half a million less per year. The prospect of having three superstars spurred a run on season ticket packages, even before the players signed with the team. The Heat froze prices for season ticket plans to encourage their regular customers to sign before the inevitable increase in prices.

These examples highlight the importance of planning and the potential effect if only several hundred dollars or as much as several million dollars are either saved through facility-related policies or raised by adapting marketing strategies. The Rangers thought that Alex Rodriguez would be their winning and financial savior, but after several years they realized that they had miscalculated both expectations.

Sound financial planning is also necessary when a company undertakes an advertising campaign; the company needs to develop an advertising budget that incorporates forecasts of future advertising expenditures. Table 3.4 is an example of an advertising budget worksheet that could help a company establish priorities for future advertising campaigns. This information is critical for financial planning because sales forecasts are based on the anticipated advertising campaign and the anticipated resulting sales. If a new product is launched and only a small marketing budget has been provided, the anticipated sales could be severely

Table 3.4 2011 Advertising Budget Categories

Category	Priority	Number of insertions	2010 budget ($)	2011 budget ($)	% difference
Magazines	2	200	8,000,000	5,500,000	−31.2
Newspaper advertisements	7	40	1,000,000	1,000,000	0.0
Newspaper supplements	5	26	2,000,000	2,300,000	15.0
Radio	11	900	1,300,000	850,000	−34.6
Television	8	150	2,500,000	2,000,000	−20.0
Endorsements	1	10	1,000,000	8,500,000	750.0
Posters	4	50,000	60,000	140,000	133.0
Special media	3	100	800,000	1,000,000	25.0
Agency fees	16	N/A	1,200,000	1,000,000	−16.7
Trade media	6	60	700,000	750,000	7.1
Consumer incentives	9	100,000	500,000	500,000	0.0
Sales conferences	10	12	230,000	250,000	8.7
Merchandising material	12	400	130,000	150,000	15.4
Trade allowances	13	N/A	100,000	100,000	0.0
Trade free goods	14	2,000	1,000,000	1,050,000	5.0
Sundries	15	N/A	120,000	130,000	8.3
Totals	N/A	153,898	20,640,000	25,220,000	22.2

compromised. At the same time, a large marketing budget that is misspent on the wrong advertising medium can be counterproductive.

If a sport manufacturer, such as Under Armour, decides to switch from advertising primarily in magazines to using athletes as endorsers, this planning decision will be shown on a completed form that lets management know how the strategy will be implemented (see table 3.4). The worksheet would help a company develop appropriate strategies that reach the desired audience but takes into consideration the financial cost and value of each advertising option.

The marketing budget highlighted in table 3.4 reflects a new emphasis on endorsing athletes, along with a dramatic cut in the magazine advertisement budget. Note that some high-priority areas may have a lower budget than certain lower-priority items. For example, posters have one of the lowest allocations in the budget, but they are a high priority. Because the new campaign emphasizes endorsing athletes, giving away posters of the athletes may be a major initiative, but it does not represent a major expenditure. Other items that have higher budgeted amounts may have a lower priority. For example, the company might purchase certain ads even though they are not a major part of the marketing effort because they have a long-standing relationship with the advertising medium or wish to avoid an image backlash. The major declines in the marketing budget are in radio (−34.6%), magazine (−31.2%), and television advertisements (−20%).

Advertising variables may not be as clear to upper management if different segments of the business submit different marketing budgets. A large business may have several segments, each with its own budget; if these budgets are not consolidated into a final marketing budget, upper management will not have a correct picture of the marketing goals and associated costs. For example, a professional sports team might have separate marketing budgets for ticket sales and for the team's web page or souvenir store. If the various budgets are not consolidated into a simple-to-read document, management will make decisions without all the relevant facts. The planning process cannot be accomplished without this information, and the information paves the way for the overall corporate budget. Although it might appear that examining individual budgets might be easier for some executives, the inability to compare and contrast each budget in a synthesized manner can reduce the effectiveness of various techniques such as zero-based budgeting (see the Internal Data section). Thus, some executives like to examine the budgets for individual units but insist on examining a consolidated budget to see what effect any changes in one budget will have on other units.

Management can examine the chart shown in table 3.4 to determine where the marketing emphasis will be in the coming year and what areas will have the greatest spending growth and decline. This information can be correlated with sales forecasts to help management understand why a certain advertising strategy is being suggested. For example, if sales stemming from magazine advertisements increased 20% in the past year, it would make sense for the advertising campaign to show an increase in magazine ads to help spur additional sales from that outlet. But if the sales force informed management that using athletes as endorsers was expected to produce the greatest surge in exposure, management could understand why magazine advertising was declining even though they might expect additional magazine advertisements to increase sales. Thus, the marketing budget chart serves as a tool that management can use to make a logical plan for the future. The marketing budget, along with any other budgets, is critical for financial planning.

DETERMINING FINANCIAL OBJECTIVES

For many managers, making the highest profit possible is a financial objective. But profit is not the only criterion for financial success. Most corporate managers are interested in one primary overall objective—keeping stockholders happy. If a manager is interested in keeping stockholders happy, then she should focus more on earnings per share than on total corporate profits (Brigham & Gapenski, 1994). A company that earned $10 million and had over 100 million outstanding shares would generate earnings of $0.10 per share. In contrast, a company that earned $1 million but had only 100,000 outstanding shares would generate earnings of $10 per share. The shareholders of the second company would have higher earnings per share and would probably think that they had a better investment. This evaluation assumes that the criterion for analysis used by the shareholders was earnings per share rather than stock price appreciation or total earnings.

Earnings can also be reflected in increased stock value. Especially for stocks that do not pay dividends, the increase in share value will be the hallmark for determining financial success. Thus, if two companies (company A and company B) have earnings of $50 million each, the hallmark of yearly success could be the companies' stock values. If company A's stock rose $2 per share from $28 to $30 and company B's shares rose $1 from $4 to $5 per share, most analysts would consider company B more successful. Because the earnings were identical, the focus turns to increased stock value, and company A's 7.125% increase in stock value pales in comparison with company B's 25% rise.

Earnings per share is just one of the factors that influence the health of a corporation. A corporation is a business entity that is incorporated under state law and is entitled to issue ownership interests in the form of stock certificates (see chapter 4 for a thorough analysis of business structures). People interested in investing in stocks, also called shares in a corporation, want to know whether their investment will generate a return, such as dividend payments or an increased stock price. Besides knowing whether the stock will pay a dividend, a potential investor might want to know the following:

♦ How often the dividends are paid
♦ How risky future earnings might be
♦ How much debt the company carries
♦ What the corporate policies are (e.g., whether they are going to try to purchase a competitor or what dividend rate they pay)

All these questions become critical for financial analysis because corporate policies concerning stocks and bonds help dictate stockholder and analyst interest in the stock. Stocks are only one criteria of success. Nonprofit sport organizations will have different financial objectives. But every organization has a financial objective, and the planning process is designed to help an organization reach those goals.

Every sport organization will also go through good financial times and difficult financial times. Through preparation, a sport manager can possibly position an organization for the rough times by stashing away money. For years, high school sport programs have been facing financial challenges. These challenges seem to occur almost every 10 years, as evidenced by incidents in the 1980s, 1990s, and more recently from 2008 to the present. Financial planning can help high school athletic administrators prepare for what they know will be tough times in the future. When the years are good, expenses start increasing as more services or programs are offered. When times become

rough, administrators cry foul and ask for help in balancing their budgets. This example shows that slow, steady growth is much easier to plan for than a yo-yo cycle of rapid growth and rapid decline.

An example of appropriate financial planning entails large colleges bringing in small schools to play in the larger school's stadium or arena without a corresponding return contest. Traditionally, teams play home-and-home series in which each team hosts a game. But football teams such as the Ohio State University Buckeyes can hold a crowd of around 100,000 at their home stadium, and a return game at the home field of a rival might be played in front of a crowd of just 40,000, the capacity of their opponent's stadium. To generate greater revenue for both, teams often agree to play in the larger stadium without a return game being scheduled. For example, in 2009 Ohio State paid Navy to come to Columbus, Ohio. For larger universities, this kind of scheduling generates revenue and usually results in a win before a tough conference schedule begins. The strategy has worked well for Ohio State, which in 2009-2010 generated $123,174,176 in revenue and $122,739,754 in total expenses to produce a surplus of $434,422 ("Most big-time schools winning the profit game," 2011). For smaller programs, playing an away game in a big arena gives them significant revenue and helps them recruit better players by letting them know that they will play against national-caliber competitors. Thus, both sides in such an arrangement generate significant revenue and other benefits. The best financial plans benefit both sides to an agreement.

Budget

Revenues and expenses are included in various types of financial statements, such as budgets, income statements, and balance sheets. A budget is a road map that shows where the sport business intends to spend its money. The budget helps show the right path for a business, but it is much more. A budget helps anticipate the future, so it is a strategic planning tool. The budget also gives a clear picture of the resources that are needed, indicates where revenue shortfalls might arise, allows for better financial monitoring, helps communicate plans to various stakeholders, and allows more precise measurement of financial performance.

All members of the business can use the budget to help make decisions. If the budget allocates a certain amount of money for marketing and the marketing department reaches that limit halfway through the year, it may be difficult for the department to receive additional funds for the rest of the year. The only way that additional funding is likely to become available is if sales exceed the sales forecast or if another area in the budget, such as customer service, is reduced to free up money for the marketing department. A good example associated with sport budgeting is the process of going to a postseason football bowl game. Most schools would love to have a chance at a bowl game and the resulting positive publicity, but if they do not properly budget for such an opportunity, it can quickly change from a blessing to a curse. The university will generate some appearance fees and possible broadcasting revenue that is shared with their conference. Expenses include transportation, housing, food, and related expenses. Often excluded from this analysis is the cost to purchase tickets. Every major bowl game requires participants to purchase a certain number of tickets at a set price to participate in the game. For that reason bowl games prefer to have strong universities such as Big Ten or Pac-12 schools that have large numbers of loyal alumni who will travel to games and buy tickets. Such was not the case with some schools that have had the financial misfortune to make it to a bowl game. In 2011 the University of Connecticut, as the Big East champion, was invited to play a New Year's bowl game against the Oklahoma Sooners. UConn was supposed to sell thousands of tickets. They were able to sell only 4,600 tickets for around $646,000 against a guarantee of $3.35 million. Only 2,771 of those tickets went to the general public, who paid from $105 to $255 per ticket. The remaining tickets were given to fulfill sponsorships or given to athletes' families. Many fans did not want to pay the high list price and instead purchased tickets on the secondary market where tickets were plentiful and cheap. When all the dust settled after the game, UConn generated around $3.2 million from the game but incurred $4.86 million in expenses, resulting in a loss of $1.66 million ("Bowl no bonanza for UConn," 2011).

Budgets are often developed by examining existing business successes or failures. These business stories are found in income statements and balance sheets. An income statement highlights a company's income and expenses over the past year. A balance sheet shows the worth of a company at a specific time. These documents are just two of the types of financial statements discussed in detail in chapter 6. Investors, stakeholders, analysts, and government officials are the primary readers of most financial statements. The examples in the Two Budgets sidebar illustrate the stories that can unfold when one critically analyzes income statements, as well as

show how budgets influence sport businesses. By examining past income statements, a business can help plan for its future budget and also determine whether or not its prior budget was accurate.

Almost all businesses need to start the budgeting process by initially developing a rough budget based on assumptions. These numbers will normally be a best guess, so the first-year budget for most organization or business units will be vague and often inaccurate. After one or several years, however, the organization will be able to craft a more accurate number based on information received through the process. Businesses have to track compliance closely with a budget to make sure that expenses are not running away or that revenue is not growing too quickly. Although increased revenue might always appear to be a favorable outcome, it can spell doom for a business. For example, a sport manufacturing company might develop the latest must-have product and see sales skyrocket. With increased sales the company might have to increase production. To do so, it will have to find a larger manufacturing location, hire more workers, and purchase more raw goods (inventory). If sales drop significantly, the company will have assumed significant new expenses and will not have the revenue stream to pay for all its growth. Thus, a budget helps an organization manage growth in a more effective manner.

The same concern can be raised with overspending or not timing spending accurately. One such issue that often affects public schools and university athletic departments is that a budget might need to be spent by a given date, often June 30 if the budget year is from July 1 through June 30. To meet the expenses allocated for their programs, many managers spend every penny they have on June 30 purchasing office supplies and other items. This annual dance occurs because managers want to show that they need all the money that they were allocated. If they had any money left over the organization might cut their budget in subsequent years, surmising that the department does not need as much money. To avoid this penalty, departments often spend every penny in their budget. One way to deal with this issue is to have an incentive and a penalty. If a department exceeds their budget one year, the money would be taken out of their next budget. But if the department was able to spend less than what was budgeted, the amount would roll over to the next year, offering the department an incentive to save and giving them more money to work with in the future. This process can occur only if a department has a budget and has properly documented all their revenue and expenses.

TWO BUDGETS

Many universities have a separate nonprofit [501(c)(3)] foundation in charge of raising money through hosting various events and fund-raising drives. Assume that an athletic foundation reported $7.1 million in income and expenses in its 2011 annual report. The 2011 Athletic Foundation Income Statement shows how the numbers could break down in amounts and percentage of total funds for various categories.

Among the stories these numbers tell are the following:

- More than 50% of all moneys raised helped pay for program services.
- Investment income will increase on an annual basis if the foundation continues increasing its net assets, because the primary assets are investment securities that will generate future income.
- Only 6.6% of expenses were dedicated to managerial tasks, whereas 26.5% of expenses helped raise operating funds. Thus, over a quarter of the expenses were used to raise money.
- Although direct mail and telemarketing costs were $634,965, this investment was successful in helping to raise almost $2 million.
- The greatest revenue source came from fund-raising efforts and donations by individuals to the annual campaign.

Based on these numbers, a budget could be developed for 2012 highlighting possible additional anticipated revenue from programs that are doing well. Future expenses also might increase if priorities are different or if additional expenses are anticipated such as a significant increase in the cost of postage. If those working in the fund-raising area anticipated a major gift, the future budget could reflect that opportunity. But if they anticipate a change for the worse, such a decrease in gifts brought about by a tough economy, they might have to reduce the budget. If they anticipate a 10% decline, the income and possibly the expenses will both be reduced by 10% in the next budget.

The 1996 Atlanta Olympic Organizing Committee's Income Statement tells a story completely different from the athletic foundation example. The sheer magnitude of the billion-dollar budget presents a sharp contrast to the relatively small budget of the fictitious athletic foundation budget. Most sport-related budgets are for midsized companies and range from $2 million to $8 million. Budgets of professional sports teams often reach into the range of hundreds of millions of dollars.

The numbers for the Olympic Games indicate that revenue is derived primarily from broadcasting rights, ticket sales, and national sponsorship programs. Construction and venue operating

2011 Athletic Foundation Income Statement

INCOME ($)	
Fund-raising and annual campaign (45.4%)	3,220,266
Direct mail and telemarketing (27.2%)	1,936,589
Investment income (11.8%)	838,773
Program services (5.6%)	395,540
Game sponsors (5.2%)	366,930
Foundations and grants (3.0%)	215,007
Souvenir sales (1.8%)	126,895
Total income	7,100,000
EXPENSES ($)	
Program services (52.8%)	3,742,385
Revenue development (17.6%)	1,252,106
Net asset increase (14.1%)	1,001,196
Direct mail and telemarketing (8.9%)	634,965
Management and general (6.6%)	469,348
Total expenses	7,100,000

1996 Atlanta Olympic Organizing Committee's Income Statement

Revenue and support	Millions ($)
Broadcast rights	568.3
Ticket sales	427.2
Joint marketing: USOC	426.7
Top III sponsorship	81.1
Rate card rentals	63.2
Merchandising margin	34.6
Interest	19.4
Local sponsors	14.8
Housing	14.2
Ticket fees	12.6
Contributions	10.2
License plate sales	9.5
Parking and transportation	9.3
Disposal of assets	8.0
Other	30.0
Total revenue	**1,729.14**
Less royalties	6.4
Net revenue	**1,727.0**
Expenses	**Millions ($)**
Salaries and wages	315.7
Benefits	21.1
Professional services	209.7
Construction and venues	541.2
Contracted services	94.5
Rent and occupancy	147.2
Equipment	197.1
Materials and supplies	68.5
Insurance	25.2
Conference, travel, hospitality	55.0
Interest and other financing	19.0
Other	10.3
Reserve: liabilities	10.3
Reserve: operations	7.9
Total expenses	**1,723.0**

Data from Glier 1997.

expenses dominate the Atlanta Olympic Organizing Committee's (AOOC) expenses. The human resource expenses are fairly large and compose a significantly higher percentage than the human resource expenses generated by the athletic foundation example. The budget also highlights that although the AOOC earns interest income from excess cash reserves invested in various interest-earning accounts, it also has to pay interest on various loans. The interest earned ($19.4 million) and the interest paid ($19 million) are almost equal, but the strategy did generate an additional $400,000 in revenue. Any budget using such large numbers would be impossible to follow without proper documentation to track all the funds.

As highlighted earlier, a budget is a map. Every map has the points that the traveler wants to reach. Normally, various routes could be taken. Some of these routes might be scenic, whereas others might get the traveler to the destination quickly. Some people might use tools such as a GPS to help, but a GPS might lead a driver astray or might not highlight specific concerns such as road construction or accidents. Furthermore, a map has a legend that shows what various symbols or colors mean on the map. This information helps the map reader understand the issues that might affect the planned trip. Note that just as GPS devices have revolutionized travel, computerized budgeting has changed the way that budgets are developed and changed. Electronic systems make it easier to track and predict trends for planning purposes.

Sport organizations can use several types of budgets. The two primary budgets are operational budgets and capital budgets. An operational budget reflects the day-to-day operations of the organization and lists sales and expenditures for normal operations. A capital budget is oriented more to the long term and often focuses on future expenditures such as spending for a new building or purchasing other major assets.

An operational budget often uses a line-item approach in which each revenue and expenditure amount is highlighted on a separate line. Some companies use a numerical code to reflect each line item so that aggregating similar revenues and expenses is easier. For example, all revenue from ticketing sources might start with a 100 code and be further specified with a code of 101 for season tickets and a code of 102 for individual game-day tickets. Such a breakdown facilitates the identification of out of place or inconsistent reporting in budgets.

Budgets can also be organized based on programs, such as an athletic department budget that is separated by sports. A program budget can also evolve into a performance budget in which each revenue or expenditure is related not just to a program but also to how it furthers an organization's strategic plan.

By collecting all the appropriate data (see the next section), an organization can conduct a variance analysis to determine whether the budget is being followed or whether they are overspending or not generating enough revenue. The key to collecting data is to identify the proper classification of data. As an example, expenses are often categorized as either **variable or fixed costs**. Variable costs are those costs that change in direct relation to the number of items or products that might be consumed or the number of fans in attendance. Concession food costs might fall into this category. Fixed costs remain constant and are independent of the level of organizational activity. Using the concession example, the fixed costs would include the refrigeration and cooking equipment that incur an expense regardless of how many food items are sold.

Budgets are not only analyzed for compliance but also can be manipulated based on change. Incremental budgeting takes an existing budget and increases it based on expected changes. If sales are expected to increase 5% in the future, then the incremental process would increase all line items in a budget (both revenue and expenses) by 5%. A decrement budget is one in which the revenues and expenses are decreased based on expected lower revenues. A sport manager can really stand out in this circumstance. Sport managers who can properly administer and maintain a budget to avoid financial losses will set themselves apart from others in the industry. The key for sport managers is to have a system in place to track costs. Having such a system is contingent on obtaining and properly analyzing appropriate data.

Data

Companies and organizations cannot develop financial plans without appropriate data. Planning data should be compared against internal projections and external projections such as industry standards. The information from which spending and revenue sources can be identified includes internal data and external data. Internal data are often referred to as primary data because the business itself generates the information. External data, or data obtained from other sources, have already been developed and published and are referred to as secondary data. As an example, a professional sports team could develop its own data on ticket prices for other entertainment venues in the area to price their tickets appropriately. The team could then identify revenue for the future budget based on such research. This source of information is an example of internal data. In contrast, secondary data could be obtained from industry research that might track how much game tickets are sold for on the secondary market. If a report published by a local business magazine highlights that tickets are selling for significantly less on the secondary market, the team might be pricing the tickets too high compared with the demand.

Internal Data

As the Two Budgets sidebar highlights, forecasting cannot be accomplished without reliable internal data. An internal audit could have significant value, but if it is not accurate, then any reliance on the data would be erroneous. Having reliable internal and external data is critical to making good decisions. Internal data can include past balance sheets and income statements, audited financial records, annual reports, research and development reports, and countless other documents generated by employees or consultants. Paper trails should not be used to the exclusion of other data. For example, e-mails may contain valuable data that researchers may miss if they examine only printed materials.

Internal data can come from various other sources. Information can be derived from personal observation or through conversation around the water cooler. Additional sources may include surveys conducted by the business to analyze customer concerns. Many sports teams conduct fan surveys to determine why people attend games and how the organization can provide more valuable services. Information about how much and what types of soft drinks or beer are sold can be useful. By analyzing the sales figures in the grandstands and at concession stands, a team can plan its strategy for increasing beverage sales. Similarly, by breaking its operation down into its basic elements, the team can develop a more appropriate budget. This process is often seen in **zero-based budgeting**.

Many companies use zero-based budgeting as a technique to justify future expenditures. In zero-based budgeting (ZBB), every expenditure is justified in comparison with other potential projects. If a team will have $1 million for its marketing budget, every department that wishes to receive some of that money needs to indicate how much money it is requesting and provide justification for the request. If a department has been successful in a particular campaign, those numbers can be used as a justification for receiving a given amount of the funds. Each unit, division, or department might be required to produce formal documentation to justify requested expenditures.

Objective documentation is the key. If the existence of a department could be under review, there may be a temptation to manipulate data to ensure continued employment. For example, if the National Aeronautics and Space Administration (NASA) operated under ZBB principles, its entire Mars program might be under review after several major disasters costing millions of dollars. People in an affected program might try to paint a picture that is better than what really occurred. But objective data can help eliminate potential bias or distortion. An excellent way to uncover objective information is to go to external sources.

As part of the information-gathering process, defining the target markets of the business is imperative. Key questions that must be answered include the following:

♦ How big are the target markets?

♦ What is the business' penetration of these markets?

♦ What is the potential that is remaining for the business to exploit in these markets?

♦ Who are the competitors, what are their market shares, and what is their pricing strategy?

Answers to these questions are important in generating accurate revenue forecasts.

As the business projects its revenues, including a reality check is important. In particular, is the future projected sales growth truly sustainable? High growth will consume substantial sums of internal cash and capital, as well as any capital provided by lenders and investors. Managers need to determine whether the firm has sufficient resources to sustain the level of growth built into revenue forecasts.

Information also needs to be obtained about the extent to which expenses vary directly with revenues. If the expenses of the firm are primarily variable, profitability may be improved significantly by reducing the costs per unit produced.

Although we often use Speedway Motorsports as a real-world example, here we use the fictitious Sport Manufacturing Company (SMC). Inventory numbers are rarely publicly available because companies do not want their competitors knowing what manufacturing cycles they are following. In this example, SMC manufactures and sells golf clubs and skis. **Variable costs** for SMC include the cost of labor and material. If the company finds that it is selling fewer golf clubs, it will reduce production. As production is reduced, SMC can reduce the number of people employed in production as well as the purchase of materials used to manufacture the golf clubs.

As for **fixed costs**, we assume that SMC has extensive machinery and equipment in its manufacturing facilities. The machinery and equipment, along with the manufacturing premises, are long-term capital assets whose costs are considered fixed over any particular period. If the machinery and equipment are used in a facility that fabricates golf clubs, the annual expense is incurred even if no golf clubs are produced and sold to customers. When expenses are mostly fixed, higher profitability will be associated with higher sales because the cost per unit sold will fall as sales increase. If we assume that most of SMC's expenses are the fixed costs associated with its machinery and equipment, the company needs to maximize golf club sales to boost profitability by lowering the cost per golf club sold.

In the short run, a major constraint in SMC's attempts to maximize profitability through increased golf club sales is the maximum production capacity of the manufacturing facility. A production constraint is also a sales constraint. If SMC can produce only 800,000 golf clubs in a given year, it will be unable to sell more than 800,000 golf clubs annually. Even if the demand for golf clubs is one million per year, SMC will be unable

to sell that many golf clubs unless it can find some way to increase production.

In contrast to a manufacturing company that has numerous variable costs, the major cost for a professional sports team is the salaries of players and coaches, which are fixed costs. No matter how much revenue is derived from attendance at games or broadcast rights, the team will be paying the same salaries, so it needs to make sure that the budget covers at least those expenses.

External Data

The Two Budgets sidebar highlights the importance of internal data for decision making. By knowing how successful internal operations are, a business can plan more appropriately. External data can serve the same purpose. External data and documentation are critical for successful planning. External data can be used to help shape various decisions to reflect the true business environment. For example, the data in the sidebar table shows

---

CONCEPTS INTO PRACTICE

When a sport organization examines a budget, managers must use the right information and compare apples with apples. Under the Equity in Athletics Disclosure Act (EADA) of 1994, the United States Department of Education requires all colleges that receive federal funds and have intercollegiate athletics to report their spending on an annual basis. The problem is that the information can have errors or omissions and is not specific. After years of work a database is now available for NCAA Division I and II called the Financial Dashboard. The database uses EADA data to examine 26 indicators in multiple formats and what-if scenarios (Goldstein & Alden, 2011). Colleges can examine other colleges in their conference or across the nation to get a better idea of how they are spending and earning money.

Comparison is critical to understanding what it takes to be competitive. Sport administrators can use the information to be proactive rather than reactive and to construct a better strategic plan. The numbers are useful, however, only if they are analyzed correctly. For example, one school might list every expense associated with recruiting in the

recruiting budget whereas another might put air travel for recruiting in a travel budget. Other differences include salaries that likely vary with the cost of living at colleges in large cities compared with those located in rural areas. Several other areas need to be carefully examined:

- Team travel. Some programs take buses everywhere, some take commercial air carriers, and others might take chartered flights.
- Equipment and supplies. Although some schools need to pay a lot for equipment and supplies, other schools might have a contract with a sports apparel company and would not have to buy any equipment.
- Ticket sales. Every college is different. Some have large facilities and huge ticket demand, whereas other schools let students in free.
- Donations. Every school has different ways of documenting donations. Some let the athletic department record the gift, whereas others record the donations for a general institutional fund (Goldstein & Alden, 2011).

BALL TEAM

The following are excerpts from an interview with Chris Canetti, the general manager of a minor league baseball team at the time of the interview several years ago. The information reflects the importance of internal data and how the internal data can generate strategies for future growth.

I receive a lot of resumes where someone says in the cover letter that they love sports, and that's great. You have to love baseball to work in baseball, and you have to love sports to work in sports, but the bottom line is that it is a business. When I have to hire someone I couldn't care less if they played Little League baseball; I want to know what positives they can bring to my business and me and how they can benefit the bottom line. This might encourage or discourage you, but when I went to college I was a communications major. I never took an accounting, marketing, or finance course. For a bachelor's degree in my school the only thing I needed was Economics 101. I wish differently now that I had taken those courses, but a few years ago before I became general manager, the former GM came to me one day and said, "I want you to do the budget." A minor league baseball team makes millions a year in revenue, and I have to make a budget. You can't tell your boss no, so you have to figure it out. I wish I had a course like this [sport finance]; it would have made my life a lot easier.

A budget is a model that is set by the team to try to forecast the goals they want to meet for the coming year . . . . If you look at some budgets, they might show a cash-positive year. However, if the team has debt service that is amortized out over the course of time, it will show up as an expense, even though it is not a hard cash expense. With the debt service expense included in the budget, the budget could show a loss. I use a piece-by-piece approach to developing the numbers in this budget. The primary source for these numbers is from historical data. History describes what occurred last year and serves as the base for predicting what might happen in the coming year. For example, if we look at fictitious numbers for last year, we see that the team had $1.4 million in (game-day) concession sales. Assume 200,000 fans attended games last season. By dividing the $1.4 million by the 200,000 fans, we can calculate that an average fan spends $7 each game on concessions. If we anticipate a 10% increase in attendance, then our budget should also reflect that 10% increase. Our ticket sales would increase 10% and our concession sales would also increase. If fans once again spend on average $7 each, then we can multiply $7 by 220,000 fans (200,000 fans plus the 10% increase in fans), resulting in a budgeted $1.54 million for concession revenue for next season.

A team's stadium lease will always be a major factor in determining an organization's financial picture. The lease is a key consideration when going through the budgeting process. The lease outlines how the parties involved will split the responsibility and control of major expense and revenue categories. These elements often include things such as concession revenue, suite revenue, parking revenue, ticket taxes, stadium maintenance, and utilities. The factors within a lease are unique in almost every team's case. In some instances, a team's lease is written so that a percentage of annual revenues are used to pay debts incurred from stadium construction or renovation. Such cases will affect the team's annual financial statement.

When asked about profit centers, Canetti responded:

> Concessions represent one of the greatest profit centers for a team. While a minor league team makes a significant amount on ticket revenue and does not pay players' and coaches' salaries, which are paid by the parent club, concessions are still the best profit center. A team can generate between 50% and 60% profit on concession sales. A team could possibly outsource concessions to another company but then would only receive 35%. This significant potential decline in concession revenue has encouraged us to keep taking care of concessions ourselves to maximize the revenue and flexibility.

(continued)

Hypothetical Minor League Baseball Team Budget for the 2012 Season

Category	($000)
Revenue	6,140
Direct costs	1,758
Gross profit	**4,382**
Park and game expenses (schedule 1)	992
Team expenses (schedule 2)	196
General and admin. expenses (schedule 3)	2,422
Debt service (schedule 4)	840
Total expenses	**4,450**
Operating income	**−116**
Sources of revenue:	
Ticket revenue	2,000
Direct ticket costs:	
Facility fee	200
Payment to MLB	60
Ticket production	14
Total costs	**274**
Gross profit	**1,726**
Advertising revenue	1,400
Direct costs:	
Paint/Material	–
Printing	–
Radio	10
Promotional spots	200
Total costs	**210**
Gross profit	**1,190**
Game day concessions	1,400
Group concessions	600
Total concession revenue	**2,000**
Direct costs:	
Food	380
Soft drinks	70
Beer	80
Supplies and uniforms	60
Equipment leasing	8
Payroll	240
Payroll taxes	30
Total costs	**868**
Gross profit	**1,132**
Merchandise revenue	340
Direct costs:	
Beginning inventory	70
Purchases	130
Payroll	14
Total costs	**214**
Ending inventory	48
Final costs	**166**

	($000)
Gross profit	**174**
Other revenue:	
Parking	40
Programs	40
Other	320
Total other revenue	**400**
Direct costs:	
Program	80
Other	160
Total costs	**240**
Gross profit	**160**
Total gross profit	4,382
Departmental gross profit margin	
Ticket department	1,726
Advertising department	1,190
Concessions department	1,132
Merchandise department	174
Other departments	160
Total gross profit	**4,382**
Gross profit margin	**71.37%**
Schedule 1—Park and game expenses	
Stadium rent	150
Real estate taxes (waived)	0
Utilities	130
Maintenance—grounds	280
Security	110
Umpires	70
Game day payroll	190
Game day payroll taxes	18
Equipment rental	16
Miscellaneous	28
Total park and game expenses	**992**
Schedule 2—Team expenses	
Transportation	80
Lodging	96
Laundry and clubhouse	10
Uniforms	10
Total team expenses	**196**
Schedule 3—General and administrative expenses	
Salaries	800
Payroll taxes	74
Office operations	4
Dues and fees	60
Promotion and advertising	550
Other (schedule 5)	984
Total general and admin. expenses	**2,422**

Schedule 4—Debt service plus other expenses		Professional fees	60
Interest	180	Miscellaneous	2
Depreciation	260	Outside services	16
Amortization of contracts	400	Postage	40
Total expenses	**4,450**	Rent	2
Schedule 5—Other expenses		Repairs	16
Amortization	370	Supplies	32
Auto expenses	18	Taxes—others	60
Bad debt expenses	10	Telephone	80
Bank service charge	40	Travel	16
Contributions	2	**Total other expenses**	**934**
Entertainment	10	**Total debt service plus other expenses**	**840**
Insurance	160		

the extent to which marketing efforts are succeeding. If the team were facing financial trouble, it could examine prior expenditures to see what efforts were and were not successful (e.g., was the $550,000 spent on promotion and advertising profitable, or is a different campaign needed based on customer response to the prior campaign?). In addition, if the stadium landlords were having trouble with the local officials, as evidenced by news stories and city hearings, the team could attempt to renegotiate the lease both to save money and to project a positive public image for the landlords. These are only two examples of the use of external data to help shape sport business decisions.

External data can help shape decisions in many other ways as well. The following are examples of gathering external data:

♦ Monitoring international terrorist activities to determine whether an event needs to be canceled

♦ Analyzing industry trends to develop appropriate pricing for concession items

♦ Tracking culinary advances to determine the most effective means of packaging and selling food items

♦ Reading current articles in trade publications to stay abreast of industry changes

♦ Attending conferences to hear what other executives are saying about the industry

♦ Reviewing government census reports to understand demographic changes in the possible fan base

Publications such as *Barron's, Forbes, Business Week,* and the *Wall Street Journal* provide useful general information. More specific information can be obtained from such sources as *Dun & Bradstreet's Key Business Ratios,* which analyzes 14 key ratios for various industries. Both state and federal governments produce significant useful data such as statistical abstracts. Industry trade groups can also produce valuable data to assist with financial planning. The Suggested Resources section contains information on these publications and how to access them.

Among the best information sources for the sport industry are industry publications such as *Athletic Business, Athletic Management, Fitness Management, NCAA News,* and a host of other specialized publications. Each has unique special features, reports, and surveys that can provide invaluable assistance. One of the premier publications in the industry is *Street & Smith's SportsBusiness Journal.* This weekly publication has special sections devoted to attendance numbers, a stock market index for sport-related companies, and information on sponsorship deals, among other features.

Regular newspapers often list the payrolls for every professional team in leagues such as the NFL, MLB, and the NBA. Such data can help a team compare itself with others, which is called **benchmarking**. Benchmarking allows a business to see whether it is paying more for similar work or results. For example, a basketball team can compare their salary range with other teams in the league or examine specific statistical variables such as the cost per rebound or assist for each player.

Organizations regularly research specific industry benchmarks that can help establish criteria for success or failure. Although the data are only as good as the techniques used to retrieve them, the information can help shape many financial decisions. Numerous managers focus on the bottom line, and the bottom line can be examined by looking at what others in the same industry do to determine whether a facility is operating effectively compared with similarly situated facilities.

Industry-related data come from a variety of sources and appear in a variety of formats. The Small Business Administration (SBA) publishes free business plan formats online to help businesses understand what data they will need and what to do with the data. More specific data are often needed from specific industry groups or associations.

Regardless of the type of external data, the reader of such reports needs to compare apples with apples. Some publications calculate return on equity as net income divided by average common equity, but others divide net income by the year-end common equity. Comparing data that have been obtained using different equations will lead to inaccuracies. Referring back to NASA's trouble with its Mars program, one expensive blunder occurred, in part, because of human error in which measurements were not converted correctly from the metric system to the traditional English system. This simple mistake led to the crashing of a spaceflight. Similarly, incorrectly analyzing an internal rate of return or price–earnings ratio can destroy an investment decision. Thus, all financial statements should be carefully scrutinized to determine what equations and measurement techniques were used and when the data were collected to ensure proper comparisons.

Proper Documentation

The key to success in data collection is proper documentation. Although record keeping is stressed throughout this text as an integral component of financial success, record keeping should not be seen as an end in itself. It is simply a tool. If too much emphasis is placed on developing the right documents, managers will not be able to see the forest for the trees and may make decisions that look great on paper but become major disasters. Nevertheless, the documentation process is critical and is highlighted throughout this text. At the same time, documentation is only one of the many functions required by law or contract for obtaining necessary funds. For that reason analyzing revenues and expenses is critical. Finance necessitates analyzing the financial feasibility of various projects based on the projected revenues to be gained, the expenses that will be incurred, and the availability of moneys to fund the project through to completion. When potential income from a project is properly documented, a potential investor is more inclined to back that project.

The ability to make appropriate financial decisions is predicated on proper documentation. The Atlantic Olympic Organizing Committee had to pay an accounting firm to develop an audited financial statement that could be shown to the government and other stakeholders. When a sport business finds itself in a financial plight, the only way that it can analyze the situation accurately is through proper documentation. Did someone fudge the sales numbers? Is someone embezzling money? Is the company carrying too much inventory? Are the costs of employee benefits out of control? Is extra cash just lying around in unknown accounts? Proper documentation enables you to find the answers to these types of questions. Thus, when examining a balance sheet or income statement, people need to ask themselves if they can trust the numbers. If the financial statements are not audited or otherwise certified by an independent party as accurate, the reader should be cautious.

FINANCIAL PLANNING PROCESS

After data are obtained, from whatever source, they need to be evaluated. Data will be evaluated based on organizational mission, goals, and objectives as well as any competitive analysis that could help shape future organizational activities. The data combined with potential future directions will help in developing a financial plan, which is a budget. Financial planning requires two major activities: forecasting potential revenues and budgeting for future expenses. After the appropriate data are collected, management must act on the data. They cannot hide behind the numbers and fail to make a decision. Stockholders and voters demand that a business or government entity make decisions that will maximize their investments. The most common managerial decisions have to do with maximizing revenue sources and minimizing expenses.

Financial planning is often based on behavior learned from previous bad habits or mistakes.

Failing to turn over inventory quickly enough or not collecting overdue bills in a timely manner leads to reduced income and higher expenses. Both inventory levels and uncollected accounts can significantly decrease profitability if they are high. If excess inventory and uncollected accounts receivable appear on the balance sheet, then a significant amount of money may be tied up and unusable. Both of these problems can be corrected through the implementation of efficiency control mechanisms such as posting systems (based on the due dates of outstanding accounts receivable) or the establishment of guidelines for inspecting the inventory. Many steps that people might categorize as financial planning are just commonsense tactics. For example, American Express Small Business Services promotes the following simple tactics to help manage cash flow ("Steps for improving," 1998):

- Organize billing schedules so that overdue bills can be flagged for quicker follow-up.
- Stretch out repayment to suppliers to the maximum time allowed by contract.
- Try to pay bills earlier if suppliers offer incentives for early repayment.
- If suppliers do not offer an incentive program for early payment, ask for such a program.
- Do not hesitate to raise prices; clients are accustomed to small but regular increases.
- Eliminate any unnecessary inventory, which just wastes money.
- Consider leasing rather than buying to free your credit line and to take advantage of tax write-offs.
- Buy from various suppliers to prevent harm if a supplier faces a problem and to take advantage of special offers that other suppliers might make.

These simple strategies are in fact decisions that can be reached through the planning process. A business can decide to pay bills within 10 days if a discount is offered and then reinvest the savings into interest-bearing Treasury bonds. Such a planning process appears simple, but numerous managers live by the seat of their pants when making decisions and do not consider the long-term consequences. Planning helps determine potential long-term ramifications.

One of the most important planning issues is determining the capital structure for a business. Chapter 11 explains the importance of determin-ing the capital mix, or target capital structure. The planning process can help determine the most appropriate structure for a given year based on economic variables and countless additional pieces of information acquired in the data-collection process. If Nike is overburdened by bond obligations, it might not be able to generate enough return to interest potential stockholders. But if Nike's equity is overdiluted, the company may find it difficult to buy back its shares. Nike could be in trouble if it has issued so many shares that its equity is composed primarily of shareholders' equity rather than retained earnings. This situation could be a problem if Nike ever wanted to buy back its stock to go private or buy back some of its shares to reduce the number of shareholders and increase the share value for the remaining shareholders.

Economic conditions are an excellent example of the concerns raised in the planning process. Inflation and prosperity typically cause a sharp need for corporate capital so that the company can continue to produce more. If bonds and preferred stock are issued too quickly, however, a company can go bankrupt if the economy changes and the company owes too much in interest, principal, and required dividend payments. Furthermore, during periods in which interest rates are low, bank borrowing may be more economical than issuing bonds. If a bank loan is obtainable at a relatively low interest rate, the main savings will be the costs associated with issuing bonds (versus the minimal costs associated with obtaining a bank loan). If the long-term bond interest rate is lower than the obtainable bank interest rate, then it may be worthwhile to issue the bond because the issuing cost can be recouped over the long term. The opposite result is seen when interest rates are high, in which case a business would have more difficulty issuing long-term bonds. The business would have trouble selling long-term bonds to investors if the interest rate is lower than what an investor might be able to obtain in the short run from other investments. Planning helps prevent making the wrong decision and issuing securities that might not be attractive to investors.

Forecasting

Forecasting is the key to financial planning. If a plan is to work, the sport organization will need to look toward the future. The more distant the forecast period is, the greater the difficulty is in making the forecast and the lower the likelihood is that the results will be accurate. Thus, a 1-year forecast will be much more accurate than a 5- or 10-year forecast. Forecasts also involve uncertainty and historical performance. They are usually less accurate than desired, and experience is often the best teacher of what really works (Schmidgall, Singh, & Johnson, 2007). Information for forecasting can come from quantitative data (such as regression analysis, econometrics, naive estimation, and smoothing) or qualitative data (market research, sales force estimates, and focus groups). The most common approach for forecasting is the prior year's actual revenues adjusted subjectively. This somewhat naive approach is one of the most commonly used approaches. Thus, if the budget for one year entails revenue of $1,000,000 from ticket sales and sales are supposed to increase 10%, then the next year's budget would have estimated revenue of $1,100,000. Smoothing is another key technique in which a sport organization uses an estimated percentage for future growth (or decline). Instead of applying it for one year, however, the manager uses several years of past sales data for a more realistic estimate. Thus, if over three years the team sold $1,000,000, then $1,100,000, and lastly $900,000 in tickets, the average smoothed over three years would be $1,000,000. If sales are projected to increase 10%, the estimate for the next year would be $1,100,000 in revenue.

To generate sales forecasts for an established business, the starting point is sales from the most recent full year. It is useful to list sales separately by product line, by sales distribution method (e.g., direct sales, retail sales, online sales), or by geographic market.

Assume that Under Armour sold four million apparel units in 2011. If Under Armour charged $15 per unit sold, its 2011 total revenues for those units would be $60 million. In table 3.5 Under Armour's 2011 revenues of $60 million are broken down by sales distribution channel (i.e., by the method for distributing the products to the final customers). As shown in the Hypothetical Minor League Baseball Team Budget for the 2012 Season (see Ball Team Sidebar), Under Armour, in this hypothetical example, relies heavily on sales to retail chains, with 60% of sales through that distribution channel. Sales to independent stores and abroad are also significant. Under Armour has invested in distribution on the Internet, although online sales in 2011 were only 6% of total sales.

After sales force and marketing executives analyze potential sales from various projections, historical sales are examined to project future sales. At a minimum, three to five years of the most recent sales figures should be reviewed. This approach allows analysis of recent trends that can be useful in forecasting future sales growth.

The research process, specifically an examination of historical sales data, has shown that over the last 10 years Under Armour has maintained its position as a sporting goods manufacturer with seasonal sales patterns, and those sales have grown an average of 8% per year. In individual years, sales have been dependent on the strength of the U.S. economy. The forecasts for year 2012 sales will be based on the historical information, supplemented by the experience and research of Under Armour's analysts.

In table 3.6 three scenarios are presented for forecasting purposes. These include a best-case scenario, a worst-case scenario, and a most likely scenario. The most likely scenario is based on pulling together the best and worst cases. The two extreme cases give the analyst a way to understand opportunities as well as potential barriers to success (Koller, Goedhart, & Wessels, 2005).

The worst-case scenario assumes that most of Under Armour's sales are stable and that 90% of 2011 sales is a reasonable assumption. The 90% range is designed as a cushion in case sales are

Table 3.5 Under Armour's 2011 Sales (hypothetical)

Distribution channel	2011 sales ($)	Percentage of total
Chain stores	36,000,000	60%
Independent stores	12,525,000	21%
Individual (direct)	375,000	1%
Internet	3,750,000	6%
Foreign	6,000,000	10%
Other	1,350,000	2%
Total	60,000,000	100%

Table 3.6 Under Armour's Sales Forecast for 2012 (hypothetical)

Distribution channel	2011 sales ($)	Worst-case sales ($)	Most likely sales ($)	Best-case sales ($)	Most likely sales ($), percentage change
Chain stores	36,000,000	32,400,000	38,880,000	43,200,000	8%
Independent stores	12,525,000	11,272,500	13,527,000	15,030,000	8%
Individual (direct)	375,000	375,000	375,000	375,000	0%
Internet	3,750,000	2,250,000	6,525,000	9,375,000	74%
Foreign	6,000,000	5,400,000	6,480,000	7,200,000	8%
Other	1,350,000	1,350,000	1,350,000	1,350,000	0%
Total	60,000,000	53,047,500	67,137,000	76,530,000	12%

lower in a subsequent year. If Under Armour's historical sales had fluctuated substantially from year to year, a worst-case scenario could involve sales of even less than 90% of 2011 sales. In the case of sales over the Internet, that distribution channel is still in its infancy and is subject to greater risk, particularly if other manufacturers decide to use the Internet as a distribution medium. Thus in a worst-case scenario, sales over the Internet are shown as a 40% decline. Sales to individuals are expected to remain the same, even in a worst-case scenario, because Under Armour does not devote any marketing effort to individual sales and annual sales to individuals have stayed relatively constant over the last decade.

Note that historical sales were used to determine the worst-case scenario. In the event of a new trend that is not reflected in the historical sales information, the potential sales decline under the worst-case scenario would be easy to underestimate. For example, if a new movement toward consolidation took place in the retail sporting goods sector and certain retail chains that had been Under Armour customers went out of business, Under Armour's sales might be subject to unforeseen declines. Furthermore, if Under Armour made nothing but snowboarding and skiing jackets and winter snowfall was poor or if it missed the snowboarding jacket trend, then sales could plummet.

The best-case scenario assumes that with properly focused marketing efforts, chain store, independent store, and foreign sales can increase by 20%. By contrast, because the Internet distribution channel is still new, a best-case scenario includes Internet sales growing by a multiple of 2.5 in the event that Under Armour's efforts to enter this market segment begin to bear immediate fruit.

The increase of 2.5 times is an estimate based on either an educated hunch or market expectations.

The most likely scenario represents a composite of the worst-case and best-case scenarios. The best- and worst-case scenarios do not have to be weighted evenly. Instead, the weight applied to each should represent subjective judgment about the relative likelihood that each of these scenarios will occur. In terms of a reasonableness check, note that Under Armour's sales in its traditional chain store, independent store, and foreign distribution channels are expected to grow at rates that match recent historical growth rates for the business as a whole. Because the Internet is an entirely new distribution channel with a lot of upside potential for growth, Internet sales are projected to grow 74% in 2012 under a most likely scenario. The Internet sales growth causes overall projected sales growth to be 12% for 2012, which will surpass the 8% historical norm.

So far, we have developed a sales forecast using a bottom-up approach. Essentially, we have separately forecasted each component of sales and then summed up the total sales across components (or distribution channels in our example) to determine total sales.

Short-Term Planning

The Under Armour example is a short-term forecast for one year out. Short-term planning dictates how a business should proceed within a short time frame, usually less than two years. Short-term planning cannot be undertaken without examining the potential implication of current decisions on the long-term profitability or success of any business. Long-term planning is more oriented toward the future and allows executives to be more creative because many options and uncertainties play into such decision making. Short-term planning is based on specific research and requires people to meet specific goals.

Regardless of the time frame used for planning, accuracy and the ability to interpret internal and external data properly are the keys to success. For example, if the short-term analysis does not adequately examine internal debt-related issues and the external borrowing environment, a business may not last more than several months before creditors file for involuntary bankruptcy.

The short-term planning process requires close scrutiny of internal variables such as cash flow and debt-related issues. Key aspects of short-term planning include knowing how to make decisions based on working capital, net working capital, current ratio, acid test ratio, and the cash budget. These ratios are discussed in chapter 6.

Deciding whether to hire a new basketball coach is normally a long-term planning process. Most coaches are not hired for the short term; they are hired to build a program using their skills and strengths. This intention does not mean that short-term planning will not influence the decision. Ticket sales and player recruiting still need to be undertaken during the hiring process to ensure continued success or prevent falling further behind rival programs. Thus, the hiring process, like almost all planning decisions, entails a blend of short- and long-term planning.

For example, the University of Houston hired a former star basketball player at the university and one of the top 50 players in NBA history, Clyde Drexler, as the head basketball coach. Almost immediately thereafter, the university spent a considerable sum to remove several rows of seats and install luxury boxes. Although the initial demand for the boxes was high based on the prospect that the new coach would develop a winning team, those hopes quickly faded. The team performed unremarkably during Drexler's tenure, and after two years he resigned. This account serves as an example of poor short-term planning and inadequate capital management. The athletic department was hoping for a miracle with a new coach, but it would have been better served by waiting for the coach to succeed and then grow rather than hoping that growth would be immediate.

Effective planning would have included a cost–benefit analysis of installing the luxury boxes based on the possible failure of the coach rather than just on the expectation that a miracle would occur

and that the hiring would erase years of debt. In fact, attendance had been abysmal for years before the hiring, and during the two years thereafter it improved. Still, there were no guarantees that attendance would not return to its previous level if the basketball team did not deliver a high-quality product. Short-term planning might have focused on examining the attendance trends associated with the new coach for at least several years after he came to the University of Houston to see whether his hiring would in fact increase attendance. After collecting some empirical data based on actual ticket sales and revenue for a one- or two-year period after the coach's hiring, the university could have made a more accurate short-term plan for capital expenditure during a deficit.

The University of Houston example highlights how most business decisions entail an element of both short- and long-term planning. Another example of how short-term planning can blend into long-term planning is the futures market. The futures market primarily involves commodities such as metals, meats and other foods, and currencies. Most commodities sales are conducted in the spot market, where an item is bought and sold for cash and the exchange is completed immediately.

But in the futures market, transactions involve delivery and payment at some future date. A sports team could pay a significant amount of money for a player, but the player might be delivered at a future date because of other contractual obligations. This future obligation often happens with foreign athletes who might be drafted and signed by North American teams but still have to complete their contracts with their foreign teams. If a player is playing in Europe, the payment amount could be affected by fluctuations in the value of the U.S. dollar against the European currency during the waiting period.

Floating means paying a certain amount to buy future dollars or other currencies on the currency markets. Some people are betting that currency values will increase, and others are betting that the values will decrease. A similar type of gamble occurs when people buy stock with the expectation that the shares will either increase or decrease in value. This process is often called hedging, which entails purchasing futures contracts in situations in which a price change could positively or negatively affect profits. A business could purchase a long hedge when it anticipates a price increase. With a short hedge, a business sells futures contracts to guard against price declines (Brigham & Gapenski, 1994).

The short sale is also used in the stock sale context when someone sells short with the intent of borrowing the stock from a broker and waiting for the price to decline before he actually buys the stock. The difference between the value of the borrowed stock and the final amount he paid for it when the stock price declined is the profit generated by this short sale. But if the stock increases in value, the investor will have to pay the higher price, which could result in a significant loss for the investor. Purchasing stocks is covered in greater detail in chapter 9.

When purchasing a futures contract, the purchaser does not have to put up the full amount. The purchaser needs to put up only an initial margin, which for certain Treasury bonds is only $3,000 for each $100,000 in contracts (Brigham & Gapenski, 1994). Although the purchase price is low, investors need to maintain a certain value in their margin account, called a maintenance margin. If the contract value declines, the futures owner is required to pay more money to cover the maintenance margin.

A futures contract can be satisfied by the actual delivery of the commodities. A farmer could sell a futures contract for 5,000 bushels of oats for a September delivery. A sport nutrition-bar company might buy the contract in March so that the company knows how much it will need to pay for ingredients and the farmer knows how much he will be paid for the future delivery of oats. Thus, a futures contract is a definite agreement on the part of a given party to buy something on a specific date and at a specific price. No matter how the price might change, the contract guarantees that the purchaser has locked in a price to protect against such price fluctuations. Futures can be used speculatively or for hedging. People buy speculative futures if it appears

that a price might decline or rise, resulting in profits.

By carefully examining financial markets, a business can increase its profitability and reduce its chances of losing money through inactivity. For that reason, a business needs to scrutinize short-term strategies related to all facets of its operation. Long-term strategies also help guide businesses, as discussed next.

Long-Term Planning

In contrast to short-term forecasts, long-term goals are often less clear because the large number of variables reduces the accuracy of projections. Even so, obtaining additional research on which to base decisions can result in projections that are more accurate. Long-term planning focuses on planning for the future and places greater emphasis on external variables, such as industry trends and technological advancements. A fitness center's long-term analysis might focus on developing new exercise techniques or programs that combine some of the hottest fitness trends.

The long-term plan serves as the backbone for developing the documentation needed to secure capital support. Potential lenders such as banks or venture capitalists look to the managerial foresight highlighted in the plan. But no matter how much information the plan contains, a lender will not invest a penny without getting a picture of the business' future profit potential. The profit potential is reflected in the pro forma budget.

Earlier we examined a one-year hypothetical sales forecast for Under Armour. Most companies develop both a short-term forecast (for sales and other parts of the business) and a longer-term forecast. Typically, lenders and investors require at least a three-year projection, as shown in table 3.7.

Table 3.7 Under Armour's Three-Year Sales Forecast (hypothetical)

Distribution channel	2011 actual sales ($)	2012 estimated most likely sales ($)	2013 sales ($)	2014 sales ($)
Chain stores	36,000,000	38,880,000	41,990,400	45,349,632
Independent stores	12,525,000	13,527,000	14,609,160	15,777,893
Individual (direct)	375,000	375,000	375,000	375,000
Internet	3,750,000	6,525,000	9,135,000	10,962,000
Foreign	6,000,000	6,480,000	6,998,400	7,558,272
Other	1,350,000	1,350,000	1,350,000	1,350,000
Total	60,000,000	67,137,000	74,457,960	81,372,797

In the case of Under Armour, we assume that in the chain store, independent store, and foreign distribution channels, sales will continue to grow at their historical 8% average annual growth rate. In the case of the Internet, we assume that growth will decline from 74% in 2012 to 40% in 2013 and 20% in 2014. This projection is consistent with the notion that a new business line will demonstrate extremely high sales growth that declines over time (Ross, Westerfield, & Jaffe, 2008). We also continue assuming that sales to individuals and other sales will remain constant over time.

As discussed earlier in this chapter, numerous decisions in the sport industry entail both short- and long-term planning. An excellent example involves the Extreme Football League (XFL), launched by World Wrestling Entertainment (WWE) in 2001. WWE went public in 2000 and is listed on the New York Stock Exchange. The launch was undertaken with a broadcast partner, NBC, and had the intent of capitalizing on the young male audience that dominates in wrestling. The games, scheduled for prime-time Saturday nights, were a complete disaster. The shows had declining ratings each week, and the experiment ended with the WWE taking a $37 million charge to earnings (Grover & Lowry, 2001). A charge to earnings is a fancy term for a loss. Instead of a steady loss from poor sales, a charge represents a one-time loss that the business does not expect to occur again in the future.

Wall Street did not take the news well. Some analysts were skeptical about how the WWE could expand in a saturated market after the XFL collapsed (Grover & Lowry, 2001). The concern was also reflected in a drop in the stock price from $21 per share to around $12 per share after the XFL folded. By November 2001 the company had laid off almost 10% of its employees because lower-than-expected revenues resulted in year-end losses ("WWF fires COO," 2001). In 2011 shares of WWE were selling for around $10 per share.

This example highlights how a long-term plan, such as attempting to increase revenues by launching a new football league to compete with existing leagues, can backfire. With a significant amount of hype and planning, the league had a decent first night because of the novelty of the event. When advertisers started complaining about the low ratings and the general lack of interest in the new league, a short-term exit planning process had to be undertaken. As the XFL crumbled, WWE had to engage in short-term planning to find other options for continued growth. WWE started pursuing other projects such as music sales, cookbooks, and children's storybooks. It expanded overseas broadcasts and launched a two-hour magazine-style show (Grover & Lowry, 2001). Thus, when the long-term plans failed, WWE was forced to pursue short-term plans to fill the financial void left after the XFL failed to generate the expected future revenue streams. WWE was not resting on its laurels and was pursuing long-term growth through new consumer product launches, new television programming, and international growth. The company was also exploring the acquisition of entertainment content companies and the outsourcing of WWE's core competencies—television and film production, live event production, and licensing.

Special Situations

In our discussion of preparing sales forecasts, we have not considered the following special situations:

- Start-ups
- Ownership changes
- Fast growth

Start-Ups

Sales forecasts for start-ups are particularly difficult because the business has no established track record. In addition, trade group and industry data comprise sales figures for ongoing and successful businesses, which are not necessarily relevant for a new business. New businesses tend to have lower sales than those of an established business but have the same level of expenses. In addition, new businesses tend to be strapped for the capital necessary to generate sales sufficient to translate into profitable financial results. Consequently, pro forma balance sheets and income statements for new businesses are speculative.

Ownership Changes

When an ownership change occurs, the operating history of the business may not be a useful guide for developing future sales forecasts. If the ownership change resulted from poor business performance, new ownership is probably going to institute changes in management. The business must halt its negative momentum and engineer a turnaround before sales growth can occur. Ownership changes can also result in the loss of customers or key employees, especially in smaller, closely held businesses in which the company's success is tied to the efforts of a key person. Under these circumstances, businesses tend to need to reexamine their product lines and markets.

To avoid possible conflict with a previous owner, buyers of existing small businesses often insist that the sales agreement includes a noncompete clause. Noncompete clauses prevent the sellers from competing in the same line of business from a location within the same geographic region for a specified number of years. Another way around this problem is for the buyer of the business to retain the seller of the business as a consultant for a specified time after the sale is completed.

Fast Growth

Businesses characterized by fast-growing sales should not assume that this fast growth will continue forever into the future. For example, if corporate sales in the economy have been growing annually at a rate of 6% per year over the past five years and a particular business has been growing at a rate of 20% per year, it is unreasonable to assume that this divergence will continue. Typically, successful start-ups have extremely high growth rates that slow as the business matures. Businesses seizing new market niches or entering new and growing markets are typically the ones associated with abnormally high growth. These businesses are at risk as other entrants, having witnessed the explosion in growth, try to steal market share (Pratt & Niculita, 2007).

DEVELOPING A PRO FORMA BUDGET

As highlighted in chapter 6, budgets represent the key to financial planning. Financial planning is accomplished through the development of budgets as a road map for a business' financial success. Budgets help establish a means to forecast future performance based on past results and expected external changes such as changes in the market or the economy. The budget also helps management establish goals and objectives for the business. Thus, a budget is first and foremost a financial plan for the future. The financial plan highlights what results are anticipated if certain financial actions are taken. For example, if you want to buy a car, you might examine your financial position and determine that you can afford only $100 a

month. You can develop a financial plan based on how much of a down payment you can make and your $100 a month available for monthly payments.

A financial plan is often a key component of a pro forma budget and a business plan. A pro forma budget is simply a future budget based on past financial results and expected future financial results. The pro forma budget contains a financial plan for the business, and the two are often combined to help complete the business plan. The business plan is the road map for the business; it contains financial analysis along with other key components such as marketing and production that help an executive or lender determine the potential for future success of the business.

Before considering the pro forma budget as part of the planning process, we should note the significant difference between forecasting and budgeting. A forecast is an estimate of anticipated operations, such as how many hours given machinery will operate. The sales force could be asked what sales they would forecast for the coming quarter. In contrast, a budget is a target agreed on by management as an indicator of success; for example, management might agree that a successful year would entail selling one million tickets. On the basis of this distinction, it is often best to view profit planning and appropriate budgeting from a product or division perspective in which less profitable products or divisions can be isolated for more thorough analysis.

Typical extensive pro forma budgets might incorporate the following:

- ♦ A sales budget
- ♦ A promotion budget
- ♦ A materials, labor, and overhead budget
- ♦ A cash budget
- ♦ A capital appreciation budget

All the previously listed documents or components are contingent on developing a focused strategic plan. All the numbers in the world are meaningless if the business has no direction. Although this book does not focus on strategic planning, note that the hallmark of any business is a concise corporate purpose. This overall mission for the business leads to the development of the corporate scope—a definition of the business' area of concentration. The area of concentration is further refined through developing corporate objectives, strategies, and plans that focus on how the business can achieve its corporate purpose. The financial plan is a key document produced after significant foresight has shaped the future direction of the business.

The financial plan can be developed in five steps. The first step is to develop a system of projected financial statements, which can help a company analyze how the operating plan will affect the projected profits. The next step requires analysts to determine the funds that will be needed to help support the long-term plans. The third step entails forecasting what funds will be available over the long term and how much of the funding will be generated internally and externally. The fourth step requires a business to establish and maintain a system of controls governing how funds are allocated and used. The last step requires analysts to examine the results and develop procedures for adjusting the plan if the forecasts are not met (Brigham & Gapenski, 1994).

INCORPORATING THE PRO FORMA BUDGET IN THE BUSINESS PLAN

The hallmark of a successful business involves a detailed business plan that accentuates the pro forma budget. This chapter has focused so far on developing a financial plan, or road map. After this plan is developed, it has to be communicated. Some individuals with a strong financial background can examine the pro formas and get a decent picture of a business, but most people need a little more guidance. That guidance comes from a business plan that expands on the financial plan and communicates the business' vision using both words and pro formas. Thus, a business plan blends a financial plan and a business strategy analysis to examine both long- and short-term goals and objectives.

Although a business plan can be written in several ways, the following framework provides the most critical elements of a business plan that you might write to submit to a bank or other investors. Within the business plan, the pro forma budget is the concise document used to show that the plan makes financial sense and is viable and accurate. An example of the first page of a pro forma budget is shown in figure 3.1.

The following components found in a typical business plan were developed by Florida Atlantic University's Small Business Development Center. Potential variations are countless, however, and software to help with writing business plans is available. The Small Business Administration also offers sample forms for writing a business plan at www.sba.gov.

▶ The plan summary should be written after all other sections are finished. It describes

- the purpose of your plan,
- the product or service that you will sell and why it is unique,
- second- or third-generation products or services to help maintain sales,
- the market potential,
- specific highlights in the marketing plan,
- the skills provided by the management team,
- the financial projections for the first several years,
- your funding needs, and
- an exit strategy to be implemented if the business does not succeed.

▶ The industry section should highlight the economics in the industry, industry trends, and potential legal or regulatory concerns, and it should critically analyze the competitive forces that you might face. This section requires objective, verifiable information. Most of the information should be documented through secondary data from reliable sources. Sources of secondary data could include government reports, Better Business Bureau reports, reports from national or international trade organizations, research conducted by competitors, and even magazine or newspaper articles. Primary data, as discussed earlier, are data generated by the business itself (e.g., results of a customer satisfaction survey of a competitor's customers to determine whether the customers would prefer a different option or service). Any data used to substantiate statements in the industry section should be copied and attached to the business plan as exhibits.

▶ The company section describes the history and background of the business. It can include the mission statement, objectives, goals (long term and short term), and strategies. This section should also list the current principal owner or owners or majority stockholders, all members of the board of

Profit and loss summary ($000) * CONFIDENTIAL *	Year 1	Year 2	Year 3	Year 4	Year 5	Year 6	Year 7	Year 8	Year 9	Year 10
Net revenue: sports core (schedule A)	0	0	6,167	8,543	10,334	11,183	11,252	11,265	11,265	11,265
Leasing (schedule B)	0	0	1,782	2,158	2,214	2,247	2,278	2,310	2,310	2,310
Total net revenue	**0**	**0**	**7,949**	**10,701**	**12,548**	**13,430**	**13,530**	**13,576**	**13,576**	**13,576**
Net margin	0	0	4,210	6,659	8,288	9,013	9,007	8,947	8,947	8,947
Net margin %	**0**	**0**	**53.0%**	**62.2%**	**66.1%**	**67.1%**	**66.6%**	**65.9%**	**65.9%**	**65.9%**
Period costs:										
General and administrative (worksheet 2)	486	709	1,183	1,227	1,245	1,245	1,245	1,245	1,245	1,245
Depreciation (worksheet 2)	51	586	1,139	1,157	1,174	1,192	1,068	937	816	684
Vacancy cost (worksheet 2)	0	0	99	46	42	44	45	47	47	47
Total period costs	**537**	**1,294**	**2,421**	**2,429**	**2,461**	**2,481**	**2,359**	**2,230**	**2,108**	**1,976**
Income from operations	(537)	(1,294)	1,788	4,230	5,827	6,532	6,648	6,717	6,838	6,970
Other income/(expense) (see schedule E)	0	(1,446)	(218)	(834)	(720)	(553)	(371)	(178)	12	209
Charge-out to capitalizing organizational costs (except depreciation)	486	709	0	0	0	0	0	0	0	0
Pretax income	(51)	(2,031)	1,571	3,395	5,106	5,979	6,278	6,539	6,851	7,179
Provision for taxes (N/A due to LLC status)	0	0	0	0	0	0	0	0	0	0
Net income	**(51)**	**(2,031)**	**1,571**	**3,395**	**5,106**	**5,979**	**6,278**	**6,539**	**6,851**	**7,179**
Ratios and valuation (assumes owning land vs. leasing)										
ROE	N/A	N/A	30.0%	46.7%	49.4%	42.9%	35.5%	30.2%	26.6%	23.9%
ROA	N/A	N/A	22.5%	36.8%	40.9%	37.0%	31.5%	27.4%	24.5%	22.3%
Net income/net revenue	N/A	N/A	19.8%	31.7%	40.7%	44.5%	46.4%	48.2%	50.5%	52.9%
Book value	449	3,668	5,238	7,276	10,339	13,927	17,694	21,617	25,727	30,035
Liabilities to net worth	2.28	5.09	0.33	0.27	0.21	0.16	0.13	0.10	0.09	0.07
Interest coverage	N/A	N/A	16.26	38.45	52.97	59.39	60.44	61.06	62.17	63.37
Debt service coverage	N/A	N/A	25.64	42.38	58.10	66.19	67.88	68.97	70.69	72.48

Notes

Information on this and accompanying pages is confidential. It is being provided to the reader with the understanding that it shall not be shared with others without express permission.

As of this date, the numbers provided here are preliminary and still undergoing analysis and revision. They are best, current, conservative estimates. We are in the process of refining the financial model and testing the investment, revenue, and expense projections as well as exploring various capitalization strategies.

Interest expense based on assumption that mortgage principle payments are level over life of notes, with interest payments declining.

Pro forma assumes organization as an LLC. In future years the company may elect to change to a corporate structure.

Figure 3.1 The first page of a pro forma budget.

Adapted from The Peak Experience, LLC.

directors (if applicable), and all key executives. Last, this section should include the business' address; form of organization (sole proprietorship, partnership, limited liability company, or corporation); and any pertinent local, regional, or federal license requirements (such as requirements for handling pool chemicals).

▶ Any special circumstances concerning the company should be specified in this section, such as what stock purchase options exist if the company goes public or whether key employees have non-compete contracts. Any data that an investor would need to make an investment decision should be included. For example, if a company-owned patent is about to expire, meaning that competitors could start manufacturing the previously protected item, the company could face significant hardships. Similarly, if a fitness center is leasing a fitness facility and the lease is about to expire, meaning that the center could be without a facility, that fact would need to be disclosed. The plan needs to highlight such hardships even if they hurt the prospects for raising capital. The failure to include critical data can lead to allegations of fraud or of negligent or intentional misrepresentation.

▶ The analysis of the product or service is a thorough analysis of the unique qualities of the product or service, which will help distinguish the product or service from those offered by competitors. You want to analyze the risks associated with the product or service and the reasons that purchasers might not buy your product or service. You will need to analyze any market surveys or other research that helps you draw conclusions about your product or service or that of the competition. Last, this section should identify any ancillary products or services that might be produced to develop a more expansive product or service line. If you were developing an indoor rock-climbing facility, for example, you would examine that facility in relation to

- any home-based climbing apparatus,
- any club-based climbing apparatus,
- options available at health clubs,
- the uniqueness of the industry,
- the demand for leisure sports or recreational activities in a given community,
- the availability of other climbing facilities within a 20-mile (32 km) radius of the proposed facility,

- the availability of natural climbing areas nearby and how weather patterns will affect usage,
- the availability of safety-related products, and
- the availability of trained instructors to work with patrons.

▶ The market section focuses on the demographic characteristics of the proposed market. Who is the target market? What is its size? Can those people be reached? And do they have the funds necessary to purchase the product or service? You will need to examine the market critically to determine whether the potential customers or clients buy on a regular basis or seasonally, whether they respond to sales or coupons, and whether other locations can more effectively reach the intended market. Look through a general telephone directory such as the Yellow Pages and identify the competition by name, address, and phone number. Visit the competition to see how big they are, what products or services they offer, whether they are busy, and when they are busy. After you analyze the potential market and the competition, you should establish one-year and five-year sales goals.

▶ The marketing strategy section of the business plan applies the product or service characteristics to the customers' demands. This section focuses on how to sell or distribute the product or service to potential buyers. It requires applying the four Ps of marketing—place, product, price, and promotion. Sample brochures, advertisements, announcements, product packaging, product or service guarantees, and related materials should be included. The price for the product or service should be clearly explained and compared with prices charged by competitors. This section should include all relevant information obtained through the marketing research process and used as a basis for the marketing decisions.

▶ The operation section describes how the product will be developed and produced or how the service will be delivered. Here you should discuss critical dates, such as when production will begin, as well as who will produce the products, where the inventory will come from, what shipping schedule will be followed, how the products will be delivered to clients, and so on. Writing this section requires that you have analyzed the financial and managerial control mechanisms for tracking production, inventory, and shipping, as well as accounting procedures and the like. This section should conclude by specifying the steps that will be taken if the sales goals are not reached (e.g., inventory liquidation) and the revenue that such procedures can realize.

▶ The management and personnel section lists all the key individuals necessary for the business to be successful, including brief biographies of accomplishments and potential references. This section should highlight the key skills required for the business to succeed and indicate how the key individuals fit within the necessary skill areas. In addition to discussing qualifications, you will typically analyze the compensation packages that key individuals are receiving or will receive.

▶ The financial projections section addresses when investors can make their money back and what profit they can realize. Anyone who might be interested in investing in your business will probably view this as the most important section of the business plan. Although the product or service, marketing strategy, and personnel are critical areas, investors are likely to be most interested in the return on their money. Projected cash flow needs to be calculated on a month-to-month basis for the first year until a positive cash flow can be realized and then maintained. The cash flow should also be calculated annually for five years. These projections should be augmented with pro forma income statements and balance sheets. From these pro forma statements, the potential investor can start making calculations to determine critical points for business growth and expansion, such as the break-even point or return on investment.

▶ The capital needs section covers what funds will be needed to launch the business and when the funds will be needed. To help establish potential collateral, the plan should highlight what the funds will be used for. Thus, if the funds will be used to purchase a building, a lending institution will probably be more willing to extend the loan knowing that the loan proceeds could be secured by the building. This section also needs to detail how the money will be repaid, over what period, and what penalties might apply for late payments. Last, this section should cover any ownership potential that might be available. If you are willing to sell a 10% stake in the business to the right investor, you need to explain the potential deal in great detail. Details are required, especially if someone else

can purchase a controlling interest or can assume liability for financial obligations.

▶ A miscellaneous section can be added that contains relevant pictures, price lists, facility diagrams, a listing of necessary equipment, or a discussion of any unusual risks (Pounds, 1997).

Business plans are written every day, but most never receive funding. Most business plans fail because of lack of research, preparation, and presentation. The following is a top-10 list of characteristics seen in successful business plans:

1. Clear and realistic financial projections are the most important element.
2. The plan contains detailed and documented objective market research.
3. The plan includes a detailed analysis of all competitors.
4. The plan demonstrates that the management team is more than capable of leading the company.
5. The plan has a "killer" summary of two or three pages that includes critical projections such as income statements.
6. The plan provides proof of the writer's vision by clearly differentiating the product or service from that of the competition.
7. The document follows a clear plan and, most important, is written in proper English that is clear, precise, and free of grammatical mistakes.
8. The most effective plans are short, rarely exceeding 40 pages. Documents longer than this can become too cumbersome to read.
9. The writer clearly explains the bottom line—why the money is needed and how investors will be repaid.
10. The writer has taken the time to make the plan her own. When people write business plans using their own words, instead of hiring an outside writer or using canned computer software, the reader has a better feel for their sincerity (Elkins, 1996).

CONCLUSION

Every organization needs an accurate plan, and the budget serves as the plan. The previous chapter highlighted various forms of revenues and expenses; this chapter discussed how to examine revenues and expenses in a way to plan for the future. Vigilance is the key to effective financial planning. Managers must take the time to research all prior actions and potential future actions. Planning cannot focus just on the past; it also requires a critical analysis of the future. By doing their homework, managers can learn a great deal about their businesses. The research required to prepare budgets and develop business plans can provide a significant education about a company. All the people in the planning process have valuable information about the business.

Their insight can be of great help. If chief financial officers meet with individual salespeople, they may uncover reasons why certain products do not sell as well in particular regions and can use this knowledge to help allocate resources more effectively. Thus, the planning process is not designed just to keep employees busy; it is the only technique available to prepare a business for the future. The hurdles and opportunities identified in the planning process lead to finalizing the capital budgeting process, which is covered in chapter 11.

Class Discussion Topics

1. Discuss a rough budget for your personal finances. What hurdles might you face in preparing and following the budget?

2. Discuss a short-term plan for a perennially losing team and identify specific steps that could be taken to increase income or generate victories.

3. Discuss a long-term plan for a perennially losing team and identify specific steps that could be taken to increase income or generate victories.

4. What things can prevent a team from meeting its budget projections?

5. What do you think is the most important primary data for a sport business to develop, and how can the business find this information?

6. What do you think is the most important secondary data for a sport business to develop, and how can the business find this information?

7. Develop a sample survey you believe could be used to obtain critical information on which financial decisions could be made.

8. What is the value of budgeting?

9. Analyze the revenue and expense projections for a local college or university and try to determine some of the potential financial objectives for the athletic department.

10. Compare the team expenses for a baseball team in the 1930s against the expenses for a team today and identify the greatest differences.

11. What key items need to be documented so that a business can accurately analyze its financial performance?

12. What are some of the difficulties that can be encountered when trying to project the future profitability of a team-sport franchise?

13. Why is it advisable to use multiple scenarios to project the future financial profitability of a business?

Government and Other Influences on Finance

Now that you know the basics of finance (revenues, expenses, and budgeting), you can start to analyze some of the variables that can influence the financial strengths and weaknesses of a business. Part II will give you a perspective of the primary influences and environmental issues that affect sport businesses and organizations.

Chapter 4, "Financial Systems and How They Operate," covers the basic systems that allow finance to occur. For example, if there were no standard currency, how would people buy and sell items? For the economy to function, we need stable markets that everyone accepts. The financial world includes markets (such as stock exchanges) and financial institutions (such as banks), and it requires government oversight to make sure that honesty and accountability are present. The chapter ends with a review of some environmental conditions that influence the various markets.

Chapter 5, "Business Structures, Bankruptcy, and Taxation," highlights the various types of businesses that exist in the sport industry. Business structure is important because it determines how government rules can affect a company and influences the financial strategies that a business can undertake. For example, a sole proprietorship cannot issue stocks and become a publicly traded company without changing its structure. Furthermore, recent rules such as the Sarbanes-Oxley reporting requirements affect C corporations but not many other businesses at this time. Business structures covered include sole proprietorships, general and limited partnerships, subchapter S corporations, C corporations, limited liability corporations and partnerships, and nonprofit organizations. This chapter also covers some of the legal and government influences affecting sport such as taxes and bankruptcy, and it discusses strategies that can be followed to address risks.

chapter 4

Financial Systems and How They Operate

Chapter Objectives

After studying this chapter, you should be able to do the following:

- Describe a financial market.
- Compare the various types of financial markets and the way in which they affect the sport industry.
- Understand the differences among marketable securities such as stocks and bonds.
- Explain how sport businesses can acquire needed capital through institutions such as banks and savings and loans.
- Comprehend government's role in influencing financial systems and sport industries.
- Understand the forces that propel the stock market and the various publicly traded sport-related stocks.

This chapter deals with the key elements in various financial systems and institutions and the way in which they interact to help sport businesses. Financial markets and systems play a critical role in the management of sports organizations. For example, a person or group that is interested in buying a professional sports team must decide how to raise the necessary capital. It may be done through equity (stocks), debt (bonds and bank loans), or both. The primary focus of this chapter is on what constitutes value and how value can be exchanged to help facilitate sport business transactions. Financial systems are affected by financial markets, financial institutions, government influences, and environmental factors. Financial **markets**, such as stock markets, are the arenas in which value is transferred. Financial institutions, such as banks, are entities that help transfer value. **Interest rates** are controlled by a combination of economic factors and government regulations. Two final sections of this chapter address government's greater role in regulating businesses, through such strategies as taxes, and the effect of environmental conditions on a sport investment.

Financial systems are mechanisms that allow anything of value to be exchanged between parties. Financial systems are involved when people receive their paychecks from an employer, such as when a sporting goods store pays its managers and clerks. The employer draws the check from a bank, credit union, savings and loan, or other type of financial holding entity. The money that is drawn may have been received from the employer's customers or from other sources such as borrowed funds or extra cash in the employer's accounts. The paycheck will have some taxes withdrawn, reflecting participation by various government units in the financial exchange. Various financial institutions are also used when the employee deposits the check and starts paying bills, such as credit card bills and the **mortgage** on a home loan.

This oversimplified example illustrates some financial systems and institutions at work. The financial systems work in a cyclical manner, and the same types of transactions occur on a regular basis. Many sport businesses face the same cyclical patterns in their financial dealings. Each month new orders are received, meaning that new funds are generated. Some debts are paid immediately, whereas others might not be paid for several months. Money will be trickling in from accounts receivable while the sport business attempts to pay its own **obligations**, which are **accounts payable**. If sufficient money is not on hand to pay outstanding debts, the sport business may need to turn to financial institutions such as banks, the bond market, the **stock market** (**stock exchange**), or possibly venture capitalists to obtain money.

FINANCIAL MARKETS

Businesses and individuals that need funds are brought together in financial markets. Funds can be obtained from numerous financial markets, and every business will have several markets from which to choose. The following are the primary types of markets (Brigham & Ehrhardt, 2011):

- Tangible or physical markets involve items of value such as products or property. Examples of items in these markets are golf clubs, tennis rackets, golf courses, race cars, and manufacturing machinery.
- **Financial asset** markets involve evidence of value or ownership such as stocks, bonds, loans, and mortgages.
- Spot markets involve assets that are bought, sold, and delivered within several days. Precious metals such as gold and silver are examples of such assets.
- Futures markets involve assets that are bought, sold, and delivered at a later date, which could be six months or several years later. A sport drink company might buy ingredients for its drinks, such as sugar or salt, on the futures market if the company anticipates that certain ingredients might increase in cost and wants to lock in a lower price. In the past few years, futures markets have even been developed for tickets to sporting events like the Super Bowl and Bowl Championship Series national championship collegiate football game.
- Money markets are for **debt securities**, such as loans with a low risk of default, that mature in a shorter time period—usually less than one year.
- In **capital markets**, long-term debt (e.g., bonds) or ownership rights (e.g., stocks) are traded.
- In the mortgage market, residential loans or business loans backed by real estate are traded.
- International markets allow people in one country to tap financial resources in another country. As an example, Canadian professional teams that have to pay players in U.S. dollars may wish to exchange currency on the international market to obtain good exchange rates.
- **Primary markets** are markets in which businesses raise new capital by offering securities

for sale. A primary market exists for a particular security only when the security is issued and sold for the first time.

♦ Secondary markets exist after a security has been sold in the primary market. Thus, the first time that a sport company such as Speedway Motorsports, Inc. issued its stock, it was offered in the primary market. After the initial issues were sold, someone who wanted to buy shares from other owners could acquire the shares only in the secondary market.

This listing indicates the numerous arenas in which sport businesses can obtain or sell assets. Businesses are not required to use only one market exclusively. The various financial markets overlap because some financial assets are also capital assets and are part of both markets. Businesses can use several markets, and most businesses use several markets concurrently. Furthermore, most businesses use several markets when raising capital.

A sport business may raise money on the capital market, or possibly from foreign markets. The markets listed earlier are primarily based in the United States, but a business can also raise money from markets anywhere in the world, such as the London Stock Exchange or the European currency market. A financial manager's job could include constantly tracking these markets to minimize borrowing expenses or raise additional funds. No matter what market is used, the key to funding business growth and facilitating movement within all financial markets is money.

Money

Money is the means by which commerce can occur. A bill or coin has no value in and of itself without agreement on the part of the government and people that it has value. We are accustomed to taking a dollar or two out of our wallets and buying a sports drink or energy bar. We probably do not think twice about such a transaction. But the situation is different if we are buying something for $1 million. No one would expect us to bring in $1 million in small bills. Over time, the growth of commerce necessitated the creation of instruments that functioned like money but were easier to use for conducting business. Checks are an everyday example. Although money is the backbone of most financial transactions, numerous individuals and businesses are now using other payment options, such as automatic withdrawals and bill payments through electronic funds transfers (EFTs).

Money, credit, and checks are not the only instruments of commerce. Wealth can be transferred and documented through other instruments as well. A deed to a piece of land demonstrates that you own the land and have certain rights that may include the right to transfer the land. For example, Washington Redskins owner Daniel Snyder owns the land where FedEx Field is located. Similar rights are conferred by marketable securities, which represent documentation of ownership or indebtedness that can be transferred to others under the right circumstances. Stocks and bonds are typical examples of marketable securities and are discussed in the sections to follow.

Marketable Securities

Marketable securities are instruments so widely accepted and purchased by others that they are almost like cash (Brigham & Ehrhardt, 2011). Any asset that is easy to convert to cash is called a **liquid asset**. For example, common stock in a publicly traded company like Under Armour can be sold through a broker and the resulting cash deposited into the seller's account within a day. In contrast, **hard assets** are assets that a company might not be able to convert to cash as quickly but that can still have significant value. For example, an office building that Under Armour owns and uses to operate its business has significant value but might take a year to sell. This item is an example of a hard asset.

Accounts receivable (A/R) and **inventories** lie between these two extremes. An A/R is an owed obligation. If you have a yearly membership to a new fitness center that requires a payment of $50 a month, a missed payment becomes a receivable owed to the club. The fitness center may develop a group of similar obligations that are past due; these obligations are categorized as accounts receivable. Although significant value exists in A/R and inventories, a business may need several months to collect these funds, and some funds will be lost because of spoilage or because they are uncollectible.

Marketable securities are the most liquid assets available for investment because of their shorter maturity periods (Treasury bills), their ability to be sold on a daily basis (stocks), or their status as relatively risk free (certain bonds and government securities). Relatively risk free means that the chances of the borrower's not paying are negligible. The U.S. government is considered one of the most risk-free investments because of the extremely low risk that the government will collapse. Examples of marketable securities include the following:

▶ Treasury bills: **Treasury bills**, or **T-bills**, are direct obligations of the U.S. government that mature in 3 to 12 months. Direct obligation means that the U.S. government must repay the debt itself when the loan comes due, which is called the maturity date.

▶ Treasury notes: Similar to T-bills, **Treasury notes** are obligations of the U.S. government that mature in 1 to 5 years.

▶ Government agency securities: The maturity on these obligations can be up to 30 years. These securities differ from Treasury notes, however, in that although individual government agencies can issue them, the taxing authority of the U.S. government does not directly back them.

▶ Certificates of deposit: **Certificates of deposit**, or **CDs** as they are commonly called, represent cash deposited in commercial banks, savings and loans, and credit unions. CDs normally mature in 1 month to 5 years. **Jumbo CDs** are for deposits of more than $100,000. These investments have extremely low risk, especially if they are maintained in a federally insured savings institution.

▶ Commercial paper: **Commercial paper (CP)** is a **short-term debt** obligation issued by a large corporation for an amount over $25,000. These debt obligations can have maturity dates ranging from one day to a year. Most of these promissory notes mature in 90 days and carry an interest rate around the prime rate based on the company's credit rating. A promissory note is a simple contract in which the borrower agrees to repay the **lender** for money borrowed. The **prime interest rate** is the interest rate charged by banks on loans to their best customers (those with minimal credit risk).

Table 4.1 lists liquid securities as well as investments or securities that are not as liquid. Riskiness represents the potential that a borrower will default on an obligation. A default-free investment is guaranteed, so the lender is certain to be repaid. A low default risk is the next best protection; with this level of risk there is potential for the borrower to default. When a risk is identified as based on the insurer, the risk of default is contingent on the entity that borrowed the money. Some companies are so strong that the risk of default is minimal, but other companies have a high default risk. See chapter 10 for a discussion of the role of credit ratings in assessing credit risk.

Table 4.1 Securities From Risk Free to High Risk

Security	Typical maturity	Riskiness
LIQUID INVESTMENTS FOR NEAR-CASH RESERVES		
U.S. Treasury bills—sold by the U.S. Treasury	91 days to 1 year	Default free
Banker's acceptance—promise to pay backed by a bank	Up to 180 days	Low risk if backed by a strong bank
Commercial paper—issued by large firms	Up to 270 days	Low default risk
Negotiable certificates of deposits (CDs)	Up to 1 year	Low default risk
Money market mutual funds—investment in T-bills, CDs, commercial paper, and so on	Various maturity dates	Low degree of risk
Euro market time deposits	Up to 1 year	Based on issuing bank
Consumer credit loans—banks, credit unions, finance companies	Variable	Based on issuing bank
Floating rate and market auction preferred stocks	Variable	Based on issuer
LIQUID INVESTMENTS NOT SUITABLE FOR NEAR-CASH RESERVES		
U.S. Treasury notes—price can change based on interest rate changes	3 to 10 years	Default free
U.S. Treasury bonds	Up to 10 years	Default free
Corporate bonds (rated AAA)	Up to 40 years	Based on issuer
State and local government bonds (rated AAA)	Up to 30 years	Based on issuer
Preferred stocks (rated AAA)	30 years to perpetual	Based on company
Common stocks in corporations	Unlimited	Variable

Most CP is highly liquid; only the top corporations with strong credit histories can effectively issue this type of security. Commercial paper is an effective funding source in that it can be issued inexpensively compared with bonds and stocks, which take considerable time and money to issue. Commercial paper also entails less governmental regulation, can help raise significant cash, and does not require the issuer to maintain any compensating balances with a bank. (A **compensating balance** is a required amount of cash kept with the lending institution that serves as a type of security. Because the corporation itself issues the CP, there is no need for any compensating balance to protect the lender.) A final benefit associated with CP is the prestige that a company can generate from being financially strong enough to issue this type of instrument (Griffin, 1991). Thus, as with government-issued securities that can be treated much like **cash**, a corporation's CP can inspire a high level of investor confidence.

This section has covered the types of investment vehicles that are the most liquid, which are almost like cash. But other assets also considered liquid assets are not as liquid as cash or cash-equivalent assets. Thus, ownership of a sport business can also be considered a liquid asset if the ownership is evidenced through publicly traded stock. But in contrast to the situation with cash, T-bills, or CDs, which all have a definite value, the value of stock is uncertain. If you have ever owned stock and sold it, you may have obtained less than the stated value of the stock. Stock redemption refers to the process of selling stocks back to the open market or to the original issuing company. A stock may be hard to sell if investors are not interested in it. Furthermore, market volatility can affect the value of the investment. When times are good, as they were in the early 2000s, and a bull market keeps driving up the value of stocks, more companies put excess cash into acquiring shares in various other companies. If a balance sheet indicates $1 million in investment assets such as stocks, that value will drop $100,000 in one day if the stock price declines 10%. When investors redeem their shares of stock, they may receive less than they originally paid for the shares. Thus, the **liquidity** of stocks is lower than cash or cash equivalents because of the volatility of the stock market.

In October 2011 Under Armour had a market capitalization of $3.87 billion, shares were selling at about $75 each, and the 52-week range for the stock price was $45 to $84. As of March 31, 2011 (a few months earlier), the company had total current assets of more than $558 million. The company also had over $80 million invested in property, plant, and equipment. Under Armour's net tangible assets, combined with the total shareholders' equity, totaled more than $1.1 billion and included $281 million in retained earnings (Under Armour, 2011).

On the same day in October 2011 Speedway Motorsports, Inc. had a market capitalization of $539 million. Shares were trading at $13, and the 52-week range was $11.37 to $16.54. The company had $172 million in current assets, including $90 million in cash and $975,000 in short-term investments. Speedway Motorsports had more than $1.1 billion in total liabilities as of their last reported quarter at that time (July 2011). The stockholders' equity was about $827 million (Speedway, 2011).

These examples highlight the fact that two stocks can be trading at far different price ranges but represent similar pictures. Both companies have significant levels of assets and shareholders' equity. The financial positions of companies can change based on numerous factors, from investor sentiment to ownership changes to legal changes. A perfect example of a legal change was the U.S. law passed in 2006 prohibiting banks from interacting with online gambling establishments. Within hours of the law's passing, the stock value of numerous offshore companies (i.e., companies based in other countries) dropped significantly because of investor perception that the companies were going to lose a significant amount of their customers.

Stocks

Obviously, value can be demonstrated in vehicles other than money. One of the strongest value indicators is stocks. A stock certificate is a document demonstrating ownership interest in a company. This ownership interest is often referred to as equity value. The equity value in companies in general increases over time. The **Dow Jones Industrial Average** (Dow), one of the major **market indexes** (**market averages**) is the average of 30 large, publicly traded companies such as Walmart, DuPont, IBM, and McDonald's, just to name a few. Charles Dow established the Dow in 1896 as an index to be used in the *Wall Street Journal*. The Dow closed its first day at 40.94, and almost 10 years passed before the index reached 100. The stock market went through some tumultuous times in the early 1900s; large drops occurred in 1901 and 1907, and the famous Black Thursday occurred on October 24, 1929. The Dow started to rise in the World War II period and soared through the 1950s, reaching 500 in 1956. In 1970 the Dow ended the year at 838.92 (Dunphy, 1998). In 1972 the Dow surpassed 1,000 points. In 1979 the index ended at 838.74, and in 1987 it passed the 2,000-point mark, having entered a bull market that would push the index past 10,000 by mid-1999.

But even during the good times of a bull market, when prices advance at an aggressive pace, a bear market, or even a day of large losses, can significantly alter such a run. In 1987 Black Monday occurred on October 19 when the index collapsed 508.32 points, which represented a 22.6% drop in one day. This drop was approximately twice as large, in percentage terms, as the drop in 1929. But the prospect of war pushed the Dow up again in 1991, and the Persian Gulf War fueled a rise past 3,000 (Yip, 1999). These highlights suggest the volatility of the Dow in relation to financial, political, and global concerns. For example, right after the attacks in New York and Virginia on September 11, 2001, the Dow dropped to 8,235, but it rose 20% within four months ("Dow Jones continues," 2002). The Dow moved steadily upward in the first part of the 21st century and peaked in October 2007 at the record level of 14,198. It had risen over 3,000 points in less than two years. The bull market that led to this large increase ended in 2008 with the onset of the global recession. The Dow quickly plunged on news of the world financial crisis. By March 2009 the Dow had dropped to 6,547, its lowest level in 12 years. In only 6 weeks in the spring of 2009, it lost 20% of its value. The Dow rebounded somewhat in 2010 and was back over 12,000 by February 2011. The recession, however, brought a great deal of uncertainty to the economy, which resulted in large fluctuations in the Dow Average. Single-day gains or losses of 100 points or more are now common (Rosenberg, 2010).

The Dow has undertaken a number of renovations to reflect more effectively the change in the economy from smokestacks to high tech. Several major corporations were removed from the Dow in 1999, including such household giants as Chevron, Goodyear, Sears Roebuck, and Union Carbide. These businesses were replaced by Intel, Microsoft, Home Depot, and SBC Communications to complete the 30-stock list. The change marked the first time that the Dow included two stocks (Intel and Microsoft) from the NASDAQ ("High-tech injection," 1999). By 2004 the Dow had changed again when AT&T, Eastman Kodak, and International Paper left to be replaced by Verizon Communication, American International Group, and Pfizer (Isidore, 2004). American International Group was dropped from the Dow after its financial difficulties in 2008. Most recently, companies like Bank of America, Kraft Foods, and Cisco have been added.

The Dow does not value stocks. It is only a tool to measure investor confidence in the stock market. Investors hope that the company they invest in will do well enough that the stock will increase in value and any profits will be split with the stockholders through dividend payments or increased share values. The value of the Dow increases as the values of the businesses that compose the Dow increase. Conversely, if the stocks of companies on the Dow decline, so will the Dow. This visible volatility helps dictate whether analysts consider the market to be a bull or bear market. A **bear market** is a stock market in which investors are scared and prices drop approximately 20%, as they did in 2008-2009. A **bull market**, on the other hand, occurs when investors are optimistic and the stock market increases more than 20%. Instead of analyzing all stocks, analysts can look to the Dow and other market indexes such as the Standard & Poor's 500 (S&P 500) to develop a quick barometer of market conditions.

Similar to what happened with the Dow, the NASDAQ index also showed significant weakness in 2008-2009. In October 2007 the NASDAQ had reached a six-year high of over 2,860 points. By March 2009 the NASDAQ had lost almost 55% of its value and was hovering at around 1,275 points. The NASDAQ, however, rebounded nicely in 2010 and regained most of its losses from the recession. It was trading in the 2,500 range by the end of 2010. As of fall 2012, the index was at about 3,100 and the Dow was trading in the 13,000 range.

Bonds

Bonds represent another measure of value. Unlike stocks, which denote ownership interest in a company, bonds represent an obligation owed by a company or institution. The entity issuing the bond is the **debtor**, and the purchaser of the bond is the **creditor**. Creditors are interested in investing their money in bonds that provide a reasonable **yield** (**rate of return**) with the lowest possible risk level. Similar to the situation with CP, the greater a company's financial strength, the easier it is for that company to issue bonds. A company that has a poor financial picture has to pay investors a premium to interest them in buying their bonds. Bonds issued by established companies normally pay lower interest but present a significantly lower default risk.

Bonds are not as frequently seen in the sport industry as in the consumer goods or manufacturing industries. But sport businesses have issued bonds in a few cases. For example, the New York

Yankees and the New Jersey Nets merged and undertook a bond offering through YankeeNets LLC that raised $250 million. Proceeds were used to help purchase the New Jersey Devils. Analysts thought that the YankeeNets offering was unusual and that most bond offerings would still come from stadium and arena construction projects because facilities have a more predictable revenue stream than teams, whose revenues can be volatile based on their win–loss record ("Corporate debt," 2000). The YankeeNets merger ended in 2004, and the Nets were sold to an investor who wanted to move the team to New York. More recently, in 2009, controlling interest in the Nets was sold to Mikhail Prokhorov, a Russian billionaire. In 2012 the team moved to Brooklyn, New York.

Marketable securities, stocks, bonds, and other methods used to finance a business are discussed in detail in chapters 8, 9, and 10. They are relevant in this chapter as vehicles that help facilitate financial transactions. An issuing company can use these instruments to raise money, or companies can buy these instruments in an effort to acquire another business or as an investment vehicle to earn a return. The only limits regarding which corporations can issue stocks and bonds are internal or external variables such as a corporation's articles of incorporation or its credit rating. If a corporation's bylaws allow the corporation to issue only one million shares, then after that number is reached no more shares can be issued without amending the bylaws. No matter who issues or acquires value, institutions need to facilitate the flow of value through these documents.

FINANCIAL INSTITUTIONS

Several major types of financial institutions facilitate the transfer of capital. These institutions are involved in the process either to obtain an interest in the transaction or to be paid a fee for their services. For example, seats on the New York Stock Exchange (NYSE) are sold to companies wishing to engage in buying and selling listed stocks. A seat gives the seat owner the right to trade stocks on the NYSE. A seat is similar to a personal seat license (PSL) for a sports team. After you buy a PSL you can use it, sell a game-day ticket to someone else, or leave the seat empty. Similarly, a seat on the NYSE allows the owner to buy and sell shares personally or to have others do the buying and selling on his behalf. Thus, a seat is the right to be able to do business. Other institutions such as banks charge various fees for services, and they also obtain revenue by acquiring money at a low

interest rate and then turning around and loaning the same money to others at a higher rate.

Banks

The Babylonians are often credited with developing the first true banks sometime around 2000 BC. These banks were run by the Babylonian temples and were involved both in lending and in safekeeping of valuables. The temples charged as much as one-sixth of the deposits for the safekeeping of gold, silver, and other valuables entrusted to them. A temple then charged people who borrowed deposits about 20% interest, compounded monthly (Rodgers, 1966). Fifteen hundred years later, the Greeks also turned their temples into safes for the wealthy. Athens developed a specific body of law covering banking transactions, as well as a court system, which required repayment of debts within 30 days (Rodgers, 1966).

The first publicly owned bank was the Bank of Venice, founded in 1171 AD. The success of the Bank of Venice in its limited lending role spawned future banks such as the Bank of Barcelona in the 14th century, the Bank of Amsterdam in 1602, and the Bank of England in 1694 (Rodgers, 1966).

Banking in the American colonies experienced numerous failures in the early years. In 1791 Alexander Hamilton convinced Congress to charter a national bank called the Bank of the United States, which failed shortly thereafter (FDIC, 2002). Banking history has had numerous success stories, such as the Bank of England, which started as a 1,200,000-pound loan to the English government in 1694 and is still around today. Many disasters befell the French banking system, which collapsed numerous times from unbridled spending and abuses. Banks as we know them today have learned many lessons from the past, but greed has crept into the system at various times and led to problems such as the Great Depression and the savings and loan scandal of the 1980s. Most recently, the banking industry has been cited as one of the major causes for the 2008-2009 recession. Multiple failures in the worldwide banking system contributed significantly to the global economic downturn.

Even with all the faults seen in the commercial banking system, the system is essential for economic and financial survival. For example, if bankers start reducing the credit offered to businesses, which we saw happen almost overnight in 2008, then economic growth slows and the standard of living for all citizens decreases. Conversely, if too much credit is extended to the business community, the rate of growth and the standard of living

HISTORY OF FINANCIAL INSTITUTIONS

Date	Activity
600 BC	Lydia, a Greek state in Asia Minor, uses coins for the first time.
600-200 BC	The Athenian drachma and Roman denarius are first used.
54 AD	Roman emperor Nero is the first official to start reducing the amount of gold and silver in coins.
1409	The first stock exchange is established in Brussels.
1587	One of the first public banks is established in Venice, Italy.
1661	The first paper money is printed by the Swedish National Bank.
1816	England introduces gold as an official currency.
1918	The international gold standard ends.
1925	England returns to the gold standard.
1929	All major international currencies are again linked to gold, and that link continues until the Great Depression ends the influence of gold.
1945	After World War II the world's monetary systems start operating on a standard linked to the U.S. dollar.
1978	The European monetary system is introduced.
1999	Euro coinage is phased in for most nations in the European Union, although the currency was not adopted by all EU members.

Data from "Coins to credit cards," 1999, *Connecticut Post*, F4.

will rise significantly, but at a pace that is not economically sustainable. For example, when the demand for money is great but not enough money is available to meet the demand, competitive pressure causes higher interest rates. These two examples of banks' influencing the economy in the direction of success or failure are commonly referred to as boom and bust (Rodgers, 1966).

Capital

A bank's capital can come from money initially used to start the bank. For example, several major investors may each contribute $100 million to create a bank, and publicly traded banks may issue stock to raise more capital. Capital can also take the form of retained earnings accumulated from income generated by the bank. A bank may choose not to pay dividends and instead use the accumulated earnings as capital. Banks need extra capital to pay daily bills and to extend credit to a broad base of individuals and businesses that need to use that capital. The amount of capital required by any bank for its own reserves is set by law. Capital reserves are also analyzed by the **Federal Deposit Insurance Corporation** (**FDIC**) when

a bank makes a request to reduce its capital stock, establish a new branch, merge or consolidate, or move its main office (*Who is the FDIC?* 2006).

The amount of capital available for issuing loans is affected by the risks associated with other loans, the liquidity of other assets, whether deposits are increasing, and whether enough profit is being made to sustain shareholder confidence. For example, during the recent recession, many banks failed because of their exposure to the real estate market. Banks loaned large amounts to homeowners who could not repay their mortgages when the recession hit. Thus, these banks lost significant amounts of money when they were unable to recover their investments. These losses depleted the banks' available capital because money would be spent covering losses and paying attorneys to help recover as much of the investment as possible. As a result, some banks were forced to file for bankruptcy and close their doors. Therefore, banks need to analyze every loan decision to ensure that the investment will not jeopardize their loan portfolios or their available credit reserves.

One of the primary reasons that banks are required by law to maintain adequate capital reserves is to prevent a run on the bank. If depositors think that their money is at risk, they can pull out their deposits, and the bank must have enough capital to repay all such demands. Before depositing funds, people need to feel comfortable that the bank's management will take care of their money. Although any bank or savings and loan may potentially face financial hardships, investors have federal protections that have been designed to help safeguard their deposits. This protection includes reserve requirements, which are funds that cannot be loaned out, and can include account insurance offered by the federal government, which is discussed later in the chapter.

Federal Reserve System

The **Federal Reserve System**, established by Congress after 1913, comprises 12 Federal Reserve district banks, 25 branches, and more than 5,800 national and state banks (see figure 4.1) (Federal Reserve System, 2006). The Fed, as it is commonly called, was established to provide central banking facilities for the entire United States. The system operates to manage the nation's money supply by

raising or lowering the reserve amount that banks need to keep on hand, changing the discount rate (which is the rate charged to commercial banks for borrowing money), and purchasing and selling government securities (Siegel, Shim, & Hartman, 1992). The Fed has jurisdiction over the following activities (Spiro, 1996):

◆ Commercial bank regulatory function
◆ Reserve requirements and bank discounts
◆ Selective credit control
◆ Open market operations
◆ International operations

The Fed is responsible for conducting field audits of member banks but typically conducts such audits only for state-chartered banks. Nationally chartered banks are under the statutory domain of the Office of Comptroller of the Currency (OCC) and can be examined by that office rather than the Fed. The OCC also audits banks under its charge and works with the Fed in controlling the practices and procedures of nationally chartered banks. The Fed

Figure 4.1 The 12 Federal Reserve districts.

is responsible for administering the Bank Holding Act of 1956, which was enacted to prevent bank monopolies while permitting banks to expand into some nonbank endeavors such as the credit card business or investment management (Spiro, 1996). Another federal law that the Fed is responsible for promulgating and enforcing is the **Consumer Credit Protection Act** (**CCPA**) of 1968 (also called the **Truth in Lending Act**), which requires lenders to provide user-friendly information about the true terms and interest rates on loans.

The Fed is responsible for some regulations concerning credit-related borrowing and lending. For example, the Fed can specify which securities can be purchased on credit and the amount or percentage of credit that lenders are able to extend to purchase the securities. Although the Fed engages in significant policy making, its decisions and actions do not require any governmental approval from either the executive or the legislative branch. The Fed is run by a board of governors who are appointed by the president of the United States with the Senate's consent. After being appointed, the governors and the Fed chairperson work autonomously but report on a yearly basis to Congress. The current Fed chairman is Ben Bernanke. The six other members of the board of governors serve staggered terms, and no member can be reappointed.

The Fed operates similarly to a bank in that member banks can deposit funds with and borrow funds from the Fed. Member banks are required to keep a specific fraction of their deposits as a cash reserve. The money can be kept by the banks in their vaults or can be deposited with the Fed. The Fed determines what percentage needs to be kept on reserve and varies this amount to help stimulate the economy. The Fed can also influence the economy through its discount window. A discount window is the range of interest rates at which a bank can borrow money from the Federal Reserve. The discount window allows banks to borrow against their loan portfolio to raise additional money for offering more loans. By changing the discount rate that it charges commercial banks, the Fed can either encourage more loans (by offering a lower rate) or discourage more loans (by increasing the rate that banks need to pay to borrow the funds) (Spiro, 1996). During the recession of 2008-2009, the Fed drastically cut the discount rate in an effort to encourage banks to make more loans. By 2011 the discount rate had dropped to a historically low level of below 1%. As recently as 2006, the Fed discount rate had been above 6%.

Primary Deposits

Primary deposits are deposits in a bank that come from other banks. Banks that have excess cash but not enough borrowers may deposit the extra cash in another bank to obtain some interest. If the funds just sit in a bank, that bank is forced to pay interest to the depositors but the funds do not generate any revenue. Depositing the funds in another bank makes it possible to obtain some interest, but the funds can also be quickly withdrawn if other borrowers need the money.

These funds can be used to increase reserves with the Fed, which frees more capital for investing. The Fed can also affect bank reserves. The Fed is responsible for maintaining the nation's money supply, and one technique entails purchasing securities. When the Fed buys securities, the funds used to pay for the securities end up as increased deposits in the banking system, which ultimately translates into higher reserves. Thus, Fed member banks can increase their reserves without having to deposit any more cash into their reserves. During World War II the Fed purchased more than $22 billion in securities to help create reserves to finance the war. Banks throughout the nation had more capital that they could loan, but they did not need to do anything to acquire the extra capital. More recently, in an effort to grow the economy after the 2008-2009 recession, the Fed bought more than $1 trillion of bank debt, mortgage-backed securities, and U.S. treasury notes. This move was done to pump more cash into the economy and spur economic growth.

Bank Deregulation

After the 1930s, banks were heavily regulated to prevent them from engaging in other business enterprises such as selling insurance or providing investment advice. But new laws passed in the late 1990s resulted in bank deregulation. Commercial banks are now allowed to establish or acquire investment banking and merchant banking subsidiaries that can engage in extending loans, purchasing ownership interests, or underwriting bond offerings. Banks can now invest in as much as 5% of a company outright or purchase up to 49% of a company through bank-owned subsidiaries. This opportunity to own other businesses has fueled significant investment by banks in high-tech start-ups. Banks can derive significant profit from venture capital investment, which is one of the first stages of investing in a new business. By 1999 Chase Manhattan's venture capital arm had

$2.5 billion in revenue and generated $1.4 billion of Chase's profits (Mclean, 2000).

Deregulation created an environment with significant banking investments in potentially riskier businesses, which resulted in the threat that banks could lose a large amount of their deposits. The Fed was called in to analyze this concern, and it developed policies in 2000 to address the situation. Banks are now required to set aside more capital to cover riskier equity investments. An **equity investment** is not a loan but a purchase of an ownership interest in a business. Because a business can increase or decrease in value, it is a riskier investment compared with most bank portfolios, which contain a large number of commercial and personal loans (Sapsford, 2000). Despite these changes, many critics cited bank deregulation as a major cause of the financial disaster that played a key role in the economic collapse of 2008-2009. Many banks engaged in highly risky investments such as mortgage-backed securities and credit default swaps. When these risky investments went bad, several major financial institutions such as Goldman Sachs, Bear Stearns, Bank of America, and Lehman Brothers were put into financial distress. In the case of Lehman Brothers, the result in 2008 was the largest bankruptcy filing in U.S. history. Lehman held about $600 billion in assets. Ultimately, in 2008 and 2009 the risky investments led to the need for the U.S. federal government to infuse billions of dollars in capital through the Troubled Asset Relief Program (TARP) into those banks for them to remain solvent.

Bank Lending Rules

The various rules and regulations enforced by the Fed can also interact with a bank's own written or unwritten rules. All banks use a loan-to-deposit ratio: They will not loan money as freely after their loans reach more than a certain percentage—often 70% to 75%—of all deposits. The remaining percentage is kept in reserves or invested in short-term or other liquid investments such as **Treasury bonds**. If the loan-to-deposit ratio is reaching the tip of a bank's comfort zone, a borrower could be caught in a credit squeeze. A credit squeeze occurs when a business borrows too much money and a bank or other lending institution will not loan the business any more money unless it repays previously incurred obligations. This situation is similar to a bartender's refusal to serve alcohol to a person who has had too much to drink. A bank will put a credit squeeze on a company if it believes that the

company is overextended or cannot repay debts as they become due. A credit squeeze could be caused by a bank, lender, borrower, the economy, or any other external conditions. To avoid such a problem, most financially astute managers develop multiple banking relationships so that they can approach several sources for the same loan. In 2009 Tom Hicks, the owner of the Texas Rangers and Dallas Stars, was caught in a credit squeeze. He eventually was forced to declare bankruptcy on the teams as his debt mounted to over $525 million. The team was sold in auction in 2010 to a group headed by businessman Chuck Greenberg and former MLB pitcher Nolan Ryan (*Rangers owner Hicks agrees to sell team*, 2010).

Banks may also establish specific rules about the types of loans that they may entertain. Banks typically do not want to issue capital loans because the repayment period for loans to help start a business is much longer than the repayment schedule for typical commercial loans. Thus, a sport business such as a new fitness center would have much more difficulty obtaining initial financing from a bank than would an established business such as Speedway Motorsports or Under Armour. Banks can demand a security pledge from someone who wants to obtain a loan. These **secured loans** can use anything of value as a pledge from which repayment can be extracted if a borrower defaults. Sport loans are often secured by the item purchased. If a golf course borrows money to purchase new golf carts, the carts themselves can become the collateral that secures the loan repayment. Each bank has specific rules about each facet of a loan, from the application process through repayment requirements. These rules are designed not to waste valuable paper but rather to reduce the risks associated with collecting the loan.

Bank Services

Besides providing loans and facilitating economic growth by making money available to borrowers, banks perform various additional services. These services include

♦ allowing people to deposit their money in a bank account for safekeeping,

♦ allowing checking account holders to write checks demanding that the bank pay another party a specific amount,

♦ providing clients with cashier's checks or certified checks,

◆ providing numerous specialty savings accounts for customers, and

◆ acting as general depositaries for U.S. Treasury funds.

These services are provided at various costs, depending on the bank and the special programs offered by each bank. Many banks charge a fee for every check written; other banks provide interest payments to customers who write fewer checks. The costs or interest rates available are based on supply and demand factors as well as competition from other banks. When rates are nearly equal among banks, the banks often engage in sales promotion strategies to encourage business and may offer potential customers various prizes, from stuffed animals and piggy banks to toasters or other kitchen appliances. For example, in 2006 Wachovia Bank (now Wells Fargo) offered two free tickets to a Philadelphia 76ers game to all new customers who opened a checking or savings account. All sport businesses use checking accounts, and a business that has significant money in an account can negotiate how much it will pay for the services that it receives.

Protecting Deposits

Banks can use numerous gimmicks to win clients, but the depositors' primary concern is probably whether their money will be safe. Through the 1930s the history of banking caused depositors to be skeptical about their ability to remove funds. Several early attempts to protect deposits failed.

In 1933 the first form of federal **deposit insurance** was developed as an attempt to facilitate better banking (Rodgers, 1966). The Banking Act of 1933 helped establish the FDIC as a government unit charged with insuring bank deposits. In 1950 the law was superseded by the Federal Deposit Insurance Act. The FDIC is now owned by the banks rather than the government. Similar to the Fed, the FDIC is run by a board of directors that includes the comptroller of the currency and two other individuals appointed by the president with the Senate's consent. The FDIC has a strong weapon to help ensure compliance with safe banking practices. If a bank engages in and is found guilty of unsafe, unsound, or illegal banking activities, the FDIC can terminate that bank's insurance. Part of the insurance termination process involves contacting all depositors to let them know that insurance coverage will be terminated.

If a bank cannot cover withdrawals, the FDIC can pay all claims and liquidate the bank's assets.

This extreme measure produces negative publicity. If possible, the FDIC tries to find another bank willing to assume the deposit liabilities of the defaulting bank. Furthermore, under the 1950 act, the FDIC can purchase assets from, extend a loan to, and make deposits in any insured bank facing financial hardships.

The insurance covers funds based not on the depositor but on the account, covering the first $250,000 in any account. Thus, if a depositor has $1,000,000 in an account, only the first $250,000 is insured. In contrast, if a depositor has four accounts each of which contains $250,000, each is fully insured. The insurance level was increased from $100,000 to $250,000 in 2008.

Account protection through insurance is critical to ensure the availability of funds. For example, suppose a sports team kept all revenue from ticket and broadcasting sales in one account at a bank that closed because of financial problems. Even if the team had $40 million in the account, only $250,000 would be insured. Thus, the team could face significant financial trouble and be unable to cover bills because of the bank's closing. To avoid this problem, the team could keep smaller amounts in each bank (a maximum of $250,000 per account), do business only with the largest and strongest banks, or keep a smaller amount in the bank and invest more of the money in marketable securities. Such exercises in distributing money—constantly juggling money to provide the greatest return and protection—are among the key duties of financial managers.

Quasi Bankers

The discussion so far has focused on commercial banks. But many other banking-related businesses provide needed capital for corporations and individuals. These entities range from savings and loans, which are similar to banks, to mortgage companies, which are discussed later.

Investment bankers specialize in raising long-term funds for both corporate expansions and capital needs. Insurance companies, based on their large cash reserves, can also provide significant capital for corporations seeking additional funds. **Pension funds** and retirement accounts are often used as borrowing sources. The largest teacher pension and retirement fund in the world, TIAA/CREF, has provided significant financial support to several major stadium construction projects ("Top holders," 1997). Credit unions can also provide substantial capital based on their large membership numbers. Because credit unions receive money from members and loan money only to members, they are often the least expensive source for borrowing funds. Joining a credit union, however, is sometimes impossible without being affiliated with a specified employer or social group. But a small sports business owner who also works for a company affiliated with a credit union may be able to secure a loan at favorable terms.

Other sources of funds include **consumer finance companies**, sales finance companies, pawnbrokers, and even unlicensed lenders such as loan sharks. An example of consumer financing is a car purchase agreement in which the car serves as the collateral for the amount financed by the purchaser. If the purchase price of the car is $20,000 and the down payment is $5,000, then $15,000 is the financed amount. The $15,000 note could be sold to a large finance company that purchases millions of dollars in loans to consumers for numerous products. A sales finance company sells items such as photocopiers, or even Zambonis, and instead of accepting cash can finance the items through loans secured by the equipment.

Mortgage companies loan money to people willing to pledge their homes as collateral. Mortgage companies rarely receive deposits except for initial capital infusions by investors. Because mortgage companies are specialized, they can offer additional services and can often provide comprehensive benefits.

Stock Exchanges

Established stock exchanges have specific requirements for admission and regulations concerning who can **trade** the shares. Only firms that are members of a particular exchange can trade stocks on that exchange. This policy was established when the **securities exchanges** were chartered. Because the exchanges are owned and operated by their members, they can establish rules for future members. One rule is that any company wishing to buy a seat (place) on a particular exchange must purchase the seat from a departing member and must pay the prevailing market rate for the seat, which can exceed $3 million on the New York Stock Exchange. Having a seat makes the company a member of the exchange. Someone who wants to purchase shares of a stock listed on an exchange contacts a member to purchase the shares. Nonmembers cannot purchase shares.

Three major stock exchanges exist in the United States. The most prestigious is the **New York Stock Exchange** (NYSE), which was founded in 1792 and became publicly traded in 2006. Approximately 2,300 companies that have a combined market value of over $13 trillion meet the stringent requirements for size and profitability that a company must fulfill to be listed on the NYSE (Dunphy, 1998). To be listed, a company typically must have at least 400 U.S. shareholders, a market value of its public shares of at least $40 million, a stock price of at least $4 at the time of listing, at least 1.1 million outstanding public shares of stock, and a record of profitability for the last three years with earnings of at least $10 million (*NYSE rules*, 2011). Normally, only the most prestigious companies can be listed on the NYSE.

The **National Association of Securities Dealers Automated Quotations** (NASDAQ) system is a computerized national trading system for more than 2,800 publicly traded companies. The NASDAQ began operating on February 8, 1971, and included several larger companies such as American Express and Anheuser-Busch (Ip, 2000, March 10). Both companies are now listed on the NYSE. Some companies listed on the NASDAQ, such as Google, Microsoft, Intel, Starbucks, and Apple Computer, have become big and profitable enough to be listed on the NYSE but for various reasons have not moved their stock from the NASDAQ. One reason may be that because many start-up and high-tech companies are launched on the NASDAQ, companies listed there are considered more cutting edge than their more established counterparts trading on the NYSE. The NASDAQ is also the primary U.S. market for trading securities in overseas companies such as Fujifilm. In the past the NASDAQ has also been the trading home for other overseas companies such as Canon, Cadbury Schweppes, Toyota, and Volvo. All those companies have either merged with other companies or been delisted from the NASDAQ.

Besides listing major national and international companies, NASDAQ also has several ancillary services that help people trade securities in smaller companies. The OTC (over-the-counter) Bulletin Board is an electronic market for securities not listed on NASDAQ or any other U.S. exchange. Bid and ask quotations are captured and displayed in real time so that trades can be accomplished almost instantaneously. The **ask price**, or **offer price** is the price that a seller would like to receive for the item that he or she wishes to sell. The **bid price** is the amount that a potential buyer wants to spend to acquire the item. Somewhere between these two amounts a compromise might be reached. But numerous deals are based on firm asking prices or bid prices in which the party making the firm offer refuses to budge. Similar to what occurs with bidding on eBay or other Internet auctions, the highest

MAJOR INTERNATIONAL EXCHANGES

Market or exchange	Year founded	Average daily number of shares traded	Average daily trading volume	Market capitalization	Largest stocks
NYSE	1792	1.46 billion	$36 billion	$14 trillion	Exxon-Mobil, Walmart, Chevron
NASDAQ	1971	1.44 billion	$39.5 billion	$4.44 trillion	Microsoft, Apple, Google
London	1801	580,000	$9.5 billion	$3.2 trillion	BHP Billiton, Royal Dutch Shell, HSBC
Tokyo	1878	1.5 billion	$6.2 billion	$3.325 trillion	Softbank, Mitsubishi, Canon
Australian	1837	1.2 billion	$3.48 billion	$1.2 trillion	BHP Billiton, Commonwealth Bank of Australia
Toronto	1878	250 million	$5.2 billion	$2 trillion	Potash Corp. of Saskatchewan, Barrick Gold, Canadian Natural Resources

Data from Calian and Latour 2000.

price offered at the designated time wins, and the item is automatically shipped or transferred after the payment is verified.

The **Financial Industry Regulatory Authority (FINRA)**, previously known as the National Association of Securities Dealers (NASD), regulates the NASDAQ and other **over-the-counter exchanges**. Regulation is accomplished through education programs, on-site examination of member firms, automated market surveillance, registration and testing of security professionals, review of members' sales and advertising practices, an arbitration program to resolve disputes, and review of underwriting arrangements associated with new offerings (Financial Industry Regulatory Authority, n.d.). Automated market surveillance and reviewing of underwriting arrangements are undertaken through close examination of the launching and selling of stocks to ensure that no improprieties are occurring. For example, the system can track whether weird spikes in stock prices are caused by manipulation or insider trading. These powers are derived through federal legislation such as the 1938 Maloney Act amendments to the Securities Exchange Act of 1934, which established the NASD, later to become FINRA. The NASD was organized through the joint effort of Congress and the Securities and Exchange Commission. Although the NASD, or later FINRA, was given significant power by federal legislation, it is a privately financed and managed company. It oversees nearly 4,400 brokerage firms, about 163,000 branch offices, and approximately 630,000 regis-

tered securities representatives (Financial Industry Regulatory Authority, n.d.).

Another exchange is the NYSE Amex Equities (AMEX), formally known as the American Stock Exchange, which lists over 500 small to midsized businesses, a large number of which service the oil industry. AMEX merged with the NASD at the start of the 21st century, which shows that the exchange was evolving based on technological demands. Several years after the merger, however, the AMEX spun off on its own again. In 2008 NYSE Euronext bought AMEX for $260 million in stock.

Technology may have an effect on various other exchanges, which may become obsolete in the future. Smaller regional exchanges operate throughout the United States, such as the Boston, Cincinnati, Chicago, Pacific, and Philadelphia stock exchanges and specialty exchanges such as the Chicago Board Options Exchange and the Chicago Mercantile Exchange. Among the most prominent international exchanges are those based in Tokyo, London, Madrid, Paris, Tel Aviv, and Hong Kong.

Exchanges list the prices of their shares on a daily basis in a variety of sources from financial websites such as cnbc.com to financial newspapers such as the *Wall Street Journal*. Typical daily newspaper business sections list only the most active shares from the biggest exchanges. In most cases, stock listings show the bid and ask prices, the difference from the prior day if any, the 52-week high and low prices for the shares, and possibly the price–earnings ratio (PE ratios are covered in chapter 6).

The major stock exchanges operate in different ways. The NYSE and the AMEX use an auction style in which investors send orders through their brokers to the stock exchange floor. The floor is the trading area where buyers and sellers swap stocks or other commodities. Brokers on the floor gather in groups to buy and sell stock of a particular company. The brokers use the time-honored negotiation tool of supply and demand to develop a fair market price for the stock. If someone asks too much for her shares, the shares will go unsold. If someone offers to sell a stock at a low price, numerous brokers may try to buy. Through negotiations the parties reach a mutually acceptable price. If a block of shares is offered for sale or purchase and no one steps forward to make a deal, an exchange specialist can sell or purchase from his company's own account (Dunphy, 1998). An exchange specialist typically sells shares from a range of stocks sold on a specific exchange. If someone wishes to purchase the shares, a deal is concluded and the shares exchange hands. Actual stock certificates are not exchanged on the floor; instead, slips of paper evidencing the deal are exchanged, and ownership changes are recorded at a different time.

The NASDAQ and OTC markets operate differently from the NYSE in that there is no trading floor. Brokers do not gather in any specific location but instead negotiate with others through computers. Thus, NASDAQ is a computer-driven dealing system in which orders are bought and sold based on prices posted by various buyers and sellers (Dunphy, 1998). An OTC brokerage operates as a normal securities retailer and wholesaler and trades in select securities from its own accounts (Spiro, 1996). Securities retailers and wholesalers buy and sell whatever stocks are being demanded in either small or large lots. Brokers are often called market makers; they advise other brokers and the investment community at large of the price at which they are willing to buy or sell shares. With the speed of today's computers, buying and selling stocks can occur in tenths, or even hundredths, of a second.

Electronic trading has become popular among investors over the last decade. They use Internet-based trading companies to buy and sell stocks at the touch of a button. Commissions on these trades are often lower than traditional commissions, which run approximately $50 and up depending on the volume traded; electronic commissions are often less than $20 per trade. For example, if you purchase 100 shares of Nike for $50 a share, you are buying an entire lot, or **even lot** (100 shares). In addition to the $5,000 paid for the stock, you might have to pay an extra $20 to possibly $200 to compensate the broker who purchased the stock

for you. You would also need to pay a commission when you sell the stock. If you were to purchase an **odd lot**, which is anything but an even lot (1-99 shares), you might have to pay a higher commission because the broker may find it harder to find a seller. Commissions can be negotiated with the brokerage house based on the number of stocks traded, the number of trades each month, or the dollar value of your account.

Various techniques are used to assess market conditions and track stock movement. As discussed earlier in this chapter, the most famous barometer of the stock market is the Dow, which includes 30 large U.S. companies. The representative mix of companies ranges from computer giant IBM to Disney. The primary benefit of the Dow is that it has an established track record. The primary disadvantage is that the average represents only a small spectrum of all available stocks.

Another indicator is Standard & Poor's 500 Composite Index, which tracks the 500 largest companies based on market capitalization. Because the Standard & Poor's index has more stocks than the Dow does, it is considered a more reliable indicator of market movement. The only indices that provide more in-depth coverage are the Russell Indexes, which cover 1,000, 2,000, or 3,000 stocks. The NASDAQ also has a composite to track its shares. The NASDAQ Composite Index first closed above 1,000 on July 17, 1995. Because of the skyrocketing prices of Internet offerings, the index shot up to over 5,000 by the year 2000 (Ip, 2000, March 10). The opening months of the 21st century saw a rapid decrease in the technology-heavy NASDAQ. The collapse of the dot-com economy from overspeculation caused the NASDAQ to lose more than 3,000 points ("Dow Jones continues," 2002). The NASDAQ also fell below 1,300 points during the 2008-2009 recession. These downturns represent one of the major concerns associated with exchanges that specialize in a given industry segment. If that industry segment experiences a downturn, the exchange will suffer significantly.

Examples of sport-related stocks available on the NYSE include Comcast, Disney, Time Warner, Under Armour, NIKE, and several other companies in the golf, shoe, fitness, and auto and horse racing industries. The NASDAQ system includes similar prestigious companies. Table 4.2 highlights some of the major sport-related companies that are publicly traded on various exchanges.

The securities industry is regulated by its own rules, but it also needs to comply with federal regulations. In the following section we consider how the government affects financial systems.

Table 4.2 Major Publicly Traded Sport-Related Companies

Company symbol	Company name	Primary sport product	Exchange
AASP.OB	All-American SportPark	Sport parks	OTC
ADDYY	Adidas AG	Shoes, apparel, and equipment	OTC
ADGF	Adams Golf	Golf clubs	OTC
ALDA	Aldila	Golf clubs	OTC
AGPDY.PK	Amer Sports Oyj	Sporting goods (Wilson, Salomon)	OTC
BC	Brunswick Corp.	Bowling, billiard, and motor boats	NYSE
BFT	Bally Total Fitness Holding	Fitness centers	OTC
BLLY	Cannondale	Bicycles	OTC
BOLL.PK	Bollinger Industries	Fitness equipment	OTC
BOOT	LaCrosse Footwear	Sports shoes	NASDAQ
CCMO	Clear Channel Communications	Media and entertainment	OTC
CHDN	Churchill Downs	Thoroughbred racing	NASDAQ
CMCSK	Comcast	Broadcasting	NASDAQ
CVC	Cablevision	Broadcasting	NASDAQ
DAKT	Daktronics	Scoreboards	NASDAQ
DIS	Walt Disney	ESPN, ABC	NYSE
DVD	Dover Downs Entertainment	Motor sports	NYSE
ELY	Callaway Golf	Golf	NYSE
ERTS	Electronic Arts	Video games	NASDAQ
FINL	Finish Line	Apparel	NASDAQ
FTAR	Footstar	Shoes	NYSE
GET	Gaylord Entertainment	Media and resorts	NYSE
HEDYY	Head N.V.	Manufacturing and marketing	OTC
HIBB	Hibbett	Apparel retail	NASDAQ
HSPO.OB	Healthsports	Manufacturing	OTC
ISCA	International Speedway	Motor sport	NASDAQ
KSWS	K-Swiss	Athletic footwear	NASDAQ
LCAPA	Liberty Media Corp	Broadcasting and Atlanta Braves	NASDAQ
MSG	Madison Square Garden	Teams, media, and events	NASDAQ
MTN	Vail Resorts	Skiing	NYSE
NICH	Nitches	Sports apparel	OTC
NKE	Nike	Shoes	NYSE
NWS	News Corp.	Sports media	NASDAQ
PERY	Perry Ellis	Sports apparel	NASDAQ
SIX	Six Flags	Amusement parks	NYSE
PMMAF	Puma	Footwear, apparel	OTC
SGMS	Scientific Games	Technology	NASDAQ
SMDI	Stratus Media Group	Mixed Martial Arts Events (MMA)	OTC
SPCHB	Sport Chalet	Sporting goods retail	NASDAQ
SPOR	Sport-Haley	Golf apparel	NASDAQ
SSTR	Silverstar Holdings	Fantasy sports	OTC
TRK	Speedway Motorsports	Motor sports	NYSE
UA	Under Armour	Sports apparel and shoes	NYSE
WWE	World Wrestling Entertainment	Wrestling	NYSE
ZQK	Quicksilver, Inc.	Sports apparel	NYSE
ZUMZ	Zumiez, Inc.	Outdoor sports apparel	NASDAQ

NASDAQ = regular NASDAQ; NYSE = New York Stock Exchange; OTC = NASDAQ's Over-the-Counter Bulletin Board.

GOVERNMENT INFLUENCE ON FINANCIAL MARKETS

In addition to the Federal Reserve Bank, discussed earlier in connection with banking, numerous federal and state government units can exert considerable influence over financial systems. Various regulatory bodies at the state and federal level make laws in many areas, from how to incorporate to what taxes are to be paid. One such federal regulatory agency is the **Securities and Exchange Commission** (SEC), which was formed after the 1929 stock market crash and started operating in 1934. The SEC's initial primary emphasis was ensuring accuracy in the underwriting of stock offerings and proper disclosure (Spiro, 1996). The goal was to ensure equal access among investors to information from companies. Activities of the SEC have evolved into analyzing practices at the private exchanges and monitoring the accounting practices used by companies in their initial security offerings and subsequent annual reports.

The SEC's current primary focus is proper disclosure. The scandals affecting private and publicly traded companies such as Enron, WorldCom, Madoff Investment Securities, Lehman Brothers, and AIG highlight the importance of following the SEC's disclosure rules. Proper disclosure often centers on **annual reports**; proxy statements; audited financial statements, including management's analysis of operating and financial conditions (Form 10-K); and quarterly reports, including unaudited financial statements (Form 10-Q) prepared by the corporation but not verified by an independent auditor (*About the SEC*, 2011). With the passage of the Sarbanes-Oxley Act of 2002, corporate executives now need to certify these filings to attest to their truthfulness. The SEC faced harsh criticism during the 2008-2009 recession because of its failure to uncover several cases of financial fraud.

The most noteworthy of these cases involved Bernie Madoff. The Madoff fraud continued for more than a decade before being uncovered in part because of the SEC's failure to conduct an adequate investigation of the financial information that Madoff supplied to his investors. Ultimately, the affair became the largest financial fraud case in U.S. history. The fraud also had a major effect on the Wilpon family, the majority owners of the New York Mets baseball franchise. Mets' co-owner Fred Wilpon invested millions of dollars of his own wealth and channeled the money of others, through the Sterling Equities Group, into Madoff Investment Securities. In December 2008 when news of the Ponzi scheme went public, it was estimated that Fred Wilpon and his companies had over 300 accounts and $550 million invested with Madoff. To make matters worse, the bankruptcy trustee for Madoff Securities, Ira Picard, sued Wilpon in federal court claiming that he "willfully turned a blind eye to every objective indicia of fraud before them." Picard sought to reclaim millions in earlier profits made by Wilpon through Madoff as repayment to other investors who lost money from the Ponzi scheme (Toobin, 2011).

A federal judge in 2011 threw out 9 of 11 counts brought by Picard and limited the trustee to clawing back money withdrawn in just the two years before Madoff came clean. The two-year limit would cap the amount that Picard could recover from the Mets at $386 million. Picard had been seeking $1 billion, including $300 million in alleged profits and $700 million in principal based on the life of their Madoff investment (MacIntosh & Whitehouse, 2011). In 2012 the parties settled for $162 million, which could be reduced by the bankruptcy court to nothing coming out of the owners' pockets. Financial fraud will be discussed in more detail in chapter 15.

Certain decisions made by a corporation's board of directors, such as election of new board members or a change in the bylaws, are subject to shareholder voting. At a corporation's annual meeting, stockholders who cannot attend are allowed to vote by proxy. A **proxy** enables someone else to vote in the shareholder's place. The proper disclosure of proxy-related issues is designed to ensure that all stockholders have the opportunity to air their ideas or concerns. A proxy statement needs to disclose the date, time, and location of the meeting; which types of stockholders (those holding class A or class B stock) are allowed to vote on certain issues; information about directors, including their compensation; and any significant decisions to be made such as changing the charter, issuing new securities, or discussing mergers and acquisitions ("Securities regulation," 1994). Although most annual meetings are not contentious, companies going through tough times or internal strife may need to discuss critical issues at the annual meeting. The government steps in to ensure that the competing groups provide appropriate and accurate information to all shareholders.

Insider Trading

One key concern addressed by the SEC is **insider trading**. Pursuant to Section 1b of the Securities Exchange Act of 1934, insider trading is illegal. The definition of an insider has expanded over the years. Initially only the top corporate officials had confidential information that could guide their buying or selling practices associated with the company's securities. Over the years, the definition of an **insider** has come to cover other investors, even those not associated with the company, who acquire confidential information and use that information for their own or another's financial gain.

A good example of an insider trading case was publicized in 2000. A former temporary employee with several securities trading firms used his position to find information in garbage cans, in desks, and on computer printers (McMorris, Smith, & Schroeder, 2000). This incident was the first case of an insider trading ring on the Internet, in which information on 23 corporate deals was discussed with friends who met in chat rooms. In all, 19 people were charged with insider trading for their activities, which generated $8.4 million in profits. Some of those charged were fairly distant from the initial illegal tip. The case showed that the government was serious about all people involved in insider trading. The government was willing to go so far as to prosecute individuals who had heard the news from others who had heard the news from another source who could be traced to the original insider. Thus, the government does not care where people might have heard the inside information; the fact that they used inside information makes them liable (McMorris et al., 2000). Note that one of the most prominent insider trading cases did not involve a conviction on that charge. The Martha Stewart case involved actions associated with using inside information to sell stocks, but Stewart was convicted of obstructing justice and lying to investigators about her alleged insider trading activity. The sports world is not immune to insider trading. In 2005 Reebok stocks rose 30% on the news that Adidas was going to make an all-cash purchase of Reebok. Nine people were accused by the SEC of making more than $6 million in profit after placing suspicious stock and option trades based on inside information (Shell, 2005).

Power of the Securities and Exchange Commission

Congress tracks the securities industry through the Committee on Banking, Housing, and Urban Affairs in the Senate and the Committee on Energy and Commerce in the House of Representatives. The Securities Exchange Act of 1934, mentioned earlier, concerns the sale and trading of existing securities and created the Securities and Exchange Commission (SEC). In contrast, the Securities Act of 1933 primarily concerned the issuing of new securities. The 1934 act provided the primary underpinning for rules governing brokers and dealers, financial responsibility requirements, regulations restricting borrowing to purchase securities, and rules for manipulation of security prices. The numerous regulatory requirements are beyond the SEC's scope. Thus, the SEC has delegated significant regulatory authority to several self-regulatory organizations that oversee their respective markets. The NYSE, NASDAQ, and AMEX are examples of self-regulatory organizations.

State Regulations

In addition to federal regulations, state regulations apply to any company issuing securities. A company issuing securities needs to ensure first that it follows all corporate laws in the state in which it is issuing stocks. Next, the certificate of incorporation needs to comply with all applicable state laws. The certificate of incorporation is the formal application and approval form from the state, authorizing the corporation's formation and ability to operate. Last, the corporation's bylaws must not conflict with either state laws or the certificate of incorporation ("Securities regulation," 1994).

State laws can cover such diverse areas as classes of stocks that can be issued, limitations on dividend policies, restrictions on transferring stocks, the rights and obligations of officers and directors, amending corporate charters to change capital structure, mergers and consolidations, selling corporate assets, and final corporate dissolution. Some laws are similar in the federal and state systems but provide for different legal conclusions. For example, state laws can cover mergers or consolidations, but many mergers require federal approval to avoid antitrust violations. Similarly, although state laws cover corporate dissolution, most dissolutions revolve around bankruptcy proceedings, which are covered by federal laws.

Government regulations affecting financial systems abound. Chapter 5 covers additional issues such as laws affecting business structures, tax considerations, and bankruptcy protection. Government units can also work to shore up failing financial systems. After the stock market crash in 1929, states as well as the federal government tried to protect the banking industry. In late 1932 and early 1933 several governors instituted banking holidays, which prohibited depositors from removing their funds. Congress followed the lead and passed the Emergency Banking Act (Klise, 1972). The strategy could not save all banks, but it saved a large number of banks that were able to use the holiday closures to reorganize and strengthen. Although the government is supposed to protect the public, the sport finance examples in the following section might point to the scenario of the wolf guarding the sheep. More recently, banking and financial regulations were closely examined after the financial crisis of 2008-2009. Congress enacted several new laws such as the Dodd-Frank Act in an effort to regulate the banking industry more tightly. The goal of this legislation was to minimize the possibility of a future financial meltdown. Some of the provisions highlighted in the act include creating the Consumer Financial Protection Bureau, developing stronger investor protections, and making sure that corporations followed rules already passed by Congress.

In God We Trust

Government entities are elected to represent the interests of citizens within their jurisdiction, but government interaction with sport can produce mixed results that affect the bottom line. A good example of such a connection is the Olympic bribery scandal that unfolded in 1998 and 1999. Officials within the Salt Lake Olympic Committee were accused of misappropriating funds to bribe International Olympic Committee members involved in the host-city bidding process ("Briefly," 2000). Some officials considered such payments justified to help secure an event that could bring tremendous growth and income to Utah. Others considered such actions an affront to the notion of amateurism and fair play. Moreover, such conduct can also be illegal as a violation of federal or state laws, or both, against corruption and bribery.

Financial wrongdoing was also alleged in a case involving the Tampa Bay Lightning. Former city and Lightning officials were cleared of criminal charges after team officials allegedly altered their balance sheets before city officials reviewed them (Gilpin, 1998). Charges were dropped by the prosecutor, possibly because of the perceived difficulty of prosecuting the case. City officials backed a $160 million arena deal and agreed to guarantee $1 million per year in the package. Former Lightning executive David LeFevre allegedly ordered the removal of $1.1 million in short-term liabilities from the balance sheet and transferred the funds to another building project that did not become

active until nine months later (Gilpin, 1998). Thus, the balance sheet did not accurately reflect all the team's debt. The criminal probe failed because there was no proof that the city had relied on the altered documents to make the decision (Gilpin, 1998).

As highlighted earlier, a number of scandals have occurred recently. One of the bigger scandals involved Adelphia, one of the nation's largest cable operators and owner of the Buffalo Sabres. Adelphia and Sabres owner John Rigas was convicted of embezzling billions of dollars and using the Sabres to secure millions of dollars in loans. During the bankruptcy proceedings in 2002, the team was taken over by the NHL, which eventually found a buyer in 2003.

In another case, plaintiffs alleged in a lawsuit against the city of San Francisco that city officials failed to comply with voting secrecy requirements and allowed early voting at four public housing projects during the elections that would decide on the proposed San Francisco 49ers' new stadium (Chiang & Wilson, 1998). The two propositions authorized $100 million in lease revenue bonds for the proposed stadium and changed some land zoning restrictions. A state court of appeals dismissed the suit (Chiang & Wilson, 1998).

More recently, in 2009 William "Boots" Del Biaggio III pleaded guilty to one charge of forging financial documents to obtain $110 million in loans from several banks and two NHL owners. Del Biaggio III used the funds to purchase a controlling interest in the Nashville Predators hockey franchise. Del Biaggio III had falsified account statements by cutting out the names of the account owners and pasting his name into those statements. He then used those account statements, which showed that he had millions of dollars in assets, as collateral to acquire loans to purchase the team. In September 2009 a tearful Del Biaggio III was sentenced to eight years in jail by a federal judge in San Francisco (*Predators*, 2009).

ENVIRONMENTAL CONDITIONS

Professional teams might seem like a solid investment considering how some franchises have increased in value over the past two decades. However, a financial winner is never guaranteed. Numerous environmental concerns can affect any sport investment. The following quote from a Baltimore Orioles annual report highlights the various threats.

Escalating player salaries have become our most serious problem; baseball is experiencing a rapidly changing environment. We have entered a period of financial extravagance and, while it lasts, salaries will continue to escalate wildly and the stability of our game will be put to a severe test. (Much, 1997, December 1, p.1)

The rapidly escalating salaries for professional athletes have fostered the tremendous boom in new arena and stadium construction because new revenue streams are needed to fund salary increases. The previous quote might have appeared in a press release from MLB concerning the aftermath of the player strike in 1994 and 1995 and the continuing increase in player salaries over the two decades. But the quote appeared in the 1977 Baltimore baseball club's annual report. Baseball salaries in 1977 averaged $76,066 (Ruxin, 1989). By 1998 the average baseball salary was $1.4 million, and 750 players earned more than $1 million (Singer, 1998). By 2011 the average salary in baseball was $3.3 million, and three teams (New York Yankees, Philadelphia Phillies, and Boston Red Sox) paid an average of more than $5.9 million per player on their rosters (*USA Today*, n.d.). The team with the lowest payroll in 2011 was the Kansas City Royals, which averaged $1.338 million per player and had an overall payroll of $36.1 million. The next closest team was the Tampa Bay Rays, which had a payroll of $41 million (*USA Today*, n.d.). The New York Yankees had the top payroll for the 11th consecutive season at $201.7 million. Interestingly, that figure was 2.3% lower than their 2010 payroll amount of $206.3 million. The Texas Rangers, the defending American League champions, had the largest one-year jump when they raised their payroll from $55.2 million to $92.3 million, a 67.1% increase (*USA Today*, n.d.). Player salaries represent just one internal constraint that affects a professional team's financial bottom line.

Internal constraints are factors within a business that can be controlled. Player personnel issues can involve both internal and external constraints. A baseball team may have a farm system to help train young players, as well as gifted scouts who can help sign top talent. The team can also carefully plan the payroll to optimize bonuses and planned player retirement or free agency. These internal variables must be contrasted with external variables such as whether baseball is losing popu-larity, whether fewer high school teams are being formed, whether other sports are drawing greater fan support, whether other teams are paying their players more, and whether a municipality taxes the team or athletes in an unreasonable manner.

CONCLUSION

Every business has to balance the internal and external constraints in its financial environment. Sport organizations such as Speedway Motorsports or Under Armour need to deal with their banks, their customers' banks, and possibly the financial institutions of their suppliers or landlord. Speedway Motorsports can face a multitude of other financial systems and concerns, from having to manage their accounts to ensure that they are protected from a bank default to understanding the SEC's authority if they wish to sell shares in their business. Although the number of entities involved is limited, the interactions can be highly complex. The interactions are that much more complex for a pro sports team such as the Boston Celtics or the Los Angeles Dodgers. Imagine the millions of interactions each season that relate to attendance alone. Fans buy their tickets with cash, bank **drafts**, or credit cards, and each transaction requires the involvement of at least two financial institutions.

Every successful sport business at one point or another handles money, stocks, bonds, and other assets, ranging from liquid to hard assets. Similarly, every sport business needs to be concerned about the inner workings of all the financial institutions. No business can know where it might need to obtain its next round of capital infusion. One year a sport business might obtain necessary funds from a bank or a public offering. The next year the same sport business might have to borrow from an insurance company or pension fund. The options are limited only by the various internal and external constraints. These constraints can include such elements as the corporation's own bylaws or articles of incorporation (discussed in chapter 5) or its credit rating (discussed in chapter 8). Government regulations can dramatically affect the options if interest rates rise or if borrowing regulations are tightened. No matter what capital criteria might arise, businesses need to be proactive in their capital funding operations to help reduce borrowing or capital acquisition expenses and to increase their ability to raise any necessary funds.

Class Discussion Topics

1. What is the difference between the NYSE and the NASDAQ?
2. What determines value?
3. Why would the price of a stock increase or decrease?
4. What is the difference between stocks and bonds?
5. Should governments control banks?
6. Should governments control monetary policies?
7. Why would a bank want or need to borrow money?
8. Should banks be allowed to sell insurance, securities, and related products or services?
9. Discuss some of your positive and negative banking experiences, such as bouncing a check.
10. What is the difference between a bank and a savings and loan?
11. If you were going to take a minor league baseball team public, what stock exchange would you try to get it on and why?

chapter 5

Business Structures, Bankruptcy, and Taxation

Chapter Objectives

After studying this chapter, you should be able to do the following:

- Understand why a business structure can affect a company financially.
- Define the requirements for each type of business structure used in sport.
- Compare the advantages and disadvantages of sole proprietorships, partnerships, corporations, and limited liability corporations or limited liability partnerships.
- Understand some of the tax concerns affecting the sport industry.
- Describe the importance of tax planning in sport.
- Understand how tax law is applied to athletes.
- Understand the basics of financial risk management.
- Describe the techniques that can help spot financial trouble.
- Understand how to reorganize a troubled business.
- Compare the types of bankruptcies available.

The previous chapter highlights the financial systems that come into play when we examine financial issues, but the structure of a sport business can also generate particular financial benefits or hardships. Thus, understanding business structures is just as important as understanding financial systems. A sport organization could form a business as a sole proprietorship, a partnership, an S corporation, a C corporation, or a limited liability corporation; and each business type would have different tax and legal concerns or benefits. Companies such as Under Armour and Speedway Motorsports need funds to expand and grow, and corporations have the ability to issue stocks and bonds as a vehicle for acquiring additional funds. Thus, one of the most important decisions for any sport business is what form the business entity should take.

The various options for raising funds highlighted in chapters 8 through 10 are often contingent on the type of business structure that is seeking funds. This chapter covers the various types of business structures that exist and considers the advantages and disadvantages associated with each structure type.

Most businesses start as small single-owner companies and expand from that point if they are successful. The owner of a sporting goods store could invest her life savings in a business and own the entire business with no obligations to any lenders. But if the business is not structured properly, it could be lost through litigation.

The various types of business entities that exist include governments, nonprofits, sole proprietorships, partnerships, limited partnerships, limited liability corporations (LLCs) or limited liability partnerships (LLPs), subchapter S corporations, and C corporations. This text does not focus on government structures; although they can be found throughout the sport industry, they are not highlighted here. Government entities can run numerous sport entities such as park and recreation departments, high school athletic departments, community centers, public college athletic programs, and other programs sponsored in whole or in part by the public. In fact, most sports organizations throughout the world are owned or operated by government entities. Because such programs are government entities, their liability and financial status are significantly different from those of traditional private businesses. For example, a business that exceeds its budget may need to borrow funds to survive but will still owe the funds even if it goes out of business. In contrast, if an institution such as a public university exceeds its budget by millions, traditionally the state will assume the obligation and pay the bills, even if the expenses were not authorized, because the state government is ultimately responsible for the debts of its own agencies.

NONPROFIT ORGANIZATIONS

In most countries the Olympic programs are run by the government. In the United States, however, the federal government passed a law (the Amateur Sports Act of 1978) that allowed for the creation of the United States Olympic Committee (USOC), which is supposed to be a nonprofit organization. The USOC can use its nonprofit status to receive gifts from donors who would possibly give money only if they were able to write off the donation from their tax obligations. Nonprofits can own and operate sport businesses. Examples include the New York City Marathon, Special Olympics, Pop Warner Little Scholars, Little League Baseball, and health clubs associated with YMCAs and hospitals.

Nonprofits can also own professional sports teams. For example, the Massachusetts attorney general investigated the sale of the Boston Red Sox in 2002 to ensure that charities received the largest amount possible under the proposed sale. The Yawkey Trust, which was the majority owner of the team, benefits numerous charities, and the state examined the sale to make sure that the highest price was received so that the **trust** would be able to give the greatest amount back to those charities ("Attorney general," 2001). The sale proceeds were used for various purposes, including a multimillion-dollar donation by the Yawkey Trust to Boston College for construction of an athletic department building attached to the football field.

Nonprofits face different financial concerns, primarily in relation to raising funds. Although some nonprofits can use traditional bank lending, the primary fund-raising options for nonprofits are donations and the selling of various items, from memberships and registration fees for special events to television and sponsorship rights.

Although it may seem that only large entities can be nonprofits, any group of people can form a nonprofit (usually at least two people are needed to form a nonprofit organization because at least two different officers are required, such as a president and vice-president). Chapter 4 includes additional discussion of the tax consequences of raising funds for nonprofits.

SOLE PROPRIETORSHIPS

A sole proprietorship is a business entity owned by a single person. If a sport organization decided not to form a partnership but to have one person as the sole owner, then the business would be classified as a sole proprietorship. The primary benefits of this business structure are that no formal paperwork is needed to start the business, the cost of organizing the business is not significant, and profits and organizational control do not need to be shared with anyone else. The primary disadvantages are that a single individual has limited ability to raise significant capital, the owner can face unlimited personal liability, and the business ends when the owner dies (Cheeseman, 2010). Unlimited personal liability means that a sole proprietor's personal property such as a home or car can be taken to cover debts if the sport business entity faces financial bankruptcy. Another disadvantage is that a sole proprietorship is normally a single-person operation without access to support from partners. This lack of support can render decision making more difficult.

Other advantages and disadvantages associated with a sole proprietorship are listed here:

Advantages

- Total control over decision making
- Revenues taxed only once
- Great flexibility
- Easy to form
- All profits retained by owner
- Less concern about confidentiality
- Easy to sell
- Fewer government restrictions

Disadvantages

- Limited managerial experience
- Unlimited personal liability
- Lasts only as long as owner lives
- Limited access to capital funds

Most businesses in the world are sole proprietorships (Cheeseman, 2010). In the sports world, many entities fall under this classification. In thinking about sole proprietorships in sport, you may envision small mom-and-pop businesses such as a specialized sporting goods store, a bowling alley, or a small fitness center, but this view leaves out another entire classification of sole proprietorships. Independent contractors are often sole proprietors and are prevalent in many sports (e.g., professional bowlers, golfers, figure skaters, and race car drivers). These people have a minimum of expenses apart from travel and entry expenses and often live on meager purses won at events or appearance fees. After they become more successful and have larger income streams and expenses, they can become incorporated (incorporation is discussed later in this chapter).

GENERAL AND LIMITED PARTNERSHIPS

If two people decide to run a sport business equally and if each owns 50% (or any other division of ownership) of the business, they are considered partners. A partnership's primary benefits are minimal formation costs and few government regulations. The primary disadvantages are difficulty in raising capital, unlimited personal and business liability for all partners, and immediate termination of the partnership when one partner dies or withdraws from the partnership (Cheeseman, 2010). The advantages and disadvantages associated with a partnership are highlighted here:

Advantages

- Some control over decision making
- Revenues taxed only once
- Great flexibility
- Easy to form
- All profits retained by owners
- Easy to sell
- Fewer government restrictions

Disadvantages

- Limited managerial experience
- Joint personal liability
- Limited access to capital funds
- Lasts only as long as the partnership survives

There are two primary types of partnerships. In a general partnership, individuals or groups combine their resources to share in operating, managing, and controlling a sport business and also share in all profits and liabilities. This type of partnership has several advantages. General partnerships have greater access to capital than sole proprietorships do, profits are taxed only once when distributed to the partners, and the combination of at least two parties helps enhance managerial decision making. The primary disadvantages are that this type of partnership has a limited longevity based on each partner (e.g., a human partner may die, or a partner that is a corporation or other business structure may be terminated by dissolution or by court order); partners are jointly and severally liable for partnership debt or liability; capital acquisition is limited compared with that of corporations; and the managerial talent pool is often limited to only those individuals who are partners, whereas corporations may have many more voices from which to harness expertise.

A general partnership can be created in one of two ways. An express partnership is developed through a written contract. An implied partnership is created through the actions of the parties.

In contrast to a general partnership, a limited partnership involves a general partner who is responsible for managing the company and one or more limited partners who provide only financial input (Cheeseman, 2010) A **limited partner** is entitled to share profits but is not engaged in day-to-day management. Because the limited partner's stake in the company is purely financial, her liability is limited to her financial contribution. Limited liability provides a strong incentive for people to invest in a partnership. Other benefits associated with a limited partnership include the ability to generate more capital than sole proprietorships, maintenance of a pass-through benefit for the profits paid to a limited partner (i.e., limited partners are paid their profits without the partnership being taxed first), and the fact that limited partners can invest in several businesses without exposing themselves to significant liability. The two biggest disadvantages of a limited partnership are the lack of managerial involvement by the limited partner and the fact that the general partner is still subject to unlimited liability.

Both general and limited partnerships can be ended through express language in the partnership agreement or through addition or subtraction of a partner. By law, a partnership ends when a partner dies, a partner goes bankrupt, or the partnership engages in any illegal activity. A partnership can also end if a partner is adjudicated insane by the courts, if a partner can no longer perform his or her duties, if a partner engages in improper conduct, or if the partnership can never make money (Cheeseman, 2010). Some sport businesses, no matter how hard they try, may not make any money. If a partnership has entered this trap and cannot make any money, a partner can ask the court to dissolve the partnership. This action is a last alternative if the other partners refuse to close the sport business

and one partner does not want to invest any more money because of the inability of the business to make a profit. The partner who wants to exit the partnership will need to prove that there is no likelihood that the partnership will ever make money.

C CORPORATIONS

Corporations are entities whose formation complies with specific state laws. Thus, corporations are fictitious legal entities that exist only through the rights given to them by specific statutory law. Corporations are often referred to as C corporations to distinguish them from S corporations. Corporations need to develop bylaws and articles of incorporation that specify how they will conduct business. The articles of incorporation typically contain the corporate name, the number of shares that the corporation will issue, the corporation's initial address, and the name and address of each of the initial incorporators (Cheeseman, 2010).

A corporation can be formed in any state as long as it complies with specific rules. Rules may relate to activities such as conducting annual meetings, keeping minutes from each meeting, and electing boards of directors. Delaware is the "friendliest" corporation state and has laws that assist a company in fending off a takeover attempt. The Delaware business laws are favorable to corporations and contain numerous advantages compared with laws in other states (see Advantages of Forming a Corporation in Delaware sidebar).

Corporations have several major advantages and disadvantages. The primary advantage sought by those seeking to incorporate is the liability protection available to the owners (shareholders). The primary disadvantages of incorporating are double taxation, the costs involved in forming the corporation, and the complexities associated with complying with all pertinent government regulations. The various advantages and disadvantages associated with incorporating are highlighted here:

Advantages

- Unlimited life of the corporation
- Liability of the corporation limited to the extent of corporate assets
- Creditors not permitted to go after individual investors for payment over and beyond their equity investment
- Ownership interest easily transferable in the form of shares
- Ability to hire a broad base of talented managers

- Tax benefit: dividends paid to corporation are 70% tax free
- Greater bargaining position with vendors who are more willing to provide credit to a corporation versus a single owner
- Ability to issue publicly traded debt and equity

Disadvantages

- Complex formation process
- Need to answer to shareholders who might have ulterior motives
- Sometimes onerous government regulations
- Double taxation

The paperwork associated with incorporating can be voluminous, including initial filings, annual reports, Securities and Exchange Commission filings (for public corporations only), and so on. The expenses associated with documentation make up only one cost and do not include the costs associated with state filing fees (which can be thousands of dollars), hiring entities to represent the corporation in each state where the corporation conducts business (called an agent for service of process), preparing audited financial statements, and a host of additional fees. The other major financial drain for any corporation is the prospect of double taxation.

SUBCHAPTER S CORPORATIONS

Subchapter S corporations (often called S corporations) had significant popularity in the 1990s. S corporations can have up to 100 shareholders and can own subsidiaries, and S corporations that are tax-exempt organizations such as charities can own shares. The primary advantage of S corporations is that their income flows through the corporation to the shareholders, who pay taxes as personal income. This avoids the double taxation inherent in C corporations, in which the corporation is taxed and dividend income to the shareholders is also taxed. The option of owning subsidiaries allows S corporations to insulate themselves further from liability (Nelson, 2011).

A major disadvantage for an S corporation is that the corporation can issue only one form of stock. A

ADVANTAGES OF FORMING A CORPORATION IN DELAWARE

The following advantages are available for corporations domiciled in Delaware:

- Delaware has a court of chancery dating back to 1792, which is a business court that hears only business cases, without a jury and with appointed judges.
- Delaware has a highly developed body of case law that is considered the standard for corporate law nationwide (Black, 2007). Fees are low; corporate formation charges can be as little as $89, and franchise taxes can be as low as $75 a year.
- Because of the large number of companies that have incorporated in Delaware, the state has realized that incorporation is a significant revenue stream and has invested heavily in technology and processes. This investment has ensured that filings are dealt with quickly and professionally.
- Shares of stock are not subject to Delaware taxes if the owner lives outside the state.

- Delaware-based corporations do not have to pay taxes on income earned outside the state as long as no income is earned in the state (*Delaware Intercorp*, 2000).

Favorable laws have helped develop Delaware as the premier state for incorporating businesses; close to a million business entities have made Delaware their legal home. Additionally, more than half of the Fortune 500 companies and half of publicly traded U.S. companies are incorporated in Delaware (Black, 2007). These favorable laws include a dedicated judge that handles only business-related cases; such cases are not heard by a jury. In part because of these legal advantages afforded to businesses incorporated in Delaware, a research study indicated that Delaware-based businesses from 1991 to 1996 were worth 5% more than corporations formed in other states (Lipin, 2000). Nevada has also become a frequently cited state for new corporations because it has adopted similar business-friendly laws.

traditional corporation can issue various types of shares that entitle shareholders to different **voting rights**, or it can issue preferred stock that entitles stockholders to better dividends. An S corporation must be based in the United States, and no more than 20% of its income can be derived from passive investments (providing financial resources without any other assistance). Furthermore, corporations, partnerships, and international investors cannot invest in an S corporation. Last, an S corporation cannot own 80% or more of another corporation's stock (Cheeseman, 2010).

The S corporation fell somewhat out of favor through advancements in limited liability corporations (LLCs) in the 1990s. LLCs, as discussed later, are simpler to form and manage than S corporations. Thus S corporations have decreased in popularity over the last decade or so, and many S corporations have been converted to LLCs. At the same time, numerous S corporations still exist in the sport industry and in other industries.

Another concern is the potential for shareholders to rebel and demand a managerial change. If the shareholders are dissatisfied with the corporate strategy or management team, they can vote to change corporate direction or management. Most major companies have departments that work exclusively with shareholders to address their concerns and to help produce shareholders' reports.

LIMITED LIABILITY CORPORATIONS AND PARTNERSHIPS

Forming a traditional corporation can be complex, expensive, and time consuming. Adding the further burden of going public can encourage entities to form a limited liability corporation in place of a traditional corporation. LLCs and LLPs are attractive forms of business structure in the United States because of their simplicity. The primary benefit for LLCs and LLPs is their classification as a partnership for federal income tax purposes (*Revenue Ruling 88-76*, 1988). Besides the tax benefit, LLCs and LLPs obtain the liability protection afforded to corporations.

In contrast to an S corporation, which cannot be owned by either a corporation or a partnership, an LLC or LLP can be owned by another corporation or partnership. Thus, a sport business that is an LLC can purchase another business that is an LLC and keep that unit separate as an LLC. The major disadvantage of LLCs is their newness. No national standard is in place, and each state has unique rules and regulations that are still working their way through the legal systems. After all the legalities are settled, LLCs and LLPs will become a primary business structure for new businesses (Cheeseman, 2010).

An LLC or LLP is created through the filing of articles of partnership in the state where the business will be organized. Although the SEC typically does not regulate LLCs and LLPs, it can regulate some of their activities, such as issuing publicly traded debt. When it was a publicly traded stock, the Boston Celtics were an example of a partnership that had to file reports with the SEC because of having publicly traded securities. Now that the team is privately owned it does not need to file any reports with the SEC. The lack of SEC oversight can save a significant amount of money, especially if the LLC or LLP does not need to pay for audited financial statements and other related expenses.

Pacific Sports LLC is a sports consultation, event production, management, and corporate sports marketing development firm. They have produced over 300 sport events in the United States, including the 1996 Triathlon World Championships and 12 U.S. championships. They also own several major events such as triathlons in Eugene, Dallas, Cleveland, and Los Angeles. By being an LLC the company can have legal protection while not having to go through a complicated incorporation process or expensive accounting procedures.

TAXATION ISSUES IN SPORT BUSINESS

Legal issues abound in the finance field. SEC regulations are voluminous. Legal issues can apply to the wording of the prospectus and to footnotes added to financial statements to provide details on transactions. Legal issues involve not only federal law but also numerous state laws. For example, blue-sky laws in almost all states regulate securities dealers or the selling of securities in the state. We will start by focusing on the legal and tax ramifications of the structure of a sport business and then expand on the earlier discussion of corporations and partnerships. This section deals with various tax-related concerns such as tax planning, the effect of taxes on both teams and athletes, and financial risk.

Benefits of Corporate Status

Corporations have several distinct advantages that can aid sport businesses, and professional sports teams have benefited from these opportunities for many years. Corporations and some partnerships can use losses to offset tax liabilities that occur in other business enterprises. Former San Francisco 49ers owner Edward DeBartolo Jr. transferred ownership in the team to his father's real estate company to create additional tax losses (Euchner, 1993). The New York Yankees reorganized in 1991, and the structural changes allowed limited partners to claim losses on their personal income taxes (Euchner, 1993). Although these examples are not recent, they represent specific attempts to use a corporate structure to gain a competitive or business advantage. Additional recent examples are highlighted later in this section.

In 2004 Congress passed a new law that could boost teams' values by about 5%, which equaled millions of dollars in some cases. The new corporate tax law let teams deduct the entire franchise value (including concession, player, and broadcast contracts) over a 15-year period; under the prior law, only player contracts could be written off, and only up to half the franchise's value ("Provision could boost," 2004). Thus, corporate status offers specific and valuable advantages over other ownership forms.

Proper business and financial structuring can save millions of dollars. The **estates** of NFL team owners George Halas and Paul Brown were both assessed more than $100 million in back taxes by the IRS. Through shrewd business reorganization efforts, however, the estates in fact received an aggregate IRS refund of $2.5 million (Much, 1997, September 9). The tax benefit was established through the creation of minority ownership rights in the teams and the resultant lower value attributable to the minority interests. An example will clarify how this worked. Let's suppose that a company has 100 shares of stock. If numerous people own the shares, anyone interested in buying the company needs to buy a majority of the shares, but she will not have complete control unless she buys all 100 shares. If someone owns 49 shares, that person's shares represent 49% of the business. The reason for the lower value is that not as many people would be interested in buying a minority interest because they would not be the primary owner and could never sell the entire business. As explained later, by giving away shares to various relatives or colleagues, a team owner can dramatically reduce the book values of all shares.

In the case involving the estate of the late Paul Brown, former owner of the Cincinnati Bengals, the IRS sought over $40 million in estate taxes. The controversy that brought the dispute before U.S. Tax Court judge John O. Colvin entailed a 1983 stock option transaction that the government claimed was a scam. In that transaction, Brown had transferred 117 of his shares in the team to John Sawyer (another stockholder) for $30,000 per share. The sales contract allowed Brown to keep one share and still maintain complete control over the team. Another contract required Sawyer to sell, if Brown's sons exercised an option to buy, 329 of the now 330 shares Sawyer had for $25,000 each in 1993. The IRS unsuccessfully argued that the stock shares were sold significantly below their true market value. The court ruled against the IRS based on the fact that even though the contract allowed the sons an option to buy back the team at a lower price, there was potential risk that the team would be worth less in 1993 than it was in 1983 (Much, 1997, September 9). If there had been no possibility that the value could go down and the sons could have bought back the team at a lower price than what had been paid for the team, then the IRS would have prevailed.

Another key component in the Bengals' deal involved the minority ownership interest. A minority owner traditionally does not have significant pull in any business; a minority share, however, does have the ability to decrease the value of the team drastically, as previously mentioned. Suppose you own 99% of a house, and your parents own the remaining 1%. If the house is worth $100,000, no one would ever pay $100,000 for it because that individual would never be the complete owner. Someone might pay $70,000 for the house with the intent to buy the remaining 1% from your parents. There is no requirement that your parents in fact sell their percentage share of the house, so the buyer would be taking a risk. This risk element reduces the value of the majority share.

The same concept applies to a professional sports team and other sport businesses. Although more people are willing to take a risk in buying a professional team, minority shares can still reduce the value of the majority shares. This reduced value can drastically decrease taxes that might be owed either on capital gains or on an inheritance, because the minority interests reduce all other values.

Although team values have significantly increased over the past two decades, the value for some teams' minority owners has not necessarily increased. Anyone interested in purchasing a business would attempt to pay a higher amount for the largest share and then pay a lower amount for smaller shares. A potential purchaser might be willing to pay more for a larger share, after which he could assume managerial control and make life miserable for minority owners.

In contrast, if a minority owner is a holdout, the majority shares can decrease in value. Assume that the developer of a stadium wants to buy 10 houses that are located on the land where the playing field will be. Nine homeowners are willing to sell, but the 10th owner refuses. The other owners will receive either reduced offers for their houses or a revocation of the offer, because the missing house reduces the value of the deal. The developer will not want to build a stadium if a house will sit on the 50-yard line. Thus, not owning all 10 houses reduces the value of all the houses. Similarly, not owning an entire team can reduce the team's value and save on taxes.

Although the Bengals' deal held up in court, not every attempt to avoid estate taxes is successful. The Robbie family faced a $47 million tax bill after the death of former Miami Dolphins owner Joe Robbie. The family did not have the money and were forced to sell the team to Wayne Huizenga (Much, 1997, September 9). On the basis of these tax issues, the NFL has on several occasions over the last decade changed the amount that a general partner needs to own, having the aim of helping families reduce estate tax concerns. In 2000 a general partner in an NFL team was required to own at least 30% of a team. A new rule enacted in 2004 lowered the amount that a general partner must own to 20% as long as that person had been the team owner for at least 10 years and another 10% of the team had been owned by family members.

Most recently, this rule was amended in 2009. The new requirement for a general partner lowered the ownership level to 10%, and at least 20% had to be owned by other family members. The new rule is in place only for existing owners. New owners must wait a decade to become eligible, and an active succession plan for ownership must be in place if the general partner passes away. The NFL passed this rule because of the large number of aging owners within the league and the increasing value of franchises. With the high franchise values comes a higher level of estate tax burden for family-owned teams such as the Chicago Bears, New England Patriots, and Dallas Cowboys when the eldest family member passes away. This rule allowed families to maintain ownership in a franchise by reducing the ownership level of the eldest family member, thus lowering the estate tax burden when that person passes away (Kaplan, 2009).

A more recent death of a team owner led to a unique situation regarding estate taxes and professional teams. In 2010 the long-time owner of the New York Yankees, George Steinbrenner, passed away at age 80. At the time of his death, the Yankees were one of the most valuable franchises in the world. *Forbes* estimated the value of the Yankees at over $1.5 billion (Brown, 2010). But unlike so many team owners in the past, the Steinbrenner family was poised to avoid paying any estate taxes on the team. In 2010 there was an unplanned yearlong gap in the estate tax, which meant that no taxes had to be paid on estates of those who died in 2010, the first year since 1916 in which estate taxes were not required to be paid. Steinbrenner's estate was valued at about $1.1 billion. With the 35% estate tax that had been in place, the debt burden on his family would have been about $400 to $500 million. Instead, the family would pay zero dollars in estate taxes. But in December 2010 the Tax Relief Unemployment Insurance Reauthorization and Job Creation Act of 2010 was passed into law by the federal government. Part of this law called for the retroactive payment of estate taxes for those who died in 2010. The new law allowed heirs several options for paying the uncollected state taxes. Thus, in the end it appears that the Steinbrenner family may be forced to pay estate taxes for the Yankees (Tanner, 2011).

Taxes

No matter what organizational structure is chosen for a business, every manager needs to know some tax basics. The value of any financial asset or instrument is contingent on the cash flow produced by the investment. This cash flow is subject to taxation when disbursed and when received. If the tax rate on a given investment cash stream is too high, the investor will opt for a different investment that may have a lower return but also lower taxes. For example, cautious investors often purchase tax-free bonds rather than stock or other types of investment vehicles. Although the interest rate is lower, tax-free bonds may be more practical than investments that pay a higher interest rate because taxes on a taxable investment may cancel out any benefit derived from the higher interest rate.

An example will help show why this is so. If an athletic department that is part of a state university starts building a stadium and issues a $1,000 tax-free bond that pays 5% interest each year, the investor will take home $50 each year. In contrast, if the investor buys a $1,000 face-value bond issued by Under Armour that pays 7%, her $70 per year interest will be subject to taxation. If her tax rate is 30%, then instead of taking home $70, she will take home only $49 after taxes. Although the difference is only $1, the purchaser of the tax-free bond also has the comfort of owning a secure investment; most tax-free bonds are issued by government entities and have a low default rate. The difference could be much more significant when riskier bonds, such as junk bonds, are being purchased.

Two formulas can help an investor determine which of two investment options would return the most after taxes. Assume that Jane Doe wants to invest $10,000 in bonds. She is taxed at a rate of 31%. She is considering investing in government municipal tax-free bonds (a "muni") with a 10% yield. Munis are attractive investment vehicles because they help communities grow and pay their holders interest that is tax free. Doe wants to determine the **tax-equivalent yield** for a taxable bond that would produce the same rate of return as the muni. The formula is as follows:

tax-equivalent yield = yield on muni / (1 − marginal tax rate)

= 10% / (1 − 0.31)

= 14.5%

This formula determines the equivalent taxable bond yield, but what if we know the taxable bond yield and want to determine the equivalent muni yield? Another formula determines the desired minimum muni yield (Brigham & Houston, 2013):

yield on muni = (taxable bond yield) × (1 − marginal tax rate)

= 14.5% (1 − 0.31)

= 10.0%

The formulas illustrate the types of calculations that an investor or business needs to make to do tax planning. Making the wrong choice can cost an investor a significant amount of money, but by undertaking a simple analytical step, an investor can save a significant amount of money. The difference between the bond returns would entice most investors to choose a taxable bond if the return is over 14.5% when tax-free bonds are paying less than 10% interest. Careful tax planning is not just an exercise in trying to keep the government happy or to avoid an audit; it gives people or businesses information about various investment options to help them maximize revenues.

Tax Planning

Almost everyone is familiar with taxes. We pay taxes at the gas pump in the form of gas taxes. We pay sales taxes at the cash register. We may pay a surcharge on a ticket to a game or other event. We also may pay income tax at the federal or state level or both. Thus, the average person is often all too familiar with taxes. Corporations and businesses, however, have unique tax concerns. We may not feel the effect of tax withholdings when our employers pay our taxes and we readjust the amount paid when we complete our tax forms. But sport businesses often have to pay sales, employee, transportation, property, income, and possibly numerous additional taxes. If a sport business does not properly plan for all potential tax liabilities, it can lose significant revenue.

In 1958 the Federal Tax Code had 650 pages. By 2010 the Federal Tax Code had swelled to over 70,000 pages ("Tax numbers," 2000). Although it

TAXING VISITING ATHLETES

To help raise income tax revenues, many cities across the United States have enacted professional athlete taxes. The taxes are based on a "duty day," which is calculated by determining what percentage of the athlete's income is earned in the city that is imposing the tax. If an athlete played in a city on 10 of the 200 days on which he played or practiced his sport over the year, then the taxable income would be based on 10 days. Let's assume that the tax rate for visiting players is 4%. For a player who earned $1,000,000 a year to play on 200 days, the tax due to that city would be $2,000 a year. The tax on athletes is not unique; the same tax applies to any nonresident who earns money in a given state or jurisdiction. Thus, the athletes are not being targeted, but enforcing the law on this group is easy because everyone knows when athletes are in the state or jurisdiction and basically how much they are earning there (Baxter, 2009). The tax can be somewhat problematic for the athletes. They must pay taxes in numerous cities in which they play.

is not clear how many pages are in the latest tax code, some estimates put the number at more than 70,000 (Cary, 2010).

Sport businesses that fail to analyze tax implications properly can overstate anticipated income, which can lead to litigation from shareholders based on the inaccurate information. Numerous taxes can apply including sales, property, and ad valorem taxes. Although some taxes are direct pass-through taxes to the ultimate consumer, other taxes are borne by the company that manufactures the product. If a bicycle manufacturing company is based in Europe, the host country may impose a value-added tax, which is a tax applied to the value added at every stage of production. When the raw aluminum is transformed into a bicycle frame, a tax may be imposed. This type of tax may be charged at all phases of the manufacturing process and is incorporated into the sales price. But no separate sales tax is imposed on the bicycle when it is sold. Furthermore, many European countries offer travelers a value-added tax refund as they leave the country. This tax example applies only to European countries.

The two key concepts for analyzing taxing structures are marginal and average tax rates. The marginal tax rate is defined as the percentage tax liability imposed on the next dollar of income earned by the company or individual (Spiro, 1996). In contrast, the average tax rate is the total tax liability imposed on all taxable income. Suppose that a tax structure calls for a tax of 20% on all income under $100,000 and a 25% tax on income between $100,001 and $200,000. If a sole proprietor sport business earned $140,000 in income, the taxes would be $30,000 ([0.20 × $100,000 = $20,000] + [0.25 × $40,000=$10,000]). The marginal tax rate is 25% for all income over $140,000 (i.e., the next dollar of income earned). To calculate the average tax rate, we divide the $30,000 total tax burden by the $140,000 income, which produces an average tax rate of 21.4%. The average tax rate is important for historical purposes (e.g., if you want to know how much of your income has been paid in taxes over the past five years).

The more critical point of analysis for financial managers is the marginal tax rate, the rate on the next dollar earned. If a sport company knows that the next $100,000 earned will be taxed at a very high rate, it might decide not to earn that extra money because the resulting tax obligation would negate some added value from raising the next $100,000 in income. But if additional income adds to the corporation's bottom line, then the corporation should attempt to earn that additional income even if a large percentage will go to taxes.

Taxing Sport

It is beyond the scope of this text to analyze all tax-related issues, but in this section we overview some significant tax issues that affect the sport industry.

Various tax implications are associated with purchasing a professional sports team. For example, a major legal battle arose in connection with a 1997 tax court decision about whether stadium leases could be amortized when a professional team with a good facility lease is purchased ("Portions of New Orleans Saints," 1998). The case involved the New Orleans Saints, sold in 1985. When a team is sold, the primary assets are the players' contracts, franchise rights, and possibly a favorable lease. A business' goodwill is a Section 197 amortizable asset that can be amortized over 15 years. However, Section 197(e)(6) specifically excludes a sports franchise from such **amortization**. Thus, the team, or more specifically the expenditure directly attributable to the sports franchise rights, is not amortizable.

But if the team has switched some of the value away from the team franchise and allocated that sum to the lease, the lease value can be amortized over the time remaining on the lease. The cost of acquiring a leasehold is a capital expenditure recoverable through amortization. Such a benefit can be taken only if someone is willing to pay for the lease, which would occur only if the fair value exceeds the rent obligation established under the terms of the lease agreement. For example, if the team has been paying $100,000 a year to lease a facility and the fair market value for leasing the facility under a new lease would be $200,000, then the $100,000 value could be amortized over the remainder of the lease term.

The Saints were purchased for more than $70 million. The team and the IRS took different approaches in establishing whether the lease was amortizable, but they agreed that if it were, the value would be $16 million. The court concluded that the lease agreement, modified in 1975, was a premium lease and as such was amortizable. But the court also held that if new lease terms are negotiated at the time that the team is purchased, such new lease terms cannot be amortized ("Portions of New Orleans Saints," 1998).

Besides potential tax implications associated with lease values, tax issues can arise as they relate to benefits generated for team owners through public tax dollars. This concern can arise when a team negotiates a favorable contract that might be "too good." For example, Charlotte Hornets owner George Shinn was sued by a community activist for $4.1 million ("Shinn faces suit," 1998). The suit concerned the revenue that Shinn had received from the Charlotte Coliseum based on parking and concession profits. Originally, the lease between the Coliseum and Shinn had given the coliseum 100% of parking and concession profits during Hornets games. This arrangement was changed in 1995 to give Shinn 50% of the profits, which over three seasons had totaled $4.1 million.

The suit claimed that the lease agreement was unconstitutional because it conferred "privileges upon private parties without public benefit" ("Shinn faces suit," 1998, p. 5B). The activist was in essence claiming that in getting a change in the contract terms without public input, approval, or benefit, Shinn was receiving an unconstitutional benefit and that the benefits of the contractual change should revert back to Charlotte citizens. Thus, tax implications can benefit team owners or can raise the specter of public coffers being raided by the wealthy, creating a legal backlash.

Potential legal backlashes associated with favorable stadium financing deals were addressed by Congress in the 1986 Tax Act. Before passage of the act, municipalities were able to issue tax-exempt bonds for sports facilities. Tax-exempt bonds are more attractive for investors and might carry a better rate than taxable bonds. The interest coupons are tax-exempt, but any capital gains from the bonds are taxable. The benefit associated with tax-exempt bonds became problematic when the main tenant of the public building was a professional sports franchise. The government viewed such facilities, even if they were run by the local government, as private-purpose facilities and therefore not qualified for tax-exempt status (Greenberg & Gray, 1996).

One loophole in the legislation allows bonds to retain their tax-exempt status. Under the private-activity test, a bond is not tax exempt if 10% of the facility's use is controlled by a private business or if 10% of revenues to repay the bonds are derived from private use. This loophole has been used by numerous stadium and arena projects. Deals have been structured in such a way that a primary facility user will be charged less than 10% of the required principal and interest repayment amounts (Greenberg & Gray, 1996). Thus, many lease agreements limit the payment from the primary user to minimal amounts such as parking revenue, which

normally would not come close to covering 10% of the annual debt service.

Additional attempts to prevent the raiding of public coffers or to deny a major advantage to a sports team can be seen in legislation proposed by Illinois congressman William O. Lipinski titled the Taxpayer's Right to View Act of 1992 (H.R. 4736, 1992). The bill, which was not passed, was based on the premise that most sports facilities are funded by taxpayers and that it is unfair for taxpayers to pay for a facility but not be able to enjoy watching events broadcast from there if the events are aired on pay TV instead of "free" TV. The legislation also focused on nonprofit educational institutions that receive significant tax incentives and then try to broadcast events to taxpayers on a pay-per-view basis. The legislation called for taxpayers to have free access to events that are sponsored by nonprofit organizations and held in taxpayer-financed facilities. The bill also would have prohibited cable operators from charging or collecting a fee for pay-per-view broadcasts of an event held in a facility built, renovated, or maintained with taxpayers' financial support.

Although the Taxpayer's Right to View Act of 1992 was not successful, the IRS has been able to develop some equity by forcing nonprofit educational institutions such as schools involved in bowl games and some athletic departments to pay taxes if they are in fact engaged in a business enterprise. Two college football bowl games faced this issue in 1991 when the IRS ruled that Mobil's contribution to the Cotton Bowl ($1.5 million) and John Hancock Mutual Life Insurance Company's $1 million payment to its bowl constituted unrelated business income (Lederman, 1991). The primary mission of the bowl games is educational, but the IRS concluded that the sponsorship payments were made in essence for advertisements whose benefit is not educational. Thus, because the advertisements were not "substantially related" to the primary mission of education, the revenue was taxable at about 34% (Lederman, 1991).

Another example of taxation with sport has recently arisen with intercollegiate athletic conferences and their television networks. The Big Ten Conference, a nonprofit organization, established the Big Ten Network in 2006 as a separate LLC. The network airs Big Ten sporting events and other conference-related programs. Although the Big Ten and its members may not pay taxes on much of their income as nonprofit organizations, the Big Ten Network is a commercial interest and is taxed as such.

Nothing Is Free So far we have considered just a few tax-related issues, but the IRS has developed so many complex rules that it is almost impossible to engage in any revenue-generating project without raising a potential tax-related concern.

For example, let's assume that a local charitable group wants to raise money through a fund-raising event such as a walk-a-thon and automobile raffle. They will also just ask people for donations and give donors gifts based on the size of the donation.

The IRS rules are fairly straightforward for the walk-a-thon; because there is no expected return to the donor, the donor may deduct the entire donation. Those who have lost money on the car raffle can claim a donation for charitable purposes. The winner of the car will need to claim the gift on his or her tax return. The complexity arises with the last fund-raising option. As of 1998 the IRS requires people to reduce their donation amount by any premiums (gifts) they receive if the premiums are valued at more than 2% of the donation or $71, whichever is less (McAllister, 1998). Thus, if a person gives $100 and receives a $10 gift, the total donation is only $90 (because $10 is greater than 2%, it cannot be disregarded). If a donor gives $4,000 and receives a plaque, the plaque can be disregarded if it is worth less than $71 (because $71 is less than 2%, which is $80 in this example) (McAllister, 1998).

These rules are further complicated by additional rules that provide for disregarding low-cost logo premiums if the donation is over $35.50 and the total cost for the premium is under $7.10. The amounts applied to logo premiums are adjusted annually for inflation. Clarity becomes the key to helping donors understand their gifts, and the IRS requires charitable organizations to give donors a breakdown of deductions that may be claimed whenever they contribute more than $75 and receive something of value (Blum, 1993).

Charitable Planning Various techniques can be used to raise funds for nonprofit organizations. An important concern relates to large donations and the various tax ramifications associated with such charitable gifts. All nonprofits try to attract large donations. Although small gifts are helpful, running larger programs is usually impossible without some large gifts. The manner in which those gifts are given significantly affects the amount that the recipient can receive and the total benefit that the donor receives.

Assume that a University such as Florida State University or the University of Texas has an alumna who wishes to give $500,000 to the university. But she does not want simply to hand over the money because she bought the asset for $100,000 and would have to pay capital gains taxes on the $400,000 increase in value. The university could suggest using a charitable remainder trust to provide a benefit to the university and give the donor the option of reducing her tax liability. A charitable remainder trust (CRT) allows donors to give gifts at a future date but retain during their lifetimes the interest income from the asset. The donor receives a current tax deduction, whereas if the gift was transferred after the individual's death, the estate would receive the deduction. The assets deposited in the trust can appreciate, the donor does not have to pay tax on the income from the trust, and the donor does not need to pay capital gains taxes if the trust increases in value.

Using the $500,000 figure, assume that the donor currently receives a 3% return on the asset ($15,000 a year), that her tax bracket is 30%, and that the estate tax bracket is 55%. From the CRT the donor wishes to receive a 7% return, or $35,000 a year, over the course of her life. Table 5.1 shows the analysis for the options available to the donor if she deposits the asset in the CRT, keeps the asset, or sells the asset.

Table 5.1 shows that the lifetime net spendable income increases 181% when the CRT is compared with selling the asset and increases 256% when compared with keeping the asset (Fagan, 1999). If the donor kept the asset, she would have a lower income level but would be able to pass more money on to her heirs. If she sold the asset, she would receive the greatest up-front return, but her heirs would get a smaller amount because of the high

Table 5.1 Analysis of Donor Options

	Charitable remainder trust	Keep	Sell
Market value ($)	500,000	500,000	500,000
Capital gains ($)	0	0	112,000
Charitable tax deduction ($)	162,295	0	0
Income for donor ($)	576,122	225,000	407,400
After-tax income ($)	403,285	157,500	299,180
Value to heirs ($)	0	225,000	174,600

estate tax rate. If the donor's goal was to raise the highest amount of after-tax income over the life of the gift, then the CRT would be her best option. The example shows that proper tax planning can help educate donors about opportunities that can maximize their potential gifts.

Athletes and Taxes Although nonprofit organizations and their donors need to be concerned about tax implications of donations, professional sports teams can face the same challenges. For instance, in 1988 the Philadelphia Phillies gave Mike Schmidt a $2,150,000 contract that included a $100,000 charitable donation made in Schmidt's name but with the tax deduction to go to the club ("1988 baseball salaries," 1988). Under this arrangement, Schmidt would have to include the $100,000 in his income even though he did not receive the money and the club took the deduction, pursuant to Federal Regulation 1.61-2(c). Teams used to provide such bonuses to players as a means of increasing the player's take-home pay without increasing the player's salary. The additional amount usually is not counted against any salary cap constraints if it is an earnable bonus. Players appreciate the bonus because it can help their marketing and public relations effort, even if they have to pay taxes on the amount. Many athletes today have created their own nonprofit organizations. Because teams can reduce their own taxable income through funding such organizations, they now rarely give donations in an athlete's name.

Numerous additional tax-related concerns can also arise for an athlete, such as how to categorize income. For example, a professional athlete's salary is subject to income tax withholdings, but signing bonuses are not considered remuneration for services and generally are not subject to the employer's withholding taxes. But the tax law clearly indicates that bonuses paid to baseball players that are predicated on continued employment are subject to withholding (*Revenue Ruling 58-145*, 1958). Numerous other revenue rulings issued by federal tax courts have addressed bonuses, notably whether a player can give part of a bonus to a parent and claim the payment to the parent as a business expense. In one case a player gave $40,000 of his $70,000 bonus to his mother, but the tax court did not allow the expense deduction (*Allen v. Commissioner*, 1968). But in another case the tax court allowed the expense. In that case the player had paid his father a portion of the bonus, in part for his father's shrewd handling of the contract negotiation process and the years that his father had spent coaching and training him (*Hundley v. Commissioner*, 1967).

Business expenses for a professional athlete can be highly diverse. The following are some of the expenditures that are classified as business expenses for athletes (*Robinson v. Commissioner*, 1965):

♦ Game tickets for individuals who train with the athlete to help improve the athlete's skills

♦ Expenses for operating a training camp or for off-season conditioning

♦ Dues for a players' association

♦ Expenses for tax planning and investment advising

♦ Agent fees

♦ Fines imposed by a league or team for misconduct

Although the case involving fines is more than 35 years old, it is still the law of the land, and all the items listed are still considered valid expenses to reduce an athlete's tax obligations. Interestingly, although game tickets for individuals who train an athlete are considered a business expense, a player is required to pay tax on the value of tickets that he or she leaves for friends or family who have not helped improve the athlete's skills.

As the list suggests, careful planning by an athlete can reduce potential tax obligations. A professional athlete can run a summer camp and his own off-season training regime at the same facility using the same personnel. Through legal but creative accounting techniques, the expenses can be covered either under the athlete's personal business expenses or on the camp's tax return to help minimize tax obligations. The failure to plan properly can destroy an athlete as easily as it can destroy a business. Former Dallas Cowboys great Tony Dorsett became so involved in ill-advised tax shelters that by 1985 the IRS had taken his paychecks and put liens on his homes to satisfy a $414,274 tax obligation (Rosenblatt, 1989).

The same tax issues associated with bonuses and business expenses also affect various other monetary matters, such as

♦ deferred income and nonqualified deferred income plans for player salaries,

♦ local and city taxes charged to players who earn money by playing in a given area or city such as Pittsburgh, and

♦ the creation of nonprofit charities by players that are designed to give family members jobs and provide the players a qualified tax deduction.

Taxing the Teams

Tax planning requires analyzing a company's or institution's long-term plans to determine the most appropriate path toward minimizing tax obligations. For example, to maximize potential tax savings, a company expecting significant future profits may want to wait until the next tax year to purchase expensive equipment. The long-term plan can also help determine whether buying or leasing produces the greater tax benefit. In addition, long-term planning can help a business develop an appropriate strategy for categorizing income and expenses.

Depreciation of Assets

The way that costs are categorized can help determine the total allowed tax benefits. Teams can incur current expenses and capital asset expenses, and they can purchase nondepreciable assets. Current expenses can be written off the year in which they are incurred. Thus, if the Minnesota Timberwolves spend $10,000 on office supplies, those expenses can be used to decrease income earned that year and ultimately reduce the tax burden.

Capital assets are expensive assets that have a longer life. Machinery is a good example of a capital asset; a truck used by Speedway Motorsports at one of its racetracks may be expensive and may last longer than five years. The government allows companies to reduce their tax burden to save money so that they can purchase another truck in the future. If a truck lasts about five years and costs $50,000, Speedway Motorsports can depreciate it by $10,000 a year for five years. If the truck is sold after five years to another business for $25,000, the new owners can keep depreciating the truck. These owners will be able to depreciate $5,000 a year for five years.

Capital assets typically exclude salaries, which are normally classified as current expenses. This holds true for all industries except the sport industry. The salaries of athletes involved in professional sport are the only type of salaries that are depreciable (Euchner, 1993). The owner of a professional franchise can claim depreciation for five years after purchasing a franchise. In 1976 Congress passed the Tax Reform Act, which limited 50% of the franchise purchase price to players' salaries. Before that, a team buyer could claim 90% of the purchase price toward depreciable player salaries.

In 1986 Doubleday sold the New York Mets to two major stockholders, Nelson Doubleday, Jr. and Fred Wilpon (Euchner, 1993). The new owners did not change the management structure, but technically a new ownership group was in place. When the transfer occurred, exactly six years after Doubleday had bought the team, the company had just exhausted the player depreciation benefits. The new owners were then able to start the five-year depreciation clock again.

Players are not the only assets that can be depreciated by a professional team. Other capital assets that can be depreciated include (Euchner, 1993)

♦ the franchise itself,

♦ lease contracts,

♦ concession contracts,

♦ broadcast contracts, and

♦ customer lists.

All these contracts and marketing assets, as well as the goodwill inherent in the team, are assets that have value. The revenue stream available from luxury box lease contracts, concession contracts, and broadcast contracts can diminish over time, and although these are income-earning assets, they can be depreciated, like all other major capital assets. In 2004 Congress passed a law allowing teams to deduct the entire franchise value over 15 years.

As previously indicated, the methods by which assets, expenses, and income are categorized in the planning process significantly affect all tax decisions. Income taxes can be markedly reduced on the basis of how income is classified. Active income is classified as **earned income**. Passive income is income derived from transactions such as renting that do not involve regular work activities.

Tax-related issues can be highly diverse and can cover every possible facet of a business. Even when money is paid to others, tax issues arise. An employee's withholding and Social Security taxes are just two of the many taxes that an employer needs to consider. Pension plans also involve significant tax-related issues. Contributions to an approved pension plan are tax deductible for the employer. Thus, an expensive employee relations technique can be less costly when tax advantages are analyzed. We cannot consider every conceivable tax benefit or cost in this text. Instead, the aim is to indicate the broad range of tax and legal constraints that affect sport businesses.

Financial Risk Management

Risk management is the process designed to identify problems and produce solutions for various risks ranging from tax concerns to litigation-based issues. One solution that any risk management plan must include is insurance, which can save a sport business a tremendous amount of money. Insurance protection represents an attempt to shift the risks associated with a financial loss.

Some people prefer to run a business without insurance. Their thinking may be based on the calculation that if they do experience a loss, the cost of the loss will be lower than the premium payments that would have been required if they had purchased insurance. Others might base their gamble on the implementation of a significant risk management program that might reduce future claims. Although some managers are willing to take such risks or do not have the capital needed to buy insurance, most are much more risk averse and prefer to ensure predictable outcomes through insurance or other risk reduction tools (Williams, Smith, & Young, 1997).

Risk management is designed to help reduce or eliminate potential hazards. A hazard is a condition that increases the likelihood of a loss. An example of a physical hazard is a defective gym floor; a moral hazard involves an effect on a person's behavior (Williams et al., 1997). A moral hazard is present, for example, if the owner or manager of a gym might not know whether a closet has been properly locked and thus does not know whether a student could enter the closet, remove a trampoline, and get injured. Having an insurance policy to cover such an accident decreases the concern that the person might have.

Insurance represents a finance technique termed *risk transfer*. The risk of a financial loss is transferred to another party. If a sport business does not have any insurance coverage, it is retaining the risk of any potential loss. Risk financing is a passive activity compared with risk management. Risk management is designed for **loss prevention**. Risk financing is designed to help settle a financial dispute after a loss has occurred—it establishes who will pay. Regardless, though, of whether the financial risk is transferred or retained, a sport business needs to allocate money for both risk financing and risk management.

CONCEPTS INTO PRACTICE

One element of financial risk management that is unique to the sport industry is the risk of serious injury to the players. A team is always concerned that a player may suffer an injury that can be career threatening or involve the loss of significant playing time. Historically, many teams purchased insurance policies for the contracts of some, if not all, of their players.

For example, a Major League Baseball team may purchase injury insurance for several of its players; teams usually take out insurance policies only on the top salaried players. In this example, a team would purchase an insurance policy from a provider and that policy would stipulate the types of injuries and the amount of playing time missed for which the policy would be paid. Let's suppose that the Minnesota Twins sign a player to a five-year, $100 million contact. The team may also buy an insurance policy on that contract that will be paid if the player is seriously injured. If that player were to suffer a career-ending injury with three years left on his contract, the insurance policy would likely cover the remainder, or a portion thereof, of the salary that he is owed. The team can then use that insurance payment to cover the injured player's salary and use other sources of revenue to acquire a new player.

The insuring of players, especially in Major League Baseball, was common until the early 2000s. But because of the career-ending injuries of several high-priced players such as Albert Belle, the premiums charged by insurance companies skyrocketed. In some cases, the premiums increased by as much as 400%. In response to the spiraling cost of insurance, some teams have elected not to insure contracts, have greatly reduced the number of player contracts for which they purchase insurance, or have elected to self-insure their players' contracts by placing funds in a separate account that is used only to pay the salaries of injured players.

Lost Income

The risks that a sport business or organization can face could include various categories of decreased revenues (Williams et al., 1998):

♦ Lost rent if a subtenant does not pay the rent on time

♦ Interruption in business services through theft or vandalism of company property

♦ Interruption in the delivery of supplies (e.g., when a power outage occurs)

♦ A reduced amount recovered from accounts receivable when debtors do not pay their accounts on time

Other sources of lost income include competition, environmental restrictions, legal changes, and numerous other internal and external variables. A risk management program can help identify all these potential ways in which income can be lost. Organizations can then develop proactive strategies to help reduce the potential effect of any given loss.

Legal Challenges

One risk management concern that any financial analysis must cover relates to potential future legal ramifications from any decision. For example, government entities can develop unique financing schemes to help build a facility. But the fact that the government is involved does not guarantee that a legal challenge cannot invalidate provisions that might have made the deal financially beneficial. For example, a 1,500-acre (600 ha) cow pasture was converted into the 150,000-plus-seat Texas Motor Speedway. The developer and city entered into an agreement that the privately owned track would not have to pay any property taxes. A local school district sued the city to terminate what it called a sweetheart deal that deprived the school district of badly needed tax revenue.

The deal was founded on tax incremental financing (TIF). As noted earlier in the text, TIF is a financing vehicle whereby taxes for a facility such as a stadium are deferred. The municipality is gambling that with the new development, property around the stadium will increase in value, thus increasing the tax base. When the tax base increases, the municipality will receive higher taxes, which presumably will offset the tax savings given to encourage the stadium owners to build in a neighborhood with depressed property values. Tax incremental financing represents a potential win–win for all parties; the stadium owner receives a tax break, local citizens see increases in property values, and the municipality earns more tax revenue.

In the case of the Texas Motor Speedway, however, the school district claimed that the TIF led to unfair competition—it allowed developers to receive undeserved government charity, which would eventually hurt homeowners. Homeowners would be forced to pay higher property taxes because of losses in the city's tax income resulting from the deal. The Texas Motor Speedway cost approximately $204.5 million. Tax money covered $9 million in road improvements, $20 million for land acquisition, and $100 million in waived property taxes (Gibeaut, 1999). The developer was required to make only $2.2 million in total lease payments and after 30 years could buy the facility from the city (Fort Worth) for $500,000. The dispute led to litigation and every facility needs to understand that every action can result in potential litigation from an unhappy constituent.

Financial Risk Analysis

So far we have focused on business structure concerns affecting the bottom line, tax considerations, government regulations affecting sport financing, and risk financing. In addition, risk management can rely directly on financial ratios. For example, leverage ratios help measure the extent to which an organization is in debt. The more a sport business borrows, the higher the leverage ratio becomes. A highly leveraged sport business is more vulnerable to changes in the business environment. A business facing significant leverage may be forced by a debt holder to buy insurance to help protect pledged assets. Two specific techniques that can help identify leverage-related financial risk are the long-term debt to net worth ratio and the times interest earned ratio discussed in chapter 6 (Williams et al., 1998).

Liquidity ratios measure the ability of a company to raise cash in the short run. If a company does not have the ability to raise cash for emergencies, it is not on strong footing to deal with fiscal risks. Several ratios that can be used to evaluate the ability of a sport business to cover short-term obligations are the net working capital to assets ratio, the current ratio, and the acid test ratio (Williams et al., 1998). These ratios are also covered in chapter 6.

Risk managers in sport also examine ratios to determine whether a team is in financial trouble. According to Fitch IBCA, an international rating agency, several measures can help determine the soundness of a professional sports team. Using collateral coverage, Fitch IBCA expects collateral to cover team debt at least two times over (*Changing game*, 1999). The analysts also think that team debt to contractually obligated revenue should not exceed two times. Last, they recommend as a general guideline a minimum ratio of operating income to annual debt service of 1.5 times for investment-grade franchises in 1999 (*Changing game*, 1999).

Another financial measure for risks associated with a sport business is based on how stockholders view the business and whether they perceive the business as facing significant risks. Market valuation ratios such as the price to earnings (PE) ratio can provide a barometer of confidence. A high PE ratio is a strong sign that investors expect the organization's earnings to grow at a high rate. Another ratio is Tobin's q ratio, which analyzes how efficiently a business has invested its assets. Tobin's q is calculated by dividing the market value of the business by the replacement value for the assets of the business. A ratio above 1.0 implies that assets are worth more within the firm than if they were invested elsewhere. This number can be critical in risk management analysis when a buyer acquires a business and has to determine whether to liquidate the assets. If Tobin's q ratio is under 1.0, then an acquiring business might decide not to replace broken machinery because the added investment would not generate enough revenue to increase the value of the business (Williams et al., 1998).

BANKRUPTCY

This section examines the primary legal strategy to take when a business faces financial hardship. The federal government has created a means by which a company and individuals can discharge or reduce their current or future financial obligations. One of the major techniques for resolving financial hardships includes Chapter 7, 11, and 13 **bankruptcy** as well as involuntary bankruptcy.

CONCEPTS INTO PRACTICE

Although bankruptcy is not common in the sport industry, especially in team sports, a team has recently filed for bankruptcy. In June 2011 Frank McCourt, the majority owner of the Los Angeles Dodgers, filed for a much-publicized bankruptcy. At the time McCourt was going through a divorce from his wife and had mounting debt on the team. Other teams such as the Phoenix Coyotes, Chicago Cubs, Texas Rangers, and Buffalo Sabres have all filed for bankruptcy in the 21st century. In 2009, an entire league, the Arena Football League, filed for bankruptcy. After not playing in 2009, all assets of the AFL were eventually sold through a bankruptcy auction, and the league resumed play in 2010.

Bankruptcy Protection

Bankruptcy is the primary technique used by sport business owners when they are facing mounting obligations and do not have the resources to finance continued operations. The U.S. bankruptcy laws were first passed in 1898. The laws were developed to prevent a creditor from racing to the courthouse against debtors. Before the bankruptcy laws were enacted, creditors would make a mad dash to the courthouse in an effort to be the first to file so that they could establish a higher repayment priority over subsequent filers. The bankruptcy laws are designed to give all creditors with equal standing (secured and unsecured creditors) the right to be put into a common pool in which each creditor has the same rights. All secured creditors are entitled to have their obligations repaid first with the sale of the secured assets. The unsecured creditors would then together receive proportional repayments of their loans based on what moneys remain after the secured creditors are paid.

Bankruptcy petitions hit a new high in 1988 at 1.44 million. That number declined 8.5% to 1.3 million petitions in 1999. Personal filings, which account for most bankruptcy petitions, declined 8.3%, and business filings declined 14.6% between 1998 and 1999 (Dreazen, 2000). The numbers rose sharply in 2005 before the new laws that make bankruptcy filing more difficult took effect. An all-time high of 1.78 million petitions were filed in 2005, but the number dropped 37.6% to 1.1 million in 2006. Most of the cases filed were no-business cases, numbering 34,222 business filings in 2005 and 27,333 business filings in 2006. Most of the filings are Chapter 7 (personal liquidation) cases, totaling 833,147 in 2006. That was followed by Chapter 13 (personal debt reorganization) filings, totaling 272,937; Chapter 11 (business) at 6,003; and Chapter 12 (family farmers), numbering only 376 cases in 2006 (*Bankruptcy filings decline*, 2006).

More recently, over 1.4 million bankruptcies occurred during the 12-month period that ended on September 30, 2011. This amount was 8% lower than the number of bankruptcies in 2010. The number of 2010 bankruptcies, slightly over 1.5 million, was the highest since the new bankruptcy laws were enacted in 2005. In 2010, 1.036 million of those bankruptcies were Chapter 7 filings, and 434,839 of them were Chapter 13 bankruptcies (*Bankruptcy filings down*, 2011).

In the United States 291 bankruptcy courts serve 90 judicial districts throughout the country (Brigham & Houston, 2008). Although newspapers do not typically report smaller bankruptcies, several major sport-related bankruptcies occurred in the past several years. Some of the highly publicized petitions include those of the Arena Football League, the Chicago Cubs, and the Phoenix Coyotes.

The Bankruptcy Reform Act of 1978 produced the bankruptcy system used through 2005. Major reforms went into effect on October 17, 2005, with regard to who can file for Chapter 7 (personal debt liquidation) or Chapter 13 (personal debt reorganization) bankruptcy. The new laws make filing for bankruptcy harder and more time consuming. Under the new law, all debtors need to get credit counseling before they can file a bankruptcy case ("The new bankruptcy law," 2005). All potential filers must complete their counseling with an agency approved by the U.S. Trustee's office. Unlike in previous years, some filers with higher incomes will not be allowed to use Chapter 7 (which extinguished almost all debts owed) but will instead have to repay at least some of their debt under Chapter 13.

The bankruptcy code contains nine chapters, but the chapters are not numbered consecutively. Chapters 1, 3, and 5 contain general provisions; Chapter 9 applies to municipalities that declare bankruptcy; Chapter 12 deals with family-owned farms; and Chapter 15 establishes a system of trusts to administer bankruptcy proceedings. Three primary bankruptcy options are available to debtors to obtain court protection from creditors, depending on the existing circumstances; these are provided for in Chapters 7, 11, and 13.

CONCEPTS INTO PRACTICE

If a sport organization such as Speedway Motorsports, Inc. owes several lenders $10 million, it might be possible to develop a workout in which the company pays 25% of the debt immediately and 20% a year for the next three years. Thus, in four years Speedway Motorsports will have repaid 85% of the original debt, and the debt will be discharged.

Even though lenders might not receive the entire amount that they are owed, most lenders would be happy to recover 85% of the original loaned amount rather than nothing or a much smaller amount if the borrower goes bankrupt. Not all banks are willing to engage in workouts, but most understand the value of negotiating the best deal that they can to receive the largest possible share of their initial loan. The lenders might demand interest payments during the payback period to help cover the extension and might also demand additional security, such as personal pledges or asset-backed pledges.

Chapter 7 Bankruptcy

Chapter 7 bankruptcies entail a procedure for the orderly liquidation of the debtor's assets to repay creditors based on a priority established by statute. A trustee is appointed to gather and liquidate assets and then distribute the proceeds to creditors.

One of the many benefits associated with having a trustee to administer the bankruptcy estate is the power that the trustee can wield. A trustee can invalidate a transaction made by the debtor if the trustee believes that the transaction was preferential or fraudulent. For example, if the owner of a sport organization pays her son-in-law $50,000 for some consulting work two weeks before the team declares bankruptcy, the trustee may invalidate the payment if the son-in-law in fact did not do meaningful work.

Chapter 7 is designed to ensure that the debtor does not engage in fraud, to provide an equitable distribution of the debtor's assets among the creditors, and to allow the debtor to clean the debts and start from scratch. Distribution of the assets is based on preference. Preference is allocated from the most- to the least-secured creditors such that assets are distributed in the following order (Brigham & Houston, 2009):

1. Proceeds of sold items pledged for a lien or mortgage to which secured creditors are entitled
2. Trustee-incurred costs associated with administering the bankrupt business
3. Expenses that were incurred after an involuntary case had been filed but before a trustee was appointed
4. Wages due to workers earned within three months before filing for bankruptcy
5. Claims related to unpaid contributions to employee benefits plans that should have been paid in the previous six months
6. Any unsecured claims for customer deposits
7. Any taxes due at the federal, state, or local level
8. Liabilities associated with unfunded pension plans
9. Payments to general or unsecured creditors
10. Preferred stock
11. Common stock

Chapter 11 Bankruptcy

Chapter 11 bankruptcy provides an outline for a formal business reorganization supervised by the court. When a business owner files a voluntary

Chapter 11 petition, he becomes a debtor in possession of the business, and the business becomes a property of the bankruptcy estate (Kupetz, 1998). The debtor is authorized to keep running the business and make all necessary business decisions until otherwise ordered by the bankruptcy court. The reason that the debtor is allowed to continue running the business is that Chapter 11 bankruptcies are designed to rehabilitate the debtor, make sure that all creditors are treated equally, and maximize the value of the business to help pay as much of the debt as possible (Kupetz, 1998). A debtor can be issued debtor-in-possession financing for short-term liquidity purposes; these loans are given preference for repayment because they are made with the knowledge that the borrower is in bankruptcy and with the hope that the funds may help him out of bankruptcy. The sport team bankruptcies mentioned earlier (Phoenix Coyotes, Texas Rangers, Chicago Cubs, Los Angeles Dodgers, and Buffalo Sabres) are all examples of Chapter 11 bankruptcies.

Specific protections are afforded a debtor in Chapter 11 proceedings, including an automatic stay that prohibits the commencement or continuation of any legal action against the business (Cheeseman, 2010). Creditors can obtain relief from the stay, but courts traditionally attempt to assist the debtor as much as possible, including limiting the distractions caused by creditors pursuing litigation, by vigorously enforcing the stay.

Although the debtor is authorized to sell assets and enter into transactions in the ordinary course of business that benefit the company, creditors can petition the court to appoint a trustee. A trustee can be appointed if the creditors can show that some improprieties are evident. Such improprieties can include debtor fraud, dishonesty, incompetence, or gross mismanagement (Kupetz, 1998).

The debtor has the obligation in Chapter 11 proceedings to file a reorganization plan within 120 days after filing for bankruptcy protection. Such a plan gives a debtor the opportunity to try to turn the business around in four months. The debtor can stop making interest and principal payments until the plan is approved. Each creditor must be addressed in the plan, and the creditors have a final vote on whether they wish to accept the reorganization plan. Creditors have the right to vote against the plan, but this right is severely limited if the plan provides the creditors with at least as much as they might have obtained if the debtor had filed under Chapter 7. Such a reorganization effort involves all creditors regardless of the amount that each is owed. This effort differs from the situation with a workout, which normally entails only the largest creditors. Workouts are more informal and, as discussed earlier, are generally voluntary actions taken by a creditor to reduce its losses or costs or to help create a future business opportunity with the same debtor at a different time.

Creditors can also be coerced into accepting an extension agreement, which does not reduce the obligation but delays repayment for a specified period. A standstill, or moratorium, agreement allows the debtor to delay repayment for a given period without facing interest charges or penalties.

Chapter 13 Bankruptcy

Chapter 13 bankruptcy is designed only for consumers, so we will just touch on it. A debtor needs to file a petition voluntarily indicating that she is insolvent or unable to pay her debts as they come due. The trustee who administers the plan is paid 10% of the debts paid under the plan (Cheeseman, 2010).

Involuntary Bankruptcy

A business owner may think that he can turn the business around, but creditors can force his hand if they think otherwise. An involuntary bankruptcy occurs when three or more unsecured creditors who hold bona fide debts of at least $10,000 combined file a petition against the debtor. If fewer than 12 creditors in all are involved, only one needs to file a petition for involuntary bankruptcy against the debtor. When a petition for involuntary bankruptcy is filed, a summons is issued to the debtor requiring the debtor to respond to the claims within 20 days. If the debtor does not respond in a timely manner, the court can enter an order for relief against the debtor. The order for relief might entail a creditor's being allowed to seize some of the debtor's property. If the debtor responds, the court will grant relief only if the debtor does not pay his obligations as they become due. In most instances, the debtor is allowed to keep operating the business. But if the creditors who petitioned for involuntary bankruptcy are concerned about the debtor's actions, under certain circumstances they can ask the court to appoint a trustee to take possession of the business (Kupetz, 1998).

Bankruptcy issues often arise in the health club industry as a result of mismanagement, although bankruptcy actions can also take place in the professional sport arena. The American Basketball League, the first women's professional basketball league to show strong box office success, folded in its third year after competition arose from the Women's National Basketball Association. More recently, the Los Angeles Dodgers filed for Chapter 11 bankruptcy in 2011. According to the bankruptcy filing, the Dodgers owed more than $500 million to creditors. Some of these creditors included players such as Manny Ramirez, Andruw Jones, and Hiroki Kuroda, who had guaranteed contracts. Ramirez alone was owed nearly $21 million at the time of the bankruptcy filing. Even longtime and beloved Dodgers radio announcer Vin Scully was mentioned in the filing because of his claim of $150,000 in guaranteed salary (*Dodgers file*, 2011).

CONCLUSION

This chapter covered the various business forms that exist and some of the positive and negative aspects of each. Although the form of a business is typically a legal issue, it also involves important financial considerations. A sole proprietorship can never issue stock, so its capital acquisition options are limited. In contrast, a corporation can go public, but such an action raises numerous financial reporting requirements. Thus, you must consider the business structure before you examine what financing options are available or what industry ratios might serve as appropriate frames of reference for comparing one business with another. As highlighted throughout the rest of this book, industry benchmarking standards might exist, but they are irrelevant if you are comparing two different types of business structures.

In closing, the list of potential legal concerns is practically endless. The breadth of legal challenges facing a sport finance manager is equally significant. As seen in this chapter, when dealing with taxation and bankruptcy a sport manager faces countless potential legal hurdles that are either self-imposed or imposed by external entities. Luckily, as with hiring accountants and financial advisors, a company can hire skilled lawyers to help navigate the potentially confusing legal maze.

Class Discussion Topics

1. If you were going to operate a small sport business such as a fitness center or sporting goods store, what type of business structure would you try to establish and why?

2. The NFL currently does not allow any team other than the Green Bay Packers to have any shareholders. Should the NFL change this rule?

3. Give the pros and cons of public ownership of a sports franchise. Should more teams be publicly owned so that fans can be owners?

4. With all the money that the NCAA generates, should it still be considered a nonprofit organization?

5. Would you ever want to start your own business? If so, what do you think you would need to be financially successful?

6. Do you think that the LLC structure gives too much flexibility to business owners, who can hide their assets and avoid financial judgments by claiming that the LLC has no money and is just a shell?

7. Should a business be able to choose what business structure it wants to adopt, or should the government decide?

8. Should professional team owners be allowed to depreciate players' salaries? Take the pro or con side of this question.

9. Should athletes have to pay tax in states that they play in but do not live in?

10. Should the heirs of team owners have to pay taxes if they inherit a team? If so, should they pay taxes on the value of the team when originally purchased or at the appreciated value?

11. What is financial risk management, and how can it be used by a sport business?

12. What risk management strategies do you take on a daily basis to protect your finances (everything from insurance to preventing identity theft)?

Principles of Financial Analysis

Now that you know the basics of finance and financial systems, you can start to analyze a business' strengths and weaknesses. Part III will give you the tools to do that analysis.

Chapter 6, "Financial Statements, Forecasts, and Planning," introduces you to the types of financial statements produced in the financial decision-making process. The chapter then outlines the various financial ratios that can be used to compare one company with others in that industry. The process for preparing financial forecasts and budgets is then described. Through forecasts and budgets, a company can plan for the future based on sound financial reasoning. The chapter concludes with break-even analysis, which helps a company determine whether its financial planning was realistic.

Chapter 7, "Time Value of Money," highlights a simple concept integral to all financial planning: Money loses value over time, and a dollar today is worth more than a dollar tomorrow. Because of the risk associated with the changing value of money, a company must plan for the future (budget) based on realistic assumptions covered in this chapter.

chapter 6

Financial Statements, Forecasts, and Planning

Chapter Objectives

After studying this chapter, you should be able to do the following:

- Identify the elements of the balance sheet.
- Identify the elements of the income statement.
- Discuss the cash flow statement and relate it to the income statement and the balance sheet.
- Define common financial ratios used to assess an organization's liquidity, activity, financial leverage, profitability, and inventory as well as the firm's collection cycle.
- Understand the information that must be gathered before beginning forecasting.
- Forecast sales as well as profit and loss.
- Understand what drives the need for capital.
- Forecast the balance sheet.
- Relate the projected profit and loss and balance sheet to industry norms as a reasonableness check.
- Discuss how to use break-even analysis as a planning tool.

To achieve success in their ventures, sport managers must know how to analyze financial statements and develop skills in financial forecasting and planning. In this chapter, we discuss the nuts and bolts of financial statements and show how cash flow is derived from these basic financial documents. We also introduce you to the steps involved in financial forecasting and planning. In addition, we describe the basic accounting statements that businesses use for reporting purposes. The techniques that we discuss are critical for starting new businesses, investing in new equipment, and making appropriate operating decisions. The chapter addresses the following key concepts underlying financial analysis:

♦ Types of financial statements
♦ Interpreting financial statements
♦ Preparing financial forecasts and budgets
♦ Break-even analysis

TYPES OF FINANCIAL STATEMENTS

Financial statements are compiled from a firm's accounting records. These financial statements include the balance sheet, income statement, and statement of cash flows. Financial statements are intended to provide information about a business in a consistent manner as a result of efforts by accountants to follow generally accepted accounting principles (GAAP). Two private organizations, the American Institute of Certified Public Accountants and the Financial Accounting Standards Board, as well as the Securities and Exchange Commission, an agency of the federal government, are the authoritative bodies determining GAAP. For example, GAAP establish policies concerning how to categorize depreciation or properly record losses. However, although GAAP are considered appropriate standards, they were criticized because of loopholes that allowed accounting scandals involving such companies as Enron, WorldCom, and Tyco to occur. Consequently, the Sarbanes-Oxley Act was passed by Congress in 2002 to make the financial operations of public companies more transparent to the investing public.

The balance sheet displays the financial condition of a business at a single point in time, offering information about assets, liabilities, and owners' equity. The income statement describes a business' profit or loss over a given length of time, such as a month, quarter, or year. It provides information about a business' operating performance over that period. The statement of cash flows indicates how the cash position of a business has changed over a given period. For example, the firm may see its cash position depleted through the purchase of machinery or supplies. The firm's cash position can also be diminished through the paying down of debt or the paying of dividends to stockholders. For example, the income statement may show that a business had a profitable year, yet the company's cash holdings can decline. The statement of cash flows can be used to determine what happened to the business' cash. When examining financial statements, note that some terms are interchangeable whereas others are not. For example, sales and revenues are interchangeable; profits, earnings, and income are the same; but costs are different from expenses. Costs refer to money spent on manufacturing a product or service, whereas expenses refer to money spent on developing, producing, selling, and managing the product or service.

Balance Sheet

The balance sheet is used by accountants to give a picture of the business at a single point in time, as if the business were standing still. Here is the basic equation that all balance sheets follow:

$$\text{assets} = \text{liabilities} + \text{owners' equity}$$

Because this basic definition must always hold, capital provided by investors is always equal to the assets of the firm minus the liabilities of the firm. The left side of the balance sheet (debit side) is what a company owns; the right side (credit side) indicates how the assets were financed. Given the preceding equation, when any two variables of the equation are known, we can always solve for the third using basic math.

In a balance sheet the assets of the firm are listed according to the length of time needed to convert them to cash. The asset side is normally determined by the nature of the business, the industry that it operates in, and financing and operational decisions made by management. In many businesses, management has to decide whether sales are cash or credit transactions, whether equipment should be purchased or leased, and whether cash balances should remain as cash or be invested in short-term securities that can earn a return.

Liquidity refers to the degree of ease and quickness of converting assets to cash. The entries listed under current assets are the most liquid because they are expected to be converted to cash within one year or less. Examples of current assets appearing on balance sheets are cash and short-term financial assets. In addition, current assets include accounts receivable, consisting of the dollar amounts not yet collected from customers for goods and services sold to them (after adjustments for bad debts). Inventory consists of raw materials used for manufacturing, work in process, or for finishing goods. Current assets are discussed in more detail in Chapter 12. **Fixed assets** are the assets on the balance sheet with the least liquidity. These assets include real estate, plants, and equipment. Unlike current assets, fixed assets normally are not converted to cash for such day-to-day activities as meeting payroll or paying vendors. The balance sheet also lists intangible assets including goodwill and patents.

A balance sheet for Speedway Motorsports is shown in figure 6.1. Most of the current assets consist of cash and cash equivalents. An additional major category of current assets is accounts receivable. Speedway also reports prepaid expenses as a current asset. Prepaid expenses are listed as an asset because the good or service that has been paid for but not yet received by Speedway is expected to earn income for the company in the future. Speedway Motorsports reports equipment and property as fixed assets. Other fixed assets include intangible assets and goodwill, which account for the value of the business that cannot be directly tied to specific physical goods that the company owns. An example of an intangible asset is the value of a company's brand name.

In the liabilities section of the balance sheet, liabilities are listed in the order in which they must be paid. Current liabilities consist of obligations that must be paid down in one year or less, and long-term liabilities consist of items that will not be paid for within one year. The liabilities and stockholders' equity (capital provided by investors) portions of the balance sheet typically reflect decisions about the sources of financing for the business. For example, decisions concerning the mix of financing provided by debt versus stockholders' equity, as well as short-term versus long-term debt financing, are reflected in the entries shown in the liabilities and stockholders' equity section of the balance sheet.

CONCEPTS INTO PRACTICE

Speedway Motorsports' primary current liability is accounts payable, composed of unpaid bills to vendors. In addition, Speedway lists the current portion of its long-term debt as a current liability because it must be paid within the year. Typical long-term debt includes land leases, mortgages, and loans exceeding one year. Because Speedway is not required to pay all of their long-term debt immediately, they disclose exactly how much of it must be paid in the current year and report that amount as a current liability.

For Speedway Motorsports, the investment in the business by its owners is denoted by the term *stockholders' equity*.

The net working capital, or working capital, of any business is current assets less current liabilities. When net working capital is positive, the firm expects that the cash paid out over the next year will be less than the cash that will become available over the next year. Speedway Motorsports had positive net working capital of $56,124,000 in 2010 and $53,189,000 in 2009, indicating that the company's short-term assets have been exceeding the company's short-term obligations. Positive net working capital is an indication of strong liquidity.

The term *investment in working capital* refers to an increase in net working capital between points in time on the balance sheet. See the case study in the "Concepts into Practice" sidebars that follow throughout the chapter.

CONCEPTS INTO PRACTICE

Between December 31, 2009, and December 31, 2010, Speedway Motorsports' positive net working capital increased from $53,189,000 to $56,124,000, representing an increase of $2,935,000 in net working capital.

Income Statement

The income statement measures a business' profitability over a specific period, such as a year or a quarter. Income is defined as follows:

$$income = revenue - expenses$$

Speedway Motorsports Balance Sheet	As of December 31	
Assets (in thousands, except share amounts)	2010	2009
Current assets:		
Cash and cash equivalents	$92,200	$97,651
Short-term investments	975	975
Accounts and notes receivable, net	42,509	40,435
Prepaid income taxes	11,431	15,333
Inventories, net	9,382	11,224
Prepaid expenses	4,317	3,961
Deferred income taxes	291	459
Current assets of discontinued operation	2,150	101
Total current assets	163,255	170,139
Notes and other receivables:		
Affiliates	4,412	4,754
Other	4,623	6,857
Other assets	27,655	32,220
Property and equipment, net	1,169,281	1,179,055
Other intangible assets, net	394,972	394,983
Goodwill	187,326	181,013
Total	$1,951,524	$1,969,021
Liabilities and stockholders' equity	2010	2009
Current liabilities:		
Current maturities of long-term debt	$2,381	$1,219
Accounts payable	14,182	11,288
Deferred race event income, net	67,084	78,566
Accrued interest	3,865	3,978
Accrued expenses and other current liabilities	19,619	20,885
Current liabilities of discontinued operation	—	1,014
Total current liabilities	107,131	116,950
Long-term debt (note 15)	626,316	671,143
Payable to affiliate	2,594	2,594
Deferred income, net	6,587	7,795
Deferred income taxes	333,947	309,722
Other liabilities	8,712	12,604
Total liabilities	1,085,287	1,120,808
Commitments and contingencies (notes 2, 6, 8, 10, 14, and 15) **Stockholders' equity:**		
Preferred stock, $.10 par value, shares authorized—3,000,000, no shares issued	—	—
Common stock, $.01 par value, shares authorized—200,000,000, issued and outstanding—41,621,000 in 2010 and 42,266,000 in 2009	450	449
Additional paid-in capital	243,132	241,379
Retained earnings	702,558	674,851
Accumulated other comprehensive loss	(72)	(64)
Treasury stock at cost, shares—3,398,000 in 2010 and 2,655,000 in 2009	(79,831)	(68,402)
Total stockholders' equity	866,237	848,213
Total	$1,951,524	$1,969,021

Figure 6.1 Speedway Motorsports balance sheet.

Reprinted, by permission, from *Speedway Motorsports Annual Report*, 2011. Available: http://phx.corporate-ir.net/phoenix. zhtml?c=99758&p=irol-sec.

Whereas the balance sheet provides us with a snapshot at a single point in time, the income statement can be viewed as a film portraying how the organization performed between the single snapshots depicted on two balance sheets. Speedway Motorsports' income statement is shown in figure 6.2.

The income statement typically consists of three sections. The first section includes the revenues and expenses from the company's operations. Second, a nonoperating section of the income statement includes financing costs and any income earned by financial investments. For Speedway Motorsports, the interest expense represents financing costs.

Speedway Motorsports Income Statement	As of December 31		
Year ended (in thousands, except per share amounts)	2010	2009	2008
Revenues:			
Admissions	$139,125	$163,087	$188,036
Event-related revenue	156,691	178,805	211,630
NASCAR broadcasting revenue	178,722	173,803	168,159
Other operating revenue	27,705	34,827	43,168
Total revenues	502,243	550,522	610,993
Expenses and other:			
Direct expense of events	100,843	100,922	113,477
NASCAR purse and sanction fees	120,273	123,078	118,766
Other direct operating expense	21,846	26,208	34,965
General and administrative	85,717	84,250	84,029
Depreciation and amortization	52,762	52,654	48,146
Interest expense, net (note 6)	52,095	45,081	35,914
Equity investee losses (earnings)	76,657	(1,572) Impairment of intangible assets (note 5)	7,273
Other expense (income), net	(2,378)	337	(1,077)
Total expenses and other	431,158	516,460	432,648
Income from continuing operations before income taxes	71,085	34,062	178,345
Provision for income taxes	(25,822)	(40,220)	(72,442)
Income (loss) from continuing operations	45,263	(6,158)	105,903
Loss from discontinued operation, net of taxes	(782)	(4,145)	(25,863)
Net income (loss)	$44,481	$(10,303)	$80,040
Basic earnings (loss) per share:			
Continuing operations	$1.08	$(0.14)	$2.44
Discontinued operation	(0.02)	(0.10)	(0.60)
Net income (loss)	$1.06	$(0.24)	$1.84
Weighted average shares outstanding	41,927	42,657	43,410
Diluted earnings (loss) per share:			
Continuing operations	$1.08	$(0.14)	$2.44
Discontinued operation	(0.02)	(0.10)	(0.60)
Net income (loss)	$1.06	$(0.24)	$1.84
Weighted average shares outstanding	41,928	42,657	43,423

Figure 6.2 Speedway Motorsports income statement.

Reprinted, by permission, from *Speedway Motorsports Annual Report*, 2011. Available: http://phx.corporate-ir.net/phoenix.zhtml?c=99758&p=irol-sec.

Typically, the nonoperating section of the income statement includes all taxes paid by the enterprise. The third section of the income statement is the net income of the business.

Under GAAP, revenue is generated when an exchange of goods or services occurs. In addition, revenues and expenses are reported when they occur, although cash inflows or outflows may or may not have occurred. For example, when goods and services are sold for credit, associated sales and profits are reported even if payment has not yet been received. This system is known as accrual basis accounting as opposed to cash basis accounting (discussed in chapter 2), in which revenues and expenses are not recognized until actual cash inflows and outflows occur.

The value of a firm's assets is linked to the future incremental cash flows that they will generate, but cash flows do not show up on the income statement. As a result, some expenses that appear on the income statement are not actual cash outlays. One such expense is depreciation. Depreciation represents an estimate by the firm's accountants of the cost of equipment and property that are used up by the organization in the process of producing and distributing goods and services.

CONCEPTS INTO PRACTICE

Speedway Motorsports has a noncash expense that is related to the amortization of their property plant and equipment and intangible assets. Intangible assets are nonphysical fixed assets of the business that provide value, such as patents, licenses, trademarks, and copyrights. Unless one is ready to assume that an intangible asset has unlimited life for accounting purposes, amortization must be claimed over a reporting period because of either obsolescence or the "wearing out" of the intangible asset. As with depreciation, this amortization of intangible assets does not result in a cash outflow for Speedway Motorsports.

Companies report as the cost of goods sold those expenses that are directly related to the production and distribution of goods and services. Such costs include raw materials, direct labor, and manufacturing overhead. Other costs are allocated by the accountants preparing the financial statements to the period covered by the income statement. Such costs are reported separately as selling costs and as general and administrative costs.

CONCEPTS INTO PRACTICE

Speedway Motorsports separately reports general and administrative costs but reports no cost of goods sold. Speedway does not report cost of goods sold because the company offers a service as opposed to a product. The company is engaged in the business of entertaining their customers with racing events As a result, Speedway reports costs and expenses associated with conducting races over the regular season, which can be viewed as the company's productive activity.

Statement of Cash Flows

From the perspective of financial analysis, the importance of financial statements lies in their ability to provide information about an organization's cash flows. Firms have value when they generate cash flows for investors. By cash flows, we are referring directly to cash flowing into the business as well as cash flowing out of the business. To see this distinction between cash flows and accounting measures of income, recall that income statements include noncash expenses such as depreciation. The amount of depreciation reported on a business' income statement has no effect whatsoever on the cash generated by the business. When the business reports depreciation, the dollar amount reported as depreciation is not directly paid to any vendors or employees, as would be the case with other operating expense categories. The statement of cash flows is a financial statement that reports changes in a company's cash holdings over a particular period. Speedway Motorsports' statement of cash flows is shown in figure 6.3.

Speedway Motorsports has three primary sources of cash flows as a result of business activities. These include cash flows from (used in) operating activities, cash flows from (used in) investing activities, and cash flows from (used in) financing activities. Cash flow refers to the difference between what a company brings in and what it pays out. Thus, cash flow from (used in) operating activities refers to both positive and negative cash flows resulting from the firm's basic operating activities. These include operating revenues less all operating expenses other than noncash operating expenses, such as depreciation. When a firm earns revenue, positive cash flows occur, whereas cash expenses are associated with negative cash flows. In addition,

Speedway Motorsports Statement of Cash Flows	As of December 31		
Year ended (in thousands)	2010	2009	2008
Cash flows from operating activities:			
Net income (loss)	$44,481	$(10,303)	$80,040
Loss from discontinued operation, net of tax	782	4,145	25,863
Cash used by operating activities of discontinued operation	(3,845)	(1,513)	(4,803)
Impairment of intangible assets	—	7,273	—
Adjustments to reconcile income (loss) from continuing operations to net cash provided by operating activities:			
(Gain) loss on disposals of property and equipment and short-term investments	(2,304)	131	820
Deferred loan cost amortization	3,584	3,101	1,772
Interest expense accretion of debt discount	1,527	1,120	—
Depreciation and amortization	52,762	52,654	48,146
Amortization of deferred income	(1,534)	(1,680)	(1,536)
Deferred income tax provision	24,168	29,826	12,936
Equity investee losses (earnings)	—	76,657	(1,572)
Share-based compensation	1,979	1,585	1,538
Changes in operating assets and liabilities, net of business acquisitions:			
Accounts and notes receivable	(1,770)	2,174	3,999
Prepaid and accrued income taxes	3,902	1,968	(3,752)
Inventories	1,842	2,737	1,346
Prepaid expenses	(356)	(91)	20
Accounts payable	(1,789)	(1,733)	350
Deferred race event income	(11,482)	(26,826)	(23,348)
Accrued expenses and other liabilities	(1,787)	(483)	(3,782)
Deferred income	389	312	580
Other assets and liabilities	(3,935)	(3,251)	2,298
Net cash provided by operating activities	106,614	137,803	140,915
Cash flows from financing activities:			
Borrowings under long-term debt	—	296,271	300,000
Principal payments on long-term debt	(51,505)	(311,509)	(48,446)
Payments of loan amendment and debt issuance costs	(88)	(11,007)	(452)
Dividend payments on common stock	(16,774)	(15,352)	(14,748)
Exercise of common stock options	—	—	740
Tax benefit from exercise of stock options	—	—	91
Repurchases of common stock	(11,429)	(12,792)	(9,921)
Net cash provided (used) by financing activities	(79,796)	(54,389)	227,264
Cash flows from investing activities:			
Capital expenditures	(37,218)	(42,551)	(75,004)
Kentucky and New Hampshire speedway business acquisitions, net of cash acquired	—	—	(392,411)
Increase in short-term investments	—	—	(1,365)
Proceeds from (payment for) other non-current assets	1,500	(1,570)	(1,387)
Proceeds from:			

(continued)

Figure 6.3 Speedway Motorsports statement of cash flows.

Speedway Motorsports Statement of Cash Flows	As of December 31		
Year ended (in thousands)	2010	2009	2008
Sales of property and equipment	2,755	98	393
Distributions of short-term investments	—	4,503	7,610
Increase in notes and other receivables	—	—	(3,646)
Repayment of notes and other receivables	694	1,079	1,258
Cash used by investing activities of discontinued operation	—	—	(7,222)
Net cash used by investing activities	(32,269)	(38,441)	(471,774)
Net (decrease) increase in cash and cash equivalents	(5,451)	44,973	(103,595)
Cash and cash equivalents at beginning of year	97,651	52,678	156,273
Cash and cash equivalents at end of year	$92,200	$97,651	$52,678
Supplemental cash flow information:			
Cash paid for interest, net of amounts capitalized	52,584	45,239	38,137
Cash paid for income taxes	1,616	11,856	63,308
Supplemental noncash investing and financing activities information:			
Increase (decrease) in accounts payable for capital expenditures	4,443	(6,145)	4,195
Net liabilities assumed for Kentucky and New Hampshire speedway acquisitions	6,313	—	11,174

Figure 6.3 *(continued)*.

Reprinted, by permission, from *Speedway Motorsports Annual Report*, 2011. Available: http://phx.corporate-ir.net/phoenix.zhtml?c=99758&p=irol-sec.

operating cash flows include the positive cash flows resulting from increasing current liabilities (other than short-term debt) and the negative cash flows associated with increases in current assets (other than cash).

Most companies choose to use the indirect method of cash accounting, and Speedway is no exception. Rather than add up every cash revenue and expense, the indirect method begins with the year's net income, adds back noncash expenses, and deducts noncash revenues. This approach saves considerable time and effort because all the cash revenues and expenses are already accounted for in the net income figure.

Speedway Motorsports reported positive cash flows from operating activities for the years ending December 31, 2009, and December 31, 2010. The cash flows from investing activities are associated with the business' making additions to fixed assets. Purchases of current and fixed assets lead to negative cash flow resulting from the use of cash to purchase those assets. When current and fixed assets are reduced (i.e., sold or disposed of) during the year, a positive cash flow occurs because of the cash generated by the sale of the assets. In addition, when current liabilities are increased, a positive

cash flow occurs from investing activities because of the postponement of cash use.

The cash flows associated with financing activities are cash flows to and from creditors and owners. Such cash flows include changes in the firm's debt and equity. When the firm increases its borrowings, the cash that is created is a positive cash flow. By comparison, paying off a loan results in negative cash flow. When dividends are paid out to stockholders, negative cash flow occurs, whereas proceeds from stock issues (i.e., new owners purchasing stock) result in positive cash flow.

TYPES OF FINANCIAL RATIOS

Information from financial statements is used to compute financial ratios that provide insight into the condition of a business. Specifically, we define commonly used financial ratios focusing on the following areas:

- ◆ Liquidity
- ◆ Activity
- ◆ Financial leverage
- ◆ Profitability
- ◆ Firm valuation

Financial ratios are important for companies because they serve as a barometer against three different benchmarks:

♦ Previous company ratios

♦ Competitors' ratios

♦ Ratios of other firms of similar size and scope

Liquidity

The liquidity ratios measure the ability of a business to meet short-term financial obligations. Liquidity ratios are associated with the firm's net working capital. A common liquidity ratio is the current ratio (CR), which is computed by dividing current assets by current liabilities.

$$\text{current ratio} = \text{total current assets} / \text{total current liabilities}$$

CONCEPTS INTO PRACTICE

The current ratio for Speedway Motorsports as of December 31, 2010, is 1.524.

$$\text{current ratio} = \$163,255,000 / \$107,131,000 = 1.524$$

The company's current ratio is greater than 1, indicating that current assets can cover current liabilities. If the current ratio drops below 1, the company may be unable to pay their bills on time without borrowing more money or receiving more cash from the owners. For manufacturing companies, a ratio of 2.0 or greater is favorable.

For a service company such as Speedway Motorsports, the current ratio can drop below 2 and still be considered strong because inventory, a major current asset in manufacturing companies, is nonexistent in the service sector.

A second measure of liquidity is the acid test ratio, or quick ratio, which is obtained by subtracting inventories from current assets and dividing the resulting difference by current liabilities. Because inventories are the least liquid of any current assets, the quick ratio indicates whether a firm can pay its current liabilities without relying on the sale of inventories.

$$\text{acid test ratio, or quick ratio} = (\$163,255,000 - \$9,382,000) / \$107,131,000 = 1.436$$

(total current assets − inventories) / current liabilities

Because Speedway Motorsports carries minimal inventory, its quick ratio is similar to its current ratio. Net working capital is not a ratio, but it helps highlight the available current assets after all the current liabilities are paid. Net working capital shows how much cash or other liquid assets might be available if the business had to repay all the liabilities that are due in the next several months. Net working capital is calculated as follows:

$$\text{net working capital} = \text{current assets} - \text{current liabilities}$$

Activity

Activity ratios measure how effectively a firm manages its assets. The total asset turnover ratio is computed by dividing total revenues for a particular accounting period by the average total assets for that period.

$$\text{total asset turnover ratio} = \text{revenues} / \text{total assets}$$

CONCEPTS INTO PRACTICE

For the year ending December 31, 2010, the total asset turnover ratio for Speedway Motorsports was 0.256. The average level of assets was obtained from their balance sheet shown in figure 6.1. We need to compute the average of Speedway Motorsports' assets in the period ending December 31, 2010, and the period ending December 31, 2009, to obtain the average level of assets during 2009-2010. The average level of assets is equal to ($1,951,524,000 + $1,969,021,000) / 2 = $1,960,272,500.

$$\text{total asset turnover ratio} = \$502,243,000 / \$1,960,272,500 = 0.256$$

The asset turnover ratio gives an indication of how effectively a firm uses its assets to generate sales. If the asset turnover ratio is relatively high, the firm is efficiently using its assets to generate sales. If the ratio is relatively low, the firm is not using its assets as effectively and may wish to consider selling off assets if sales do not increase.

The inventory turnover ratio is equal to the cost of goods sold over a particular period divided by the average inventory level during that same period.

inventory turnover ratio = cost of goods sold / inventory (average)

The inventory turnover ratio tells us how many times during the year the inventory is purchased and sold. A relatively high turnover ratio is usually preferable, although the appropriate ratio is industry specific. For a manufacturing company, the inventory turnover ratio can be easily affected by the technologies used to produce the goods that it sells, as well as by distribution techniques. Inventory management is covered in more detail in chapter 13.

To calculate the receivables turnover ratio, we divide revenues by average receivables during the collection period. The ratio of receivables can then be used to derive the average collection period, which is the number of days in the period divided by the receivables turnover ratio. The values of these ratios are highly dependent on a firm's credit sales policies. A firm with generous credit terms will have a higher amount of receivables.

receivables turnover ratio = total revenues / average receivables

average collection period = number of days in the period / receivables turnover ratio

CONCEPTS INTO PRACTICE

Speedway Motorsports' receivables turnover ratio and average collection period for the year ending December 31, 2010, are 12.11 and 30.14 days, respectively. The average level of receivables is obtained from the balance sheet shown in figure 6.1. We need to compute the average of Speedway Motorsports' receivables in the period ending December 31, 2010, and the period ending December 31, 2009, to obtain the average level of receivables during 2010. The average level of receivables is equal to ($42,509,000 + $40,435,000) / 2 = $41,472,000.

receivables turnover ratio = $502,243,000 / $41,472,000 = 12.11

average collection period = 365 days / 12.11 = 30.14 days

Financial Leverage

Financial leverage ratios provide information about the extent to which a business relies on debt (loans) rather than equity (stocks) for financing. Firms with high financial leverage ratios relative to other firms in their industry have a greater likelihood of financial distress and bankruptcy. One measure of financial leverage is the debt ratio, which is total liabilities divided by total assets.

debt ratio = total liabilities / total assets

CONCEPTS INTO PRACTICE

The December 31, 2010, debt ratio for Speedway Motorsports was 0.556.

debt ratio = $1,085,267,000 / $1,951,524,000 = 0.556

Speedway Motorsports is not highly leveraged because their total assets are greater than total liabilities. The term *leveraged* refers to the extent to which a company relies on borrowing to finance its operations. Because Speedway is not highly leveraged, they are paying lower interest costs relative to the value of their assets than those companies that are highly leveraged. Most businesses cannot survive with high debt ratios relative to their competitors. A higher debt ratio means that a company is effectively paying more for its assets than its competitors are.

An alternative to the debt ratio is to measure the extent to which a company is leveraged by calculating the ratio of long-term debt to net worth. The difference between the debt ratio and the ratio of long-term debt to net worth is that the ratio of long-term debt to net worth excludes current liabilities. Similar to the debt ratio is the debt–equity ratio, which also analyzes a business' leverage but from the standpoint of the owners' equity rather than all assets. The debt–equity ratio is calculated as follows:

debt–equity ratio = total debt / total shareholders' equity

This ratio highlights how much of the debt is financed by shareholders. The higher the ratio is, the greater the reliance on shareholder support is.

A low ratio might indicate that the debt is being purchased through retained earnings or internal sources rather than through shareholders.

An additional financial leverage measurement is the interest coverage ratio. To calculate the ratio of interest coverage, we divide **earnings before interest and taxes (EBIT)** by interest. This ratio provides insight into whether a firm has sufficient earnings to cover its interest expense.

interest coverage ratio = earnings before interest
and taxes / interest expense

The interest coverage ratio is also commonly referred to as the times interest earned ratio.

CONCEPTS INTO PRACTICE

Speedway Motorsports' interest coverage ratio for the year ending December 31, 2010, was 1.365.

interest coverage ratio = $71,085,000 /
$52,095,000 = 1.365

Profitability

One of the most critical figures for examining a company's success is corporate earnings. The bottom line for companies is their ability to generate sufficient earnings to continue growth and reward shareholders. Earnings are calculated by subtracting total costs from total sales. The earnings or the corporate losses if costs exceed sales are the key point of analysis for future progress, dividend payments, bankruptcy, and any other potential corporate decisions. In the year ending December 31, 2010, Speedway Motorsports had a profit, as measured by net income, of $44,481,000.

Several measures of profitability are commonly used. These include profit margin (gross and net profit margin), return on assets, return on equity, and return on investment. Profit margins are calculated by dividing profits by revenues. Net profit margin is computed using net income (earnings after interest and taxes) as a proxy for profits; gross profit margin uses earnings before interest and taxes to represent profits.

Net profit margin = Net income / Revenues

Gross profit margin = Earnings before interest
and taxes / Revenues

CONCEPTS INTO PRACTICE

Speedway Motorsports' profit margins for the year ending December 31, 2010, follow:

net profit margin = $44,481,000 / $502,243,000
= 8.86%

gross profit margin = $71,085,000 / $502,243,000
= 14.16%

When a firm's net profit margin is high relative to other firms in its industry, the firm is able to provide its products at either a low cost or a high price. Speedway has an 8.86% net profit margin, but a competitor has only a 4.50% net profit margin. Specific reasons could account for the difference; it could be attributable to better local television rights contracts, a better track revenue-sharing deal, payroll differences, or simply that some markets can command higher ticket prices for any number of reasons.

Stockholders are primarily concerned about the return on their investment; thus the dividend per share is an important calculation. If the stock price increases, stockholders can realize a gain only if they sell the stock, known as capital gains. In contrast, if the corporate board of directors decides to issue a dividend, then stockholders can earn an immediate return on their investment without having to sell.

Other measures of profit do a better job than profit margins in reflecting the investment in capital by the firm or its shareholders. One such measure of profitability is **return on assets (ROA)**, which is defined as profits divided by average assets for the reporting period in question. The average assets can be found on the balance sheet.

return on assets = net income / total assets

CONCEPTS INTO PRACTICE

For the year ending December 31, 2010, the return on assets for Speedway Motorsports was the following:

return on assets = $44,481,000 / $1,951,524 = 22.79%

Return on assets (often referred to as ROA) is also known as return on investment because it reflects the amount of profits earned on the investment in all assets of the firm. Any new asset purchased by the firm should be able to generate increased returns over and beyond what could have been earned had the funds been placed in an equally risky financial investment.

A profitability measure related to ROA is the **return on equity (ROE)**, which is net income divided by average stockholders' equity. Return on equity measures profitability in terms of profits earned on investment in the firm's assets by stockholders only—as opposed to ROA, which measures profitability earned on investments in a firm by all providers of funds, including lenders and creditors as well as stockholders.

return on equity = net income / stockholders' equity

return on equity = $44,481,000 / $866,237,000
= 5.13%

Determining the Company's Value

As we have seen so far, financial statements give information about the basic condition of the firm, but they do not tell us anything about the firm's market value. **Market value** is based on what stock buyers and sellers establish when they buy and sell shares in the business. For a publicly traded company, the market value is simply the price per share of common stock, based on reported prices of shares traded on stock exchanges, multiplied by the number of shares of common stock outstanding.

market value = price per share of common stock × average number of outstanding shares

On December 30, 2011, Speedway Motorsports traded at $15.44 per share. Because 43.8 million shares of common stock were outstanding, the market value of the company can be expressed as follows:

market value = $15.44 × 43.8 million outstanding shares = $636.21 million

Whereas market value tells an investor what the investing public thinks a company is worth, a company's book value presents a different version of the company's worth. **Book value** is based on the historical cost of assets minus accumulated depreciation. Although book value represents the value of assets on paper, it does not necessarily represent the true value because an asset might have a replacement cost that is higher than its book value. An asset might cost $1 million to replace, but the book value could be only $500,000 ($2 million purchase price minus $1.5 million in accumulated depreciation). Book value is calculated by subtracting total liabilities from total assets.

book value = total assets − total liabilities

For Speedway Motorsports, the book value on December 31, 2010, was $866,237,000.

The book value of a company is also called owners' equity because it represents the value that the owners have in the business. Owners' equity is also calculated by adding retained earnings and the value of common stocks. Because owners' equity is a measure of a company's value, it is also called the net worth.

Book value per share is another measure of a company's value based on the owners' equity obtained from the balance sheet.

book value per share = owners' equity / total outstanding shares

The calculation for Speedway Motorsports on December 30, 2011, is as follows:

book value per share = $866,237,000 / 43,800,000 = $19.77

Techniques to Determine the Value of an Investment

Besides all the calculations that a corporation can make concerning its value, earnings, liquidity, and so on, investors can use several techniques to determine whether it was profitable to invest in the company. These techniques include annual return, holding period return, simple rate of return, and dividend payout ratio.

The annual return per share and the annual rate of return for an investment analyze whether any increase or decrease occurred in the value of a stock and whether any dividends were distributed to stockholders. Assume that an investor purchased a stock on January 1, 2012, and sold it on December 31, 2012. The stock was purchased at $8 per share and was sold for $10 per share. During the year the company paid dividends of $0.04 per share. The annual return per share and annual rate of return would be calculated as follows:

annual return per share = increase or decrease in value + dividends = ($10 − $8) + $0.04 = $2.04

annual rate of return = annual return / initial investment= $2.04 / $8.00 = 25.5%

The 25.5% return highlights how profitable the investment in the stock was that year. But this analysis is useful only for a quick snapshot in time and only if the stock was sold. If the stock price fell the next day, then the annual return would still be an accurate reflection of the value for the prior year but would not reflect the true value of the investment. The relevant concept here is paper profit (because the profit is shown only on paper). That is, the stock might have produced an excellent annual return, but if the stock is not sold the profit could vanish in an instant if the stock price declines.

In contrast to annual return, the holding period return takes into consideration the fact that the stock was possibly not sold. For the stock being analyzed, the holding period return indicates what happened to the investment, independent of what might happen in the future. Because the return on the investment during the one-year holding period was 25.5%, that is the holding period return rate. The dividend payout ratio examines the dividends per share relative to how much the company earned per share. The formula is as follows:

dividend payout ratio = dividends per share / earnings per share

If dividends per share are $0.50 and earnings per share are $3.00, the dividend payout ratio is 16.67 ($0.50 / $3.00). This number means that 16.67% of earnings were repaid to the stockowners as dividends.

To get a sense of how the stock market is valuing a company, we can compute the **price–earnings ratio (PE ratio)**. The PE ratio is equal to the price per share of common stock divided by the earnings per share of common stock. Earnings per share (EPS) is calculated as follows:

earnings per share = net income / average number of shares outstanding

If Speedway Motorsports (SM) and a competitor each reported earnings per share of $5, but SM's shares sell for $15 and its competitor's shares sell for $20, then the PE ratio for SM is 3 and its competitor's PE ratio is 4.

price–earnings ratio = price per share / earnings per share = $15 / $5 = 3

By contrast, the PE ratio for SM's competitor is 4.

price–earnings ratio = $20 / $5 = 4

Note that the stock market is valuing SM's competitor's shares at a higher multiple of earnings than it is valuing SM's shares. This disparity in PE ratios is usually related to differences in how the financial markets view the quality of earnings, past profitability, expected future earnings growth, or a combination of two or more of those factors.

Besides noting the PE ratio, some financial analysts also report a company's PEG ratio (price–earnings growth ratio). Although the PEG ratio and traditional PE ratio have similarities, they conceptually have one fundamental difference. Specifically, the PEG ratio estimates what the future quarterly earnings will be besides using the previous three trailing estimates.

Financial statements provide important information about the condition of a firm. By using numbers in financial statements, we can get key information that allows us to summarize an organization's liquidity, activity, financial leverage, and profitability. These ratios also allow a firm to examine its operations and ratios in comparison with publicly traded firms in the same industry. But when appropriate information is available, the market value of the firm should be used as a supplement to these accounting-based ratios. Market value is the true street value for a business (i.e., what someone would pay for a business today). Such a value is based on investor perceptions and the quality of available information about the company.

REVISITING FINANCIAL PLANNING

Now that we have introduced the basics of financial scorekeeping as it relates to income statements, balance sheets, statements of cash flows, and financial ratios, in this section we apply some of the tools of basic financial measurement to track financial results and prepare financial forecasts. Chapter 3 highlighted how budgets use financial data to plan and how to develop appropriate data to make decisions. By creating appropriate financial statements and analyzing financial ratios, a sport manager can plan in detail and possibly again evaluate an organization's budgetary and financial needs. The basic financial statements are probably the most important source of numbers for managing any organization. Any organization, regardless of size and complexity, must develop a solid accounting and financial information system and compile up-to-date information. An accounting and financial information system generates detailed financial reports, including income statements, balance sheets, and statements of cash flows. An accountant must be available to help interpret the data provided by the accounting and financial information systems.

Although developing accounting and financial information systems may sound like a daunting task for small organizations, in part because of the elaborate record keeping and report-generating activities required, many bookkeeping and accounting packages for businesses that can be operated on personal computers are available. Thus, even sole proprietors can generate monthly income statements and current balance sheets with minimal effort. These systems also offer a convenient way to archive past records. Having a historical record of income statements and balance sheets is useful in helping a business prepare budgets and projections of future financial results.

One of the hallmarks of financial planning is planning for future financial needs, which is covered in the following section about how companies attempt to determine their capital needs.

Determining Capital Needs

After sales and profit forecasts are complete, the next step is to see whether the forecast sales and profits can be accomplished with the firm's current assets. If the forecast sales and profits grow at too high a rate in the future, a company may need to obtain additional capital or assets in the form of inventory and fixed assets. These assets can be acquired only with money obtained through either increased borrowing or the issuance of stock. If the company cannot raise the money to obtain the capital, it can face a crisis caused by the inability to finance the high growth.

To determine capital needs, sustainable growth rate analysis is used. If the annual sales growth rate exceeds the sustainable annual growth rate, then external capital is needed to finance the necessary growth. The sustainable growth rate is calculated as follows:

$$g^* = [P (1 - D) (1 + L)] / [T - P (1 - D) (1 + L)]$$

g^* = sustainable growth

P = net income / sales

D = target level of dividends paid out to stockholders / net income

L = total liabilities / net worth

T = total assets / net worth

As an example, if a company's net sales were $60 million in 2011 and net income was $7.2 million, then P was approximately 12%. Assume that a board sets D at 50% and that the calculations for L and T are 50% and 80%, respectively. Note that L and T are hypothetical numbers to simplify the example.

$$g^* = [0.12 (1 - 0.50) (1 + 0.50)] / [0.80 - 0.12 (1 - 0.50) (1 + 0.50)]$$

$$= 0.09 / 0.71$$

$$= 0.1268, \text{ or } 12.68\%$$

Based on this projected 12% sales growth rate, this company will barely miss needing a capital infusion to fund growth. Suppose that the company's actual annual growth in sales ended up averaging 14% per year over the next several years instead of the forecast 12% per year. The company's growth rate would exceed the 12.7% sustainable growth rate, so the company would require additional capital to fund its growth. The company's options for obtaining new capital would be to issue new common stock, reduce dividend payouts to current stockholders, or increase borrowing (see chapters 8 through 10). The sustainable growth rate formula also implies that the company can reduce its assets to sales ratio by renting and leasing fixed assets, as opposed to owning them, because doing so will reduce the need for capital. In addition, if the company is a closely held business, another option is to reduce compensation to owners.

Sustainable growth rate analysis suggests that when planning for high rates of sales growth, businesses need to factor in the likelihood of further capital infusions. High sales growth uses up cash and capital.

Break-Even Analysis

So far this chapter has covered various financial calculations to determine strengths and weaknesses and has examined forecasting and planning. A key concept embodying all three elements is break-even analysis. Because of its relevance to inventory and production management in addition to its usefulness for guidance in financial forecasting and planning, break-even analysis is also covered in chapter 13.

Break-even analysis is used to determine the level of unit sales required for the business to just cover its expenses. In other words, break-even analysis provides the base sales level needed to ensure profitability. The break-even point occurs when EBIT equals zero (i.e., when pretax operating profits, independent of financing considerations, are zero). The break-even point can be expressed in the following way:

$$EBIT = revenues - variable\ costs - fixed\ costs\ of\ production = 0$$

The preceding equation can also be expressed as follows:

$$EBIT = PQ - VQ - F = 0$$

EBIT = earnings before interest and taxes

V = variable cost per unit sold

P = selling price per unit sold

F = fixed costs of production

Q = sales

The break-even point of unit sales (QBE) follows:

$$QBE = F / (P - V)$$

QBE = break-even point of unit sales

P = selling price per unit sold

F = fixed costs of production

V = variable cost per unit sold

The break-even formula states that the break-even point of unit sales will be higher if fixed costs are higher. The difference between unit price and unit variable cost (P − V) can be viewed as the gross profit per unit sold. The higher the level of gross profit per unit sold, the lower the number of units that need to be sold to break even.

The break-even formula can be demonstrated using assumptions about Under Armour Apparel Company. To illustrate, assume that the company's per unit price (P) is $15 and that the per unit variable cost (V) is $8.25, which is the sum of the direct manufacturing costs ($7 per unit) and the selling and administrative costs ($1.25 per unit). The fixed cost of production is $15 million, which is the sum of the $10 million depreciation expense and the $5 million interest expense. Plugging these values into the break-even formula, we get the following:

$$QBE = \$15,000,000 / (\$15 - \$8.25) = 2,222,222\ units$$

Note also that Under Armour's per unit gross profit margin on each sale is equal to $15 minus $8.25, or $6.75 per unit sold. If fixed costs remain at $15 million per year, the per unit gross profit margin would have to fall to $3.75 for Under Armour to be breaking even at four million units. This calculation indicates that Under Armour is in good shape because any reduction in per unit profits could come about only through severe price reductions, significantly reduced sales, or substantial increases in variable costs.

CONCLUSION

In this chapter we discussed the rudiments of financial statement analysis as well as financial forecasting and planning. Specifically, we provided an introduction to financial statements. We discussed the elements of the balance sheet, which summarizes the firm's financial condition at a particular point in time, and the contents of the income statement, used to measure the profitability of a business over a specified period. The balance sheet and the income statement provide a lead-in to explain changes in the cash position of a firm over a given period. Specifically, we describe changes in cash flows resulting from operations, investing activity, and financing. The elements of the balance sheet and income statement are used to compute financial ratios that summarize the firm's liquidity, activity, financial leverage, profitability, and market value.

Understanding the information contained in financial statements is critical to projecting future profits. When we forecast future sales and profits, we make various assumptions that require extensive analysis of company financial statements, as well as knowledge of typical financials in the industry that the company is part of. This analysis is especially important because sales and profit forecasts are used in the planning process to determine capital needs and break-even sales.

Class Discussion Topics

1. Discuss the pros and cons of using the various measures of profitability to examine a company's performance.

2. Discuss the pros and cons of using measures of leverage to assess whether a company faces financial distress.

3. How would you finance the high growth of a business such as Nike if you were not willing to borrow or raise additional capital?

4. Financial ratios can serve as benchmarks for comparisons. Specifically, discuss three comparative benchmarks that a company can use to evaluate its financial performance.

chapter 7

Time Value of Money

Chapter Objectives

After studying this chapter, you should be able to do the following:

- Understand the concept of future value, including its calculation for a single amount of cash received today.

- Understand the concept of present value, including calculation of the present value of a single payment at a particular time in the future.

- Calculate the present value of multiple payments received in the future, including perpetuities and annuities.

- Describe basic concepts of risk and return and their relationship to computing the present value of future payments.

- Use risk statistics to define risk, including those relating the performance of financial assets to risk.

The book to this point has highlighted the importance of finance in making business decisions and the issues associated with determining value based on various ratios or industry benchmarking standards. But no analysis can be complete without examining the time value of money. It is impossible to examine a $1 investment today versus one from 25 years ago without realizing that $1 from 25 years ago might be worth $10 in today's dollars. This chapter highlights why money is sensitive to time and how to calculate changes in value based on time constraints.

HOW MUCH IS MONEY WORTH?

In chapter 6 we discuss how to analyze sales and costs, evaluate cash flows, measure profitability, and prepare financial forecasts. A key issue in valuing these flows is their timing. A dollar received today is worth more than a dollar received in the future. **Time value of money** represents the concept that money in today's dollars decreases in value the further out into the future it is expected to be received. With this concept in mind, any investor or business needs to examine the time in which investment decisions will be made and critically examine how that time frame will ultimately affect the invested amount and projected payout.

Future Value More Than One Period Into the Future

So far, we have looked at the concept of present value and future value in the context of cash flows over a single period. We will now show how this can be generalized over more than one period. This process is critical because most business deals do not start and end in one year, but rather last several years.

CONCEPTS INTO PRACTICE

Assume that Speedway Motorsports (SM) has a parcel of real estate that it wishes to sell and has lined up two prospective buyers. One buyer, RaceCar Enterprises, is willing to enter into a contract to pay $1,000,000 immediately for the parcel of land. A second buyer, Sports Unlimited, has offered to pay $1,025,000 for the land but will make the actual payment in one year's time. At first glance, it may appear that Speedway Motorsports should take the Sports Unlimited offer, because Sports Unlimited is willing to pay more for the land, but looks can be deceiving!

The way to evaluate which offer Speedway Motorsports should accept is to note that if SM accepted the offer from RaceCar Enterprises, it could hypothetically deposit the funds in a one-year certificate of deposit (CD) that earns 5% interest per year. Speedway Motorsports would start out with $1,000,000 in the bank (principal) and would earn interest equal to 0.05 multiplied by $1,000,000. As a result, SM would have the following on deposit in one year:

$$\$1,000,000 + (0.05 \times \$1,000,000) = \$1,050,000$$

or

$$\$100,000 \times 1.05 = \$1,050,000$$

In other words, SM would have on deposit its initial $1,000,000 principal plus $50,000 in interest, which equals $1,050,000. Factoring in the interest earned during the year, the initial principal is multiplied by 1.05 (i.e., 1 plus the interest rate) to obtain the $1,050,000 on deposit at the end of the year.

By contrast, if SM accepted the Sports Unlimited offer, it would have only $1,025,000 available in one year, compared with the $1,050,000 it would have on hand in one year if it accepted the RaceCar Enterprises offer. By taking the offer from Sports Unlimited, SM would have $25,000 less than if it had invested the initial $1,000,000 in the one-year CD. Clearly, SM is better off taking the offer from RaceCar Enterprises.

In working through this example we made use of the concept of future value. **Future value** (FV) is the value of an initial lump sum of money after it is invested over one or more periods. The future value in one year's time of the $1,000,000 received from RaceCar Enterprises is $1,050,000. Note that the future value of any given investment income reflects the interest earned on that investment.

Another way of looking at this example is to examine how much money SM must deposit in a one-year CD that earns 5% to have $1,025,000 in one year. The amount of money that would yield $1,025,000 if invested today at a 5% interest rate is the **present value (PV)** of $1,025,000 received in one year. We can solve for PV as follows:

$$PV \times 1.05 = \$1{,}025{,}000$$

Solving for PV gives us the following:

$$PV = \$1{,}020{,}500 / 1.05 = \$976{,}190$$

So, if SM has $976,190 today, this lump sum can grow to $1,025,000 in one year as a result of earning interest.

In general, the formula for the present value can be written as shown in the following:

$$PV = C_1 / (1 + r)$$

PV = present value

C_1 = cash flow received at the end of one year

r = appropriate interest rate

The variable r, the interest rate or percentage return that can be earned on an initial amount of money, is also known as the **discount rate.** In our example, the 5% annual return that SM earns on its financial investment (i.e., a one-year CD) is used as the discount rate to value the $1,025,000 received in one year.

Our analysis of present value indicates that a payment of $1,025,000 received in one year from Sports Unlimited has a present value of $976,190 today. In other words, at a 5% interest rate, SM would find receiving $976,190 today from Sports Unlimited or $1,025,000 in one year equally acceptable alternatives. Given $976,190 today, the company can deposit the funds in a one-year CD that will allow it to receive $1,025,000 in one year.

Because RaceCar Enterprises offered to pay $1,000,000 today, this offer has a present value of $1,000,000. Thus, our present value analysis suggests that SM should take the RaceCar Enterprises offer.

CONCEPTS INTO PRACTICE

Assume that Joe Smith owns shares of SM common stock, and the return on the stock is 6%. To keep things simple, let us also assume that Smith paid $1 per share for SM's common stock. At the end of one year, he will have $1 plus the return on that dollar at r% for each share. Because r is 6%, he will have $1.06 at the end of one year.

$$\$1 + \$1r = \$1 \times (1 + r) = \$1 \times 1.06 = \$1.06$$

r = expected rate of return

At the end of the year, Smith has two choices. He can cash out his stock and take the $1.06 per share or hold the stock for a second year. The process of holding the stock and accruing a further return over the second year is referred to as **compounding**.

If Smith decides to hold the stock for another year, then at the end of two years he will have the following:

$$\$1 \times (1 + r) \times (1 + r) = \$1 \times (1 + r)^2 = \$1 \times (\$1.06)^2 = \$1.1236$$

At the end of two years, he will have transformed $1.00 into $1.1236. Notice that at the end of two years, he will generate $0.1236 in **compound interest** or return. That is, each payment of interest or return that is reinvested earns a return also.

This process can be generalized over many periods of time (t) with the following formula for the future value (FV) of an investment:

$$FV = C_0 \times (1 + r)^t$$

FV = future value

C_0 = initial amount of cash that is invested today

r = interest rate or rate of return

t = number of years over which the cash is invested

We can do this calculation by hand or with the help of a table. Table A.1 in appendix A presents future values of $1 at the end of t periods, a variable number of periods into the future over which the $1 is earning interest. Traditionally, t periods on a future value chart range from 1 year to 20 or 30 years. To use the table, locate the appropriate interest rate or return on the horizontal axis and the appropriate number of periods on the vertical axis. For example, you could find that the future value of $1 that is received two years into the future is $1.1236. This figure is reached if you assume a 6% rate of return. If you started out with $500 and earned a 6% annual return over two years, then the future value at the end of two years would be $561.80.

$$FV = 500 \times 1.1236 = \$561.80$$

As another example, suppose that an investor buys a $1,000 bond issued by SM. The bond pays 10% interest and is redeemable in 20 years. Going to table A.1, you can find 20 years as the t period and then move across to the column labeled 10% interest. The number on the chart is 6.7275. Thus, FV = $1,000 multiplied by 6.7275, which yields a future value for the $1,000 investment after 20 years of $6,728. Through compounding interest, the bond increases more than six fold if it is kept for the entire 20 years. This example highlights how the federal government can sell U.S. bonds for $50 now and guarantee payment of $100 in 10 years. Through compounding, the $50 investment can produce a four to five times greater return in 10 years while still allowing the government to pay the investor double his or her money.

Present Value Over More Than One Period Into the Future

Assume that a professional athlete such as Alex Rodriguez has signed a contract including $2 million in deferred compensation that will be paid at the end of two years. Assume that if he were to receive compensation today, he could invest that money in a financial vehicle (such as a CD) that earns a 4% annual return. We would like to know how much money received today would be worth $2 million after earning a 4% annual return for two years. This can be written as follows:

$$PV \times (1 + r)^t = FV$$

PV = present value
r = annual rate of return
t = number of years
FV = future value

$$PV \times (1.04)^2 = \$2,000,000$$

In this equation, PV stands for present value, the amount of money that would need to be invested today to grow to $2 million in two years.

Solving for PV gives us the following:

$$PV = \$2,000,000 / (1.04)^2$$
$$= \$2,000,000 / 1.0816$$
$$= \$1,849,200$$

This equation indicates that if Alex Rodriguez received $1,849,200 today, invested it, and earned a 4% annual return, he would have $2 million at the end of two years. This process of obtaining a present value is known as **discounting**. The $2 million is discounted by a **discount factor**, or **present value factor**, which equals 1 divided by $(1.04)^2$, or 0.9246, in this example. Using this discount factor, we can calculate the present value as $2,000,000 multiplied by 0.9246, or $1,849,200.

An alternative way to calculate the results obtained from this equation is to use table A.2 in appendix A to obtain a present value factor. This table shows the present value of $1 to be received after t periods. To use the table, locate the appropriate number of periods on the vertical axis and the interest rate on the horizontal axis. In our example, the number of periods is 2 and the interest rate is 4%. Thus, the present value factor is 0.9246. If we multiply $2 million by the present value factor, we find that the present value of $2 million received in two years is $1,849,200.

In general, the present value of a sum of money received t periods in the future can be written as follows:

$$PV = C_t / (1 + r)^t = C_t \times PVF_{r,t}$$

PV = present value
C_t = cash flow received at the end of t periods
r = annual return of interest
$PVF_{r,t}$ = the appropriate present value factor for $1 received t periods into the future

Table 7.1 Present Value of Diana Taurasi's Cash Flows Over Several Years

Year	Cash flow ($)	Present value factor	Present value ($)
0	100,000	1.0000	100,000
1	110,000	0.9615	105,765
2	115,000	0.9246	106,329
Total			312,094

We can extend this example to finding the present value of multiple payments. Assume that Diana Taurasi, a player in the Women's National Basketball Association, has signed a contract that will pay her $100,000 immediately, $110,000 at the end of one year, and $115,000 at the end of two years. Assume that she can earn a 4% annual return investing the money. The present value of the cash flows is shown in table 7.1.

The present value of the cash flows under this contract equals $312,094. In other words, the payment structure under this contract is equivalent to paying Taurasi $312,094 in one lump sum today.

Perpetuities and Annuities

For certain types of finance problems, shortcuts can be used to calculate present values. In particular, we discuss shortcut methods for two types of cash flow streams:

1. Perpetuities
2. Annuities

Perpetuities

A **perpetuity** consists of a single cash flow per year forever into the future. Although perpetuities may not seem to have any real-world relevance, certain financial instruments are in effect perpetuities. These instruments are called consols, which are bonds issued by the British government. The holder of a consol receives yearly interest from the British government forever into the future. As a hypothetical sport example, imagine a solid company such as Speedway Motorsports agreeing to give the founder and her family, for an unlimited number of generations, a $1 million per year payment for eternity. The concept of a perpetuity comes into play when valuing preferred stock because the price of a preferred share is equal to the present value of expected constant dividends that will be paid each year forever into the future.

The present value of a perpetuity is equal to the following:

$$PV = C / (1 + r) + C / (1 + r)^2 + C / (1 + r)^3 + \ldots$$

PV = present value

C = a constant annual cash flow

r = interest rate or rate of return

The dots at the end of the formula indicate that an infinite number of terms complete the formula. The equation is an example of what math texts call an infinite series. Based on mathematical formulas used to solve infinite series, the equation can be simplified:

$$PV = C / r$$

In other words, the present value of a perpetuity is simply the annual cash flow divided by its discount rate (Brigham & Ehrhardt, 2011). Assuming that the perpetuity pays $100 per year at an interest rate of 8%, the present value of the perpetuity is as follows:

$$PV = \$100 / 0.08$$

$$= \$1,250$$

If interest rates fell to 6%, the present value of the perpetuity would rise.

$$PV = \$100 / 0.06$$

$$= \$1,666.67$$

Note that the preceding formulas indicate that the value of the perpetuity rises as the interest rate declines and falls as the interest rate increases. This point illustrates a general principle: The present value of any stream of cash flows (whether or not it is in the form of a perpetuity) is inversely related to the discount rate. At higher interest rates, the present value of any future cash flows declines because the holder can start with a smaller initial lump sum; as this sum earns a return, it will grow to equal the future cash flow.

Annuities

An **annuity** is a constant stream of payments that is received for a fixed number of periods. Annuities are common in the real world. Home mortgages, leases, student loans, and pensions paid at retirement are all examples of annuities. When evaluating annuities, we use the following formula:

$$PV = C / (1 + r) + C / (1 + r)^2 + C / (1 + r)^3 + \ldots + C / (1 + r)^t$$

PV = present value

C = a constant cash flow per period

r = annual rate of return

t = number of periods during which the cash flow will be received

This equation is cumbersome, but fortunately it can be simplified to yield the following formula for an annuity that is paid over t periods (Brigham & Ehrhardt, 2011):

$$PV = C\{1 - [1 / (1 + r)^n]\} / r$$

PV = present value

C = a constant cash flow per period

r = annual rate of return

n = number of periods during which the cash flow will be received

CONCEPTS INTO PRACTICE

An example of an annuity is the compensation package received by Nick Saban, the head football coach of the Alabama Crimson Tide. In August 2009 Saban signed a new contract that would pay him approximately $4,000,000 in salary for nine years (Low, 2009). For our purposes, this is treated as a nine-year annuity, effective August 1, 2009. If the appropriate discount rate is 7%, then by plugging these values into the equation we obtain the following:

$$PV = \$4,000,000 \times \{1 - [1 / (1.07)^9]\} / 0.07$$

$$= \text{periodic payment} \times \text{annuity factor}$$

$$= \$4,000,000 \times 6.5152$$

$$= \$26,060,800$$

The present value of Saban's contract, as of August 1, 2009, when he signed it (and assuming a 7% discount rate), equaled $26,060,800. The numbers in braces in the equation are the present value factor for an annuity. In this example involving the value of Saban's salary, the present value factor for the annuity equals 6.5152. Table A.3 in appendix A is titled Present Value of $1 per Period for t Periods. Again, interest rates are shown on the horizontal axis, and number of periods is shown on the vertical axis. Consulting the table, you will see that for an interest rate of 7% and an annuity that is received for nine periods, the present value factor is 6.5152, which we obtained in the calculation.

In calculating the value of Nick Saban's contract at the time it was signed, we have not factored in any potential uncertainty about his receiving the salary in the future. This uncertainty can be viewed as risk, which is our next topic.

RISK

When we calculated the present value of future cash flows, we did not discuss how to choose a discount rate. As we explain here, the choice of discount rates is tied to the risk of the future cash flows. By risk, we are referring to uncertainty about the future cash flows.

Whenever we compute the present value of a stream of future cash flows, we do not know with 100% certainty that those cash flows will be received. In the sidebar we calculated the present value of Nick Saban's nine-year contract, signed August 1, 2009, as the Alabama Crimson Tide's head football coach. In that example, we calculated the cash flows without making any allowances for future uncertainty about whether Saban would receive all of that compensation. As it happens, the job security of head coaches in college football is tenuous at best.

A common way to adjust for uncertainty is to use a discount rate that reflects the riskiness of the cash flows. As we will show, the higher the level of risk of a financial instrument, the higher its rate of return. This relationship implies that we need to use higher discount rates when there is greater riskiness associated with the cash flows being valued.

Returns

To measure risk, we need to examine the behavior of returns on various types of financial assets. Thus, before we go any further, we need to focus on the meaning of the term *return*. As a first step, we want to distinguish between dollar returns and rates of return.

In general, **capital gain** is defined as the dollar amount by which a financial instrument (e.g., shares of stock) increases in value over a given period. The term **capital loss** is used when the value of the financial instrument declines.

CONCEPTS INTO PRACTICE

Assume that you bought 100 shares of stock in Speedway Motorsports (SM) at $10 per share. Your initial investment is $1,000.

$$100 \text{ shares} \times \$10 = \$1,000$$

Suppose that SM paid an annual dividend to all shareholders of $0.50 per share. During the year, you would receive the following dividend income:

$$100 \text{ shares} \times \$0.50 = \$50$$

In addition, assume that the price of SM's stock increased over the year to $11 per share. Because the stock increased in price, you would have a capital gain equal to the change in the stock price over the year multiplied by the number of shares held:

$$\text{capital gain} = (\text{current price} - \text{initial price}) \times \text{number of shares}$$

$$= (\$11 - \$10) \times 100 \text{ shares} = \$100$$

The capital gain is equal to the dollar increase in the value of the SM stock.

Conversely, if the stock declined in price to $9 per share, there would be a capital loss (the negative change in price over the year):

$$\text{capital loss} = (\$9 - \$10) \times 100 \text{ shares} = -\$100$$

Because the stock declined in value over the year, the capital loss is equal to the dollar decline in the value of the stock.

The capital gain or loss, like the dividend income, is part of the total return earned by stockholders. In general, the total dollar return on a security is calculated as follows:

$$\text{total dollar return} = \text{capital gain or loss} + \text{dividend income}$$

In our first example, where the stock price increased, the total dollar return is positive.

$$\text{total dollar return} = \$100 + \$50 = \$150$$

In our second example, where the stock price decreased, the total dollar return is negative.

$$\text{total dollar return} = -\$100 + \$50 = -\$50$$

Rates of return allow us to measure gains and losses in percentage terms. In particular, they provide us with a means of standardizing the measurement of the performance of a financial asset, regardless of the dollar amount invested, which is useful for comparing the performance of different financial assets. Going back to our earlier example, assume that the initial price of the stock (P_0) is $10, that at the end of one year the price of the stock (P_1) is $11, and that the dividend paid per share (D_{t+1}) is $0.50. The return represented by dividends paid to the stockholders of the company, called the dividend yield, is equal to the dividend divided by the initial price of the stock:

$$\text{dividend yield} = D_{t+1} / P_0$$

D_{t+1} = dividend paid per share in a given year
P_0 = price when the stock was initially purchased

In this example, the dividend yield is $0.50 divided by $10, which equals 0.05, or 5%.

The rate of return resulting from the capital gain is equal to the change in the price of the stock over the year divided by the initial price.

$$\text{rate of return} = (P_1 - P_0) / P_0$$

P_1 = stock price at the end of year 1
P_0 = price when the stock was initially purchased

If the stock price increases to $11 per share, then the rate of return resulting from the capital gain is equal to 10%.

$$\text{rate of return} = (\$11 - \$10) / \$10$$
$$= \$1 / \$10$$
$$= 0.10, \text{ or } 10\%$$

We now combine our results to obtain the total return, from both the dividend payout and the capital gain, as follows:

$$\text{total return} = \text{dividend return} + \text{return resulting from the capital gain}$$
$$= 5\% + 10\%$$
$$= 15\%$$

Risk Statistics

Now that we have discussed how to measure returns, we need to define what we mean by risk. In a nutshell, the risk of any financial asset can be measured by examining the extent to which the returns on that asset fluctuate over time. In particular, we want to measure the performance of the asset with reference to the extent to which the returns fluctuate relative to their average value. This undertaking requires us to develop some statistical measures of performance and risk.

The stock returns shown in table 7.2 are for the portfolio of stocks that make up Standard & Poor's (S&P) 500 Composite Index. With data such as those shown in table 7.2, we can calculate the average, or mean. To compute the mean, we add up all the annual returns and divide by 44 because we have 44 years of data. If R_t is the rate of return in year t, then the formula for the average rate of return R over t years is as follows:

$$R = (R_1 + R_2 + \ldots + R_t) / t$$

R = average rate of return

R_1 = rate of return in year 1

R_2 = rate of return in year 2

R_t = rate of return in year t

t = number of years

The mean of the returns from 1967 through 2010, shown in table 7.2, is 11.38%. The mean tells us the average of the annual returns for a particular period. In other words, in our example, annual returns on average were 11.38%. But an examination of table 7.2 reveals that in any given year, the return can be either far above or far below the average. For example, although the average return was 11.38% over the 44-year period from 1967 through 2010, in 10 of those years the return was negative.

Because returns in any year of a historical period can differ from the average, we want to measure the extent to which this occurs for a sample of returns. The most common measures of dispersion or variability are the **variance** and its square root, the standard deviation. The variance (s^2) of a sample of annual returns over t years is calculated as follows:

$$s^2 = [1 / (t - 1)] [(R_1 - R)^2 + (R_2 - R)^2 + (R_3 - R)^2 + \ldots + (R_t - R)^2]$$

Table 7.2 S&P 500 Composite Index Returns From 1967 Through 2010

Year	Annual percentage return	Year	Annual percentage return
1967	23.98	1989	31.69
1968	11.06	1990	−3.10
1969	−8.50	1991	30.47
1970	4.01	1992	7.62
1971	14.31	1993	10.08
1972	18.98	1994	1.32
1973	−14.66	1995	37.58
1974	−26.47	1996	22.96
1975	37.20	1997	33.36
1976	23.84	1998	28.58
1977	−7.18	1999	21.04
1978	6.56	2000	−9.10
1979	18.44	2001	−11.89
1980	32.50	2002	−22.10
1981	−4.92	2003	28.69
1982	21.55	2004	10.88
1983	22.56	2005	4.91
1984	6.27	2006	15.79
1985	31.73	2007	5.49
1986	18.67	2008	−37.00
1987	5.25	2009	26.46
1988	16.61	2010	15.06
Average			**11.38**
Standard deviation			**16.00**

To calculate the variance, we take each of the individual annual returns, subtract the average return R, square the result, and add all the years together. We then divide the result by the number of years minus one. The standard deviation (**s**) is the square root of the variance:

$$S = \sqrt{S^2}$$

The standard deviation is a measure of the spread, or dispersion, of a sample. The significance of the standard deviation is that unlike the variance, it is measured in the same units as the returns in our sample. Statistical theory suggests a probability of approximately two-thirds of the observations in a sample are in a range between the mean less the standard deviation and the mean plus the standard deviation. Going back to our example, there is a probability of approximately two-thirds that the returns lie between 0.1334 minus 0.1990 and 0.1334 plus 0.1990 (i.e., between −0.0656 and 0.3324).

CONCEPTS INTO PRACTICE

To see how the calculation of these statistics is used to analyze the performance of financial securities, assume that Speedway Motorsports (SM) issues common stock and that its returns from 2008 through 2011 are 0.1170, 0.1236, 0.3896, and −0.0965, respectively. The average return for SM from 2008 through 2011 is calculated as follows:

$$\bar{R} = (R_1 + R_2 + R_3 + R_4) / 4$$

$$= [0.1770 + 0.1236 + 0.3896 + (-0.0965)] / 4$$

$$= 0.5337 / 4$$

$$= 0.1334 \text{ or } 13.34\%$$

The variance in SM's returns over this four-year period is calculated as follows:

$$S^2 = [1/(4-1)] \left[(R_1 - \bar{R})^2 + (R_2 - \bar{R})^2 + \right.$$

$$\left. (R_3 - \bar{R})^2 + (R_4 - \bar{R})^2 \right]$$

$$= [1/(4-1)] [(0.1170 - 0.1334)^2 + (0.1236 - 0.1334)^2 + (0.3896 - 0.1334)^2 + (-0.0965 - 0.1334)^2]$$

$$= [1/3] [(0.1170 - 0.1334)^2 + (0.1236 - 0.1334)^2 + (0.3896 - 0.1334)^2 + (-0.0965 - 0.1334)^2]$$

$$= (1/3)(0.1189)$$

$$= 0.0396$$

The standard deviation, which is the square root of the variance, is 0.1990.

$$s = \sqrt{0.0396} = 0.1990$$

We have assumed here that the population (theoretical distribution) of returns for SM (i.e., all possible outcomes over all possible years) follows the normal distribution, which is the bell-shaped curve that many students are familiar with. Because we are working with a sample that is drawn from a population, there is no guarantee that the annual returns will cleanly fit on the bell-shaped normal distribution. Statistical theory does suggest that as one analyzes larger samples of annual returns (i.e., covering more years), the historical data will begin to resemble the theoretical distribution. If we look at SMC's stock returns over a long time, we know that there may be some sampling error in our individual sample of returns, but this error is small relative to that for a sample consisting of four years of data. Students interested in going beyond the thumbnail sketch in this footnote should consult a business statistics text, such as Siegal's *Practical Business Statistics* (2000).

As shown in table 7.2, the standard deviation of the annual returns in the S&P 500 Composite Index is 16.00% from 1967 through 2010. That measure tells us that for the years 1967 through 2010, there is approximately a two-thirds probability that the annual returns for the S&P 500 Composite Index lie between (11.38% minus 16.00%) and (11.38% plus 16.00%), or between −4.62% and 27.38%.

Average Returns and Risk

Table 7.3 shows summary statistics of annual returns for the portfolio of stocks that make up the S&P 500 Composite Index. In addition, the table includes summary statistics for three-month U.S. Treasury bills. What stands out in table 7.3 is that the standard deviation of the returns on three-month U.S. Treasury bills is extremely small relative to that for common stock. Treasury bills, which are sold once per week by the federal government at an auction, typically mature in less than a year. Because the federal government can use its taxing power to pay its debt obligations, this debt has little likelihood of default. As a result, we can think of the return on Treasury bills as **risk-free return**.

Table 7.3 Means and Standard Deviations for U.S. Treasury Bills and Common Stocks From 1967 Through 2010

	Annual yield on newly issued three-month Treasury bills	Return on the S&P 500 Composite Index
Mean	5.53%	11.38%
Standard deviation	2.94%	16.00%

The lower standard deviation is a reflection of the virtual nonexistence of risk for Treasury bills. Because the annual returns on Treasury bills have a low standard deviation, they do not fluctuate substantially from their average value. Individual investors have much more certainty that they will receive the return on an investment in Treasury bills.

By contrast, the standard deviation of the annual returns on common stock is 16.00%, which is substantially higher than the 2.94% standard deviation of the annual returns on Treasury bills. This higher value results from the greater year-to-year fluctuation in the annual returns of common stock, which means that the annual returns on common stock can deviate substantially from the long-term average in any given year. Although the average return on common stock was 11.38% from 1960 through 2006, a large negative return in any given year is far more likely to occur with common stocks than with Treasury bills, as we saw with the recent recession of 2007-2008. The larger standard deviation or variance in annual returns is an indicator of greater risk.

Table 7.3 indicates that Treasury bills have less risk than common stock but that common stock on average outperform Treasury bills, as shown by a comparison of the average annual returns of the S&P 500 Composite Index with the average yields on three-month Treasury bills. From 1967 through 2010, an investor on average could have earned 11.38% per year by holding common stock but would have earned only 5.53% per year by holding Treasury bills. In other words, an investor in the portfolio of stocks included in the S&P 500 Composite Index earned an excess return of 5.85%, based on the difference between the average returns on stock and the yields on Treasury bills. This excess return can be viewed as a **risk premium** (i.e., the additional annual return that the holders of common stock earned relative to that for a risk-free asset, Treasury bills).

The data in table 7.3 show that investors in the stock market are rewarded with much higher returns than are investors in relatively risk-free Treasury bills. This comment is not to suggest that a person should not invest in Treasury bills. Instead, the information in table 7.3 suggests that investors in riskier assets are rewarded with higher average returns. By contrast, investors in Treasury bills receive lower returns because the investment is virtually without risk.

A way to understand the choice of risk undertaken by an individual investor is from the standpoint of the length of time that the money is to be invested. If the investor plans to use the proceeds of the investment to buy a house in one year, it would be prudent to purchase Treasury bills, because a riskier investment has a higher likelihood of resulting in a capital loss over the year. For example, if that investor had bought the average S&P stock in 2008, he or she would have lost 37% of the investment. In contrast, an investor who is saving for retirement and will not retire for another 30 years may find the greater risk of investing in a stock portfolio acceptable because of the potential for higher expected returns over a longer time horizon.

Risk and the Choice of a Discount Rate

Up to this point, we have discussed the concept of risk and the ways that investors are compensated for taking on more risk in the financial markets. This brings us full circle, to the issue of putting a value on cash flows that will be received in the future when the cash flows have an element of uncertainty, or risk. As we discuss next, risk is dealt with by choosing a discount rate that factors in risk. We consider this issue under two assumptions:

1. Risk is the same as that for the overall stock market.
2. Risk is different from that for the overall stock market.

Risk Is the Same as That for the Overall Stock Market

For argument's sake, assume that at the time Nick Saban signed his long-term contract to serve as the head coach of the Alabama Crimson Tide, he viewed the riskiness of the cash flows as equivalent to that of the overall stock market. In that case, Saban would have used the current expected return for an index of stock market performance, such as the S&P 500 Composite Index. The expected return on the market index (S&P 500 Composite Index) can be expressed as follows:

expected return on the market index = risk-free rate + expected risk premium

We can look at the return on the S&P 500 Composite Index as the sum of the risk-free rate of return plus a premium for taking on the risk of investing in a stock portfolio. The risk premium is what investors must receive in the financial markets to be induced to take on the additional risk associated with holding a diversified stock portfolio such as the S&P 500 Composite Index.

The estimation of the expected return on the market portfolio is straightforward. Assume that the current three-month Treasury bill rate is 4.50%. We can then use 4.50% as our estimate of the risk-free rate. Table 7.3 shows that from 1967 through 2010, the average Treasury bill rate was 5.53%, whereas the average annual return on the S&P 500 Composite Index was 11.38%. Thus the historic risk premium from 1967 through 2010 is 5.85% (11.38% minus 5.53%). The historic risk premium is a common estimate of the expected risk premium in the future (Brigham & Ehrhardt, 2010). Adding the historic risk premium of 5.85% to the estimated 4.50% risk-free rate, we end up with an estimated expected return on the S&P 500 Composite Index equal to 10.35%. The estimated 10.35% return on a portfolio of stocks contained in the S&P 500 Composite Index can then be used as the discount rate for these cash flows.

Risk Is Different From That for the Overall Stock Market

So far we have assumed that the risk of the future cash flows being valued is equal to the overall risk of the stock market, as represented by returns on the S&P 500 Composite Index. If the risk of the cash flows differs from that for the overall stock market, then we cannot use the expected return on the S&P 500 Composite Index as the discount rate. To decide which discount rate to use, we look at the risk that matters to individual investors.

The S&P 500 Composite Index is a highly diversified stock portfolio that contains 500 common stocks. The standard deviations of the returns of individual stocks tend to be considerably higher than the standard deviations of the returns of the S&P 500 Composite Index. The reason for the difference is **diversification**. With diversification, individual stocks can be combined into portfolios. As long as the stocks in the portfolio do not completely move together over time, stocks in the portfolio that earn poor returns are offset by other stocks that earn higher returns. As a result, returns on the portfolio fluctuate less than the returns on individual stocks. Because people have the ability to diversify their portfolios, we can argue that when analyzing the risk of an individual security, we are concerned about the effect of an individual security on the overall risk of a well-diversified portfolio such as the S&P 500 Composite Index.

Specifically, when we measure the risk of an individual security, we are interested in how the risk of a well-diversified portfolio is affected by adding that security to the portfolio.

Under the assumption that investors hold well-diversified portfolios, the capital asset pricing model (CAPM) shows that the risk of an individual security can be represented by its beta coefficient. Beta tells us the extent to which the return on the individual security moves with the overall market (the S&P 500 Composite Index). The S&P 500 Composite Index itself has a beta of 1. The beta of a stock that is less risky than the overall market is less than 1. A stock that is more risky than the overall market has a beta exceeding 1.

Under the CAPM, the expected return on an individual security is as follows:

expected return on an individual security =

current risk-free return + (beta of the individual security × market risk premium)

CONCEPTS INTO PRACTICE

Assume that Speedway Motorsports has a beta equal to 1.20, that the current risk-free rate is 4.50%, and that the historic market risk premium is 5.85%.

SM's expected return = 4.50% + (1.20 × 5.85%)

= 11.52%

If SM is valuing the cash flows of an individual project funded entirely by common stock, then 11.52% is an appropriate discount rate. The CAPM and the choice of an appropriate discount rate when firms obtain funding through issuance of bonds, loans, internally generated cash, or new equity issues is discussed further in chapter 11.

CONCLUSION

In this chapter, we covered principles of financial analysis that we will use throughout the rest of this textbook. In particular, we use the time value of money to place values on future expected cash flows. This concept is particularly important for sport organizations that must look at valuing a future stream of lease payments to make decisions about whether to own or lease an asset. The proper analysis of risk is important because a faulty analysis can yield bad estimates of the discount rate used to estimate present value. As a result, in our example of choosing whether to lease or buy an asset, mismeasurement of risk can result in incorrect valuation and ultimately faulty decisions about the course of action to pursue. As a result, understanding the time value of money, as well as risk, will be shown to be important to financial decision making throughout the rest of this book.

Class Discussion Topics

1. Evaluate the following statement: "Because a well-diversified portfolio of stocks tends to outperform U.S. Treasury bills, there is no reason to invest in Treasury bills."

2. Increased criticism has been directed to corporate executives for being too short-term oriented and not focused enough on the long-run performance of their companies. Should companies place an emphasis on maximizing long-term profits?

3. What happens to the present value of an annuity if the discount rate is increased? What happens to the future value if the discount rate is increased?

4. Assume that two athletes sign 10-year contracts that pay out a total of $100 million over the life of the contracts. One contract will pay the $100 million in equal installments over the 10 years. The other contract will pay the $100 million in installments, but the installments increase 5% per year. Which athlete received the better deal?

5. A professional sport athlete—let's call her Sue—has a nonguaranteed (meaning that she receives no salary if she is cut from the team or injured) contract that pays her $5 million per year for the next five years. Sue has been severely injured in an automobile accident and will no longer be able to work, let alone play for her team. When Sue sues the driver of the other vehicle in court, the jury awards her $25 million to cover the loss of earnings over the next five seasons. Given what we have learned in this chapter, was the jury correct?

6. The returns in table 7.3 have not been adjusted for inflation. What would happen to the expected return if we adjusted the annual returns for inflation?

7. Table 7.3 demonstrated that stocks outperform Treasury bills over long periods. If that is the case, why do some people avoid the stock market and invest only in Treasury bills over long periods?

8. What kind of asset would have a beta of zero?

PART IV

Capital Structuring

Without capital, a business cannot operate successfully. Part IV explores where the money is and how businesses find the capital that they need to operate.

Chapter 8, "Obtaining Funding," highlights where the money to start a business comes from. To pay their bills, people who start a business sometimes use their savings, their credit cards, or investment dollars from others. This chapter highlights the various areas where money can come from and how to continue receiving money after a business takes off. Issues such as open markets and other short-term borrowing strategies are compared with various long-term borrowing options. The chapter ends with an analysis of the strategies that can be used to obtain funds from various sources such as the government.

Chapter 9, "Capital Stocks," covers the complex world of stocks. Stock certificates represent ownership interest in a company, and a company will sell stocks to raise needed funds. The chapter covers what types of stocks are sold, what rights a stockholder has, how to take a company public, and how to increase stock value. The chapter contains a significant list of publicly held sport businesses.

Chapter 10, "Bonds," covers the concept of corporate borrowing to raise necessary funds. Besides borrowing from banks or issuing stocks, a corporation with a strong credit rating can issue corporate bonds. When issuing bonds, a corporation needs to consider how much it will cost to issue the bonds, how it will repay the bonds, and how the bonds fit into the capitalization effort of the business. In addition, the chapter highlights bonds issued by government entities to fund the construction of stadiums and arenas as well as how government entities can help owners fund new facilities through industrial development bonds. The chapter ends with an overview of the capitalization process and the way in which borrowing, stocks, and bonds can work together in a comprehensive financing plan.

chapter 8

Obtaining Funding

Chapter Objectives

After studying this chapter, you should be able to do the following:

- ◆ Describe where money comes from.
- ◆ Compare various short-term borrowing strategies.
- ◆ Understand how to use personal funds and private financing as a source of capital.
- ◆ Understand how government-backed borrowing can spur economic growth.
- ◆ Understand how to use existing resources to leverage the financial position of a business.
- ◆ Distinguish between leasing and other financial vehicles.

There is no one correct method to fund a sport business. Some people acquire a sport business through inheritance and do not need any funds to become owners. This is the case for many professional team owners, such as the Rooney family, who have owned the Pittsburgh Steelers for several generations. Other owners have tapped numerous sources such as their credit cards, relatives, and bank **loans** to keep a business alive. Each business is different and requires its own unique blend of financing. The various funding techniques combine to form the capital structure of a business.

The total number of options and techniques that can be used to obtain funds is limitless. Some people have made their fortunes through luck, whereas others have relied on hard work. Arthur Rooney, the famed founder of the Pittsburgh Steelers, bought the franchise for $2,500 in 1933. It is rumored that he obtained the money for the franchise by winning $250,000 at the horse track in 1932 (Pro Football Hall of Fame, 2007). John Moores, owner of the San Diego Padres, founded BMC Software in 1980. By working hard, designing innovative products, and making a strong marketing push, he made a fortune ("Company," 2012). With these funds, he purchased the Padres. Noted "bad boy" Mark Cuban, the owner of the Dallas Mavericks, and Microsoft cofounder Paul Allen, who owns the Portland Trailblazers and Seattle Seahawks, both made their fortunes in computers before buying their professional teams.

A person lucky enough to win the lottery could use his winnings to start a business. Former athletes have taken the money that they earned in professional sport and used those funds to launch or buy a business. Examples include Dave Bing, who started the Bing Group, considered one of the largest black-owned businesses (*Bing Group capsule*, n.d.), and Isiah Thomas, who purchased the entire Continental Basketball Association in 1999 for $9 to $10 million, which included a $5 million down payment and four future payments. Two years later the league was bankrupt, and Thomas' holding company owed at least $5 million to various lenders ("Left for dead," 2001). Magic Johnson turned his winning form and smile into a major fortune in real estate and movie theaters. In 2012, he became a part-owner of the Los Angeles Dodgers in a record breaking $2.15 billion deal. Another basketball legend is Michael Jordan, who turned his fortune into owning a majority share of the Charlotte Hornets. In yet another example, Mario Lemieux was owed a fortune by the Pittsburgh Penguins and was the largest debt holder for the team. He purchased the team in bankruptcy proceedings.

Although this chapter and the subsequent chapters on stocks and bonds (chapters 9 and 10) highlight for-profit businesses, we make some references to funds used by government and tax-exempt businesses, primarily in chapter 10. As with for-profit businesses, both government and nonprofit organizations can use countless techniques to raise funds. One of the major differences between government and nonprofit organizations is the opportunity to receive gifts and the potential tax consequences associated with such funding techniques. Tax issues associated with gifts were covered in chapter 5.

Most fund-raising for sport businesses follows established patterns that countless organizations have used for years. This chapter highlights the basic approaches to raising funds without necessarily having to incur significant costs or sell owners' equity. Early in the chapter we examine basic funding sources for starting a business, such as personal bank loans, credit cards, and government assistance. The chapter then covers open markets and short-term borrowing options, followed by several long-term borrowing options. The chapter concludes with an analysis of funding options for minority-owned businesses, including advice on how to obtain funding.

UNIQUE FUND-RAISING

Not all funds needed to finance sports events are derived from television rights payments, ticket sales, sponsorship contracts, or similar income-generating techniques. Someone paying money from his or her own wallet can help finance a Special Olympics event or pay a team's payroll. Organizations can put expenses on credit cards; individuals can provide collateral to back a loan; a facility can be used as collateral for obtaining a loan. Obscure revenue-generating techniques can raise significant funds or can be significant failures. Olympic stamps and coins are a good example of these extremes. Canada sold both in its effort to finance the 1976 Olympic Games.

Olympic Coin Program

The lineage of Olympic coinage is formidable. Anaxilas, a ruler of Sicily, ordered the first recorded minting of a coin struck especially to commemorate a sporting event in about 480 BC. The silver coin honored his victory in a historic chariot race and appropriately depicted the winner bearing a laurel wreath. Since the 1950s several Olympic host countries have issued a variety of commemorative

SEEKING FUNDING FOR YOUR BUSINESS

Ralph Willis, EFA Partners

In early 2009, two partners and I formed EFA Partners, an advisory firm that focuses on providing financial consulting services and arranging financing for entertainment and leisure companies. We currently have offices in New York and Atlanta and the success of EFA is due in large measure to my 25 years of previous experience in the finance sector with over 15 of those years in entertainment finance, as well as to my partners' longstanding experience and commitment to financing these industries. In 2004, I was a founder of GE Capital's sports and entertainment finance unit and I led that group from its formation through to 2009. The group started with a small team based in Norwalk, Connecticut, but grew with our success closing transactions to include personnel in New York, Atlanta, Chicago, and San Francisco. Previously, I was one of the founding members of Heller Financial's entertainment and media group and I worked on entertainment finance transactions with Gilman Financial Services, both companies based in New York.

Over the years, I have been involved in sourcing, structuring, negotiating, closing, and managing finance transactions across numerous leisure sectors. Clients have included owner–operators of sports franchises, movie theatres, theme parks, waterparks, ski resorts, family entertainment centers, casinos and others. Throughout my career, I have worked with a wide variety of organizations ranging from small start-up ventures to large mature companies providing financing proceeds that have been utilized for working capital, equipment purchases, refinancing existing debt, growth, and acquisitions. Most of my experience has been with senior debt and equipment financing; however, I have also been involved with junior capital including mezzanine debt and equity with transactions sizes ranging from relatively small financings of $1 million to larger transactions in excess of $200 million.

As groups have approached me seeking financing, they typically have provided basic company information and conveyed management's enthusiasm for their business but too often they have not provided detailed financial information. You should keep in mind the following when seeking funding for your business:

- It is extremely important to have a well thought out business plan presentation that describes your company in detail and includes historical financial performance plus realistic projections. The plan should also include the key drivers of your industry since it could be brand new to many funding sources.

- When preparing a business plan, it is essential to understand the basics of financing including such items as determining working capital needs, rate-of-return calculations, financial ratios, net cash flow calculations, and others. Funding sources will look for these, and it is best to provide them in advance with your commentary on each.

- Also understand that not all money sources should be treated alike. Funding sources vary for start-up firms as compared with mature local firms or large international companies. Funding can come from local or regional banks, national or international banks, mezzanine funds, private equity groups, high net worth individuals, and others. You need to know how each may or may not be a good fit for the capital structure of your business.

- Of course, start-up funding is more difficult to obtain than that for mature companies but such financing can be available for firms with strong business plans and management teams. Often "friends and family" funding is needed for firms in the very early stages, or you can approach venture capital groups that are looking for the next great idea. Another alternative is local banks that have programs backed by the Small Business Administration. Be prepared that personal guarantees are often a requirement for start-up funding.

- When obtaining debt financing, keep both a short- and long-term outlook. Often a revolving credit facility is needed to satisfy short-term working capital needs while long-term financing is needed for growth and other objectives.

(continued)

For long-term needs, most lenders will lend an amount based on a multiple of EBITDA (earnings before interest, taxes, depreciation, and amortization). It is important to know the appropriate multiple for your industry and current economic climate so that you can approach lenders with realistic proposals.

- Obtaining equity financing is an excellent method to start or grow your business. Understand that it is more expensive than debt financing and will involve giving up a portion of your business' ownership. Given

that, make sure you are comfortable with your potential equity partner and with the direction that partner may want to take your business.

While it's important to have enthusiasm and insight in the sports and leisure sectors, it is equally important to have a solid foundation of finance and the mechanics involved in obtaining funding. Without that, you will find it very difficult to successfully start or grow your business. Good luck!

coins to defray costs of the Games. Canada's coin program was considered one of the most successful (*Charlton Standard Catalogue*, 1990).

The program was aimed at selling collections of 28 specially minted silver $1, $5, and $10 coins. Canada was also the first Olympic host to issue a gold coin in the denomination of $100.

The margin between the cost of production and the face value of coins is known as seigniorage. According to the Canadian legislation authorizing the coins, the seignior, or issuing authority, had the right to retain that difference as profit. Profits from sales of the Olympic coins were initially expected to reach between $125 and $500 million. The coins were successful, but they were issued at the height of an internationally depressed economy. Even so, through 1977, sales of the coins had reached $386 million. Of the $386 million, $278.7 million represented the face value of all coins delivered and had to be held in reserve by the Canadian government. The expenditures over and above the face value of the coins totaled only $8 million. Thus, the program netted a profit of close to $100 million.

Olympic Stamp Program

The Olympic Stamp Program was yet another unique fund-raising effort designed to help finance the 1976 Olympic Games. Canada Post's fund-raising focused on four areas: Olympic action stamps, commemorative stamps, stamp sculptures, and stamp souvenirs. In 1974 Canada brought out its first set of semipostal issues—postage stamps that carried a surcharge. The purpose of the surcharge was to give the public a convenient

opportunity to support the Olympic Games on a voluntary basis. Germany, France, and Japan all have used semipostal stamps when hosting the Games. Additional sets were issued by Canada in 1975 and 1976 (Gandley & Stanley, 1978).

The Olympic action stamps bore two different prices, separated by a plus sign (+). The first price on each stamp indicated the postal value of the stamp, the other the amount of the surcharge; the two amounts combined gave the sale price of the stamp. Thus, a stamp with a 15 + 5 marking included $0.15 of postage and a $0.05 contribution to the Olympic effort. The post office collected $0.20 for each one of those stamps sold.

To support the Olympic Stamp Program, Canada Post developed a promotional program under the umbrella theme Help It Happen. Advertisements were published in all major Canadian newspapers and magazines and in specialized publications the world over; commercials were aired on television and radio networks. Display stands, posters, and decals were used in post offices to attract the customers' attention. In spite of all the promotion, the stamps did not generate the target figure of $10 million. Potential buyers were either opposed to the idea or hesitant to try anything new.

The United States Postal Service (USPS) used a similar approach in the 1990s to raise funds for breast cancer research. Since 1998 the USPS has sold more than 908 million semipostal breast cancer research stamps, raising $73 million. The stamp's reauthorization allows the stamp to be sold at a special 55-cent rate, which was 11 cents higher than the price of regular first-class postage in 2011.

WHERE THE MONEY COMES FROM

Most consumers have faced a financial crisis in which they needed money but found that sources of funds were lacking. Some people can approach their parents and ask for a loan. Money sometimes comes from an inheritance or in the form of a raise. Increased monetary streams are sometimes expected—such as an annual cost-of-living salary increase to keep a salary at pace with inflation. At other times money might not come in when it is expected. You might anticipate receiving an Internal Revenue Service refund by a certain date and have to change your plans significantly if a delay occurs. But what happens when you need a substantial amount of money and your likelihood of receiving a major gift is astronomically small? You need to analyze alternative approaches for raising the needed capital.

Not all capital needs arise from emergencies. Numerous capital structuring changes occur because of anticipated growth—growth that can occur only through the exploration of various capital financing options. This chapter deals with the various capital options available to those seeking to raise needed capital. We give special attention to individual borrowing, SBA loans, commercial lending, and venture capital. Subsequent chapters will cover issuing various types of stocks, issuing bonds, and obtaining capital assistance from the government. There is no one correct method of raising funds, and this chapter presents the diverse techniques available.

The same concerns that people face in deciding how to finance items such as equipment or a new business can apply to any decision requiring capital outlays. For example, an investor who wants to build a golf course would need a significant amount of up-front capital to purchase the land and develop the course. Several years might pass before the course would be suitable for use, and no income would be forthcoming during that time. Most investors would shy away from a deal that was uncertain and that would not produce revenue for several years.

A 1994 National Golf Foundation report concluded that financing for the average golf course loan requires 40% to 50% equity. Therefore, to build a $5 million course, developers need to raise approximately $2 to $2.5 million from other sources such as their own money, limited partnerships, corporate investments, syndications, pension

CONCEPTS INTO PRACTICE

Assume that a new health club wants to buy some expensive exercise equipment for their proposed facility. Through their initial research they discover four primary means of obtaining the equipment: renting, paying cash, obtaining a loan, and leasing (Haynie, 1998).

If they rent the machines no up-front cash expenditures will be required, except for a possible down payment or security deposit. The club owners will face lower upkeep and repair costs using this strategy and can return the equipment if they are not satisfied with the quality. Renting equipment, however, is normally not a good long-term option; renting for several years could cost twice as much as taking out a conventional bank loan or leasing (Haynie, 1998). Note that both rental and lease payments are 100% tax deductible as a business expense.

If the club owners purchase the equipment with cash, they can avoid **finance charges** and depreciate the equipment. But even if they had significant cash reserves and invested in machines, they could no longer use those funds to pay for additional growth that might generate a greater return in the future.

A bank loan could be an effective technique for purchasing the equipment. A bank would require background material such as a credit check, tax returns, financial statements, and collateral. Based on the potential need to sell the equipment upon loan default, a bank might provide a loan that covers only a certain percentage of the equipment's purchase price. If a new piece of equipment has a purchase price of $10,000 but will be worth only $8,000 by the end of the year, the bank might limit its exposure by lending only $6,500 toward the purchase.

If the club owners leased the equipment, they could receive flexible terms and 100% financing. Initial expenses could include 2% to 5% of the purchase price as a down payment, any applicable taxes, installation, delivery, and related "soft" costs. The key benefit of leasing involves the potential to expense 100% of the payments every month with pretax dollars (Haynie, 1998). Assume that the club owners financed $36,000 in equipment for $843 per month. If they made $5,000 profit per month, $1,500 of this amount would go to taxes if their tax rate was 30%. But if the owners reduced their $5,000 profit by $843 (their monthly payment obligation), their potential taxes would decline from $1,500 to $1,247 (30% multiplied by $4,157). The $253 tax savings, when subtracted from the $843 monthly lease obligation, would result in an actual payment of $590 for the leased equipment. When the $590 cost is multiplied over the actual term of the lease (60 months), the total cost is $35,400, which is less than the purchase price had they purchased the equipment for $36,000 (Haynie, 1998). One benefit of the **lease option** is that the small initial **capital outlay** would not encumber the cash balances. In addition, the owners would face less risk if the product broke or became obsolete, and they could obtain a service agreement to keep the machines in working condition.

funds, or possibly **real estate investment trusts** (REITs) to obtain a bank loan (Turley, 1998). Such large equity requirements are based on the competitiveness of the golf course industry, the potential resale value of the course, uncertain projected cash flow, uncontrollable factors such as weather, and other variables. Nonetheless, experienced golf course lenders search for opportunities. These lenders can use several methods to design loans that could include (Turley, 1998)

- capitalizing working capital requirements and income shortfalls;
- requiring sufficient cash reserves to cover any possible contingency; or
- offering their own equity participation to help decrease the required borrower's equity, which will help lower the debt interest rate.

Another option is to finance the golf course through the public coffers. Municipal golf courses have been built for years using standard voter-approved bonds or the newer revenue bonds that can be paid back from the course's revenue. Other means to finance a municipal course include general budget allocations (as a line item in a budget), the selling of bonds, and establishing a public development corporation, in which the city has a contractor design and construct the course on a turnkey basis (Turley, 1998). In a turnkey operation, the contractor performs all the building construction and design functions for a set price and then turns the building over to the owner when all the work is completed (Fried, 2010).

Although multiple funding techniques are available, investors are more cautious than ever about funding golf courses. Lenders are concerned because numerous courses are both being built and going under at the same time. Some analysts claim that being the second buyer of a golf course is best; the developer typically pays more to build a course, and if the course fails, the subsequent buyer pays a much lower amount. Thus, lenders are wary of investing millions in a course that might be worth less when it is completed than it cost to build in the first place (Nemeth-Johannes, 2003).

To investigate the potential value of an investment, a lender might undertake significant research to evaluate how risky the loan will be. Analyzing the golf industry could help a lender decide whether to risk loaning money to a potential course developer. When the nation's economy was at its peak from 1998 to 2000, more than 1,100 of the nation's 15,827 golf courses were built (Kaspriske, 2003). Although golf has been around for more than a century, 7% of all U.S. golf courses were built between 2000 and 2003 (Kaspriske, 2003).

The recession after the events of September 11, 2001, resulted in a decrease in leisure and business travel, leaving clubs scrambling to keep their members, even though the United States had an estimated 26.2 million golfers (Ripley & Mabe, 2003). A golf course owner was quoted as saying, "Thirty years ago, the average age [of members] was 64; if the average age of your members today isn't 54 [or slightly younger], you're in trouble" (Kaspriske, 2003). First, younger members help ensure long-term success for a country club because they are likely to be members for decades to come. More important, younger members are more inclined than older members to spend money at the club entertaining family, friends, and business associates. Furthermore, when the clubhouse needs updating and the greens need repair, those younger members will usually approve the expenditure (Kaspriske, 2003). Through 2011 the state of golf in the United States was in significant decline. A significant number of courses were closing, country clubs were going out of business, and the number of rounds played was declining.

Lenders also examine the cost of running a business to make sure that it is viable. In keeping with the golf example, the average cost percentages for club maintenance are as follows (Thornton, 2005):

Salaries and wages	63%
Chemicals	14%
Repairs and maintenance	9%
Other	14%
Total	100%

Thus, a lender considering investing in a new club could examine the projected budget and calculate whether the costs are similar to what other clubs in the industry face. By examining projections against benchmarked industry standards, a lender can get a better feel for an investment. The preceding golf course example shows that although a project can be funded in various ways, lenders are going to scrutinize any potential deals to minimize their risk. A lender who is going to pursue a riskier loan will charge the borrower a higher interest rate to compensate for assuming the higher risk.

The same options that are possible for building a golf course can be applied to building a professional sports stadium or arena. Because of the hundreds of millions of dollars required to build a stadium or arena, the financing tools used by the health club or a golf course developer would typically not generate all the necessary funds. The risk of going bankrupt is much lower for a stadium or arena than for a fitness center or golf course. Lenders will still investigate the facility funding plan, but because of the potential involvement of the government, lenders are more inclined to fund these large facilities through a variety of funding strategies. For a privately financed facility, the typical financing tools include loans, bonds, cash contribution, partnerships, equity offerings, and related investment pools. If the project is a public facility, the following financing techniques could be used (Miller, 1998):

- Loans
- General obligation bonds
- Project revenue bonds
- Tax revenue bonds
- Certificates of participation
- Tax incremental financing
- Tax exemptions
- Tax rebates

Loans are simple borrowing agreements in which the borrower agrees to repay the borrowed amount at a set time at a set interest rate. General obligation bonds are bonds issued by a municipality that agrees to use any and all tax revenue that it obtains to repay the bond. Project revenue bonds are more specific; revenue generated from the project is dedicated to repay the bond. Tax revenue bonds are backed by general tax revenue collected by the municipality, such as property taxes. With certificates of participation, purchasers buy a share of the lease revenues instead of the bond's being secured by those revenues (*Certificate of participation*, n.d.). These revenues are then usually used to construct a facility.

Tax incremental financing, discussed in detail in chapter 10, represents a municipality's decision to forgo taxes from a landowner, such as a stadium owner, to encourage that landowner to build a facility in a given neighborhood. The municipality hopes that bringing the facility into the neighborhood will increase other property values and thus increase the general tax base for the entire municipality. A tax exemption refers to a waiver of tax obligations as an incentive to attract a business or build a new facility. A tax rebate is similar to a refund: The municipality returns some or all of the money that a business has paid in whichever tax category is being rebated. Thus, a team could receive a rebate of their property taxes but still need to pay sales and utility taxes.

Note that almost every stadium or arena project involves certain government benefits such as tax abatements. The two new stadiums and one arena in New York (Yankees, Mets, and the Barclay's Center) received an estimated $1.2 billion in public subsidies, including significant tax abatements. Under existing legislation, new commercial developments in certain New York boroughs do not have to pay property tax for the first 15 years. After that the tax is phased in, so that full taxes are not paid until the 26th year of the private facility (deMause, 2005).

In 2010 some citizens in Sarasota, Florida, filed lawsuits alleging that Sarasota County promised the Baltimore Orioles $31.2 million for stadium improvements in a backroom deal. Sarasota was formerly the spring home for the Cincinnati Reds, who left to Goodyear, Arizona, after Sarasota residents rejected a referendum in 2007 that would have paid for $56 million in stadium renovations. To help avoid a referendum, the county moved forward with an $18.7 million bond to help renovate the stadium. The amount was under the $20 million threshold that would have required a referendum by law. The $31.2 million price tag was also funded with $7 million from a city-backed bond, and the remainder was to come from a tourist tax (Antonen, 2010). Because property taxes did not increase, the tourist tax would have been a major funding component. Such taxes often involve a hefty tax on hotel and motel rooms and rental cars.

Numerous techniques are available for funding business growth, whether a new gym needs to be built or a team is interested in renovating a stadium. The options are as countless as the number of people who have money to invest. Each deal can be structured to meet the needs of the parties involved. A deal might include financing from family, friends, corporate partners, government entities, or venture capitalists.

Obviously, we cannot describe every means of financing a business in this text; instead, we focus on several major sources of funds, including yourself, relatives and friends, banks, nonbank lenders, public stock offerings, bonds, and venture capitalists. Before discussing each capital acquisition method, we want to identify the three primary categories of sources of capital.

1. *Equity investors.* These investors purchase a portion of the business (e.g., in the form of stock) with the hope of obtaining future returns through capital gains or dividend payments. Because equity owners assume significant risk that a business might not succeed, they typically require a higher rate of return to offset the higher risk. This reward is evidenced through either increased stock value or dividend payments to the stock (equity) owner.

2. *Long-term debt obligations,* such as bonds. A bondholder is interested in receiving an appropriate rate of return on the investment with the lowest possible risk. Bondholders do not benefit the way that equity investors do if the corporation becomes highly successful, but the risk of losing the investment is greatly reduced because the bonds are secured by collateral.

3. *Short-term loans.* Suppliers of merchandise or raw goods are often the source of loans of this type; they sell goods on the basis that the buyer will pay within 30 days, for example.

Personal Resources

Sometimes people accumulate money from a current job with the intention of someday starting their own businesses. Often these sums are wholly inadequate for that purpose. Industry professionals highlight the need to set aside at least two years' worth of living expenses in preparation for starting your own business. This sum is necessary because most new full-time businesses take at least a year, and sometimes many years, to earn enough profit to pay the business owner a salary (Pounds, 1997). Proper financial planning can help eliminate numerous hurdles that might arise during the formative years of a business. But the planning process needs to begin long before a business starts up, and sufficient capital reserves are required to sustain the business through cyclical and seasonal downturns.

If you do not have enough cash or investments that could be liquidated to start the business, you might consider a home loan. Home equity financing requires a borrower to use her house as collateral when obtaining a loan from a bank or other lending institution. The loan amount is based on the equity that the borrower has in the home. Suppose that you have a house that is worth $100,000 on the market today. You paid $60,000 for the house 10 years ago, with $10,000 down and a $50,000 mortgage. You have paid off $20,000 on the mortgage and still owe $30,000. Thus, if you were to sell the house for $100,000, you would receive $70,000 free and clear of the mortgage ($100,000 minus $30,000 remaining on the mortgage). The $70,000 represents the equity that you have in the house and is the maximum amount that you could borrow from a lending institution.

Home equity loans are traditionally favored over other loans because they carry a lower interest rate. Furthermore, some banks are willing to lend more than 100% of a home's value, depending on what the loan proceeds will be used to purchase. New businesses are highly speculative, and only 20% of new businesses survive (Zikmund & d'Amico, 1996). Therefore, some banks require substantial equity before loaning to a new business; established businesses with significant financial history are more reliable, and owners of these businesses can obtain larger mortgages.

Although most financial advisers do not recommend borrowing on a credit card because of the high interest rates, credit cards can also generate funds from which to start a business. But anyone using this method of borrowing must be careful to repay the debt as quickly as possible because the interest charges will negate any potential benefits that could have accrued from not having to approach other lenders such as banks. Furthermore, the high rate of small business failures should serve as a warning that a business owner could be paying off debts for years after a business fails. With a high interest rate, the repayment obligation could force an individual into bankruptcy (see chapter 5).

The key to using credit cards is to maintain a good **credit rating**. Especially if using personal credit cards, borrowers need to be vigilant in ensuring that purchases and repayments do not hurt their credit rating. A credit rating can plunge if the credit card bills are not paid on time or if payment is always late (see How Credit Card Applicants are Rated).

Can the Government Help You Get a Bank Loan?

A spotty credit history might limit a person's ability to obtain bank financing. The government, however, has developed several programs to help small businesses borrow funds, even if the owner does not have an unblemished credit history. The federal government realized the need for helping small businesses in the 1950s. In 1953 it created the Small Business Administration (SBA) to "aid, counsel, and protect the interest of the nation's small business community" (SBA, 2002). SBA accomplishes this mission by working with lending institutions to encourage and promote loans and other financing to small businesses. For example, SBA started the Microloan Program with the express purpose of helping people realize the American dream of owning their own businesses (Hodges, 1997). The microloans range from $100 to $50,000; the average loan is around $13,000. These loans need to be paid back in six years at 8% to 13% interest. SBA created more than 100 loan outlets throughout the United States through various nonprofit organizations. The only requirement is that the company requesting funds must prepare a business plan that can meet the loan criteria.

SBA also offers various other programs to encourage investing in small businesses. Its 7(a) Loan Guarantee and Certified Development Company Programs provide a guarantee for approved lenders if the borrower defaults on the SBA-backed loan. SBA will not repay the loan; instead, it requires the lender to go after the borrower's collateral and then will supplement any remaining shortfall that might have been guaranteed.

HOW CREDIT CARD APPLICANTS ARE RATED

When determining whom to issue credit cards to, companies often use complex computer programs to score applicants. The scoring technique analyzes distinct credit patterns to determine the likelihood that a borrower will repay any debts. Scores range from 375 to 900; higher scores indicate lower likelihood of default (Sichelman, 1998). The key factors that can lower a score are late payments, collections, bankruptcies, outstanding debts, a short or nonexistent credit history, credit inquiries, and applications for new credit (Sichelman, 1998). AnnualCreditReport.com is the only government-authorized (Federal Trade Commission) source for a free annual credit report that is yours by law. The Fair Credit Reporting Act guarantees you access to your credit report at no cost from each of the three nationwide credit reporting companies—Experian, Equifax, and TransUnion—every 12 months. Checking your credit history is important because of the increased number of identity theft crimes that affect college students and young adults.

Table 8.1 Percentage of Points Given to Help Determine Your Credit Score

Category	Percentage
Payment history	35
Amounts owed	30
Length of credit history	15
New or attempted credit accounts	10
Variety of credit types	10

Data from "Planning for success," 2000, *CampBusiness* 8-11.

The SBA does not loan money to everyone. SBA lends money to people starting a business if they have

- ♦ excellent credit, including no collection letters in the past 3 years;
- ♦ no bankruptcies in the past 10 years;
- ♦ a business plan;
- ♦ some type of collateral, such as a home;
- ♦ up to one-third of the required capital to put into the business;
- ♦ 24 months of experience in the same field as the current business;
- ♦ at least 12 months of training or special certification required for the business;
- ♦ an explanation of hardship that caused any blemishes to personal credit; and
- ♦ a personal expense plan to satisfy the lender that the borrower can meet his or her own living expenses.

For those who meet these criteria, SBA has several lending programs available including the 7(a) and Microloan Programs, as well as 504 and Certified Development Company, Certified Preferred Lender, and Surety Bond Programs. The 7(a) Program is the most commonly used. In Hartford, Connecticut, 555 SBA-backed loans were approved in 1999, totaling $124 million. More than 96% of those loans (533) were 7(a) loans, and 50% (279) of all loans were for amounts under $100,000 (SBA, 2002). By 2006 the number had increased to more than 1,500 loans totaling $239 million, including 1,352 loans ($188.1 million) generated under the most widely used 7(a) Loan Program, which funds general business purposes. The 504 Loan Program, which is used for fixed-asset financing, accounted for 91 loans totaling $49.1 million. The Microloan Program, which provides smaller loans, produced 44 loans totaling $1.2 million (*SBA loans*, 2006). By 2011 the Hartford market had 695 business loans totaling $223.7 million. The decline in loans could be directly traced to a tougher economy that discourages many new business start-ups (Seay, 2011). The market for SBA-guaranteed loans has become so big that a secondary market has been created to sell these loans. Lenders are able to sell the guaranteed portions of the SBA-guaranteed loans to investors and increase their yield on the unguaranteed portions of the SBA loans.

Self-Funding

Funds for a business can also come from the business itself. An established business might use depreciation allowances and profits not paid out as dividends as a way of fueling further expansion. For example, if a golf cart purchased for $10,000 has a five-year life, it can be depreciated $2,000 a year. The $2,000 deduction reduces total tax obligations and represents funds that should be set aside to help purchase another golf cart in the future. Most businesses also retain a percentage of their profits, whether at regular or random intervals, for future needs. These retained earnings are for future use and are not intended to pay salaries or other current expenses.

Companies often have extra cash that might be sitting around for one day or several months. Liquid assets can be invested in a bank, in commercial paper, or in Treasury bills for a short period and then withdrawn for any fiscal needs. The interest earned from such investments can be used for future development.

Although business owners will find it difficult to finance capital growth by themselves, it can be done. Through savings, credit cards, government assistance, or internally generated funds, a business owner can find the means to grow. More often than not, however, the business owner will need help from relatives or external investors.

CONCEPTS INTO PRACTICE

Another example of a self-funding concept is raising ticket or membership prices. If a professional sport team wants to hire two new star players, they can anticipate a payroll increase of several million dollars a year. Borrowing funds from a bank or other lending institution can be risky. The Pittsburgh Penguins filed for bankruptcy in 1998, and part of their debt was attributable to players' salaries. Other teams face a similar problem when they attempt to cover their payrolls. A standard industry technique for covering such expenses is to raise ticket prices. If the team raises ticket prices 10%, the resulting increased income might be enough to fund both players. Although the funds for the new players' salaries come from customers and constitute external funds, they are generated from internal marketing efforts rather than from debt or equity sources.

CONCEPTS INTO PRACTICE

A fitness center could also try to raise funds before the center even opens. They could hold a membership drive to sign up prospective members who will be entitled to pay $500 for a two-year membership and $200 a year in subsequent years. If the center sells 200 such memberships, they will have $100,000 to pay for construction costs. Some states, however, require clubs to keep preopening revenue in escrow until the club is opened (Caro, 2000). Even if they cannot touch these initial funds, the center would have 200 membership contracts that could be used as collateral for a loan. Such collateral is often called contractually obligated revenue or contractually obligated income. Large stadiums and arenas use naming rights, pouring rights, personal seat licenses, and luxury box contracts as collateral to secure loans.

Relatives and Friends

Some people are fortunate to have wealthy family members or friends who are willing to invest in a business. But most people do not have a Daddy Warbucks in their circle, so they must go elsewhere for funding. If you are able to obtain money from a parent or relative, you should take specific steps to maximize the benefits for you and the other parties. Many people regularly borrow money from friends or relatives, and most of these arrangements are never documented. Most people do not think that their own flesh and blood or best friend would fail to pay a debt. But courtrooms are filled with people who have broken such promises.

To avoid any improprieties, a business owner should take the following steps when borrowing money from family members or friends who might have to write off a bad debt in the future (Marullo, 1998, March):

♦ Document the loan with a formal agreement.
♦ Develop a formal repayment schedule.
♦ Pledge security, or collateralize the loan.
♦ Keep accurate records of all repayments.
♦ Make sure that there is proof that the business was solvent when the loan was made.
♦ Provide the lender with a detailed business plan specifying how the loan will be repaid.

A relative or friend could also play the part of an "angel" who comes to the rescue. An angel is a major investor who can give a small amount or several million (Ambrosini, 2002). One of the most well-known angel investors in the sport industry is Paul Allen, a founder of Microsoft and owner of the Portland Trail Blazers and Seattle Seahawks. Allen operates an angel investment firm that has invested in sport-related entities such as electronic ticketing businesses and Charter Communications, a major cable operator (*Paul Allen*, 2002). Unlike venture capitalists, who want the business to go public and who invest only in larger projects, angel investors often come into a project before venture capital investors do or when they anticipate being part of a smaller but still profitable business. No matter who provides the capital, risks are always associated with accepting money from others. Some concerns are

♦ whether the lender requires an ownership interest,
♦ whether the lender will demand a say in management decisions,
♦ whether an exit strategy is in place after the business is sound enough to repay the angel and regain control, and
♦ whether interest payments will be tax deductible as a business expense.

Friends and acquaintances can also be a good source of funds. People often think that they need to approach someone with a luxury car or big house. Research shows, however, that the average millionaire does not live in grand style. In *The Millionaire Next Door*, Albert Hoffman concluded that of the 3.5 million millionaires in the United States in 1996, most owned less expensive cars such as Fords, ran mundane businesses, and lived well below their means (Stehle, 1997). Hoffman suggests that instead of trying to meet potential investors at the polo grounds or the opera house, individuals should go to industry trade shows to meet people who might be willing to invest (Stehle, 1997). Researchers have estimated that by 2020 the number of millionaires will have grown to over 20.6 million, double the current number. The country with the second highest number of millionaires is Japan, which will have 8.6 million millionaires (Strachan, 2011).

Loyal customers also represent a potential funding source. The Mad River Glen Cooperative is one of the nation's smallest (and oldest) ski resorts, but it is financially sound. Loyal skiers are willing to pay $1,750 a share for stock in the cooperative and $200 a year thereafter. These funds and the dedicated following of loyal skiers help make the single-lift facility successful. The resort's management has critically examined expenses and determined that the resort needs to be open only 90 days a year to make a profit. Because the top customers are also owners, the resort understands its investment options and maintains a lower run price than that of other resorts. The company does not invest a significant amount in new equipment, such as chairlifts or snow-making machines that could cost $1,000 an hour to operate. Customer loyalty is so strong that when a dividend was paid in 1998 ($16.43 per share), many stockholders suggested that the resort just keep the money (Goo, 2000).

Although family and friends can be a source for capital infusion, many business owners do not want to risk souring a good relationship. What happens if the initial capital infusion is not enough? What happens if more funds are needed, but the business owner does not want the initial investor to lose any money? What happens if the lender needs the money back immediately? Such issues associated with exit strategies are critical. People who do not want to make enemies of family members or friends might try to find funding through external sources such as the open market.

One of the most innovative means to raise funds is the Internet. *Crowdfunding* is the term used to describe using the Internet to gather investors into a company. Under laws in place in 2011, new companies using this approach through various web pages such as kickstarter.com, rockethub.com, and funding4learning.com can collect start-up funds from people all over the world. Some sites collect the money and release the funds to the start-up when the desired goal is reached. If the desired funding amount is not reached, the web users who donated money get their funds back. Other sites give the start-ups the money right away. In contrast, current laws do not let the start-up give any equity to these investors, so the companies give products or other items in exchange for the funding. Under proposed rules that will skirt traditional rules for private offerings (in which there cannot be more than 35 nonaccredited investors who have net worth under $1 million or yearly income less than $200,000 and cannot have more than 499 shareholders), crowdfunding would be allowed to tap as many investors as possible if they raise less than $2 million and can raise funds from numerous investors who can risk up to $10,000 or 10% of their income, whichever is less (Tozzi, 2011).

OPEN MARKETS AND OTHER SHORT-TERM BORROWING

Several effective techniques can be used for raising funds on either a short- or long-term basis. Long-term equity or capital funding techniques are discussed later in this chapter. Short-term funding techniques include borrowing to purchase inventories, supplies, or other items or to pay expenses in situations in which the repayment period is expected to be less than 90 days. For purchases that require longer funding commitments, midterm, start-up, or long-term funding strategies might be needed.

People often find short-term and long-term funds in the open market. The open market is a free-enterprise environment where anyone who wants to borrow and anyone who wants to lend money can enter into a relationship—somewhat similar to the traditional bazaar in which sellers and customers come together and negotiate the price of goods. A bank is part of the open market because anyone can enter a bank and, with collateral or a good credit history, borrow money. Likewise, a successful business can be approached by numerous lenders interested in lending it money.

A professional sports team might rely on long-term funding options such as issuing stocks or bonds to buy a new scoreboard or renovate their arena. They might require short-term funds to pay expenses or salaries if the players are on strike. In contrast, a fitness facility might need to use short-term borrowing to meet current accounts payable but need long-term funding to buy expensive equipment. A company such as Under Armour, for example, might turn to short-term funds to buy inventories or pay unexpected expenses such as settlement of a lawsuit. Such a company also might need long-term funds to buy manufacturing equipment or lease a new facility. In other words, every business at times experiences a need for long- or short-term funds.

Short-term funds may be required for a business to meet monthly, seasonal, or other temporary financial needs. A business does not want to obligate itself to several years of interest payments if the money will be available to repay the loan in several months. A major advantage of short-term borrowing is the relative ease of completing such transactions.

Banks and other lending institutions are accustomed to providing short-term loans, whether the money is required for several hours or several months. Many companies maintain a **line of credit** with a lending institution that allows them to borrow short-term funds on a preapproved basis.

Another major benefit of short-term borrowing is that this strategy can be used to postpone long-term financing. Economic conditions or interest rates sometimes do not justify issuing bonds or stock. A "bridge gap" lending option such as short-term borrowing can help cover any financial obligations until conditions are more favorable for obtaining long-term funding. Regardless of the purpose, short-term borrowing is critical for all businesses.

Accounts Payable

One of the primary techniques for obtaining short-term funding involves accounts payable. Accounts payable represent amounts owed to vendors and suppliers for services that have been rendered or products that have been delivered.

Many people use accounts payable on a daily basis. The most common approach is through a credit card. People make purchases with a promise that at the end of the month they will pay for them. Businesses do the same thing on a daily basis, whether they are purchasing items on a corporate credit card or buying office supplies and inventory with the expectation that they will pay a bill coming at the end of every month. Normally these accounts need to be repaid within 30 days of receiving the bill. This example demonstrates that accounts payable can be more complex than a credit card arrangement. Most businesses use a blend of short-term borrowing that includes accounts payable and other short-term borrowing options.

Assume that a sport business completes an account contract with a laundry service to pay the bill every month. At the end of the first month, they receive a bill for the prior month's service with specific repayment instructions. The laundry service might give a discount if the bill is paid within a week, offer no benefit if the account is paid in full within 30 days, and assess a penalty fee or an interest obligation on the owed amount if the required payment is not made within 30 days. This type of account payable is called a trade credit that one business issues to another. In this example, the trade credit is being offered pursuant to a cash discount option.

A major problem with accounts payable is that the turnaround time for repayment is often slow. If a business buys season tickets for a team's games but does not pay at the time of purchase, the team may have a problem with this receivable account if it never gets paid or is paid months later. Some suppliers may not mind slow repayment because they can obtain interest payments from the borrower. Other suppliers, however, may count on repayment to help pay other obligations. In this case the supplier may reduce the total amount owed to encourage fast repayment.

The most common technique for encouraging fast repayment is the cash discount. A supplier might provide a business with a cash incentive for paying the obligation within 10 days. Cash discounts are often expressed in the formula 2/10/30. This notation refers to a 2% discount if the buyer pays in cash within 10 days and full payment if paid after the 10th day. If payment is not made within 30 days, the buyer has to pay interest or other penalties as defined by the purchase agreement. Although a 2% discount may not seem large, calculated out for the entire year it represents 36% (Bogen, 1966). To calculate the opportunity lost by not paying early, divide the 20 days each month that you do not receive a 2% discount into 365 days a year. The resulting 18.25 is then multiplied by the 2% discount that you could have obtained to find the annualized loss of 36.5%. This discount encourages purchasers to pay their bills quickly, which can reduce collection fees for the supplier. The purchaser receives a significant benefit in obtaining a 30-day interest-free loan. For those reasons a cash discount is a popular short-term funding technique. See chapter 12 for a discussion of cash discounts in the context of accounts receivable.

CONCEPTS INTO PRACTICE

To put this into an example, assume that Under Armour needs to buy some supplies. After working out an agreement with a local supplier, Under Armour purchases 10 pieces of material for $50 each with sales terms of 10/10/30 (10/10/30 means payment in full is due in 30 days, but the buyer may take a 10% discount if payment is made within 10 days). If payment is made during the discount period, Under Armour will save $50 ($10 \times 50 \times 0.10$). If payment is not paid within the discounted period, they will owe the entire $500.

Bank Financing

As discussed in chapter 4, banks are among the cornerstones of the finance system. Banks provide numerous levels of financial assistance, whether through personal banking or comprehensive business banking services. Although accounts payable are a critical tool for commerce and most businesses use accounts payable on a daily basis, bank loans are the most economical and flexible means of short-term financing. Banks provide various services, from savings accounts and business checking accounts to night deposit and automatic bill payment services. They often offer flexible short-term loans ranging from 30 or 60 days to several months. If a 30-day loan comes due, a bank has the flexibility to renew the debt. If the loan is for a longer period, such as three to five years, it is referred to as a **term loan**. Banks prefer to issue short-term loans to get their money back as quickly as possible (Spiro, 1996). Unlike short-term loans that come due at the end of the designated period and are discharged with one payment, term loans often entail regular periodic payments and one **balloon payment**.

CONCEPTS INTO PRACTICE

If a university borrows $5 million from a bank for 5 years, the university might be required to pay $500,000 a year in principal and interest for 4 years and make a large balloon payment approaching $4 million in the fifth year. For a conventional loan, the university might make the $500,000 payment for 14 years to cover both the principal and the interest.

No matter what services are used, a bank is more willing to negotiate and customize accounts with businesses that already have an established account. Some banks require businesses with active loans to maintain an average deposit balance equal to 20% of the loaned amount. Such a deposit is often called a compensating balance. This protective balance may not seem significant, but it does represent a cost of borrowing.

A loan that is contingent on maintaining a minimum balance at a bank is a type of secured loan. Many loans require the use of collateral. Anything of value can be used to secure a loan. Some businesses pledge physical property such as land, buildings, inventory, or equipment. Other businesses pledge intangible assets such as accounts

receivable or the rights to an invention or patent. Because loans against accounts receivable or inventory are often riskier, some banks do not offer such loans, and businesses need to go to nonbank lenders for those loans.

CONCEPTS INTO PRACTICE

Suppose that a sport business borrows $100,000 from a bank but has to maintain $20,000 in a savings account at the bank throughout the life of the loan. If the business pays 10% on the loan, maintaining the $20,000 in the bank at a low interest rate or with no interest would in essence bring the cost of borrowing to 12.5%, which is calculated as follows:

$$I / (L - B) = \text{cost of borrowing}$$

I = interest paid on loan

L = amount borrowed

B = compensating balance that needs to be maintained

$$\$10,000 / (\$100,000 - \$20,000) = 12.5\%$$

Many businesses use real estate or machinery as collateral for a loan, but assets such as inventory, investment assets, or accounts receivable can be pledged if other assets are already being used for collateral. In some instances businesses do not want to encumber an asset because they want to be able to sell it. A company that has pledged a factory as security cannot sell the factory because it does not have a **clear title**—the title is "clouded." Because most debt instruments with any security (especially real property) are recorded by a city or county clerk, potential buyers can determine whether a property has a clouded title. If someone tried to buy the pledged factory, the title could not be passed as free and clear of any encumbrances. After the obligation was paid in full, however, the factory could be sold. This same process operates when people buy a house. The mortgage on the house is recorded with a government agency and is discovered when a title search is conducted. The buyer can clear the title by paying the mortgage and having the mortgage company release its claim to the property.

Using current inventories as collateral is a technique that maximizes current value while affording the option to raise additional funds. Asset-based borrowing entails a revolving line of credit secured by accounts receivable, inventories, or both (Hovey, 1998, November). Bally Total Fitness expanded its business by acquiring debt, and the debt was secured by accounts receivable (Caro, 2000). Because the chain had numerous members throughout the world, it was guaranteed a certain amount each month from dues. These dues were part of the accounts receivable and were also called contractually obligated revenue or contractually obligated income because they were required by the membership contracts. Bally could use these prospective assets to secure debt obligations, similar to the way that a stadium can use the contractually obligated revenue from naming-rights contracts as collateral for a bond or other debt instruments.

Standard & Poor's raised its corporate credit rating on Bally Total Fitness to B− from CCC+ and removed it from credit watch, after placing it on the list on August 17, 2005 (*Club hopping*, 2004). Bally obtained limited waivers relating to its 10.5% senior notes due 2011 and 9.875% senior subordinated notes due 2007 (*Club hopping*, 2004). As of September 30, 2004, Bally's debt was $747.7 million. To restore investor creditability, Bally Total Fitness was to commence a search for a new chief executive officer (CEO) as part of its financial structuring process (*Liberation Investments delivers*, 2005). Bally's indenture violations originated from its failure to file with the SEC its financial statements for the quarter end of June 30, 2004, and to deliver the financial statements to the board trustee and lenders (*Liberation Investments delivers*, 2005). By 2007 Bally had been delisted from the NYSE and was flirting with filing for Chapter 11 bankruptcy protection (see chapter 5) (Dow Jones Newswire, 2007). Bally has been listed since then on the Over the Counter Exchange (see generally chapter 9), but its legal woes about stating income and expenses continued through 2008 when it finally reached a settlement with the Securities and Exchange Commission. The commission issued a press release with the following language:

> The Securities and Exchange Commission today filed financial fraud charges against Bally Total Fitness Holding Corporation, a nationwide commercial operator of fitness centers that has recently emerged from bankruptcy proceedings under new, private ownership. The Commission alleges that from at least 1997 through 2003, Bally's financial statements were affected by more than two dozen accounting improprieties, which caused Bally to overstate its originally reported year-end 2001 stockholders' equity by nearly $1.8 billion, or more than 340%. The Commission's complaint further alleges that Bally understated its originally reported 2002 net loss by $92.4 million, or 9,341%, and understated its originally reported 2003 net loss by $90.8 million, or 845%. As a result, the Commission alleges that Bally violated the antifraud, reporting, books and records, and internal control provisions of the federal securities laws. (U.S. Securities and Exchange Commission, 2008)

Bally had been a public company and generated annual revenues over $1 billion until 2007, when it filed for bankruptcy protection. In 2009, after Bally's second bankruptcy in 17 months, J.P. Morgan received 50.5% of Bally's equity and Anchorage Advisors received 33.7% in a reorganization plan approved in bankruptcy court based on the owed debt (Goldman, 2011).

LA Fitness based in Irvine, California, acquired 171 clubs from Bally Total Fitness for $153 million in 2011. The acquisition involved Bally clubs in 16 states and the District of Columbia. After completion of the transaction, Bally will continue to operate its remaining 100 clubs. LA Fitness was ranked second behind 24 Hour Fitness on Club Industry's Top 100 Clubs list in 2011. LA Fitness had an estimated $1 billion in 2010 revenue, which was less than the estimated $1.352 billion for 24 Hour Fitness. Bally was number 5 on the 2011 list, reporting $550 million in 2010 revenue (Goldman, 2011).

If a borrower, such as Bally, defaults on secured loans, the lender can seize the assets as with any other collateral. Because of the potential difficulty that a lender might have in collecting receivables or selling inventory, the lender might loan only up to 85% of the value in receivables and 55% of the value of the inventories (Hovey, 1998, November). Asset-based loans are normally provided at the prime rate plus 2% for a creditworthy business. Although these loans are not especially hard to obtain, they do require significant paperwork. A borrower typically needs to provide three years of profit-and-loss statements, current and past financial statements, inventory aging reports, personal financial and tax return statements for the past three years, and sales projections for the coming year (Hovey, 1998, November). After receiving a loan, the borrower must comply with additional paperwork requirements such as providing monthly reports on accounts payable and receivable.

COLLATERAL VALUES

The following table shows common collateral values needed to secure credit from financial institutions. According to these industry standards, if a company has accounts receivable of $100,000 and allows the bank to monitor the receivables, it could possibly obtain an $80,000 loan secured by the receivables.

Value of Factored Assets in Obtaining Loans

Collateral	Percentage loaned
Accounts receivable, monitored	80
Accounts receivable, unmonitored	70
Inventory, monitored	50
Inventory, unmonitored	40
Owned equipment, % of book value	50
New equipment, % purchase price	80
Used equipment, % purchase price	75
Real estate	65-90
U.S. government securities	90
Investment-grade municipal bonds	80
Bonds or preferred stock	75
Stocks below AA grade	50
NYSE, AMEX, NASDAQ shares	65
Cash value of insurance policies	100
Cash	100

Data from "Planning for success," 2000, *CampBusiness* 8-11.

Some commonly used documents that provide security for an asset-backed loan are bills of lading, trust receipts, and warehouse receipts. A bill of lading pledges commodities or merchandise in transit as collateral for a loan. Goods covered by a trust receipt are held in trust for the lending institution but could be housed in a separate area at the borrower's business. After those goods are sold, the cash from the sales is first paid to the bank to satisfy the debt. A warehouse receipt performs the same function as a bill of lading, but it applies when the inventory is stored in a bonded warehouse to protect the bank's collateral. Title to the assets rests with the lender until a release document is provided to the warehouse. The warehouse can then release the specified assets. Although secured loans provide significant protection for the lender, collateral may not be required if a business has a strong credit rating or a good relationship with the lending bank.

Banks have significant flexibility, within federal guidelines, to offer various customized services. Twenty years ago, banks were typically smaller than they are today and often had strong personal relationships with customers. Banks could provide a broader range of services for business owners whom the bank employees knew and had done business with in the past. Having a "personal banker" is more unusual today. Recent mergers have consolidated numerous smaller banks into more impersonal businesses. But even with larger banks, businesses need to communicate with bank employees on a regular basis. Loan officers and their supervisors are important contacts. Knowing several bank employees in these positions provides protection if bank personnel move to different locations (Nelton, 1998, November). Developing personal relationships can help if you ever need to apply for a loan—it is to your advantage if you are more than just a name on an application, possibly a friend and someone whom the bankers would judge as highly credible.

Banks frequently expect the owner of a proposed new business to put some of his own money at risk. The underlying thinking is, Why should the bank invest in the project if the owner is not willing to risk his own money? Equity capital represents a firm commitment by the owner to work for the best interest of the business. The owner wants to succeed to avoid losing his own money, as well as the bank's money. A bank could require equity capital to approach approximately 40% of the amount needed to fund the new business (Horine, 1999). Even if no equity is required to obtain the bank loan, banks traditionally require audited financial statements to help calculate standard ratios, such as debt–equity and acid test ratios, and these figures can help determine the prospect for default. Banks might also require business plans, pro forma budgets, personnel profiles, sample products, and other information to make a lending decision. Most banks require a borrower to complete a formal application, which could include a summary of the business, profiles of the top executives, financial statements, pro forma budgets, and a detailed repayment plan (Griffin, 1991).

After the loan papers have been approved, the parties sign an agreement. This document is called a promissory note. The note specifies the amount borrowed, the interest rate to be charged, any repayment terms, whether the loan is collateralized, and all other terms and conditions that the parties have agreed on. After the note is signed, the borrower receives the loan proceeds.

THE FIVE Cs OF CREDIT

Regardless of the requested loan amount, people should not quit their jobs before obtaining a loan. A bank will check to see whether an applicant is currently employed to help establish her ability to repay, or service, the loan. The potential borrower's employment status is just one variable that banks and other lending institutions might investigate. Banks commonly refer to the **five Cs** of credit when deciding whether to loan someone money. The five Cs are character, capacity, collateral, capital, and condition.

1. *Character* refers to the applicant's credit history and truthfulness. Did the applicant disclose all outstanding debt? Did she list any prior bankruptcy? Does the applicant have favorable business or professional references? Does it appear that she is willing to repay the loan? The answers to such questions help determine whether the lender can trust the applicant.

2. *Capacity* represents the lender's determination about whether the potential business has the right management team and philosophy to become a profitable enterprise that will earn more than enough money to pay the loan.

3. *Collateral* refers to anything of value that can be pledged to guarantee final repayment of the loan. Collateral can include a home, property, equipment, collectibles, a legal judgment, or even a lottery payoff.

4. *Capital* represents the equity that the applicant will put into her own business. A lending institution will not be interested in loaning money to help launch a new business if the business owner does not think that the business will succeed. If the applicant believes that the business will be a success, she must support her conviction by investing some of her own money. Banks typically require a 30% to 35% equity or cash investment in the business by the loan applicant (Pounds, 1997). Capital also refers to any excess cash that might be available to pay unexpected expenses.

5. *Condition* is the applicant's primary opportunity to sell the lender on the value of the business. The lender will want to know whether the industry is growing, whether there are competitors, whether the product has a long life cycle, whether a location or distribution channel is available to sell the product, and so on. By thoroughly researching the proposed business and presenting the lender with a comprehensive business plan that addresses those issues (see chapter 3), the applicant greatly increases the chance of securing a loan.

Whether the loan is backed by a personal guarantee, collateral, or a mortgage, banks offer numerous financial options that make short-term borrowing fairly simple. Lines of credit are more complicated but still represent an effective use of bank resources to cover immediate fiscal needs. A lending institution charges interest only on the amount actually borrowed from the credit line but can also charge a commitment fee that could range from 0.05% to 1% (Battersby, 1999). The commitment fee can be waived if the borrower has compensating balances in other accounts. Three types of lines of credit are available:

1. A nonbinding line of credit is an open account for the business to borrow from. If the business experiences hardships and has financial trouble, however, the line of credit can be revoked.

2. A committed line of credit requires the potential borrower to pay a commitment fee to lock the line of credit into place, thus guaranteeing needed funds.

3. A revolving line of credit requires the borrower to undergo an annual review and renewal of the credit line (Battersby, 1999).

A **revolving credit** agreement is similar to a line of credit in allowing a company to borrow a specified sum, but there is a major distinction. A line of credit allows the borrower to access a certain amount of money if needed, but the bank or the company can withdraw from the agreement at any time. A revolving credit agreement is a contract whereby the borrower agrees to pay an annual commitment fee, a small percentage of the unused amount, to compensate the bank for entering into the commitment (Brigham & Gapenski, 1994). If the company uses only half the available credit, it is charged the commitment fee for the unused amount and is charged the agreed-on interest for the amount borrowed. Because the revolving credit agreement is a contract, both parties need to undertake formal contract cancellation steps to end it.

Commercial Paper

Businesses can raise short-term funds from other nonbank businesses by issuing commercial paper (CP). Commercial paper is a promissory note that might mature in one to nine months. Commercial paper is not often seen in the sport industry, but it is common among some large manufacturers and sales finance companies, such as General Motors Acceptance Corporation (GMAC). Large corpora-

tions are also among the largest purchasers of CP, which they acquire with liquid funds to earn some interest. As with other short-term lending, if a large corporation needs money to pay bills, it can sell the CP it previously purchased. The business that issues the CP determines the interest rates charged based on what rates would draw the greatest investor interest. Specialized CP dealers quote CP prices on the open market. Rates and prices change as economic conditions change, and as companies need more money, they may offer better rates.

Private Placement Through Nonbank Lenders

Various options are available for obtaining cash from other sources. **Private placement** refers to the process of obtaining funds from private parties such as investors, venture capital investors, or other companies interested in investing in a business. These investments can take the form of debt instruments, equity interest, or a blend of the two.

Nonbank lenders are the most frequent source other than banks for financing smaller businesses. These lenders do not include angel investors, family members, and friends, who can also serve as lenders. Nonbank lenders can be independent businesses or can work in conjunction with the government. Some companies that offer nonbank loans include AT&T Small Business Lending Corporation, Heller First Capital, Business Lenders, Money Store Investment Corporation, and GE Capital Small Business Finance Corporation. Nonbank loans often have a higher interest rate based on risk factors, which might have been what dissuaded a bank from providing the loan in the first place. These loans are often attached to special purchasing deals offered by suppliers (see the "Supplier Financing" section).

The list of potential lending sources is almost limitless. This section covers private companies, private investment group financing, factoring, installment sales, supplier financing, and leasing. These financing methods do not entail selling any equity position in the business. Thus, no ownership interest is given up to obtain the funds.

We discuss mergers and acquisitions in chapter 14, but every business owner has the option of selling a portion of the business or the entire business to acquire funds. Several **buyout** funds established for the sport industry provide funds to businesses or purchase entire businesses. Chase Manhattan joined with International Management Group to form the IMG/Chase Sports Capital fund. The fund had $170 million to help finance sport businesses and used some of those funds to purchase the Skip Barber Racing School in Connecticut (Tan, 2000). Although selling an entire business entails obtaining funds for the sellers, the process should not be thought of as selling out. The owner may have sold the business, but the potential cash infusion from a financially stronger business might have been what was necessary to finance further expansion. Many businesses would have failed had they not been purchased by a buyer who funded future growth.

Private Companies

Other nonbank lenders include private companies that are licensed by the U.S. SBA. These small business investment companies (SBICs) can provide either debt financing by issuing long-term loans or equity financing by acquiring an ownership interest in a company (Pryde, 1998). SBICs, however, are barred by law from acquiring a controlling interest in a company. SBIC owners are required to contribute $5 million of their own money, which makes them highly selective in picking high-quality investments. The SBICs also prefer to invest close to home and typically invest around $500,000 in each company (Pryde, 1998). Many investments are in specialized companies, which might include minority-owned businesses and socially or economically disadvantaged companies. To qualify for an SBIC loan or equity investment, a company's net worth must be less than $18 million, and the business must have had after-tax earnings of less than $6 million in the two previous years (Pryde, 1998).

Some private-placement investors, such as some venture capitalists, require significant control over managerial decisions. But some hands-off private-placement investors do not require any seats on the board of directors or any managerial involvement. These people are typically content with a 25% return per year (Reynes, 1998, October). Hands-off private-placement deals are best suited for developed companies that are already publicly traded or that plan on pursuing a public offering in two to three years.

Most cities have local brokers, bankers, or regional brokerage firms that can help coordinate private-placement deals. These individuals or firms typically are paid a percentage of the money that they help raise (5%-15%). Caution is required when working with anyone who is trying to help you raise funds. Because deals are contingent on getting funding, numerous scams and incomplete deals can cost a company both money and time. If any broker or investment banker asks for money up front, there is no guarantee that you will receive anything (Reynes, 1998, October). In contrast, people who receive a percentage after a deal has been completed are more likely to engage in prudent conduct to guarantee payment for themselves and their firms.

Through private placement, an investor might purchase convertible debentures. A convertible debenture pays a certain predetermined interest rate to the investor. After a specified period, convertible debentures can be converted into stock or maintained as a loan. The opportunity to convert the loan to stock is a choice made by the loan holder, the issuer, or both (Reynes, 1998, October). In one example involving a company that manufactured drug-screening kits, investors had the option to purchase convertible debentures in $5,000 blocks. The company's shares were selling for $0.38 each. After three years, the lenders could choose to get their money back and all interest owed or convert their debenture to stock at $0.75 a share. Converting to stocks would have been the best option for the lenders because three years later the stocks were selling for $3 to $4 per share (Reynes, 1998, October). Debenture offerings are discussed further in chapter 10.

Private Investment Group Financing

Entrepreneurs can also turn to a private investment group (PIG) for nonbank funding. A PIG can pool money from a variety of sources including individuals, endowments, pension funds, private investors, and institutional investors (Hovey, 1997). Private investment groups traditionally invest in stable companies that have shown continued growth for several years. These investors typically prefer investing in manufacturing or distribution companies rather than retail or service companies (Hovey, 1997).

Private investment groups normally invest more than $1 million in a company and buy stocks and possibly secure loans to raise the necessary capital. Such investments do not come without a hefty price. Private investment groups typically require a rate of return of 30% to 35% per year (Hovey, 1997). This rate of return may seem high, but venture capital or angel investors who invest in certain industries or products typically invest in riskier young firms and demand a higher **annual return**—often over 50% (Hovey, 1997).

A PIG deal might take 6 to 18 months to complete, and a $10 million deal might cost up to $340,000 to finalize. This figure is the sum of

$100,000 to $200,000 for the mergers and acquisitions adviser, $30,000 to $100,000 for legal fees, and $25,000 to $40,000 for accounting fees (Hovey, 1997).

Factoring Accounts Receivable

Private parties can also provide short-term funds through factoring. Factoring entails selling assets. The assets sold are either inventories or accounts receivable, and they are purchased by a specialized financing company.

Factoring of receivables can be accomplished in several ways. One way is for a company to purchase the receivables, and another is for a company to purchase only the rights without transferal of actual administrative duties. The first technique is called factoring without recourse. A factor (the company that purchases the receivables) that purchases without recourse assumes complete responsibility in debt collection. Customers are instructed to send their payments to the factor. The factor receives a commission on the accounts that are paid and charges interest on the money loaned to the business until the accounts are paid.

CONCEPTS INTO PRACTICE

Assume that a sport business is owed $10,000 and that Acme Factoring purchases the accounts receivable without recourse. Acme might receive 10% of the $10,000, or $1,000, as commission and might loan the sport business $7,000 on the remaining receivables at 5%. If Acme collects the entire $10,000, Acme profits from the $1,000 commission and from receiving 5% interest on the $7,000 loan. The remaining $3,000 might be returned to the sport business according to the negotiated contract provisions.

In the second type of factoring—factoring with recourse—the original holder of the receivables is still responsible for obtaining repayment and collects all payments but sends those payments to a finance company. This technique is also called accounts receivable financing. A finance company might advance money contingent on the borrower's agreeing to collect and manage the receivables. The factoring company might advance 70% to 95% of all receivables sold to it and then pay the remaining percentage when the last receivables are collected (Bogen, 1966). Again, the factoring

company makes money by charging interest on the money advanced to the company selling the receivables. Regardless of the technique used, factoring accounts receivable is more expensive than bank borrowing because the factor charges a higher interest rate based on the potential risk factors.

Installment Sales

Installment sales are common in the auto sales industry. A buyer makes a down payment and makes monthly payments of principal and interest for a specified number of months or years. These contracts are typically for three or four years. The purchaser's failure to make timely payments gives the installment contract holder the right to repossess the car. Thus, the person holding the installment contract has title and true ownership.

Installment sales contracts can be found in the sporting goods industry (e.g., when someone buys an abdominal workout machine seen in an infomercial for three installments of $19.99 each). The purchaser has obtained the opportunity to receive the product contingent on future payments. Similar deals are made in almost all businesses, by which a party to a contract can make several payments. If a university sells their broadcasting rights to a television station, the station might pay 33% when the contract is signed, 33% before the season starts, and 33% when the season ends.

Supplier Financing

Businesses can also obtain financial assistance from those who sell them necessary equipment or supplies. Such an arrangement can take a variety of forms, from loaning equipment to reducing purchase prices to extending credit or creating longer repayment terms (Hodges, 1997). Assistance from suppliers represents just one technique in **creative financing**. By casting a wide net, a business can find numerous potential coentrepreneurs interested in possibly joining forces. Arrowhead Pond in Anaheim is a good example of such a deal; Ogden paid a significant amount for the rights to provide food and concession services for the facility. Ogden was hoping to write off the building cost as a tax expense and generate significant long-term revenue from the exclusive contract. In 2006 the facility's sponsor changed, and the arena became the Honda Center.

An established company might also offer financing options, but the terms might not be as favorable as those of a new company or a major competitor that is trying to gain market share. This example can often be seen in consumer car sales, in which various manufacturers offer lower-interest loans to win potential customers away from a rival manufacturer.

Operating Versus Capital Leases

Leasing, whether from the selling company or from a leasing agent or corporation, can also provide the funds needed to obtain equipment or other assets. By leasing equipment, money can be saved to buy other assets or equipment.

CONCEPTS INTO PRACTICE

Fitness equipment leasing evolved in the mid-1990s, and in 1999 between 25% and 40% of all fitness equipment was being leased (Cohen, 1999). The numbers increased through the first part of 2005 because the cost of operating health clubs kept increasing, and leasing freed up additional funds to pay for other expenses. For a facility that leases equipment, the average leased amount is $40,000. This amount is based on the total equipment value, the credit rating, financial conditions, and business experience. Fitness equipment does not depreciate as quickly as other assets, such as vehicles, and thus often serves as collateral for the lease.

A fitness center could obtain either a capital lease or an operating lease for equipment. Under a capital lease, they would make their monthly lease payments and at the end of the lease term could pay a specified price, normally $1, to acquire the ownership rights for the equipment (Cohen, 1999). In contrast, an operating lease allows the lessee to return the equipment at the end of the lease or to buy it for a percentage of the original cost. Operating leases are often called service leases because the contract normally requires both financing and maintenance. Operating leases are not fully amortized, which means that the lease payments are insufficient to recover the full cost of the equipment.

A major advantage of the operating lease is a cancellation clause that gives the lessee (the fitness center) or the lessors (the equipment company) the opportunity to terminate the lease within a specified period. The cancellation clause could call for a 30-day written notice. Regardless of the time requirement, the benefit for the facility would be that they could, within 30 days, switch to a less expensive equipment supplier or one that provides equipment that is more advanced.

In contrast to the operating lease, the capital lease has one major advantage: the right to own the equipment when the lease ends. A capital lease, however, does not have any maintenance provision, the lease is not cancelable, and the lease payments will equal the cost of the equipment. A capital lease is often called a finance lease because of the nature of the lease arrangement.

Several issues require examination when determining whether to purchase or lease new assets. Leasing new assets has the following advantages (Bogen, 1966):

♦ Funds that would normally be used to purchase assets could be used for working capital and other needs.

♦ No external financing is required, or the amount of such funds would be minimal.

♦ The corporation's financial picture is strengthened because investments in fixed assets are reduced and debt service is not increased (although additional debt obligation would be required to pay for the lease).

♦ No significant capital outlay is required, because most leases do not entail a significant down payment.

♦ Corporations can often avoid a large maturity payment such as that involved when a corporation retires a bond issue.

♦ Unlike the situation with stock sales, the shareholder's equity is not diluted through leasing.

♦ The entire lease payment is deducted from **taxable income**, which often produces a significant benefit over asset ownership. Other assets such as buildings and equipment can be depreciated if purchased, but the land is not deductible.

♦ Technological obsolescence because of innovations in technology can be avoided when a company can rapidly replace older leased equipment.

♦ Leasing equipment can eliminate numerous repair and upkeep expenses that could be covered by the lease agreement.

CONCEPTS INTO PRACTICE

As an example, the fitness center might find a good piece of equipment sold by XYZ Manufacturing. They could negotiate price and delivery specifications with XYZ. The center could then apply to have a finance company buy the equipment and lease it back to them. This arrangement would be considered an amortized lease with an interest percentage built into it. If the equipment cost $10,000 and the interest rate was 10%, the fitness center would have paid $11,000 when all the lease payments had been rendered.

Although leasing assets offers significant advantages, such as lower up-front costs, tax deductibility, and a positive effect on credit rating, some distinct disadvantages are also present:

- Gross lease costs are traditionally higher than financing costs if extended over the life of the asset.

- After the point at which an asset would have been paid for if purchased, the lessee is still making regular lease payments throughout the lease period.

- Modifying the asset requires the lessor's permission, eliminating the lessee's ability to control the asset.

- A lessee loses the benefits associated with inflation, increased values, or increased salvage values because the asset is turned over after the lease period ends. The lessor gains these benefits.

- A long lease obligation may force a company to keep using older equipment covered by the lease to avoid paying penalties for breaching the lease (Bogen, 1966).

- Because leases entail no significant capital requirements, some companies may lease too much equipment, not realizing that their fixed lease obligations are growing significantly and that the lease obligations would still be owed even if their sales stopped.

- A lessor can always confiscate the equipment upon default, leaving the company without machinery.

Whichever leasing technique is used, there are specific effects on taxes and the balance sheet. The big tax benefit of a lease is the ability to deduct lease expenses as a business expense. If a company buys the equipment instead, it will be able to depreciate the equipment cost over five years only as set forth by IRS regulations. The tax benefit is available only under specific circumstances if the lease meets the following conditions (Brigham & Gapenski, 1994):

- The initial lease term cannot exceed 80% of the estimated useful life of the equipment, which means that when the lease ends the equipment still should have at least 20% of its useful life remaining.

- The residual value of the equipment at the end of the lease must equal at least 20% of its initial value.

- No party can be allowed to purchase the equipment at a predetermined price when the lease ends. This concern can be eliminated by allowing the lessee to purchase the equipment at the equipment's fair market value after the lease ends.

- The lessee cannot make any investments in or improvements to the equipment other than through the lease payments.

- No contractual provision can limit the use of the equipment until after the lease expires.

An example of the depreciation versus business expense deduction highlights the value of a lease to the bottom line.

Leases also affect financial statements. Leases were called off-balance-sheet financing for many years because neither the leased asset nor the lease liability (payment requirements) appeared on a company's balance sheet. Because leased assets and obligations did not appear on the balance sheet, an investor might not know that all the equipment in a business was leased and that the business owed over $1 million annually in lease obligations, for example. These facts would be critical for any investor. On the basis of this concern, the Financial Accounting Standards Board issued a ruling that leased assets need to be reported as fixed assets and that the present value of future lease payments needs to be recorded as a liability (Brigham & Gapenski, 1994). An operating lease is now recorded on the balance sheet. A capital lease is recorded on the books as either an asset or an obligation. An asset is considered part of a capital lease if ownership of the asset is transferred to the lessee when the lease expires, if the lease contains a bargain purchase option, or if the lease term exceeds 75% of the asset's economic life (Spiro, 1996).

CONCEPTS INTO PRACTICE

Assume that a fitness center bought $2 million in equipment with a three-year class life. They would receive a depreciation allowance of $660,000 in the first year, $900,000 in the second year, $300,000 in the third year, and $140,000 in the fourth year. If the center was taxed at 40% (federal and state taxes combined), the purchase would provide a total tax savings of $800,000. Assuming a discount rate of 6%, the present value of the tax savings would be $671,680. If the center leased double the amount of equipment for one year for a $2 million lease payment, they would likewise have an $800,000 tax savings ($2,000,000 multiplied by 40%). But because the lease option benefits are derived in the first year, the savings are $42,559 compared with the present value from the purchase option (Brigham & Gapenski, 1994). The problem with this analysis is that the $2 million lease obligation appears extremely high when the purchase price is also $2 million. The example makes sense only because we are supposing that the fitness center would lease twice as much equipment as they would have purchased. If they were to lease the same amount of equipment, the tax savings as a function of present value would be significantly less. Obviously, proper comparisons must be made between items to be leased or purchased.

LONG-TERM BORROWING

This chapter has covered various financing techniques that are often short-term solutions. Borrowing on a credit card is not a long-term option because of the high interest rates. Furthermore, factoring is a stopgap solution, and other funding options would need to be pursued in subsequent times of financial need. Other funding options, such as a bank's line of credit, can be either short term or long term. Installment contracts can be short term for a car or long term for equipment that might last longer than 10 years.

The most traditional forms of long-term funding are stocks and bonds (discussed in the next two chapters). Whereas these two options are normally available for larger businesses, smaller or new companies often do not have these alternatives. Various long-term funding options, such as mortgages or long-term loans, exist for medium-sized businesses. Mezzanine financing is also available as a bridge loan for businesses that wish to expand but are not yet ready for a public offering. This section covers mezzanine financing and venture capital financing.

Mezzanine Financing

Although raising short-term start-up capital is often difficult, the scenario for existing companies is different. A company with a successful track record has fewer problems raising money because it should be able to show sustained income. These companies can use mezzanine financing, a type of financing available to established companies that show growth potential but that are not yet ready for a capital stock offering (Hovey, 1998, March). Companies can typically use mezzanine financing to raise between $1 million and $20 million through a combination of borrowing money from an investor and selling stocks to the same investor (Hovey, 1998, March).

Financing typically works through payment of interest on the borrowed amount for about five years. After that time, the business can cash out the investor by going public or can **refinance** for a longer period. The investor has the benefit of earning a good rate of interest, typically prime plus 2 to 4 points, or, if the business has increased in value, selling the stock for a capital gain (Hovey, 1998, March). No set amount needs to be raised. So the fitness center, after operating the business for several years, could possibly raise $2 million in unsecured, partially secured, or secured debt financing and perhaps $1 million in equity financing. Such deals typically take between three and five months to complete, and the total fee cost (attorneys, accountants, and investment bankers) can equal 5% of the deal (Hovey, 1998, March).

The rule of thumb for mezzanine lending is that a company can

> leverage two to three times its cash flow in senior secured debt. It can raise total debt four to five times cash flow with a mezzanine deal. So if the company is doing $2 million in cash flow, it can probably raise $4 million to $6 million in senior debt and $4 million to $5 million more in mezzanine financing, for a total debt of $10 million or five times cash flow. (Hovey, 1998, March, p. 42)

Although mezzanine lending can help a company grow before a possible public offering, some businesses need a larger boost to expand more rapidly or to position themselves more expediently for a public offering. Whereas the previously discussed angel investor might stay with an investment for the long term, a venture capital investor normally remains with an investment until the business goes bankrupt, is purchased by someone else, or goes public.

Venture Capital

Venture capital represents an opportunity for people with marketable ideas or products to raise funds from private investors willing to take a risk in owning part of the company in exchange for their investment. Venture capital, commonly called VC, is similar to mezzanine financing in that it blends debt-based loans with the potential for equity interest if the borrower goes public. In 1996 capital investments of more than $10.1 billion were made in U.S.-based companies (Reynes, 1997). Investments went up and down over the next 15 years. Venture capitalists invested $4.8 billion in 780 deals in the third quarter of 2010. Traditionally strong sectors such as life sciences and clean technology were down, but biotechnology and software took the lead as the top generator of VC dollars in 2010 (Peterson & Brooks, 2010).

VC investors are primarily interested in technology-based industries in which a winning company can pay off many times over rather than industries in which a successful company will show only marginal profits. Venture capitalists like to see gross margins over 50%. A company that makes a 30% profit a year represents too great a risk and does not attract the strong investor interest that could make an initial public offering (IPO) successful (Evanson, 1998, January).

Venture capital investors have shied away from the sport industry in the past, but sport-related Internet companies are starting to garner VC interest. But not all Internet businesses are drawing VC interest. Venture capitalists are attracted to companies that have clear access to a channel of distribution, whether it is the company's own or someone else's (Evanson, 1998, January). A unique product with significant demand has priority over a flashy new product that might be harder to sell. The ultimate goal for any VC investment is for the company to go public. Through a public offering the VC company can make many times over their investment. A VC investor might invest in 10 companies with the hope that one will hit it big and more than make up for their initial investment in all 10 companies.

Regardless of the method used to obtain initial funding or short-term funding, any successful business will also require long-term financing. VC and mezzanine investors may pay a premium for the ability to transfer their investment from a debt instrument to an equity interest. The equity interest is developed through giving the investor a share of the business. Providing a share of the business is made easier with stock. The preferred approach is to give a VC investor one million shares of two million outstanding shares instead of a contract stating that the investor owns 50% of a business. That is, a contract indicating a 50% ownership in a business is often much harder to sell than stocks, especially stocks listed on an organized exchange.

FUNDING FOR SMALL OR MINORITY-OWNED BUSINESSES

This section expands on previous analysis to look more closely at other capital options for smaller or minority-owned businesses and indicates where to go for help if you are having difficulty finding funding.

Small Business Association Loans for the Inner City

An additional government source to look to is the SBA, discussed earlier in the chapter. The SBA can offer assistance in obtaining various types of loans, including 7(a), 504, Microlenders, Small Business Lending Company, bank-regulated Certified Development Corporation, and SBIC-related loans or programs. In addition, the SBA can provide assistance in conjunction with other capital efforts. For example, the City of Detroit obtained $100 million from the federal government to develop an empowerment zone (Detroit Empowerment Zone Transition Office, n.d.). The empowerment zone is designed to foster revitalization of a community. Businesses moving to such a zone may receive wage credits, **tax-exempt bonds**, section 179 (depreciation) expensing, and assistance in obtaining SBA-backed loans. Property taxes also were to be frozen for those new businesses for five years. In conjunction with this effort, the Detroit Recreation Department put forth an empowerment zone initiative that received more than $10 million in Title XX funding for such projects as Roving Recreation and Recreation Facilities Enhancement Project (Detroit

Empowerment Zone Transition Office, n.d.). Blending various government levels and agencies can help develop innovative capital acquisition programs and reduce operating costs, especially in the context of minority-based programs.

A Helping Hand for Minority Business Owners

Although the capital sources just mentioned all present some strong opportunities for a new or established business to obtain funds for growth, other companies might not have the same opportunities. Minorities and women have traditionally faced hardships in acquiring capital for their businesses. Some of these hardships were attributable to minimal or nonexistent credit histories for business owners who had never had credit cards in their own names or who represented too high a risk for traditional capital lenders. To prevent potential continued discrimination—whether disparate impact (unintentional) or disparate treatment (intentional)—numerous support opportunities have been established to help minorities and women obtain funding. A female-owned business could become eligible for specific government set-aside contracts.

Female-owned companies can use the Women's Prequalified Loan Program, guaranteed by the SBA, to borrow up to $250,000. Guarantees are for 80% of loans under $100,000 and 75% for loans over $100,000 (Broome, 2001). To qualify for the SBA-guaranteed loan, the business needs to be a female-owned business (at least 51% of the business needs to be owned, managed, or operated by women), have less than $5 million in sales, and employ fewer than 100 workers (Broome, 2001). If a loan under $100,000 is sought, the process requires only a one-page application. For loans over $100,000 the applicant needs to submit an expanded application, business plan, resumes of the primary officials, recent financial statements or tax returns, and a personal financial statement (Broome, 2001). Loans over $50,000 have an interest obligation at the prime rate. Loans under $50,000 can cost the prime rate plus up to 4% interest (Broome, 2001).

The following paragraphs describe some minority-oriented funding programs.

The National Minority Supplier Development Council (NMSDC) has 42 regional affiliates and works with 3,500 businesses to help minority-owned companies acquire goods and services. Such assistance is not meant to be charity. Rather, the companies involved in NMSDC participate to help generate additional sales. Through the provision of flexible payment options or collateralized sales to minorities who otherwise might not obtain such preferential treatment, new sales and potential clients can be developed. The NMSDC has proceeded one step further to create the Business Consortium Fund, which helps minority business owners obtain financing for raw materials, employee salaries, and other contract-related expenses (Nelton, 1998, June). The Business Consortium Fund limits loans to $500,000 over a maximum of four years and requires the borrower to have a purchase order specifying where the funds will be spent.

Although NMSDC aims to help minority-owned business owners, the definition of a minority has created a controversy. In 2000 NMSDC redefined the minority-owned business as a business with as little as 30% nonwhite ownership. But even if less than one-third of a business needs to be minority owned for the business to qualify as a minority business, the rules also require qualified businesses to have 51% of their voting stock held by minorities (Wynter & Thomas, 2000). The rule change was designed to give larger minority-controlled businesses that have a high number of nonminority investors the opportunity to compete more effectively with other businesses.

Apart from the Business Consortium Fund, minority-owned companies may obtain capital from specialized small business investment companies (SSBICs) licensed by the SBA. Local chambers of commerce, economic development committees, and various national associations can also help minorities and women find needed capital. The Suggested Resources section in this book lists several associations that can help in obtaining capital.

CONCLUSION

This chapter covered the basic elements of capital financing. Numerous options exist for finding necessary funds, but even people with business experience can face rejection. A businessperson may approach multiple lenders and be refused by all. This does not mean that the individual is a bad businessperson; it may mean that the economic environment is not right, that the lending market is tight, or that collateral is insufficient to secure the obligation, among a host of other things.

No matter what capital source you attempt to tap, you will need several key tools. The primary tools are either audited financial statements or pro forma statements (see chapter 3, 6, and 15). You will also need a realistic road map for your business (i.e., a business plan) that will help investors determine what direction you will be taking to guarantee a strong likelihood of success. Although the proper documentation is important, you also need a strong team of professionals to help you through the process. An accountant, attorney, and financial planner or investment banker might be critical for your capital acquisition success.

Selling investors on your project is significantly different from selling potential customers. Customers may be interested in product features, customer service, and warranties. In contrast, investors are interested in margin (profit), market size, a competitive environment, return on investment, product development opportunities, and related financial issues (Evanson, 1997). The financial planning process (discussed in chapter 3) helps identify these issues.

Persistency is the key to securing capital. This chapter focused more on short-term funding in situations in which quick decisions are necessary and when time is not available to pursue long-term funding options. Having the capital infrastructure in place, such as a line of credit, is always important in case you need money and do not have time to try various options. The next two chapters discuss long-term funding options that often require months or years of planning to be successful.

Class Discussion Topics

1. If you have ever applied for a credit card, what were you required to show to obtain credit?

2. If you have ever borrowed money to buy a car, what was involved in that process?

3. If you have ever borrowed money for college, what steps were involved in that process?

4. What would you want from a friend (e.g., collateral, a contract) if you loaned the person $1,000?

5. If a friend asked you for a $1,000 loan to start a business, what information would you want to obtain to help you make your decision?

6. Is there value in "sweat equity," or the owner's involvement in a company, to help fund a business?

7. Have you ever defaulted on a loan? What were the ramifications?

8. If you had the money, would you lend it to someone to help start a business if you knew that the business had a 75% chance of failing?

9. If you had to develop a strategy to fund building a sports facility based exclusively on borrowing funds, what sources would you pursue? What do you think your chances of success would be? What criteria could help or hurt your chances of obtaining funds?

chapter 9

Capital Stocks

Chapter Objectives

After studying this chapter, you should be able to do the following:

- Compare the different classes of stock available.
- Describe the rights of a stockholder.
- Understand how a company decides whether to go public.
- Describe how a smaller sport business can issue stock.
- Understand how stocks are issued.
- Understand the evolution of sport stocks.
- Compare the various publicly traded sport businesses.

Chapter 8 covers borrowing on the open market as a form of capital acquisition. Another major form of capital acquisition is selling the business to a group of individuals who purchase stock in the company. Stocks, which represent ownership in the business, can be sold on the open market or through private transactions. Whereas some businesses are owned by thousands of shareholders, others are owned by only one shareholder. Each business is different, and the number and types of shares sold are based on the capital needs of the company when it initially issues stock and future financial needs that might warrant the issuance of additional shares.

Stock certificates represent an investor's ownership right in a business. A stockholder pays a designated amount to acquire an ownership interest in a company. Each share represents an ownership interest, so a stockholder is also referred to as a shareholder. If you own 1,000 shares of a company's stock and 100,000 shares were issued, you own 1% of the company.

This chapter covers the types of stocks that can be purchased, the ways in which shareholders participate in a business, the process of issuing stock (often called going public), the reasons for increases in the value of shares, and the types of sport stocks available.

COMMON STOCK

As the name implies, the type of stock that is most frequently issued and used is **common stock**. Nike, for example, has issued millions of shares of both class A and class B common stock. Phil Knight, the original cofounder, owns 95.5% of the class A shares and 95,652,015 class B shares, which together make up approximately 36.1% of the outstanding shares.

Common stocks represent an equity ownership right in a company. Each share denotes a percentage ownership of the corporation. Because Phil Knight owns more than 95 million shares and Nike has in total 268 million shares outstanding, he owns 35.7% (this number differs from the 36.1% previously mentioned because of the inclusion of the class A shares) of the business. As a partial owner, Knight is entitled to a proportional share of profits earned by the company. If Nike had a $10 million profit and the board of directors decided to pay the entire amount to its common shareholders, then Knight would be entitled to a dividend of $3.57 million.

Knight has certain rights, risks, and obligations as an owner. His rights include the right to help set the direction of the corporation through voting his shares. He also faces risks, such as the possibility of losing his investment and the prospect of any recovery if Nike ever goes bankrupt and no money is left after the bondholders are repaid. Common stocks are low on the repayment list after secured creditors are repaid and holders of preferred shares are paid. Also, Knight has obligations to the business, which could include the prohibition of self-dealing or taking a business opportunity for himself.

Shares can be purchased in several ways. Online brokers allow investors to purchase stocks themselves over the Internet, usually at reduced cost. Investors can also buy shares through an investment adviser or broker. These individuals charge more than a no-frills online service does, but an investor can ask questions and possibly pay to acquire detailed research on stocks. Using either technique can expose investors to significant risk if a stock drops in value. Although some people such as day traders might make a fortune, numerous others have lost fortunes. Buying stocks is akin to gambling. Someone can have the best information about a horse race or great information about a company, but that knowledge does not guarantee a win. Investors rely on information about new product launches, the retirement of key executive, large contracts that have been signed, and numerous other factors. One of the most commonly sought pieces of information is industry ratios, which help indicate whether a stock is over- or undervalued or whether a stock is performing well compared with others in the same industry. Financial ratios were covered in chapter 6.

Because of the potential for significant losses and because investors are often risk averse (not wanting to invest in risky stocks for fear of losing precious money such as a retirement fund), investors try to minimize their risks. One technique that reduces the risk of purchasing stock is to purchase shares in a mutual fund. A mutual fund normally represents millions of dollars from investors who want to spread their risk and opportunity for gain over many stocks. Specialized mutual funds can invest in sport stocks, social equity stocks, global stocks, or aggressive growth stocks. A mutual fund might have millions of shares in hundreds of stocks, and professional administrators of each fund analyze each stock and try to pick the best time to buy or sell the fund's shares.

Another technique used to reduce the risk of investing in stocks is dollar cost averaging, in which an investor buys shares on a routine basis in the same company regardless of the price. Through this technique, an investor may purchase shares of a stock at $4.00 one month, $6.00 another, and maybe $3.00 in yet another month. Over time, this technique is one of the best ways to lower the risks of paying too much for stocks because the purchases are made at both the highest prices and the lowest prices, a practice that averages out the price paid over time.

Mutual fund and stock pickers often try to focus on key stocks, such as those in the Dow Jones Industrial Average, which lists some of the most famous stocks in the world. After Bank of America and Chevron were added in 2008, the Dow had the following industrial sectors (Shell, 2008):

Sector	Percentage of Dow
Industrials	22.2
Financials	13.9
Technology	13.0
Consumer staples	11.6
Energy	10.8
Consumer discretionary	9.5
Health care	8.7
Materials	5.3
Telecom services	4.9

This list shows that sport stocks are not considered a major player on the stock exchange. Nevertheless, sport stocks can be valuable and important. One Dow-listed stock with a direct connection to the sport industry is Walt Disney Company.

No matter what index is used, if any, those who invest in stock are often concerned about how stock prices change and whether they are truly an accurate indicator of value. Mark Cuban, owner of the Dallas Mavericks, blogged just before a large market valuation drop: "Wall Street is now a huge mathematical game of chess where individual companies are just pawns" (Mehta, Thomasson, & Barrett, 2010). The ability of the stock market to represent true value is a theory promoted by the efficient market hypothesis, which holds that stock prices reflect the best available information and as such, stocks are rationally valued. Stock market activity over the past several years has highlighted that the market might not act rationally. Computer trading has shown this flaw and has sharply changed the market. Behaviorists have another theory: Investors hang on to losing stocks not because of their value but because they do not want to admit that they are defeated. The same theory holds that people buy stock not because the company's earnings are increasing

but because the stock price is increasing (Waggoner, 2011).

PREFERRED STOCK

Preferred stock earns its name from the dividend preference that it carries in relation to common stock. Although a corporation might not issue a dividend to common stock shareholders, it may be bound to provide dividends to preferred stock shareholders. The dividend is cumulative in that if it is not paid to holders of preferred stock in a given year, the corporation will owe two years' worth of dividends the next year. The dividend to the preferred shareholders needs to be paid before common stockholders can receive their dividends. The requirement to pay a dividend, if one is issued, makes a preferred stock a blend between a bond with a required interest payment and a stock with its associated equity benefits. The requirement to pay a fixed dividend increases the issuing company's **financial leverage**. In the eyes of lenders, preferred stock represents equity and is shown in the equity section of the balance sheet.

Other benefits that are available for preferred stockholders can include (Bogen, 1966)

- the right to dividend payments before common stock shareholders receive dividend payments;
- preference as to assets in distribution;
- voting power for preferred stock, available under limited circumstances;
- strong redemption provisions;
- subscription privileges to future stock offerings; and
- the right to convert preferred stock to common stock.

Some investors rely on dividend income as their primary return on an equity investment. For these investors, preferred shares would be the most prudent investment because preferred stock shareholders are entitled to a dividend payment before common stock shareholders receive any dividends.

Regarding preference in distribution, some corporations specifically authorize preferred stockholders to receive the first of any return upon liquidation of a corporation's assets. If no such preference is provided for in the corporate bylaws, all classes of stock share equally in any distributions. Preferred stockholders often perceive their investment as riskier than bonds because the preferred shareholders' claims are subordinate to those of bondholders in the event that the company is liquidated. Furthermore, bondholders are more likely than preferred shareholders to continue receiving disbursements during hard times (Brigham & Gapenski, 1994).

The right to vote is given to preferred stockholders in limited situations, such as when the board of directors fails to pay a required dividend over a specified number of quarters. Preferred stockholders can also vote on issues affecting their status when dividends are in **arrears**.

The conversion privilege attached to some preferred stocks can be an attractive feature. Assume that Under Armour issues a preferred stock that can be converted two to one. Such a provision means that one preferred share can be exchanged at a given time for two common shares. Assume that Under Armour's common stock is selling at $20, but management decides to raise $5 million by selling 100,000 shares of preferred stock at $50 par value. At the $50 price, converting the preferred stock to common stock would not be worthwhile. If the common stock subsequently rose to $30 a share, however, converting the preferred stock to common stock would be advantageous (Bogen, 1966); the shareholder would receive two common shares valued at a combined $60, compared with the initial investment of $50 per preferred share. A $10 profit would result from the conversion.

If the conversion had occurred when the common shares were valued at only $20 per share, the shareholder would have lost $10 in the conversion process. Thus, conversion typically occurs only when the conversion process will increase the investor's return. If preferred shares are not converted to common shares, they can continue to pay the required dividends, or they might be called. Preferred shares could be issued with a **call provision**. The call provision might require that 2% of the shares be retired each year. A **sinking fund** could be established to help pay for buying back the preferred shares. Under a 2% buyback plan, the preferred shares would mature in a maximum of 50 years.

Preferred stock can also pose a risk if certain attached provisions used to help sell the stock can also be used as a weapon. In one case, a small meatpacking company sold preferred stock with a condition that no bonds could be issued without the approval of 75% of the preferred stockholders (Bogen, 1966). Although the restriction was onerous, management thought that it would be a valuable tool to help sell the stock to skeptical buyers. Years later when the company needed funds for expansion, it discovered that a larger competitor had purchased more than 25% of the preferred stock and could block the proposed sale of new bonds. This situation forced the smaller company to merge with the larger company on unfavorable terms.

SHAREHOLDERS' RIGHTS

In the United States the basic rights and obligations of stockholders are set forth in the laws of the state in which the business is incorporated. Incorporation is the formal process of applying to be registered as a stock-issuing corporation. Each state has different laws. A disproportionately large number of businesses are incorporated in several states, including Delaware and Nevada, because they offer favorable tax or liability laws designed to attract corporations. Besides being spelled out in specific state laws, stockholders' rights can also be found in the corporation's bylaws, charter, or articles of incorporation.

Stockholders have the following legal rights (Investopedia staff, 2010):

- To receive evidence of ownership such as a stock certificate (see figure 9.1)
- To transfer the stock freely, within limited rules
- To exercise the right to vote in person or by proxy as set forth in the corporation's bylaws
- To receive dividends and other disbursements on a pro rata basis according to the number of shares held
- To receive disbursements on a pro rata basis when a partial or complete liquidation of corporate assets occurs
- To bring action on behalf of the corporation against board members who do not act in the corporation's best interest (commonly referred to as stockholders' derivative actions)
- To obtain information from the corporation to help safeguard the stockholders' investment (such as an annual report)
- To subscribe pro rata to new shares of company stocks when authorized by law (commonly referred to as stockholders' preemptive right)

As an owner of the business, a stockholder has the right to participate in profits earned by the company if the board of directors approves such

Figure 9.1 Example of a stock certificate.

Reprinted by permission of the United States Basketball League, Inc.

a payment. Whether to issue a dividend is an important decision for the board. If a dividend is declared, most investors see that decision as a sign that the business is doing well because the business is able to cover its internal fiscal needs and still has money available to pay the shareholders. In contrast, some investors and analysts may view paying a dividend as a sign that the business has no good investment prospects in which to reinvest its additional capital.

The board of directors is responsible for making the final determination about where the extra funds, if any, should be invested, and shareholders assume that the board makes those decisions with the shareholders' interest in mind. The board of directors is elected by the shareholders to run the company on behalf of the shareholders. A successful board does more than just pay dividends to shareholders. A board is judged according to whether its decisions increase the value of the stock.

The **preemptive right** is one of a stockholder's most important rights. Preemptive rights protect a stockholder's power of control and prevent dilution of the stock's value. Suppose that investor A owns all 1,000 shares of outstanding stock in a fitness center and that the shares are valued at $100 each. The market value of the company would be $100,000. If the company sold an additional 1,000 shares at $40 each, the total market value would be $140,000. When the total value is divided by the total number of shares, the stock value drops to $70 per share. To prevent such a loss for the prior investor and to prevent a windfall for new investors, the preemptive right gives investor A the right to buy the new stock before anyone else.

The right to exercise control over a business is one of the primary purposes of the preemptive right. If you own 10% of the business, you are entitled to purchase 10% of the newly issued shares. You have the right to exercise the same amount of control over the business that you did before, even if new shares dilute the total number of outstanding shares. The right to control a corporation is one of the most basic stockholder rights, because if you have an investment in something you want to be able to protect that investment.

Stockholders can control a corporation's direction in several ways. These include voting power, holding companies, and defensive tactics.

Voting Power

A major right for corporate owners is the right of certain stockholders to control the corporation through their voting power. Stockholders have the right to elect board members who then hire the company's management team. Smaller companies may have their major shareholders serving as owners, board members, and even managers. Larger businesses have board members who are elected for terms of only several years to allow shareholders the opportunity to elect new board members. Board members are typically elected annually. Each shareholder is entitled to one vote for each share held. Control can be exercised by a large shareholder such as Mr. Jacobs, who controlled 99% of the Cleveland Indians' voting stock when they were publicly traded. Others can also exercise control, such as a block of family members who own significant shares in a business, a group of unrelated investors (from individuals to banks, corporations, foundations, and pension plans) that own a large voting bloc, a board member who might wield coercive control over fellow board members, or even bankers or financiers who can exercise considerable control.

Regardless of who is in direct control, most larger businesses with traded stocks rely on the proxy process for voting on key matters such as electing new board members or changing the bylaws or articles of incorporation of the business. A proxy is basically a power of attorney given by a registered stockholder, who appoints someone else to vote on her behalf. Proxies are regularly mailed to all stockholders before the meeting of the board of directors.

The Securities and Exchange Commission (SEC) has detailed laws to ensure equality and a democratic voting process for all shareholders of voting stocks. Thus, some regulations cover the process of hearing dissenting opinions or proposals and the requirement that management summarize these proposals in its proxy solicitation statement (Bogen, 1966). Although proxy fights typically do not occur on a regular basis, they can occur for a business in transition or one facing financial peril. A proxy fight can also occur when one company is trying to take over another company. A strong philosophical rift between key members of the management team can also lead to a proxy fight. Stockholders can be contacted by a marketing company that has been hired to try to sway their vote through letters, newspaper advertisements, or, in the case of large shareholders, personal phone calls.

Holding Companies

Besides controlling the board of directors, parties can obtain control by investing in a company. A company that has one million outstanding shares can be effectively controlled by anyone who owns 50.01% of the voting stock. Thus, a company can purchase 50.01% of another company and then effectively control the purchased company. A company does not even need to use its own money to acquire a controlling interest. In fact, some companies have been leveraged through another company, such as a holding company, that uses the financial resources of the company that it is trying to control to help issue bonds or nonvoting preferred stock to help finance the purchase. Through this technique, a holding company can purchase controlling shares of several businesses. A fitness center, for example, could purchase a majority share of several fitness clubs to develop a fitness network without having to purchase each club in its entirety. Thus, the fitness center could grow without spending the money to buy each club that they want in their network.

The same basic issues associated with holding companies started gaining exposure over the last several years in the form of shell companies. The shell company process occurs when a company is initially formed and incorporated under the applicable laws in their jurisdiction. The company then gets listed, often on NASDAQ's over-the-counter exchange. The company might go out of business, but instead of closing it offers itself as a shell company for another company interested in raising capital through a stock offering. Through this approach, a new company does not need to go through all the official incorporating process and resulting scrutiny, because they are not incorporating, just joining forces with an already listed company. Since 2006 more than 150 firms based in China alone entered the United States securities market through these transactions, which are called reverse mergers (McCoy & Chu, 2011). These companies have no operations in the United States and just took over companies already listed for public stock trading. To reduce fraud and investor scams, the SEC developed new rules in 2011 to strengthen requirements for international companies attempting a reverse merger.

Defensive Tactics

Other businesses or individuals often purchase sport businesses. These transactions are often amiable, as when private parties purchase the shares of a publicly traded company. This scenario occurred when Larry Dolan purchased the publicly traded Cleveland Indians by buying the outstanding shares of the team from Jacobs and other shareholders for $323 million (Kurdziel, 2000). But not all purchases or attempts to change a corporation are welcomed. An unwelcome attempt to purchase the shares of a company is called a **hostile takeover**. Hostile takeovers can be vigorously contested. Each side or even several suitors that are trying to win a bidding war can commit significant funds. At other times, the company targeted for acquisition does not have the resources to fight and has to accept the takeover without any recourse. Most hostile takeovers, however, are fought in court or financial markets if the company is not able to implement any defensive tactics.

If a company cannot change its board or acquire other companies to make itself less attractive as a takeover option, it can use other techniques to appear less desirable for a hostile takeover. **Golden parachute** contracts that require huge payments to executives if they are terminated can make a company less attractive. If a potential suitor discovers that it might be necessary to pay an extra $20 million to former executives, a deal can quickly die.

Stock purchase **warrants** can also be used as a defensive tool. Warrants that can be exercised at a price not much higher than the current market price can help discourage efforts by outsiders to acquire control. As an outside company attempts to buy shares on the open market, the price of the shares will rise. Management, however, can buy shares at the fixed warrant price, which will allow them to purchase more shares. The mere fact that management has such an option can dissuade a potential hostile takeover. The potential for a takeover can also be affected if the corporation is in financial trouble and stockholder assistance is necessary for it to survive or a suitor is needed to save it from bankruptcy.

Although shareholders can benefit from profits paid out through dividends, shareholders can also face losses that diminish the value of their investment. Stockholders cannot be punished or forced to pay more money if the business faces economic losses, but the share value can decline or the company can go out of business, rendering the stock valueless. Shareholders, much like any other business owner, have responsibilities for business losses. As discussed in chapter 4, shareholders are not personally liable for a corporation's debts, but they

ADVANTAGES AND DISADVANTAGES OF GOING PUBLIC

Advantages

- Owners are allowed to diversify their investments instead of having all their assets locked into the company.
- A liquid asset is created (a privately held company would be harder to sell).
- Going public helps raise new cash for growth.
- A value for the company is established based on the combined value of outstanding shares.

Disadvantages

- Increased operating costs are associated with quarterly and yearly reporting requirements.
- The company is required to disclose sensitive data that a competitor can use against the business.
- Self-dealing and nepotism are not allowed.
- The value of shares can drop if the market for the shares is slow and they are not traded enough, or if the company or its sector falls into disfavor.
- Loss of control of the business is possible if investors acquire enough stock.

Data from Brigham and Gapenski 1994.

can be asked to contribute additional funds to keep the corporation from going bankrupt. Although no shareholder can be forced to buy additional shares, they sometimes do so to help the business through rough times.

GOING PUBLIC

The first step for any corporation is deciding whether to go public. The decision is not simple; in fact it is expensive and time consuming. Chapter 5 (and the Advantages of Forming a Corporation in Delaware sidebar) outlines the advantages and disadvantages of the corporation as a legal entity.

Besides the advantages and disadvantages of going public, specific advantages and disadvantages are associated with financing through the issuance of common stock (see the Advantages and Disadvantages of Going Public sidebar).

After a corporation decides to go public, the second step is to determine whether the stock will be publicly traded. Going public is the process of making a company's ownership available to new potential owners and investors. But issuing stock and going public does not mean that the shares will be available to the general public. Whereas most large corporations are publicly owned and traded, small corporations are often owned by only a few shareholders, such as family members. Numerous stocks are privately held, or closely held, and only a few owners own all the shares. Publicly held stocks are made available to an unlimited number of investors as long as shares are available for purchase.

The company also has to decide whether it wants the shares listed on a major exchange or wants to have unlisted shares traded on the over-the-counter (OTC) market. Some companies prefer to avoid the regulations imposed by larger listing exchanges and thus opt for being unlisted. To be listed, a company has to pay a small fee and meet the minimum entrance requirements of an exchange. The company also needs to examine who the potential investors are. Institutional investors, such as pension funds or insurance companies, own about 55% of all common stocks and account for 80% of all stock transactions (Brigham & Gapenski, 1994).

After a decision is made to sell shares to the general public, the shares will go through three possible phases. The first phase is the **initial public offering** (**IPO**), when shares are sold on the new-issue market. The first time that shares are ever sold is called the **private offering**. The purpose of the IPO is to raise new capital for the business and put money into the owner's hands. After shares have been sold during the IPO, the shares move into the second phase, the secondary market. In the secondary market, stocks are bought and sold for all publicly traded businesses after the IPO. On the first day that Under Armour stock was issued, the stock was part of the new-issue market. Any subsequent transactions would occur in the secondary market, with one exception. If Under Armour decided to issue more shares, those shares would move into the third phase. The third phase is the primary market, which exists for companies that have already had an IPO but want to issue more shares to generate additional funds.

New shares can be sold to five possible types of buyers:

- Existing shareholders on a pro rata basis
- Investment bankers, who will then sell the shares to the general public in an IPO
- Several major purchasers in a private placement
- Employees in an employee stock purchase plan
- Buyers in a dividend reinvestment plan

Selling shares to existing shareholders is fairly simple and entails letting shareholders know when the shares will be available and at what price. Shareholders then have the opportunity to indicate whether they will subscribe. This process is called **preemption**. Through preemption a shareholder has the first right to buy new shares. Shareholders value this right because it prevents share dilution. For example, if you own 10% of Nike you hold significant power. If Nike were to issue several million more shares to expand (such as to help pay for building a new factory), you could maintain your 10% stake by purchasing 10% of the new stocks. If you pass on making this purchase, the new shares will result in share dilution, so your stake in the company might decline to 7% or 8% and you will have fewer votes at shareholders' meetings.

Investment bankers operate as intermediaries to help facilitate the marketing and transfer of stock ownership. A large investor such as a mutual fund or a pension fund might contact an investment banker to secure a large position in an IPO. These large buyers often indicate in advance that they are interested in purchasing shares. Thus, the issuing corporation knows in advance that a certain minimum number of shares will be purchased through the investment bankers.

A private-placement transaction occurs when one or more investors purchase most shares in a company. One advantage of such a sale is the lower flotation costs associated with finding potential buyers, because one major potential shareholder is already identified. Flotation costs are the costs to sell shares to the general public. If a major purchaser is identified in advance, then less effort and cost need to be expended because a majority of the shares are already sold. Another major advantage is the ability to circumvent SEC requirements, because shares do not need to go through SEC registration. Although the prospects of gaining a large partner are great, private placements do not comply with SEC requirements, so it is often hard to sell the shares except to another large investor or institutional investor. Private placements are discussed in greater detail later in this chapter.

Employees can obtain an equity interest in their place of employment by buying shares in the company. The process in which employees buy stock in a company is often referred to as an **employee stock ownership plan** (ESOP). In these plans, the company often uses its own profits to buy shares for the employees. Over time, employees buy enough shares that they eventually own the company. Because Congress believes that employees should have the right to buy into their employer, the federal tax code provides specific benefits for companies engaged in ESOPs. Besides being able to deduct the interest on debt used to acquire the stock, a company can deduct some of the principal used to acquire the stock and can also deduct the dividend payments made to the employee stockholders. In addition to offering tax benefits, an ESOP can help prevent takeovers by other firms because the employees own a significant number of shares.

Another benefit of an ESOP is that it can replace the employee retirement program. Thus, instead of pouring millions into a pension fund, the company can issue and then buy shares for its employees. The employees obtain a valuable asset that may increase over time, and the employer obtains a new avenue for selling additional shares. The final benefit associated with an ESOP is the potential for increased employee morale. Employees are more prone to work harder when they know that their productivity will benefit themselves fiscally. If employees work harder and generate increased income, the company benefits, and as owners, the employees will eventually benefit.

Although ESOPs provide significant benefits, they can also have some disadvantages. The biggest disadvantage is the dynamic shift in power within a business as employees become owners. Assembly line workers who are used to being told what to do might now have a say in how the CEO acts. Labor negotiations can become tricky because management must try to produce a fair labor agreement with union workers who might also be shareholders, and the more money that is paid in salary, the lower the profits are for the company. The government (Department of Labor) can also cancel an ESOP if it was designed to fight a takeover and was not properly developed. Another concern arises in relation to retirees and pension holders whose entire **portfolios** might be composed of shares in the company. As long as the company is doing well, everyone will be happy. If the stock declines, however, the result can be devastating. A retiree could see his portfolio decline from $500,000 to $100,000 if the stock loses 80% of its value as a result of a negative industry analysis, for example.

A **dividend reinvestment plan** allows a shareholder to transfer all dividends back into the company to obtain more shares.

Assume that a company paid a $0.50 dividend in a given quarter and that you had 20 shares and reinvested the dividend to purchase additional shares. If the shares were selling for $10 each at that time, you would receive one additional share rather than a dividend check for $10.

Because the math usually does not involve round numbers such as these, a shareholder normally obtains a percentage of a share. Thus, in a given quarter a shareholder might receive 0.756 of a share through dividend reinvestment. After the next dividend amount is reinvested, she might have built up to one complete share and started working on the next complete share.

Prospectus

Before making a stock offering, the issuer or underwriter needs to develop a **prospectus** describing the company and all the potential risks and benefits associated with purchasing the stock. The prospectus often contains information on key employees and members of the board, information on how the funds will be used and the products that will be sold, audited financial statements, the sales forecast, pro forma budgets, the dividend policy, and related documentation. The audited financial statement, prepared by an independent accounting firm, describes the business and the management structure and explains what the managers are paid, who the principal shareholders are, what the underwriting agreement is, and who is involved in the stock sales syndicate.

The SEC has to approve the prospectus before it can be sent to potential investors. But the issuer or underwriter has the opportunity to distribute rough drafts of the prospectus before SEC approval to help generate investor interest. The preapproved document is called a **red herring**. The red herring, along with company executives, is then shopped around in a marketing blitz by the underwriter through visits with potential major investors such as institutional investors. Significant oral information can be passed on in this process, but no written material other than the prospectus can be given, and no sales can be made at these meetings. After the SEC obtains all the necessary information, it can approve the prospectus for general distribution.

Selling Shares

Stocks have value only if they are purchased. New issues need to be priced at a level that will interest potential investors. If the stock is priced too high, investors may see this as a sign that the stock is out of their league. Other investors will see a high issue price as a sign of value. In contrast, people may perceive a low price either as an indication of an inferior company or as an attempt to garner ownership from smaller investors. Traditionally, stock prices for new issues are based on the average price of similar stock issues (Spiro, 1996). Issuing new shares for existing stocks is simpler because the current market value for the shares can be used as the benchmark price. If investors believe the stock is correctly valued, they can purchase at the offering price or wait to see whether investors bid the price up or down.

Current stockholders, institutional investors, investment bankers, potential investors, and even current employees can purchase stocks. Current stockholders might be the first choice for many corporations; some laws require that current shareholders have the first right to buy stocks so that they can maintain their pro rata interest in earnings, assets, and voting rights. The process of offering stocks first to existing shareholders is called a privileged subscription. Shareholders often find this privilege an important benefit, similar to receiving dividends.

Shareholders are given a right to subscribe to shares before they are offered to the general public. These shares are normally priced a little lower than the price at which the general public could purchase the same shares. The right might allow a shareholder to buy one share of the new stock for every three shares of existing stock owned by the shareholder. But shareholders do not need to purchase stocks through the right and can in fact sell their rights on the open market to others who would like to buy new shares at a lower price. No matter who exercises the right, the right becomes valueless after the subscription date expires.

ADVANTAGES AND DISADVANTAGES OF FINANCING THROUGH STOCK

Advantages

- No fixed cost is associated with issuing stock, whereas a company that issues bonds or commercial paper (see chapter 10) will have to allocate a fixed amount in the budget for debt service.
- Common stocks do not carry any fixed maturity date at which they need to be paid.
- Issuing common stock can help raise new capital without affecting the company's bond rating.
- At times, such as when interest rates are low and the demand for bonds is also low, selling common stock is easier.

Disadvantages

- Issuing bonds or commercial paper provides a predictable fixed cost for repayment. In contrast, stocks represent a stake in the company's future profits.
- The costs associated with issuing stocks and all ancillary activities can make issuing common stock more expensive than issuing preferred stock or debt instruments.
- Some investors may see issuing new stock as a negative sign that the company needs to sell more of itself to survive.

Data from Brigham and Gapenski 1994.

Although subscription rights can attract some purchases from dedicated investors, the issuer has no guarantees. Issuing stock can be like throwing a party—all the key people may be there, but perhaps no one will be there. To ensure that the stock is sold, an issuing company often uses the assistance of an investment banker to underwrite the stock offering. An underwriting is similar to an insurance policy. If sales are good and all the shares are bought, then the investment banker will not have to purchase any shares. If sales are mediocre, however, the investment banker may need to buy a significant number of shares. Investment bankers charge either a commission or a set fee for their services. Investment bankers often attempt to sell stock concurrently with the issuing company to hedge the prospect of their having to buy a large number of shares.

Investment bankers are the primary vehicle for independent sales. The services offered by investment bankers or investment houses include the following (Bogen, 1966):

♦ Giving advice on the security type to offer and the exact terms of the issue

♦ Giving assistance in underwriting a security issue

♦ Purchasing a security issue outright

♦ Helping a company comply with state and federal requirements

♦ Distributing new securities to investors

♦ Helping stabilize the price of a new issue by buying shares in the marketplace to support interest in the issue

♦ Providing additional advice after a security is issued

Private Placement

Private placement can occur in the borrowing market (the bond market, in particular) as a loan is obtained from private parties. Similarly, private placement can occur with the issuing of stocks when stocks are sold by at least one institutional investor. Life insurance companies have been involved in numerous private placements because of their strong **purchasing power**. Companies that issue stocks are often interested in pursuing private-placement sale of their shares because doing so allows them to avoid some SEC rules and reduce their marketing costs drastically.

Because the SEC knows that companies like to avoid stringent rules if possible, it has developed a two-part test for private offerings. The first is a

consideration of the potential investor's sophistication. The investor must have enough knowledge to understand the risks and rewards inherent in the offering. The second component is a limitation of potential buyers to a maximum of 35 investors. Private-placement securities have other restrictions such as being restricted from resale to the public market for at least two years. Private placements are covered in detail in the next section.

Initial Public Offering

A business needs to hit the primary market with an IPO to launch its stock activities. The IPO can range from informal to extremely formal, depending on the stock offering. Before an IPO can be undertaken, the business needs to formalize its existence as a corporation. Corporation issues are covered in detail in chapter 4. We note here that a business' articles of incorporation specify how many shares can be issued. The corporate bylaws might specify how shares can be transferred and when shareholders can inspect the corporate records, as well as delineate similar rules affecting issuing and selling shares (Cheeseman, 2010).

For a full-scale common stock issue, a company first must file a registration statement with the SEC. The registration documents are lengthy and require considerable time and expense to complete. The SEC can suspend or prohibit the offering if it finds any misleading or inaccurate statements. After filing for registration, the company and its underwriting syndicate of investment bankers distribute a preliminary prospectus. This prospectus could provide as follows:

> A registration statement relating to these securities has been filed with the SEC but has not become effective. Information contained herein is subject to completion or amendment. These securities may not be sold nor may offers to buy be accepted prior to the time the registration statement becomes effective. This prospectus shall not constitute an offer to sell or the solicitation of an offer to buy, nor shall there be any sale of these securities in any state in which such offer, solicitation, or sale would be unlawful prior to registration or qualification under the securities laws of any such state. (*IPO basics*, 1999)

After the preliminary prospectus is issued, the company's top officials must go on a road show to promote the stock sale. During this time the

SEC reviews the registration and might request additional information. If the SEC approves the registration, the company and its syndicate need to establish a price and the number of shares that will be sold. The final prospectus and any necessary amendments are distributed when the stocks are made available to the public. The IPO closes when the money is received and the stock certificates are delivered, usually about three days after trading has started. The money is received about two to three and a half months after the start of the IPO process (*IPO basics*, 1999).

The decision to issue stocks is not to be taken lightly. The costs are normally steep. In addition, determining that a stock offering is the proper direction for a company is not enough. The company also has to determine what priority will be given to stock. This prioritization can be seen in preferred stock and the various rights given to different classes of shareholders.

Failed Offerings

Every year, many companies go out of business. Even companies that have issued stock can face financial troubles. Publicly traded companies that flounder can find themselves being delisted by one of the exchanges. In 1998 Golden Bear Golf, a company primarily owned by Jack Nicklaus, faced some hard times, including suits by shareholders claiming that the company had underreported 1997 losses by $20 million (Mullen, 1998). Furthermore, the company's assets had decreased so that it no longer met the NASDAQ capital requirements (at least $4 million in assets), and it was delisted. **Delisting** meant the shares would no longer be traded on NASDAQ; shareholders would have to trade their shares on the less prestigious OTC Bulletin Board or the pink sheets (the least formal trading market for NASDAQ, which handles shares that are infrequently traded, such as private-placement or Regulation D shares) ("Nicklaus company's stock," 1998). When the stock had been initially offered in 1996, the company was able to raise $37 million. Golden Bear sold its string of golf centers in 1998 and then shut down Paragon, the golf course construction subsidiary that had generated the questionable accounting practices. After the restructuring, the company was taken private in 2000, when it was bought by Nicklaus and his family (*Golden Bear Golf*, n.d.).

Although the Golden Bear example focuses on a sport-specific stock, 17 publicly traded Internet companies were delisted by 2006. Some sport companies such as the Boston Celtics are no longer traded on exchanges, but that was a voluntary exit from an exchange. Delisting refers to the process of kicking a stock out of an exchange because it failed to meet exchange requirements. As highlighted in chapter 8, Bally was delisted for failing to meet NYSE requirements. Delisting often occurs when a publicly traded sport business files for liquidation bankruptcy under Chapter 7 of the bankruptcy code. In 2011 Cybex (a fitness equipment manufacturer) asked NASDAQ not to delist the company after it lost a $66 million jury verdict in a product liability case. At the time of writing this text, NASDAQ had not yet decided whether Cybex would be delisted, but the stock shares were selling for only 99 cents a share (Club Industry staff, 2011).

Common or preferred stocks are sold when a company is interested in selling ownership or equity rights to others for needed funds. The primary benefit of such an approach is the elimination of the need to pay a set interest payment even during rough times. But many companies do not want to dilute their ownership interest and prefer to finance growth through debt instruments. We have already discussed bank loans and various types of nonbank loans. An additional strategy for stronger companies would be to issue bonds, which we discuss in the next chapter. Note that nonprofit organizations such as college athletic departments, public schools, and public park and recreation departments cannot issue common stocks, but they can issue bonds and obtain additional funding from other sources.

INCREASING STOCK VALUES

After selling shares, a corporation and all the employees are responsible for increasing the value of the stock. One of the foremost benefits associated with buying stocks is the potential for increased equity value. If the business is doing well financially, it increases in value. A business increases in value through a rise in the value of its shares. Note that a rise in stock value does not necessarily mean that a company is healthy. After a reverse merger, shares of ProElite, Inc. rose 480% in a year to $14.50 in 2007, which represented a market capitalization of $673 million. This high valuation applied even though the company had only $2 million in revenue and $12 million in losses in the first half of 2007 (Barrett, 2007). ProElite held 21 Mixed Martial Arts (MMA) events before it collapsed in October 2008 under the weight of a $55 million debt accrued in 20 months of operations.

In 2010 Stratus Media Group Inc (OTCBB: SMDI) acquired ProElite and is now running events under the ProElite name (Marrocco, 2010).

As noted previously, the success of any management team is based on the extent to which it can increase the value of the company's stock and provide dividends to the company's owners. You can examine this success by looking at the company's PE ratio, the ratio of the stock price to the company earnings. A high ratio indicates that a company's stock is selling for much more than the per share earnings. A stock with a high PE ratio reflects strong investor demand, although the company has not produced enough earnings to justify the high stock price. Thus, a hot stock can have a high PE ratio until its earnings meet expectations or the share price declines. If the earnings of such a company decrease, the value of the stock could plummet, thus greatly affecting the PE ratio.

The rapid rise in the stock market during 2000, propelled by Internet companies, provides such an example. Most prominent stocks in the largest traditional companies were trading at 20 times their earnings in 1999. Similarly, the top NASDAQ shares in 1995 were trading at 20 times their earnings. But the demand for Internet stocks and the low earnings of Internet companies pushed the PE ratio of the NASDAQ 100 to around 90 times earnings in March 2000 (Browning, 2000). At the same time, the PE ratio for the Standard & Poor's 500 was around 25 and for the Dow it was around 20. The PE ratio of the World Wrestling Federation (now WWE) in February 2002 was 19.07 (*Yahoo! Finance—WWF*, 2002). The stock price fluctuated a bit for a number of years, and in 2011 the stock was selling at a PE ratio of 17.07.

PE ratios can show significant fluctuation. Yahoo had a PE ratio of almost 1,000 at the start of 1999, and it shot up to over 2,000 just one year later (Browning, 2000). By 2011 Yahoo's PE ratio was at 18.82, which meant that the stock price was much closer to representing the true value and earnings of the company. Although WWE was trading at a PE ratio of 25.29 in 2007 (compared with 19.07 in 2002), Yahoo had undergone significant changes, and its revenue skyrocketed so that by 2007 the PE ratio was 36.82 (compared with 236.71 in 2002). By 2002 Yahoo's PE ratio had settled at 236.71 (*Yahoo! Finance—YHOO*, 2002). Stocks can change quickly over the years. A stock might increase so much in value that the company splits the stock so that the shares are not as expensive, as some of the Internet companies did when their stocks were trading in the several-hundred-dollar range.

Shares can go up in price because of a multitude of factors. One primary category that affects stock prices is external factors. Examples of external factors that can affect the value of professional sports teams include the following:

♦ Antitrust decisions affecting the league

♦ Labor disputes and unwillingness of players to cross the picket lines to play

♦ Environmental regulations affecting the arena

♦ A change in workplace safety rules that apply to operating the team

♦ New rules related to employment practices in the workplace, such as the classification of food vendors as employees rather than independent contractors

♦ The folding of a rival league or the success of another league

Stock prices can also be affected by internal strategic policy decisions. Examples of such decisions include whether to

♦ trade a star player or hire a new coach,

♦ increase the number of preseason games,

♦ borrow money for expansion or issue more stocks,

♦ declare a dividend, and

♦ consolidate television and radio broadcasting operations in house.

Teams that go public sell shares for an attractive price (normally under $25 per share) in odd lots to fans who wish to buy a few shares and frame the certificate as part of a sports memorabilia collection (Much, 1996).

The Cleveland Indians made a splash in the stock market, but they were just as quickly taken off the market. The Tribe's shares were doing well in the 1999 baseball season until the team lost in the division series. The day after the series ended, the stock declined 4.9% ("Go figure," 1999). Several days later, a deal was announced in which an Ohio attorney (Larry Dolan) agreed to buy the team for $320 million, including assuming $35 million in debt (Walker, 1999). The planned purchase to take the Indians private only two years after they had gone public would mean a significant windfall for shareholders. At a price of over $22 per share if the purchase was approved, shareholders could have earned a 50% return on their investment in less than two years (Walker, 1999). The reward was worth the wait for investors who initially purchased shares for $15 each but then saw the stock drop to $10 per share for several months until the team's primary shareholder, Jacobs, announced his intent to sell.

Publicly traded professional teams are found throughout the world. The owners of Germany's 1995 and 1996 champion soccer team, BV Borussia 09 Dortmund, voted to become a corporation and issue stock to the public. Publicly traded soccer teams exist throughout Europe (see stock chart in chapter 4). England has a "Kick-Index" that tracks 20 soccer stocks in the United Kingdom. The index reached its highest point in 1997, but through 1999 it declined 35%. The only team that showed financial strength at that time was Manchester United, which was worth about a billion dollars before the 2000 market crash ("German soccer," 1999). Manchester was the first soccer team listed on the London Stock Exchange back in 1991. That value was proved in 2005 when American Malcolm Glazer purchased Manchester United for more than $1 billion, including debt, and delisted the team. Manchester United planned to raise US$1 billion in an initial public offering (IPO) set for October 2011 on the Singapore Exchange to expand the club's Asia business and pay down club debt. The club saw its earnings before interest, tax, depreciation, and amortization for the year to June 30, 2011, rising 9.6% on year to £110.9 million, and total revenue climbed 15.7% to £331.4 million ("Manchester United posts higher earnings," 2011). The team was hoping to grow supporters and investors in Asia but ultimately sold fewer shares on the NYSE in 2012.

Although companies interested in launching an IPO are usually financially strong, some businesses try to take advantage of a strong stock market to offer an IPO that might not be very strong. For example, a San Diego A-league soccer team, the Flash, filed preliminary documents with the SEC to go public. The announcement came even though the team was losing money (more than $795,000 in the first six months after going public), had attendance of around only 3,000 per game, and had $67,196 in the bank (Palazzo, 1999). By 2002 the shares were trading for $0.17 each ("Stock quote," 2002).

That year was the last year of the club in its publicly traded state; it was resurrected a year later as a private group playing in a lower division.

Sport entities besides professional teams also issued stock in the late 1990s to take advantage of the IPO craze. Although numerous Internet-based companies were the primary beneficiaries of such IPOs, traditional businesses were also successful. WWF (now WWE) raised almost $200 million in a 1999 public offering, fueled by its success in such programs as *Raw* and *SmackDown* on national television ("Ready to wrestle," 1999).

Some people buy shares in publicly traded sport businesses to impress their friends. The Green Bay Packers' shares are an excellent example of such a purchase because the shares issued in 1997 have little value on the open market (see next section). Other stocks have more value, but it might be harder to place a value on these shares other than the actual market value. Ancillary benefits, however, can be significant. For example, people who owned shares in the Tribune Company may have purchased them not only for their investment value but also to be eligible for the annual shareholders games at Wrigley Field for the Tribune-owned Chicago Cubs (Newberry, 2001).

SPONSORSHIPS INCREASE STOCK VALUES

Is sponsoring a major professional league worth the investment? A sales increase is one positive indicator, but stock values can also increase. According to a 2005 study, sponsoring a professional league can result in increased stock prices for the sponsors. The study examined 53 publicly traded companies whose stocks gained $257 million in market value ($13.6 billion in economic value) in the first trading week after announcing sponsorship deals with the NBA, NFL, NHL, MLB, or PGA (Howard, 2005). Companies that sponsored the NFL or MLB had slight gains (because of the high costs of such deals) compared with the larger spikes for companies that sponsored the other leagues. Smaller companies, those with smaller market shares, and those associated with products that had a clear connection to the league being sponsored had larger increases in stock value (Howard, 2005).

INFLUENCE OF INTERNAL AND EXTERNAL FACTORS ON PUBLICLY TRADED SPORTS ORGANIZATIONS

Internal and external factors have played a part in the success and failure of several publicly traded sports organizations (Much, 1996):

- The Cleveland Cavaliers went public in 1970 for $5 per share, but shares dropped to as low as $0.50 per share in 1982. The team went private in 1984 for $1.25 per share.
- The New England Patriots went public in 1960 for $5 per share and went private in 1976 for $15 per share.

- The Baltimore Orioles went on a roller-coaster ride in the 1970s; the stock price ranged from $8 to $25.50. In 1979 the team went private, and the liquidation value earned shareholders $49.60 per share over a three-year period.
- The Milwaukee Bucks went public in 1968 for $5 per share and went private for $12 per share 11 years later.

SPORT STOCKS

Stock offerings in professional sport are not new. The Green Bay Packers sold their first 1,000 shares in 1923 for $5 each (Lascari, 1998). In 1935 the company went into receivership and was reorganized as a Wisconsin nonprofit stock corporation; it then issued another 3,000 shares at $5 each. In 1950 the Packers had another stock offering that raised $118,000. By 1997 there were 4,627 stockholders, who were given 1,000 shares for every share owned, which resulted in 4,627,000 shares outstanding. After amending their articles of incorporation, the Packers were able to sell an additional 5,373,000 shares. A fourth sale was consummated in 1997. Each new share sold for $200 plus a handling fee of $15 (Lascari, 1998). (See The Case of the Green Bay Packers sidebar.)

Similar to other Packer fans, banker Nicholas Bertha said that his favorite investment was the one that he made with his heart, not his head: a $200 share of the Green Bay Packers. As a Wisconsin native, Bertha purchased the share of his home-state football team in 1997 and proclaims that he accepts this exception to the Wall Street rule of thinking before buying. The Green Bay Packers Inc. stock certificate will never appreciate in value and cannot be sold. He grew up in Milwaukee, 110 miles (180 km) south of Green Bay, Wisconsin, and remembers watching at home with his father when quarterback Bart Starr won the 1967 NFL championship game against the Dallas Cowboys with a 1-yard touchdown run. When the opportunity came in November 1997 to purchase Packers shares, he purchased five—one each for himself, his wife, and his three children.

Significant restrictions prohibited almost all transfers of the new stock except back to the Packers for $0.025 per share, to family members as gifts, or as a bequest after death. Additional rules prohibit a stockholder from making any profit or even receiving a dividend. Furthermore, to comply with NFL rules, each stockholder had to pledge that he or she had not been involved in any litigation alleging fraud, had not been convicted of a felony, and had not participated in sport gambling. Even with all these restrictions, the Packers sold 120,000 shares and raised over $24 million. Most purchasers bought the stock as a novelty to claim ownership in the Packers.

The last sale, in which Bertha was a buyer, raised $24 million to renovate Lambeau Field. The stock is illiquid and pays no dividend, and no one is allowed to own more than 200,000 shares. Also, resale is prohibited, except to the club at a fraction of the original value. The success associated with the 1997 sale spurred the Packers to issue stocks again in 2011. The Packers leveraged team interest in choosing to sell their last two offerings immediately after winning Super Bowls. Thus, after winning the 2011 Super Bowl, the team organized another stock offering similar to the 1997 offering. Fans could pay $250 per share (plus a $25 handling fee) for stocks that basically had no value, received no rights, and paid no dividends. The stock offering was designed to help the team offset an expected $143 million renovation to their stadium. In the first two days of the offering the team sold 185,000 shares, which

THE CASE OF THE GREEN BAY PACKERS

The Packers, the City of Green Bay, and the Green Bay/Brown County District financed the $295 million renovation that took place over four years (2000-2003) in four major ways: sales tax, stock sale, sale of naming rights, and PSLs. According to financial records, when the Packers sold stock in 1997, they raised nearly $24 million and increased the number of shareholders from 1,940 to 109,723. Although the Packers have not sold naming rights to the stadium itself, they have successfully sold naming-rights deals for multiple entrances to Lambeau Field (Frey, 2011). The Packers also financially capitalized on the NFL's G-3 loan program. Initiated in 1999, this program provides financial assistance to franchises using the money as collateral to issue bonds for stadium development. This money is taken from the league's national television revenue, which is shared equally among the teams. Between 1994 and 2004, the league loaned $725 million to facilitate the building or renovation of 20 NFL stadiums including Lambeau Field (Frey, 2011). Yet despite the fact that the Packers are the only publicly traded NFL

organization and have one of the most passionate fans bases in professional sport (over 81,000 people are currently on a season ticket waiting list), whenever there is public allocation of scarce resources involving professional sports franchises, opposition and controversy arises. As noted by Frey (2011), the initial resistance came from the Wisconsin legislature after the team sought legislation to create the Brown County Stadium District. Specifically, the board was to issue $160 in bonds for the stadium project, subject to voter approval of a half-cent sales tax increase. As previously outlined, a sales tax is a regressive tax; consequently, every taxpayer is charged the same amount to pay, regardless of overall income.

In addition to the challenges presented by the state legislature, the Packers were also confronted with issues locally in Green Bay. For example, several key elements within the lease kept the team and the city from reaching an agreement. Included among these issues were user fees, ticket tax surcharges, rent, and the city's usage of the stadium (Frey, 2011).

---

generated over $43 million and represented selling three-quarters of the entire offering (*Packers sell*, 2011). The stock sale occurred in December, at a time when many fans were excited about the team's outstanding play (they were 12-0), and the stocks made a perfect Christmas gift.

Because of its ownership structure, Green Bay is the only NFL team to reveal annual financial results. Consequently, the Packers offer a rare glimpse into league finances. Intuitively, NFL owners are reluctant to open their financial books for public scrutiny for several reasons including (*a*) establishing ticket prices, (*b*) trying to get stadium subsidies, and (*c*) managing payroll costs.

As noted previously in this chapter and in chapter 1, several teams are attempting to cash in on the interest of sports fans to sell parts or all of their teams to the public. Some stocks have done well, but others have not. For example, the Cleveland Indians went public (a limited ownership right with few voting rights) in 1998 at an initial price of $15 a share, which correlated to a team value of $232 million. Within seven months, however, the stock had

fallen over 50% and was trading at $7.13 a share, which translated to a team value of approximately $113 million (Much & Phillips, 1999). Each of the four million class A common shares was entitled to one vote, but each of the 2,281,667 class B shares, all owned by the owner of the team, was entitled to 10,000 votes (Lascari, 1998). Thus, Jacobs retained 99.98% control of the company and was entitled to elect the entire board of directors.

The Indians were unusually lucky with the timing of their stock offering. The year the Indians went public, they went to the World Series. The prospectus, which showed income through December 31, 1997, highlighted $140 million in revenue and $22.5 million in net income (see figure 9.2) (Much & Phillips, 1999). Those numbers were much inflated; almost 90% of the income that year came from postseason and nonbaseball activities. If interest income, gains from player transactions, league expansion proceeds, and postseason income had been removed from the team's net income, the net income would have dropped to $1.76 million (Much & Phillips, 1999).

EVOLUTION OF THE CELTICS

The Boston Celtics went public in 1986 when 40% of the team was sold for $18.50 per share. As of 1998, 5.3 million shares were outstanding and owned by more than 50,000 shareholders (Lascari, 1998). Unlike the Packers' shares, which are not approved by the SEC or covered by any federal or state laws, the Boston Celtics' shares (publicly traded from 1986 to 2002) complied with all federal laws and were openly traded on the New York Stock Exchange. The team's symbol on the NYSE was BOS. (Symbols for companies instead of company names are shown on ticker systems that display the most recent share prices.)

The Celtics have gone through several major changes over the years, including buying and selling radio and television stations. In 1998 the stock underwent additional changes forced by legislative requirements. The Revenue Act of 1987 required that a limited partnership (a business structure similar to that of the Celtics when the team was formed) be taxed at the partnership rate. On the basis of a grandfather clause, the Celtics' limited partnership would be taxed at the corporate rate beginning July 1, 1998. In June 1998, the Boston Celtics Limited Partnership reorganized into two separate entities:

1. Boston Celtics Limited Partnership II, which was formed to remain on the NYSE and be taxed as a corporation
2. Castle Creek Partners, which was formed as a nonpublic entity with pass-through tax treatment (Much & Phillips, 1999)

Each stockholder had a choice of an interest in either entity. There were 2,703,364 publicly traded units of a master limited partnership that could be traded on the New York Stock Exchange. Unlike common stock, which could entitle the owner to an equity position (ownership) in the team, the units were claims only against the company's cash flow. In September 2002 the Celtics were bought for $360 million and again became a privately owned team (Frost, 2002).

Cleveland Indians' 1997 Adjusted Net Income	($000)
Reported net income	22,570
Interest income, net of interest expense	(2,371)
Gains on player transactions	(2,696)
League expansion proceeds	(9,286)
Playoff game revenue	(5,700)
Pretax income (adjusted to highlight only traditional revenue)	**2,517**
Pro forma income taxes	(755)
Pro forma adjusted net income	**1,762**

Figure 9.2 Cleveland Indians' 1997 adjusted net income.
Data from Much and Phillips 1999.

The $15 per share IPO, which implied a $232 million franchise value, priced the stock at 131.7 times the adjusted earnings from regular-season revenue (Much & Phillips, 1999). By pricing themselves so high, the Indians provided virtually no opportunity for price appreciation. Thus, when the 1998 revenue numbers for the quarter ending September 30 showed a 37% increase in third-quarter operating profit, the stock price barely budged (Much & Phillips, 1999). As previously mentioned, Larry Dolan purchased the team in 1999 for approximately $320 million.

Stocks in professional teams have had a mediocre reception from the investing public. Pure-play investments that include only a professional sports team have several major problems, such as seasonal revenue streams, potential labor strife, limited investment liquidity, reliance on other business owners to generate a product, and intense media and government scrutiny (Much & Phillips, 1999). A pure play refers to a corporation that participates in only one industry segment. For example, the Celtics and the Indians were exclusively sports teams and thus were pure plays. In contrast, a blended company could encompass a team and other unrelated businesses; an example is the Florida Panthers hockey team and their resort holdings. Other examples include diverse companies such as Disney, Tribune, Comcast, and Time Warner. Even with blended companies, the presence of a sport team can significantly affect stock prices. In 2010 Madison Square Garden, Inc. (NASDAQ:MSG), which became its own public company in 2010, had various revenue streams, but when the team was in the running for LeBron James its share prices spiked 12% and then fell when he chose to play elsewhere (Flamm, 2010).

Although a **pure-play stock** offering for a team might not be a sound investment option for stockholders other than the primary team owner (because of significant risks), blends can produce significant revenue streams through the addition of other revenue-producing units to a professional team. In the case of the NHL's Florida Panthers, additional units were combined with a pure play, producing a comprehensive business entity capable of using additional revenue to offset potential losses associated with a professional team. In 1996 Florida Panthers Holdings (parent company of the NHL's

Florida Panthers—NYSE: PAW) sold 7.3 million shares of class A stock to the public. Team owner H. Wayne Huizenga retained 5.3 million shares (Much & Phillips, 1999). The shares sold for $10 each, which valued the team at $126 million.

Shortly after issuing the stock, the company evolved from just the team to a diversified leisure and recreation company that included six resorts, an arena management company, two ice rinks, and one golf facility. This growth was funded through additional stock sales that increased outstanding shares from 12.6 million in 1996 to 35.1 million in 1998. Compared with the sport segment, the company's leisure and recreation side brought significant economic prosperity to the parent company. Table 9.1 presents the revenue, operating income, depreciation, and cash flow for the company's two divisions in 1997 and 1998.

As highlighted in table 9.1, the $235 million increase in revenue produced by the resorts helped offset the continued losses incurred by the sport side of the company. The marriage between the leisure and sport divisions, however, would be short lived; management at the 1998 annual meeting announced the potential to spin off the sport division into a separate public company (Much & Phillips, 1999). A spin-off would indicate that in this particular attempt at blending the company was not successful. So in 2001 the team portion of the business was sold to concentrate the corporate efforts on the resort and property management side of the business. With the Panthers out of the corporate umbrella, former owner Huizenga concen-

Table 9.1 Florida Panthers Holdings' Financial Highlights

1997 ($000)			
	Sports	**Leisure**	**Total company**
Revenue	36,695	17,567	54,262
Operating income	(10,533)	4,053	(8,379)
Depreciation	4,239	1,459	5,698
Cash flow	(6,294)	5,512	(2,681)
1998 ($000)			
	Sports	**Leisure**	**Total company**
Revenue	43,586	252,603	296,189
Operating income	(17,503)	52,769	25,452
Depreciation	5,168	17,950	23,155
Cash flow	(12,335)	70,719	48,607

Data from Much and Phillips 1999.

trated his efforts on the resort side of the business and changed the **stock symbol** (ticker symbol) to RST (Boca Resorts), which is still publicly traded (*Panthers' new ownership*, 2002).

The Panthers are not alone in their inability to develop a blended structure. Poor performance has also hounded Ascent Entertainment Group, which owned several businesses including the NHL's Colorado Avalanche and the NBA's Denver Nuggets. After enduring double-digit losses for years, Ascent's parent company, Comsat Corporation, divested its remaining interest in Ascent in 1996. Ascent suffered operating losses of $42.4 million in 1997 and was facing even larger losses in 1998 (Much & Phillips, 1999).

In 1999 the Colorado Avalanche and Denver Nuggets were tentatively sold, along with their arena, for $400 million, and the buyer assumed some debt associated with the arena ("Two Denver franchises," 1999). The sale did not go unchallenged; a potential suitor sued, saying that Ascent shareholders would make more money from a different offer to buy the team and that a potential conflict of interest had not been made public (Lewis, 1999). After several suits were filed, the teams were resold. The original buyers returned with a $450 million offer, which appeared to be enough to close the deal ("Wal-Mart heir," 2000). The teams (as well as the Denver Avalanche and the Pepsi Center) were eventually purchased for $450 million by Stanley Kroenke (*Owner*, 2002).

In addition to pure-play and blended professional sport-related corporations, another variation has emerged recently—a vertically integrated combination whereby the sports team benefits other corporate units. Some examples of such combinations were Walt Disney (Mighty Ducks of Anaheim), Tribune (Chicago Cubs), and Fox Entertainment Group (Los Angeles Dodgers and a minority interest in the New York Knicks, New York Rangers, Los Angeles Lakers, and Los Angeles Kings) (Much & Phillips, 1999). The Ducks, Cubs, and Dodgers have all subsequently been sold, highlighting that sometimes a sport property will not benefit the corporate bottom line. These vertically integrated combinations were thought to be more effective than pure-play sport businesses because the broadcasting arms of each company can generate significant sport advertising income without having to pay significant fees for broadcasting rights. The sale of these teams might indicate that purchasing sport media is easier than operating a team at a profit.

Sport stocks are not focused just on professional teams, whether as a pure play or part of a larger organization. One active area for sport stocks are golf-related companies. Ely Callaway took his golf company public in 1992 and was one of the few to succeed. The landscape has been littered with various golf companies who failed in their effort to go public such as Orlimar, TearDrop, CoastCast, and Natural Golf (Foust, 2008). *BusinessWeek* had a golf stock index, which declined 15.5% from 2001 to 2008 while the Standard & Poor's 500 index declined only 10.9% during the same period. Part of the problem is that only a limited number of dedicated golfers are willing to spend money on expensive golf gear. Only 13 million golfers account for 91% of equipment spending (Foust, 2008).

Also getting into the stock market push are entities that in years past would not have considered such a fund-raising effort. One effort involved Boise State University, which started selling stocks in 2009 for $100 a share. Because the university is a nonprofit organization the athletic department started a separate nonprofit called Boise State Broncos, Inc. that has a 12-person oversight board. The fund-raising effort was designed to raise $20 million to help fund facility renovations. The shares do not pay dividends, provide any financial reward, or provide privileges for purchasing tickets. The only benefit to owners, besides pride in supporting the school, is the ability to vote on future oversight board members ("Boise State sells stock," 2009).

The history of sport stocks is reminiscent of a roller coaster. Because of strong interest in IPOs in the late 1990s, several more teams considered public offerings, but investor interest waned on new sport issues. If a team or other business does not have the ability or interest to pursue a large public offering, it can still sell stock through a smaller stock offering such as a Regulation D or SCOR offering, discussed earlier in the chapter.

CONCLUSION

The ability to reach more potential investors is a major advantage for a company issuing stock. Investors who might never express interest in a company might be willing to gamble and invest a small amount to be part of the ownership team. Large mutual funds could also purchase a large number of shares. No matter who owns the shares, a publicly traded company has greater access to capital than almost all nonpublicly traded companies.

Teams such as the Boston Celtics, Cleveland Indians, Florida Panthers, and Green Bay Packers have all flirted with issuing stock to the public or are still publicly traded because of the potential for significant capital enhancement. Furthermore, large sport businesses such as Nike, Disney (ABC and ESPN), and WWE cannot grow without the capital infusion afforded by issuing stock.

Although shareholders have some obligations and significant rights, a publicly traded company needs to comply with numerous regulations and reporting requirements, which can make the decision to go public unattractive—regardless of how much money could be raised. In fact, because of the quick decisions that often need to be made in sport, public ownership may not be an attractive option. If the issuance of stock is not available as a capital acquisition tool, a company can entertain the idea of issuing bonds (see chapter 10) or other instruments to borrow funds.

Class Discussion Topics

1. How many people in your class own stocks?
2. Have you ever purchased stocks yourself or been given stocks? If you purchased them yourself, what factors went into buying those shares?
3. Have you ever thought about buying stocks? Have you ever researched them?
4. Would you ever buy any sport stocks? Why or why not?
5. What sport stocks would you consider purchasing? Why?
6. Would you invest in a mutual fund? Why or why not?
7. Have you ever lost money on an investment? Explain what happened and what you learned from the process.
8. Do you think that buying the publicly available shares in the Green Bay Packers is a good investment?
9. What key facts about a stock might make you think that it would be a good investment?

chapter 10

Bonds

Chapter Objectives

After studying this chapter, you should be able to do the following:

- Understand how issuing bonds creates a fixed-cost solution to raising funds.
- Describe what types of bonds are available and how they are secured.
- Understand how a company repays bondholders.
- Understand the dynamics of using government-issued bonds to finance sports facilities.
- Describe capital structuring through various examples.

In chapter 8 we consider short-term funding through bank loans and other capitalization techniques such as venture capital. Chapter 9 covers equity ownership through stocks as a means of raising capital. This chapter focuses on a tool used by both the private and the public sectors—bonds. A **bond** is an obligation that needs to be repaid with interest, similar to a loan from a bank. The difference is that bonds are typically issued by larger corporations or government entities with a good repayment history and are sought after by investors because of either favorable interest rates or tax benefits. The high desirability of these bonds creates a market for their purchase and sale that is similar to the stock market. Thus, bonds have the financing characteristics of loans (covered in chapter 8), as well as a market in which they can be bought and sold, like stocks (covered in chapter 9).

This chapter first looks at the types of corporate bonds available, the costs associated with issuing such bonds, and various repayment methods. Next, we consider government bonds used to finance stadium and arena construction and related projects; this section highlights the various types of bonds issued by government entities and the manner in which they are issued. The last part of the chapter presents an example of a strategy in which various capital acquisition techniques are combined and then examines concerns associated with raising too much or too little capital.

CORPORATE BONDS

Bonds issued by businesses are often referred to as **corporate bonds** because bonds can normally be issued only by the largest corporations. Similar to a mortgage loan, a mortgage bond is a bond backed by specified real estate. If the bond issuer defaults, the **bondholders** can foreclose on the property and sell the property to satisfy the claim.

A bond is similar to a long-term loan in that it is a contract under which a borrower agrees to make specified interest and principal payments on specified dates for a specified period. Every bond has some restrictions attached. These restrictions (called bond covenants) are similar to typical contract terms that limit both parties. A company issuing bonds might attach restrictions that allow the company to pay a lesser amount if the investor tries to redeem the bond before its maturity date. Similarly, investors might demand restrictions on a company to protect their investment. These restrictions could include limiting the extent of acquisition activity and capital spending, requiring minimum levels of liquidity, restricting a com-

pany's right to issue additional equity, and limiting the size of the debt–equity ratio.

Besides the bonds already discussed, there are convertible bonds (discussed later in this chapter) and warrant bonds (not included in the scope of this book); income bonds that pay interest only when income is earned; indexed bonds whose interest rates increase if inflation rises (the index typically tracks a well-regarded index such as the **consumer price index**); and **zero coupon bonds** or original issue **discount bonds**, which carry no interest rate but are originally sold at a price lower than **par value** and appreciate in value over time (Brigham & Gapenski, 1994).

A type of bond that was popular in the 1970s and 1980s was the **junk bond**. In the late 1970s Michael Milken of Drexel Burnham Lambert analyzed the often-overlooked area of junk bonds and concluded that riskier bonds paid a higher return compared with other bonds. He concluded that junk bonds were a strong investment even though they were associated with significant risk. With the financial decline starting in 2007, the credit rating of various companies and even countries was downgraded. A junk bond is normally defined as a bond rated BB or lower because of its high default risk, which also means that it has a high yield for purchasers. The high yield encourages investors to assume risk, and for that reason junk bonds are speculative. The chance that a junk bond issuer will default is much higher than the chance that a company that issues an AAA-rated bond will default, so the junk bond issuer needs to offer a higher interest rate to attract investors.

On the basis of his analysis, Milken convinced more institutional investors to buy risky bonds, and the market for junk bonds was born. These high-risk, high-yield bonds were often used in **leveraged buyouts** in which a company used debt instruments to help buy other companies. Ted Turner offered to buy CBS by offering CBS shareholders junk bonds for their shares. The shareholders balked at the offer, which then fizzled and disappeared. Numerous savings and loans, however, invested in other junk bonds, which helped usher in the savings and loan collapse. But savings and loans were not the only victims. Investment powerhouse Drexel Burnham Lambert was forced into bankruptcy in 1989, and Milken was jailed for his activities (Brigham & Gapenski, 1994).

Milken faced a 98-count federal indictment alleging such acts as bribery, insider trading, and stock manipulation. These charges all stemmed from Milken's interest in pushing the often-riskier junk bonds. He plea-bargained to six counts of

ADVANTAGES AND DISADVANTAGES OF BOND FINANCING

Advantages

- Interest on bonds is tax deductible (versus stock dividends, which are not deductible).
- Bond financing can be reasonably inexpensive for an established company with a good credit rating.
- The market for trading and issuing bonds is strong and established.

Disadvantages

- Interest is a fixed charge that needs to be paid regardless of whether income was earned.
- The principal loaned amount must be paid in full when the bond matures.
- Issuing bonds can harm a company's credit rating and make it more difficult for the company to borrow money in the future.
- If the bond is secured by collateral, a corporation might not be able to sell or otherwise dispose of the asset without bondholder approval.
- Bondholders have the upper hand whenever a company declares bankruptcy

minor securities violations, including involvement with a client who failed to make Securities and Exchange Commission (SEC) disclosures. Although the case was weak, the judge appeared to be trying to send the message that bond manipulation would be strictly scrutinized, and Milken was sentenced to 10 years in prison. He was released after 2 years (Wanniski, 1991).

Bond Financing

People often do not appreciate how important it is to choose the right funding vehicle for a business. If an owner makes a quick decision and the business has some poor years, the debt obligation could turn a strong investment into a fiscal disaster. An example can be seen with the Memphis Redbirds minor league baseball team and their AutoZone Park. The Redbirds built an extravagant $80.5 million stadium and made ambitious attendance projections that led the team into its financial struggles. The Memphis Redbirds Foundation, which owns the team and stadium, defaulted on a $1.625 million bond payment in March 2009. In 2010 the foundation entered into a deal with bondholders for reduced annual bond payments of just over $1 million that year because they could not afford to make the payments. In 2010 the bonds were consolidated from five or six bondholders to one private equity firm, Fundamental Advisors of New York (Morgan, 2010). But even with the downside associ-

ated with a financial obligation that can last more than 30 years, bonds have significant positive attributes (see Advantages and Disadvantages of Bond Financing).

Other factors that affect the decision of a business to issue bonds include the general business environment and the prevailing interest in the specific business that is issuing bonds. If interest rates are generally low, then every business may have difficulty issuing bonds. But a specific business that is facing a potential hardship may find it impossible to issue bonds. For example, if a labor dispute arises within the players' association, the a team might face a difficult market in which to issue their bonds even though other businesses may not be having a problem in this regard. One way of avoiding such a problem is to provide some type of pledge to guarantee repayment (e.g., by issuing a secured bond).

Secured Versus Unsecured Bonds

One disadvantage of **secured bonds** is related to a corporation's ability to control secured assets. If an asset is secured by the terms of the security agreement, the corporation does not have exclusive use of the asset and might need to obtain approval before using the asset for various activities. Unsecured bonds provide the greatest flexibility for the issuing corporation but minimal protection for the bond purchaser. A secured bondholder receives preferential treatment over subsequent bondholders, whether those subsequent bondholders are secured or unsecured.

Various types of secured bonds can be issued. Collateral trust bonds are secured by stock or other bonds. The collateral security is deposited with a trust company, which holds the assets for the bondholders' benefit (Bogen, 1966). Such a bond is similar to someone taking his property to a pawnshop and receiving a loan based on the perceived resale value of the item. If the borrower fails to repay the loan in a timely manner, the pawnbroker can sell the collateral that secured the loan. The only difference is that with bonds, the security is stocks, bonds, or other investments. An equipment trust obligation is a secured transaction whereby a corporation can acquire equipment under a collateral bill of sale. Title to the equipment does not pass to the corporation until the obligation has been paid, and a trustee retains title to the equipment until the obligation is **discharged**.

In another type of arrangement, a second corporation, in addition to the original issuer, can guarantee a bond. These guaranteed bonds can be highly marketable if the backing corporation has an excellent credit rating because the bondholder has two guarantees for repayment—the original issuer and the guarantor. Guaranteed bonds are often issued in cases in which a large corporation is helping a small company expand and the companies have an existing or intended working relationship. For example, a professional sports team might guarantee the bond issued by a minor league affiliate. In another type of situation, similar to that with guarantees, a larger corporation can purchase a smaller corporation and assume the bond obligations incurred by the smaller corporation.

Debentures

A **debenture** is an unsecured bond, meaning that no assets secure the bond (guarantee repayment) if the bond issuer defaults. Normally, because of the lack of protection for debenture bondholders, only companies with the best credit rating can issue such bonds. Although debenture bonds are generally unsecured, several techniques are used to extend protection to such bondholders. To provide investors with additional security that a debenture will be repaid, some companies issue **subordinate debentures**. These bonds provide some security because assets are pledged to back them. Claims on these assets, however, are subordinate to senior claims against the assets.

For example, a mortgage bond issue could be secured by a company's manufacturing equipment, and any amount of the equipment value that is not securing the mortgage bond issue (senior claim) can be used to secure repayment of the subordinate debentures. Assume that a company backs a $10 million mortgage bond issue with property valued at $15 million. The company issues subordinate bonds in the amount of $10 million several years later, after the property has appreciated. If the company were to file for bankruptcy protection, their land and buildings might be worth only $16 million. The mortgage bondholders would recover their $10 million. The subordinate bondholders are still in a better position than unsecured creditors because $6 million is still available from the assets after the mortgage bond is satisfied. The $6 million would go to the subordinate bondholders, who would probably be paid on a pro rata basis ($600 for each $1,000 bond that they held).

Debenture bonds can be issued with clauses to protect investors. In a covenant of equal coverage, the debenture bond is treated as equal to a secured mortgage if a mortgage is ever obtained in the future. Thus, both the mortgage and debenture bonds would be secured. Additionally, a debenture can be issued with a specific condition that no dividends will be paid to stockholders unless such moneys are derived from future earnings or unless the corporate assets exceed liabilities by a specified amount (Bogen, 1966).

Regardless of the asset used to secure a debt instrument, the security helps increase the liquidity of the instrument, lowers the cost of capital to borrowers, and helps develop greater efficiency through the financial marketplace (Brigham & Gapenski, 1994). Thus, whether a homeowner pledges her home to secure a mortgage or a team uses contractually obligated revenue from their broadcasting contract, the security helps seal the deal and allows the flow of needed capital.

Whether they are secured or unsecured, bonds are covered by a contract called an indenture. The indenture is issued to a trust company that acts as a trustee for the bondholders. The indenture has to follow specific SEC guidelines related to the trustees and their duties: Trustees must have no conflict of interest and must have financial responsibility, make periodic reports to bondholders, provide appropriate default notice, protect bondholders after default, and fulfill related obligations (Bogen, 1966).

AN UNUSUAL WAY TO SECURE A BOND

In 1998, in an effort to acquire considerable cash in advance of his payday, Chicago White Sox slugger Frank Thomas, working with a New York City investment banking firm, was attempting to raise $20 million. The money would be raised through an offering of bonds in Thomas' name backed by his guaranteed annual salary of $7 million per year through 2006. The bonds would have probably paid a rate of approximately 9%. It was assumed that Thomas could earn more than 9% by reinvesting the $20 million somewhere else. Otherwise, borrowing the money would be of no benefit to him ("Thomas secures," 1998). But shortly after an attempt was made to launch the bond, the idea was scrapped because the player's contract included too many inhibitive conditions, such as a morals clause, that could limit repayment. Furthermore, players can lose their entitlement to compensation if they are injured in a non-team-related event or if players go on strike. In this case Thomas would lose his entitlement to compensation if he decided to take the bond money and not play anymore (Kaplan, 1998, November). After 1998, Thomas was often injured and he performed sporadically at times, which justified the nervousness of potential investors back in 1998.

But in 2006 the 38-year-old slugger led the Oakland Athletics with 39 homers and 114 RBIs. Thomas hit .301 with 521 homers and 1,704 RBIs in 19 major league seasons, 16 with the Chicago White Sox. His success with the Athletics prompted the Toronto Blue Jays to reach a tentative deal with the slugger for the 2007 and 2008 seasons. Under the $18.12 million contract, Thomas received a $9.12 million signing bonus, a $1 million salary in 2007, and $8 million in 2008. The deal included a $10 million vesting option for 2009 that would become guaranteed if Thomas made 1,000 plate appearances in the next two seasons or 525 plate appearances in 2008 (*Blue Jays sign Thomas*, 2006). Thomas retired in 2008.

In February 2001 William Andrews securitized the remaining $5 million that he was owed by the NFL's Atlanta Falcons. Andrews had last played in the NFL in 1996. But as part of his playing contract, he was owed $200,000 per year over 25 years. Instead of waiting for those annual payments, Andrews decided to sell the deferred compensation in the form of a bond to Hanleigh, a sport insurance company. Hanleigh paid $2 million to Andrews for the right to the future compensation stream. This deal marked the first sale of a bond securitized by an individual athlete's deferred compensation in the history of professional sport. Although the $2 million was only 40% of the amount that Andrews was to be paid over the next 25 years, the securitization gave the athlete immediate access to a large sum of money. He then had the ability to invest and grow that $2 million. The transaction was overseen by NDH Capital, a small Connecticut financing company (Kaplan, 2001).

Most bonds are **bearer bonds**, which means that the bondholder retains possession of the bond document. Bonds typically have **coupons** attached to them that the bondholder can redeem at her bank on a semiannual basis to receive the specified interest payment. Such bonds are called coupon bonds. Coupon bonds are the easiest to transfer to other purchasers because the person in actual physical possession of the bond is entitled to redeem the coupon. In contrast, a registered bond is issued in the name of the bondholder. If such shares are transferred, the registered bondholder needs to endorse the bonds to the new owner, and the new owner has to have his name added to the corporate books. Because of the registration requirement, such bonds are less marketable.

Some corporations have issued income bonds during reorganizations or in exchange for preferred stock. Income bonds pay interest only if the corporation earns income. If no income is earned, no interest is paid. Such a contingency requirement reduces the fixed costs that would normally be allocated for paying the interest on a coupon or registered bond. Thus, if a company is facing rough financial times, it does not need to worry about paying interest to the bondholders. This provision frees up a significant amount of money to help the business staff in operation. But when the company starts turning a profit, it is required to start paying interest to the bondholders. An indenture specifies the formula for calculating the required payments under an income bond. One rule typically applied to income bonds is that the interest is cumulative. If interest is not paid in a given year because income is low, it must be paid the next year, when income is greater, along with the interest for that next year.

Issue Size and Maturity

One of the primary concerns associated with bonds is determining the appropriate interest rate to attach to the bonds and determining how many bonds should be issued. When corporations are seeking millions of dollars, they do not resort to guesswork to determine the appropriate interest rate. Long- and short-term forecasting becomes a serious matter—a difference of 1/10th of a percentage point can cost millions in interest or may make an offering so unattractive that no one purchases the issue.

Several agencies rate bonds, such as Moody's Investors Service and Standard & Poor's. These entities examine the bond issuer and determine the potential for default based on factors such as the revenue stream to repay the bonds, current economic conditions, interest rates, and past repayment history. After analyzing all the relevant criteria, the rating agency establishes a rating for a bond. The highest rating is typically AAA or Aaa depending on the agency. Bonds with such a rating have the lowest risk for default and do not need to pay as high an interest rate. Bonds that have a low rating are sometimes classified as junk bonds and need to pay a much higher interest rate to attract investors. Even if Moody's and Standard & Poor's give a bond a high rating, the potential for default always exists. Investors would not have considered Enron bonds high risk, but they turned out to be. Thus, the potential for default needs to be considered; the riskier the bond is, the higher the interest rate needs to be to attract potential investors. During the economic turmoil of 2011, the rating of bonds issued by the United States government was lowered by Standard & Poor's. S&P lowered the long-term rating from AAA to AA+ because of political risks, rising debt burden, and an overall negative outlook (Beutler, 2011).

To help reduce the potential disaster associated with choosing an inappropriate interest rate, corporations appraise the supply and demand for money, which affect interest rates. Interest rates represent a true example of supply and demand in that if a glut of money is on the market, whether because of government actions or market forces, interest rates are lower than when the money supply is tighter. If the money supply is tight, however, interest rates are higher because more corporations are fighting to obtain scarcer funds, and the competition bids up the interest rates.

The demand for long-term funds arises from four major sources: mortgage borrowing, corporate bond financing, state and local government bond financing, and long-term U.S. Treasury borrowing (Bogen, 1966). The various entities that have money available and those that need funds are all affected by the Federal Reserve. As discussed in chapter 4, the Federal Reserve can control the supply and demand and affect interest rates through monetary policies. The Federal Reserve tends to relax the money supply during recessionary times and restrict money during prosperous times. Such a strategy is designed to foster stable growth without significant fluctuation (Bogen, 1966).

The diverse suppliers for long-term funds include (Bogen, 1966)

- life insurance companies,
- savings and loan associations,
- mutual savings banks,
- commercial banks that might acquire bonds,
- insurance companies (fire, property, and casualty),
- corporate pension funds,
- state and local government retirement funds,
- union retirement plans, and
- mutual funds that buy bonds.

COSTS OF ISSUING BONDS

Although bonds can raise substantial funds, they are expensive to issue. The primary cost associated with issuing bonds is the required interest payments. Such payments are due on a semiannual basis for as long as the bond is outstanding. A 20-year $100 million bond issued with 10% interest would require semiannual payments of $5 million for 20 years.

Another cost associated with issuing bonds is the discount or risk premium at which they are sold. The discount for the $100 million bond issue might be $5 million, which means that the issuing or selling entity for the bonds would take $5 million

(5%) as a fee to process and help sell the bonds. Every transaction is different, but the typical issuing fee for bonds is around 5%. This cost effectively increases the interest rate because the $10 million annual interest obligation is based on $100 million. So the company would still owe $100 million for the bonds but receive only $95 million after paying the fee. This added cost must be built into the bond's repayment schedule. Thus, the actual interest cost for such a bond would be 10.25%. The $5 million cost for the bond issue can be amortized over the bond's life by putting aside $250,000 a year for 20 years. Thus, the actual cost to the bond issuer is $10.25 million a year. Additional expenses could include legal fees for preparing the indenture, recording the mortgages, and general legal advice, as well as marketing expenses.

LOAN REPAYMENT

Up to now we have looked at the types of bonds that can be issued. In this section we turn our attention to repayment and refunding mechanisms. Normally, bond repayment occurs when the bond matures and the issuer repays all remaining obligations. Most bonds are redeemable when they mature. At that point the issuing company pays the bondholder the cash value of the bond. Some bonds are redeemable at par, at the holder's option. The par value is the arbitrary initial value that the bond was issued for, and that helps establish its value. These bonds are often sold at a lower interest rate. If the prevailing interest rate for bonds is 10%, the redeemable bonds might pay only 9.5%. The lower interest rate is justified in that the bondholder has the option of redeeming the bond before it matures and is then able to take the proceeds and invest in another bond. If the interest rate increases, then the investor may want to take the proceeds and purchase a bond with a higher rate. If the interest rate declines, the investor still has a bond paying 9.5% interest.

Sometimes a company faces hardships that can force it to pay off the bondholders before maturity. If interest rates drop several percentage points, a company may not be able to afford the prior interest rate. Normally, changes in interest rates do not affect the maturity date, and the issuer is stuck with the higher rate. But if the bond was issued with a call provision, the issuer can exercise the call provision after a specified number of years. The call allows the issuer to pay the **face value** of the bond plus a fixed payment, such as a year's worth of coupon payments. After a bond is called

and paid, the company can issue new bonds at the lower interest rate. Callable bonds have higher interest rates than noncallable bonds to compensate investors for the risk of the bonds being redeemed by the issuer before they mature.

Repayment can be accomplished through the following techniques:

◆ Sinking funds
◆ Serial bonds
◆ Bond redemption before maturity
◆ Convertible bonds

Sinking Funds

The most common technique for repaying a note is to use a sinking fund in which moneys are set aside, either in preset amounts or on a variable basis. For example, a professional team could deposit a preset amount of $1 million a year into a sinking fund account. The amount can grow to well over $20 million in 20 years, and the funds can be used to repay loans, bonds, and notes as they mature. In certain instances, the price of a bond may decline because the associated interest rates are unfavorable. In those instances, the sinking fund account can be used to buy bonds on the open market and retire them at an earlier date (Bogen, 1966). This practice can save significant interest obligations.

Sinking funds can be created through various means. Annual payments of a fixed amount or a percentage of profit can also be used. Bonds issued for the purpose of acquiring fixed assets could also be retired through the establishment of a sinking fund using annual depreciation allowances for the asset. In that case the tax savings associated with depreciating an asset can be set aside to repay the bond. No matter what approach is used, the key is that a sinking fund is a way to set aside funds to repay the bonds in the future—a much better approach than trying to obtain funds at the last minute.

Serial Bonds

Serial bonds are a series of bonds issued with maturity dates at predetermined redemption dates. These types of bonds could include $1 million in bonds due in 20 years, and a company can issue such bonds every year for a 10-year period so that the bonds would need to be repaid in a series 20 to 30 years later. Serial bonds for a $50 million bond offering could include $5 million of bond obligations that mature in the 15th year and increased retirement obligations in subsequent years until the final bonds are retired in the 30th year.

Serial bonds are often issued by states and municipalities, which have fairly reliable tax revenue. Because corporate revenue is more difficult to project in the long run, serial bonds are less popular as a way of meeting corporate funding needs. Some corporations, however, are willing to use serial bonds for short-term debt but use sinking funds for long-term obligations. Some corporations set equal serial maturities over several years and then provide a large balloon payment at the end. If a 10-year bond issue for $10 million was issued under this format, the corporation might have serial maturity of $400,000 per year for 9 years and make a final balloon payment of $5.5 million in the 10th year (Bogen, 1966).

Bond Redemption Before Maturity

The sinking fund and serial maturation are just two techniques that companies can use to redeem bonds. Corporations can also issue newer bonds with more favorable interest rates and use the proceeds to buy older bonds on the open market. Numerous corporations issue bonds on a regular basis in an effort to take advantage of favorable interest rates and avoid the potential effect if interest rates rise. Such bonds often have a call provision to allow the corporation to repurchase the bonds at a moderate premium if interest rates change drastically. Some bonds are **convertibles**, which means that they can be redeemed when the bondholder converts the bonds to stocks (see the next section). Other bonds are retired through retained earnings, the selling of assets, or the issuing of more equity. If all these techniques fail, the corporation can ask the bondholders for a voluntary extension of the bond's maturity date.

As just mentioned, a corporation may issue callable bonds that it can repurchase before the maturity date. If a bond is not callable, there are two other means of repurchasing. The company can purchase a bond on the open market or from a bondholder who is willing to exchange it voluntarily. Note that even if a corporation issues callable bonds, the callable provision typically does not take effect on a 20-year bond until at least the 10th year. Until then, the bondholder is protected from an attempt by the corporation to call the bond when interest rates decline or if the corporation

attempts to issue new bonds with a lower interest rate. The protection against having a bond called can encourage larger investors such as life insurance companies to accept a lower yield on the express condition that a bond will not be callable.

Convertible Bonds

Some corporations issue bonds that can be converted to common stock. These bonds are designed to redeem themselves and retire the debt through converting the debt to equity ownership. This approach increases equity ownership while reducing the total corporate debt. Reducing the corporate debt can dramatically increase the corporate credit rating, which can make it easier for the company to borrow additional funds or issue additional bonds. But when a bond is converted to stock, it does not bring any new funds into the business; it merely redistributes debt obligations to owners' equity.

Convertible bonds have some strong benefits for both the issuing company and the potential bond buyer. Buyers often prefer convertible bonds because investors can obtain interest payments on their investment but can also choose to switch to the equity ownership option if the corporation starts to experience significant growth. Buyers might also prefer convertibles because they retain the position of a secured creditor but also have an option to purchase stock. This feature might not be an important reason to purchase the bond, but if the stock price soars, it can suddenly become a key benefit.

Corporations can also benefit from convertibles. When bonds are converted, the conversion usually occurs at a share price that is higher than it would have been if the shares had been purchased earlier. Thus, if the conversion occurs, the corporation can lower its debt obligation by exchanging that obligation for shares that are valued significantly less on the corporate books. This helps the corporation because it can sell its own shares at a higher rate compared with the bondholder, who might buy stock on the open market that might not directly benefit the corporation. But this benefit is also one of the primary reasons that some corporations do not want to issue convertible bonds. Some corporations do not want to dilute the stockholders' equity. Furthermore, because it is uncertain whether or when a bondholder might wish to convert bonds to stocks, convertible bonds add a degree of uncertainty to the corporation's capital structure.

Convertible securities are analyzed based on their conversion ratio. The conversion ratio (CR) represents the number of shares that a bondholder will receive on conversion. Another important number is the conversion price (CP), which represents how much the company will receive when the bondholder purchases the shares. Assume that a company issues a $1,000 bond that can be converted to 20 shares of common stock. The CR is 20, because 20 shares will be received. The CP is calculated with the following formula:

$$\frac{\text{par value of bond}}{\text{shares received}} = \text{conversion price}$$

$$\frac{\$1,000}{20} = \$50 \text{ CP per share}$$

The CP can conversely be used to calculate the CR, as follows (Brigham & Gapenski, 1994):

$$\frac{\text{par value of bond}}{\text{conversion price (CP)}} = \text{conversion ratio (CR)}$$

$$\frac{\$1,000}{\$50} = \$20 \text{ shares}$$

The issuing price for a convertible security is normally set at 10% to 30% above the prevailing market price for shares. Thus, the $50 CP would be appropriate if the shares were currently selling at the $35 to $45 price range. Most convertibles have fixed CPs and CRs for the life of the bond. Some convertibles contain step-up clauses that allow the CP to increase over time. Thus, a bond could be issued with a $50 CP during the first five years of the bond, and the CP is able to rise to $55 per share thereafter. The step-up is allowed if the conversion instrument contains specific language authorizing the increased cost for converting the bond to shares.

Almost all convertibles have specific clauses designed to protect the convertible holder from stock splits (discussed later in this chapter) and the sale of common stock below the CP. If the sales price decreases, then the CP must also be lowered. If the CP for a convertible was stated as $50 per share and the stock was selling for $35 per share, there would be no incentive to convert. If the stock price rose, there would be an incentive. Conversely, if the stock value drops significantly and the company has to issue new shares at $25 each, the company will renegotiate the CP and reduce it to keep the bondholders happy. Similarly, if a stock split occurs and bondholders have the right to convert the bond to 40 shares at a CP of $20, they will receive 80 shares at $10 each if they exercise the conversion (Brigham & Gapenski, 1994).

Investors may not want to exercise a conversion, but a company can force a conversion if the bond issue had a call provision. Assume that a sport company issues a $1,000 bond with a $50 CP, a 20-share CR, a share price of $60, and a call price of $1,050. If the company wants to exercise the call provision, the bondholder will have to calculate under which scenario he would make the greatest income. If he accepts the call, he will receive $1,050. If he converts the bond, he will receive 20 shares valued at $60 each, or $1,200 (Brigham & Gapenski, 1994). Most investors would take the $1,200 even if they did not favor equity ownership, because they could always sell the shares on the market.

GOVERNMENT-ISSUED BONDS

Bonds are documents representing a loan agreement and specifying the terms of the agreement. Corporations and government entities are the most frequent issuers of bonds. Government-issued bonds for building sports facilities have several unique attributes. Special laws, elections, or referendums are often required for the bonds to be issued. After the legal hurdles have been overcome, numerous additional steps need to be taken, from entering into a lease agreement with a professional team to acquiring funds for infrastructure repairs. The following example depicts this complex process.

In a general election, the citizens of Houston, Texas, voted to authorize a sports authority to issue bonds for the construction of a baseball and football stadium. The sports authority had been created after passage of a law by the Texas legislature providing for formation of the authority to raise taxes and issue bonds. The Harris County–Houston Sports Authority agreed to borrow $236.5 million to construct a new downtown baseball stadium (Williams, 1998). The money was to be borrowed in two ways: $34.7 million was to be raised through a zero-interest loan from business leaders, with repayment due starting in 2009. The remaining $201.8 million was raised through **revenue bonds** at an interest rate of 5.61%, with debt service to start at $10.3 million in 1999 and increase to $22.8 million by 2028 (Williams, 1998). The revenue bonds are secured from revenue collected through special hotel and rental car taxes.

Only $180 million of the offering was to go to stadium construction; the remaining $21.8 million was to be used to cover other finance-related costs such as issuing the bonds. The $21.8 million also went to purchase bond insurance, which helped increase the **bond rating** (Aaa from Moody's and AAA from Standard & Poor's). In turn, this feature allowed the bonds to be issued at a lower interest rate (Williams, 1998). The bond underwriters included Salomon Smith Barney; Chase Securities of Texas; Goldman, Sachs & Company; Samuel A. Ramirez & Company; Siebert Brandford Shank & Company; Artemis Capital Group; Estrada Hinojosa & Company; J.P. Morgan & Company; and Paine Webber. Bond issues of this magnitude by government entities often have numerous companies helping to underwrite them, including some minority-owned firms and local firms that are involved for political reasons.

Not all bond deals need to be complex. In 2006 the Hennepin County Board approved a 0.15% increase in sales tax to fund $350 million in bonds. The funds were to be used to help build a baseball stadium for the Minnesota Twins. The county was to pay $350 million of the $522 million construction cost, and the Twins picked up $130 million of the bill (*Hennepin County*, 2006). When Target Field was finally finished in 2009 (in time for the 2010 baseball season) at a cost of $544.4 million (including site acquisition and infrastructure), the public bond offering had increased to $392 million and the team's owner contributed private financing of $185 million.

Types of Government-Issued Bonds

Numerous types of bonds can be issued in the sport industry. Earlier sections of this chapter cover several types of bonds that can help sport corporations. This section centers on bonds issued by various government entities. Bonds represent the most likely funding source for publicly financed projects such as stadiums and arenas.

Although bonds for stadiums and arenas are the type of bonds most typically studied, sports facilities are low on the list of total expenditures for bond proceeds. Other public projects garner a greater amount of bond dollars. The greatest amount of funding is directed to school projects. Other major projects funded by bonds include park and recreation departments, convention centers, and administrative offices. This section focuses on stadiums and arenas financed with bonds. The same principles that relate to securing and repayment of bonds apply to all projects funded with government-issued bonds. The primary types of bonds considered here are general obligation bonds and revenue bonds. Other financing techniques, such as lease-backed financing (lease revenue bonds) and certificates of participation, can be used by the government entity, which then leases the facility to another government entity or sports authority (Greenberg & Gray, 1996).

General Obligation Bonds

General obligation bonds (GOBs) are among the instruments most commonly used to fund facilities. These bonds are often called **full faith and credit** obligations because the city, county, municipality, state, or other government unit pledges to repay the obligation with existing tax revenues or by levying new taxes (Greenberg & Gray, 1996). General obligation bonds and other bonds are rated by independent companies such as Moody's and Standard & Poor's based on the issuer's ability to repay the loan. General obligation bonds are often highly rated because currently existing and future sources of tax revenue can be tapped for repayment. Bond ratings can be influenced by a multitude of factors, including (Greenberg & Gray, 1996)

- the level of coverage (ability to repay the loan with existing revenue streams);
- the strength, breadth, and reliability of the tax base;
- the historical performance of the revenue stream;
- the risk associated with the project;
- the underlying economic strength of the stadium or arena or the community;
- political volatility; and
- whether the project is economically viable.

The strength of the tax base is one of the most important criteria for GOBs. A small city with a low tax base might suffer significantly if property values decrease or sales drop significantly. In contrast, a large city with hundreds of thousands of properties can experience downturns in the economy but still have a large enough tax base that the damage could be minimal.

Raters often look at the purpose of the project and the anticipated long-term benefits. Projects such as Camden Yards or Coors Field revolutionized the manner in which stadiums were viewed. These stadiums could be seen as catalysts for change that could revitalize an entire downtown community. If the downtown was revitalized, property values would increase. The increased property values would result in higher tax revenue, which would generate additional funds from which to repay bonds. The Florida Marlins built a stadium in 2009 (which opened in 2012) with an oft-cited price of $515 million to $644 million, and the stadium was to cost taxpayers more than $2.4 billion in debt service over the next 40 years. The project looked at three bond-backing strategies from general obligation bonds to convention center tax-backed bonds and sports tax bonds. About $91.2 million in convention development tax-backed bonds was to cost almost $1.2 billion in debt service (principal and interest) by 2047. Of the $91.2 million, $80.8 million was structured to go to the stadium. The rest covers expenses such as debt service reserve deposits. An additional $319.3 million in professional sports tax bonds was to be used for the project, which would cost a total $1.3 billion by 2049. The project required an additional $50 million in county general obligation bonds for the stadium. The county commissioners approved up to $563 million in bonds to back the planned ballpark. The county planned to sell about $454.6 million in new and refunding bonds. The total county contribution was estimated at $347 million just for the new stadium. The City of Miami was scheduled to contribute $23 million, and the team owners were supposed to contribute $155 million. The county had a hard time selling all the bonds within the commission-set 7.5% interest cap. Professional sports tax bonds sold below the ceiling. In contrast, the convention development tax-backed bonds went for nearly 8.2%, yielding proceeds $6.2 million short of what the county was hoping to raise (Polansky, 2009).

Revenue Bonds

A more specific type of bond is the revenue bond; here the tax revenue to support repayment may come from the project itself. For example, an entrance tax of $1.50 per ticket could be charged, and all revenues from this tax would first be allocated to repaying the revenue bond. These bonds traditionally have a lower credit rating than other bonds because significant financial risks are associated with limiting repayment requirements to a specific tax source. This concern arose during the 1998 NBA strike. If games were canceled and admission revenue was lost, some bond issuers might not have had any of their anticipated revenue sources to repay revenue bondholders whose bonds were secured by attendance taxes or other revenue sources ("Securitizing sports," 1998). Because NHL teams are not the anchor tenants at most arenas, the threat of defaulting on bonds was not a major concern during the 2004-2005 NHL lockout. This

concern arose again during the 2011 NBA lockout when the Orlando Magic had just finished their first season in the new Amway Center. The Magic were to receive all proceeds from ticket sales for Magic games, and the city was to receive all proceeds from ticket sales for all other events. The Magic were to contribute at least $50 million in cash up front, pick up any cost overruns, and pay rent of $1 million per year for 30 years. The City of Orlando paid for the land and infrastructure. The remaining money was to come from bonds that would be paid off by part of the Orange County, Florida, Tourist Development Tax, collected as a surcharge on hotel stays. The tourist tax was raised to 6% in 2006 to start generating income as soon as possible, even before ground was broken on the arena. The Magic were to guarantee $100 million of these bonds. Without any NBA games, however, a default or inability to comply with other contractual terms was possible. This concern expands on other concerns that Orlando was facing, as highlighted by the following quotation from the *Orlando Sentinel* back in 2010:

> The city could default on the bonds used to pay for the construction of the Orlando Magic's new arena just two years after the $480 million building opens, according to a leading financial-rating service.

> In the latest sign of how the recession has squeezed Orlando's $1.1 billion plan for new and updated community venues, Fitch Ratings downgraded the bonds sold to finance the arena to "junk" status. The firm's analysts also offered a dire warning: As soon as November 2012, there might not be enough money to cover debt payments. (Schlueb & Damron, 2010)

Thus, the City of Orlando was in fear of a default before the facility even opened. With less revenue because of the NBA lockout, the city could take advantage of the open dates by bringing in new events to generate additional income that they could use to repay the bonds. But the dates needed to be left open in case the strike was resolved, and most events require months of marketing to be successful.

Sometimes a public entity targets a specific tax to finance a bond. Cleveland used a sin tax on alcohol and tobacco sales to help finance Jacobs Field and Gund Arena. San Antonio used a sales tax–based bond issue to help finance building the Alamodome. **Special tax bonds** are repayable from a specific pledged source and are not backed by the full faith and credit of the issuing entity. Thus, if the specific revenue source is inadequate, tax revenue may be insufficient to repay the bondholders. Tax and revenue anticipation notes can be issued to fund the project before revenue starts arriving. Similarly, a bond anticipation note or tax-exempt commercial paper can help bridge the gap during construction until revenue is generated to repay the interim note and start repaying special tax bonds (Greenberg & Gray, 1996).

Bond Acquisition Process

Bond acquisition is a complex process for sports facilities that can take several years. The first step often entails determining whether tax revenue can be raised from alternative sources. For example, the proposal for an arena in Denton County, Texas, included "calling" a half-cent sales tax to raise some of the required funds. This process starts with calling the election, which entails applying for the tax to appear on a future election ballot. After an election is held and the half-cent tax is approved, the municipality needs to close the bond backed by the half-cent tax. With the prospect for the sales tax bonds, the municipality can then proceed with calling an election for the GOB. The GOB goes through the same process of being put on a future ballot. If the voters approve the GOB, the next step is closing the bond. The voting process alone can take 10 months to complete (*Overview*, 1995).

Repayment Sources

Whichever type of bond is issued, repayment will always be the key concern for investors. Other factors can be important to a potential investor, such as whether the bond is tax exempt (see chapter 5 for tax-related factors), whether the government entity purchased bond repayment insurance, and whether contractually obligated revenue (COR) is sufficient to repay the bond. Even with these variables, investors will look toward a stable and adequate repayment source as an additional assurance that the bond will be paid. Significant funding sources include (Greenberg & Gray, 1996)

- utility taxes,
- ticket surcharges,
- car rental taxes,
- real estate taxes,
- specific sales taxes,
- possessory interest taxes,

- tourist development taxes,
- restaurant sales taxes,
- excise or sin taxes,
- lottery and gaming revenue,
- nontax fees such as permits,
- general appropriations, and
- general sales and use taxes.

A utility tax, for example, is a cost added to an electric, water, or gas bill to help pay for the debt service of the bond. In the 1990s the San Francisco Giants were considering a move to San Jose, California. The proposed stadium was to be partially financed by a utility tax. Opponents of the stadium distributed light-switch covers to communicate the idea that every time people turned on the lights, they would be paying for the proposed stadium. The stadium ballot measure was defeated by the strong activists against the tax.

A possessory interest tax designed to tax the primary facility user is charged to whoever possesses control of the facility. Tourist development taxes and car rental taxes are designed primarily to tax out-of-towners who visit the city. This technique is popular because it is easy to tell a voting population that out-of-towners will pay for the facility (Howard & Crompton, 2004).

Excise taxes are general taxes added to various products; sin taxes are more specifically set up to be added to the cost of alcohol and tobacco products. Sin taxes were used to help finance building the arena and stadium in Cleveland.

Nontax fees are special expenses passed on to particular parties (e.g., raising the permit costs for other developers in the city). Such a tax can stimulate a backlash from citizens who do not want to pay a greater share of the funding for the facility than others are paying. General appropriations are among the most favored funding options.

Appropriations are funds that are set aside for specific purposes. Through political dealings a municipality might convince the state legislature or federal government to give a "gift" appropriation from the budget to help pay the facility construction expenses or to fund bond repayments. The San Antonio Alamodome was built as a bus stop to help secure a federal appropriation for interstate transportation. In March 1994 VIA Metropolitan Transit started collecting a five-year half-cent sales tax to help fund the $197 million construction of the Alamodome in 1990 to 1993. Part of the construction included a bus stop, allowing the project to collect federal transportation funds.

Although these revenue sources can often support significant repayment obligations, CORs can also provide a significant guarantee that a debt will be repaid. Contractually obligated revenues are any contract whereby a party agrees to pay a specific sum for a guaranteed number of years. Typical long-term contracts that form the basis of COR backing include (Greenberg & Gray, 1996)

♦ premium seat contracts,
♦ luxury box contracts,
♦ concession and novelty rights contracts,
♦ naming rights contracts,
♦ pouring rights (beer and soft drink) contracts,
♦ personal seat licenses, and
♦ parking rights contracts.

Contractually obligated revenues have two primary functions. They can be used as a source of revenue to guarantee repayment of bonds or other loans. They also can be used as an independent funding source. If the bonds are all covered through other revenue streams, the team or facility may be able to sell the naming rights and use those funds to enhance its bottom line.

Several examples will suggest how stadium and arena builders can use a blend of bonds and CORs to finance a stadium. The Rangers Ballpark in Arlington opened in 1994 at a cost of $190 million. Most of the project (71%) was financed through a 30-year 5% sales tax that was projected to raise $11 million yearly. The public sector also contributed 13% to the deal through a $1 per ticket surcharge. The Texas Rangers contributed 16% to the project by selling $30 million in luxury suite contracts (Greenberg & Gray, 1996). More deals are being pursued using blended projects. One of the primary contributions often provided by team owners is a large lump sum that represents how much the owners were able to sell naming rights for. Thus, an owner who agrees to contribute $100 million toward constructing a facility might include in that sum $80 million from a naming-rights contract that could be paid over a number of years. The city or county building the facility might need to take out a bond and pay interest on this amount until the owner is paid by the right's holder.

The Gateway project in Cleveland was financed through a tax-exempt county bond offering that raised 45% of the $152 million needed to build the Gund Arena (now the Quicken Loans Arena). Liquor and cigarette taxes (sin taxes) covered another 42%, and private naming rights covered the remaining 13% (Greenberg & Gray, 1996). The bonds were sold to various investors, and the income stream used to repay the bonds came from state capital improvement funds and a countywide sin tax. The sin tax taxed alcohol at $3.00 per gallon of liquor and $0.16 per gallon of beer, and cigarettes were taxed at $0.045 per pack. These taxes were to be in place for 15 years (Greenberg & Gray, 1996). More than $238 million was raised in the 15 years since the sin tax was adopted to help fund Jacobs Field and Gund Arena. Cuyahoga County ended up paying $87 million to help build the facility. In 2005 voters approved a 10-year extension for the sin tax to help pay off the debt for the Cleveland Browns Stadium ("'Sinners' as saints," 2005). In 2011 the Columbus Blue Jackets were attempting to sell Nationwide Arena to Franklin County because the team was having to dip into their hockey budget to fund the building. A sin tax was suggested as a way to fund the purchase (Wyshynski, 2011).

The Ice Palace in Tampa may be one of the most complex projects in terms of the multitude of funding sources used to cover the $160 million needed to complete the facility in 1996. The Tampa Bay Lightning's parent company issued private-project revenue bonds to cover 30% of the costs. The Tampa Sports Authority issued tax-exempt bonds backed by a state sales tax rebate, estimated at $2 million annually (19% of the costs), and a county tourist tax bond backed by non–ad valorem revenue, which would also generate $2 million annually. Another $750,000 per year (7%) was backed by city parking bonds. The sports authority also issued taxable bonds that included a requirement for a ticket surcharge of $0.50 per ticket, which was projected to generate $1.5 million annually (11%) and backed by a county loan or pledge. Additionally, the city issued a surcharge bond backed by a $0.25 surcharge per ticket, which was expected to generate $250,000 yearly (2%). Last, the city provided 2% of the construction costs through public land acquisition, which was accomplished through use of eminent domain (Greenberg & Gray, 1996).

Eminent domain is the process by which government units can take land from individual landowners. Land or property can be taken if the seized land will be used for the public good. Government units have to pay the fair market value for the land and use this process to build roads, new schools, or even new arenas or stadiums. In addition, eminent domain can be used to take more than just land. The city of Baltimore attempted to invoke eminent domain to take the Baltimore Colts, which prompted the team to pack all their belongings into trucks and move to Indianapolis in the middle of the night (*Eminent domain*, 2002).

After it has been determined where potential tax revenue can be found to repay the bonds, a public entity considering issuing bonds needs to examine the potential municipal bond rating. Bond ratings for stadium projects are normally fairly high because of the backing of major cities that presumably will not go bankrupt. Lenders, however, have become more leery of these deals in recent years because of the possibility that the oversaturated television market will reduce future broadcast contracts. Lenders can also be concerned when teams and leagues face a multitude of challenges, from fickle fans to legal challenges of league policies. For example, suppose that a public university issues $50 million in bonds to fund new buildings and a new stadium. If bond repayment is tied to student tuition revenue, the university could be in serious trouble if student enrollment decreases significantly. If student tuition drops by 20%, the effect on bonds could be significant, and the lender might speed up the repayment schedule.

GOVERNMENT ASSISTANCE: INDUSTRIAL DEVELOPMENT BONDS

So far, this chapter has focused on debt- and equity-based capital acquisition. Companies and organizations can use any one or several of the capital acquisition techniques that we have considered. But many small businesses, including minority-owned businesses, need some additional help to acquire needed capital while still relying on bonds.

Although most bond offerings are cost prohibitive for smaller companies to issue, businesses can secure other bond-based funding options with local government assistance. Government units in each state have the authority, through sport authorities, economic development commissions, and similar divisions, to offer small-issue **industrial development bonds (IDBs)**.

Federal law allows a business owner to raise up to $10 million using IDBs. The IDBs carry an interest rate ranging from one-half to three-quarters of the prime interest rate, with a 30-year maturity. The one drawback to IDBs is the transaction costs (ranging from 2% to 5%), which can erase all interest savings and make smaller bonds uneconomical (Hovey, 1998, July). In 1996 over $2.7 billion was raised for businesses through this financing method, and these funds were used to

create new jobs (Hovey, 1998, July). The process requires a significant amount of paperwork, and company owners must compete with other projects (such as public housing and urban renewal) that are trying to secure tax-free bonds. The key to obtaining these bonds is for the business to show that it can generate jobs. A rule of thumb is that every $50,000 in bond funding should create one full-time-equivalent job (Hovey, 1998, July).

CONCEPTS INTO PRACTICE

Assume that a fitness center wishes to build in a rundown part of town that they think will turn around and become a prime location for young professionals. The owners could approach city hall with a request for assistance to help revive the area. Working with the city's economic development commission and planning committee, they could present a deal to city hall that gets approved. The city can then issue the IDB, which is really a corporate bond for the fitness center but appears to be a tax-free municipal bond issued by the city (Hovey, 1998, July). The proceeds from the bond can be used to buy equipment or purchase the building.

Although these tax-free bonds have significant benefits, the owners of the fitness center would need to examine some rules and regulations to determine whether an IDB would be appropriate for their project. If they used the IDB-generated funds to pay for equipment, the money would go further than if they used the funds for construction because many states require people who use funds obtained from IDBs to pay union or prevailing wages. Union wages might need to be paid for construction, but wages are not relevant to equipment purchases. Another issue is that borrowers may need to contact a bank to secure a letter of credit guaranteeing repayment of the bond, and the letter of credit could cost around 1% of the borrowed amount (Hovey, 1998, July). Such added costs or restrictions might make IDBs impractical for some borrowers.

CAPITALIZATION PROBLEMS AND ISSUES

As highlighted throughout this chapter and chapters 8 and 9, a company must carefully examine its funding needs. Capital or debt structures are not random acts of choosing numbers. The consequences of issuing too many shares or bonds can have a significant negative effect. Likewise, the failure to issue enough shares or bonds can be a disaster. This section covers the concerns associated with overcapitalization, undercapitalization, and recapitalization.

CONCEPTS INTO PRACTICE

Assume that a fitness center has been operating for two years and decides to expand. Investors may be interested if the prospective earnings are high enough to meet their investment needs. Many of the issues raised throughout this chapter come into play in determining exactly how the owners would pursue obtaining the funds. An attorney friend has suggested that the owners incorporate to take advantage of liability reduction benefits. The owners decide not to issue bonds but instead to have preferred stock issued to themselves, with a dividend requirement of $50,000 a year. Their business plan shows that future earnings before taxes should be $400,000 a year, but even in a poor year their contractually obligated revenue (COR) will produce a minimum of $200,000 in pretax earnings. Therefore, even in a poor year, and even if they received only $100,000 after-tax profit, they still could cover dividend obligations twice over.

The fitness center owners therefore decide to issue 20,000 shares of 5% preferred stock at $50 par value. Based on these figures, the yearly dividend will be $2.50 per share. The owners did not base their calculations on pie in the sky; they analyzed the worst possible earnings scenario and calculated how much they could withdraw from the business while still maintaining owner equity return. If the company has a strong year with $400,000 in earnings, reduced to $200,000 after taxes, they will have a $50,000 obligation for their preferred stocks and $150,000 for common stocks. The owners decide to sell common stock valued at 12.5 times expected earnings ($150,000), or $1,875,000 in potential value. If stocks at that time are selling for 10 times earnings on average, then the stock would be selling on the market for $1,500,000 in total.

The owners' next step is to determine a selling price for the stock. On the basis of the $1,875,000 valuation for the common stock, they choose to sell the stock for $10 per share. If they wanted to price the stock higher, at $50, for example, then they would not issue as many shares. To arrive at the

requisite $1,875,000 value, they would issue only 37,500 shares at the $50 price. Using the $10 stock price, the initial capital structure for the business is as follows:

20,000 shares of preferred stock ($50 par value) = $1,000,000

187,500 shares of common stock ($10 per share) = $1,875,000

The fitness center's net assets would total $2,875,000 in this scenario. Using this strategy the owners would have funded their business entirely through stocks.

Overcapitalization

A critical concern that needs to be discussed is overcapitalization. A company can raise too much money and not have the financial means to pay everything off. The most serious form of overcapitalization entails issuing too much bond-backed capital. Interest payments are due even if excess cash is lying around and not gaining any return. Too many cumulative preferred shares can also represent a significant cash flow problem, especially in periods of depression. Overcapitalization can also occur with stocks when too many shares are on the market, which reduces the earnings per share.

CONCEPTS INTO PRACTICE

If the fitness owners issued one million shares and earned only a $150,000 profit from which to pay common stockholders' dividends, then the dividend would amount to only $0.15 per share. On the basis of the 12.5 times earnings figure used in the previous analysis, the stock would now have a market value of only $1.87 per share (Bogen, 1966). A stock price that low could scare away many investors who might think that the stock was too speculative.

Undercapitalization

Besides having too many financial obligations, a company can issue too few shares or bonds in relation to the expected earnings. If a company becomes valuable and only a few shares are available, the cost per share might be extremely high. Individual shares for various companies or partnerships have been worth several thousand dollars. Highly priced shares often scare away potential investors.

CONCEPTS INTO PRACTICE

Suppose that the fitness center owners issued only 10,000 shares of common stock and had $150,000 in earnings. The entire amount was to be used to pay dividends. Each stock would receive $15 per share in dividends. If the stock sold at 12.5 times earnings, the shares would sell for $187.50 each (Bogen, 1966).

Another concern with undercapitalization is that if most of the funds for growth come from internal sources such as retained earnings, the business may have a hard time raising funds externally. As with the situation for consumers, a business needs to borrow through accounts payable and bank loans to develop a credit history. Some consumers prefer to pay for everything with cash. Although you might think that these people are being fiscally responsible, in fact they are hurting themselves by not developing a history of borrowing and paying debts in a timely manner. A business also needs to borrow enough from a variety of lenders to establish a credit history. Undercapitalization hampers the ability of a business to develop a strong credit history.

Recapitalization

A key technique in capitalization is recapitalization, which can be performed through a **stock split**. If shares are trading at an excessive price, the corporation's board of directors may decide to bring down the price by issuing a large number of shares in exchange for outstanding stock. Stock splits can be two for one, or three for one, or any other variation, including fractions. Stocks can be split from common stock into either just common stock or common stock and preferred stock.

Recapitalization can occur with bonds as well, but the process is more elaborate. To recapitalize bonds, a corporation needs to go to the bondholders and ask them for approval before changing interest or principal payments. Any changes that do not affect principal or interest payments can be made by amending the indenture, if the indenture provides for changes. This process might seem complex, but it is basically a change in the contractual terms, and contract changes are not that difficult if all the parties agree to the changes.

To help encourage bondholders to extend the principal repayment period, the corporation can offer to raise the interest rate, establish a sinking fund for retirement of the bonds or provide additional security as collateral (or both), or make the bond convertible (Bogen, 1966). If recapitalization does not appear feasible and the interest owed on the bonds is excessive, the corporation can ask bondholders to agree to postponing payments for a given period or have the bonds "stamped," indicating that interest will be paid only when earned (Bogen, 1966).

CONCEPTS INTO PRACTICE

Preferred stocks can also be recapitalized. For example, if a sport manufacturing company had to pay a 5% dividend on preferred stocks and had not paid the dividend in several years, the company might ask the shareholders to return the shares. The shareholders would receive in exchange additional shares that could include a higher dividend rate to make up for the unpaid dividends.

CONCLUSION

This chapter highlighted various capital acquisition techniques. Sport businesses, whether for-profit or nonprofit, need to acquire funds to keep operating or to expand. Finding capital is often the most difficult task for new as well as established businesses. Capital can be acquired in various ways, but no technique is guaranteed. Issuing bonds is among the most difficult ways to raise funds.

A significant amount of work is required to issue a bond, and typically only the largest companies do so. Most sport businesses use stock or bank financing rather than bonds. But major privately financed construction projects, such as stadiums or arenas, can be financed through bonds secured by the facilities. Furthermore, stadiums and arenas built with public funds are almost always built using bonds guaranteed by a variety of taxes or revenue streams. Thus, bond financing is often the most visible form of capital acquisition in the sport industry.

Class Discussion Topics

1. Should the general population pay the debt service for bonds issued to pay for a stadium or arena that is used primarily by a privately owned professional team? Debate the topic, citing all the pros and cons associated with the question. What innovative ideas could be used to help repay the bonds?

2. What is the value of bonds versus stocks?

3. What happens when a company defaults on paying a bond?

4. Is a bond a safer investment for an investor than other investing options such as stocks?

5. Should companies be allowed to sell junk bonds?

6. Besides the various backings for bonds highlighted in this chapter, what other resources can be tapped to help repay government-backed bonds to build stadiums and arenas?

7. What do you think the biggest problems are with under- and overcapitalization?

PART

V

Financial Management

After a business gains capital, it has to know how to spend that capital wisely. Part V looks at the various options that businesses have to manage their money.

Chapter 11, "Capital Budgeting," starts by identifying the goal of capital budgeting and gives a brief overview of capital spending. The chapter then provides an analysis of how much it costs to acquire capital. After a company knows how much capital costs, it can develop a capital-budgeting decision analysis to see which method is most beneficial. No decision is without risk, so risks need to be considered, and the final analysis will produce a realistic cash flow based on the identified assumptions.

Chapter 12, "Short-Term Financial Management," highlights various strategies for funding short-term growth. The first step involves a review of current assets and liabilities. After these variables are understood, a company can examine both cash and credit management to make sure that it is maximizing its cash flow while not losing money by granting credit to weak borrowers. By using a strong collections management program, a company can make sure that it receives payment in a timely manner or obtains additional revenue by charging interest on short-term lending to others.

Chapter 13, "Inventory and Production Management," highlights how money can be either lost or preserved through effective management of the production and inventory process. The chapter first highlights the cost of doing business and then examines the process of inventory and production management. This chapter also covers newer trends such as just-in-time inventory and the balanced scorecard to help save money and make businesses more efficient.

chapter 11

Capital Budgeting

Chapter Objectives

After studying this chapter, you should be able to do the following:

- Define capital budgeting.
- Distinguish between the various techniques of capital budgeting.
- Understand the process of calculating the cost of capital.
- Calculate and use the weighted average cost of capital and the capital asset pricing model formulas.
- Understand how to make capital decisions.
- Distinguish between present value and net present value calculations.
- Understand payback rules such as the internal rate of return.
- Describe cash flow and the way that it works.

Sport managers have many decisions to make with respect to financial management. One of the most important decisions involves the use of funds for long-term projects such as purchasing equipment, constructing a new facility, or renovating an existing structure. The process of making investments toward these types of fixed assets, both tangible and intangible, is known as capital budgeting. Capital budgeting is a key component of long-term success for a sport organization. **Capital** is the long-term funding necessary for the acquisition of fixed assets (Brigham & Ehrhardt, 2011). With respect to the sport industry, the largest area of capital spending is facility construction and renovation. Each year, billions of dollars are spent on facility projects such as stadiums, arenas, fitness facilities, and youth sport complexes. New income streams are also an important component of capital budgeting. A sport manager must decide whether the positive future cash flow from a capital project will be large enough to offset the cost of the project.

This chapter focuses on the basics of capital budgeting. We discuss the cost of capital, the methods of making capital-budgeting decisions, and ways of projecting future cash flows from capital projects.

GOAL OF CAPITAL BUDGETING

The goal of capital budgeting is to select investment opportunities that are worth more than they cost. Also, sport businesses should initially invest in those projects that provide the greatest return for their investment. Given the long-term effects associated with any investment, we can see why capital budgeting is a primary focus for sport organizations.

A sport business can raise and spend capital funds in countless ways. An integral part of financial management is determining the best capital sources. Efficient capital spending leads to growth and success for a sport business. To grow, a business must invest some of its available capital in fixed assets such as land, equipment, or machinery. For example, a fitness center cannot improve its recreational offerings without investing in new equipment and facilities. Although a for-profit business should invest in those projects that will result in the largest return on investment, this concern may not always be true for government or nonprofit organizations.

CAPITAL SPENDING

Before critically analyzing capital budgeting, we must focus on the meaning of capital spending. **Capital spending** is the net spending on fixed assets. Net spending is the total money that a business uses to acquire **real assets**, less the sale of previously owned real assets (Brigham & Ehrhardt, 2011). During the decade of the 2000s many businesses invested heavily in fixed assets. This trend carried over into the sport industry as well. A boom occurred in construction of new sport stadiums and arenas such as Citizens Bank Park in Philadelphia and Heinz Field in Pittsburgh, just to name a few. The construction boom was fostered by several circumstances. On the financial side, team owners believed that capital expenditures for facility amenities such as luxury suites, club seats, concessions, and parking would result in new income streams. Additionally, new facilities were needed to replace older structures that required major repairs, such as Veterans Stadium in Philadelphia and Busch Stadium in St. Louis. The building boom ended, however, with the recession of 2007-08 because many teams either had trouble securing financing for these projects or decided to wait until the end of the recession.

Capital budgeting and purchasing capital items are long-term endeavors. When we refer to items as long term, the period involved is usually greater than one year. Long-term assets such as equipment and facilities have a productive life that is longer than one year. With respect to capital, a business is usually unable to allocate the amount of money necessary for purchasing high-priced fixed assets in a single year. Therefore, the business must develop capital budgets that detail how the funds will be raised and allocated over an extended period. For this reason, current, or short-term, items are separated from capital items in financial statements.

The funding mix required for capital expenditures is referred to as the capital structure. In general, the traditional corporate capital structure includes debt (bonds and long-term loans), preferred stock, and common stock (Ross, Westerfield, & Jordan, 2008). These capital vehicles are discussed in part IV, but they are referred to again in this chapter within the context of analyzing their budgeting implications. All these capital sources have an accompanying cost. If a sport business wishes to borrow funds from a bank to construct a new facility, it must pay interest on the borrowed amount. The interest that is paid in addition to the principal being borrowed is referred to as the cost of the debt. The next section deals with each form of capital and covers methods to measure the accompanying costs.

For nonprofit organizations such as university athletics departments, additional sources of funding include donations and gifts. Supporters of nonprofit organizations often make financial donations toward new capital projects. For example, a university alumnus may donate a significant amount of money toward constructing or renovating a sports facility, such as when T. Boone Pickens donated over $175 million to the Oklahoma State University Department of Athletics. Many nonprofit organizations rely on these donations for a portion, or all, of the funds necessary to complete capital projects. These donations are important to nonprofit organizations because unlike corporations, they cannot raise capital through equity ownership.

COST OF CAPITAL

Sport businesses can use four traditional forms of capital to fund growth: debt, common stock, preferred stock, and retained earnings. The four traditional forms of capital are known as capital components. They all have one common trait: The persons or institutions that provide the capital expect, or demand, a return on investment (Brigham & Ehrhardt, 2011). A bank or financial institution that loans money to a sport business expects to be repaid the loan principal plus interest. A common stockholder or investor expects the firm to invest in capital-spending projects that will increase the value of the company and ultimately result in increased stock value. This expected return on the investment means that the business incurs a cost to acquire the capital funds. In the case of a bank loan, the cost of capital is the amount of interest owed to the creditor. This section develops methods to measure the cost of capital for debt and equity. Sport businesses need to understand and appreciate the fact that any capital acquisition technique has a cost, and that cost will dictate how much capital can be raised.

We must make a quick point about retained earnings before moving forward. **Retained earnings** are funds that are kept by a business to be used for reinvestment in the company. This reinvestment often takes the form of capital spending. Management believes that the stockholders will benefit more from this reinvestment than from having the money returned through dividend payments. Because the retained earnings can be used by the

sport business to purchase additional stock, the cost of retained earnings is considered the cost of common stock. Therefore, we will discuss the cost of retained earnings along with the cost of common stock.

Note that companies develop strategies for structuring their capital. For example, Speedway Motorsports may have 50% of their capital in the form of debt, 30% in preferred stock, and 20% in common stock. These proportions, referred to as a target capital structure, may vary greatly across businesses and industries (Ross et al., 2008). Within some professional sports leagues, capital structure is controlled by the league to some extent. For example, the NFL has restrictions on the level of debt that each team can maintain. The NFL set the debt limit as a financial safeguard to ensure that none of its teams has excess debt that will lead to future financial difficulties. The debt limit was increased from $125 million to $150 million in 2005. This increase was made possible by the increases in league revenues from media contracts and team valuations (*Fitch affirms*, 2005). If a league member is at its debt limit, it must raise capital through other sources, perhaps by attracting new equity investors.

Most sport businesses finance their capital budgets through a combination of debt and equity. Each form of capital has an associated cost. Some businesses may decide to structure their capital budgets such that they rely on one form of capital, but this approach is uncommon for large corporations. For government-owned and -operated institutions such as a university athletic department, the sources of capital are primarily debt and money raised through gifts and donations. State-funded universities such as Florida State University or the University of Iowa have no individual private ownership rights. Their income comes from sources such as donations, ticket sales, sponsorships, student fees, and broadcast fees. These funds are used to cover the current expenses involved in operating a collegiate athletic program. The university usually raises money for capital projects from donations or the issuance of debt. The state government is ultimately responsible for paying the bondholders if the university defaults.

Privately held sport businesses such as fitness centers, pro sports teams, and apparel companies can also raise capital by selling equity ownership rights or borrowing funds. For example, Under Armour may raise money by issuing common stock to the public, but they may also borrow from banks or issue bonds.

Several factors can influence capital-structuring decisions. For example, a weak stock market such as that seen in 2007 and 2008 may make the issuance of stock less attractive than it might be otherwise. As stock prices fall, a business needs to issue more shares to raise the necessary capital funds. In addition, a cost is associated with issuing new stock. Most businesses work with a financial institution to help with a public offering, and they pay for those services. The expenses related to issuing new stock are known as flotation costs (Ross et al., 2008). Immoo, Lochhead, Ritter, and Zhao (1996) found that a company that wants to raise $2 to $10 million in capital through a common stock offering will have flotation costs of approximately 13.28% of the total amount of capital being raised. Thus, if a business wants to have $2 million in capital, it will need to raise approximately $2.26 million. The additional $260,000 will be needed to cover the flotation costs.

Immoo et al. (1996) also found that the average flotation cost is significantly less when capital is raised through debt. In the $2 to $10 million debt range, the average flotation cost is 4.39%, one-third the level of flotation costs for common stock. Whether debt or equity is used, many of the flotation costs, such as attorneys' fees, are fixed and are not greatly affected by the amount of capital being raised. Therefore, most businesses do not like to raise capital in small quantities. Other businesses also elect to raise capital through a single source, debt or equity, each year in an effort to minimize flotation costs (Ross et al., 2008).

A professional sports team example will illustrate average cost of capital for debt. Assume that the Atlanta Braves decide to go public by issuing stock. The team raises $300 million in its initial public offering. If the average flotation cost for such an offering is 8%, then $24 million will be paid to float the shares, and $4.5 to $6 million of that amount might represent attorneys' fees that need to be paid even if only $100 million had been raised through the offering.

Selecting one capital source each year has short-term effects on a target capital structure, so maintaining the target structure is difficult. A business' target capital structure may also be affected by outside economic forces such as the stock market or interest rates. Interest rates have an effect on the cost of issuing debt. Therefore, a business may want to select debt as its capital source (to maintain its capital target), but issuing new stock may be more cost effective, especially when stock prices are relatively high.

Thus far, we have discussed the general principles of capital, the forms of capital, and the importance of capital cost. The next step is to develop a method for accurately measuring new capital costs. The most commonly used method to measure the cost of capital is the **weighted average cost of capital** (WACC). The WACC focuses on determining the average cost of each capital component and weights each based on its contribution to the total capital amount. In general, a sport business will maximize its value when it minimizes its WACC (Ross et al., 2008).

To calculate the WACC, we must separate capital into each of the three potential capital sources available for a business: debt, preferred stock, and common stock. As stated earlier, the cost of retaining earnings and the cost of issuing common stock are calculated similarly. In doing the calculation of the WACC as outlined in this chapter, retained earnings are implicitly included in the value of common stock. Whether new shares of stock are issued or whether retained earnings are used to finance a capital project, the cost of funds is identical (ignoring underwriting and flotation costs). The following sections deal first with the cost of debt, then with the cost of equity, and finally with the cost of combining the capital mix in the WACC.

Cost of Debt

Debt is important because many smaller businesses raise most of their capital through this capital component, usually in the form of bank loans (Brigham & Ehrhardt, 2011).

Many large corporations also issue debt through bonds and debentures. A bond is a long-term promissory note issued by a business. For most bonds, the business agrees to pay back the amount borrowed at a specified future date (usually 10 to 30 years for long-term bonds) in addition to a coupon payment, which is a percentage of the bond's value. The coupon payment for most corporate coupon bonds is made semiannually (twice per year). For example, a sport business can sell 25-year bonds with a value of $1,000 and a semiannual coupon payment of 6%. Anyone who purchases a bond will receive semiannual payments of $60 for 25 years. Also, at the end of the 25 years, the creditor will receive $1,000. In this example, the annual cost of debt for the life of the bond would average around 12%.

CONCEPTS INTO PRACTICE

Suppose that you own a relatively small business, such as a local health and fitness center. You may borrow money from a bank or similar financial institution to fund new capital spending. The principal amount that you borrow must be repaid over time with interest. The interest is the cost of borrowing the funds. If you borrow $200,000 at an interest rate of 8%, the cost of debt, excluding taxes, is also 8%. But, the cost of debt is misleading unless the potential tax implications are extracted. Because the debt repayment of 8% is probably tax deductible, you will not pay 8% per year (see more about taxes in chapter 4). The true cost will be $16,000 (8% multiplied by $200,000) minus what tax savings can be generated by reducing your income by $16,000. Assuming a 40% combined federal and state tax rate for the business, the potential cost could drop from $16,000 to $9,600 ($16,000 minus 40%).

As discussed in the previous chapter, a debenture is a long-term bond. But unlike regular bonds that are secured by corporate assets, a debenture is unsecured. The only protection that a debenture holder has to guarantee repayment is the good name of the company that issues the debenture. If the corporation faces financial hardship, the debenture holders are similar to all other unsecured lenders in that they are often the last group to be repaid, if they are paid at all.

From these examples, measuring the rate of return required by debt holders appears to be relatively straightforward. How much will debt holders demand in future payments to make the necessary funds available today? For a small business like an independently operated sporting goods store, ascertaining this number may be as simple as determining the annual interest rate on a bank loan. But the process can be a bit more complex for a large corporation such as Speedway Motorsports or Under Armour. Given that the WACC is used in the planning process for the issuance of future debt, a financial manager is making a prediction or estimation of the future cost of debt. Determining the coupon payment that must be offered to attract future bond purchasers is not always easy. A business that issues a new bond at a time when interest rates are on the rise will have a hard time selling the bonds without increasing the interest

rate paid to purchasers. Therefore, determining the appropriate rate of return is not an exact science. Nevertheless, by using the correct information the analyst can make a credible estimate.

What Is the Correct Information?

A financial manager can analyze historical data on debt instruments to make a prediction about the future. Suppose that Speedway Motorsports wants to issue new 25-year bonds to raise capital. Through experience, the financial manager knows that similar bonds have been issued for each of the past five years. She also knows that the financial position of the business has not changed over that period and that the previous bonds were issued with a 10% coupon rate. Additionally, the financial manager would look at the current yield on a bond with the same maturity and credit rating, as determined by Moody's or Standard & Poor's, as well as the current debt costs for similar businesses. For example, suppose Speedway Motorsports is investigating the issuance of debt to build a new racetrack. The financial manager would gather information on the cost of debt incurred by other businesses that have recently financed facility construction.

Calculating the Cost of Debt

One other important debt feature is crucial to the cost-of-debt calculation. To encourage capital investment in the United States, the federal government and most state governments provide a tax deduction on the interest payments made to debt holders. For most corporations, the federal tax rate for interest deductions is 35%. Most states also give tax allowances for interest deductions, usually at about a 5% rate (Brigham & Ehrhardt, 2011). In total, the average tax rate for interest deductions is approximately 40%. This tax savings reduces the overall cost of debt for a sport business.

Assume that we want to calculate the cost of debt for Speedway Motorsports. The cost of debt can be written as a mathematical formula:

$$D = R - (R \times T)$$

D = cost of debt

R = interest rate paid to debt holder

T = marginal tax rate on interest payments

The rate of return required by debt holders is the interest rate, or **R**, that is paid on the debt. The tax savings is the rate of return required by debt holders multiplied by the **marginal tax** rate on interest payments, which we will abbreviate as **T**. We can rewrite the cost of debt this way:

$$D = R \times (1 - T)$$

CONCEPTS INTO PRACTICE

In our example, we assume that Speedway Motorsports borrows $1,000,000 at an interest rate of 6% and has a marginal tax rate of 40%. Their cost of debt is calculated as follows:

$$D = 6\% \times (1 - 0.4)$$

$$D = 3.6\%$$

Therefore, Speedway Motorsports' cost of debt is 3.6% annually. Multiplying 3.6% by $1,000,000 shows that the cost of debt in dollars is $36,000. The tax deduction associated with making interest payments will save Speedway Motorsports 2.4%, or $24,000 each year, of the original $1,000,000 that was borrowed.

Cost of Equity

Capital can also be acquired by selling ownership in the business, also known as the issuance of equity. Equity is separated into two different classifications: preferred stock and common stock.

Cost of Preferred Stock

Preferred stock has a few unique characteristics that are important when calculating its cost. First, dividend payments on preferred stock are not tax deductible for the corporation paying the dividends. Additionally, individual investors must pay tax on the money that they receive from being preferred shareholders. Corporations are permitted to claim that 70% of the funds they receive from being preferred shareholders in other corporations are tax deductible (Ross et al., 2008). Tax savings such as we saw with debt are not available for firms that issue preferred stock. In addition, although firms have no legal requirement to pay yearly dividends on preferred stock, they usually make every attempt to do so. If a company misses a dividend payment, it has to pay the back-owed dividend the next time that a dividend payment is

declared. Dividends must be paid on preferred stock before they are paid to common stockholders. In addition, in some cases preferred stockholders have the right to take control of a company if they do not receive dividend payments. To avoid defaulting on required payments, management attempts to pay dividends regularly to keep preferred stockholders happy. The failure to make dividend payments to preferred stockholders is a signal that a firm may be in financial distress. This circumstance may eventually lead to difficulty in issuing future capital in either the debt or the equity market (Ross et al., 2008).

As discussed in chapter 9, preferred stocks pay a fixed dividend to the investor, similar to the coupon payment of a bond. Dividends can be postponed until future years; the firm's board of directors is responsible for making this decision (Ross et al., 2008). Also, as stated earlier, preferred stock dividends are not tax deductible, so we do not need to include a tax savings component in our cost calculation.

All preferred stock has a predetermined share value, called the par value, and a fixed dividend payment per share. For example, Nike preferred stock has a $1 par value and an annual fixed dividend payment of $0.10 (*Standard & Poor's*, 1999). The cost of preferred stock is the dividend payment, which we abbreviate as **v**, divided by the issuing price, **P**. In our calculations, we also abbreviate the cost of preferred stock as **S**.

As stated earlier, flotation costs are associated with issuing new stock. The flotation costs decrease the amount of cash that the firm receives from the sale of new preferred stock. For example, if Speedway Motorsports issues new preferred stock for $100 per share and the flotation cost is 6%, Speedway will receive only $94 per share. Therefore, we should include the flotation cost in the calculation of P and redefine P as the net issuing price. Given the information that we have, the cost of preferred stock can be written as follows:

$$\text{Cost of preferred stock} = \frac{\text{preferred stock dividend}}{\text{net issuing price}}$$

or

$$S = \frac{v}{P}$$

S = cost of preferred stock
v = preferred stock dividend
P = net issuing price

Cost of Common Stock

The last capital component to be considered is common stock. With respect to common stock, a sport business can raise capital through two methods. First, it can issue new common stock. To attract new common stock shareholders, the sport business must sell the stock shares at an attractive price. Prospective stockholders will buy the stock if they believe that the value of the stock will increase in the future. The annual percentage return (holding period return) associated with annual dividend payments and increases in the stock price must exceed the returns on investments of equivalent risk. If it does not, people will invest their money in other opportunities.

During the 1990s a number of initial public offerings (IPOs) occurred for sport-related businesses, but the recession in 2001 and 2002 slowed the growth rate of sport business IPOs considerably. In fact, several public sport businesses such as the Boston Celtics returned to being private entities. Since the 1990s we have seen few IPOs for purely sport-related companies, Under Armour being an exception. For sport teams, the inability to achieve substantial growth and the onerous financial reporting requirements seem to make the option of going public unattractive. As we saw in chapter 9, an initial public offering is the first offering of a stock to the public. The shares that are made available can be primary offerings (new shares that are sold to raise additional capital) or secondary offerings, which occur when the company ownership sells a portion of their existing shares (Brealey, Myers, & Marcus, 2009). After being issued, the stock is bought and sold through a public market such as the New York Stock Exchange or the NASDAQ.

A sport business can also raise capital through retaining earnings that would otherwise be used to pay dividends to common stockholders. By not paying dividends, the firm is retaining funds for use in capital spending. The capital-spending goal is to increase the value of the business. If the value of the business grows because of the capital spending, the common stock price should also increase. Most common stockholders will gladly forgo current dividend payments if the retained earnings will lead to an increase in the firm's stock price that is greater than the expected dividend payment.

Dividend policy is an important part of corporate finance. Financial managers continually struggle with the trade-off between dividend payments and retained earnings. They are looking for the appro-priate levels of each that will both keep the stockholders happy and allow the firm to grow. Making every investor happy is impossible, and there are never any guarantees. For example, Speedway Motorsports could pour $100 million into retained earnings and build a new racetrack. Investors might be ecstatic with the prospects of future increased value as new track revenues develop. But a year after the track opens a competitor may build a better facility and send Speedway's stock into a dramatic tailspin. Thus, retained earnings represent a potential risk, but all business decisions contain an element of risk.

Ultimately, the important aspect of common stock is that common stock shareholders require a return on their investment. This expected return on investment is vital for calculating the cost of common stock. In the simplest terms, the cost of common stock is the rate of return demanded by stockholders.

We must include several factors in calculating the cost of common stock. As with preferred stock, flotation costs are incurred when new common stock is issued. Likewise, issuing new common stock increases the overall supply of common shares available in the market. The increased supply of stock will cause the price of all shares to drop. The price decline often forces the firm to sell the new stock at a lower price and reduce the amount of capital that is raised. All these additional costs discourage some businesses from issuing new common stock. Most established larger businesses do not regularly offer new common stock on the open market. Instead, they elect to raise capital through retained earnings that would otherwise be paid as dividends or by issuing bonds or commercial paper.

Shareholders incur an **opportunity cost**, also known as **implicit cost**, if a business retains earnings to raise capital. The shareholders are forgoing dividends when earnings are retained. Shareholders could have reinvested those dividend payments in stocks, bonds, and other opportunities that may have resulted in a positive return. Therefore, the retained earnings should result in an increase in the value of a business that is greater than the amount that a shareholder can expect to earn if the money is paid out as dividends. The difficult task for a financial manager is to calculate this amount in dollars and cents. As with issuing new stock, the amount that shareholders could make by investing their dividend payments in the best alternative can serve to help measure the cost of common stock. Thus, the cost of common stock involves many factors, such as dividend payments, flotation costs, the rate of return of other investment opportunities, and the risk involved in investing in common stock. We now present three methods for measuring the cost of common stock.

Capital Asset Pricing Model

The first method of measuring the cost of common stock is the **capital asset pricing model** (CAPM). This method is the most commonly used approach for measuring the cost of capital (Brigham & Ehrhardt, 2011). It begins by estimating the rate of return on a risk-free investment such as a U.S. Treasury bond. Within the mathematical formula for the CAPM, we refer to the rate of return on a risk-free investment as **F**. Besides buying risk-free investments, the shareholder can also purchase riskier investments such as corporate stocks and bonds. The CAPM builds this into the calculation of the common stock cost. The most obvious investment decision would be for the shareholder to buy more shares in the same business. Given this, we want to develop a measure of the expected return on the firm's stock. The return is based in part on the risk of the stock.

Risk is an important component of common stocks. Stocks with large price swings are considered more volatile than others and therefore have a higher risk level. Stocks with a high level of risk must have the potential for a large increase in value. Several measures of a stock's level of risk are in common use. The CAPM incorporates the most commonly used measure, which is known as the beta coefficient. The beta coefficient is a measure of the volatility of an individual stock. A stock with volatility similar to that of the overall stock market has a beta coefficient of 1.0. A stock that is half as volatile as the stock market has a beta of 0.5, and a stock that is twice as volatile has a beta of 2.0. The risk of a stock increases as the beta coefficient increases. Information on the beta coefficients of stocks is readily available in publications such as *Value Line Investment Survey, Standard & Poor's,* and *Moody's.*

Another key component of CAPM is estimating the expected rate of return for the overall market. We want to develop the overall average return that can be expected from investing in the stock market. Using all this information, we develop an equation that will measure the expected cost of common stock:

$$C = F + [(M - F) \times B]$$

C = expected cost of common stock

F = expected rate of return from a risk-free investment

M = expected rate of return for the overall market

B = the company's beta coefficient

This equation attempts to measure the cost of common stock in two ways. First, it estimates the cost of a safe investment through F, defined as the rate of return on a risk-free investment. In addition, the model builds in an additional measure of cost for the individual corporation being analyzed. This is done by first deducting the rate of return for a risk-free investment, F, from the overall stock market rate of return, M. This amount is then multiplied by the beta coefficient of the stock of the individual business. The result is a measure of the additional cost, above that of a risk-free investment, for the common stock of an individual business. This amount is then added to F, the cost of a risk-free investment. The sum is the total cost of common stock using the CAPM method. This method is popular because it incorporates several important variables (risk-free investment cost, overall market cost, and the individual stock's level of risk) into the computation of the cost of common stock.

CONCEPTS INTO PRACTICE

Assume that Under Armour (UA) wants to raise capital by forgoing dividend payments to its stockholders. It will retain the earnings and use the funds to build a new distribution center. The company must determine its cost of raising the capital through retained earnings. Under current economic conditions, a risk-free investment will return 5%, Under Armour estimates the expected rate of return for the overall stock market to be 8%. The firm's beta coefficient is 1.2. To summarize, F = 5%; M = 8%; and B = 1.2. The CAPM equation is as follows:

$$C = F + [(M - F) \times B]$$
$$= 5\% + [(8\% - 5\%) \times 1.2]$$
$$= 5\% + 3.6\%$$
$$= 8.6\%$$

The estimated cost of common stock for UA is 8.6%.

The CAPM is not a perfect measure. Although it arrives at an exact percentage, some unpredictability is present in the various components used to calculate the final CAPM figure. We are making an estimate of the overall stock market performance that may be inaccurate. Predicting the future performance of the stock market is extremely difficult. In addition, the beta coefficient is a measure of the risk of the individual stock, which can change over time. Last, selecting the appropriate risk-free investment may be difficult. The many types of short- and long-term Treasury bonds have different rates of return. Any change in these variables greatly affects the result when we are using the CAPM.

Bond Yield Plus Risk Premium Model

The second method of estimating the cost of common stock is much simpler but also much more subjective. Some financial analysts believe that the cost of common stock is closely related to the firm's cost of debt. The cost of common stock will be several percentage points higher than the firm's cost of debt because of the higher level of risk associated with stock. Intuitively this makes sense: Firms with low-risk, low-interest-rate bonds should also have a low cost of common stock. Conversely, firms with high-risk and high-interest-rate debt should have a higher cost for issuing common stock.

Based on these concepts, the bond yield plus risk premium model was developed. It measures the cost of common stock as the yield from the firm's bonds plus some risk premium. The risk premium is usually in the 3% to 5% range and is selected by financial analysts (Brigham & Ehrhardt, 2011). One shortcoming of this model is that the risk premium is not an exact measure based on available financial data.

CONCEPTS INTO PRACTICE

To return to the example of Under Armour, we may find that the company has outstanding bonds that were issued at 7%. We would add some risk premium to the 7% to arrive at the cost of common stock. If we say that the risk premium is 4%, we will estimate the overall cost of common stock as 11%. As with the CAPM, we cannot state that 11% will definitely be the cost of common stock for Under Armour. We are making an estimation of the cost.

Dividend Growth Model

A third method for determining the cost of common stock is the dividend growth model. The price of common stock and its expected rate of return are related in part to the expected dividends that will be paid on the stock. Stockholders expect to earn some level of dividends, usually the amount paid in past years. But stockholders also expect that the annual dividend payments will increase in the future. Therefore, the cost of common stock is the sum of these two values (Griffin, 1991). We can represent the dividend growth model through the following equation:

$$C = \frac{E}{N} + G$$

C = required rate of return for stockholders (this serves as a measure of the cost of common stock)

E = annual dividend payment (for simplicity, we assume that these payments are fixed at the same level each year)

N = current price per share of the stock

G = annual growth rate of dividends

The equation captures the notion that investors expect to receive a certain level of return from purchasing a common stock. That return is the **dividend yield**, as measured by the annual dividend payment divided by the current stock price, plus the expected annual dividend growth rate. For a firm to invest capital in projects, capital that would otherwise go to common stock shareholders, it must assure stockholders that the capital investment will result in a higher return than C, the required rate of return for stockholders. Although this method seems straightforward, there are some problems. Accurately predicting the annual growth rate of dividends (G) can be difficult. Security analysts spend countless hours analyzing company financial data to determine future performance and profitability. Despite such efforts, they are often wrong. Errors are especially common for companies whose past financial performance is abnormal or erratic.

Economic cycles and industry trends can also influence the future performance of an individual business. These factors often come into play in sport segments that rely on products with short life cycles. For example, before 2003 few people had even heard of professional poker or Texas hold 'em. Despite this lack of visibility, poker events have seen tremendous growth over the past several years. TV networks such as ESPN, NBC, Fox Sports, and the Travel Channel have all dedicated airtime to poker events, and players such as Phil Ivey and Annie Duke have become celebrities. Although the popularity of poker is unlikely to continue for years to come, predicting these consumer trends is often difficult. Who would have predicted 10 years ago that people would prefer to watch poker rather than sporting leagues such as the NHL and MLS?

Calculation of the Weighted Average Cost of Capital

We now have measures for the three primary components of capital: debt, preferred stock, and common stock. The next step is to combine these measures to develop an overall cost of capital. As stated earlier, the most common method is the weighted average cost of capital, or WACC. The WACC uses the targeted levels, or proportions, of the three components along with the cost measures developed for each. Most firms have a targeted capital structure. The target is the proportion of debt to preferred stock to common stock that the business believes will be best for its future success. The proportions of target capital are represented by weights that are given to each capital type. When added up, the weights must equal 1. For example, if the debt portion has a weight of 0.1, then 10% of the business' targeted capital structure is funded through a debt instrument.

We can use any of the three previously discussed methods to calculate C, the cost of common stock. In the following example the CAPM is used. The equation that follows solves for the WACC.

$$WACC = (W_D \times D) + (W_S \times S) + (W_C \times C)$$

WACC = weighted average cost of capital

W_D = target weight for debt

D = cost of debt

W_S = target weight for preferred stock

S = cost of preferred stock

W_C = target weight for common stock

C = cost of common stock

Also, remember that we have already identified methods to measure D, S, and C, as highlighted by the following formulas:

$$D = R - (R \times T)$$

$$S = \frac{V}{P}$$

$$C = F + [(M - F) \times B]$$

If we were to start from the beginning, we would first develop the costs of debt, preferred stock, and common stock and then weight each component, based on the target capital structure, to determine the WACC.

CONCEPTS INTO PRACTICE

Assume that Speedway Motorsports has a targeted capital structure in which 20% will be in the form of debt, 55% will be in preferred stock, and 25% will be common stock. In addition, using the measures described earlier, Speedway Motorsports has found that its after-tax cost of debt (D) is 8.5%, its cost of preferred stock (S) is 9.2%, and its cost of common stock (C) is 10.2%. The company needs to raise $10 million in new capital to make major renovations to its administrative offices. Management wants to know what the average cost of the capital will be if the targeted capital structure is followed. The best way to show this is to solve the formula for WACC.

$$WACC = (W_D \times D) + (W_S \times S) + (W_C \times C)$$

$$WACC = (0.20 \times 8.5\%) + (0.55 \times 9.2\%) + (0.25 \times 10.2\%)$$

$$= 1.70\% + 5.06\% + 2.55\%$$

$$= 9.31\%$$

To summarize, the weighted average cost of capital for Speedway Motorsports in this example is 9.31%. This amount is what Speedway Motorsports can expect to pay in after-tax costs when it wants to raise money for capital projects such as the construction of new racetracks or corporate offices. For example, if Speedway wants to raise $100 million in capital through a combination of debt, preferred stock, and common stock, it should expect to pay an additional $9.3 million in financing costs. Additionally, for every $1 of new capital that is raised, 20% should be in the form of debt and have an after-tax cost of 8.5%; 55% should be preferred stock and have a cost of 9.2%; and last, 25% should be raised through common stock and have a cost of 10.2%.

Note that the WACC is for the cost of new capital only. We are attempting to develop cost measures as part of the capital-budgeting process. This estimate should not be used to make statements about the cost of previously issued capital. Previous capital was raised under different economic and financial circumstances, and such circumstances can greatly influence the cost of capital. Last, note that the weights used are based on a targeted capital structure. If the firm raises capital in proportions that vary from the targets, the WACC will vary as well. Again, the WACC is a method used to estimate the cost of capital. Any changes in the variables used in the model will change the WACC.

As with any estimations of the future, the WACC will not be accurate in every instance. As stated earlier, outside factors such as interest rates and tax rates play a role in determining the WACC. Any changes in these factors would obviously affect the cost of capital. Additionally, a firm may change policies related to dividend payments, investment strategy, or capital structure. Any changes in these areas would influence the WACC. For example, a change in investment assets may markedly affect the risk premium for the company, which may ultimately affect the cost of common stock.

Our discussion of WACC and the cost of capital has focused primarily on publicly held businesses. Numerous businesses in the sport industry are small businesses or privately held companies (or both). Neither of these types of businesses has stocks that are openly bought and sold. This circumstance presents some unique problems when determining the cost of capital. The price of preferred and common stock is not easily obtainable because the stocks are not traded on the open market. Overall, the same principles for the cost of capital determination apply for small businesses and privately held companies. Obtaining accurate and usable financial data, however, is difficult. Moreover, many small firms do not pay any dividends. Earnings are often retained and used to grow the company, adding to the difficulty of calculating accurate costs of preferred and common stock.

In addition, most small businesses do not have publicly traded bonds. The bond yield plus risk premium method for determining the cost of common stock relies on knowing a business' bond yield. Applying this method to small businesses is usually not appropriate.

We have now developed a method for measuring the cost of capital. The next step is to develop a method for making capital-budgeting decisions.

Sports managers are continually presented with a number of capital projects. They must decide which projects are worthy of being undertaken and which should be bypassed. The next section develops several different methods for making these capital-budgeting decisions.

CAPITAL-BUDGETING DECISION METHODS

Sport businesses have a variety of options with respect to spending funds. Capital spending on fixed assets such as equipment, facilities, and new technology is common. This section presents several methods for making decisions about how to allocate capital funds. Before examining decision making, we must consider the importance of time. Then we look at net present value, the payback rule, the discounted payback rule, and the internal rate of return. The first point of analysis needs to be the present value of an income stream as determined through the time value of money.

Importance of Time

An important element of capital budgeting is time. Capital spending and obtaining the returns from capital projects occurs over many years. Therefore, the timing of the costs and revenues is critical. In chapter 7 we discuss the time value of money and the importance of determining the present value of a future stream of income. The following case study can help explain the importance of understanding time, but feel free to skip it if you think that you have a good grasp of the concept. For those wishing a quick review, please read the following example.

CONCEPTS INTO PRACTICE

Let's assume that a university athletic department, such as the one at the University of Virginia, is approached by a wealthy philanthropist who would like to make a large donation. The philanthropist offers two options for how the money will be paid:

1. The athletic department can receive a $500,000 check today.
2. The athletic department can receive a $550,000 check in one year.

The decision is based on which option is more valuable. If the present value of $550,000 in one year is greater than the present value of the $500,000 check received today, the athletic department should select option 2. But how do we determine which option is more valuable? Obviously, $500,000 today is worth more than $500,000 a year from now, but is $500,000 today worth more than $550,000 a year from now? The athletic department can invest the $500,000 today in an interest-bearing account and have more than $500,000 in one year. But can it make an additional $50,000 from the investment? Suppose that it investigates the payoff from the best risk-free investment opportunity, probably a U.S. government security, and learns that the annual interest rate is 7.0%. Therefore, $500,000 invested in a U.S. government security will give the athletic department $535,000 in one year. Under these circumstances, the university should obviously select option 2 and take the $550,000 in one year.

Another method for making this decision is to calculate the present value of option 2. Using this process, the athletic department will determine the current dollar value of receiving $550,000 in one year. To make the decision, the university will need to know the expected rate of return. The rate of return is the reward demanded by investors for waiting one year to receive a payment. Assume that the athletic department would expect no more than a 7.0% return from its best alternative risk-free investment. Therefore, we will use 7.0% as the rate of return. The rate of return is then used to develop a discount factor. Mathematically, the discount factor is expressed as follows:

$$\text{discount factor} = \frac{1}{1+r}$$

r = the expected return

The discount factor is then used to determine the present value of the $550,000 that will be received in one year. The future payout, in this case $550,000, is represented by FP. The following mathematical formula represents this concept.

$$PV = R \times FP$$

PV = present value
R = discount factor

$$PV = \frac{1}{1.07} \times FP$$
$$PV = \frac{1}{1.07} \times 550,000$$

FP = future payout

Here is the calculation for our example:

$$PV = 0.9346 \times \$550,000$$
$$PV = \$514,030$$

As you can see, $514,030 is the present value of receiving $550,000 in one year. Because this number is greater than $500,000, the athletic department should select option 2. If we go through the same process but assume that the expected rate of return is 15%, the present value of option 2 would become $478,280. In this instance, the university should select option 1. The rate of return is important in the determination of present value. In general, it represents the reward that investors demand for accepting a payment made later. This concept has obvious ramifications for capital spending—the investment of money today in an effort to receive future cash flows.

Although the calculations in this example help establish which choice will be the most beneficial, they do not take into account other variables. For example, if the athletic department does not build a park with the $500,000 this year, inflation and increased building costs might force the university to pay $575,000 next year. Furthermore, the future contains numerous variables that might make budgeting decisions more difficult. The athletic department might approve an additional $500,000 for a new field, but those funds might not be available if the athletic department waits a year to receive the $550,000 from the philanthropist.

Net Present Value

The calculation of present value leads us to the next important facet of capital budgeting. For all capital investments, a sport manager should calculate the present value of the expected future income related to the project. An investment is considered wise if the present value of this future income is greater than the necessary investment. The financial term associated with this process is **net present value** (NPV). The NPV is the difference between the present value of the future income and the required investment. It can be represented as follows:

$$NPV = PV - RI$$

NPV = net present value

PV = present value of future income

RI = required investment

The following case study example highlights how to apply NPV.

CONCEPTS INTO PRACTICE

The same university athletic department from the previous example must decide whether it wants to spend $1 million to construct 10 new luxury suites in their basketball arena. Each suite will last for 10 years. At the end of 10 years, we will assume that the suites will need to be replaced and will have no salvage value. For simplicity, we will also assume that each luxury suite can be rented for $30,000 per year and that no other income will be made from the suites. The construction project will take one year. Therefore, the first income from the suites will be earned one year from today. If we think of one year from now as the end of year 1, income will flow into the athletic department at the ends of years 1 through 10. Even though this example is not completely accurate, it offers a good depiction of the concept of NPV.

The athletic department must calculate the NPV of this investment opportunity before making the decision. So starting next year, it will have $300,000 in income for the each of the next 10 years. Overall, the project will generate $3 million in income, but the present value of the income stream must be calculated. Unlike the situation in the previous example, in which one **payoff** was to be received one year into the future, here there is a stream of future payoffs. Thus, the present value of the payoff in each future year must be calculated. The following mathematical formula is used to calculate cash flows in future years (Brigham & Ehrhardt, 2011):

$$PV = \left(\frac{1}{1+r} \times FP_1\right) + \left(\frac{1}{(1+r)^2} \times FP_2\right) +$$
$$\left(\frac{1}{(1+r)^3} \times FP_3\right) + \ldots + \left(\frac{1}{(1+r)^{10}} \times FP_{10}\right)$$

FP_1 = future payoff one year from now

FP_2 = future payoff two years from now and so on

These calculations will continue up to the end of year 10. We will assume that the rate of return for the athletic department is 8%. We can rewrite the equation as the following:

$$PV = \left(\frac{1}{1.08} \times \$300,000\right) + \left(\frac{1}{1.08^2} \times \$300,000\right) +$$
$$\left(\frac{1}{1.08^3} \times \$300,000\right) + \ldots + \left(\frac{1}{1.08^{10}} \times \$300,000\right)$$
$$PV = \$2,013,000$$

The present value of $2,013,000 can then be used to calculate the NPV of the capital expenditure. Note that these calculations can be done manually, but if the rate of return and stream of income are constant throughout a project, an annuity table, such as table A.3 in the appendix, can be used. The table will save a great deal of time and frustration by allowing the user to arrive at the correct amount without the need for mathematical calculations because the math has already been done. As stated previously, the initial investment is $1 million, and the present value of the stream of income is $2,013,000. So, we can calculate the NPV as follows:

$$NPV = \$2,013,000 - \$1,000,000 = \$1,013,000$$

The NPV of the construction of 10 luxury boxes is positive and slightly over $1 million. The project definitely is worth more than it costs the athletic department.

Net present value is an important capital-budgeting component. Any project that has a negative NPV should not be undertaken because the cost of the project is higher than the projected income—financially, it is a losing proposition. But not all projects that have a positive NPV must be undertaken. We will return to the selection of capital-spending projects in a later section.

Next, it is important to note other methods besides NPV can be used for making capital-budgeting decisions. All these methods have strengths and weaknesses. The NPV method was presented first because it is the most often used and is regarded as the best. Although it is important to recognize and discuss these other methods, the NPV method is strongly recommended.

TRENDS IN STADIUM FINANCING

The period from 1989 to 2009 saw an explosion in the construction of professional sports stadiums and arenas. New facilities opened for teams such as the Houston Texans, Cincinnati Reds, Philadelphia Phillies, Arizona Cardinals, Charlotte Bobcats, and St. Louis Cardinals, just to name a few. This trend in sports facility construction came about for several reasons. Because of changes in facility design, a stadium such as FedEx Field in Washington, D.C., can produce substantially more revenue for the Redskins franchise than their previous home, Robert F. Kennedy Stadium. For example, FedEx Field has 208 luxury suites that bring in more than $15 million annually, as well as 15,000 club seats that sell for $1,000 to $2,000 per year.

The new income generated from the facility is critical for the financial success of the Redskins. As operating costs increase, due in part to rising player salaries, teams must find new income streams. Stadium revenues along with ticket sales, national broadcast rights fees, and team merchandise revenues are the main sources of income. Unlike other revenue sources, however, most stadium income is not shared equally among all franchises. In the four major professional leagues, teams keep 100% of revenues from parking, concessions, advertising, and stadium naming rights. New facilities are often built to maximize these revenue sources.

Another important aspect of new professional sports facility construction is the source of funding. New facilities can cost over $500 million. The new facilities for the Dallas Cowboys and New York Yankees each cost approximately $1.5 billion. In contrast, the Los Angeles Forum was built in 1967 for $15 million (Howard & Crompton, 2004). Given these high construction costs, the recent trend has been for new facilities to be jointly financed between the team ownership and the public sector. A popular financing method is for local and state governments to issue debt, through municipal bonds, that will be repaid later. The public sector can use financing sources such as state lotteries, sales taxes, and ticket surcharges to raise the funds for debt repayment.

Cities and states have been involved in sports facility construction since the inception of professional sport. But the end of the 20th century saw a new trend of franchise free agency. Team owners were willing to move to a city that would build a new stadium mostly financed by the public sector. Along with having a new stadium, team owners were allowed to keep a significant share of the stadium revenues. Many cities and states were willing to make such deals because of their strong interest in acquiring a professional franchise. The decade of the 1990s saw the relocation of several franchises. Art Modell moved his NFL franchise to Baltimore when the City of Cleveland refused to build a new publicly financed football stadium. Baltimore was willing to build Modell a new stadium as well as allow the team to play rent free. Modell also received all revenues from concessions, parking, and in-stadium advertising. In addition, the city permitted Modell to keep up to $75 million from the sale of permanent seat licenses (PSLs). The money from the sale of PSLs was to be used to cover the costs associated with the team's relocation and the construction of a new practice facility in Maryland. In return, Modell agreed to sign a 30-year lease and cover all operational and maintenance costs associated with the new facility, estimated at $3 to $4 million annually (Stellino, 1995).

A similar deal was signed by Georgia Frontiere, the owner of the St. Louis Rams, when she moved the team from Los Angeles. The City of St. Louis spent $260 million to build a new domed stadium for the team. In addition, the city covered the Rams' operating losses from their last season in Los Angeles and paid off $30 million in debt that the team owed to southern California. St. Louis also paid a $29 million league relocation fee and constructed a $15 million training center for the team. All these benefits allowed the team to remove itself from its financial difficulties and become profitable (Stellino, 1995). This new financial success may have played a major role in the Rams' ability to acquire the necessary talent to win Super Bowl XXXIV in 2000.

As the 20th century drew to a close, taxpayers in several cities began to rebel. Legislators in North Carolina rejected a stadium project that would have used public subsidization to build a new baseball facility for a Major League Baseball team. Even so, we have seen some teams relocate. For the 2005 season the Montreal Expos relocated to Washington, D.C. In the NBA, the Vancouver Grizzlies moved to Memphis and the Seattle Supersonics relocated to Oklahoma City. One of the reasons for these moves was the promise of new or renovated sports facilities.

In most cases, team owners must contribute some funds for constructing the new facilities. In a few cases such as FedEx Field in Washington, D.C., and Wells Fargo Center in Philadelphia, the team ownership contributed most of the funds and retained facility ownership. Usually, the capital necessary for these projects is financed through debt. Several trends in the issuance of private stadium debt occurred in the 1990s and early 2000s. Historically, financial institutions viewed these projects and the accompanying revenue streams as high risk. As a result, the team owners' cost of capital was relatively high. Owners were usually forced to use existing assets as collateral to secure the necessary loans. In some instances, team owners had difficulty finding financial institutions that would provide the capital. But as facilities such as Baltimore's Camden Yards, Denver's Coors Field, and the Palace of Auburn Hills near Detroit proved to be great sources of revenue, financial institutions loosened their purse strings. Creditors began to issue debt based on the future revenue streams from the facilities. Some owners secured loans with the expectation of future revenue streams, as opposed to existing collateral.

Another recent trend has been the refinancing of facility debt. The late 1990s and early 21st century saw some of the lowest interest rates in decades. The interest rates issued in the late 1980s and early 1990s for facility debt were significantly higher. As a result, several sports organizations refinanced their preexisting facility debt and, in some instances, saved millions of dollars. For example, in 1999 the New Jersey Sports and Exposition Authority used a complex financial technique known as a "swaption" to refinance its debt. The authority saved $9.1 million, which was used to help pay for renovation of the New York Giants' practice facility and the Continental Arena (Kaplan,

1999). The United States Tennis Association (USTA) used a similar technique to refinance a 1994 debt issuance that was used for renovations made to the National Tennis Center in Queens, New York. The USTA was able to save $3.25 million as the interest rate of its debt dropped from 6.4% to 5.94% (Kaplan, 1999). In a trend similar to that seen with American homeowners who refinanced their mortgages in the late 2000s, several sports organizations took advantage of low interest rates to save millions of dollars.

Another trend in sports facility financing is giving teams cash payments to stay in older facilities. For example, under the terms of a 10-year $186 million agreement reached in 2001, the New Orleans Saints were being paid millions to stay in the Superdome. The 2005 payment was for almost $13 million, and a large percentage of that sum had to be borrowed by the state ("Louisiana forks over," 2005). This arrangement was in danger of coming to an end because of the effects of hurricane Katrina. New Orleans was in no condition to keep making payments to keep the team in town, which was part of the impetus for the Saints to investigate a move to San Antonio. Ultimately, the city, state, Saints' ownership, and NFL were able to reach an agreement to keep the team in the New Orleans Superdome after its post-Katrina renovation.

The sports facility construction and renovation sector was greatly affected by the global recession of 2007-2008. Despite low interest rates, financial institutions became more reluctant to finance stadium deals. In addition, the recession was devastating to many local and state governments, so these groups were less willing to participate in stadium financing projects. Several projects such as the New Cowboys Stadium in Dallas, Target Field in Minneapolis, and Yankee Stadium in New York were completed postrecession; but the funding for these facilities was finalized before the downturn. Few new sports facilities projects have been initiated since 2008. One exception is the new ballpark for the Miami Marlins. The funding for this facility, which opened in 2012, was approved in March of 2009, just about the time that the global recession took hold (deMause, 2009).

Payback Rule

A second method of analyzing the value of a capital project is through the use of the payback rule. The payback rule analyzes how long it will take a business to receive its money back after investing in a capital project. The money is paid back through the stream of future income related to the project. The payback rule may be best explained through the following case study example.

As you can see in the example, the capital-budgeting decision method that is used can have a major effect on the decision. The difference occurs because the payback rule weights all cash flows equally, ignoring the importance of time. This rule centers on which investment option will repay the initial outlay in the shortest time. The NPV method discounts future cash flows based on the opportunity cost of capital. It also looks at the entire cash flow over the life of the project, in this case four years. The university's payback rule of three years means that only the cash flows in the first three years are important; even if project A had a cash flow of $1 billion in the fourth year, it would not be selected. The cash flow in the fourth year is meaningless in this example if we are using the payback rule. This characteristic is another obvious weakness of the payback rule; it ignores the cash flows after the arbitrarily selected payback date.

To account for the failure of the payback rule to recognize the time value of money, the discounted payback rule has been developed.

CONCEPTS INTO PRACTICE

Assume that an athletic department has $1 million that it wants to invest in a capital project. The initial investment will result in a future cash flow into the university. The university has two possible capital projects that cost $1 million each. It must decide which one to select. These are the two choices:

Project A is a new outdoor aquatics facility. The facility will produce $250,000 in revenue in the first year and $300,000 per year for two subsequent years. In the fourth and final year, the cash flow will be $400,000. For simplicity, we will assume that there are no other costs or revenues. The total revenue for the next four years will be $1.25 million.

Project B is a new recreational gymnasium to be used for adult and youth sports leagues. This facility will produce $100,000 in the first year and $450,000 per year for the two subsequent years. Because of a decrease in future demand, the cash flow for the fourth year will be only $100,000. The total revenue for the next four years will be $1.1 million.

The question is, Which capital project should the athletic department select? The university is going to use the payback rule to make this decision. The university has decided that all of the initial $1 million investment must be paid back within three years. If this cannot occur, capital funds will not be allocated for the project. Table 11.1 depicts the cash flows over time, the expected **payback periods**, and the NPV for each project.

Examining table 11.1, we see that it will take four years for project A to repay the investment, whereas the investment for project B will be repaid within three years. Given the university's payback rule of three years, project B is the one to select. The cash flow from this project can repay the $1 million initial investment in three years.

The decision would change dramatically if we used the NPV method. To determine NPV, we assume that the opportunity cost of capital is 8%. We find that the NPV of project A is $20,842, and the NPV for project B is –$90,880. Using the NPV method, project B would be rejected and the athletic department would select project A.

Table 11.1 Time Line of Cash Flows for Projects A and B

Project	P_0	P_1	P_2	P_3	P_4	Payback period	Net present value at 8%
A	–$1 million	$250,000	$300,000	$300,000	$400,000	4 years	$20,842
B	–$1 million	$100,000	$450,000	$450,000	$100,000	3 years	–$90,880

CONCEPTS INTO PRACTICE

To return to our previous example, table 11.2 shows the cash flows when the athletic department applies the discounted payback rule, incorporating an 8% rate of return.

Using the discounted payback rule, the payback period remains at four years for project A. Project B does not produce enough cash flow in four years to cover the initial investment. Therefore, using the discounted payback rule and a predetermined three-year maximum payback period, both projects are rejected. But remember that using the NPV method would lead to the selection of project A, and the original payback rule would result in the selection of project B. Again, which capital-budgeting decision method is used has a major effect on the disbursement of long-term capital.

Table 11.2 Time Line of Discounted Cash Flows for Projects A and B

Project	P_0	P_1	P_2	P_3	P_4	Payback period	Net present value at 8%
A	–$1 million	$231,481	$257,210	$238,150	$294,009	4 years	$20,842
B	–$1 million	$92,593	$385,802	$357,225	$73,502	>4 years	–$90,880

Discounted Payback Rule

The **discounted payback rule** discounts the future cash flows based on the opportunity cost of capital, as highlighted in the sidebar.

Internal Rate of Return Method

The last method for making capital-budgeting decisions is to use the **internal rate of return** (IRR). As with NPV and the discounted payback rule, IRR relies on the opportunity cost of capital and the time value of money. As stated earlier, the opportunity cost of capital is the return obtained by investing the capital in the next best alternative. For example, if you can place $100,000 in an interest-bearing investment that will result in you having $110,000 at the end of one year, the rate of return is 10%. Therefore, you would invest only in projects that can return more than $110,000. The IRR method emphasizes finding the rate of return for which NPV equals zero. Table 11.3 displays a situation in which a $1,000 capital investment results in a $750 cash flow in one year and a $500 cash flow in two years.

Table 11.3 Time Line of Cash Flows

Time 0 (P_0)	In one year (P_1)	In two years (P_2)
–$1,000	$750	$500

The goal of the IRR method is to find the rate of return for which NPV equals zero. The mathematical model for our example in table 11.3 is as follows:

$$\text{NPV} = P_0 + \frac{P_1}{1+r} + \frac{P_2}{1+r^2} = 0$$

P_0 = cash flow at time zero

P_1 = cash flow in first year

r = rate of return

P_2 = cash flow in second year

To complete the formula, we need to solve for r, the rate of return. This can be difficult without the proper computer software. If you attempt to solve the formula manually, it will be a matter of trial and error. The trial-and-error process for manual calculation requires you to estimate for r and keep lowering or raising r until the equation equals zero. With a computer you can perform the analysis almost instantaneously. If we input the information from table 11.3, the equation can be rewritten as follows:

$$\text{NPV} = \$1.000 + \frac{\$750}{1+r} + \frac{\$500}{1+r^2} = 0$$

We must now solve for r. Using trial and error, let's start with a 10% rate of return. If we solve the equation when r = 0.10, we find that the NPV equals $95.10. We now know that the IRR for which NPV will equal zero is greater than 0.10. We continue this trial-and-error process until we find the rate of return at which NPV equals zero. In our example, NPV will equal zero when r equals 0.175. A wise sport manager will undertake this capital project if she believes that its opportunity cost of capital is less than 17.5%. In other words, she will go ahead with the project if no other investment choices have an expected rate of return greater than 17.5%.

RISK AND CAPITAL BUDGETING

CONCEPTS INTO PRACTICE

Let's start with an example. Should a small business owner construct a new $3 million health and fitness center that will result in an annual increase of $300,000 in profit? Initially, you might answer yes, noting that an additional $300,000 in profit, a 10% return on investment, is fairly high. But what if the owner can also take that $3 million and purchase U.S. Treasury bonds that are guaranteed to provide a 5% return each year? Initially, the new fitness center still appears to be the best opportunity. But is the 10% return guaranteed? No. The 5% return from the U.S. Treasury bonds is a sure thing. The expected return on the new fitness center is greater, but there is no guarantee that the return on investment will be 10%. It is an expected, not guaranteed, return.

This example illustrates the importance of risk and uncertainty. When you are calculating the return on investment for capital expenditures, risk is important. Different capital projects have different levels of risk. To accept a higher level of risk for a project, the investor must expect the returns to be higher. In every case, a wise sport manager faced with the choice of selecting one of two capital investment opportunities with equal returns will select the one with the lower risk.

All capital projects have some level of risk. Calculations of expected returns on investments and pro forma budgets are forecasts of future costs and revenues. Therefore, when discussing capital investment, we refer to expected payoffs and expected rates of return. Pro forma budgets are discussed in chapter 3.

PROJECTING CASH FLOW

The discussion to this point has centered on capital budgeting from the cost side. The calculation of capital costs is an integral part of capital budgeting, but it is only half the story. The other half deals with income and with developing methods to estimate future income that results from capital investment. The combination of expenses and income is known as cash flow. The accurate projection of cash flows, both expenses and income, is a key to making wise capital-budgeting decisions. Although no projection of future income will be totally accurate, a sport manager needs to make the best and most accurate attempt.

Chapter 6 covers the use of financial tools such as balance sheets and income statements to explain the current and past financial positions of a business. Projecting cash flow also relies on financial tools, but the emphasis shifts to pro forma statements, discussed in chapter 3. Pro forma statements are important to capital budgeting because an organization is investing capital today that will result in future cash flows.

The future cash flows that result from capital investment depend on many business factors. For example, if an athletic department plans to spend $100 million on a new 30,000-seat football stadium, the future cash flow resulting from this spending may be difficult to estimate accurately. The following is a list of factors that may affect future cash flow for such a project:

♦ Is there demand for 30,000 tickets to the football games? Before construction, an in-depth **market analysis** should be undertaken to determine spectator demand.

♦ How important is ticket price to the spectators? Would an increase in the ticket price affect spectator demand?

♦ The athletic department cannot assume that it will always put a winning team on the field. How will winning and losing affect spectator attendance?

♦ If the project succeeds and the 30,000 seats are filled on a regular basis, can the stadium be expanded in the future?

♦ If the capital is raised, in part, through booster donations, how will fund-raising efforts for other parts of the athletic program and university be affected? Will other projects or budgets be affected by the stadium project?

♦ How much additional cash will flow into the athletic department? If the new stadium is built, will it have an effect on future cash flow as compared with the current cash flow from football games?

♦ Besides football games, what other uses would the facility have, and what would the cash flow be from those uses?

♦ If luxury seating or boxes are included, is there a demand from corporate clients for those seats? What is the fair price for the luxury seating or boxes?

♦ How much will it cost to maintain and repair the stadium after it is built?

♦ What will the cost be for the capital required to construct the facility?

All the factors listed are important when projecting the cash flow from a new university sports facility. It is necessary to ask questions related to market demand, sales projections, operating costs, and capital costs when attempting to project future cash flow. Again, remember that projecting future cash flow is not an exact science. A financial manager makes the best possible estimation based on available data and research.

We will define the cash flow of a project as the net cash inflows and investment expenditures associated with the project (Brigham & Ehrhardt, 2011). Again, projecting future cash flow is the most difficult facet of capital budgeting.

For a sport organization, many people and departments should be involved in any major capital projects. For example, when a university athletic department constructs a new stadium, several departments will be involved in the process. The ticketing and marketing departments need to make projections about ticket sales and ticket pricing. The university's construction planners and outside construction firms need to estimate construction costs. The university's physical plant department should be consulted to estimate maintenance costs. An event planner or promoter can help determine what revenues will be generated from other events being held in the stadium. The university's advancement or fund-raising office can estimate the effect of stadium fund-raising on other university fund-raising endeavors.

Several capital-budgeting methods such as the payback rule, discounted payback rule, NPV, and IRR have already been presented. Remember that all these financial techniques are worthless if poor cash flow projections are made. Poor decisions will result if cash flow estimations are inaccurate.

An organization's financial staff must play a prominent role in projecting the cash flow. The financial managers have the job of taking all the information obtained from other departments and developing accurate projections. Several common pitfalls must be avoided. For a number of reasons, such as career advancement, emotional ties, or possible benefits to their departments, some people in other departments may be strong supporters of specific capital projects. This bias may affect the accuracy of the information that they provide to the financial staff. The financial staff needs to ensure that projections are as accurate as possible. Unfortunately, doing this is not always easy.

All businesses have a limited capital budget and many alternatives for capital spending. Each project must be evaluated on its own financial worth and needs to be compared with other options. Those investment opportunities that fit within the capital budget and have the highest NPV are the most attractive. In the real world, the process of quantifying the NPV of investment choices is not this easy. Many confounding factors come into play. One capital-spending project may affect another, and some may need to happen simultaneously to be successful. Management has the job of deciphering all this information.

Measuring Relevant Cash Flow

The first step in projecting cash flow is to measure the relevant cash flow for a capital project. All existing firms have a cash flow. The key to obtaining an accurate measurement of the cash flow of a single project is to include only new cash flow. The new, or incremental, cash flow is the additional future cash flow, either internal or external to the business, that results only from the decision to undertake a project. Any cash flow that occurs regardless of the presence of a new project should not be included in the calculation of relevant cash flow. You need to remember this important concept throughout this discussion. With respect to measuring incremental cash flows, financial managers make several common errors.

The first common error relates to measuring sunk costs. **Sunk costs** are costs that have already occurred and do not change regardless of the decision to undertake a project. Let's go back to the example of a university. The university may pay $20,000 for a feasibility study on the construction of a new student recreation building. If because of this report the university decides not to construct the building, it would still have to pay for the feasibility study. The cost is incurred regardless of the outcome. According to our definition of incremental cash flow, the $20,000 is not important in making the capital-spending decision. The money has already been spent, and it should not be included as a cost when the university is projecting cash flow for the capital project.

The second common error concerns opportunity cost, another important aspect of projecting relevant cash flow. Opportunity cost refers to the most valuable alternative that is forgone if a particular capital project is undertaken. Returning to the university example, the recreation building must be built on a piece of land. The university has a parcel of land that can be used, but the land could also be used for new playing fields or a swimming pool. Initially, you might think that the cost of land is zero because the university already owns it. This assessment is not accurate. An opportunity cost is associated with using that piece of land; the university is forgoing its next best alternative use of the land. The next best alternative may be to build a swimming pool. The university must estimate the value of the land and include it in its projection of project costs. This point is especially important if the university will need to buy a new piece of land in the future to build a pool.

Failure to analyze the effect of any funding decision is a third common error. Most new capital-spending projects have an effect on the overall organization. If the athletic department elects to build the new student recreation building, other parts of the university may feel some side effects. Perhaps student fees will increase for activities that do not take place in the new recreation center. Visitors to the new facility will learn more about other activities at the university and might pay to attend them. This result is an example of a positive side effect, also known as a spillover effect. But negative spillover effects can also occur. Students may decide to decrease their activities at other university venues or events to go to the new facility. This drop in attendance, and most likely a loss in income, at other locations is directly related to the new project. These types of spillover effects must be factored into projecting cash flows.

The failure to appreciate the effect of a decision on net working capital is another common error. New projects normally result in an increase in net working capital. Most projects need some cash on hand to pay for short-term expenses that arise. For our example, the university may need to buy a scoreboard for the new facility using net working capital. Additional net working capital must be allotted for any new project. We could expect the increased investment in net working capital to be recouped by the university at the end of the project's life span. If the new facility has a life span of 30 years, at the end of that 30 years the scoreboard will no longer be needed. The scoreboard can possibly be sold for scrap value, and some of the initial investment in net working capital can be recouped. The increase in net working capital could be viewed as a loan that will be repaid at the end of the project's life span.

The last common error is including interest payments in the cash flow projections. We are interested only in the cash flows, both income and expense, that result directly from the project's assets. Interest payments and dividends are payments to creditors and shareholders. They are not expenses that result from the assets themselves. But perhaps more important, as already discussed, interest and dividend payments were included in calculating capital costs. If we also include them as cash outflows, we would be double counting these payments. They have already been accounted for in the cost of capital, so they do not need to be included as expenses (Brigham & Ehrhardt, 2011).

As you can see, some aspects of projecting cash flow are complex. The easiest way to explain the projection of cash flow for a capital project is probably through an example.

Example of Projecting Cash Flow: New Fitness Facility

Pro forma financial statements must be developed to project cash flow for a small business owner who wants to construct a new health and fitness center. Pro formas are the easiest and most convenient method for projecting cash flow. To develop these statements, we need estimates of items such as fixed costs, variable costs, unit sales, and sales price per unit. Information must also be obtained on the change in net working capital and the total required investment. For our example, several numbers will be simplified. We will limit the life span of the facility to four years. A four-year life span is somewhat unrealistic (the facility would probably last much longer than that), but it will make our example of projecting cash flow much easier to understand. The important thing is to understand the concepts of projecting cash flow.

Several assumptions will be made for the new facility. The new facility will be built on land valued at $250,000. The fitness center owner currently owns the property and has already had an offer from another business to buy the land for this amount. The construction cost of the building will be $400,000. The equipment that will be required, such as fitness machines, weights, and computers, will cost $100,000. The equipment can be fully depreciated over four years. For simplicity we will assume that the new facility can be constructed in one year and will open for business the following year. Therefore, all the land, building, and equipment costs will occur in the same **fiscal year** (2012), and income from the facility will occur from 2013 to 2016. This assumption is also somewhat unrealistic, but it will make the example easier to understand. Table 11.4 provides an overview of the investment costs for the project.

At the end of the building's four-year life span, the land will still have a value of $250,000 and the building will be worth $200,000. Therefore, straight-line depreciation will be used to depreciate

the $200,000 loss in value over the four years. The value of the equipment will be equal to the cost of removing it from the site; therefore, we will state that the overall value of the equipment in four years will be zero.

The owner believes that 1,000 memberships can be sold at an average price of $500 per year. She estimates that they will incur about $100 per person in variable costs (e.g., staff salaries, benefits, and supplies such as towels). For a membership level of 1,000, fixed costs such as rent, electricity, and water will be approximately $70,000 per year. Again, for simplicity, we will assume that there is no inflation and that the level of sales will remain at 1,000 memberships for each of the four years of operation.

To open the new facility, the owner must initially increase her net working capital. The net working capital for the entire organization will be increased from its prior level of $65,000 to $75,000. The additional $10,000 in the first year must be included as a cash flow. The $10,000 will be retained at the end of the project, and that sum must also be included in the projections of total cash flow. The new facility will be subject to federal, state, and local taxes. The total cumulative tax rate will be 35%. Last, the WACC for the owner is 9.5%, and we will assume an interest rate (r) of 5%.

From all this information, we can construct our pro forma statement of cash flows as shown in table 11.5. As you can see, a pro forma cash flow statement is complex. But it does capture the

Table 11.4 Investment Outlays for 2012 (Year 1)

Fixed assets	Cost ($)
Land	250,000
Building	400,000
Equipment	100,000
Total initial investment	$750,000

Table 11.5 Net Cash Flows

	2013 (year 2)	2014 (year 3)	2015 (year 4)	2016 (year 5)
Unit sales	1,000	1,000	1,000	1,000
Sales price	$500	$500	$500	$500
Net sales	$500,000	$500,000	$500,000	$500,000
Variable costs	$100,000	$100,000	$100,000	$100,000
Fixed costs	$70,000	$70,000	$70,000	$70,000
Depreciation (building)	$50,000	$50,000	$50,000	$50,000
Depreciation (equipment)	$25,000	$25,000	$25,000	$25,000
Earnings before taxes	$255,000	$255,000	$255,000	$255,000
Taxes (35%)	$89,250	$89,250	$89,250	$89,250
Projected net operating income	$165,750	$165,750	$165,750	$165,750
Add back noncash expenses*	$75,000	$75,000	$75,000	$75,000
Cash flow from operations	$240,750	$240,750	$240,750	$240,750
Investment in net working capital	($10,000)			$10,000
Total projected cash flow	$230,750	$240,750	$240,750	$250,750

*Depreciation is used for tax purposes. However, it is not a cash flow, and therefore the $75,000 is added back into the cash flow statement.

expected inflows and outflows of cash for the new facility during its four-year operational life span? Several important aspects must be discussed here. First, notice that depreciation is added back into the calculation of cash flow. Depreciation is an item that is included as part of the balance sheet of a business to calculate its accounting value. But depreciation is not a flow of cash into or out of a firm. Therefore, although it is initially deducted in the cash flow statement, depreciation is ultimately added back into the cash flow.

Depreciation is used for tax purposes, but it is not a cash flow, and therefore the $75,000 is added back into the cash flow statement.

This important point is worth reemphasizing—the cash flow statement measures the inflows and outflows of cash for a firm, and depreciation is not a cash flow. The important result from the cash flow statement is that it provides a projection for the amount of cash that will accrue from operating the new facility. The cash flows range from $230,750 in 2013 to $250,750 in 2016. The difference in cash flows occurs because the owner must increase her net working capital in 2013 to start the operation. She will get this $10,000 back in 2016 when the facility closes.

The next step for fitness center owner is to make the decision about undertaking this project. At this point, she has a projection on the cost of construction for the facility and the projected cash flows during the life of the operation. The importance of the time value of money must be mentioned. The owner is using capital today to construct a facility that will increase future cash flow. The future cash flow must be discounted to account for the time value of money. Review this process in the following Concepts Into Practice sidebar.

A financial manager can use all these measures—IRR, NPV, and the discounted payback method—in making the capital-budgeting decision for this project.

You should note that a project should not be undertaken solely because it has a positive NPV or an IRR that is higher than the WACC. Capital budgeting is one part of a sports organization's overall financial management strategy. The capital project must fit into the organization's long-term objectives. A sporting goods company may have an opportunity to invest in a capital project involving athlete representation that will result in a positive NPV, but if this project does not fit into the overall organizational objective, it should not be undertaken.

CONCEPTS INTO PRACTICE

In this example, we will assume that there is no inflation. The time line in table 11.6 captures the cash flow analysis. Additionally, the value of the land must be included in the cost of the project.

Using the assumptions that have been made and the projected cash flows that are presented in tables 11.5, 11.6, and 11.7, we can calculate the net present value, internal rate of return, and discounted

Table 11.6   Time Line of Net Cash Flows (2012-2016)

Year	Net cash flow ($)
2012	–750,000
2013	230,000
2014	240,740
2015	240,740
2016	250,740

Table 11.7   Discounted Payback Period (5% interest rate)

	2012	2013	2014	2015	2016	Discounted payback period
Cash Flow	–$750,000	$230,750	$240,750	$240,750	$250,750	
Discounted cash flow	–$750,000	$219,062	$218,367	$207,969	$206,293	
Aggregate discounted cash flow		–$530,938	–$312,571	–$104,602	$101,691	Approximately 4.5 more years

payback period. You should be able to make these calculations on your own.

Net Present Value

$$NPV = P_0 + [P_1 / (1 + r)] + [P_2 / (1 + r)^2] + [P_3 / (1 + r)^3] + [P_4 / (1 + r)^4]$$

Assume r = 5%.

$$NPV = -\$750,000 + [\$230,750 / (1 + 0.05)] + [\$240,750 / (1 + 0.05)^2] + [\$240,750 / (1 + 0.05)^3] + [\$250,750 / (1 + 0.05)^4]$$

$$NPV = -\$750,000 + [\$230,750 / 1.05] + [\$240,750 / 1.1025] + [\$240,750 / 1.1576] + [\$250,750 / 1.2155]$$

$$NPV = -\$750,000 + \$219,762 + \$218,367 + \$207,969 + \$206,293$$

$$= \$102,391$$

Internal Rate of Return

$$NPV = P_0 + [P_1 / (1 + r)] + [P_2 / (1 + r)^2] + [P_3 / (1 + r)^3] + [P_4 / (1 + r)^4] = 0$$

$$NPV = -\$750,000 + [\$230,750 / (1 + r)] + [\$240,750 / (1 + r)^2] + [\$240,750 / (1 + r)^3] + [\$250,750 / (1 + r)^4] = 0$$

Through trial and error, we find that for NPV to equal 0 in the previous equation, r must equal 0.1066, or 10.66%.

Table 11.7 presents the calculations for determining the discounted payback period. For each period, the discounted cash flow values, which were calculated when determining the NPV, are deducted from the initial investment. The discounted payback period is the estimated length of time required to repay the investment after discounting the value of the cash flows because of the passage of time. In this case, approximately 3.5 years is needed to generate the cash flows necessary to repay the initial $750,000 investment.

As the calculations show, the NPV of this project is $102,391. Because the NPV is positive, it appears that this capital project could be undertaken. Additionally, the IRR is higher than the weighted average cost of capital (WACC), 10.7% versus 9.5%. Therefore, a sport manager who uses IRR as a basis for capital-budgeting decisions would also accept this project. Finally, through use of the discounted payback method, the manager would learn that it would take approximately 3.5 years to pay back the initial capital outlay of $750,000. Thus, someone basing her decision on the discounted payback method may elect to pass on this project and search for other business opportunities. As stated earlier, the owner wants to recoup her investment within 4 years. As this example clearly shows, the various capital-budgeting decision techniques can support different conclusions.

CONCLUSION

Capital spending is an integral part of financial management. Ultimately, it ensures the long-term success of the organization. Sport businesses must develop capital budgets that will increase the stock value. The primary sources of capital for private or public sport businesses and organizations are debt and equity. Equity can take the form of preferred stock, common stock, and retained earnings. Government-owned and nonprofit sports organizations do not have ownership rights and therefore cannot raise capital through the sale of equity ownership interests. But these organizations can raise money through donations and gifts. Many college athletic departments rely on donations as a major source of capital for spending in areas such as facility construction and equipment.

The cost of capital is a primary concern for all sport businesses. A capital project should be undertaken only if the projected revenue is greater than the projected cost. Otherwise, the funds can be more efficiently used in other ways (e.g., redistributed to shareholders or owners). The costs of the various capital components can be calculated in several ways. The CAPM, bond yield plus risk premium model, and dividend growth model can all be used to calculate the cost of common stock. After the cost of each capital component has been determined, the WACC method is most commonly used to calculate the overall cost of capital.

The cost of capital is only one piece of capital budgeting. Managers must also determine the additional revenue that will be generated from a capital project. Only new or marginal revenue should be considered when making this projection.

Because of risk and uncertainty, the best approach is to establish a range of expected revenues. Best-case, worst-case, and most likely (also called middle-of-the-road) estimates of future revenues are recommended.

The next step is to use the cost and revenue estimates to project cash flow statements. These pro forma statements are critical for making a final capital-budgeting decision. They allow a sport manager to organize and analyze a wealth of data related to a capital project.

A wise sport manager must analyze the validity of the projections that are included in calculating cash flows. If poor or inaccurate projections are used, the results are worthless. Accurate financial data are critical for the success of capital-budgeting decisions. Businesses often develop several measures for projecting cash flows. For example, they might make several projections based on different economic conditions. Perhaps a business develops worst-case, best-case, and most likely projections. The worst-case projection would capture a situation in which sales are low, economic conditions are poor, and costs are larger than expected. Calcula-

tions of the WACC, NPV, and IRR would provide the financial manager with the absolutely worst result. This information is valuable to have when making a capital-budgeting decision. Similarly, it is beneficial to know what the best-case scenario is. This projection provides a measure of the projected return when all variables are at their best. As you can probably guess, the most likely scenario would be the most realistic one based on the available information. Although the most likely scenario is the most realistic, having projections for the range of other possible outcomes is valuable.

The final step is to make a decision on the capital project. The capital-budgeting decision will affect the future direction of the sports organization. For example, constructing a new facility, signing a professional athlete to a long-term contract, or purchasing new technology can have a major effect on the future value of a sport business. Three models used in capital budgeting are NPV, the discounted payback rule, and IRR. Each has inherent strengths and weaknesses. Financial managers should use the method or methods that they believe are most appropriate for their organizations.

Class Discussion Topics

1. Why is the capital structure of a business important?

2. What would happen if a business had too much in bonds or stocks as part of its capital structure?

3. Which funding option would be the most economical to issue if you were trying to raise $200 million?

4. What does flotation cost mean?

5. Why is the time value of money important?

6. Why is the payback rule important when analyzing financial issues?

7. What does IRR mean?

8. If you were to make a capital-budgeting decision based on project cash flows, would you prefer to use NPV, the IRR method, the payback rule, or the discounted payback rule? Why would you use the method that you have selected? What is the advantage of using multiple methods?

9. There are several methods for determining the cost of common stock. Which method do you think is the best, and why?

10. What is the present value of receiving $10 million in five years assuming that the discount factor is 3%?

Short-Term Financial Management

In chapters 7 and 11, we focus on long-range financing, particularly capital budgeting. In this chapter, our focus is the management of working capital (i.e., the current assets and liabilities of a business).

Working capital management can be viewed as short-term financial management because it centers on current assets and liabilities that generate inflows or outflows of cash to or from a business within a year or less. For example, short-term financial management is occurring if Under Armour buys raw materials, pays for them in cash, and then uses the raw materials to produce and sell sweatshirts within one year for cash. By contrast, capital budgeting is not considered short-term financial management because it tends to focus on projects of several years' duration. For example, if Under Armour buys machinery to produce sweatshirts, the machine may be used for several years until it either becomes obsolete or wears out. The analysis of the decision to buy the machinery relies on the tools of capital budgeting that were introduced in chapter 11.

In this chapter we focus on several key areas of short-term financial management. These areas include cash management, credit management, and collections management. But first we briefly review current assets and liabilities.

REVIEW OF CURRENT ASSETS AND LIABILITIES

Figure 12.1 provides a breakdown of current assets and current liabilities for all manufacturing corporations in the United States in the second quarter of 2011. Current assets include cash and other assets expected to be converted to cash within one year.

Current assets total $2,249.6 billion, and current liabilities total $1,558.4 billion. Net working capital (current assets minus current liabilities) equals $691 billion.

As shown in figure 12.1, accounts receivable are an extremely important current asset based on their value relative to other current assets. Accounts receivable consist of unpaid bills for goods and services that have been sold to customers.

CONCEPTS INTO PRACTICE

To operate a fitness center, an entrepreneur bills the patrons for membership dues. When the patrons are initially billed, accounts receivable increase. As membership dues are paid, the account balance in accounts receivable declines, and the balance in cash increases.

Inventories consist of raw materials, work in progress, and finished goods awaiting shipment to customers. Inventories are discussed in more detail in chapter 13. Cash consists of currency, funds in checking accounts, and funds in savings accounts. Marketable securities include commercial paper, short-term unsecured debt that is sold by other firms, U.S. Treasury bills, and state and local government-issued debt.

Other current assets include prepaid expenses (such as rent, utilities, and insurance) that have been purchased for use within one year. Prepaid expenses are items of value that have future usefulness in business operations. For example, all businesses purchase various types of insurance

Current assets ($ billions)		Current liabilities ($ billions)	
Cash	344.1	Short-term debt	166.0
Marketable securities	172.3	Accounts payable	510.6
Accounts receivable	669.6	Accrued income taxes	31.4
Inventories	672.3	Current payments due on long-term debt	117.8
Other current assets	391.2	Other current liabilities	732.7
Total	2,249.5	Total	1,558.5

Figure 12.1 Current assets and liabilities for all U.S. manufacturing corporations in the second quarter of 2011. All numbers are in billions.

Data from U.S. Department of Commerce 2011.

policies for protection against burglary, fire, personal injury, business interruption, and injury and death to employees (e.g., workers' compensation policies). Insurance premiums (i.e., the cost of insurance) are typically paid in advance. The unexpired portion of the already paid insurance policy is a current asset.

One of the key issues for financial managers in a sport business is choosing how much cash to hold. This choice involves various trade-offs. On the one hand, holding large amounts of cash reduces the likelihood that the sport business will run out of cash and need to raise funds on short notice. On the other hand, there is a cost in the form of lost investment income as a result of holding cash balances rather than investing those proceeds in marketable securities that can earn a return.

From a balance sheet perspective, the assets of one business are the liabilities of another. As an example, suppose that a wholesale supplier bills Under Armour for a shipment. Until Under Armour pays the bill, the balance owed by Under Armour is part of the wholesale supplier's accounts receivable, a short-term asset. At the same time, the unpaid bill is a short-term liability for Under Armour. Accounts payable are outstanding payments owed to other companies and are a major short-term liability for firms.

To finance investments in current assets, a company must rely on various types of short-term debt (i.e., loans). Commercial banks are the most common source of short-term loans (Ross, Westerfield, & Jaffe, 2008). Issuing commercial paper is another technique that large corporations use to borrow needed funds. Although many short-term loans are unsecured, companies may offer inventories or receivables as security or may sell inventories or accounts receivable to financial institutions at a discount. Short-term loans, including bank lending, commercial paper, secured loans, and inventories or receivables sold at a discount to financial institutions are discussed in chapter 8.

When businesses either issue long-term debt or take out a loan that is paid down over more than one year, all payments due any time within the next year are classified as current payments on long-term debt. Current payments on long-term debt are viewed as a current liability.

Another current liability is accrued income taxes. This category results from differences in the way that revenues and expenses are reported for income tax purposes and the way that they are accounted for to prepare an income statement. These differences in reporting income for

tax purposes and for the objective of preparing financial statements are particularly prevalent in large publicly traded companies. Larger companies often try to claim all available expenses to reduce tax liabilities while showing stockholders the largest amount of reported income possible under generally accepted accounting principles (GAAP; see chapters 4 and 15) (Fraser & Ormiston, 2009). Because of the differences in reporting income for tax purposes, as opposed to GAAP, a company's net income on an income statement can differ from what is reported to the IRS. Other current liabilities include accrued liabilities and unearned or deferred credits. Accrued liabilities result from the recording of expenses at the time they are incurred but before the time they will be paid. Thus they are liabilities because there will be an eventual outflow of cash to satisfy particular obligations.

CONCEPTS INTO PRACTICE

As an example of an accrued liability, professional sports teams such as the Philadelphia Eagles might report deferred compensation owed to players as a current liability. Any player salaries that would be paid within a one-year period would be a current liability.

Numerous companies record advance payments for services or products as a liability when the cash is received. When advance payments are recorded this way, they are recognized as unearned, or deferred, credits.

CASH MANAGEMENT

In August 2011 the top 50 global corporations held roughly $1.1 trillion in cash (Collinson, 2011). Cash does not earn interest, yet individuals and corporations hold large amounts of it anyway. This was especially true after the recession of 2007-2008 when corporations were hesitant to make large investments during a period of global economic uncertainty. The reason for holding cash is the need for liquidity—having an asset on hand for immediate transactions.

As a part of cash management, financial managers face decisions about how much liquidity their sport business should retain. If the sport business decides to keep excessive amounts of cash in the bank, then it loses interest that it could have earned

RED BULL ROARING INTO SPORTS WORLD

Dietrich Mateschitz is widely known for creating Red Bull energy drink, also known as "speed in a can." His energy drink sold 4.2 billion cans in 2010, and revenues showed a 7.9% increase from the previous year. Red Bull is a privately held company, so they do not need to disclose their financial numbers, but their revenue increased by 15.8% in 2010 to €3.79 billion, propelled not only by stronger sales but also by currency and price effects. Sales increased significantly in global markets. Increases exceeded 80% in Turkey and Japan and reached 11% in the United States. The next market that Red Bull intends to tackle is China. With skyrocketing profits, Mateschitz has decided to keep expanding in the sport industry (McDonald, 2011).

The beverage now has its own magazine called *Red Bulletin,* created by media company Red Bull Media House, which was launched in 2007. In addition, Red Bull has stretched over TV programs on ESPN, films, its website, and web videos of athletes and action-packed events. Future projects include a documentary and reality TV ideas for Red Bull athletes. Mateschitz stated that multimedia plays a major role in communicating the product and brand, and although the media sectors are not yet profitable, they carry great value to the brand (McDonald, 2011).

Red Bull has employees in over 161 countries, and Mateschitz owns four soccer teams around the world: New York's Red Bulls, Red Bull Salzburg, Red Bull Brasil, and RB Leipzig. He also owns a NASCAR team and two Formula 1 racing teams. His business strategy involved building Red Bull into a philosophy or way of life. After preparing the contents, slogan, and packaging, Red Bull was ready to take off globally. Its marketing campaign to improve athletic performance assisted in gaining market share in the sports world. Red Bull's communication strategy involves producing an innovative product and proving that the brand is current and unique. Its target market is customers who are opinion leaders, particularly in sports. Red Bull uses event marketing and sampling to advertise its product. It uses over 250 endorsement agreements with leading athletes, but has no written contract with those athletes. Its event marketing efforts include sports and culture consisting of Flugtag, Creative Contest, Music Academy, and Local Hero Tour (Kastner & Partners, n.d.). Red Bull is also affiliated with specific sporting events such as BASE jumping, windsurfing, motocross, and the Red Bull Soapbox Race. Red Bull generates and arranges its own events and avoids sponsoring other events. Mateschitz's many achievements transpired because he diversified his product and was the first to execute his plan. Red Bull's strategies have allowed it to become the most expensive nonalcoholic beverage. It has applied the concept of diversification, so if any one sport segment declines, they have Red Bull tentacles in numerous other segments.

through investing that cash in marketable securities. If the sport business keeps too little cash in the bank, it will be forced to make repeated sales of securities to pay its bills. These repeated sales of securities will also saddle the sport business with excessive brokerage and other costs associated with each transaction. Too little cash can also lead to frequent trips to banks to obtain loans or use lines of credit.

Besides dealing with trade-offs between holding cash and holding marketable securities, cash management involves the efficient collection and disbursement of cash. This aspect of cash management requires an understanding of the relationship between sport businesses and their banks.

Liquidity

A simple way of looking at the trade-offs between holding cash and holding marketable securities was developed by William Baumol in 1952. In Baumol's framework, a firm must choose between holding cash and holding U.S. Treasury bills. Baumol viewed cash as something that is steadily depleted to pay bills. When the sport business runs out of cash, it replenishes its cash supplies by selling Treasury bills that it holds. For each additional dollar of cash held, interest that could have been obtained through holding Treasury bills is lost. If too little cash is held, a brokerage expense is associated with selling Treasury bills to replenish cash.

In the Baumol model, the cash management problem is shaped in terms of the optimum amount of Treasury bills sold each time the cash balance has to be replenished. The optimum amount of Treasury bills sold, Q, is equal to the following:

$$Q = \left(\frac{2 \times a \times c}{i}\right) 0.5$$

Q = optimum amount of Treasury bills sold

a = annual disbursements

c = cost per sale of Treasury bills

i = interest rate

Assume that the interest rate on Treasury bills is 5%, the cost per sale is $30, and the business pays out $1 million per year in cash. The optimum Q is then $34,641.

$$Q = \left(\frac{2 \times 1,000,000 \times 30}{0.05}\right) 0.5$$

$$= \$34,641$$

The firm will sell $34,641 of Treasury bills approximately 29 times per year ($1,000,000 / $34,461), or slightly more often than once every two weeks. The average cash balance held is equal to half the amount of Treasury bills sold. In our example, the average cash balance is $17,321.

$$\$34,641 / 2 = \$17,321$$

Note that in the Baumol formula the optimum amount of Treasury bills sold decreases as the interest rate rises. In other words, it pays to hold lower cash balances as interest rates increase. On the other hand, as the brokerage cost per sale of Treasury bills increases, the Baumol model implies that the sport business should hold higher cash balances to avoid the cost of selling Treasury bills, which would be greater than the interest earned.

Although the Baumol model demonstrates the analytical issues involved when we consider trade-offs between holding cash and marketable securities, it is simplistic relative to real-world sport business decisions. Unlike the situation described in the Baumol model, sport businesses do not deplete their cash reserves on a steady basis. Firms may find that over a one-month period they have a net inflow of cash as customers pay bills, whereas in the next month they have a net outflow of cash as

suppliers are paid. Other more complicated models allow for more unpredictable outflows and inflows (see Ross et al., 2008).

Another limitation of the Baumol model is its assumption that the only option other than holding cash is to invest in Treasury bills. In the real world, firms can invest in other assets such as stocks. As discussed in detail in the section "Marketable Securities" in chapter 8, stocks are risky relative to Treasury bills.

CONCEPTS INTO PRACTICE

Assume that Speedway Motorsports (SM) is finding that its outgoing cash is currently exceeding incoming cash by $500,000 per week. The company's financial managers need to determine the appropriate amount of cash for SM to have on hand. If SM begins the current week with $1 million in cash, its cash balance will drop to zero in exactly two weeks because $500,000 of the firm's initial cash will be consumed each week. Speedway Motorsports average cash balance will then equal $1,000,000 divided by 2, or $500,000.

By contrast, if SM started with $3 million in cash, cash would last exactly six weeks because SM consumes $500,000 per week in cash. The average cash balance over the six-week period would be $3,000,000 divided by 2, or $1,500,000. This scenario illustrates that if SM sets the initial cash balance at a higher level, it will not have to replenish cash as frequently. As a result, SM's brokerage expenses will be reduced. The trade-off is that by maintaining higher cash balances, SM sacrifices interest income that could have been earned on marketable securities.

To use the Baumol model to determine the optimum cash balance, assume that the cost per sale of Treasury bills equals $1,000 and that the interest rate on Treasury bills is 3%. Annual disbursements are $500,000 per week for 52 weeks, or $26,000,000. Using the Baumol model, Q equals the following:

$$Q = \left(\frac{2 \times \$26,000,000 \times \$1.000}{0.03}\right) 0.5$$

$$= \$1,316,561$$

SM, based on this calculation, will liquidate Treasury bills approximately 20 times per year ($26,000,000 divided by $1,316,561).

In our discussion of cash management, we have ignored another possibility for cash replenishment, which is borrowing rather than selling marketable securities. Some sport businesses draw on bank lines of credit when cash reserves are low. With borrowing, the analysis becomes more complicated because the interest rate paid to the bank is likely to be higher than the rate earned on marketable securities. If you were the financial manager of Speedway Motorsports or Under Armour, you would face a trade-off between the interest that would be sacrificed on sold-off marketable securities and the interest rate that would have to be paid on borrowings. If the interest charged on borrowed funds is substantially above the rate earned on marketable securities, selling off marketable securities as a means of raising cash would be preferable to borrowing additional amounts.

As a matter of practice, sport businesses that have idle cash invest in marketable securities with maturities of one year or less (i.e., money market instruments). Sport businesses may put their cash into money market mutual funds, which invest in short-term securities for a management fee. One of the benefits is the diversification provided by the fund manager's investment in numerous short-term instruments. In addition, banks offer "sweep accounts" for corporate customers. The bank takes all available funds in a sweep account at the end of each business day and invests them for the corporate customer. Thus, the rate of return is higher than it is in traditional bank accounts.

The reason that businesses invest idle cash balances in money market instruments is that for any given change in interest rates, the values of longer-maturity debt securities change more than those of shorter-maturity debt securities. Thus investors holding instruments with longer-term maturities face greater risk because of greater fluctuations in value associated with interest rate swings. This risk is known as interest rate risk. Given that the invested excess cash balances of the business may be needed at a moment's notice for large disbursements, businesses invest in money market instruments so that they are less subject to interest rate risk. As discussed in chapter 10, the expected returns on the debt instruments with shorter maturities are also lower because of the reduction in risk.

Collection and Disbursement of Cash

When sport businesses pay bills or receive payment for debts, they have the possibility of earning additional revenue or of losing the opportunity to earn additional revenue. Because of the time delays associated with writing, depositing, and cashing checks, some money can be lost. Checks that are written by the firm but have not yet cleared represent payment **float**. Checks that are received by the firm and deposited but have not yet cleared represent availability float. Net float represents the net effect of checks in the process of collection and is equal to the difference between payment float and availability float. With the increased use of electronic transfers, especially web-based transactions, float can be reduced. The next example illustrates net float.

CONCEPTS INTO PRACTICE

Although we have discussed the liquidity of a sport business, it is necessary to be more precise about how cash enters and exits the corporation and how the available cash balance is computed. Assume that SM has $1 million on deposit in a bank checking account. Suppose also that SM writes a $300,000 check to a supplier of concrete for its racetracks and mails the payment to a supplier. Immediately, SM will adjust its ledgers to show a cash balance of $700,000. The company's bank will not learn about this check until the supplier has received the check, the supplier has deposited the check at the supplier's bank, and that bank has presented the check to SM's bank. While waiting for the check to clear, SM's bank continues to show in its ledger that the company has $1 million in its account. Thus SM gains the benefit of an extra $300,000 in the bank while the check is clearing. This extra $300,000 is the payment float.

Although the float sounds like something that SM can take advantage of, it is a two-way street. Assume that at the same time SM writes the $300,000 check, the company receives a $100,000 check from the purchasing department of Sports Authority, which buys SM-branded apparel for its national chain of sporting goods stores. Speedway Motorsports deposits the $100,000 check, and both the company and bank ledger balances are increased by $100,000. Unfortunately for SM, it does not have access to the $100,000 immediately; SM's bank does not actually have the $100,000 until it has sent the check to and received the payment from Sports Authority's bank. While SM's bank is waiting for the check, SM has to wait to have access to the $100,000 payment. Under current Federal Reserve regulations, this wait can be anywhere from one to five business days for most checks. While the bank waits for payment, the bank will show that SM has an available balance of $1 million and an availability float of $100,000.

In effect, SM gains from the payment float of $300,000 but loses as a result of the $100,000 availability float. The difference between payment float and availability float is the net float. In our example, the net float is $300,000 minus $100,000, or $200,000. Float can be important because if the net float exists for five days and the bank pays interest of 5% on the account, SM will gain approximately $140 in interest during the five-day period. Although this sum may seem insignificant, if SM is able to maintain an average of $200,000 per day in float because of the timing of all its transactions, the interest earned per year would be $10,000. Note that this analysis does not include the additional interest earned because of compounding.

Both SM and Sports Authority can reduce availability float by encouraging vendors to make electronic payments. For example, a website that includes online ordering and payment collection capabilities that are convenient and easy for a potential customer to use can eliminate a substantial portion of availability float. Electronic funds transfers are available for use as soon as the funds are transferred to the vendor's bank from the customer's bank.

If you are a financial manager for SM, your true concern is the available balance rather than the balance recorded on the bank ledger. If you know that a one- or two-week delay may occur before some of the checks written to suppliers are presented for payment, then you may be able to get by on a smaller cash balance. This practice is known as playing the float.

In effect, you can increase your available cash balance by increasing your net float. Checks received from customers should be cleared rapidly, and checks to suppliers should be cleared more slowly. Net float can be increased even more by encouraging instantaneous electronic funds transfers. Although managing float may not seem like an important activity for a business, for a large company it can be significant. Assume that a company averages $100 million per day in sales. If it can increase collections by one day, the business frees up $100 million, which is then available to the shareholders or for capital projects.

Several techniques can be used to accelerate collections. One technique that many large companies use is concentration banking. Customers make pay-

ments at a local office as opposed to corporate headquarters, and the local branch office then deposits the checks into a local bank branch. Surplus funds from the local bank account are then periodically transferred to a concentration account at one of the company's main banks. These transfers can be made electronically, which allows for next-day availability of the funds at corporate headquarters.

Concentration banking reduces float for two reasons. First, because the branch office is closer to the customer, mailing time is reduced. Second, because the customer's check is more likely to be drawn on a local bank, the time needed for the check to clear is lessened.

Concentration banking can also be combined with a lockbox system. In a lockbox system, the company pays a local bank to handle the administrative chores, so establishing a branch office to handle receipt of payments is not necessary. A company with a national market establishes a collection point in each region of the country. Within each region, the company rents a locked post office box. All customers within the region are required to send payments to the specified locked post office box. The local bank, on behalf of the company, empties the box regularly and deposits the checks in the company's local bank account. Surplus funds are transferred periodically to one of the company's principal banks. The number of collection points, or regions, that are required depends on how quickly the mail is delivered.

CONCEPTS INTO PRACTICE

Assume that Speedway Motorsports (SM) decides to work with a West Coast bank in setting up a lockbox in San Francisco, California, for handling payments from customers in the western half of the United States. Suppose that the average number of daily payments to the lockbox is 500, the average payment size is $1,000, the rate of interest per day that can be earned on funds invested in marketable securities is 0.02%, the savings in mailing time is 1.4 days, and the savings in processing time is 0.5 day. The lockbox would result in SM's increasing its collected balance by 500 items per day at $1,000 per item times 1.9 (1.4 plus 0.5) days saved, or $950,000. The $950,000 invested at a return of 0.02% per day (950,000 multiplied by 0.0002) equals $190 per day. Typically, the bank's charge for providing the lockbox service will be on a per check basis. If the bank charges $0.30 per check, the daily charge would be

$150 per day (0.30 multiplied by 500). Thus, SM gains $190 minus $150, or $40, per day, which does not include additional savings that result from SM's not processing its own checks.

Slowing down disbursements is another technique for increasing net float. In extreme cases, businesses maintain disbursement accounts in several locations around the country. These businesses then use computer algorithms that look up each supplier's zip code so that a check is drawn on the most distant disbursement account.

CONCEPTS INTO PRACTICE

Under Armour's (UA) corporate headquarters are in Baltimore, Maryland. If UA pays its suppliers with checks drawn on a Delaware bank account, it may find that when the check is deposited by the supplier, only one to two days passes before the check is presented to UA's bank for payment. UA can set up disbursement checking accounts in various parts of the United States (e.g., by arranging to write checks drawn on banks in such remote locations as Helena, Montana; Pierre, South Dakota; or Abilene, Texas). In these cases, it may be three to four days before each check is presented for payment. This system would allow UA to gain additional float days.

Historically, collection and disbursement activity involved movement of paper checks. Over the past decade, companies have moved toward electronic collection and disbursement. In the past, the main hindrance to paperless activities was that many smaller businesses and consumers were unable to operate electronically. This circumstance has changed as the Internal Revenue Service and state and local tax authorities have implemented electronic transmission of payroll, income, and sales tax payments. As businesses and individuals increasingly use electronic funds transfers to pay bills, collections will be faster and availability float will be reduced. Almost all businesses now have websites that allow customers to authorize immediate electronic payments by transfers from customer bank accounts. The method of these payments can take many forms.

One of the most popular methods of payment for small online businesses is PayPal. PayPal is used by thousands of online retailers. The most popular and recognizable to consumers is probably eBay which now owns PayPal. Customers of PayPal may be both the purchasers of goods and the sellers of products. PayPal allows for the instantaneous transfer of funds from one account to another. PayPal accounts are usually connected electronically to a person's or business' bank or credit card account. Account holders can also use their PayPal account like a debit account and deposit money into it. The balance then decreases or increases as payments or collection are made. PayPal has grown quickly in popularity as the number of purchases made through the web has increased. All PayPal information is encrypted to insure security.

CONCEPTS INTO PRACTICE

Although we have discussed the liquidity of a sport business, it is necessary to be more precise about how cash enters and exits the corporation and how the available cash balance is computed. Assume that SM has $1 million on deposit in a bank checking account. Suppose also that SM writes a $300,000 check to a supplier of concrete for its racetracks and mails the payment to a supplier. Immediately, SM will adjust its ledgers to show a cash balance of $700,000. The company's bank will not learn about this check until the supplier has received the check, the supplier has deposited the check at the supplier's bank, and that bank has presented the check to SM's bank. While waiting for the check to clear, SM's bank continues to show in its ledger that the company has $1 million in its account. Thus SM gains the benefit of an extra $300,000 in the bank while the check is clearing. This extra $300,000 is the payment float.

Although the float sounds like something that SM can take advantage of, it is a two-way street. Assume that at the same time SM writes the $300,000 check, the company receives a $100,000 check from the purchasing department of Sports Authority, which buys SM-branded apparel for its national chain of sporting goods stores. Speedway Motorsports deposits the $100,000 check, and both the company and bank ledger balances are increased by $100,000. Unfortunately for SM, it does not have access to the $100,000 immediately; SM's bank does not actually have the $100,000 until it has sent the check to and received the payment from Sports Authority's bank. While SM's bank is waiting for the check, SM has to wait to have access to the $100,000 payment.

BENEFITS OF ELECTRONIC FUNDS TRANSFERS

One of the most important developments in collections management over the past 20 to 30 years has been electronic funds transfers (EFTs). EFTs are now used by 80% to 90% of all health clubs in the United States. The EFT systems withdraw funds automatically from a customer's bank account. Because the withdrawals are done electronically and at set times, such as the fifth day of each month, the process streamlines the collection and accounting process (Ernest, 2002). This process can save a significant amount of time and lost cash caused by payment delays. A third party, which can also provide additional support such as membership retention and marketing assistance, often admin-

isters the process. A health club could also use EFTs to establish an accurate flow of revenue on which a bank loan or other borrowing could be secured.

Another benefit of such a payment system is the time lag for terminating the service. If someone wants to cancel the service, she has to give advance notice; otherwise she would have to make an additional payment, which represents additional cash that the health club might not otherwise have received from that customer. Furthermore, if a customer breaches the contract, the health club could keep collecting the disputed amount until the matter is resolved without incurring a significant collection problem.

Under current Federal Reserve regulations, this wait can be anywhere from one to five business days for most checks. While the bank waits for payment, the bank will show that SM has an available balance of $1 million and an availability float of $100,000.

In effect, SM gains from the payment float of $300,000 but loses as a result of the $100,000 availability float. The difference between payment float and availability float is the net float. In our example, the net float is $300,000 minus $100,000, or $200,000. Float can be important because if the net float exists for five days and the bank pays interest of 5% on the account, SM will gain approximately $140 in interest during the five-day period. Although this sum may seem insignificant, if SM is able to maintain an average of $200,000 per day in float because of the timing of all its transactions, the interest earned per year would be $10,000. Note that this analysis does not include the additional interest earned because of compounding.

Both SM and Sports Authority can reduce availability float by encouraging vendors to make electronic payments. For example, a website that includes online ordering and payment collection capabilities that are convenient and easy for a potential customer to use can eliminate a substantial portion of availability float. Electronic funds transfers are available for use as soon as the funds are transferred to the vendor's bank from the customer's bank.

CREDIT MANAGEMENT

The amount of accounts receivable held by the business is determined by the extent to which that business sells on credit, as opposed to cash. In addition, the terms of credit become important in determining the amount of accounts receivable appearing on the balance sheet. For example, if Under Armour (UA) offers its customers the terms of net 30 days, customers have 30 days from the date of purchase to pay the amount owed. Under these circumstances, most of UA's customers will pay near the end of the 30 days. To encourage its customers to pay earlier, UA may offer terms of 1/10/30 (1%/10, net 30), which means that customers have 30 days to pay the balance owed, and they receive a 1% discount if payment occurs within 10 days of purchase. Another formula for credit terms is 2/10/30, which means that the discount is 2% if payment occurs within 10 days.

CONCEPTS INTO PRACTICE

In the case of 1/10/30, the customer who pays after 10 days is in effect receiving 20 days of credit at interest equal to the 1% forgone discount. Because about 18 such periods occur in a year (360 days a year divided by 20 days in each period), the annual interest equals 18 times 1%, or 18%. If UA changed the terms to 2/10/60, the cost of credit for 60 days minus the cost for 10 days (for paying early) would equal the cost for 50 days, which is 2% in lost discounts. About 7.2 periods would occur each year (360 divided by 50), so the annual interest would be 7.2 multiplied by the 2% forgone discount, or 14.4%.

To summarize thus far, the terms of a sale define the amount that the cash customer pays for the merchandise. In addition, the terms of sale set the interest rate charged for credit. If UA increases the discount from 1/10/30 to 2/10/30, the price for the cash customer has been reduced, but the interest rate charged to the credit buyer has been increased.

If a customer has a poor credit record, UA may insist that the buyer pay either COD (cash on delivery) or CBD (cash before delivery). UA can assess the creditworthiness of a customer in various ways. One way is to have a credit agency perform a credit check. The most prominent of the credit agencies is Dun & Bradstreet. Credit agencies typically report the experience that other firms have had in collecting payments from the customer. Credit bureaus also provide this kind of information. Similar information is available over the Internet through sites such as www.businesscreditusa.com.

The business' own bank can do a credit check by contacting the customer's bank, which will provide information on the customer's average bank balance, access to bank credit, and reputation.

If the customer is a publicly traded firm, there are inexpensive ways of collecting information about how this customer is assessed in the financial markets. Although a precipitous drop in a company's stock price does not imply that the firm is going into bankruptcy, it indicates that the company's future prospects are no longer as bright as they were previously.

CONCEPTS INTO PRACTICE

UA may be supplying its sporting goods apparel and shoes to a publicly traded chain of sporting goods stores and can easily look up the company's Moody's or Standard & Poor's rating. Moody's and Standard & Poor's rate the outstanding bonds of publicly traded companies in terms of the likelihood of default. Given the availability of stock price data on the Internet through such sites as Yahoo! Finance, UA can look at the recent behavior of the customer's stock price.

COLLECTIONS MANAGEMENT

Besides managing credit, sport businesses need to manage collections. Collections management focuses on converting receivables to cash and refers to efforts made to obtain payment of past due accounts. In addition, the credit manager needs to have records of the collections experience of the company in dealing with customers who currently have credit terms. This information is relevant for determining whether credit should continue to be extended in the future.

A sport business also needs to monitor its general collections experience to determine whether its terms are appropriate. One reporting tool involves the average days sales outstanding, or days in receivables. Our example involving Under Armour can illustrate the use of this tool.

CONCEPTS INTO PRACTICE

Assume that the terms on all UA sales to customers are 1/10/30. Assume that 65% of the customers take the 1% discount and pay on day 10 and that the remaining 35% pay on day 30. The average days sales outstanding is 65% multiplied by 10 days plus 35% multiplied by 30 days, or 17 days ([0.65 × 10] + [0.35 × 30]).

Because payments to a business tend to arrive more sporadically than in our example, calculating average daily sales is necessary. To make our calculations simple, let's assume that UA's annual sales are $4 million. Obviously, UA's sales are much larger than this, but these numbers will make the example easier to understand. Thus, its average daily sales are $10,959 per day ($4,000,000 divided by 365 days). That number is divided into the existing accounts receivable to obtain the average daily sales outstanding. If accounts receivable is $186,300, then average daily sales outstanding is 17 days ($186,300 divided by $10,959). This means that when making a purchase, the average UA customer pays in 17 days.

If UA analyzes daily or weekly data on sales and accounts receivable and finds that average daily sales outstanding stays at 17 days over a 1-month period, then some customers are paying later. In addition, some accounts may be overdue. With sales outstanding staying at 17 days, a significant number of UA customers are not paying their bills immediately or taking advantage of early payment discounts. Although some customers may pay early, it appears that more customers are waiting longer than the discount period. Keep in mind that for a company such as UA that has seasonal sales patterns, the calculated average daily sales outstanding will fluctuate during the year. For such businesses, receivables are low before the major selling season and high afterward. As a result, average daily sales outstanding on a particular date may need to be compared with past averages for the same date.

An aging report, which tabulates receivables by the age of accounts, can provide more detailed information. Table 12.1 presents an example. Note that a significant number of customers are past due (40% of accounts are outstanding more than 30 days). Any sport business that displays a report like the one shown in table 12.1 has serious collections problems and should be reviewing its collections policies.

The rules governing the deduction of bad-debt losses are complicated. Whether a company has to go to court to obtain a judgment against the debtor depends on the particular situation. For example, if the company can show that the court would return a judgment of uncollectible, then going to court is unnecessary. Bankruptcy is generally considered evidence by the IRS that at least a portion of the debt can be viewed as bad. The deduction of bad-debt losses is summarized in IRS Publication 535, *Business Expenses* (Internal Revenue Service, 2010).

Table 12.1 Sample Aging Report

Age of account	Percentage of total accounts receivable
0 to 30 days	60
31 to 60 days	15
61 to 90 days	15
90 to 120 days	6
121 days or more	4
Total	100

For smaller businesses, employing someone in credit management and collections may be too expensive. Under these circumstances, the business may sell its accounts receivable directly to a financial institution, called a factor. The factor buys the receivables of the firm at a discount, which is typically 1% (Brealey, Myers, & Marcus, 2008). The company and the factor agree on credit terms for each customer. The customer sends payments to the factor, which bears the risk that the customer will not pay. Factors are discussed in chapter 8.

CONCLUSION

This chapter outlined the various types of current assets and liabilities, known on a company's balance sheet as working capital, including cash, marketable securities, accounts receivable, inventories, short-term loans, accounts payable, accrued income taxes, and current payments due on long-term debt. Net working capital refers to current assets minus current liabilities, as highlighted in chapter 6.

Financial managers face trade-offs between holding cash and holding interest-bearing securities. If interest rates are high, holding relatively less cash is desirable. Borrowing serves as an alternative to liquidating securities to replenish cash in the event of a deficiency. The cash that appears in company ledgers is not the same as the available balance in the company's bank account. The difference is net float. We discussed how sport companies can play the float to reduce their required cash holdings, as well as how companies can manage the float by speeding up collections and slowing down payments.

The chapter also described the intricacies of credit management, specifically establishing the length of the payment period and the size of any cash discounts. We discussed sources of information that can be used to assess a customer's creditworthiness, as well as collection measures and procedures. All these steps help create a plan for the effective use of a sport business' cash reserves for reinvestment or to pay expenses such as manufacturing and inventory costs, which are discussed in the next chapter.

Class Discussion Topics

1. How should a business monitor collections activity?

2. How has the advent of greater volumes of electronic funds transfers affected the accumulation of float by a business?

3. Businesses can increase cash flow by stretching out payments to vendors by an additional 15 days. If this is so obvious, why is it that companies do not necessarily do this?

4. If a company has excess cash available, should it use that cash to pay its vendors more quickly?

5. Is it better business practice to require all customers to pay before receiving a product, as opposed to having receivables?

6. For a professional sport organization such as an NFL team, list some of the financial activities that may be classified under short-term financial management.

chapter 13

Inventory and Production Management

Chapter Objectives

After studying this chapter, you should be able to do the following:

- Distinguish between variable and fixed costs.
- Understand how to determine product costs, set prices, and reduce costs.
- Understand inventory management.
- Understand how to forecast inventory needs.
- Understand the costs associated with managing inventory.
- Calculate the optimum economic ordering quantity.
- Describe inventory turnover and inventory obsolescence.
- Calculate manufacturing costs, including labor costs.

This chapter focuses on inventory and production management, which are critical components of the manufacturing analysis process. All companies that manufacture products need to examine how they use their inventory to ensure they are using resources efficiently. Similarly, companies need to examine how they produce products to maximize efficiency and minimize waste. Although we primarily use Speedway Motorsports as an example throughout this chapter, the principles illustrated apply to other sport-related businesses.

Although finance is not exclusively about expenses, managing and controlling expenses are primary financial disciplines. Controlling expenses is an important element of inventory and production management. If inventory is not effectively used, money is wasted and expenses for storage costs increase. For example, if a machine sits idle, the business loses money from the lack of production and expenses increase for machine downtime. This chapter deals first with business costs and then examines the entire inventory management process, including forecasting demand, purchasing optimum quantities, storing inventory, auditing inventory, and using inventory. We then discuss production analysis, focusing on manufacturing costs, break-even analysis, variance analysis, and labor cost concerns.

BUSINESS COSTS

As highlighted in chapter 3, a business needs to plan for various expenses. Expenses can include office supplies, raw inventory, facility costs (from mortgages to electrical bills), corporate perks such as season tickets, and an endless number of other expenses. Given the complexity within some organizations, categorizing every dollar spent by a business is difficult because some expenses are grouped into a generic category called general expenses instead of being recorded separately. General expenses for a sport-related business can be highly diverse, as seen in the next Concepts Into Practice example using Speedway Motorsports.

One question often raised relates to ticket prices and player salaries. For example, what effect did the Los Angeles Angels' 2011 signing of free agent Albert Pujols have on ticket prices? Player salaries are a fixed expense—at the start of the season, the team knows what its total salary obligation will be except for possible bonuses and reductions in salaries if players are injured, cut, or traded. Furthermore, the team can then predict other expenses based on their level of salary expense. Similarly,

the team can determine the potential revenue from broadcast rights, luxury seating, and sponsorship income. Considering these potential income areas, the team can examine how much it might need to charge ticket holders to ensure that it can cover its costs. Thus, expenses have a direct effect on prices of various items, from tickets to concessions.

CONCEPTS INTO PRACTICE

Speedway Motorsports has significant expenses over and beyond those related to merchandise and facilities. The following are some of the possible operating expenses for the business:

- Sanctioning fees for staging races
- Cleaning the facility after a race, including seating areas, locker rooms, bathrooms, team offices, pressrooms, concession areas, and the racetrack
- Race-day personnel, including ticket takers; ushers; security officers; and traffic control, police, fire, EMT, and related personnel (either directly hired or outsourced to an outside vendor)
- Ordinary repair and maintenance costs for everything from computers and photocopiers to leader boards

These expenses can be diagrammed in the same way as the expenses faced by any sport business. An expense map is similar to a road map and identifies what areas of the business are incurring expenses and where possible cost savings can come from. A partial expense map could resemble the following:

Expenses

Personnel	Legal
Maintenance	Travel
Player salaries	Accountant
Storage	Media
Coaches	Insurance
Marketing	Media food table
Scouts	Facility
Advertising	Media guides
Administrative	Utilities
Graphics	

We all know basic costs such as the price of going to McDonald's and spending $5 for a meal. When you do this, the cost to you is $5. If you earn $10 per hour, you can calculate your cost as 50% of your hourly wage. On the basis of an eight-hour day, you could calculate your $5 meal as 6.25% of your daily wage. Cost analysis is similar for a sport business.

Types of Business Costs

All businesses face several types of costs. An example of a variable cost for a sport business might be salaries for the ushers, which could change from one game to the next according to the expected attendance. Comparatively, an example of a fixed cost is a team's lease payment to a city, which needs to be made no matter how many tickets are sold. The following sections deal with the various types of costs occurring in businesses.

Variable Costs

Variable costs vary with each unit produced as seen in the following Speedway Motorsports case study example.

CONCEPTS INTO PRACTICE

If Speedway Motorsports acquired $2 million in rubber in 2011, the company bought raw materials classified as variable costs. The company might need to purchase more rubber or might have too much. If Speedway Motorsports sees an increase in orders and needs to make 1,000 more tires than previously planned, the total variable costs would increase. But even if Speedway Motorsports buys more rubber, the variable cost per tire could decrease because the company might be able to buy the greater quantity of rubber at a discount, reducing the variable cost per tire.

Semivariable Costs

Costs can also be classified as semivariable. These costs vary with the amount of activity, but they are not directly proportional to the amount of the activity. A good example of semivariable costs is maintenance. Some uniformity is normally seen with regard to the cost of regularly maintaining a piece of machinery. But if a Speedway Motorsports track-cleaning machine is running three hours more than usual each day, maintenance will probably need to be conducted more frequently. The costs of health care premiums paid by an employer could also be semivariable. The cost of a premium may be constant, but the total amount paid by the employer may vary with the number of employees covered by the plan.

Fixed Costs

Fixed costs are the last major cost category. Fixed costs stay constant no matter what changes occur in usage or sales. Property taxes and depreciation expenses are just two examples of fixed costs. Thus, a university has a fixed cost associated with using its gym. Whether 10 or 50 people show up for a game, the operating and maintenance costs still need to be paid. One of the biggest fixed costs for a sport business is salaries, because athletes are paid regardless of the number of people attending a game.

Other Ways of Classifying Costs

Through cost accounting, which is the method used to tease out the true costs associated with any given activity, costs could be identified or classified according to additional levels other than variable, semivariable, and fixed. Some of these additional categories include material, manufacturing, labor, factory overhead, general, and administrative costs. Material costs are the costs of the material used to make a given product.

For Speedway Motorsports the rubber identified earlier as a variable cost can also be classified as a manufacturing cost. The company needs the rubber to make its tires. Labor costs are the costs needed to transform the material into the finished product. Factory overhead is the cost associated with the equipment and buildings used as the material is converted to a finished product. Factory overhead traditionally includes rent or mortgage, machine costs, depreciation, electricity, and other expenses that cannot be directly linked to individual units of output but still aid in the production process. The last major category is general and administrative costs. These costs typically include salaries for employees in the sales department or other nonmanufacturing departments, marketing expenses, research and development, and related expenses not associated with manufacturing.

Before we discuss costs further, note that many businesses use terms such as *overhead* or *indirect costs*. Overhead refers to all the additional costs (over and beyond all the combined manufacturing costs) associated with getting a product to market, such as administrative, legal, marketing, and related costs. An indirect cost is a cost associated with, but not necessarily part of the process of, converting raw materials to the finished product. A good sport example of an indirect cost is scouts for a pro team. The scouts do not coach the athletes to become better or in any way enhance the value of a player, but without scouts a team would not be able to put the best product on the field. Businesses should not use the terms *overhead* and *indirect* because they are misleading; all expenses, whether variable or fixed, add a cost component to the product. For example, we should not use the term *indirect labor* because either the labor is productive and needs to be accounted for or it is unnecessary and needs to be eliminated. Nonetheless, because executives frequently use the terms *overhead* and *indirect expenses*, we briefly discuss them here.

Although indirect expenses are not the most accurate measure for analyzing costs, people typically refer to direct and indirect labor costs when discussing the manufacturing expenses of a given product or service. Examples of **direct costs** are such items as raw materials for Speedway Motorsports tires. **Indirect costs** could include employee salaries and benefits associated with office personnel who do not design, manufacture, or distribute the tires (e.g., secretaries). Traditionally, indirect costs are added directly to the cost of a manufactured item, even if those costs are wholly unrelated to the manufacturing process.

Hidden Costs

Some costs are "hidden" and thus hard to appreciate when making financial decisions. Building a new facility involves numerous costs that are not obvious. These hidden costs can significantly affect such issues as building change orders or cost increases based on the material used and passing through under the contract to build a new sport facility. For example, Speedway Motorsports could consider building a new stadium with an $80 million budget. A construction company starts the building process, and then a local homeowner sues everyone for diminishing the value of his property. The suit will cost money but will not add any value to the facility or help pay for its construction. Thus, it was hidden in the initial budget because it was not anticipated. Most construction projects have 10% of their budget put aside to cover such

contingencies, but various issues can increase such expenditures.

Additionally, hidden costs related to unexpected environmental issues could arise. An environmental impact analysis as part of the due diligence process is a standard expense. Due diligence entails a thorough investigation of a proposed business deal to determine whether any potential legal or financial problems will surface. The environmental impact analysis is designed to determine whether the land is contaminated or whether any environmental remediation might be required. Issues other than contamination (e.g., endangered species issues) may also arise. These issues can undercut an entire project.

Local laws may require development of wetlands to replace areas converted by construction. Creating or maintaining wetlands may be impossible if a stadium needs space for parking lots, so a facility project may be unable to comply with the law. This issue was recently raised when a new baseball stadium was proposed for construction on the waterfront in St. Petersburg, Florida, for the Tampa Bay Rays. Nevertheless, government entities still require compliance. To address this conflict, some companies have developed wetland mitigation banks from which a business can buy its share of acreage without having to retain wetlands at the construction site. For example, Speedway Motorsports might be required to leave 2 acres (.8 ha) as wetlands. Instead of losing all the possible parking spaces, the stadium can go to the mitigation bank and buy 2 acres that might be located near a city park. The bank owners then assume the responsibility of keeping the wetlands in good shape and allowing wildlife to use the space. The cost of buying the space is offset by the high cost that would be involved in developing and maintaining the wetlands at the stadium site. Such a project was built outside Houston on 580 acres (230 ha). The government granted credits for the acreage, and the owners sold the credits to private companies that did not want to develop wetlands or wanted to avoid time delays associated with building a wetland project (Breyer, 1998).

Analyzing Costs

Regardless of how costs are classified, fully appreciating the cost of an item is impossible without developing a cost summary sheet. The cost summary sheet breaks down all the costs incurred in the manufacture of an item. A company can also price services in this manner by calculating the labor cost for each activity that is part of the service.

Speedway Motorsports' cost sheet shows the various categories of costs over and above the raw materials used to create an item such as a premium tire, including taxes, depreciation, profits, and related expenses. Numerous pro forma budgets fail investor scrutiny because the pro forma does not identify these cost categories. A cost sheet makes it more difficult to overlook any cost category.

CONCEPTS INTO PRACTICE

Using the Super Tire cost sheet here would help Speedway Motorsports determine the most profitable optimum pricing strategies and allow management to identify where cost reductions can be made.

The cost sheet establishes several key variables that help Speedway Motorsports determine its profitability and related standards:

- Speedway Motorsports' profit is $12, which is built into the cost analysis.
- Profit as a percentage of target sales price is 8% ($96.25 target price divided by $12 profit).
- Gross margin is net sales price ($104) minus the material costs ($25), or $79.
- Value added is the net sales price ($104) minus total purchases ($27.50), or $76.50.
- Cash flow is after-tax profits ($12) plus depreciation ($10), or $22.
- Contribution margin is the net sales price ($104) minus total variable cost ($57.75), or $46.25.

The value-added component is the key point for a specialized company such as Speedway Motorsports. Although this tire example is fictitious, it does represent a unique area where a racing company can leverage its racing experience to provide value-added for those who want auto-related products. Exploiting this uniqueness, the company is able to charge more than other tire manufacturers. The uniqueness adds value to the product, in the same way that winning a championship would add value to a sports organization. After winning a championship, a team would be able to charge a higher ticket price because people would be willing to pay more to see them.

Super Tire Cost Sheet

Description	Cost per packaged unit ($)
Part A	20.00
Part B	1.00
Whitewall paint	2.00
Packaging	2.00
Material costs	**$25.00**
Supplies and repairs	1.50
Utilities	1.00
Total purchases	**$27.50**
Cost at step 1	14.00
Cost at step 2	5.00
Cost at step 3	1.50
Quality-related losses	4.00
Sales and distribution costs	5.00
Short-term interest	0.75
Total variable costs	**$57.75**
Manufacturing	7.25
Distribution	3.50
Research and development	2.50
Administrative	2.00
Long-term interest	1.25
Total manufacturing cost less depreciation	**$74.25**
Depreciation	10.00
Total cost	**$84.25**
Net profit	12.00
Target price after tax	**$96.25**
Provisions for taxes	7.75
Net target selling price	**$104.00**
Discount and terms	6.00
Total target price	**$110.00**

Reducing Costs

Besides analyzing costs, organizations need to examine techniques to reduce costs. Systematic cost reduction can be accomplished through various techniques, such as engineered standards and cost control reports. These techniques can help identify waste and appropriate remedial measures. For example, instead of having a secretary for each executive, an organization could centralize the secretarial staff so that five executives share three secretaries—saving two salaries while still accommodating the executives' needs. Other cost reduction techniques are discussed elsewhere in this text, such as reissuing bonds at a lower interest rate when the market is favorable.

Companies use capital cost reduction techniques to reduce the cost of issuing stocks or bonds. A company can issue more stock than it actually releases to the public (reserve stock) to reduce future issuing expense. If the company needs to release the additional shares, the capital costs have already been covered, so most of the proceeds from sales of the additional shares go directly to the corporation.

Although capital cost reduction produces significant benefits, cost reduction can also occur in other areas, such as inventory and the manufacturing process. First, we discuss ways to reduce costs in the manufacturing process; then, in the next section we consider inventory management, through which a company examines the length of time that inventory sits idle in storage and wastes the company's money. Examining such costs gives a business an opportunity to identify where costs might be excessive and thus reduce those costs.

The simplest means to meet a production and sales budget is to increase selling price. This strategy, however, may lead to lost sales and jeopardizes customer relationships. Reducing internal costs can also help make the budget. Cost reduction can result from various strategies, such as reducing labor costs or streamlining the manufacturing process. As an example, various cost reduction strategies can be undertaken to reduce utility expenses. Businesses can change the wattage of light bulbs or reduce the amount of water used to flush a toilet. The electricity and water usage can be plotted, and the benefits associated with conservation efforts can be tracked.

Although many sport-related products are services, numerous products are manufactured and companies such as Under Armour need to make sure that their machinery is working well to ensure standard production rates and reduce operating costs. Numerous cost reduction strategies also apply to running machinery. Businesses using machinery can identify ways to save in this area by doing the following (Feiner, 1977):

- Analyzing costs based on machine centers (a group of similar machines working together) or groups versus product runs or other evaluation methods
- Establishing preventive maintenance programs prolonging machine life and reducing costly repairs
- Evaluating utility conservation programs to determine whether machines are using energy as effectively as possible

- Ensuring that employees are not misusing the machines
- Analyzing true equipment requirements to reduce the need for certain equipment or reallocate floor space for more effective income generation
- Setting aside money (e.g., in a sinking fund) to help purchase new or refurbished equipment to replace outdated equipment

INVENTORY MANAGEMENT

Most college, semiprofessional, and amateur sports facilities have similar costs. For example, each facility has maintenance, personnel, electricity, construction, and related costs. Similarly, each facility tries to minimize the operating costs while still providing the best services. No matter where expenses might arise, financial managers need to track expenses carefully to ensure that money is not being misspent.

Inventory management is an effective tool for managing variable and semivariable costs. If excess inventory sits in a storage facility, the company not only loses the use of the money tied up in the inventory (and might even need to pay financing charges if the inventory was purchased with borrowed funds) but also has to pay inventory storage expenses. Conversely, if sufficient inventory is not available, customers may not receive items that they have purchased, which can result in lower sales and loss of customers. To avoid these problems, managers use techniques such as order forecasting to determine when they might have to purchase inventories or when certain expenses will arise.

Key Components of an Inventory Management System

The key components of any inventory management system are forecasting, purchasing, storing, auditing, and utilizing inventory. These five components are discussed in the following sections.

Forecasting Inventory

Here we briefly examine forecasting in general and then focus on one of the most critical forecasting areas, inventory forecasting. For example, we can develop a thorough forecast by analyzing what activities occur to generate a sale. A 35-point cost-of-sales questionnaire designed to solicit the information needed to develop a comprehensive forecast identifies some of the dynamic issues

35-POINT COST-OF-SALES QUESTIONNAIRE

Material Costs

1. What percentage of sales are direct materials?

2. How is the standard cost for materials established?

3. How often are these costs reviewed and by what procedure?

4. Are "free stock" items included as a direct or indirect cost?

5. How effectively and accurately are purchase parts invoiced and material (stores) requisitions processed?

6. Is a part-numbering system maintained?

7. Does cost accounting's purchase price agree with purchasing's current record and if not, what corrective action is required?

Direct Labor Costs

8. What percentage of sales is direct labor?

9. What percentage of total salary and wages is direct labor?

10. Which departments (cost centers) are being measured by performance reports, and are line managers making effective use of these reports?

11. Are standard labor hours based on historical actuals or industrial engineering standards?

12. How current are these standards?

13. How accurate are the standard dollar labor rates, and do they reflect shift differentials?

14. How is cost accounting notified of changes in the labor rate or in the standard hours?

Overhead Costs

15. What percentage of sales is overhead?

16. What percentage of overhead is classified as indirect labor, and is it all truly indirect?

17. What percentage of the overhead represents variable, semi-variable, and fixed costs?

18. How is overhead applied, and is there more than one rate?

19. Is any of the overhead pool applied to materials, and is the rate sufficient to fully absorb actual expenses?

20. Do overhead expenses exist by department?

Variances

21. How are variances reported—by job, by standard production runs, or on an exception basis?

22. Are material variances segregated from labor variances?

23. Are labor variances segregated by rate and efficiency factors?

24. Are material variances segregated by price and usage?

25. Are variance results oriented so that causes can be quickly identified and corrected?

26. How effective are variance reports? Who receives, reviews, and analyzes these reports?

27. Are sufficient data provided so all jobs can be adequately reviewed?

28. Who determines which jobs or production runs will be reviewed?

29. Is cost estimating plugged into the variance reporting?

30. Can any of these variances be honestly billed to the customer to reflect changes?

Inventory Related

31. Are book to physical adjustments recorded as discovered?

32. Are inventory cycles conducted, and if so how often are they conducted?

33. How are production losses and shrinkages controlled, reported, and booked?

Other

34. Are gross profit margin analyses performed on a regular basis?

35. Are product line profit-and-loss statements prepared and shared with those who can make a definite contribution toward improving future results?

Reprinted from R.R. Feiner, 1977, *Operational financial analysis: A practical handbook with forms* (Englewood Cliffs, NJ: Prentice Hall), 45-46. By permission of R.R. Feiner.

associated with determining the potential costs of manufacturing an item. Some people think that manufacturing expenses can be reduced simply by cutting costs, but they need to identify exactly where or how to reduce costs. The questionnaire poses questions that any manager needs to ask and answer to identify variables that may represent a potential area for cost savings.

Forecasting involves a little of both science and art to set the stage for determining optimum sales, inventory, production levels, and manufacturing costs. Forecasts for some variables are simple, such as yearly property tax or insurance obligations; in these cases the business knows what the expenses will be and when they must be paid. Comparatively, whereas a business may be sure of certain expenses such as rent, they cannot know when a sound system will break or whether they will suffer any theft. Unpredictable variables can positively or negatively affect projections, but by developing a competently researched forecast, managers can either avoid or account for variability. Inventory forecasting helps establish the inventory purchases that will need to be made throughout the year and the most effective techniques for reordering additional inventory.

Purchasing Inventory

Purchasing needed materials might appear to be a relatively easy process for most businesses. If you examine your own individual buying patterns, however, you may discover inefficiencies that cost you significantly. If you wait too long to buy gas on a highway, you may be stuck paying several more cents per gallon than you would otherwise. If you have a headache and buy a pain reliever at a convenience store, you will pay much more than if you had purchased it at a discount drugstore. Similarly, the failure of a business to manage purchases and material costs can cost a company millions of dollars. Some of the commonplace inefficiencies facing a company are (Feiner, 1977)

- intermittent, ineffective, or short production runs (a production run is the manufacture of a predetermined amount of product), such as if a company has a production run of 1,000 clubs planned for February);
- double handling of materials because some materials were not available when needed;
- inadequate development of proper tooling methods because the production runs are too short;

- failure to realize quantity discounts;
- failure to define economical order quantities; and
- downtime of machines that are waiting for parts but still incur all fixed operating costs.

Inventory Turnover Ratio

The problems identified in the preceding section are just some of the concerns associated with poor management of the raw goods required to manufacture the final product. Identifying a machine that is not in use is easy, and it is obvious when you have to pay a premium for a small order. But it is often difficult or even impossible to notice when raw materials are just sitting in storage for extended periods and out of a manager's view. Inventory **turnover** is a method used to determine whether in fact inventory is just sitting around. The inventory turnover ratio also helps identify whether management is adequately managing resources.

An inventory turnover ratio can be applied to both finished goods and raw goods. The calculation for finished goods turnover is as follows:

finished goods turnover ratio = cost of goods sold / average finished goods inventory

Assuming that the cost of goods sold is $385,000 and the average finished goods inventory is $65,000, the turnover ratio will be $385,000 divided by $65,000, or 5.92. This number can also be expressed in working days: 42.7 days of unsold finished goods sitting in inventory. To calculate the number of working days, divide the number of working days in the year (253) by the turnover ratio (5.92) (Feiner, 1977). The number of working days (253) is constant for any company that is closed on weekends and federal holidays. There is no correct ratio for inventory turnover, but the faster the inventory is turned over, the more money will be made. Some sport businesses are likely to have a high inventory turnover rate (e.g., concession items are typically bought and sold frequently). On the other hand, a yacht sales company might sell only a few boats each year, but the profit margin on each boat can sustain the business. We can do the same calculation for raw materials using the following formula:

raw materials turnover ratio = raw materials consumed / average raw materials inventory

Using the preceding formula, if a company spends $135,000 on raw materials and maintains an average inventory of $17,000 in raw goods, the company's turnover ratio would be the following:

$$\text{raw materials turnover ratio} = \$135,000 / \$17,000 = 7.94$$

The 7.94 ratio translates to 31.9 days that raw materials are generally in inventory before they are consumed. The more quickly that raw materials are consumed, the lower the inventory handling costs are. This number is important because it serves as a benchmark to help identify potential waste. Management must vigilantly monitor whether this number increases or decreases. Knowing about any decreases will help the manager identify what is being done correctly to maintain the success. Any increases represent a trouble sign that raw materials are sitting around incurring unnecessary expenses.

CONCEPTS INTO PRACTICE

Assume that Speedway Motorsports has incurred costs of $400,000 for their Super Tires that they produced and $125,000 for the raw materials consumed. Also, assume that the average finished goods inventory is $50,000 and that the average raw materials inventory is $15,000. Based on those numbers, the inventory turnover ratios would be as follows:

$$\text{finished goods} = \$400,000 / \$50,000 = \text{a turnover ratio of } 8$$

$$\text{raw materials} = \$125,000 / \$15,000 = \text{a turnover ratio of } 8.33$$

Thus, in our example, the number of working days required to turn over the inventory is 31.6 days for finished goods (253 divided by 8) and 30.4 days for raw materials (253 divided by 8.33). The data obtained through this calculation can be compared with ratios from similar companies to determine whether Speedway Motorsports is storing and selling its inventory effectively. Comparison data can be obtained from banks and trade associations (Feiner, 1977).

Purchasing Concerns

Purchasing concerns arise when inventory is not ordered in a timely manner, is ordered too quickly, or is ordered in incorrect quantities. Centralized purchasing is one technique for reducing these potential problems. Centralized purchasing moves the decision making and execution away from individual departments. Centralizing the purchasing function provides benefits such as the following (Feiner, 1977):

- Managers can focus on their specialties rather than on administrative issues surrounding purchasing.
- Responsibility is given to a single person rather than numerous individual managers.
- Clerical effort and inventory control problems can be reduced.
- Problems of potential shortages can be identified early.
- Price negotiation can be improved because of the ability to buy bigger lots and redistribute the materials throughout an organization.

Purchasing is only the second step in the inventory management process. Inventories are typically not purchased on an as-needed basis because the costs for ordering small amounts would be prohibitive. Thus, a business places larger orders, and excess inventory needs to be stored for future use.

Storing Inventory

As you have already seen, inventory-related costs can be significant over and beyond the cost for the storage facility itself. Inventories can be classified as raw materials, work-in-process, and finished goods. At each level the inventory needs to be stored, moved, modified, shipped, packaged, and sent through related processes; and all these steps cost money. Some of these expenses can be reduced through joint warehousing with other businesses or through the development of automated systems to move the right parts at the right time.

Raw materials can pose unique storage concerns when in liquid or bulk form. If Speedway Motorsports has purchased a large amount of rubber for making tires, the rubber might take up significant space or may need to be stored in special areas. Work-in-process is a term for

INVENTORY CONCERNS IN THE NFL

The National Football League (NFL) accumulates $3.2 billion in retail sales each year, making it the largest sports brand and the seventh-largest brand in the world behind the likes of Coca-Cola. Approximately 31% of sports fans over age 12 own some type of NFL product. Although the items of some teams are popular sellers, other products go unsold. Manufacturers need to produce enough goods from each team to cover fan needs, especially in case a team does well. No retailer wants to be without a team's merchandise if the team is having a great season. Manufacturers need to play a guessing game, and when a team does well they must ramp up production and shipment—even though the team might tank later in the season. In fact, all championship events have T-shirts produced with the winning team's name on them. How can they be available so quickly that they are worn within a minute of the game's ending? The manufacturer prints two versions of the shirts, one for each team. The winning team receives their shirts, and the other team's shirts are destroyed or given away to charity organizations.

refined raw materials that have not yet reached the finished product stage. These materials need to be stored in a location from which they can easily be moved to the finishing area. In a typical manufacturing plant that produces millions of products each year, the amount of goods classified as work-in-process can be significant, especially if the manufacturing process takes more than a week and products are manufactured in a cycle in which new runs are started each or every other week. If the product takes three weeks to manufacture and a new production run is launched every other week, a significant amount of work-in-process is being stored at various stages of completion.

Inventory Storage Costs

Inventory management is the process of lowering the total costs associated with all the inventories required to sustain efficient operations (Brigham & Gapenski, 1994). In other words, by effectively tracking inventory costs, a company can reduce costs while continuing to operate efficiently. Costs can be broken down into four main areas: carrying costs, ordering costs, shipping and receiving costs, and costs associated with running out of inventory. The carrying, or storing, costs are the most expensive component of the inventory costs. These costs generally rise in direct proportion to the average amount of inventories carried. Thus, the more inventory that is being stored, the greater the carrying costs are, as the following example shows.

CONCEPTS INTO PRACTICE

Assume that Speedway Motorsports sells S units of tires each year and that the company has to place equal-sized orders N times a year for the raw materials needed to build the tires. The ratio of S to N (S divided by N) will indicate how many units are purchased with each order. The average inventory level (A) can be expressed with the following formula (Brigham & Gapenski, 1994):

$$A = \text{units per order} / 2 = (S / N) / 2$$

A = average inventory level
S = units of tires sold in a year
N = number of orders of raw materials in a year

The number of units purchased per order is divided by 2 to obtain the "average" number of units to be ordered. If Speedway Motorsports sold 120,000 tires and placed four orders a year for raw materials, the formula would be completed as follows:

$$A = (120,000 / 4) / 2 = 30,000 / 2 = 15,000 \text{ units}$$

Thus, Speedway Motorsports would carry an average inventory of 15,000 units. The company orders 30,000 units at a time, so when a shipment is received, the inventory level should be close to 0 units; after the order is received, the inventory level will be slightly over 30,000 units. By knowing the average inventory level, we can calculate carrying costs.

If Speedway Motorsports pays $2 per unit, then the average inventory value is $2 multiplied by 15,000 units, or $30,000. Many businesses have a cost of capital based on having to borrow money to purchase inventory. If Speedway Motorsports has a cost of capital of 10%, then the inventory carrying costs for one year will be $3,000. This cost needs to be added to the storage costs, including space, utilities, security, taxes, and so on. These annual costs come to $2,000 a year. In addition, the following annual costs also need to be added to the total carrying costs: $500 for insurance and $1,000 for inventory losses. Speedway Motorsports' total carrying costs for carrying the $30,000 average inventory are $3,000 plus $2,000 plus $500 plus $1,000, or $6,500 total (Brigham & Gapenski, 1994). We can calculate the $6,500 cost as a percentage (C) by dividing it by the $30,000 average inventory: $6,500 divided by $30,000 equals 0.217, or 21.7%. The annual percentage cost can be used in subsequent forecasts to determine potential carrying costs.

$$TCC = C \times P \times A$$

TCC = total carrying costs
C = carrying costs divided by value of average inventory
P = product cost
A = average inventory

If Speedway Motorsports increased its average inventory value to $40,000—which would change A to 20,000—and the price (P) remained at $2, the carrying costs would be calculated as follows:

$$TCC = 0.217 \times \$2 \times 20,000 = \$8,680$$

The TCC of $8,680 is a $2,180 increase over the previous cost of $6,500. This example highlights how the carrying costs increase when larger inventories are ordered. The increase would be reduced if the turnover rate was much greater. Thus, if 240,000 units were sold each year, the 100% increase in sales coupled with larger inventory purchases could reduce some of the carrying costs, resulting in increased profits or having funds to pay the capital costs earlier.

As noted previously, four types of costs are associated with inventory. Carrying costs are the largest, but ordering costs, shipping and receiving costs, and the cost of running out of inventory are also important. These costs are often fixed and include such items as the cost of research on purchase options, interoffice memos, phone calls, taking delivery, and moving raw materials. The fixed costs associated with inventory ordering are represented by F. To calculate the total ordering cost, we multiply F by N, with N representing the number of orders per year. The equation is often written as follows:

$$TOC = F \times N$$

TOC = total ordering costs
F = fixed cost of inventory ordering
N = number of orders per year, which is calculated as follows:

$$N = S / 2A$$

S = total units sold in a year
A = the average inventory

Thus, TOC can also be written as F × (S / 2A). This equation can be applied to our Speedway Motorsports example.

CONCEPTS INTO PRACTICE

Using Speedway Motorsports' previous number of 120,000 units sold and average inventory of 15,000 units, the total ordering costs would be calculated as follows if Speedway Motorsports incurred $100 in expenses to place an order:

$$TOC = \$100 \times 120,000 / 30,000 = \$400$$

Thus, the total ordering cost is $400 a year based on the four orders. By knowing TOC and TCC, we can calculate the total inventory costs. In this case, Speedway Motorsports' total inventory cost is $400 plus $6,500, or $6,900.

The numbers in the examples presented do not include certain other costs such as lost sales, loss of consumer goodwill, and the disruption of production schedules associated with not having enough inventory in storage (Brigham & Gapenski, 1994).

Inventory Valuation

Purchase costs, **replacement costs**, and the proper accounting technique to measure true revenue are components necessary for determining the effects of storing inventory over extended periods. This process is often called the cost-of-goods-sold method, analyzing the replacement cost for sold inventory. Two basic techniques can be used to value inventory: LIFO and FIFO. LIFO, standing for **last in**, **first out**, values inventory based on the current price of replacing an item. When finished goods inventory is sold (first out), the cost of those units are accounted for based on the most recent price paid for the required materials (last in). FIFO, standing for **first in**, **first out**, reports valuation based on the price paid earlier for an item. When finished goods are sold (first out), the cost of those units are represented by the prices paid for the oldest raw materials available at the time (first in). Corporations prefer to use LIFO because any increase in inventory prices results in less reported income and a corresponding lower tax obligation. Shareholders prefer FIFO because the increased price generates additional revenue and possibly larger dividends. Currently generally accepted accounting principles allow companies to choose which type of inventory valuation system to use, but they must consistently use this method in all their financial statements throughout the year.

CONCEPTS INTO PRACTICE

Assume that a sports organization buys souvenir gold cups for their future championship celebrations. They pay $300 per cup in 2011 and buy a supply that could last five years. But by year 2013 when the team uses all the cups, the cost to purchase the cups increases to $500 per cup. When the last of the gold cups are used by 2016, they are valued at $700 and sell for $1,200 each. The income statement for the mythical team souvenir store, selling nothing but the cups, might be as shown here for the LIFO and the FIFO methods.

Stars Souvenir Store Income Statement

LIFO	
Sales (100 units at $1,000 each)	$100,000
COGS (100 units at replacement value $500)	50,000
Gross profit	$50,000
Selling expense	20,000
Net profit before taxes	$30,000
FIFO	
Sales (100 units at $1,000 each)	$100,000
COGS (100 units at replacement value $300)	30,000
Gross profit	$70,000
Selling expense	20,000
Net profit before taxes	$57,000

COGS = cost of goods sold.

CONCEPTS INTO PRACTICE

Another example should help highlight the difference between LIFO and FIFO. Assume that Under Armour has three identical inputs valued at $5, $6, and $7. The three inputs were purchased in the order listed, and the selling price of all three items is $8. Two items are sold for a combined $16 ($8 each). Under the FIFO method, the items costing $5 and $6 would be sold first. This transaction would result in a $5 profit ($16 minus $11) and leave $7 in the closing inventory T-account. In contrast, under the LIFO method, the two items sold would be the $6 and $7 items. Under this scenario Under Armour would generate only a $3 profit ($16 minus $13), and the closing inventory would be the $5 item.

Most accountants would want to recognize the loss associated with decreased inventory values in the current accounting period. Two valuation techniques can be used to do this: cost valuation and market valuation. The following example shows how the two values can be compared to help determine a decrease in inventory value. Assume that an item costs $5, the replacement cost is $3.50, the selling price is $6, the disposition cost is $2, and the normal profit is $1. The disposition cost is the cost to dispose of an item in inventory. Some items cannot just be thrown into the garbage. Bulk items, for example, may need to be hauled to a dump, and the cost of hauling them is their disposition cost. The replacement cost ($3.50) is lower than the net realizable value (NRV), which is $6 minus $2, or $4. Because the replacement cost is lower than the NRV, the $3.50 amount is used. Because the initial cost was $5 and the lower number (between cost and market) is $3.50, the loss that would be reported is $1.50 ($5 minus $3.50). If the company buys another item at the $3.50 cost, the new item will generate a $0.50 profit. We calculate this profit by subtracting the replacement cost ($3.50) and the disposition cost ($2) from the $6 selling price. Thus, the higher-cost item would result in an initial loss, but the lower replacement cost will generate a profit in the long term.

CONCEPTS INTO PRACTICE

The sports organization from the prior example would earn a much higher rate of return if the FIFO method was used to calculate the pretax profit, but the potential tax liability is also significantly higher. In the LIFO example, the income would be lower and taxes would be lower, but a more realistic estimate of the pretax profit is shown because any new cups would need to be purchased at the $500 price. Either technique is valid, and both conform to generally accepted accounting practices. But after a company chooses one method they have to be consistent and use it for both accounting and tax purposes. A company has to decide which treatment of a given transaction is most appropriate for its needs. The FIFO method may be more appropriate if the company wants to show a higher rate of return for investors. Such financial maneuvering is not dishonest, because the company's annual report indicated that the FIFO method was used to calculate the value of the inventory. Because the method used to report income does not change the actual income received by the company, managers tend to prefer limiting their tax liability and choose the LIFO method.

Lost Inventory

One of the consequences of storing inventory is the possibility of losing it. Inventory can be lost for various reasons, from simple misplacement to theft, spoilage, or obsolescence. Inventory is an asset. As with any other asset, if care is not taken it can be lost. For example, if Speedway Motorsports does not properly track tires they could lose tires because of misreported sales or even theft (e.g., by the cleaning crew). Employee honesty can be greatly enhanced when the employees know that inventory management practices are in place.

Besides costing money for storage, inventory can have significant costs because of obsolescence. A store carrying LeBron James jerseys from the Cleveland Cavaliers will find them a tough sell compared with his Miami Heat jerseys. Although some consumers might be interested in buying a Cleveland jersey as a collector's item, the costs associated with carrying the jersey for a possible infrequent sale might not justify keeping the jerseys. Factors coming into play when analyzing whether to carry an obsolete product include

- the potential activity or lack of activity in relation to the item,
- the amount of storage space required,
- the amount of physical activity required to move the item,
- the replacement cost of the item if a replacement were ever required,

- the likelihood of finding replacement parts and their potential cost, and
- the significance of the item for the overall business operation.

If these considerations indicate that the item is expendable, then the cost analysis should determine whether the company is wasting money by keeping it. Suppose that an item would cost $100 a year to keep in inventory based on the cost of space for storage, utilities, human resources, and so on. If the replacement cost is $500 and there is a 50% chance that the item could be used or sold in the next 10 years, then disposing of the item would be a low-risk choice.

If inventory becomes obsolete (e.g., a professional sports team relocates, such as when the Seattle Supersonics became the Oklahoma City Thunder), the inventory can be given away to charity or sold at a significant markdown. If the company is a corporation, it can usually take a tax deduction for the cost of producing the donated goods or inventory cost adjusted by a percentage of the difference between the cost and the fair market value of the goods (Marullo, 1998, August).

Auditing Inventory

A key component of any inventory management system is taking a physical inventory. Whether counting production parts or supplies, taking a physical inventory is a critical step in controlling inaccurate inventory purchasing behavior or determining the true value of a business. People often just count physical units, which is an ineffective way to take inventory. You may see this in supermarkets where an inventory taker counts the number of potato chip bags on the shelf. In other settings, some people use a "line" system, drawing a line on a box and placing another order when items in the box dip below the line. Others use a two-bin system. They have two bins of parts, for example, and when one bin is emptied, they place an order, using the items in the second bin while waiting for the order to arrive.

As an alternative to just counting units, an inventory-taking protocol can help accurately determine the value of inventory units that might otherwise be difficult to track. An effective inventory-taking protocol could require the following steps (Feiner, 1977):

- Analyzing the degree of obsolescence in the inventory
- Identifying fast- and slow-moving items

- Properly classifying the inventory based on need, value, or other variables
- Identifying the cause of lost or stolen inventory items
- Identifying techniques to help move slow inventory

Numerous inventory management systems exist to help reduce carrying costs and optimize the production process.

Point of Sale

One important inventory management technique is the point-of-sale inventory management system. These systems are used at stores such as supermarkets, drugstores, and sporting goods stores. The system uses bar codes on packages. The bar code is scanned when an item enters a store and when it is sold. Computers track the item's movement, and sophisticated systems can identify when the items are selling, at what price they are sold, how often they need to be reordered, and related information.

Just in Time

Just-in-time (JIT) inventory systems are often found in the manufacturing industry when numerous suppliers are required to provide multiple and flexible inventory options for a manufacturer. Japanese manufacturers developed the JIT system so that needed components could be delivered at the exact moment they would be needed to complete the production process. By using such a strategy, businesses thought that they could dispense with having a buffer, or safety inventory, and all the associated costs.

The JIT system is timing based. Everything has to be calculated to within minutes so that an entire assembly line is not shut down because of one missing screw. The JIT system was designed based on highly predictable requirements, real-time communications between all parties, and coordinated suppliers (Spiro, 1996). Just-in-time systems can save money, but if they are not perfectly coordinated, the process does not work. For example, the manufacturer must have strong faith that each supplier's deliveries will be at least 98% defect free. A shipment with too many defects would hinder the entire process because the manufacturer would not have the benefit of possibly testing every component while in storage.

Another concern relating to JIT systems is the effect of sudden emergencies on the system. In the wake of the September 11, 2001, tragedies, according to a major study conducted by the trucking industry, 39% of companies surveyed experienced major disruptions in their supply chain because of the attacks (*Managers rethinking*, 2001). Similar major disruptions occurred after the horrible hurricane season in 2005. Because of these disruptions, many companies started developing a new mind-set and looking toward just-in-case (JIC) systems. These systems are designed to maintain a safety stock so that the company can eliminate as much inefficiency as possible. Thus, JIT should not be taken as a directive to remove every item in inventory. Rather, a safety stock should be kept to guard against a major disaster or other concerns, while at the same time efforts are made to monitor and reduce inefficiencies.

Economic Order Quantity

Another important element in the inventory auditing process is tracking how much to order. Determining the optimum order quantity is important for reducing storage and ordering costs.

Because the JIT system is not right for every manufacturer, other techniques need to be adopted to help reduce inventory costs while maintaining adequate reserves. One such technique is a mathematical model called the economic order quantity (EOQ) model. The EOQ model attempts to determine the optimum number of units to be ordered whenever an order is placed. Large inventories mean increased warehousing costs, interest expenses, insurance costs, and larger amounts of obsolete inventory. At the same time, the larger the order, the less often the orders need to be placed, which reduces ordering costs. By knowing the optimum numbers of components to order, a manager can reduce the number of orders needing to be placed and the number of extra units kept in inventory. The equation for the EOQ model is as follows:

$$EOQ = \sqrt{\frac{2(F)(U)}{C}}$$

In the model, F stands for the costs associated with placing an order, such as paperwork or personnel time to place an order or write a check, which are activities independent of the order size. U stands for the sales in units per year of the item that will be placed in inventory. C represents the costs per year associated with carrying the units in inventory, including storage rental costs, insurance, and handling charges. The model works only in cases in which the inventory and sales numbers behave in a predictable manner. The formula shown is based on the assumption that, on average, half of each shipment is carried in inventory. If the fixed cost per order (F) is $5, the number of units sold each year (U) is 5,000, and the carrying cost per unit per year (C) is $0.80, the formula would be completed as follows:

$$\sqrt{\frac{2 \times \$5 \times 5,000}{\$0.80}} = 250 \text{ units}$$

If the managers of this hypothetical company used sound inventory management practices, they would place orders in lots of 250 units at a time (Spiro, 1996). Some companies have a hard time identifying the exact cost of carrying an item, and it is easier for them to calculate the EOQ based on industry norms. Here is the formula for calculating EOQ based on industry norms or an internally generated percentage of a product's selling price:

$$EOQ = \sqrt{[2(F)(S)]/(C)(P)}$$

Under this version of the formula,

F = fixed cost of placing and receiving orders,

S = units sold annually,

C = annual carrying costs expressed as a percentage, and

P = purchase price of the inventory.

CONCEPTS INTO PRACTICE

Assume that Under Armour orders 26,000 shirts each year. Under Armour calculates that the carrying costs are 25% of the inventory. The shirts are sold for $9 each, but the inventory cost is only $4.92 each. The fixed cost per order is $1,000. Plugging these numbers into the EOQ formula produces the following results (Brigham & Gapenski, 1994):

$$EOQ = \sqrt{[2(\$1,000)(26,000)]/(0.25)(\$4.92)}$$
$$= \sqrt{42,276,423}$$
$$= 6,500 \text{ units}$$

Dividing the 26,000 annual inventory by the EOQ of 6,500 units gives a total of four orders annually. Dividing 26,000 by 52 weeks gives a weekly usage rate of 500 shirts. Thus, after an order of 6,500 is received, 500 units will be subtracted from the inventory each week. Based on these numbers, the average inventory level will be 3,250 shirts at a cost of $4.92 each, producing an inventory value of about $16,000. Economies of scale could be achieved if Under Armour sold 52,000 shirts each year, representing a 100% increase in sales. Economies of scale represent the most beneficial purchasing or ordering quantity to receive a price reduction. Thus, through more efficient ordering or by ordering larger quantities, a business can significantly reduce the per unit cost. Economies of scale can also be accomplished when companies join together to buy products when individually they might not be able to order a large enough quantity to obtain a break. The EOQ would increase from 6,500 to 9,195—a 41% increase.

Although these ordering points provide an exact number to order, the world is not exact. Under Armour will not sell 500 shirts each week. Some weeks they might sell several thousand shirts and other weeks sell no shirts at all. This reality forces us to set an order point with flexibility. For example, a lag period needs to be built in because an order may not be received for several weeks. Thus, a several-week supply needs to be reached before a reorder is placed. In addition, a safety stock should be maintained. A safety stock might be necessary to avoid delays in receiving orders or to meet demand when sales suddenly increase. This concern is highlighted in the following example.

CONCEPTS INTO PRACTICE

Although the preceding example showed an EOQ of 6,500 shirts, Under Armour might order 7,500 shirts to help maintain a 1,000-shirt safety stock. The company might also place an order when 1,000 shirts are still in inventory to maintain the EOQ and the necessary safety stock (Brigham & Gapenski, 1994). Note that any safety stock will increase the total carrying cost. If an additional

1,000 shirts are ordered, the additional carrying cost is calculated as follows:

$$\text{additional carrying cost} = \text{safety stock} \times P \times C$$

P = the purchase price for the inventory
C = the annual carrying costs expressed as a percentage

Using the definitions and numbers already given, the additional carrying cost for Under Armour is $1,230.

$$\text{additional carrying cost} = 1{,}000 \times \$4.92 \times 0.25 = \$1{,}230$$

The 1,000 additional shirts will increase Under Armour's carrying costs from $4,000, as we will see, to $5,230 (Brigham & Gapenski, 1994).
The information we have can be plugged into the TOC and TCC formulas to calculate the total inventory costs (TIC). Remember,

$$\text{TOC} = F \times (S / Q) \text{ and TCC} = C \times P \times (Q / 2)$$

Thus, the equations would be calculated as follows (Brigham & Gapenski, 1994):

$$\text{TIC} = \text{TOC} + \text{TCC} = (\$1{,}000 \times 26{,}000 / 6{,}500) + (0.25 \times \$4.92 \times 6{,}500 / 2) = \$4{,}000 + \$4{,}000 = \$8{,}000$$

This example shows that the total inventory costs, excluding the cost of the shirts, is $8,000.

Quantity Discounts

Another wrinkle can be added to the Under Armour example. The EOQ is fine if no discounts are offered for larger orders. Most suppliers, however, provide larger purchasers with a discount to attract their business. Any discount can change the optimal ordering quantity because the discount can provide a tangible savings over and above any additional storage costs that might be incurred from having to store the extra inventory. The question then becomes, What would the optimum ordering quantity be if the supplier provided a discount for larger orders?

CONCEPTS INTO PRACTICE

Assume that Under Armour's supplier offered a 2% discount for orders equal to or greater than 10,000 shirts. Based on an order of 6,500 shirts in the previous example, the TIC was calculated at $8,000. We can rewrite the TIC equation using the 10,000-shirt order size and decreasing the price from $4.92 per shirt to $4.82 based on the 2% discount (Brigham & Gapenski, 1994).

$$\text{TIC} = (\$1{,}000 \times 26{,}000 / 10{,}000) + (0.25 \times \$4.82)$$
$$(10{,}000 / 2) = \$2{,}600 + \$6{,}025 = \$8{,}625$$

The carrying cost increases because the average inventory is larger, but the ordering cost declines because fewer orders are placed. Based on these numbers it would seem that adding 4,000 more shirts to the inventory increases inventory costs by only $625 per year. But this analysis fails to consider the savings of approximately $0.10 per shirt. The total yearly savings based on the 2% discount is $2,558. Thus, even after reducing the savings in shirt prices by the added inventory carrying cost ($625), Under Armour would generate a net savings of $1,933 each year by taking advantage of the larger-order discount (Brigham & Gapenski, 1994).

Inventory Conversion Period

Another calculation, one that is similar to the finished goods or raw materials turnover ratio, is the inventory conversion period (ICP) (Feiner, 1977). The ICP is the average length of time required to convert the raw materials to finished inventory and then sell the goods. We calculate the ICP by dividing inventory by the sales per day.

CONCEPTS INTO PRACTICE

If we estimate that Under Armour has $5 million in inventory and will have $20 million in sales in the coming year, the calculation is as follows:

$$\text{ICP} = \text{inventory} / \text{sales per day} = \$5{,}000{,}000 / (\$20{,}000{,}000 / 360 \text{ days})$$

$$= 90 \text{ days}$$

The equation indicates that 90 days pass from the time that raw materials are received until the shirts are manufactured and then sold.

The shorter the ICP is, the more money the business will make if it makes a small profit on each item. For expensive items, the ICP may not be as relevant, because building one stadium might generate $20 million in profits for a builder but take three years to complete.

Regardless of the technique used to monitor inventory levels, a purchasing plan needs to be developed to optimize expenditures and carrying costs. This chapter provides several suggestions that will help with this decision. One of the best techniques to optimize purchasing and inventory control is centralized purchasing. Imagine what would happen if a collegiate athletic department allowed each team to buy its own office supplies. Each team might have several hundred pens sitting in a drawer unused. In contrast, if the entire department bought several boxes of pens at a time, it could reduce total purchases. Centralized purchasing is designed to facilitate more effective purchasing, but it also allows a business to use inventories more effectively. The other benefits associated with centralized purchasing were addressed earlier in this chapter.

Using Inventory

Businesses need to answer numerous questions to determine whether raw materials are being effectively used. The following are some of the key questions.

- How effective has management been in increasing the inventory turnover rate?
- How is purchasing controlled to make sure that purchases are in economical quantities that do not unduly increase inventory carrying costs?
- Are any components of the manufacturing process sent to external sources for finishing, and can any such steps be completed internally?
- What is the relationship between direct and indirect labor costs?
- What steps are taken to reduce the need for overtime labor?

- Are the labor and materials costs clearly defined to allow accurate tracking?
- Are accurate records kept concerning equipment maintenance and repair costs?
- Who contracts for equipment rental or leasing, and how is that process supervised?
- What control mechanisms are in place to reduce pilferage and deterioration of supplies?

These are just some of the questions raised when a business starts putting the forecasting and inventory systems together with production and manufacturing. Before the manufacturing process can begin, Speedway Motorsports needs to develop a production budget.

CONCEPTS INTO PRACTICE

Assume that Speedway Motorsports had forecast an ending inventory of 1,000 tires in 2011. The beginning inventory for 2011 was 500 tires, meaning that after the 2010 sales year ended, 500 tires were left in inventory. The company sold 10,000 tires in 2011. The formula can be calculated as follows:

$$\text{total production} = 10,000 + 1,000 - 500 = 10,500 \text{ tires}$$

Thus, Speedway Motorsports needed to produce 10,500 tires to serve all sales and to maintain an inventory of 1,000 tires.

Production Analysis

The production budget combines the desired inventory levels with forecast sales projections. The total manufactured production run can be calculated by means of the following formula (Griffin, 1991):

$$\text{total production} = \text{sales in units} + \text{desired ending}$$
$$\text{inventory} - \text{projected beginning inventory}$$

This formula can help a company determine whether it needs to reduce the number of units produced if sales are low or if the inventory level is too high. The formula can be applied to calculate Speedway Motorsports' total production needs.

Another important component related to utilization is determining whether a business is properly using the workforce. Employers can calculate whether employees are performing their jobs

AMAZON FLOATS

Amazon.com uses a different inventory management system, which is referred to as a minimal inventory system utilizing a negative operating cycle. People also call the system a float, as highlighted in chapter 12. The key to the system is that inventory is available through other suppliers so that the vendor does not really carry an inventory. The Internet bookseller Amazon carries only a small number of books in its inventory. Most book titles are not ordered until a customer places an order with Amazon. The result is that Amazon turns over the inventory 26 times a year compared with booksellers such as Barnes & Noble, which has an inventory turnover of 10 (Mayer, 1998). As such, Amazon has remained a viable company, while bricks-and-mortar businesses such as Borders filed for bankruptcy in 2011.

The negative operating cycles are what really separates Amazon from other booksellers and general retailers. Most companies need to buy a product, stock it, and move it to a different sales location before selling It. Amazon charges a customer's credit card account when the order is placed. The book distributor or publisher sends the book directly to the purchaser within days after it has been ordered. The credit card company pays Amazon within a day. Amazon then takes on average 46 days to pay its suppliers, the book distributors. Thus, instead of having to pay to finance sales (through borrowing money to purchase the books it sells—its inventory), Amazon makes even more money by having the customer's money for 45 days to reinvest and earn interest on (Mayer, 1998).

efficiently. Time–motion studies undertaken by Frank Gilbreth (1868-1924) were conducted by industrialists to determine how long it would take an assembly line worker to perform a given task (Bridges & Roquemore, 1996). Similarly, Speedway Motorsports could ascertain that an average tire takes 4 hours to manufacture. Thus, in a 40-hour workweek, an employee should manufacture 10 tires. Employees not reaching that goal are not using their skills effectively. Management can track employee performance and engage in retraining or other steps to work with employees who are not effectively using their time.

The two steps outlined represent just two types of measurement techniques that management can use to identify costs associated with the production process. But the manufacturing process entails unique components and costs that are necessary to transform the inventory, using the standards set forth in the production budget. Production management is the topic we turn to next.

PRODUCTION MANAGEMENT

This chapter focuses primarily on financing inventory and the costs associated with holding and liquidating inventory. Most businesses, however, do not maintain inventory in the same condition in which it was purchased unless they are in the wholesale business. Most companies use the inventory to develop some other marketable item. A professional team would have a useless inventory of players unless they competed on the field or in the arena. A golf club manufacturer must transform metal into a club to generate revenues. This transformation process costs money. Conversion costs entail direct materials, direct labor, and factory overhead. Direct materials are all the raw goods used to make the product. For a golf club, the direct materials might include the metal as well as rubber for the grip. Direct labor entails the personnel time required to turn the metal and rubber into the club. The factory overhead involves the proportional costs of machinery and energy that are used to transform the metal and rubber into the club. Conversion costs do not include any nonmanufacturing costs such as administrative, advertising, and selling-related expenses.

The conversion costs associated with any manufacturing process are fairly simple to calculate. We can calculate direct material by dividing the cost of all the materials by the number of units manufactured.

CONCEPTS INTO PRACTICE

If Speedway Motorsports employees can manufacture one tire in four hours, the calculation to determine labor costs is simple. The biggest mistake that people make in determining labor costs is failing to include benefits in the calculation. If a production line worker earns $10 per hour, the direct labor amount might not be $40 per tire. If we assume that the employee's benefits amount to 40% of wages, the actual cost is $56 per tire.

The last component necessary for calculating conversion costs is factory overhead (FO). To determine factory overhead, a manufacturer calculates all the costs associated with the production process not including direct material or direct labor. Typical factory overhead costs could include lease expenses on equipment, interest payments owed for financed equipment, depreciation of factory equipment, utilities, insurance, maintenance, taxes, and any other expense that can be directly linked to the manufacturing process.

Break-Even Analysis

The manufacturing process involves several key financial issues. One of the most important entails calculating an appropriate production run to maximize profits. To achieve the lowest production cost per unit, companies normally need to undertake large manufacturing runs. The setup cost per unit is the measurement tool used to determine whether the manufacturing process is economical. Break-even analysis can also be used to calculate the number of additional items necessary to make a certain profit. Break-even analysis is discussed in chapter 5, but the context there is the financial statement rather than manufacturing. Although the concepts are similar, break-even analysis associated with manufacturing focuses on specific manufactured items versus the business overall.

Instead of conversion costs, the following break-even analysis uses fixed costs. Fixed costs are the costs incurred no matter how many units are manufactured, whereas variable costs change with the quantity being produced. The formula to calculate the break-even point follows:

$$\text{sale price} \times N = F + (\text{variable costs} \times N)$$

N = quantity

F = fixed costs

Quantity, often referred to as N as in this formula, denotes the number of units needing to be sold to break even. The break-even point is calculated in the next example.

CONCEPTS INTO PRACTICE

If Speedway Motorsports paid $300,000 for rubber and can produce 100,000 tires with the materials, then the direct material cost is $3 per unit. Direct labor can be calculated in a similar manner. Assume that Speedway Motorsports pays $20,000 annually for factory overhead costs for their specialty tires and that they make one run of tires. Furthermore, assume that the factory operates for 4,000 hours to produce a run of tires. By dividing the $20,000 by the 4,000 hours, we can determine that the factory overhead cost per hour is $5. Because it takes 4 hours to make a tire, the FO is $20 per tire. By adding the direct materials, labor, and FO, we can calculate the manufacturing conversion costs for producing one tire.

Direct material	$3
Direct labor	$56
Factory overhead	$20
Total	$79

The $79 conversion cost is critical because Speedway Motorsports needs this number to determine the lowest price that it can charge a distributor for the tires. Nonmanufacturing costs need to be added to the $79 to determine the break-even point. If the total nonmanufacturing costs are $8 per unit, the break-even point for tires is $87.

Planning and pro forma budgets, discussed in chapter 3, also apply to manufacturing break-even analysis. We cannot perform a break-even analysis without referring to projected budgets for such items as sales and production runs. These data are critical for identifying how many units may be sold and how many units must be produced to meet the sales demand. A company can manufacture enough units to meet the break-even point, but if the units are not being sold, the company will not break even and will in fact be losing money as a consequence of having inventory sit on shelves.

All the factors addressed throughout this chapter help establish the numbers needed to create a realistic sales budget. The sales budget represents the number of units that the company expects to sell in an upcoming period. A sales budget is based on a multitude of factors or techniques. The unit costs, anticipated demand, the competition, consumer interest, and a host of additional variables help create the sales budget. In addition, salespeople can be asked what they expect future sales to be, and customers can be asked how much they might order in the future. A company can also estimate a specific percentage growth over the sales volume in the prior period.

CONCEPTS INTO PRACTICE

Assume that Under Armour has $100,000 in fixed costs for making a tennis uniform. The variable cost per uniform is $5. If these uniforms sell for $10 each, we can calculate how many units need to be sold to break even. Applying the numbers, the equation is as follows:

$$\$10 \times N = \$100,000 + (\$5 \times N)$$

$$\$5N = \$100,000$$

$$N = 20,000$$

Thus, Under Armour needs to sell 20,000 of these uniforms to break even. But what if Under Armour needs to make $40,000 from the uniforms to undertake manufacturing them for an acceptable profit? The equation is as follows:

$$\$10 \times N = \$140,000 + (\$5 \times N)$$

$$\$5N = \$140,000$$

$$N = 28,000$$

The company would need to manufacture and sell 28,000 units to make the profit margin desired from this product line. Because the fixed costs are covered after 20,000 units have been manufactured, each unit over 20,000 has a $5 profit based on the $10 sales price minus the $5 variable costs.

Variance Analysis

Calculating the break-even point or the optimum manufacturing run for making a specific profit is relatively simple, but these numbers are meaningless if the actual production runs are not monitored to ensure that the costs conform to the projections. Variance analysis is the process of establishing performance standards. After the standards are established, a business needs to determine whether it is reaching the standards. Are the actual fixed costs higher than projected? Why are they higher? For example, are energy prices higher than expected? Are variable costs above expectations? These costs could be higher because of an unanticipated increase in the price of iron if iron is one of the metals that the business needs. If the costs are below expectations, the business will generate a greater profit than expected. If any cost is too high, the business must lower costs to meet the production budget. Cost reduction strategies might need to target a specific cost area or the entire production process. If costs are increasing across the board, a business may consider reducing some costs by taking drastic steps such as terminating employees or taking one day off from production each week.

Labor Costs

One of the greatest expenses associated with the manufacturing process is personnel cost. Although most people do not consider people to be machines, they in fact are a part of the manufacturing process. Similar to a sewing machine that might help make a shirt, a person can help make a sports product. To produce the product of a baseball game, you need to have players who can produce the game. Depending on the quality of the product, the human machines producing the games can be either expensive or cheap. Thus, baseball players in the major leagues might be paid a significant amount for the product that they produce, whereas players in the minor leagues might be paid very little for their product; although both sets of players are producing the same product, they are producing at different quality levels. Whether for players or administrative personnel, expenses can be significant, and businesses need to track labor costs carefully. Salaries are among the primary components of labor costs, and these costs can be higher in the sport industry compared with other labor markets.

Salaries for some positions may be straightforward (e.g., minimum wage positions paying

$7.25 an hour). This wage is the current federal minimum wage rate, but some states have higher rates. New York's minimum wage mirrors the federal rate, but California's rate is $8.00 per hour and Connecticut's rate is $8.25 per hour. Salaries in sport, however, can be extremely complicated. Professional athletes have numerous clauses in their contracts calling for benefits several times over and beyond the base salaries. Athletes are not the only individuals having complicated salaries, because coaches have complicated salary packages too.

The costs associated with labor can be immense. The biggest budget item for most businesses is salaries and benefits. Many companies attempt to boost their bottom line by reducing salaries through terminations. Businesses are also reducing benefits and requiring employees to pay a greater share for health insurance to help decrease employee-related costs. Because labor is expensive, businesses often need to determine whether they are paying too much for their employees. This question can be answered through examination of a company's earnings per hour (Feiner, 1977). A way to calculate earnings per hour is to divide total sales by the expected total number of hours worked. The earnings per hour ratio helps management determine how effectively a plant is running. The next example involves this ratio.

CONCEPTS INTO PRACTICE

Assume that Under Armour forecasts sales of a given product to total $200,000 and that direct and indirect labor will entail 13,000 hours. By dividing the total sales by the expected total hours, we can develop the earnings per hour. Here, the earnings per hour are $200,000 divided by 13,000, which is $15.38 per hour. If the labor costs are less than $15.38 per hour, Under Armour will be able to cover its labor costs. Note that this analysis does not include raw materials and other fixed costs that are over and above the labor costs.

Labor costs are such a significant component of the manufacturing process that the costs need to be compared with those for other companies in the same industry. Management can use such a benchmark as a negotiation tool if the competitors have a lower labor cost. If the competition pays more, a business can use its creativity to make up

any difference. Through innovation, a company can reduce labor costs and increase its profitability. In the hot Internet market of the late 1990s, many companies moved away from traditional salary-based motivation and toward stock options and other incentives that did not require a significant capital outlay. Although stock options can be a strong benefit, some observers thought that such deals helped lead executives to push for increasing their share value over true growth. This result was seen in the WorldCom and Enron scandals.

Employers have often attempted to reduce employee-related costs. Employers need to reduce labor costs to maximize profit, which is one reason why they fight hard against unionization. Unionization might mean sharing power, but more important, when employees can negotiate as one, they normally can generate a higher per-employee salary and larger group benefits. To combat rising employee-related expenses, employers are resorting to various tactics that they hope can lower costs.

Several universities, most notably the University of Pennsylvania, Stanford University, and Tufts University, have outsourced facility workers such as custodians (Nicklin, 1997). Outsourcing can allow the universities to concentrate more fully on their primary strengths (education and research), and it can reduce benefit costs. A university employee earning $30,000 per year and receiving significant benefits, including tuition reimbursement, can cost the university well over $50,000. But if the custodian is terminated and then signs with a janitorial service that has an exclusive contract with the university, the cost for the same worker could decrease to under $40,000. The $10,000 savings can be magnified by economies of scale; the janitorial service can hire more people for less money and still make its profit. According to the principle of economies of scale, the larger the number of individuals involved, the greater the savings are. Thus, although a $10,000 savings may not seem significant, if the university requires the services of 100 janitors, the savings could be over $1 million. Outsourcing is just one technique that organizations consider when attempting to reduce labor costs. By lowering these costs, overall manufacturing costs can be reduced. Thus, if inventory or manufacturing costs are too high, a business can consider reducing costs by controlling other expense areas such as labor costs.

This chapter discusses various ways to examine costs to help determine profits. Some manufacturing costs, however, will be hard to quantify. To help develop a better appreciation of the entire production process, some managerial accountants rely on the balanced scorecard approach. The balanced scorecard examines a business from four key perspectives: financial, customer, internal process, and learning and growth perspective. Although financial perspectives can be numerical, customer feeling about a product or company might be hard to quantify.

The balanced scorecard attempts to use non-financial measures to assess performance and anticipate future results. A sports team might look at its win–loss record similar to the way that it views a financial statement to determine overall success. The record highlights how the team did on the field and represents one way of measuring success. But what will happen if the team accomplishes other major goals that are not reflected in the win column? What will occur if a player dramatically improves and wins the MVP award? What will happen if a star player is lost for the year because of an injury but the team is still able to perform well? These questions highlight the need to know exactly what is being measured so the right measurement tools can be used. The balanced scorecard process

is typically tied to the mission statement or vision of a company or organization. If a company strives for happy customers then such a result might not be seen in any financial statements, but could be seen if inventory problems are delaying delivery of products and customers are upset because they have to wait for the item they ordered.

CONCLUSION

Some of the material in this chapter, such as the information on manufacturing-related costs, does not apply to all businesses. All businesses, however, need to manage their resources, and the tool used to achieve that is inventory management. Carrying and ordering costs need to be included in any budget. Even businesses that do not manufacture products in the traditional sense do manufacture value. Thus, even teams need to analyze manufacturing-related costs and determine whether employees are working together cohesively. If players on an NFL team are not working well together, if team chemistry is flawed, then the formula for producing a winning season will need to be overhauled.

Class Discussion Topics

1. What do you think is the most effective way to manage inventory?
2. What forecasting strategies would you use if you were managing a ski resort that dealt with uncontrollable weather elements?
3. What strategies do you think might be useful in reducing employee theft if you ran a team's gift shop? Would your strategies change if you were managing a concession stand and employees took food or beverages?
4. What cost reduction strategies could be used by Speedway Motorsports?
5. If you overproduced T-shirts for a given team and could not resell the remaining shirts, what would you do with them?
6. Develop a list of all the fixed costs that you can imagine for a NBA team.
7. Develop a list of all the variable costs that you can imagine for a nonprofit sports event such as a 5K road race.
8. How should professional sports teams handle their high labor costs, especially when fans are upset that they have to pay so much to attend games?

Profits and Losses

If a business successfully manages its money, it should be able to make a profit through its investments. Part VI takes a closer look at how businesses can grow their profits.

Chapter 14, "Spending Earnings," explores how after a company has paid its taxes it can reinvest its earnings or pay its owners. If the company wants to reward its owners, it can pay them a dividend of cash or additional ownership shares. Profits can also be reinvested (e.g., by building new factories) to make the company more valuable, or they can be used to buy or merge with other companies to increase future profits. The chapter offers specific sport industry examples of successes and failures involving mergers and acquisitions.

Chapter 15, "Auditing," covers the important process of ensuring the accuracy of a company's financial numbers. The chapter begins by outlining why auditing is undertaken and describing the types of audits. The chapter then moves on to cover types of internal controls that can help prevent financial fraud. Through independent audits a company can show external investors, lenders, and others its true financial state. By understanding the auditing process, readers receive a better grasp of the information that auditors analyze and the methods that they use to find fraud.

Chapter 16, "Exit Strategy," first covers how to detect red flags that indicate financial distress. If a company is in trouble, it can try to reorganize informally or sell its assets through the liquidation process. A company can also seek bankruptcy protection from the courts to allow it to pay its bills or to avoid paying obligations already owed. Some companies also sell their assets to pay bills because they might not have any other valuable items to sell. A company can also try to sell itself and find a new owner with deeper pockets to pay for future growth. The chapter ends by discussing several techniques that can be used to value a business that is being sold.

chapter 14

Spending Earnings

Chapter Objectives

After studying this chapter, you should be able to do the following:

- Describe various types of dividend policies and the way in which they are used.
- Outline the dividend payment process.
- Describe how a business uses retained earnings.
- Understand how mergers and acquisitions are a way for a sport business to expand.
- Describe the legal concerns associated with mergers and acquisitions.
- Calculate the value of a consolidated business after a merger.

In earlier chapters we focus on learning the fundamentals of sport finance and understanding the sources of revenues and expenses. If all goes well, a sport business will have the **ability to pay** all its costs from income. If income equals costs, the business will break even. The goal for a profit-driven sport business, however, is not only to cover costs but to maximize profits. If a business generates positive earnings, it then must decide how best to distribute the excess earnings. For a sport business, the earnings distribution process is a major decision that has significant short- and long-term ramifications.

The options that a sport manager has with respect to distributing earnings differ depending on the business. Sport entities such as Speedway Motorsports and Under Armour are publicly traded with shareholders, whereas many other sport businesses either are not yet publicly traded or cannot be publicly traded because of their structure. Given that this chapter centers on how earnings are distributed and used to increase the value of a firm, we focus primarily on for-profit corporations similar to Speedway Motorsports and Under Armour.

Before discussing the earnings of for-profit organizations, we should note that nonprofit sports organizations, such as collegiate athletic departments, charitable foundations, and the YMCA, might also have revenues that exceed costs. These organizations have several options for their earnings. They may elect to reinvest those funds back into the organization. For example, an athletic department at a university such as Ohio State or Michigan may elect to add new sports, increase funding for athletic scholarships, or improve sports facilities. Some major college athletic departments with excess funds, such as Notre Dame, have established scholarships for students who are not athletes. A local YMCA may decide to increase the size of its staff or add new activities. In some cases nonprofit sports organizations elect to save those excess funds to protect against future financial difficulty. Although nonprofit organizations have a variety of options, they cannot show an accounting profit for the fiscal year.

In general, for-profit sport businesses have three choices for using earnings:

1. Pay dividends to shareholders, if the business is a share-issuing entity
2. Retain earnings for reinvestment in the business
3. Reinvest in other firms by purchasing a percentage or acquiring other firms outright

Retained earnings are used primarily for long-term financial planning and capital budgeting. Retained earnings are discussed briefly in this chapter, but the major focus is the payment of dividends and mergers with and acquisitions of other firms.

The key to making the right decision about earnings distributions is to select the option that will produce the greatest value to the ownership or, in the case of a publicly held company, the shareholders. Although shareholders directly benefit from receiving a dividend payment, they may derive the greatest long-term value from forgoing dividend payments and allowing the earnings to be reinvested back into the firm. The reinvestment may be used to research and design a new product line, buy new equipment, or hire additional human resources. Management may also attempt to increase the value of the sport business by using the earnings to acquire another firm. Management has the responsibility of making those critical decisions. At all times management must choose the option that is best for the shareholders or ownership, as highlighted in the following sidebar.

CONCEPTS INTO PRACTICE

Speedway Motorsports may decrease dividend payments to their shareholders and use such funds to construct a new racetrack or renovate an existing facility. Although the reinvestment for capital improvements decreases the dividends received by shareholders, Speedway's management believes that the end result will be an increase in the stock value.

DIVIDEND PAYMENTS

A dividend is a payment made out of earnings, in the form of either cash or stock, to the owners or shareholders of a business (Brigham & Ehrhardt, 2011). Dividends are paid to reward stockholders for staying with the corporation. Some stocks steadily appreciate in value, and that capital appreciation is the reward that stockholders need to justify their investment. Other corporations may have a steady stock price but reward stockholders by paying a regular dividend payment. Thus, although Speedway Motorsports has not had a significant increase in its stock value over the years, it has paid steady dividends that sometimes amounted to about $0.33

per share. But for the 2010 and 2011 fiscal years, quarterly dividends were at $0.10 per share paid to stockholders.

Paying dividends is one method of distributing profits. For many corporations, it is a major cash expenditure. Large companies such as IBM and Microsoft spend millions of dollars in making dividend payments to their shareholders. Many other companies, however, elect to make no dividend payments. A firm's board of directors determines the amount of dividend payments and makes all other dividend decisions not otherwise specified in the corporate bylaws or on the stock certificates.

Initially, you would think that a firm would want to give as much money back to its shareholders as possible. But it also makes financial sense for the firm to take the money and invest it for the shareholders. Deciding which option to select can be both difficult and controversial for financial managers. Shareholders and financial analysts can be critical if they believe that management is pursuing a poor dividend policy. Such negative feelings can affect a stock's performance.

A sport business may also make distributions to its ownership. A distribution is similar to a dividend, but it is paid out of sources other than current or accumulated retained earnings. For simplicity, we refer to any payment by a firm to its shareholders as a dividend. Typically, dividends are most commonly paid by large corporations. Smaller corporations often need to reinvest the money so that they can grow. For example, in the late 1990s Speedway Motorsports was a growing company involved in the motor sport industry. It owned and operated several racetracks across the United States. In its 1998 annual report the company stated that it would not pay dividends for the foreseeable future so that it could reinvest money for company growth. By 2003, however, Speedway Motorsports had enough cash on hand to feel comfortable in paying dividends to its shareholders. The company paid out dividends of $0.31, $0.32, and $0.33 respectively for the years 2004 through 2006 (Speedway, 2011). As stated earlier, more recently Speedway has made quarterly dividend payments of $.10 per quarter. In contrast, Nike paid a $0.36 quarterly **dividend per share** in December 2011 (Nike, 2011).

Dividend policies can be somewhat confusing. A corporation may have many good reasons to pay high dividends, but there are as many good reasons to pay relatively low dividends. This section covers the ways that dividends are paid, the various types of dividends, and reasons for the payment of high and low dividends.

Dividend Payment Process

The process of paying dividends is well defined. The following hypothetical example, adapted from an example in another industry (Ross, Westerfield, & Jordan, 2008), shows how the process works.

CONCEPTS INTO PRACTICE

- On June 1 Sport Merchandising Company passes a resolution to pay a dividend of a specified amount, let's say $2 per share. The date of the announcement, June 1, is referred to as the declaration date. Sport Merchandising Company's board of directors also announces that the dividend will be paid on June 30 to all shareholders of record as of June 18.

- An important date in the process comes up four business days before June 18. June 14 is the ex-dividend date, which is used to determine those shareholders who are eligible to receive dividends so that the dividend checks are distributed to the appropriate parties. Before June 14 the stock is traded "with dividend," meaning that shareholders are eligible for a dividend payment. After June 14, the stock trades as **ex-dividend**, meaning that the purchaser will not receive a dividend payment. This date is important for ensuring there is no confusion as to who is to receive the dividend payment.

- June 18 is the record date, the date on which all shareholders of record are designated to receive their payment. The firm will prepare a list, based on the ex-dividend date, of those individuals who are believed to be shareholders. These persons are the **holders of record** and will receive dividend checks. Errors occasionally occur, and dividend checks are mailed to the wrong persons. But the ex-dividend date helps minimize such errors.

- June 30 is the payment date. Dividend checks are mailed to the people who are believed to be the shareholders of record.

Cash Dividends

The most common type of dividend is a regular cash dividend. Some publicly traded companies pay cash dividends on a quarterly basis as a regular business practice. Besides paying the regular cash dividend annually, semiannually, or quarterly, a business may also make special one-time payments. These special or additional dividend payments are called extra cash dividends or special dividends. For the most part, the extra payments differ from the regular dividends in name only. As the name implies, these dividends might not be repeated in the future. Last, a liquidating dividend is a payment made to shareholders as a result of some part of the business being liquidated, or sold off. All or part of the cash from the sale is distributed to the shareholders. Regardless of the name, a cash dividend payment reduces the firm's cash and retained earnings (Ross et al., 2008).

As discussed later, not all corporations pay dividends, and even if a dividend is paid one year, the board of directors is not obligated to authorize a dividend the next year. But any interruption in the payment cycle can have a chilling effect on analysts and shareholders, who may view the suspension of dividends as a sign of economic hardship.

Stock Dividends

Corporations have alternatives to a cash dividend if they wish to distribute earnings back to their shareholders. A firm may elect to buy back stock or issue new stock to existing shareholders. The payment of a dividend in stock can have a dilutive effect on share price, which is not the case with cash dividends. There are also some differences between cash dividends and **stock dividends** in regard to tax policies. Dividend payments are taxed as income for shareholders, whereas the money earned from the sale of stock is taxed as capital gains.

In recent U.S. history, the tax rates for income have been higher than the tax rate for capital gains, but the 1986 Tax Reform Act reduced the gap. As of December 2011 the capital gains tax rate was 15% for stocks owned for more than one year and 25 to 35% for stocks owned for less than one year depending on a person's annual income level. For tax purposes the tax is recognized the year in which the stock is sold. With respect to the payment of taxes on dividends, which are treated by the U.S. Internal Revenue Service as income, table 14.1 provides details on the taxes paid based on a person's or family's level of income in 2011. As you can see, although the gap has decreased since before 1986, a gap remains between the capital gains and income tax rates for most people. Thus, because of taxation policy, many stockholders prefer the repurchase of stock over dividend payments (Brealey et al., 2009).

The decision to buy back shares is made by the corporation's board of directors, but the board considers market conditions and the effect on the shareholders. Typically, a board with extra cash might buy back stocks when the value is depressed to help increase the stock value. When the company buys back stock, the number of shares outstanding decreases, and the book value per share can increase.

Distribution of earnings is not the only reason for a company to repurchase stock. A sport business may also repurchase stock when it wants to change its capital structure. A business may borrow money, in other words, go into debt, to repurchase stock from shareholders and lower equity. This action will have the final effect of changing the firm's capital structure (WACC). The WACC was discussed in chapter 11 as a tool to measure the effectiveness of a corporation's capital structure.

Table 14.1 Taxes Paid Based on a Person's or Family's Level of Income

Single filer	Married, filing jointly	Married, filing separately	Tax rate
Up to $8,500	Up to $17,000	Up to $8,500	10%
$8,501-$34,500	$17,001-$69,000	$8,501-$34,500	15%
$34,501-$83,600	$69,001-$139,350	$34,501-$69,675	25%
$83,601-$174,400	$139,351-$212,300	$69,676-$106,150	28%
$174,401-$379,150	$212,301-$379,150	$106,151-$189,575	33%
$379,151 or more	$379,151 or more	$189,576 or more	35%

Created from Federal Tax Brackets 2011.

Determining the Appropriate Dividend Level

Another important aspect of dividend policy is arriving at the appropriate dividend level. According to Brealey, Myers, and Marcus (2009), there are three traditional views with respect to paying dividends. The groups of people who hold these views are the rightists, the leftists, and the middle-of-the-roaders.

The rightists believe that a business should pay the highest possible dividends. This group notes that the perceived business value increases as the level of dividend payments increases. Financial analysts believe that the perception of a business becomes more positive as higher dividends are paid, and this in turn increases the stock value of a business. In addition, dividends are cash in hand, whereas a capital gain is risky. Uncertainty always surrounds the reinvestment of earnings, and the investments selected may not increase the value of the business. This uncertainty and risk are eliminated if the excess cash is paid directly to the shareholders in the form of dividends.

Like investors, financial analysts and researchers can fall anywhere on the spectrum, but some may be rightists because they believe that an efficient and free capital market does not exist. That is, these researchers do not think that it matters whether high or low dividends are paid. In contrast, the leftists believe that capital markets are imperfect and do not perform efficiently. Dividend policy is therefore important. This analysis is important for investors because boards of directors that follow the leftist ideology would be more inclined to pay dividends to ensure that shareholders are happy. Note that some investors use their stock portfolios as a source of cash income. The quarterly dividend payments allow them to receive this cash. Without the dividends, these investors would need to sell some of their stock periodically and incur the transaction costs associated with those sales. Also, these investors are more susceptible to the ups and downs of the stock market because they are selling pieces of their portfolios at different times. This circumstance was especially notable during the global recession of 2007-2008 when many investors saw their stock portfolios incur significant losses. Investors who sold their stock for income during this period suffered major financial setbacks.

Shareholders often demand that management make high dividend payments. The rightists have explained and justified this in several ways. The best justification may simply be that many shareholders do not trust management to spend the earnings properly. The shareholders may not believe that management has their best interests at heart and would prefer that the earnings be paid out through dividends. This policy gives shareholders the power to control the money, but it limits the business' flexibility in making investment decisions.

The leftists hold the opposite view of dividend policy. They strongly believe that dividend payments should be low. The focus of their argument is based on a single issue: taxes. As stated earlier, dividends are taxed as income, not capital gains. Therefore, the leftists believe that whenever income tax rates are higher than capital gains tax rates, the only viable option is to pay low dividends. The excess cash can be used in one of two ways.

First, the cash can be used for investment opportunities that will allow the value of the business to grow. The company can engage in capital projects that will increase the value of the business and ultimately its stock price. If a shareholder wants cash, she can sell her stock at the higher price and pay the capital gains tax, which is lower than the income tax. Second, the firm can use the excess cash to repurchase stock. The shareholders will receive cash for the shares that they sell and will be taxed at the lower capital gains tax rate.

With respect to dividend policy, middle-of-the-roaders believe that the smart dividend policy lies in a middle ground between the two sides. This group believes that the value of a company is not affected by dividend policy. Proponents of this approach claim that if either raising or lowering dividend payments could increase the value of a business, companies would already be using such strategies to affect their stock price. In fact, some businesses do use this strategy in an attempt to influence their share price. Most middle-of-the-road managers do not believe that stock prices can be manipulated simply through changes in dividend policy. Each company arrives at some level of dividends that is appropriate for most of the shareholders. This middle-ground dividend payment satisfies the greatest number of shareholders and has no effect on business value. According to this view, smart managers would adjust the dividend policy if they believed that the change would positively affect business value.

The dividend policy is an important issue for publicly traded sport companies. It is closely related to several other financial management decisions such as borrowing, capital structuring, and investment decisions. For example, if a sport business decides to use its excess cash to pay dividends, it must rely on more borrowing for investment opportunities. This activity will significantly affect its capital structure and long-term planning. Dividends can be controversial. As we have discussed, people hold divergent views on the importance of dividends to the sport business and the appropriate dividend policy for a company to follow.

REINVESTMENT

As stated earlier, an alternative to distributing earnings to shareholders through dividends is to reinvest the funds back into the business. **Reinvestment** is a key component in financial management. A sport business must continually reinvest if it hopes to thrive and grow. One method of reinvesting funds is through retaining earnings. The business forgoes payment to stockholders and keeps the earnings for capital investment. The board of directors decides whether to cancel dividends and often sends out a press release when it files the quarterly report on the company's earnings. The suspension or canceling of a dividend is also reported in the corporation's annual report. As stated in chapter 11, the expected return from capital projects must be greater than the return that stockholders receive from investing the dividend payments. If it is not, then the funds should be paid out as dividends.

The level of earnings that should be retained for capital investment is closely tied to a sport business' capital structure, capital budgeting decisions, and dividend policy. Obviously, businesses that prefer

UNDER ARMOUR PROTECTING ITSELF

Kevin Plank started as a walk-on football player at the University of Maryland. During practices he wanted a T-shirt that would reduce the amount of visible perspiration. Plank spent months finding the right combination of material that would eventually become known as the iconic brand Under Armour. He spent $460 for a tailor to design a T-shirt that used the wick-away material (Carey, 2006). It was the first T-shirt to be branded as form fitting and moisture wicking, creating a no-drip T-shirt.

He spent the next four years working in his grandmother's house pitching his product to college and NFL teams. Plank had a few friends who made it to the NFL, so he sold them the idea and they started to wear his T-shirts. Retail stores like Dick's Sporting Goods starting selling the brand. Since then Under Armour has expanded to additional lines of clothing including women's and children's lines and has added products like shorts and mouth guards. They have gone global, reaching Hong Kong, London, and Toronto (Lyster, 2006). In 1996 Kevin Plank became Under Armour's founder and CEO.

Under Armour's success exploded when it became the first official supplier to the NFL and appeared in a Warner Bros. movie. They hit the big screen by supplying clothing to the movies *The Replacements* and *Any Given Sunday.* In 2000 Under Armour had 8,000 retail locations and sold to MLS, MLL, NHL, USA Baseball, and the U.S. Ski Team. By 2005 they had reached over 100 division 1A football programs and 30 NFL teams, and were represented in the Super Bowl (Lyster, 2006).

They are currently expecting to compete against their top competitors in the shoe category. Under Armour is launching a marketing campaign called "Footsteps" featuring Heisman Trophy winner Cam Newton and quarterback Tom Brady (Olson, 2011). Plank reached his goal in 2010 by surpassing the $1 billion revenue mark and is optimistic that sales will continue to grow. The company's stock reflects the founder's enthusiasm. In 2011 the company had 51.56 million shares outstanding. Its 52-week high-low ranged from a low of $34.20 to a high of $82.95. The company's market capitalization was $3.06 billion. Under Armour's earning per share was $1.47, and its price–earnings ratio was 47.63. In contrast, Nike's market capitalization during the same general period was $41.21 billion, its earning per share was $4.40, and its PE ratio was 20.06.

To help steal market share from its rivals and generate more income, the company launched several initiatives in 2009 including being more selective in launching new products, signing new endorsement deals, opening new retail stores, and investing internationally. Thus, although in the past the company engaged in free spending to grow its name, they had to reposition their financial resources to focus only on the deals that would add the most to the bottom line.

to pay relatively high dividends retain a smaller percentage of earnings. Note that legal restrictions govern the amount of dividends that can be paid. On the balance sheet of a business, dividend payments cannot exceed retained earnings. This policy, known as the impairment of capital rule, was established to protect creditors. It prohibits a business that is in financial distress from liquidating its assets through dividend payments. In the absence of this legal stipulation, a business could distribute all its capital assets, and creditors would have nothing to reclaim (Brigham & Ehrhardt, 2011).

The size of a business also plays a role in the amount of funds that should be used for reinvestment. For smaller businesses, such as a local sporting goods store or fitness center, other capital sources such as debt or the issuance of new common stock may be relatively expensive. Thus, a smaller business would most likely elect to finance capital spending through retained earnings. Larger businesses can issue finance capital, such as stocks and bonds, at a much lower cost compared with small businesses. Therefore, they are more likely to pay higher dividends and retain a smaller percentage of earnings than are smaller businesses.

As discussed in chapter 11, businesses also have a target capital structure. The target is the proportion of debt to equity that is believed to be best for increasing shareholder value. The level of reinvestment in the company is often a product of this capital structure. A business may lower retained earnings if it wants to repurchase stock. The result will be an alteration in the capital structure and level of reinvestment.

Last, managerial control may affect the level of retained earnings. Some sport businesses with the need for additional capital are hesitant to issue new stock. In issuing new stock, management always faces the possibility of relinquishing control. To avoid this situation, management can take the option of retaining a higher level of earnings. The earnings are then used to reinvest in the business.

MERGERS AND ACQUISITIONS

In a **merger**, one business blends its business with the acquired business. Thus, company A can merge with company B, and the new entity could be called company C. In contrast, in an **acquisition**, the acquiring company maintains control of the acquired company and serves in a dominant position over the acquired company. Thus, in an acquisition, company A can acquire company B and still be company A. A merger can be part of an acquisition, such as the merger of accounting departments from two different companies.

A merger is an investment, made under uncertainty, in which the goal of the acquiring business is to increase its value or its shareholders' wealth. As with other investment opportunities, a business should acquire another business only if it believes that a positive gain in net present value will occur. Unfortunately, given the level of uncertainty, calculating the net present value of an acquisition candidate is extremely difficult (Ross et al., 2008). Unlike the situation when a company decides to invest in long-term capital, placing a value on the additional expenses and income associated with a merger is difficult.

CONCEPTS INTO PRACTICE

For example, an independent owner of a single sporting goods store may eventually turn his small business into a much larger and highly successful operation. But the growth potential for a single location is limited. If he wishes to increase the size of the business, he may look to expand into new locations. One method of expansion is to acquire and operate other small sporting goods stores. After acquiring other stores, the owner would have the ability to increase income and grow the company.

Selected Sport Holdings for Major Sport-Related Corporations That Grew Through Acquisitions

Corporation	Selected sport and entertainment holdings
Madison Square Garden	New York Knicks, New York Liberty, New York Rangers, MSG Network, Madison Square Garden, Radio City Music Hall, Fuse Network, Connecticut Whale
Disney	ESPN, ESPN2, ESPN Classic, ESPNU, ESPN International, ESPN.com, ESPN News, ESPN Zone restaurants, ABC Sports, *ESPN the Magazine*, Walt Disney Wide World of Sports Complex
Comcast	51% stake in Universal Sports Channel; The Golf Channel; NBC Sports Network; ownership interest in Comcast-Spectacor, which operates the Philadelphia Flyers, Wells Fargo Center, Comcast SportsNet, Flyers Skate Zone, New Era Tickets, Front Row Marketing, Paciolan, Global Spectrum, Ovations Catering

A number of important mergers have occurred in the sport industry over the past decade. For example, sport and entertainment companies such as Disney and Comcast acquired other companies to increase the scope of their operations. These acquisitions have been somewhat controversial and may have a large effect on the future financial landscape within the sport industry. A listing of sport holdings for some of the major corporate entities in the sport industry is shown in the previous sidebar.

Not only the largest entities do well in mergers and some companies can lose significantly from over extending themselves financially to swing a merger. One example that shows how the little guys can win is the merger of the NBA with the ABA in 1976. The NBA absorbed four ABA teams (the Nets, Nuggets, Pacers, and Spurs) which meant the ABA had to eliminate two teams (the Kentucky Colonels and the St. Louis Spirits). The Colonels owner was paid $3.3 million and walked away. The Spirit owner refused that deal and worked out a deal where they were paid $2.2 million up front and a percentage of future TV revenue. At that time the NBA received very little in TV revenue. However, the deal allowed the owners and their kids and all future generations to receive a percentage of the TV revenue for as long as the other ABA teams are in the NBA. This amount has totaled over $180 million so far, even though they only owned the franchise for several years (Pells, 2006).

Aside from the major acquisitions, hundreds of smaller mergers and acquisitions occur each year within the sport industry. In 1995 alone, 9,030 mergers and acquisitions totaling more than $500 billion were reported (Crow, Phillips, & Gillentine, 2000). The number of mergers skyrocketed between 1995 and 2000. In the first three quarters of 1998, a total of 10,104 mergers were reported to the Department of Justice, with a combined value of $1.3 trillion (Crow et al., 2000). Merger mania subsided in the early 21st century because of an economic slowdown in the United States. In 2002 the value of all U.S. mergers dropped to $500 billion. The number rebounded in 2004 when more than $750 billion in mergers occurred (Rosenbuh, 2004). The recession of 2007-2008 also led to a significant drop in mergers. The merger market rebounded again in 2010 when over $822 billion in mergers occurred (De La Merced & Cain, 2011). Of course, most of these were not sport mergers, but they indicate a trend. Several sport mergers are discussed throughout this chapter.

Company acquisition for the sole purpose of diversification is normally not a wise financial strategy. Companies normally should merge only if they believe that the new company will result in some additional value that is not possible if separate enterprises are maintained. If no additional value is earned through a merger or acquisition, the action may not be in the best financial interests of either side. But not all mergers have financial growth as the goal. Some companies want to eliminate or reduce competition by purchasing a competitor and then shutting it down. Other companies may buy a competitor for leverage with unions so that the unions cannot use the other business as an example of concessions that they want. Still other businesses may merge to avoid a takeover by another company.

We need to remember that many mergers are unwelcome. Although the purchase of a small corporation by a large corporation may make the owners of the small company wealthy, some owners do not want to sell. In this circumstance a **hostile takeover** may occur. Hostile takeovers can also occur when one corporation is trying to buy another one and a third corporation arrives on the scene, offering more money. In December 2001, Monster.com offered to pay $355 million for Hot Jobs.com, and the companies worked on a merger for six months. At the last minute, Yahoo! upped the ante by $81 million, offering $436 million for HotJobs. Within three weeks, HotJobs agreed to Yahoo!'s hostile bid (Thornton, 2002). This is just one example of a hostile takeover. Other examples have occurred in all industries.

Not all hostile takeovers are successful, however, because companies can undertake various steps to protect themselves (see later discussion). Among these steps are issuing new shares to dilute the market, selling key assets, and approaching a "white knight" to make a counteroffer (Cheeseman, 2010). Other approaches include adopting "poison pills" that require the would-be buyer to pay executives a large fee if it purchases the company or require the would-be buyer to pay more for the shares. In fact, poison pills have increased the value of the companies that have adopted them by 35.9% versus only a 31.9% premium for companies that did not have them (Thornton, 2002).

A successful sport manager must be attentive to the possibility of acquiring other companies or possibly becoming the target of an acquisition attempt. The discussion in the remainder of this section focuses on the types of mergers, justifications for mergers, the legal forms of acquisition that occur within sport, and other forms of acquisition.

Types of Mergers

Ross, Westerfield, and Jaffe (2008) separate mergers into three categories: horizontal, vertical, and conglomerate.

Horizontal Mergers

A **horizontal merger** takes place when two companies in the same line of business are joined. The sports shoe industry has seen two mergers that have dramatically changed the business landscape. In 2003 Nike spent $350 million to acquire one of its competitors, Converse. This merger brought together two traditional shoe manufacturers. In a much bigger deal, adidas-Salomon spent $3.8 billion to acquire Reebok in January of 2006. Reebok and adidas together have about a 15 to 20% market share in the sports shoe industry. In deals such as these, management believes that the new merged company will have a higher value than the two separate businesses. Other examples of horizontal mergers in the sport industry include Aramark's acquisition of both Volume Service America in 1999 and Ogden Corporation's entertainment division for $236 million in 2000. IMG Worldwide, a sport marketing and athlete representation company, acquired ISP Sports, a collegiate sport marketing firm, in the summer of 2010 (Smith & Muret, 2010).

Vertical Mergers

In a **vertical merger**, a buyer expands operations forward toward the final consumer or backward in the direction of the source of raw materials. Livingstone (1997) refers to these different market levels as upstream and downstream. A downstream market is further along in the production process, whereas an upstream market is closer to the original raw materials. In either situation, a business expands by acquiring other companies that are part of the production process. In 1998, Intrawest, the operator of several mountain resorts in North America, acquired two companies, Breeze and Max Snowboards. Both companies rented ski and snowboard equipment. By acquiring these two businesses, Intrawest was able to extend its operations upstream because rental equipment is a necessity for many consumers who want to ski. Intrawest not only has control of the ski mountains and the corresponding income streams but also rents the equipment needed to ski on its mountains ("For the record," 1998, September). But given that sporting events are simultaneously produced and consumed, the frequency of vertical mergers is much less common in sport than it is in other industries.

Conglomerate Mergers

A **conglomerate merger** occurs when companies in unrelated lines of business come together. The merged companies can be involved in businesses that have no business link. One example of a company that was involved in conglomerate mergers was SFX Entertainment during the late 1990s. SFX had traditionally been in the entertainment industry through the ownership of amphitheaters and concert halls, as well as through participation in the music promotion business. With its acquisitions of the Marquee Group, Integrated Sports International, and FAME, SFX expanded into sport marketing, sports event production, and athlete representation. It appeared that with these deals SFX was attempting to become the largest integrated sport and entertainment conglomerate in the world. In 2000, however, SFX was bought by an even larger entertainment company, Clear Channel. Another conglomerate merger occurred in 2005 when Quicksilver, a famous surfboard manufacturing company, bought Rossignol, a ski company, for $320 million. Although the deal involved different sports, both are outdoor sports, and both companies had various lines of equipment and apparel (Grant, 2005).

Credible Justifications for Mergers

Credible justification must be in place for a merger to occur. As stated earlier, if no additional value is generated through a merger, then maintaining the status quo and keeping the companies independent is probably wiser. Perhaps the best justification for a merger, especially in the case of a horizontal merger, is **economies of scale**. A company achieves economies of scale by increasing its size. The adage "bigger is better" is a good way to sum up the idea of economies of scale. Two companies that duplicate activities may be more profitable if they merge operations. If a fitness center owner acquires another fitness center, economies of scale may result. Corporate responsibilities such as accounting, staff development, and office management for the two facilities could be combined, offering the potential for substantial cost savings. Although the consolidation of these operations would have little effect on revenues, it would likely lead to

A SHORT-LIVED FITNESS MERGER

In December 2001 Bally Total Fitness merged with Crunch Fitness. The total purchase price was estimated at $90 million for the 19 Crunch Fitness clubs in five states. The merged company increased Bally's size to approximately 420 clubs throughout North America, serving more than four million members ("Bally," 2001). Several years later, when Bally was facing financial hardship, it sold its Crunch Fitness interest.

a decrease in expenses. The result would be an increase in earnings and in the value of the merged company. The recent acquisition of NBC Universal by Comcast is an example in which economies of scale may be achieved through a merger.

Another credible justification for a merger in the sport industry is the prospect that a company can save on costs not related to economies of scale. For example, Cablevision, the New York–based broadcasting company, had paid over $40 million annually for the local television broadcast rights of the New York Yankees. The 12-year $486 million broadcasting deal between the Yankees and Cablevision ended in the year 2000. In fall 1998 Cablevision made a reported bid of $525 million to purchase 70% of the Yankees (King & Brockington, 1998). Part of the rationale for the acquisition was that it would allow Cablevision to save $40 million per year. Instead of annually paying local broadcast fees to the Yankees, Cablevision wanted to purchase part ownership of the team and use the ownership rights to reduce or eliminate the broadcasting payments. Cablevision would have owned both the television outlet and the team. Ultimately, the two sides were unable to agree on some details regarding the acquisition, such as team control, and the deal was abandoned. Ironically, the New York Yankees then decided to begin their own regional sports network, the YES Network. So Cablevision was not only unable to acquire ownership interest in the Yankees but also lost the television rights to broadcast Yankees games.

A merger or acquisition is also a wise financial endeavor if the merged entity can generate revenues that are not possible if the firms remain separate. Two firms may have complementary resources or products that when combined will result in substantial revenues. As a consequence of the merger, the combined company may have a very successful future. For example, the merger of IMG and ISP Sports Marketing that was discussed earlier has allowed IMG to be involved at a much greater level in collegiate marketing and sponsorship sales. Although IMG had a small interest in these activities before the deal, they are now the largest player in collegiate sport marketing.

A corporate acquisition may also be a wise maneuver if a business believes that the targeted company is poorly managed. A business may view the other company as underperforming because of poor management and believe that it can transform the targeted company into a financially successful business. Through acquisition, the business believes that it can improve its own value by instituting more effective management in the underperforming company.

Last, a merger can be the most effective way to invest surplus funds. As mentioned earlier, a successful business with a substantial amount of net income has several options. It can distribute the income to shareholders by increasing dividend payments, or it may repurchase its stock. A third option is for the business to invest its surplus cash by purchasing the stock of other companies. Often, businesses with surplus cash and a lack of good alternative investment choices redirect their capital toward purchasing other companies. The strategy may be wise in that a business that fails to redirect its cash may itself become a target for takeover. Businesses with significant excess cash face the possibility of acquisition because other companies may believe that they can acquire the business and redirect the cash in a profitable manner.

Mergers and Antitrust Law

Within the legal system, mergers and acquisitions are regulated by antitrust law. Three primary statutes come into play. The first statute, passed in 1890, is the Sherman Antitrust Act, which decrees that "every contract, combination . . . or conspiracy, in restraint of trade" is illegal (Sherman Antitrust Act, 2012). It was enacted in response to the monopolies that developed in the middle to late 1800s in industries such as steel, iron, and the railroads. The goal was to protect consumers from large corporations that controlled entire industries. The wording of the statute was vague, however, and thus the law was difficult to enforce.

The Federal Trade Commission Act of 1914 was a step toward tightening the restrictions on monopolies and collusive behavior. It prohibited unfair methods of competition as well as unfair or deceptive acts or practices (Blair & Kaserman, 1985). The act also established an agency, the Federal Trade Commission, that was given the responsibility of enforcing the antitrust laws. The third and most enforceable of these statutes was the Clayton Act of 1914. Section 7 of the Clayton Act addressed mergers and acquisitions. It prohibited the acquisition of another firm's stock in cases in which the result would be to lessen competition and create a monopoly (Blair & Kaserman, 1985). But the Clayton Act had one obvious loophole: It did not prohibit the acquisition of another firm's assets. The loophole was used extensively until 1950, when it was closed with the passage of the Cellar-Kefauver Act. Section 7 of the Clayton Act was amended to the following:

> No corporation engaged in commerce shall acquire, directly or indirectly, the whole or any part of the stock or other share capital and no corporation subject to the jurisdiction of the Federal Trade Commission shall acquire the whole or any part of the assets of another corporation engaged also in commerce, where in any line of commerce in any section of the country, the effect of such acquisition may be substantially to lessen competition, or to tend to create a monopoly. (Blair & Kaserman, 1985, p. 226)

The improved Clayton Act not only forbade mergers that constrained trade or greatly lessened market competition but also prohibited any merger that potentially restrained trade. Thus, the Clayton Act has been the primary statute used to stop mergers that could have created a monopoly within an industry.

Antitrust law is enforced by two federal government agencies: the Federal Trade Commission (FTC) and the U.S. Department of Justice. The Department of Justice has the power to file a civil suit to block any merger, and the FTC can initiate an official proceeding to analyze the effect of a merger on competition within an industry. Ultimately, either department can use legal means to attempt to stop two firms from merging if it believes that the result will decrease competition and harm consumers.

Since the passage of the Hart-Scott-Rodino Act of 1976, all firms are required by law to inform the government of any acquisitions of stock that exceed a certain dollar amount. Originally, that dollar amount was $15 million, but that number has been increased over the years. As of January 2005, the amount is $53.1 million. The government must also be informed if greater than 15% of the targeted firm's stock is purchased (Woodworth & Sher, 2005).

Few mergers are contested by the Department of Justice or the FTC. Within the American sport industry, no major antitrust cases have arisen from a corporate merger. As the industry continues to develop and more mergers occur, some acquisitions will likely be closely scrutinized by federal agencies such as the FTC. In 2011 the merger of Comcast and NBC Universal was examined closely by both the Federal Communications Commission (FCC) and the U.S. Department of Justice. The merger, in which Comcast paid $30 billion for a 51% ownership interest in NBC Universal, was rigorously scrutinized because of the possible monopoly power of the newly merged company within the communications industry, specifically television. Specifically, the FCC and Department of Justice were concerned with the possible monopolization of online video content by the merged company. Ultimately, both agencies allowed the merger to occur after mechanisms were put in place to ensure that online video content would be shared with industry competitors such as Apple and Netflix (Arango & Stelter, 2011).

Historically, although no significant challenges have been organized against sport mergers, the government has become involved in several transactions. For example, when the NFL merged with the American Football League (AFL), Congress reviewed the proposed merger to assess its effect on broadcast football games. In response to the inquiry, the legislature passed the 1968 Sports Broadcasting Act, which allowed the merger to proceed as long as professional football did not air games on Saturdays during the college football season. Thus, even today, no NFL games are played on Saturday during the college football season. After the regular college football season ends, the NFL starts airing games on Saturdays. This legislation was developed to prevent professional football from overrunning college football.

NFL–AFL MERGER

The NFL–AFL merger was not the first merger for the NFL. In 1949 the NFL merged with three teams from the rival All-America Football Conference, bringing Cleveland, San Francisco, and Baltimore into the NFL (Crow et al., 2000). The NFL–AFL merger was originally inked in 1966, but four years of political wrangling occurred before Congress approved the deal and the merger was completed (Crow et al., 2000).

Various Forms of Acquisition

An acquisition can take many forms. Numerous issues play into how a company acquires another company. For example, is the acquisition friendly or will it be strongly contested? The merger between Hewlett-Packard and Compaq is an example of a merger that became contentious. Millions of dollars were spent to convince people that the merger was right or wrong for the shareholders. This section examines some acquisition concerns, such as whether it is better to purchase another business' stock or just their assets.

A company can legally acquire another business using any of three methods. The first of these methods is the merger of two companies; the other two methods are purchasing voting stock and purchasing assets.

Merging Two Companies

A merger occurs when one company is completely absorbed by another. The advantages of mergers are that they are legally simple and relatively inexpensive. There is no title transfer of property or assets. One disadvantage is that a merger must be approved by a stockholder vote within each company. The management team of the business being sold must cooperate and approve the deal. Achieving this agreement is sometimes problematic because the merger may result in the termination of some high-level managers. These managers may make a concerted effort to block the merger. Because of this concern, some deals include clauses that guarantee management positions in the new company or provide for golden parachutes. A golden parachute is a large monetary payoff to a top-level manager in exchange for her support of a merger.

Purchasing Voting Stock

In a second form of acquisition, a company purchases the voting stock in another company in exchange for cash, stock in the existing company, or both. This is achieved through a tender offer, or a public offer by one company to buy the stock of another directly. An advantage of this acquisition method is that shareholders' meetings do not have to take place and management can be bypassed. The buyer can go directly to the shareholders for their approval. If a majority of the shareholders agree to sell, the purchaser will have control of the company. In 2007 French luxury goods maker, PPR SA (owner of Gucci and Yves Saint Laurent) bought 27.1% in Puma AG, the third largest sporting goods maker in the world. The initial purchase was the start of an offer to buy all the shares at a price of 330 euros per share ($441.11), which placed a value of $7.1 billion on Puma (Moulson, 2007).

Management sometimes fights the stock acquisition, and conflict can result. The process has the potential to be much longer and more expensive if management attempts to block the acquisition. Shareholders may also hold out in an effort to increase the stock's acquisition price. If current shareholders can force up the sale price of the stock, they will receive more money when they ultimately sell the stock. As highlighted in chapter 9, several shareholder groups sued Ascent over the proposed sale of the Denver Nuggets, based on the shareholders' opinion that the bid was too low and that higher bids had been rejected. The higher bids would have earned the shareholders a greater return. Any conflict typically raises the acquisition price for the purchasing firm. Note that many stock acquisitions ultimately become mergers. Management from both sides negotiates for a merger, usually protecting the self-interests of both.

WHAT'S IN A NAME?

Sports executives in a merger might overlook the effect of a merger on naming rights. If bank A has its name on a stadium under a 20-year contract, will that name change if bank A is purchased by bank B? The answer is yes. But the potential costs of making such a changeover can be significant. A naming-rights company may have to spend millions of dollars to change the corporate images on the signage in a sports facility. Areas of change may include advertising stickers on walls, seats, cup holders, stairs, concession products, and building exteriors. Philadelphia's CoreStates Center was renamed First Union Center after CoreStates Financial was purchased by First Union in 1999. In 2001 First Union then merged with Wachovia Bank. The facility in Philadelphia was then named the Wachovia Center. In 2010 Wachovia Bank was purchased by Wells Fargo. Thus, the name of the facility was again changed to the Wells Fargo Center, which is its current name, for now!

Likewise, the new Boston Garden that opened in 1995 was originally supposed to open as the Shawmut Center. However, Shawmut National Group was purchased by Fleet Financial Group, which renamed the facility the Fleet Center. Fleet Bank was eventually bought out by Banknorth in 2005, and the facility was renamed the TD Banknorth Garden. In 2008, after a merger with Commerce Bancorp, TD Banknorth was renamed as simply TD Bank. Thus, the facility name was again changed, this time to TD Garden.

Not all name changes go well after a merger. The name can be changed only if the contract provides for such a change. A dispute arose concerning Buffalo's Marine Midland Arena when Marine Midland was acquired by HSBC Holdings. The Buffalo Sabres initially did not want to change the facility's name. They argued that the contract with Marine Midland did not allow the name to be transferred ("Business bulletin," 2000). Today, that facility is named First Niagara Center, after the First Niagara Bank purchased the upstate New York and Connecticut bank branch network of HSBC.

At other times management might lead the charge to purchase a company. The growth of investment bankers and private equity in the sport industry grew significantly in the first couple years of the 21st century. Once such purchase involved the CEO of Aramark, Joseph Neubauer, and other investors taking the public company private through a leveraged buyout (LBO; see chapter 10). Aramark was sold for $6.24 billion, but its debt increased under the deal from $1.76 to $6.2 billion, which meant that the company's interest payments increased from $139.9 million to $590.9 million annually. Because of this increased debt, Aramark's corporate credit rating was decreased into junk bond status by Standard & Poor's (Simon & Yao, 2007).

Purchasing Assets

The last acquisition method to consider is the purchase of one company's assets by another business. This method, the least common of the three forms, requires voter approval by the acquired company. The benefit of purchasing assets is that the acquiring company can increase its inventory or capital assets without acquiring potential liability, debt, or other concerns from the seller. The legal process of acquiring assets such as real estate, production sites, and machinery can be costly.

Merger Accounting

With respect to accounting issues, mergers and acquisitions can be highly complex. Using generally accepted accounting principles (GAAP), mergers are handled as either a purchase of assets or a pooling of interests. The two methods have little effect on the real value of the merged firm, but we discuss here some differences between the two. The results of a pooling of interests are shown in figure 14.1, a through c. With the pooling of interests method, the two companies are merged, and their balance sheets are simply added together to form the balance sheet for the new company. The new

Assets (in millions)		Liabilities and shareholders' equity (in millions)	
Working capital	$30	Equity	$130
Fixed assets	100		
Total	$130	Total	$130

a

Assets (in millions)		Liabilities and shareholders' equity (in millions)	
Working capital	$20	Equity	$80
Fixed assets	60		
Total	$80	Total	$80

b

Assets (in millions)		Liabilities and shareholders' equity (in millions)	
Working capital	$50	Equity	$210
Fixed assets	160		
Total	$210	Total	$210

c

Figure 14.1 (a) Company A's balance sheet, (b) company B's balance sheet, and (c) their combined balance sheet.

company is jointly owned by all the stockholders in the previously separate companies. The pooling of assets method is simple, and the total assets are unchanged by the merger.

The purchase of assets method is somewhat more complex. This method requires applying the fair market value to the acquired company's assets. In addition, an asset category called goodwill is created for accounting purposes. Goodwill is the difference between the acquisition price and the fair value of the acquired business' assets. Figure 14.2, a through c, provides an example of the purchase of assets method. The balance sheets used in figure 14.1, a and b, are again displayed. Assume that company A is going to acquire company B for $150 million in cash. The money is raised through borrowing from a financial institution. On its balance sheet, company B has reported $60 million in fixed assets. At the time of acquisition, however, company B is appraised at $10 million. Because company B also has $20 million in working capital, the balance sheet assets are $120 million. Therefore, company A is paying $30 million in excess of the estimated market value of company B's total net assets. The difference is represented on the combined balance sheet as goodwill. Figure 14.2c shows the new firm's balance sheet after acquisition.

To recap, the total assets of the combined companies are $280 million, $70 million more than when the two company balance sheets were separate. Of that $70 million, $40 million is from the revaluation of company B's fixed assets, and $30 million is from goodwill. The goodwill is the amount paid in excess of the fair market value of company B. A buyer may pay an additional amount such as this because a number of intangible assets are not included on the balance sheet—assets such as employee talent and future growth opportunities. The additional $30 million pays for such assets.

Which of the two methods is best? As you can see, the major difference between them is goodwill. Goodwill has several important tax ramifications. Goodwill must be amortized over a period of years, not to exceed 40 years. The goodwill amortization expense is then deducted from reported income. But unlike depreciation, goodwill is not tax deductible. Given the goodwill expense, the purchase of assets method usually results in lower reported income than the pooling of assets method. Also, because the fixed assets are revalued using the purchase of assets method, the overall value of the merged company often increases. The combined larger book value and lower reported income can have a negative effect on company performance measures such as return on equity (ROE) and return on assets (ROA). The resulting lower measures may paint a picture that is not as strong as when the pooling of assets method is used (Brealey et al., 2009).

Note that the choice of accounting methods used for acquisitions has no effect on tax-deductible

Assets (in millions)		Liabilities and shareholders' equity (in millions)	
Working capital	$30	Equity	$130
Fixed assets	100		
Total	**$130**	**Total**	**$130**

a

Assets (in millions)		Liabilities and shareholders' equity (in millions)	
Working capital	$20	Equity	$80
Fixed assets	60		
Total	**$80**	**Total**	**$80**

b

Assets (in millions)		Liabilities and shareholders' equity (in millions)	
Working capital	$50	Equity	$150
Fixed assets	200	Debt	130
Goodwill	30		
Total	**$280**	**Total**	**$280**

c

Figure 14.2 (*a*) Company A's balance sheet, (*b*) company B's balance sheet, and (*c*) their combined balance sheet

expenses or cash flows. Therefore, the net present value of the merged firm is not affected by the selection of merger accounting methods. Also, no evidence exists to suggest that more value is created for the acquiring business under one method or the other (Ross et al., 2008). The differences are in the accounting methods only.

CONCLUSION

Successful sport businesses must determine how to use their positive earnings. Companies use these funds in three primary ways: paying dividends to stockholders, acquiring other firms, and reinvesting in themselves. Paying dividends is often a popular choice with stockholders, but this method may not be in the best long-term interests of the stockholders or the firm. People have three views on dividend payments. The rightists believe that the highest possible level of dividends should be paid to stockholders. The leftists think that dividend payments should be relatively small. The middle-of-the-roaders believe that dividend payments should be at a level that satisfies the greatest number of stockholders. Paying dividends is a complex process. The process has been established to ensure that the proper parties receive dividend payments in a fair and timely manner.

Another option for using earnings is to reinvest in the business. This reinvestment usually takes the form of spending on capital projects such as purchasing new equipment, investing in talent, or constructing new facilities. Sport is unique in that capital spending can take the form of hiring coaches and players. For example, the Boston Red Sox signed Carl Crawford to a seven-year, $142 million contract in December 2010. This contract is definitely a form of capital spending. In other industries, long-term employment contracts do not normally make up a large portion of a business' expenses. Reinvestment allows for growth and future financial success. It is an integral part of capital budgeting and long-term financial planning.

Last, earnings can be used to acquire other businesses. Acquisitions can entail horizontal mergers, vertical mergers, or conglomerates. For a merger to be successful, the value of the merged companies must be greater than the value of the two businesses if they were to remain as separate entities. Recently, mergers and acquisition activity has increased in the sport industry. Companies such as Comcast, IMG, and Creative Artists Agency have acquired other businesses in an attempt to expand their presence in the sport and entertainment industries. The use of business earnings can play a major role in determining long-term business success.

Class Discussion Topics

1. Is consolidation in the sport industry good?

2. Do you think that it would be worthwhile to create another football league similar to the United Football League or the Arena Football League? Would another baseball, hockey, or basketball league be a better investment?

3. If you could make 10% from a government bond or 10% from investing in a professional sports team, which one would you invest in and why?

4. Why should a business set a record date when issuing a dividend?

5. If you had this responsibility within a corporation, under what circumstances would you make a decision to reinvest rather than issue a dividend?

6. Which group (rightist, leftist, or middle-of-the-roader) has views that you believe make the most sense?

7. Explain the fundamental accounting difference between using the pooling of interests method versus the purchase of assets methods when dealing with the merger of two sport organizations.

8. What are the primary components of the Sherman Antitrust Act of 1890 and the Clayton Act of 1914? What is their significance to the management of the sport industry?

9. Explain the differences between horizontal, vertical, and conglomerate mergers.

chapter 15

Auditing

Chapter Objectives

After studying this chapter, you should be able to do the following:

- Define the purposes of auditing.
- Understand the problems associated with poor auditing.
- Describe the types of audits.
- Understand the importance of selecting competent and unbiased auditors.
- Understand how the auditing process works.
- Understand how sport fraud can occur through sloppy financial analysis.

Auditing is one of the most important areas within the field of accounting. Although this textbook focuses on financial management, a sports manager can benefit by being knowledgeable in the basics of auditing. The importance of knowing how income or expenses can be excluded from financial statements was made abundantly clear by the numerous corporate scandals that occurred in the early 21st century. Well-known companies such as Enron, Adelphia, Tyco, and WorldCom made news with their accounting scandals. These scandals led to criminal charges against some prominent corporate executives such as Dennis Kozlowski, John Rigas, and Kenneth Lay. Although such scandals are not common in sport businesses, they can occur.

The goal of this chapter is to provide you with an introduction to auditing. If you wish to find out more about the field, you should consult a textbook devoted to auditing. This chapter deals primarily with the principles of auditing and their applicability to the sport industry.

PURPOSES OF AUDITING

Auditing has two fundamental roles. First, auditing ensures that all financial statements accurately portray the financial position of a firm. Second, audits allow managers to analyze the efficiency of their operation.

Ensuring Accuracy of Financial Information

The primary role of auditing is to ensure the accuracy of financial information. The purpose of auditing is to investigate and determine whether the financial statements produced by the sport business have been prepared in accordance with appropriate financial reporting practices (Holmes & Burns, 1979). This matter may seem like a relatively simple task, but it can be extremely complex.

Looking at financial information and making solid decisions may appear to be easy. For everyone who has balanced a checkbook, the prospect of an error is a daunting thought. Was a number recorded incorrectly? Did someone transpose a number and enter $69.88 rather than $96.88? Did someone fail to enter a deposit? Did someone intentionally record incorrect information? What happens if a check is not cashed for over six months? What happens if all deposits were not recorded? All these concerns affect every business as well. Although you might be able to control what you do with your checking account, most businesses need to rely on the truthfulness of their employees when multiple people are entering in deposits, writing checks, paying vendors, issuing payroll, and so forth. To avoid problems, money needs to be properly tracked. The professional athletic landscape is littered with former athletes who made a fortune and then had nothing shortly after they retired. In 2009 and 2010 former Celtic great Antoine Walker and New Jersey Nets first-round pick Derrick Coleman filed for bankruptcy protection. Such scenarios are not unique. An estimated 6 to 8% of NBA players end up broke, and a staggering 60% are in serious financial trouble within five years of retirement (Wachter, 2010). This concern does not apply just to NBA players. Within two years of retiring from the NFL, 78% of former players have either gone bankrupt or are under financial pressure because of issues such as joblessness and divorce (Torre, 2009). The list of Hall of Fame sport stars who have lost money in various investment schemes include Brooks Robinson, John Unitas, Rollie Fingers, Kareem Abdul-Jabbar, and Tony Gwynn (Torre, 2009). The reason for all these bankruptcies, financial hardships, and poor investments can often be traced to a lack of diligence in monitoring, spending, and investing money. Auditing can help minimize such problems.

In this text we discuss numerous financial measures that are predicated on accurate financial data. The ratios are only as good as the numbers used to calculate them. Auditing is not limited to analyzing financial statements. To ensure that the financial statements are accurate, an auditor must study the entire business. This procedure often involves analyzing the internal processes of a business to see whether the business successfully controls the flow of financial information. For example, an auditor must examine the processes involved in functional areas such as employee payroll, the purchase of goods and services, and inventory control to determine whether the financial statements accurately represent the auditee. Additionally, an auditor must have knowledge of the industry being examined. One benefit of auditing is discouraging and detecting fraudulent activities or mistakes. Note that all businesses and organizations, regardless of size, scope, and mission, must undergo some type of periodic audit.

CONCEPTS INTO PRACTICE

Assume that a local YMCA offers a weekly drop-in basketball program and collects $5 per night from members and $8 per night from nonmembers during peak playing times. These funds need to be recorded in a meaningful manner so that someone can ensure that everyone has paid to play. The YMCA can check the totals collected every day to determine whether any errors have been made. If 15 players are participating and $90 is on hand, then an employee can do the math and determine that 10 members and 5 nonmembers are playing. If the player records indicate that 7 nonmembers and 9 members are playing that day, then she knows that $11 is missing. This example highlights how auditing is similar to the investigation process.

Honest and candid public disclosure of financial information is required of businesses and organizations, both public and private. Publicly operated sports organizations, such as university athletic departments, have the same need for accurate financial records as private companies do, such as professional sports franchises and sporting goods manufacturers. Auditing is designed to identify problems and ensure investor confidence in a company's financial statements. But if the independent auditors help manipulate the numbers, as is alleged to have occurred in the Enron scandal, the entire rationale for independent auditing is lost. The manipulation concern arose in the previously discussed scandal involving Bally Total Fitness in which their auditor Ernest & Young failed to catch the manipulation. Ernest & Young (a large accounting firm) agreed to pay the Securities and Exchange Commission (SEC) $8.5 million stemming from Bally's accounting fraud from 2001 through 2003. The settlement was reached in part because the company had failed to find and report fraud despite the fact that Bally was considered a high-risk client and because former Ernst & Young auditors had become Bally executives who were aggressive in selecting principles and determining estimates (Securities and Exchange Commission, 2009).

Analyzing Operational Efficiency

Audits may detect areas in which a sport business could operate more efficiently, which could lead to an increase in profits (Arens & Loebbecke, 2006). For nonprofit organizations, this increased efficiency may allow the organization to do more with its available resources. For example, the athletic director at a university is given a fixed yearly budget. Efficient use of these funds will allow that athletic director to maximize the number of opportunities for the coaches and student-athletes. The athletic director also needs accurate and timely information to make effective managerial decisions. Therefore, an athletic director needs to audit the organization to increase efficiency, just as the manager of a multibillion-dollar private corporation does.

CATEGORIES OF AUDITS

Audits can be separated into two general categories: internal and independent. Internal audits are completed by staff members within a business. Most large businesses have a financial department that oversees internal audits. An internal auditor serves several functions. Usually the internal auditor is involved in preparing an organization's financial statements to ensure their accuracy. The auditor is also involved in the establishment of internal controls for the organization. An auditor may develop an internal control system to track the purchase, receipt, and distribution of inventory for a retail sales company such as Modell's or Dick's Sporting Goods. Without a system that tracks the use and physical location of equipment, an employee may be able to steal business property with ease. As another example of establishing internal controls, an internal auditor for Under Armour (UA) could develop a bar code system to track the use and physical location of office equipment such as computers, fax machines, and telephones. A phone tracking system for UA might require a telephone user to enter a special code to make a long-distance call. The system can then track all calls to show whether an employee is using the phone excessively or for personal purposes.

Independent audits, as the name implies, involve an external review of the finances by individuals who are not directly involved with the documents being reviewed. Thus, an independent audit can be performed by someone from another division in the company who has not been involved in generating the document in question. Likewise, an independent audit can be performed by external entities, such as public accounting firms, that can verify the truthfulness of the documents being reviewed. The latter is the type of audit most commonly seen in corporate finance. Independent audits are discussed in detail later in this chapter.

A third general category of audit is outside the scope of this textbook. The IRS can request an audit of any business. Usually, the IRS audits a business to determine whether the correct amount of federal taxes has been paid. Businesses that fail to pay or that underpay taxes can face substantial monetary fines and penalties. In this chapter we focus on independent audits because they are the most common, and this type of audit most directly affects sport finance managers.

INTERNAL CONTROLS

As stated earlier, auditing involves more than verifying the financial statements of a business. An auditor must also examine a business' system of internal controls. Internal controls are the processes and mechanisms used in the management of a business (Meigs, Whittington, & Meigs, 1982). For example, all businesses have employees who are compensated for their labor. Paying employees

EXAMPLES OF FINANCIAL FRAUD IN THE SPORT WORLD

There are numerous examples of financial fraud in the sport industry. We have highlighted just some of these cases.

In 2009 a major embezzlement case was uncovered at the United States Coast Guard Academy. A senior Coast Guard Athletic Department official embezzled over $1.4 million between 1999 and 2000 and between 2004 and 2009. The money was used to fund his gambling debts and was taken from the academy's athletic association fund, which helped support the athletic department from annual contributions by former cadets. The fund had been operated for over 50 years without significant internal controls, and the fraud was detected only after Washington received an anonymous complaint. The former employee admitted his crime and then committed suicide (Mahony, 2009).

High school athletic booster club treasurer Tonya Yannaki transferred $48,000 from the club account to her own account over a 12-month period. This incident occurred right after another Michigan high school faced the same situation when their booster club president was charged with stealing $17,000 (Popke, 2008). Other high school incidents include a Lake Forest high school athletic director who stole $204,000 in 2007 and a former employee responsible for ticket sales at a Dallas high school who stole $95,000 from the booster club. Such actions are not unusual because many of the country's 1.3 million booster clubs do not even have bylaws or objectives.

In 2009 a husband and wife team had stolen several hundred thousand from the Reaction Fitness Club chain in Texas and Oklahoma. The wife had been a bookkeeper for a number of clubs and used her position to sign checks payable to cash and to herself and her husband. She also paid personal credit card bills from the chain's accounts and purchased numerous personal items, clothes, furniture, and airline tickets. The wife was ordered to pay $600,000 restitution and her now former husband had to repay $15,000 ("Texas man sentenced for embezzlement," 2009).

A former accounting clerk from a Washington, D.C., YMCA pleaded guilty to stealing $142,000. The clerk stole 33 blank checks and forged the name of Y officials before making the checks out to 14 accomplices ("Man steals $142,000 from Metropolitan Washington YMCA," 2009). A few years earlier a former bookkeeper at a YMCA in Lead, South Dakota, was sentenced to seven years in prison for issuing paychecks to herself, her daughter, and her husband and increasing her wage by $3.80 an hour. The theft was caught when the Y almost closed because of financial problems. The bookkeeper was serving on the committee looking into ways to save the facility (Shaver, 2007).

Larger organizations also suffer from fraud. The former payroll chief for the Los Angeles Dodgers was sentenced in 1987 to 16 months in state prison after he pleaded guilty to conspiring with six other former employees to embezzle $332,583 from the baseball club. He was accused of conspiring with other employees between 1983 and 1985 to add extra money to their paychecks by crediting themselves for hours that they did not work. He also added fictitious names and names of employees' girlfriends to the club's payroll. He ended up splitting this money with his coconspirators (Pristen, 1987).

involves many steps. Each of our sports organization cases must develop a system to calculate the number of hours worked by each employee and the wage rate at which each will be compensated. In addition, deductions must be made for expenses such as income taxes, health benefits, and retirement plan payments. Last, paychecks must be processed and distributed to employees. An efficient, consistent, and accurate system must be developed for this process. An inferior system will mean a lack of internal control, increasing the probability of financial errors. These errors could mean that an employee is not paid or is paid an inaccurate amount.

A strong internal control system is a means to avoid many financial errors. Therefore, those developing procedures for managing financial matters should stress internal control. A good example could be Speedway Motorsports' parking lot attendants. Assume that Speedway has a large parking lot, and two employees help process people through the gates. They might use two attendants because parking revenue is split between the event and the municipal entity that owns the lot. To guarantee accuracy, Speedway employs a person to take the money, and the municipality employs a person who has a counter to register how many cars have entered the parking lot. The number of cars clicked can be reconciled with the amount of money collected to make sure that both sides have the correct number. A system of strong internal controls also makes it easier for managers to pre-pare for financial audits because they will have the materials needed by the auditor.

Poor internal controls may increase the likelihood of fraud. For example, if one person oversees the entire payroll system for a small sports organization, say 20 employees, that employee could commit a fraud rather easily. Such a scenario could happen to nonprofit sport organizations and athletic departments. If an organization hires a bookkeeper to process all revenue and expenses, policies and procedures must be installed to make sure that the bookkeeper does not embezzle money. A procedure must exist for ensuring the accuracy of this person's work; without oversight, a fraudulent act can easily occur. Perhaps the bookkeeper could overpay employees or place people on the payroll who are not working for the entity. In a study of 1,000 cases involving workplace fraud, the median loss was suffered by smaller companies (with fewer than 100 employees) and the average amount stolen in these cases was $200,000 (Leukhardt, 2009).

INDEPENDENT AUDITS

Independent auditors are not associated with the business being audited. Although they are hired by the business, their responsibility is to provide assurance that the business' financial information is reliable and accurate. The issue of independence is important. The audited business may not be pleased with the findings of an independent

---

LEGAL BUT NOT NECESSARILY HONEST

Many companies "play games" with financial statements to present an interpretation of the data that shows the company in the best light. The auditor's role is to make sure that these tricks are properly recorded and communicated to all interested parties. Some of the legal, but not necessarily honest, tricks include the following:

- Companies might promote their earnings by publicizing a pro forma figure that excludes many normal expense items such as interest and marketing expenses.
- If the earnings are low or negative, a company might list instead EBITDA—earnings before interest, taxes, depreciation, and amortization.
- Companies might not report the potential effect of stock-options grants on their earnings.
- Especially in the late 1990s, some businesses reported large earnings acquired through selling their investments in start-ups. Although these are real earnings, they are the earnings of an offshoot rather than of the core business, and there is no guarantee that any future similar earnings might ever be realized (Scherreik, 2000).

auditor, but the auditor has an ethical duty to report the findings honestly (Whittington & Pany, 2006). For public corporations, auditors must complete an auditor's report that summarizes their findings. As in the general field of accounting, auditors use standard procedures to analyze and report their findings. Several professional associations oversee the auditing field, some of which are shown in the following list:

Abbreviation	Name
AAA	American Accounting Association
AICPA	American Institute of Certified Public Accountants
ASB	Auditing Standards Board
FAF	Financial Accounting Foundation
FEI	Financial Executives Institute
IIA	Institute of Internal Auditors
NAA	National Association of Accountants
PCAOB	Public Company Accounting Oversight Board
SSCPA	State Societies of Certified Public Accountants

The accuracy of an auditor's report is crucial. Under U.S. common law and securities law, third parties such as investors, creditors, and government agencies can sue independent auditors. Monetary damages may have to be paid if it is determined that the independent auditor is guilty of a crime (Whittington & Pany, 2006). In March 2002 the accounting firm of Arthur Andersen was indicted in a federal court for its involvement in the Enron scandal. The U.S. Department of Justice claimed that Andersen obstructed justice by allegedly aiding Enron in the destruction of key financial documents. Deputy Attorney General Larry Thompson stated in *USA Today* that "Andersen personnel engaged in the wholesale destruction of tons of paperwork and attempted to purge huge volumes of electronic data or information. . . . At the time, Andersen knew full well that these documents were relevant to the inquiries into Enron's collapse" (Farrell, 2002). In June 2002 Andersen was found guilty in a U.S. Federal Court of obstructing justice by shredding Enron documents. As a result of the conviction, the Securities and Exchange Commission forced the firm to surrender its accounting licenses. Andersen's business quickly disappeared, and the company reduced the number of employees from a high of 85,000 to about 200. In May 2005 the court decision against Andersen was overturned by

a U.S. appeals court. But the decision came far too late to help Andersen, which had lost almost all its clients.

In response to the accounting scandals of the early 21st century, the U.S. Congress moved quickly to enact new legislation that addresses the ethics and behavior of accounting and auditing firms. In summer 2002, Congress passed the Sarbanes-Oxley Act and President Bush quickly signed it into law. Sarbanes-Oxley includes a series of reforms restricting the types of consulting that certified public accountants may perform for audit clients. In addition, the Public Company Accounting Oversight Board (PCAOB) was established. The PCAOB tightened federal regulation of accounting practices and has developed stricter rules for the auditing process (Whittington & Pany, 2006).

Types of Independent Audits

Audits are of four distinct types. The first, the audit of financial statements, is the most common, and this type of audit receives the bulk of attention in this chapter. The three other types of audits—operational audits, compliance audits, and integrated audits—are usually referred to as audit activities (Whittington & Pany, 2006). Although attestation and assurance are provided through these audits, as discussed later in the chapter, the central theme is to analyze the efficiency and regulatory compliance of a business. What follows is a brief description of each of the four types of audits, which are also characterized in table 15.1.

1. Financial statements audit. This type of audit is done to determine whether the financial statements of a business meet generally accepted accounting principles. Most often, these financial statements include income statements, statements of cash flows, and the statement of financial position (i.e., balance sheets).

2. Operational audit. An operational audit reviews some part of a business' operating methods and procedures. The goal is to determine whether the business is operating at its maximum efficiency and effectiveness. Usually, an operational audit assesses efficiency and yields recommendations for improved effectiveness. For example, assume Speedway Motorsports underwent an operational audit to analyze the efficiency and effectiveness of its product distribution system. The result may be that the business uses the auditor's recommendations to develop new methods for transporting products from the production site to retailers.

Table 15.1 Types of Audits

Type of audit	Role of audit	Audit tasks
Financial statement audit	Ensure the accuracy of financial statements	Review documents, records, and other sources of financial evidence
Operational audit	Evaluate the efficiency and effectiveness of organizational activities	Interview employees; analyze processes and written reports
Compliance audit	Determine if specific rules, procedures, or regulations set by higher authorities are being met	Analyze written materials, stated regulations and standards, and methods for meeting these regulations and standards
Integrated audit	Assure both the effectiveness of internal financial reporting and the accuracy of completed financial statements	Document both the accuracy of the financial statements and the management's effectiveness in internally controlling the accounting processes

3. Compliance audit. The goal of the compliance audit is to determine whether the auditee is following the specific rules, regulations, and procedures set by some higher authority. Within collegiate athletics, the NCAA periodically visits member institutions to audit their operations. For example, the association may analyze the system that a college or university uses to ensure student-athlete eligibility. The NCAA has specific rules and regulations with respect to eligibility. Failure to follow these guidelines may lead to rules violations and probation. In an attempt to minimize these violations, the NCAA works with member institutions to develop effective mechanisms for following rules and regulations. In addition, the NCAA has instituted five-year self-studies and peer reviews for collegiate athletic programs as a method of instituting compliance audits.

4. Integrated audit. Because of the Sarbanes-Oxley Act, all publicly traded companies are required to complete an integrated audit. This type of audit includes assurance of both the effectiveness of internal financial reporting and the completed financial statements. The independent auditor must report on both the accuracy of the financial statements and the management's effectiveness in internally controlling the accounting processes. As a public company, Speedway Motorsports must undergo an annual integrated audit.

Materiality and Meaningfulness

One of the most important concepts within auditing is materiality. **Materiality** concerns the levels of misstatement that are allowable in financial information. Because no financial system is perfect,

misstatements do occur. The auditor must determine the level of misstatement that will affect the fairness of the information. For example, a large sport manufacturing company such as Under Armour may have millions of dollars in revenues and expenses. For such an organization, a financial misstatement of $10,000 may be considered immaterial with respect to the overall financial position of the business. A $10,000 misstatement for a small sport business, however, would probably be considered material. In each situation, the auditor must determine where to draw the line.

CONCEPTS INTO PRACTICE

One strategy that some investors use to examine the strength of a company is how much the company pays in audit fees. Audit fees need to be reported in Securities and Exchange Commission filings. Most company's auditing fees are relatively constant unless the company has undergone a major change such as an acquisition or a sale of major assets. Increased audit fees can also show that the auditors have found something requiring additional accounting attention or that they have identified a major concern for the future. Investors can examine similar companies in the same industry to ascertain the normal range of audit fees. Any audit fees that fall outside that range may indicate potential problems.

In general, a misstatement can be considered material if knowledge of the misstatement affects a decision made by a reasonable user of the statements (Arens & Loebbecke, 2006). A misstatement that is relatively small or one that does not affect the overall fairness of the financial statements is considered immaterial. If misstatements are relatively large or pervasively affect the financial documents of an organization, an auditor may not be comfortable in issuing an unqualified auditor's report (see "Receiving the Auditor's Report" later in this chapter). In this case, the auditor may issue a qualified opinion or an adverse opinion about the documents. Obviously, an auditee wants to avoid this result. Such a finding may dramatically decrease the confidence that investors and creditors have in the company's financial statements.

Role of Technology

Technology has drastically changed how businesses acquire, process, and manage financial information. As a result, auditors have changed the manner in which they organize and analyze information. Here we examine two technological advances that have greatly affected auditing.

Electronic Data Processing Systems

Electronic data processing (EDP) systems allow businesses to simplify operations such as accounts payable, payroll, and inventory control. This technology has increased efficiency and accuracy in the reporting of financial information. At the same time, businesses must take steps to make sure that information produced through use of an EDP system is accurate. First, they must ensure that the EDP systems themselves do not have errors. A poor EDP system can result in more misstatements than the old system of human recording and calculating. Second, as always, an EDP system is only as good as the data inputted. Errors in the inputting of data can be costly.

The increased efficiency gained through EDP may, in some cases, result in a loss of internal control. Too often, managers assume that financial information is accurate because it has been generated through an EDP system; this assumption can be costly. For example, a fitness center may use an EDP system to produce a monthly statement of the revenues generated through membership fees. This procedure would appear to be simple, but problems may occur if the payment amounts are inaccurately entered by employees or are not entered in a timely fashion. If membership fees received on the last day of the month are not processed for several days, the monthly statement will not be accurate. An EDP system cannot recognize a discrepancy such as this, yet it is still an obvious accounting error. As the saying goes, "Garbage in, garbage out."

EDP can offer a significant benefit, but if technological hurdles arise, the systems can quickly become worthless. The Y2K scare of the late 1990s is a great example of the possibility of errors caused by technology. Many businesses invested substantial resources toward Y2K compliance in areas such as payroll and finance. As we all know, the investment was wise. January 1, 2000, came and went with few problems attributable to computers and technology. But without instituting precautions and safeguards many businesses could have had substantial technological problems.

Today, more than ever before, businesses rely on computer technology and the Internet. When EDP was first developed, its cost made it attractive to only the largest businesses. Now it is cost-effective for even the smallest businesses. For a relatively low investment in software, any business can have an EDP system that is both powerful and user friendly. These systems have revolutionized the means by which businesses collect, process, and analyze financial information.

Because of the threat of computer viruses and breakdowns, all EDP systems must be backed up. Managers should be able to feel confident that if their primary EDP systems become inoperable, a backup system is in place. Auditors can help with this process. First, through their work with the financial statements, auditors can analyze a client's EDP and make recommendations for ensuring the safety and accuracy of financial information. In addition, businesses should undergo periodic operational audits to ensure the efficiency and effectiveness of their EDP.

Internet and Electronic Mail

Other technological advances that have changed organizational finances and audits are the Internet and electronic mail. Organizations with multiple locations can now communicate much more efficiently. A sporting goods retailer with multiple stores can use technological advances to have the sales from each store automatically sent to a central location so that management can track revenue. If sales are lower on one day as compared with other days, management can investigate what caused the decline to prevent its occurrence in the future. Transactions such as multiple electronic funds transfers from numerous bank accounts now occur without the use of paper and without human contact. Although this process increases efficiency, it leads to new types of problems. Computer fraud is a new concern, and new internal controls have been developed to ensure the accuracy of transactions and processes.

Technology has also had a significant influence on how sports products are bought and sold. Organizations such as professional sports teams, collegiate athletic programs, and sporting goods manufacturers sell their products over the Internet, place orders online, and market their products through websites. Electronic commerce has dramatically changed the sport industry. With the increase in ticket sales through the web, the threat of counterfeit tickets arises. One recent innovation in ticket sales is the use of bar-coded tickets. Most large sports facilities today use handheld bar-code scanning devices to permit entry. This system helps minimize counterfeiting and has reduced costs for sports organizations by permitting customers to print their own tickets. Sports managers must ensure that their systems can track these sales effectively. Auditors must be able to attest to the accuracy of these transactions and the financial statements that result from them.

Added to the problems caused by viruses is the increasing incidence of computer-related crime. Several major computer-related extortion cases have occurred in the last decade when hackers broke into retail websites and stole credit card numbers, threatening to publish the numbers if they were not paid a specified amount. Customers will purchase with confidence only if a website protects financial transactions.

Technology has greatly changed the landscape of auditing and will continue to do so. A sports manager must be prepared to use new technologies not only to make money but also to track these funds effectively.

Benefits of Independent Audits

Companies derive several significant benefits from undergoing periodic independent audits, including societal benefits. Poor decisions that businesses make based on inaccurate financial information can have a negative effect on society. Resources may be mistakenly allotted to inefficient or unworthy projects, thereby decreasing overall economic productivity. Additionally, individual and institutional investors may make poor decisions in selecting investment options. In most instances, investors use corporate financial statements in their investment decision-making processes. Although the positive effect of independent audits on individual businesses is obvious, the societal benefit of audits must not be overlooked. Accurate financial information about businesses is vital for maintaining an efficient economy. Holmes and Burns (1979)

separated the benefits from accurate independent auditing into three categories based on who derives the benefit:

1. Benefits primarily for auditees
   - Independent audits provide credibility and reliability to financial statements.
   - Audits dissuade management and employees from committing acts of fraud.
   - Audited financial statements lessen the likelihood of government audits by ensuring that the basis for the preparation of tax returns and other financial documents is accurate.
   - Audited financial statements increase investor or creditor confidence and broaden the sources of outside financing.
   - Independent audits uncover errors in the auditee's financial records, which may lead to the recovery of lost revenue or may decrease costs.
   - Independent audits ensure that the business is consistently following stated policies and procedures.
2. Benefits primarily for other members of the business community
   - Audited financial statements give vendors and other creditors a credible basis for making decisions about extending credit.
   - Audited statements are a credible basis on which potential and current investors can evaluate investment and management performance.
   - Audited statements provide insurance companies a credible and accurate basis for settling claims for insurance-covered losses.
   - Audited statements provide labor unions and the auditee an objective basis on which to settle disputes over wages and fringe benefits.
   - Audited statements provide the buyer and seller a basis for negotiating the terms for the sale or merger of business entities.
3. Benefits primarily for government entities and the legal community
   - Government agencies gain additional assurance concerning the dependability and accuracy of tax returns and financial reports.
   - Independent audits of financial statements from public interest organizations such as banks and public utilities provide

government agencies with an independent means to focus their special examination resources.

- Audited financial statements give the legal community an independent basis for settling bankruptcy actions.

AUDITING PROCESS

This section of the chapter covers the process of conducting an audit. The first step is to select the appropriate auditor. After describing the selection process, we discuss how a business should prepare for an audit, the various types of audits that can be undertaken, and the auditor's report.

Selecting the Auditor

As stated earlier, an independent auditor plays a vital role in managing the finances of a sport business. Despite any temptation to do so, the auditee should not influence the independent character of the audit. The auditor's report attests to the accuracy of financial statements. Creditors and stockholders have more confidence in organizations that have audits completed by credible auditing firms. Therefore, the selection of an auditor is important. A business should seek out an auditor who has experience in the industry in question. Although audits can be expensive—typical audits for medium-sized firms cost more than $100,000—a specialized auditor in the sport industry is well worth the investment. The top accounting firms such as PricewaterhouseCoopers, Deloitte, and KPMG have departments that specialize in the sport industry.

Each industry has unique characteristics that a specialized auditor can understand without needing to do as much research as other auditors would. For example, professional sports teams have several unique financial traits. Under federal tax laws, new team owners are permitted to depreciate the value of player contracts over five years. The players are treated as a capital investment similar to plants and equipment. Also, the pay structure for players can be complex because of signing bonuses, performance incentives, and deferred payments that are not seen in other industries. A professional team should seek out an auditor with experience in analyzing these types of financial documents.

PROFITS AND LOSSES FOR PRO SPORTS TEAMS

Are the revenue and expense figures of professional sports teams accurate? To obtain concessions from municipalities or labor unions, numerous teams and leagues are claiming that they are losing money. The accuracy of these numbers was called into question a number of times in the early 21st century in both baseball and hockey. Before the 2004-2005 NHL lockout, the league owners claimed that they had lost $224 million in the previous year. *Forbes* magazine, however, analyzed NHL finances and concluded that the league lost only $96 million. When former Securities and Exchange Commission chairman Arthur Levitt Jr. audited the financial records for the 2002-2003 season, he concluded that the league lost $273 million. Thus, the question must be asked: Who is correct? Note that the NHL owners did not cooperate with *Forbes* in their research, and therefore unofficial financial records were used to determine that the NHL lost only $96 million. The players' union, relying on the *Forbes* number, concluded that the league was not negotiating in good faith and that the NHL was not as financially distressed as the league owners claimed. The problem with this stance is that even when using the *Forbes* numbers, the league was still losing almost $100 million a year.

Major League Baseball faced similar auditing-related concerns when Nelson Doubleday accused Bud Selig of allegedly conspiring with a former Andersen consultant to manufacture "phantom losses" for the New York Mets. Doubleday claimed that MLB wanted to devalue his ownership share because another co-owner was trying to buy him out. If the shares could be devalued, the co-owner may have been able to buy out Doubleday at a reduced price. Before that situation, MLB had another financial controversy when 14 former limited partners of the Montreal Expos sued Commissioner Selig, claiming that he conspired to dilute their investment in the team ("Doubleday," 2002).

An inexperienced auditor could make an error that would call into question the accuracy of the team's financial statements.

Public companies need to meet certain requirements as they select their auditing firms. The New York Stock Exchange requires its member corporations to establish a committee to select their auditing firms (Holmes & Burns, 1979). This committee must consist of nonemployees of the corporation. Most firms elect to have their boards of directors choose their independent auditors. The goal of not having management select the auditing firm is to ensure objectivity from the audit. The possibility of fraud within the auditing process would be increased if management selected the auditing firm.

Preparing for the Auditor

After selecting the auditing firm, a business must prepare for the audit. An auditor needs specific types of information to do her job. The following are some of the organizational materials that should be collected in preparation for the auditor.

1. Internally prepared documents. These include operating documents such as sales invoices, purchase orders, general ledgers, payroll records, receiving forms, and other standard accounting worksheets.

2. Externally prepared documents. These include documents such as bank statements, loan documents, and vendor statements.

3. Nonfinancial records. Auditors often need corporate information that is not financial. Documents in this category include articles of incorporation, minutes of organizational meetings, past internal or independent auditors' reports, organizational charts, and job descriptions.

Additionally, independent auditors may need to verify assets physically. For example, they may need to see direct evidence of assets such as inventory, equipment, computers, and office furniture. The auditor may walk through an office to verify that the organization has items such as chairs, desks, and computers that it claims as assets in financial statements.

An auditor may also wish to obtain oral testimony from management, employees, or customers to ensure that the organizational information is accurate. Arrangements should be made so that these people are available to the independent auditor. In general, there are no problems with oral testimony unless there are misstatements—accidental or fraudulent.

The audit examines various business segments. We now focus on the areas of operation that are most important for a sports organization when it is undergoing an internal or independent audit.

Cash Auditing

For many sport businesses, cash is the most important current asset. For example, a fitness center may bring in a large amount of cash on a daily basis through collecting user fees. Businesses or organizations such as a university athletic department that produce sport events also have many cash transactions. Items such as game tickets, team merchandise, and concessions are largely sold through cash transactions (debit cards and credit cards are normally treated similarly to cash transactions). Although customers are using credit cards more often than in the past, sports organizations such as college athletic departments, professional teams, and sports facilities must develop systems to control cash.

Unfortunately, cash is the asset most susceptible to theft and fraud. It is easily transferable, liquid, and difficult to trace. Countless cases of fraud involving cash occur each year. In one example, a small business with two store locations had an employee who was responsible for both reconciling the organization's bank accounts and making the daily deposits. Each location would submit its daily cash amounts to the employee along with a completed bank deposit slip. The employee was then responsible for depositing the cash at the bank. This system might appear to be efficient and logical, but it made cash fraud quite easy to accomplish. The employee simply kept a portion of the daily cash receipts, completed a new deposit slip for the decreased amount, and deposited that amount. Because the employee did the **account reconciliation**, no one noticed that not all the cash made it into the company bank account. On paper, everything seemed to be in order. In reality, the employee was keeping thousands of dollars in company revenue. The person was eventually caught when another employee found an old deposit slip in the garbage. That employee notified the owner of the business, and the fraud was uncovered (Colbert & Bolton, 1998).

The role of the auditor is to ensure that cash assets are not overstated and that financial statements accurately represent the cash level. The usual method is to make sure that cash that should have been collected has been both collected and accurately recorded. For example, an audit of a sporting goods store involves matching the daily sales receipts from the cash registers with the cash deposit slips. All cash that is received through sales should be deposited into the business' bank account. Only the level of cash necessary for daily operations should be left in the cash register. Meigs et al., (1982) make the following suggestions for handling daily cash receipts:

▶ No single employee should be responsible for handling cash transactions from beginning to end. For example, the person who operates the cash register should not oversee the daily cash deposits to the bank.

▶ Cash handling should be separated from cash recording and deposit. This division can be accomplished by having one person open all letters and process all checks. Another person could be responsible for depositing the checks. Thus, each party can independently examine the cash or checks to be deposited to verify the amounts.

▶ Cash receipts should be centralized. For example, a sports facility may sell game tickets at several locations. A system should be developed to track the cash activities at each location, and the cash should ultimately be collected in one location. A lack of cash centralization increases the number of people handling the cash and the likelihood of theft.

▶ Cash receipts should be deposited on a daily basis. Cash should not be left in the place of business for more than one day. The only exception may be a small amount of **petty cash** that is necessary for emergency or relatively small purchases.

▶ When possible, the organization should make all payments by check, credit card, or debit card. Checks, credit cards, and debit cards are easier to track and minimize the likelihood of theft.

Another important responsibility for the auditor is to examine the auditee's management of cash balances to ensure operational efficiency. In some instances, a business may have too much cash on hand. An auditor may recommend that the organization reinvest the cash back into the business or invest in other opportunities. Conversely, the auditor may find that the organization has relatively low cash balances. The business may have problems if it does not have enough cash on hand to meet short-term debt obligations such as accounts payable to vendors or suppliers.

Inventory Auditing

Another large asset for most sport businesses is inventory. Chapter 13 covers inventory- and production-related issues. Apart from its conventional meaning, inventory can be defined as products and materials that have a life of less than one year. For some sport businesses, inventories are not their greatest asset. For professional teams, whose primary assets are the players, inventory exists, but it is not as valuable as the players. Minor league players might be considered inventory, but they have little value until they make it to the highest professional ranks. The value of a minor league team stems from its goodwill. Recall that goodwill is any value greater than the team's book value that others might pay to purchase the team. If the team's assets are worth $1 million, but someone is willing to pay $2 million to purchase it, then the team has $1 million in goodwill. The goodwill is value inherent in the minor league team, which might be based on the fact that the number of minor league teams is limited, that the team has a good relationship with a major league team, or that the team plays in a brand new facility that has numerous amenities.

Although calculating goodwill is difficult, auditing items such as inventory and other assets can help establish a potential value range for goodwill. For example, through auditing the inventory a team might discover boxes of old uniforms that might seem to have limited monetary value. When used as a promotional item in an old-timers game, however, they can generate significant value based on the goodwill associated with the team's history. Inventory auditing will not determine a team's goodwill, but it can be used in conjunction with other valuation techniques to develop a more accurate value.

Inventory auditing is the process of determining exactly what inventory exists and what the value of the inventory is. Tracking entails the process of identifying where inventory might be located and what the value of the inventory is. Inventory counting, on the other hand, refers to the process of identifying exactly how many units of a given item exist in inventory.

Internal control is a key to managing inventory successfully. A sports manager must develop a system that tracks all inventory from the time that it is purchased to the time that it is distributed to consumers or users. Inventory must be purchased, received, recorded, stored, and distributed. Management is responsible for developing internal systems to perform all these operations efficiently (Whittington & Pany, 2006). At any point in this process an item might get lost, broken, stolen, or become obsolete, and only through auditing can a company truly know the status of most of their assets.

An accurate inventory count, whether of retail goods or materials used for production, leads to increased efficiency. Technology has been a key in improving systems of internal control. Computerized systems allow managers to track inventory quickly. This capability is especially helpful to businesses such as Under Armour that are involved in the production of sport-related goods. Inventory is a large component of their total assets.

Two strategies in particular can be used to improve inventory control and make the process of auditing, both internal and independent, much simpler. The first strategy is to have one centralized location where inventory is received and distributed (Holmes & Burns, 1979). For example, a concessionaire may be responsible for overseeing a dozen or more sales locations in a major sports facility. The concessionaire must ensure that each location has the products that will be prepared and sold. Inventory tracking is more accurate if all products are distributed from one central area. This arrangement allows management greater control over all products.

A second strategy is to develop a computer scanning system to track inventory (see chapter 13). Sporting goods stores are an example of a business that typically uses a computer scanning system. In most sporting goods stores products are bar coded. The computerized bar codes, usually placed on products by the manufacturer, are used to track material, determine its availability, and facilitate the sale. This type of integrated system allows management to determine exact inventory levels. When stock level is depleted, management has the information and can order more inventories from suppliers. Bar codes are another example of internal controls.

Major manufacturing plants also use computer tracking systems. Intermediate goods are maintained in some type of storage facility until they are required for the manufacturing process. Most often, computer systems are used to track when these intermediate goods are received, stored, and distributed to the production line.

With respect to auditing, technology and computerization have made it much easier to ensure that financial statements report inventory accurately. Computer programs can quickly produce reports on the types, amounts, and condition of inventory. Another important aspect of inventory auditing is the determination of fair value. An auditor must base the value of inventory on its quantity, quality, and condition. Besides examining computer-generated inventory reports, the auditor may physically locate inventory within the organization. Last, operational audits may lead to recommendations that will improve the efficiency of inventory control systems.

Plant, Property, and Equipment Auditing

Plant, property, and equipment are similar to inventory in that they are physical assets. The difference is that plant, property, and equipment are physical assets that have a productive life greater than one year. Examples of plant, property, and equipment for a collegiate athletic program are computers, facilities, and equipment such as goalposts, motor vehicles, and playing fields.

In the process of auditing, the auditor ascertains that all plant, property, and equipment that are listed as assets really exist. This determination is usually not difficult for assets such as land, buildings, and heavy machinery. Often the difficult task is determining a fair value for these assets, especially with assets such as land that may fluctuate in value over time. Also, depreciation must be factored into the determination of fair value for plant, property, and equipment.

As with inventory, bar codes are often used to track equipment such as computers, copiers, and office furniture. Bar codes are usually placed on these items to identify the owners. Specialized nonremovable bar-coded stickers reduce the ability of a potential thief to hide the true ownership of the item. An auditor may periodically visit various organizational sites to ensure that items such as computers are found where they are supposed to be located.

Payroll Auditing

All sport businesses, regardless of size, scope, and mission, have one thing in common. They all have employees who are paid a wage in return for their labor. The ultimate result of a payroll system is that each employee receives a paycheck. The process of arriving at this final result can be complex. First, a system must be established to track the correct amount to be paid. For employees paid on an hourly basis, a system must be developed to determine the number of hours worked. Employees may be required to fill out weekly time cards or use computerized time card machines. Payroll auditing is the process of tracking employee compensation to ensure accuracy. The process determines whether employees are working too much overtime or whether personnel costs are in line with budgetary projections.

Computerized hand scanners are a new technology that has made auditing employee activity simpler and can improve the accuracy and reliability of the payroll process. The system requires making a handprint of all employees. A machine is then installed that identifies the handprint of each employee as she arrives for and departs from work. The computerized system can then calculate the total number of hours that each employee works. Although such systems may be expensive to install, they can dramatically decrease the probability of payroll fraud. Employees cannot fraudulently have other people clock in for them or fill out false time cards. The system also ensures that employees receive an accurate amount of pay. Other technology exists to accomplish accurate tracking, such as swipe cards, retina scanners, and computerized punch systems that can track personnel activity.

Besides determining the amount of gross pay, payroll preparation involves calculating income tax deductions; Social Security payments; and deductions for benefits such as retirement, union dues, and health insurance. An efficient and accurate system must be used to determine these payments. Failure to make payments for items such as federal or state income taxes will quickly lead to government audits.

When possible, the various payroll duties should be handled by different people. For example, within Under Armour's payroll department one person should not be responsible for the timekeeping system and the determination of employee wages. This person could fraudulently overpay employees.

With respect to distributing paychecks, a system must be in place to ensure that employees receive their proper paychecks. One central location should be used to distribute all paychecks. Also, employees should be required to sign a document verifying that they have received their checks. In large organizations, employees should be required to show proper identification. Additionally, unclaimed paychecks should not be left in the business' offices for an extended period because they are subject to possible theft. The paychecks should be deposited in a special bank account for unclaimed wages. To reconcile the firm's accounts, efforts should be made to distribute the unclaimed checks to the people to whom they were issued.

Most large sports organizations now require employees to have a checking or savings account with a bank or other financial institution. The employees' pay is electronically wired to these accounts on payday. This system limits the likelihood of any type of fraud because no physical paycheck is produced. Employees are then issued paper receipts of their pay and deductions, or these records are accessible through a secure online computerized system.

Last, at no time should employees be paid with cash. Tracking cash is extremely difficult. An employee may claim that he did not receive his pay and request additional money. In addition, little documentation is associated with most cash distributions, so auditing a payroll department is difficult. Checks are much easier to track because the employer receives the canceled checks and the withdrawals appear on the bank statements of the business.

Receiving the Auditor's Report

For public corporations, the auditor is required to submit an independent auditor's report that is unbiased. Auditors usually provide a report when completing an audit for private corporations, nonprofit organizations, and government agencies. Of the several types of auditing reports, the standard unqualified auditor's report is the most common (Arens & Loebbecke, 2006). The report is unqualified if no information is lacking and nothing that differs from the standard accounting practices set forth by the Auditing Standards Board is found. The standard unqualified auditor's report has seven parts. Can you identify these seven parts in the auditor's report example?

1. Report title. Auditing standards require that a report have a title that includes the word *independent.*

2. Audit report address. The report is usually addressed to the auditee, its board of directors, or stockholders.

3. Introductory paragraph. This paragraph explains management's role and responsibilities as they apply to the auditor (i.e., that management helped provide documentation or access to facilities). It also lists all the financial statements that were audited and the periods of those statements.

4. Scope paragraph. This paragraph describes the nature of the audit and the scope of what the auditor did in the audit. It also outlines the business areas examined by the auditor.

EXAMPLE OF A STANDARD UNQUALIFIED INDEPENDENT AUDITOR'S REPORT FOR A SPORT ORGANIZATION

Brady, Kelsey, Adams, Delong,
   and Crimmins, PC
Certified Public Accountants
Box 324
Noelle Trunfio Park Central
Philadelphia, PA 18360
312-555-4433

Independent Auditor's Report

To the Stockholders
Under Armour

We have audited the balance sheets of Under Armour as of July 31, 2010 and 2011, and the related statements of retained earnings, income, and cash flows for the years then ended. These financial statements are the responsibility of Under Armour's management. Our responsibility is to express an opinion on these financial statements based on our audits.

We conducted our audits in accordance with generally accepted auditing standards. Those standards require that we perform the audit to obtain assurance about whether the financial statements are free of material misstatement. An audit includes examining, on a test basis, evidence supporting the amounts and disclosures in the financial statements. An audit also includes assessing the accounting principles used and significant estimates made by management, as well as evaluating the overall financial statement presentation. We believe that our audits provide a reasonable basis for our opinion.

In our opinion, the financial statements referred to above present fairly, in all material respects, the financial position of Under Armour as of July 31, 2010 and 2011, and the results of its operations and its cash flows for the years then ended in conformity with generally accepted accounting principles.

Brady, Kelsey, Adams, Delong, and Crimmins, PC, CPAs
December 10, 2011

Arens, Alvin A.; Elder, Randal J.; Beasley, Mark, AUDITING AND ASSURANCE SERVICES: AN INTEGRATED APPROACH, 11th edition, © 2006, Pg.47. Adapted by permission of Pearson Education, Inc., Upper Saddle River, NJ.

5. Opinion paragraph. This last paragraph states the auditor's opinion. Within this section, the auditor attests to the accuracy of the financial information provided by the auditee.

6. Name of the certified public accountant's firm.

7. Audit report date.

The other possible audit opinions are as follows:

♦ Qualified opinion

♦ Adverse opinion

♦ Disclaimer of opinion

Although the use of qualified reports is common, these reports are being examined more carefully in the wake of the recent accounting scandals involving Enron, Tyco, and WorldCom. A report is qualified because information is lacking or because other problems prevented the auditor from giving a more complete report. In a qualified opinion, the auditor will state that the company has departures from standard practices or perhaps that the company did not give him full access to necessary documents. Companies, auditors, and the government are all thinking about how to develop appropriate reports that contain as much additional information as possible to move the final report from qualified to unqualified status.

RESPONDING TO FINANCIAL PROBLEMS

Every sport organization will face challenges identified either before or during an audit. The primary question is how organizations and executives will respond. Many organizations find solutions to their financial problems, but others do not and end up going out of business. For example, David Barton Gym filed for Chapter 11 bankruptcy protection in 2011. The chain filed for protection after opening high-end gyms and ran up debt of $65.5 million against revenue of $28.3 million. The chain did not get into trouble through financial fraud, but through expanding too quickly. The gym formed an alliance with a lower-end health club chain from California. Such an alliance would not stop bankruptcy proceedings, but it was designed to show that the company was proactive so that they could try to restructure their debt (Pasquarelli, 2011)

Other organizations pursue cost cutting when they discover that they are overspending. In 2011 the University of Maryland announced cutting 8 of their 27 sponsored sports to stop the financial drain. The proposal by a special commission would have canceled the sports unless the teams and alumni would be able to raise enough funds to operate the teams for the next eight years (Tkach, 2011, November).

Mergers and cutting sports are far-reaching responses, but a more common approach is to change policies and procedures. Some of these policies and procedures are imposed by government regulators, whereas others are developed by organizations in response to problems identified in an audit. One law that may prevent future problems is the Tennessee School Support Organization Financial Accountability Act, which was passed to prevent fraud and abuse with booster clubs and went into effect in 2008. The act requires every school principal to have ultimate control over booster clubs. If a club is not acting responsibly, the principal can dissolve it. The act requires booster clubs to provide officers' names, the date of their election, draft bylaws, and annual goals (Popke, 2008). Examples of policies or procedures that can help address problems include requiring all cash receipts to be deposited into a lock box or organization safe, requiring all individuals dealing with cash to be bonded, and backing up all records at multiple sites to ensure redundancy and allow more people access to records. These polices can help prevent financial fraud.

Financial fraud can be a major problem for a sport business. Fraud can take many forms. It can be as simple as theft of merchandise by a clerk in a sporting goods store or the filing of false time cards by employees in a sporting goods manufacturing plant. Inventory and payroll auditing are two of the types of auditing reviewed in this chapter that can help detect these types of fraud.

Fraud can also involve complex schemes to embezzle millions of dollars from a sport business. Later in the chapter, we look at the case of John Spano. Spano committed bank fraud in an attempt to acquire a professional hockey franchise. In part because of poor auditing of financial records submitted by Spano, several banks and the NHL were led to believe that Spano was a highly successful businessman. Ultimately, this appraisal was found to be incorrect. But Spano came close to committing one of the largest frauds in sport history.

Fraud does not always mean theft. Managers may also prepare inaccurate financial statements in an effort to misrepresent the financial position of an organization. In 1997 management of Paragon Construction International, a subsidiary of Golden Bear Golf, underrepresented its losses by more than $20 million. Management allegedly hid expenses and falsified records to conceal poor financial performance (Mullen, 1998). Shareholders and bondholders were injured when they made financial decisions about Golden Bear based on these fraudulent financial statements. The fraudulent acts were eventually uncovered, and Golden Bear filed its financial statements again. The new statements showed that the company had lost eight times the amount earlier reported. Stock in the company was eventually delisted from the NASDAQ stock exchange, and a class action lawsuit was filed on behalf of investors and creditors. In December 1999 Golden Bear settled the lawsuit and paid investors $0.75 for each of the 2.7 million shares of outstanding stock. The money was paid by Golden Bear Golf, its insurance provider, and its auditor (*Golden Bear Golf*, 1999).

Fraud can be a serious financial problem for a small sport business with limited resources. These businesses cannot easily recover from fraud. One incident of fraud could lead to bankruptcy, dissolution, or both. Additionally, small businesses are susceptible to fraud because employees usually have multiple duties, so internal control is difficult. Often, many employees have access to assets such as cash, inventory, and office equipment. Nevertheless, steps can be taken to minimize the likelihood of fraud. Colbert and Bolton (1998) make the following recommendations for small businesses:

▶ Segregation of duties. Duties such as depositing cash and reconciling bank accounts should be given to different staff members. Also, different employees should complete duties such as preparing and signing checks. This policy will allow for a system of checks and balances so that no single person has total unfettered control.

▶ Inventory of assets. To prevent assets such as plant, property, and equipment from being stolen, a business should undergo periodic inventory checks. Each item listed in the financial statements as plant, property, and equipment should be physically located. In addition, the financial statements should be cross-checked to ensure that every listed asset is physically present.

▶ Mandated vacations. Each employee should use at least a portion of her allotted vacation time each year, and vacation days should ideally be taken as a block. This policy is an effective way to detect fraud. Some fraud cases, especially with cash, occur on a recurring or daily basis. Detecting the fraud is much easier if the employee is away from the business for an extended period.

▶ Analytical procedures. Simple analytical procedures such as tracking the daily deposits, weekly sales, and monthly sales totals may be enough to uncover some fraud.

▶ Practical considerations. For a small business, the first four recommendations may be difficult to implement. Employees may not want to take their vacations in a block, or the number of employees may be insufficient to allow segregation of all duties. Besides observing these recommendations, smaller companies can take additional practical steps to minimize fraud. A small business owner may request that his bank send the business' bank statements to his home address instead of to the business. This arrangement allows the owner the opportunity to review deposit slips, bank statements, and canceled checks before other employees have access to them. This procedure not only may allow the owner to uncover fraud but also may deter employees from committing fraud.

Fraud can include simple fraudulent activities such as taking dollar bills from a cash register to

INFAMOUS FRAUD IN THE SPORT INDUSTRY

One of the most infamous cases of fraud in the sport industry occurred in 1997. John Spano, a 33-year-old Dallas businessman, bought the New York Islanders professional hockey team. He agreed to pay John Pickett, the previous team owner, $165 million. At the time, Spano claimed to have $55 million in available assets and a net worth of more than $230 million. Spano stated that he had a $107 million trust fund, $52 million in Treasury bills, and $40 million in a money market account. He also claimed to have made millions of dollars in the South African stock market (Ranalli, 1997).

To finance the deal, Spano obtained an $80 million loan from Boston's Fleet Financial Group. One of the largest lenders in the sport industry, Fleet had financed deals for teams such as the Baltimore Ravens, Washington Redskins, Phoenix Coyotes, and Los Angeles Lakers (Munroe, 1997). Unfortunately, Fleet was so enthusiastic about lending funds to Spano that it failed to

confirm Spano's net worth. As Fleet would later learn, Spano's actual net worth was less than $2 million.

Spano began by lying about his personal wealth and falsifying financial documents to obtain approval for a bank loan from the Fleet Financial Group. As part of the team purchase, on April 7, 1997, Spano was required to make a $24.4 million payment that was to cover the down payment for the team acquisition as well as interest prepayments on the bank loan. Spano did not make this payment, but he did give the bank a wire-transfer number as proof that the funds were available. The wire-transfer number, however, was a fake (Ranalli, 1997).

Shortly after the missed payment, the NHL, John Pickett, and Fleet Financial Group started to question Spano's net worth. Federal investigators quickly uncovered Spano's scheme. Spano had begun by allegedly misrepresenting his financial wealth to Joseph Lynch, an executive for

(continued)

Detroit-based Comerica Bank. On the basis of financial statements supplied by Spano, Lynch attested to Spano's claimed net worth of over $230 million. However, Lynch did not obtain independent verification of the financial documents supplied by Spano. Spano then used the support from Comerica Bank to secure the $80 million loan from Fleet Financial Group ("Rumblings," 1997).

Spano's trouble began in earnest on April 7, 1997, when he was to make the $24.4 million payment to Fleet and Pickett. Obviously, he did not have the necessary funds. At that time he provided the fake wire-transfer number to Fleet. In addition, Fleet Bank received a fax letter from Lynch verifying Spano's ability to make the $24.4 million payment. Federal investigators learned that the letter was a forgery. Spano had written the letter and reprogrammed his fax machine to make it appear that the letter had originated from Lynch's office. Investigators knew it was a forgery because it bore marks that were identical to those on a fax machine in one of Spano's companies ("Rumblings," 1997).

In July 1997 federal authorities pressed bank fraud charges against Spano. At the time, a Long Island newspaper reported that Spano was living in the Cayman Islands. But Spano eventually surrendered to federal authorities and was charged with six counts of fraud in three states—Texas, Massachusetts, and New York. If he had been convicted of all charges, Spano would have faced up to 60 years in prison ("Business briefcase," 1997). After considerable negotiations between the federal government and defense attorneys, Spano agreed to a plea bargain. He pleaded guilty to six counts of fraud, two each in Texas, Massachusetts, and New York. In January 1998 Spano was sentenced to all six counts in New York and faced up to 63 months in prison. At the time, several federal investigations were still ongoing related to alleged mail and wire fraud committed by Spano in New York and Massachusetts (Chase, 1998).

The fallout from Spano's attempt to misrepresent himself financially was considerable. On July 20, 1997, David Splaine resigned his position as senior vice president for Fleet Financial Group. Splaine was the loan officer who had approved the $80 million loan to Spano. Splaine had failed to confirm Spano's real net worth (Vennochi, 1997). In addition, investigators for Comerica Bank learned that Joseph Lynch had been a guest of Spano's at a four-star hotel on Long Island at a cost of over $2,000. The bank had clear policies stating that employees were not permitted to receive gifts, fees, or vacations from clients. In January 1998 Lynch resigned from his position with Comerica Bank ("Briefly," 1998).

As federal authorities further investigated Spano's business dealings, they uncovered several other acts of fraud. In one bizarre business deal, Spano formed a partnership with Lenco Holdings, a South African company. The partnership was formed to sell kitchen pots and pans. Spano informed Lenco that he had secured an order for the cookware from the Nordstrom department store chain. Spano then allegedly sent a fraudulent Nordstrom invoice to Lenco, and Lenco in turn sent Spano the cookware to deliver it to Nordstrom. Spano, however, failed to pay the $1.9 million due to Lenco for the cookware. The location of the now infamous cookware is still unknown (Bedell, 1997).

Spano also owed more than $250,000 to a Dallas law firm that worked for him during his attempt to acquire the New York Islanders. In addition, Spano owed more than $2.4 million to two Dallas investment companies for loans that they had made to him (Bedell, 1997).

The case of John Spano is unique in the sport industry, in which there have been few cases of financial fraud. But as the professional sport industry becomes more profitable, the likelihood of financial fraud increases. The John Spano case served as a wake-up call for all professional sports leagues. As a result, the NHL and other leagues have placed greater emphasis on verifying the financial position of prospective owners. Similar steps are now taken by MLB after a scandal involving the first owner of the Colorado Rockies. Owner Michael Monus, who was chairman of Phar-Mor pharmacies, improperly used corporate assets to acquire sports teams. He funneled $10 million from Phar-Mor into a then fledgling and now defunct basketball league, the World Basketball League (Schroeder & Schiller, 1992). Monus was convicted of a 109-count indictment, including charges of mail, wire, and bank fraud.

With a major case hitting the headlines, it could be assumed that the NHL would prevent any such future embarrassments. Several years later, however, they faced another major fraud case when William "Boots" Del Biaggio III was caught engaged in the same type of activity. He had started out by buying a minority interest in the San Jose Sharks and then bought part of a USHL team (River City Lancers). He tried to buy the Pittsburg Penguins in 2005 but failed to close on the $120 million offer. In 2007 he became a partial owner of the Nashville Predators. One year later he was charged with security fraud in the sums of millions of dollars. He ended up pleading guilty in conjunction with the $110 million loans that he took out to help buy part of the team (Mickle, 2009). Del Biaggio was sentenced to eight years in prison and responsibility to repay close to $67 million.

Del Biaggio set his crime in motion by turning to a financially strapped stockbroker friend who owed him $2 million. According to federal prosecutors and the SEC, the friend e-mailed Del Biaggio account statements from several wealthy clients showing tens of millions of dollars' worth of stock holdings. Del Biaggio then doctored the account statements by cutting out the clients' names, pasting in his own, and presenting them to the banks and NHL owners as collateral. Auditors examining the stockbroker's books uncovered the fraud in 2008 (CBS Sports.com, 2009).

elaborate schemes. The more elaborate the scheme is, the easier it is to steal large sums of money, but the most elaborate schemes are the hardest to maintain in a way that can prevent detection over the long run. Thus, some elaborate schemes continue for a couple of years. One of the most famous schemes in the past 100 years was the Ponzi scheme orchestrated by Bernie Madoff. A Ponzi scheme is named after Charles Ponzi, who convinced a large number of people in the 1920s to invest with him by promising large returns on their investment. He paid off his initial investors with new moneys coming in. Additional investors followed as people told their friends how well their investment was paying off. In this environment more and more people were investing money. As long as additional people invested, Ponzi was able to repay earlier investors. The fraud was uncovered when new investment slowed and he did not have any extra cash to pay back investors.

Likewise, sport schemes can be simple acts such as stealing money from a bake sale or highly elaborate schemes. One elaborate scheme involved a sport equipment refurbishing company. A scheme in which Circle System Group of Easton, Pennsylvania, billed clients, primarily schools in New Jersey, for work that was never done, inflated their prices, collected twice for the same work, and submitted bogus contract bids was uncovered only after a decade of deceit. The indictment against the company claimed that it curried favor with school officials by lavishing insiders with gifts such as computers, televisions, and golf outings. The company attempted to recoup their bribes by charging the schools for fake expenses (Perez-Pena, 2011). Thus, the company would send two bills for the same service, be paid twice, and then split some

of the second payment with an inside person at the school. The fraud allegedly spanned 13 states, numerous high schools, and at least two colleges.

CONCLUSION

Financial statement auditing is the objective examination of financial statements that are prepared by an organization. An auditor examines these statements to determine whether they have been prepared according to generally accepted accounting standards. Financial audits are important because they ensure the accuracy of financial statements and deter management and employees from committing theft and fraud. Audits also lend credibility to financial statements, which can increase confidence on the part of other companies and investors, making it easier for businesses to work with them. Last, accurate financial statements lessen the possibility of government audits.

Two other types of audits are operational audits and compliance audits. Operational audits examine a business' policies and procedures to determine whether they are appropriate and efficient. These audits can result in organizational changes that can affect a business' long-term efficiency and productivity. Compliance audits are undertaken to ensure that a business is adhering to rules and regulations established by an outside group such as a government agency. For example, any large employer in the United States must meet workplace regulations that have been developed by the Occupational Safety and Health Administration.

Technology has had a significant effect on auditing and financial operations in the sport industry over the past two decades. It allows businesses to process financial data quickly and efficiently and generate financial reports. Also, technology has been used to improve operational systems in areas such as payroll, inventory control, and accounting, which are critical to auditing. Last, technology has helped minimize fraud and theft. Even so, fraud can occur in any organization. For that reason, keeping track of financial records is important. A potential fraud committer will normally not undertake a fraudulent act if he knows that the business is meticulous with its monitoring of books and accounts.

Class Discussion Topics

1. What are the two fundamental roles of auditing?

2. Provide three specific examples of how the operational efficiency of an organization may be improved through the use of internal audits.

3. How would you go about auditing Speedway Motorsports, a high school athletic program, a fitness facility, and a Division I college athletic department?

4. How can you balance the need for making sure that accounts are accurate and the need to allow people to work without the fear that someone is watching their every move?

5. Why is accuracy important?

6. What are the primary benefits to an organization of using an independent auditor?

7. What are the advantages of using an independent auditor versus using an internal auditor?

8. Is it ethically correct to "permanently borrow" office supplies?

9. How would you approach someone if you thought that she had engaged in fraud?

10. Provide two examples of advances in technology that have changed the manner in which audits occur.

chapter 16

Exit Strategy

Chapter Objectives

After studying this chapter, you should be able to do the following:

- ◆ Describe the techniques that can help spot financial trouble.
- ◆ Understand how to reorganize a troubled business.
- ◆ Appreciate how a company can avoid bankruptcy by selling assets.
- ◆ Describe the process of selling a business.
- ◆ Calculate the value of a sport business.

At various times during the life cycle of a business, the going may get tough. Bills may go unpaid, debtors may not pay accounts receivable on time, shipments may be late or be canceled, or distributors may stop extending credit. A host of problems can force a business owner to think about various options. Such options are as diverse as the owners themselves. Some owners may just decide to transfer the business to a family member or a current business partner. Others may consider selling the company or just selling the assets. Still others may simply close shop or, worse, be forced to close shop. No matter what strategy or technique the owner ultimately applies, each has particular legal and financial ramifications that the individual needs to consider to avoid increasing financial obligations or to reduce potential costs.

When management is stretched to the point of no return they often try to resolve immediate difficulties rather than examine long-term financial solutions. Such short-term thinking can result in lost concessions, reduced bargaining power with creditors, or other long-term ramifications.

This chapter explains what to do at the point of no return. We start by examining red flags that might signal financial trouble. The chapter ends with an analysis of what is required to sell a business and how to determine the value of a business that is being sold.

RED FLAGS

Before deciding to terminate operations, a business needs to know when it is in trouble. Most businesses cannot just decide to close their doors; they usually have financial obligations such as accounts payable, long-term labor contracts, long-term lease obligations, repayment to equity investors, and debts. The decision to close is not an easy one, nor is it made without significant managerial forethought. Most executives take pride in their managerial skills and would not want to be remembered as the person who lost a business.

Fortunately, a number of indicators can help signal financial trouble and provide adequate warning to an executive. For example, if orders start declining significantly, a business can examine the reasons and take corrective action to avoid losing market share. If a new competitor comes into the market with a more advanced and cheaper product, then the business needs to adjust to stay competitive. Key factors associated with business failures include economic weakness, industry downturns, poor location, too much debt, too little

capital, and countless others. These concerns can lead to temporary cash flow problems that can often be worked out. Sometimes, however, the concerns indicate a permanent problem.

One sign of trouble is a lender's request for early repayment of a loan. A bank or other lender may call the loan under certain conditions; the primary reason is poor financial performance. If a sport business has been losing money steadily for several years, banks may feel uncomfortable with their loans and demand immediate repayment. The following are other conditions under which a bank might call a loan or not renew a line of credit (Broni, 1999):

- Loan covenants have been repeatedly violated.
- The bank is losing money on the relationship.
- New bank managers favor a different loan mix or institute new policies.
- The bank does not understand or is uncomfortable with the industry segment.
- The bank's credit exposure in the industry segment is too great.
- A loan guarantor's financial condition has deteriorated.
- The bank has lost faith in the business' management team.

If a bank or lending institution pulls the plug, the business needs to establish a policy to deal with the lost cash. The first step is often to negotiate a short-term extension to try to resolve any problems or secure new funding. If the business is on strong financial ground, approaching another bank might be easy. If a problem caused the bank to pull the funds, asking the bank what the problem was might be worthwhile. If the problem is one that can be fixed, such as untimely reporting, then the business owner can explain this to another potential lender and take measures to correct the problem.

If the business has assets, the assets could help secure needed funds. Asset-based loans, as the name implies, can be obtained on the basis of the existing inventory or accounts receivable. If the business owns a valuable asset such as buildings or land, these could be pledged as collateral to secure more funds. If these options are not available, the business might need to approach a commercial finance company that specializes in "unbankable" loans. Because these loans are riskier, they entail a higher interest rate. The business may also need to report earnings frequently to keep the lender abreast of financial conditions. After the business can show sustained success and compliance with loan terms for one to two years, the owner can usually apply again for conventional bank loans.

Losing a bank loan is just one sign that a business is in trouble. A business that cannot pull itself through the hard financial times may have to resort to informal or formal attempts to satisfy debt holders. Debt holders can be satisfied through informal reorganization or liquidation, bankruptcy, removal of assets, or selling of the business.

INFORMAL REORGANIZATION

Informal reorganization allows a business to recover and reestablish itself after facing a temporary financial crisis. These voluntary plans in which all parties try to come to an agreement are often called workouts. Workouts are successful only if the debtor is a good moral risk, if the debtor can show the ability to recover, and if the general business conditions are favorable for recovery (Brigham & Gapenski, 1994).

The informal reorganization process comprises extensions and composition. Extensions are extensions of the time allowed for repaying a debt. If a debt is owed and due in one year, an extension could be worked out for the borrower to repay the debt in two years instead. Composition is the process of asking to repay a lower amount. A debt holder would rather receive $900 from the company versus only $500 in bankruptcy proceedings from a $1,000 debt. Most often a workout involves a combination of these two methods.

CONCEPTS INTO PRACTICE

Assume that Under Armour (UA) owes several lenders $10 million. The company might be able to develop a workout in which it pays 25% of the debt immediately and 20% a year for the next three years. Thus, in four years, UA will have repaid 85% of the original debt, and the debt will be discharged.

Although lenders might not receive the entire amount they are owed, most lenders would be happy to recover 85% of the original loaned amount versus possibly nothing, or a much smaller amount, if the borrower goes bankrupt.

Not all banks are willing to engage in workouts, but most understand the value of negotiating the best deal they can to receive the largest possible share of their initial loan. The lenders might demand interest payments during the payback period to help cover the extension and might also demand additional security, such as personal pledges or asset-backed pledges.

INFORMAL LIQUIDATION

Informal reorganization is effective if the company can turn around, but some companies cannot fix their problems. If the company's debt is larger than its net worth, the company will probably need to go through bankruptcy protection (discussed in Chapter 5). But if the company has more assets than debt, it is "worth more dead than alive." **Assignment** is the term used for the informal liquidation process. Lenders normally obtain a greater return through assignment than through bankruptcy. For that reason, lenders should focus on encouraging informal reorganization or liquidation rather than trying to force a company into bankruptcy.

Banks and other lenders are not the only options available when times become rough. When financial concerns arise, a business can sometimes look inside itself to find an answer. One such answer lies in liquidating assets such as stocks or other liquid assets. If no such assets exist, the business might have to sell other assets such as property.

REMOVAL OF BUSINESS ASSETS

A business owner might decide to condense a business by removing assets. Selling assets can reduce business costs or raise cash. Such transactions are often highlighted on annual reports as a footnote indicating a one-time write-off. Otherwise, the transactions would appear to boost the company's income when there is no possibility of ever generating those levels of funds again. Selling assets, or downsizing, occurs frequently. The Boston Celtics once owned their own television and radio stations but sold them because those assets did not fit into the team's business plans.

Owners can use several techniques to downsize a business and remove assets so that the new business will be smaller. The primary reason that a company would want to downsize is reduced income. Instead of closing the business, a business owner might wish to downsize and hope that at a later date it could again grow. The first technique is taking out profits as dividends.

Dividends could be paid to the owner rather than reinvested into the business. Dividends can be paid at any time, but they cannot be paid if such payments would make the company insolvent (Nicholas, 1990). A business that is paying dividends must check government regulations, articles of incorporation, and bylaws to make sure that it is observing all dividend restrictions. Individual shareholders can sue and recover damages for illegally paid dividends.

Other ways in which owners can remove assets from a business include increasing their own salaries, paying themselves bonuses, and funding benefits of various kinds. If a business owner wishes to increase her salary and the business is incorporated, the board of directors, shareholders, or both might have to approve the new salary. Owners of smaller businesses such as the owners of a fitness center may be able to take out as much as they want in salaries, especially if they do not have any debt. Business owners who have outstanding debt can still pay themselves a larger salary as long as the salary is reasonable. A salary could be considered unreasonable if it leaves the company insolvent or if the IRS views it as a way to give the business a tax deduction instead of paying nondeductible dividends (Nicholas, 1990). A salary is considered reasonable if it is justified based on such variables as extra work, more duties, or exceptional service.

Business owners can also compensate themselves for independent projects in the same way that an independent contractor is paid. Owners can pay themselves commissions on sales to remove additional dollars from the business. In bankruptcy proceedings, debtors would be unlikely to contest a commission payment if it was a payment for a legitimate service. If, on the other hand, the owner did not do any work to earn the extra money, then a debtor could challenge such payments and demand that they be returned to the bankruptcy estate.

Money can also be removed through paying bonuses. The IRS might try to fight a bonus as a disguised dividend, but the businesses can tie the bonus to the compensation package to protect its reasonableness. Similarly, a business owner can receive significant fringe benefits in the form of game tickets, company cars, and travel to business conferences. Owners who are considered employees could also receive employee benefits such as insurance, pensions, financial counseling, employee stock purchase plans, and any other benefit afforded to employees.

A business owner can loan himself money from the business. The risk of being rejected for the loan is eliminated, and leisurely repayment plans can be developed. The loan could also be interest free, and the owner might not have to pay taxes on the loaned amount. Whenever self-dealing occurs, however, the potential for abuse can arise and lead to disastrous results. The Rigas family, founders of cable television giant Adelphia, was under investigation in 2002 for off-balance-sheet loans that, among other things, helped support the Buffalo Sabres to the tune of $76.5 million. At the time of the loans the Sabres were owned by the Rigas family (Grover & Lowry, 2002). Issuing inappropriate loans can cause an incorporated business owner to lose her liability shield if a debtor pierces the corporate veil. Thus, even if you are loaning yourself money, you need to document the transaction adequately.

Finally, a business owner can sell or lease property to the business (Nicholas, 1990). If the owners of a fitness center owned a vacant lot, they could sell the lot to the fitness center for a price slightly above the market value and then build a new facility on the lot. Because the fitness center is privately owned, the owners would be the primary beneficiaries of the sale. But if the land was in their name and the fitness center was incorporated, then any

HORSES HEADING OFF TRACK

Bankruptcy can provide an opportunity to grow again. In 2004 Fair Grounds horse racing track was in bankruptcy after it failed to pay Louisiana horsemen $90 million, from underpaying video poker proceeds to racing purses. The New Orleans track initially entered into an agreement to sell 86% of the track to a horse owner for $40 million, but it received an offer of $47 million from Churchill Downs ("Churchill Downs," 2004). Thus, although the ownership changed, the city did not lose the horse track as a valuable community asset.

debts owed by the fitness center could not be repaid with proceeds from selling the land, because the lot belongs to the owners as individuals and not to the fitness center.

Despite the many options for withdrawing assets from a business, most business owners would rather just sell the business in its entirety and obtain the funds immediately rather than in a piecemeal fashion.

SELLING A BUSINESS

Any business goes through ups and downs, but owners are sometimes not willing to accept the stress associated with such cyclical patterns. Business owners may decide to sell their businesses for a number of reasons, including the following:

- ♦ Wishing to retire
- ♦ Wanting to make a profit
- ♦ Wanting to change careers
- ♦ Wanting to get out while they can
- ♦ Finding the level of competition unacceptable

One trend that is helping to foster business sales is the fact that many baby boomers who own businesses are entering their 50s, 60s, and 70s and want to retire, travel, or manage their pensions or investments. Note that not all business transfers entail a sale. For example, a business owner can die and her heirs can inherit the business. Assume that a fitness center is owned by a husband and wife team. If one of the spouses passes away, the surviving spouse should value the club as high as possible because there is no federal estate tax when an asset passes to a surviving spouse. But if the surviving spouse wanted to sell the center, he would have to pay taxes on the difference between the selling price and the gym valuation when the surviving spouse took over. This will normally be a significantly lower taxable value compared with using the initial purchase or development cost (Battersby, 2003). To avoid these issues, many business owners plan for succession to allow their heirs to continue owning the business rather than being forced to sell the business. As noted earlier in the text, when some professional team owners died their children had to sell the team to pay the large tax bill.

If an owner does not want to give away the business or needs to get rid of the business, the options include shutting down or selling the business. The first step in selling any business is to gather together all relevant financial information. If an independent auditor has reviewed the company's financial condition, the audited statements are the best tool to use in selling a successful business. Having several years' worth of audited financial statements shortens the time that the buyer needs to conduct due diligence investigation and can accelerate the process of acquiring financing to buy the business.

A key component of any purchase decision is exactly what will be purchased. For example, in the year 2000 Footstar purchased some assets of Just For Feet for $66.8 million. Footstar purchased 79 Just For Feet superstores, 23 specialty stores, the Just For Feet name, and its Internet business ("Footstar," 2000). Footstar made a business decision by choosing to purchase specific assets rather than the entire company. This decision might have been based on a number of factors, such as Just For Feet's debt obligations from lease agreements or numerous other debt and liability concerns.

Four options exist for selling a business: a taxable sale of company stock, a tax-free sale of company stock, a taxable sale of company assets, and a tax-free sale of company assets (Lee, 1999). Each option involves different concerns. A cash purchase takes less time than a stock deal because there are fewer compliance issues. A sale can raise concerns for the buying company. For example, if a company issues more stock to buy another company, will the new shares give rise to preemptive rights to current shareholders? A sale can also raise concerns that are normally not considered when making a typical asset purchase such as a car, in which the only issue might be determining whether there is a clear title.

Asset Versus Equity Purchase

As already noted, one issue in selling a business is whether to sell stock, if the company is incorporated, or the company's assets. A person or another company interested in buying the business would prefer to buy assets rather than stock for various reasons. The primary reason is to reduce the purchasing company's liability—stocks convey ownership and liability for all past obligations. Thus, if the purchased business manufactured lawn dart games and parents were suing the company because kids were being injured, the new owners would be liable for all possible damages. On the other hand, if the new owners had purchased only the manufacturer's assets, the company itself and all associated liabilities would have been dissolved.

Significant tax considerations also arise for the seller and the purchaser of assets as opposed to stock. If you sell assets, the money you receive is taxed as ordinary income up to your basis (cost minus depreciation) in the asset. Any amount in excess of your basis is taxed as capital gains. Stock sales are taxed as long- or short-term capital gains. Ordinary income can be taxed up to 39.6%, in contrast to capital gains taxes for individuals, which are at most 20%. Thus, owners of a business would rather sell the stock; the difference between the buying and the selling price could be taxed at about half the rate of assets (Marullo, 1998, August). On the basis of the unfavorable tax treatment that a seller faces when selling assets, sellers can normally obtain a higher price for assets than for stock (Marullo, 1998, August).

Another significant benefit attached to selling assets involves the step-down basis for depreciable assets (Marullo, 1998, August) as illustrated in the following example.

CONCEPTS INTO PRACTICE

Assume that Speedway Motorsports purchased $100,000 worth of depreciable cameras for their broadcast booth. The cameras might have a depreciable life of five years, which means that Speedway could depreciate $20,000 a year for five years. Assume that after five years they had depreciated the entire amount allowed, $100,000, but the cameras still had a fair market value of $50,000. If Speedway sold the cameras for $50,000, the purchaser would be entitled to the step-down, which means that the purchaser could depreciate the cameras again for five years. Thus, the new owner would be able to depreciate the $50,000 purchase price by $10,000 a year over five years. If the new owner sold the cameras, the third owner would be able to depreciate the cameras from their purchase price. This process can continue as long as the cameras still have value.

The step-down provision is particularly important in the professional sport industry because players' contracts are considered depreciable assets. Buyers prefer to purchase assets if they can use the step-down basis to acquire added depreciation without assuming any liability. The step-down basis approach is covered in more detail in chapter 5.

If a business owner wishes to sell a now successful business, he faces a major challenge—determining how much the business is worth. Owners put so much sweat equity into a business that they typically think that it is worth much more than it is. Owners may have a misconception based on transactions associated with large publicly traded companies, which can sell for up to 20 times their earnings (Livingston, 1998). Sales of smaller, closely held companies rarely reach such multiples of earnings. Larger corporations have a strong track record, can maintain consistent sales for extended periods, and have significant goodwill associated with their product or service. An NFL franchise is valuable even when the team has a losing record because of the inherent value of an NFL team. The strong value of NFL teams is based on the strong broadcast agreement and shared revenue. In contrast, a small mom-and-pop gym has a less stable product, and customer loyalty might not transfer over in the same manner as it does with a large company. Some gym members might have bought memberships just because they were friends of the owner. Fans of the Dallas Cowboys or any other NFL team would still be fans even if their franchise changed ownership several times over a decade.

Calculating Business Value

Valuing a business correctly is important for entrepreneurs who are trying to acquire a sport business. Valuation is also important for current business owners, who need to make sure that they are selling a business for the right amount. A price that is too high will drive away potential purchasers, and under listing a business can result in a significant financial penalty. Last, valuation is important for lenders who are attempting to establish the borrowing ability of the proposed business owners. Thus, everyone involved in the potential sale of a sport business needs to make sure that the value is accurate.

Value represents the monetary worth of an item. Value can be expressed as what you could obtain on the open market if you had to sell an item (Siegel, Shim, & Hartman, 1992). The value that individuals place on various items will vary significantly. A family heirloom could be priceless for someone in a family, but valueless for someone buying the item at a garage sale. Similarly, a baseball card could be listed in a price guide with a $100 value, but a sports card dealer might offer only $10 for the card. This disparity in interpretation of value also affects businesses.

Valuation is the process of determining the value of a business. Although a vast amount of literature has been published about valuing businesses (e.g. Ross, Westerfield, & Jordan, 2008; Bernstein, 1993; Simmons, 2000; Pratt, Reilly, & Schweihs, 2000), little specifically addresses valuation concerns associated with the sport industry. Sport business valuation can represent unique challenges, such as determining membership numbers for service organizations, the value of intellectual property, and the value placed on a business because of the demand associated with people wishing to enter the sport industry. These concerns foster the need to conduct a critical analysis of sport businesses and their value.

Inc. magazine highlighted a recreational outfitter business for sale in northern New England in their December 2007 issue (Grant, 2007). The seller listed the asking price at $6.185 million, which included a building valued at $2.4 million, $4.5 million of inventory, $200,000 in accounts receivable (money owed the business), and $250,000 worth of furniture, fixtures, and equipment (FFE) for the business. Looking at the value of the building, inventory, and other assets might convince someone that the deal was a good buy. But the business also owed over $1.8 million, which the new buyer would have to assume. The business generated $9.4 million in sales during 2006, and the owner's discretionary cash flow (often referred to as EBITDA, or earnings before interest, tax, and depreciation and amortization) was $701,691. The company generated a gross margin of 20.3%, which represented how much profit was made from the goods sold, which can be used as a means to value the investment in the business (calculated as sales revenue minus the cost of goods sold divided by sales revenue). The higher the percentage is, the more of each dollar of sales the business retains to pay its financial obligations. For example, if a buyer could earn 4% a year investing in a safe investment, a return of 20.3% would be a significantly greater return but would have a higher risk if the business were to fail. Based on all these numbers, *Inc.'s* analyst believed that the price of almost nine times EBITDA (price of $6.185 million and EBIDTA of $701,691) was too high and that a more realistic number would be five or six times EBIDTA, or $3.5 to $4.2 million (Grant, 2007). This example highlights why having an appropriate means to determine the value for a business is important.

Effects on Sport Valuation

Sport valuations must incorporate numerous factors beyond those used to value other business, such as total risks, the competitive environment, the business' assets, the timing of the valuation, and the ownership structure. These factors can significantly alter a sport business' value even if an analysis of historic revenues and earnings suggests that two competing businesses are otherwise similar.

Total Risks Risks can significantly affect a sport business. A sports apparel company can lose a significant amount of money if its inventory is affected by a local team moving away from the area. Similarly, if a star player is traded, the apparel company might be stuck with obsolete jerseys. Although some risks develop without warning, others are foreseeable. For example, a health club that offers numerous services has a lower operating risk compared with a club that specializes in tennis or swimming. The club that specializes solely in tennis is especially sensitive to fluctuations in the economy, which can severely affect year-to-year financial performance. On the other hand, a club that has a diversified client base and provides services in a variety of areas faces less year-to-year fluctuation in profitability caused by a changing economy or altered regulatory environment.

Competitive Environment The competitive environment can affect the value of a sport business. Generally, a business will be less valuable if it is located in an area with extensive competition. A sense of competitive pressure can be ascertained by analyzing the number of businesses in the same areas as the business being evaluated. This pressure also is influenced by the number of potential customers in the area being served, the types of services offered, and the price competition between the various businesses. Although numerous businesses often share the same geographic area, the businesses can try to differentiate themselves through a broad low-cost strategy (low overall costs), a focused low-cost strategy (low costs for a specific program or item), a broad differentiation strategy (significantly different from competitors), a focused differentiation strategy (a specific program that differs from those of the competitors), or a best-cost provider strategy (providing high quality and low cost to beat competitors) (Thompson Jr., Strickland III, & Gamble, 2008). A health club can try to be known as the best place for serious weight lifters (i.e. Gold's Gym) or can differentiate itself through lowering their price to be known as the most inexpensive gym in town. Others health clubs might raise their price to become the most expensive and exclusive club in the area.

Professional sports teams often enjoy market exclusivity because a limited number of teams are allowed in a given region. This forced scarcity increases team values. For example, a National Football League (NFL) team might face competition from other entertainment options, but no other NFL teams will be located in that market to compete against. Thus, few NFL teams are available to buyers, and those who own a team would demand a significant premium to sell the team.

Business Assets Every business has assets, but some assets are more valuable than others. For high-technology firms or sport manufacturing companies, patents and trademarks might be the most important assets. For teams, fitness facilities, and health clubs, the fan or customer base is the most valuable asset. Members are important not just because they pay monthly dues or make regular purchases but also because they help grow a business by attracting additional customers or members. When comparing businesses of similar sizes, the business that generates more of its revenues from direct referrals will have a higher value (Scudder, 2001). This assessment reflects the notion that the business with the highest proportion of revenues from direct referrals has a more solid relationship with its clients, which translates into a more stable revenue stream over time. Uncertainty concerning the continuity of referrals and client growth can result in higher capitalization rates and lower values (Scudder, 2001). In a sport example, professional sports teams like the New York Giants and Washington Redskins have significant waiting lists of fans who want to become season ticket holders. This strong base of value is an opportunity to leverage the value of the business. Thus, the season ticket base is a valuable business asset.

Time of Valuation The value of a business on one date could change significantly by the next day. For example, a professional sports team that has a star athlete retire or suffer an injury could lose significant value. To avoid such incidents, a valuation can be conducted based on a time spectrum rather than a specific date. Part of the importance of determining the time for conducting the valuation is the purpose of the valuation. If the valuation is being conducted to determine the fair value, fair market value, investment value, possible purchase price, and fundamental value, then timing is important. If the valuation is conducted right after an inventory shipment has been received but before the bill has been paid, then the company would be worth significantly more than it would after bills have been paid and the inventory reduced. Similarly, a business is worth more when it is operating versus when it is being liquidated to pay off debts.

Ownership Structure Valuation can also be influenced by variables such as ownership structure. A corporation might be easier to sell than a sole proprietorship because someone can buy all the stocks in a company. Similarly, a partner can always buy out another partner or a business can change its ownership structure to increase its value or take advantage of favorable tax rules. A company with multiple owners can face the situation in which there is a majority owner (owning the greatest percentage of shares) and one or more minority interest owners. Because the primary owner cannot sell the entire business without the consent of the minority shareholders, a majority owner's interest has a lower value than if she had full control. Any purchaser of a partial interest would decrease the valuation because a percentage of a business is worth less than the entire business. Assume that a business is worth $1 million and that three owners each own 33.33% of the business. If all owners sell their shares each might receive $333,333. But if two sell their shares they might receive only $250,000 each because the buyer is not buying the entire business. The remaining shareholder's value will likewise decrease because of the new ownership structure.

As highlighted in this section, a number of variables affect the final value that can be placed on a sport business. Because these variables can be interpreted in various ways to affect the final value assigned to a business, several valuation approaches should be used to develop a potential range of values.

A typical valuation may include the following steps:

- An estimate of the future benefits of the business based on some combination of earnings, cash flow, revenues, assets, and the potential future value of the business

- An estimate of the capital required between the purchase price and expected future investments

- A risk-adjusted estimated cost of capital or discount rate to be used in the valuation

- Finally, an analysis of the timing, taxes, personalities, and other nonfinancial factors that may influence a valuation (Pratt, Reilly & Schweihs, 2000).

Critical financial information will normally come from available business reports and records. This data will probably require adjustment before they are suitable for valuation purposes. Such adjustments might be required to ensure accuracy or to reflect changes since the reports were completed. Mentioning such adjustments is important so that someone does not think that financial documents are without potential problems or blemishes.

Documentation essential for valuation purposes includes the following:

- ◆ Complete financial statements (balance sheet, income statement, statement of cash flow) for at least three years. Complete financials should include disclosures about leases, related-party transactions, and any pending legal issues. Supplemental financial statement schedules such as compensation schedules for employees and officers, ownership distributions, dividend payment schedules, and key-person life insurance policies may also be important when assembling an economic picture of the business.

- ◆ Federal and state income tax returns for the same period.

- ◆ Operating information such as company history; marketing materials; brochures; copyrights, trademarks, and patents; organizational charts; customer and supplier databases; contractual obligations; and industry-related information concerning association membership.

- ◆ Planning information regarding current budgets and forecasts, particularly of capital requirements such as future capital expenditures, deferred maintenance, and future working capital requirements.

- ◆ Business formation documents such as corporate or partnership agreements, employee contracts such as noncompete agreements, and employee stock option purchase (ESOP) agreements. (Pratt, Reilly, & Schweihs, 2000).

In addition, general economic or industry information can come from secondary sources such as various private (industry) and government entities or publications. Some examples include the U.S. Industrial Outlook, Standard & Poor's Industry Survey, Moody's Investors Industry Review, and the *Almanac of Business and Industrial Financial Ratios*.

Several techniques can be used to calculate the value of a business. The most common are asset-based valuation methods, the market-based approach, and income-based approaches. Next we briefly consider each of these.

The techniques presented here in no way represent a definite science. There is no one correct way to measure the value of a business. Someone who loves golf might be willing to pay a premium to buy a golf-related business just so she can own a golf business. This emotional element makes it almost impossible to create a foolproof valuation. Similarly, given the difficulty in valuing goodwill, a subjective element is always part of valuing a business.

Asset-Based Valuation Methods

In asset-based approaches to valuation, the value of a business is determined based on the value of tangible and intangible assets, and net of liabilities. In essence, the net worth is computed based on factoring in assets that appear on the balance sheet along with assets that might not be recorded. Intangible assets, such as goodwill, might not appear on a balance sheet because of the difficulty in determining an accurate value, but nevertheless they add value to the business. Asset-based approaches (in particular the asset accumulation approach discussed next) are most relevant for valuing an established sport business or in cases in which the valuation is being done in response to the sale of an ownership stake that exceeds 50%.

Two asset-based approaches are generally accepted for valuing sport businesses: the asset accumulation approach and the excess earnings method.

Asset Accumulation Approach

The asset accumulation approach is simply the identification and summation of the current economic values of all assets, tangible and intangible, that are controlled by the sport business as of the date of the valuation. Because the objective of the valuation is to determine the current net worth, or equity value, of the business, all liabilities existing at the date of the valuation must be deducted from the estimated value of the business' assets.

Excess Earnings Method

In the excess earnings approach, the value of net tangible assets is estimated based on the return that those assets can earn. As a separate process, intangible assets are valued based on the value of excess earnings that can be attributed to the intangible assets. The steps in the excess earnings approach can be summarized as follows:

1. Estimate the value of the tangible assets of the sport business, net of liabilities.

2. Estimate the normal level of earnings for the sport business after a historical review of the business' financial results and subject to forecast of future results. To measure normalized earnings, the compensation of all equity owners, including salary, bonus, and profit sharing is adjusted to reflect what the cost would be to hire a manager with nonownership status to perform the same tasks as owners.

3. Estimate the annual income that an owner would require to be interested in investing in the net tangible assets of the sport business.

4. Deduct the annual income computed in step 3 from the normal earnings estimated in step 2. This remainder can be viewed as the excess earnings that are attributable to the business' intangible assets.

5. This remainder is converted to an economic value by applying a **capitalization rate** that reflects the inherent riskiness in relation to the ability of the business to generate the excess earnings over the long run. Capitalization refers to the conversion of a single value of economic income to a current economic value by dividing the measure of economic income by a capitalization rate that is expressed as a percentage. As an example, if the excess earnings generated by the intangible assets equal $400,000 per year and the appropriate capitalization rate is 20%, then the value of the excess earnings equals the following:

$$\frac{\$400,000}{0.20} = \$2,000,000$$

6. The value of the tangible assets and the value of the excess earnings are added together to produce the value of the sport business.

Market-Based Approach

The market-based approach gives the value of the sport business based on a multiple of operating results, such as profits or revenues. The multiples are based on market transactions involving similar sport businesses. The inherent appeal of this approach is that the value of the business based on market-derived multiples reflects informed decisions negotiated between parties in transactions. When transactions are identified, notions of risk and return are incorporated into the multiples. Thus, the multiplier would vary within the same industry if one business has significant competition whereas a second business has no competition and is in a great location; the second business should have a higher multiplier.

For many types of closely held businesses, market multiples are derived based on multiples of earnings and revenues that are obtained either from analysis of publicly traded companies similar to the business or from data on actual transactions involving acquired or merging public and private companies. When market values of publicly traded companies are used to establish the value of a closely held business, a discount should be applied for lack of marketability to the value of the publicly traded companies. The lack-of-marketability discount results from a privately held company's being less valuable than a comparable public company because it is not as quick and easy to convert a business ownership position to cash (i.e., a private company is less liquid). The appropriate lack-of-marketability discount should be between 40% and 63% based on a recent survey of empirical studies (Pratt, Reilly, & Schweihs, 2000). For valuation analysis, limited information is available on transactions that involve sport businesses, and few sport businesses are publicly traded .

Many people believe that simple rules of thumb concerning the market multiple should be applied. This approach would mean applying an arbitrary multiple based on anecdotal information to current annual revenues, rather than analysis of empirical data. Such rules do not adjust multiples to reflect differences in operating characteristics and should not be used for any purpose other than as a reasonableness check on the values obtained from the use of other methodologies.

Income-Based Approaches

In income-based approaches, the value of a business is estimated based on the present value of all earnings and cash flow that the company provides to the owners during the time that it is owned. The appeal of this approach for valuing a sport business is that such a business is an operating entity that generates cash flow and earnings for the owners. The value resulting from the revenue- and profit-generating ability of the business is more relevant than the value that can be obtained from selling the assets of the business, because many sport businesses are not capital intensive.

One income-based approach, called the **discounted net cash flow** approach, estimates the present value of future economic income that is expected to result from the operations of the business. Also commonly used is the net cash flow to equity formula, which requires the following steps:

1. Determine net income after taxes.

2. Add noncash charges (e.g., depreciation).

3. Subtract net capital expenditures necessary to support business operations.

4. Subtract changes in net working capital necessary to support business operations.

5. Add net changes in long-term debt necessary to support business operations.

Net cash flow is used because conceptually it represents all income that an investor can hypothetically take out of the business. Generally, annual net cash flows are projected over a 5- to 10-year period into the future. At the end of the projection period, a terminal value is estimated on the basis of the cash flows that are expected to be earned after the projection period.

The value of the business is then computed as the sum of the present value of the annual net cash flows over the forecast period plus the present value of the terminal value (Shapiro, 1999). The present value of any single annual cash flow received in the future is computed by discounting the future cash flows. The concept of discounting recognizes that money received in the future is worth less than it would be today because money invested today can accrue interest over time. Under the assumption that the investor can earn an interest rate of i, the present value of net cash flow (CF) received n years (CF_n) in the future is as follows:

$$\frac{CF_n}{(1 + i)^n}$$

For example, if the interest rate (i) is 10%, the present value of $1 million received five years from now is $620,921.

$$\frac{\$1,000,000}{1.10^5} = \$620,921$$

Tables in Appendix A can help with such calculations.

A useful way to examine these various approaches is to use an example of a hypothetical martial arts studio to illustrate how a sport business valuation might be calculated in the real world. Because little inventory, capital equipment, or long-term debt is involved in this scenario, the simplified focus will use the basic income-based valuation approach.

John Lee is the owner and primary instructor at Kung Fu-R-Us Studio in New Haven, Connecticut. He started the business in 1989 and now has 200 clients. Each client signs a one-year membership agreement and pays $1,000 a year for lessons. The retention rate is high, and John often has new students wishing to join. The business is located at a strip mall, and 10 years are remaining on the lease. The lease calls for $2,000 a month in rent and includes a small yearly escalation clause. Utilities are included in the lease payment.

Staff salaries (not including Mr. Lee's salary) and benefits are $40,000, and miscellaneous expenses, such as phone, janitorial expenses, and increasingly expensive liability insurance are approximately $1,000 a month. Mr. Lee sells $2,000 each year in martial arts clothing and carries approximately $500 in inventory. He has $10,000, net of accumulated depreciation, invested in fixed assets such as protective mats, specialized martial arts equipment, lockers, and office equipment. Advertising and promotion in the community costs approximately $4,000 a year. The corporation has a $20,000 bank loan payable at a 10% interest rate.

As with many small businesses, Mr. Lee withdraws a significant amount of corporate profits as personal salary. Although many students enjoy Mr. Lee's personal instruction, he estimates that he could probably hire a high-quality instructor to teach his classes for him for about $50,000 per year. Mr. Lee estimates that a new owner could continue to grow profits by 5% per year for the next five years with minimal additional capital investments. Mr. Lee wants to enter into another business venture and is willing to sign a noncompete agreement stating that he will not open a competing business.

The balance sheet and income statement of the business are highlighted in tables 16.1 and 16.2

Because Kung-Fu R Us is clearly a service business that has few assets, an income-based approach is the most appropriate valuation technique. Adjusting net profits by replacing Mr. Lee's $110,000 compensation with a replacement instructor gives a pretax return on the business of $68,500 ($8,500

Table 16.1   Balance Sheet as of December 31, 2011

Assets		Liabilities and net worth	
Cash	$5,000	Note payable	$20,000
Accounts receivable	17,000	Accounts payable	2,000
Inventory	500	Taxes payable	500
		Other accruals	500
Total current assets	22,500	Total current liabilities	23,000
Equipment	10,000	Retained earnings	9,500
Total assets	$32,500	Total liabilities and net worth	$32,500

Table 16.2   Income Statement 2011

Sales	$202,000
Costs of goods and services sold	
Cost of goods sold	500
Depreciation expense	1,000
Staff salaries and benefits	40,000
Rent and utilities	24,000
Miscellaneous	12,000
Loan interest	2,000
Advertising and promotion	4,000
Total expenses	**83,500**
Profit before taxes and owner's compensation	118,500
Owner's compensation	110,000
Profit before taxes	8,500
Taxes	1,275
Net profit after taxes	**$7,225**

[profit] plus $110,000 [owner's compensation] minus $50,000 [new instructor's salary]). Adjusting for an expected tax burden of $23,975 (35% tax rate) leaves an after-tax net profit of $44,525 ($68,500 minus $23,975).

The next step entails assessing the value of expected future returns at present value. If a risk-adjusted 18% discount rate is used on the cash flow for a seven-year period, the net present value would be $169,708. This figure is calculated by multiplying the $44,525 net profit by 3.8115, which is found by looking up seven periods (representing seven years) at 18% on an annum table as found in appendix A

An industry rule of thumb for buying and selling businesses is five times net income, which would give a value of $222,625 (5 multiplied by $44,525). The often-used professional service rule of thumb of 1 times revenues gives a value of $200,000 (Shapiro, 1999).

Because the value of the inventory and receivables is offset by accruals and the banknote, little adjustment would be required in this example. In a situation with no debt and substantial strong receivables or valuable inventory, some adjustment should be made to increase the valuation.

The numbers highlighted demonstrate that various valuation methods can provide a wide range of values, from $169,708 to $222,625, for the buyer and seller to start the negotiation process.

Additional Considerations When Selling a Business

Besides determining the value of the business, if you are selling a business you should keep the following guidelines in mind:

- ♦ Do not let employees know too early that you might be selling; this disclosure can affect employee morale.
- ♦ Do not let competitors know too early about an impending sale; they might try to steal customers or hinder the sales process.

◆ Do not accept a purchase agreement calling for you to receive cash and a note; the note could be worthless if the new owner runs into financial hardships.

◆ Do not accept a significant bonus based on future financial success; you will remain tied to the business and its potential success or failure.

◆ Do not get so involved in the sales process that the business suffers and becomes even more difficult to sell (Livingston, 1998).

◆ Do not specifically exclude certain assets from the final sale, such as cash, past-due accounts receivable, deposits, refunds, and other valuable assets such as business records (Parrish & Maloney, 1999). Although parting with these valuable assets might be difficult, their value should be reflected in the sale price.

Despite potential problems associated with special purchasing options, if a business has a strong financial future, the potential downside might be minimal, and the seller might want to negotiate a contract attached to the company's future success. As with all contracts, the seller can negotiate a relatively risk-free deal by having the contract maximize success but minimize any losses. For example, the sales contract could specify that the seller is entitled to 10% of the company's profit for the first five years after the sale, but if the company does not have any profits, the seller will be entitled to a preferred collateral position on company assets. A preferred collateral position is a contractual agreement by which lenders can enhance their collateral positions. Thus, unsecured creditors can enter into agreements that provide them with a better position as long as such position does not harm any secured creditors or violate any bankruptcy regulations.

Selling a Business to Employees

Employee stock ownership plans give employees the opportunity to buy the business. These plans normally funnel pension or retirement funds into company stock, and at a certain point the employees can own a large percentage of the stock.

CONCEPTS INTO PRACTICE

Assume that a fitness center chain wants to sell and that the employees decide that they want to buy all the centers. The sellers could negotiate an outright purchase of the centers or undertake various strategies such as giving equity interest in lieu of some retirement benefits. The sellers could also give the employees the opportunity to purchase the centers using the lease-to-own option, in which the employees pay a lease amount for several years and then buy the centers at a set price.

External Sales Assistance

A business broker or investment banker can help focus your sales search by shopping the company only to those who have interest in buying the business and have the resources to do so. Many people would love to own a company but do not have the proper experience or the financial knowledge needed to complete the deal. External consultants can help provide an objective arm's-length opinion about a purchaser. Professionals can prequalify potential candidates to make sure that they have the necessary resources. If would-be buyers are not prequalified, another John Spano incident could occur (see chapter 15).

Business liquidators are experts in helping to establish a company's value and finding potential buyers for the entire business or just some key assets. Liquidators research businesses to find out what the best assets are and then come in, buy a business, sell all the valuables, and exit with a nice profit.

CONCLUSION

People do not want to think that their businesses will ever go under. Hard times do occur, however, and a business owner or manager needs to understand the signs of trouble. If the problem is caught soon enough, saving the business may be possible. Losses can also result from events that an owner has no way to plan for. If a team's star player suffers a career-ending injury, ticket sales could plummet and ratings for game broadcasts could drop. Such a significant loss cannot be planned for. Nonetheless, a business needs to have contingency plans.

A nonprofit organization also can face closure for nonpayment of debt. By keeping meticulous records, managers can know how much their businesses are worth. They can be aware of impacts that economic changes or competition might have on the business. They can put themselves in a posi- tion to see the writing on the wall and determine the best time to sell a business. They can tell what is happening with the competition and how their businesses might be affected. They can plan for the future and stay one step ahead of the external factors.

Class Discussion Topics

1. What is the best technique for determining the value of a business?
2. If you were facing financial hardship what signs do you think you would be able to see?
3. Is it better to buy an entire business or just its assets?
4. Is there a difference in determining the value of a large business such as a professional sports team versus a smaller business such as a health club?
5. Do you think it would be a good idea for a team owner to sell a team to the players?
6. If you were selling a sport business, what strategies would you use to try to find some potential buyers?

PART VII

Current Issues

This newest section to the third edition includes a new chapter focused on how the recession of 2007-2008 has affected sports over the past several years. The section contains an in-depth analysis of several sport industry segments to explore current issues that they are dealing with. The section ends with a sample case study focused on a Division II collegiate athletic program.

Chapter 17, "Effect of the Recession on Sport Finance," covers the basic concerns that caused past financial hardships in the sport industry and how some of these same concerns arose in 2007. By analyzing various industry segments such as public parks, high schools, colleges, professional sport, sport sponsorship, and even the entertainment industry, readers can appreciate the breadth of the current financial problems. Besides identifying signs of trouble, the chapter highlights specific strategies and solutions undertaken to address the financial hardship.

Chapter 18, "Sport Finance Trends Across Four Sectors: A Current Analysis," examines various industry segments to give readers a broader perspective of sport finance issues. Segments covered in this section include high school sports, college sports, professional sports, and international sports.

Chapter 19, "Applied Sport Finance," provides a glimpse into a year with a Division II college athletic department. This case study looks at some of the financial issues that arise when managing a college sport program. From paying coaches' salaries to generating revenue from student activity fees, the case study attempts to highlight how complicated paying bills can be as well as the difficulties associated with tracking revenue. The case study is designed to help the reader understand that budgets can play a critical role in every organization and that proper planning can help anyone plan more appropriately for the future.

chapter 17

Effect of the Recession on Sport Finance

Chapter Objectives

After studying this chapter, you should be able to do the following:

◆ Appreciate the signs that might foretell financial problems.

◆ Understand the scope of the financial problems that emerged in 2007.

◆ Analyze the effect of tighter budgets on what sport organizations could do.

◆ Develop appropriate responses and solutions after a financial problem has been identified.

No one wants to deal with financial problems, but similar to every industry, the sport industry is not immune from financial troubles. The prospect for financial troubles is not new, but every time a major financial shake-up occurs, numerous executives act as if they were unprepared for what happened. This chapter examines how to spot possible financial trouble, how various sport entities were affected by the recent financial meltdown, and how some sport entities have tried to respond to it.

The worst recession to affect the United States is considered to be the downturn associated with the stock market crash in 1929. At that time Wallace Wade was earning $25,000 a year as the head coach of Duke while average professors were earning only $3,000 to $4,000 a year. The Harvard athletic department brought in $706,000 before the depression occurred. By 1934 their revenue had declined to $292,000. Similarly, Ohio State University's athletic revenue declined from $429,000 in 1929 to $129,000 in 1932 (Whiteside, 2008). Revenue was often limited because the main source of revenue was football ticket sales. Now, athletic departments have numerous revenue sources from ticket sales to sponsorship contracts, major donors, and broadcasting agreements. The revenue from broadcast contracts has increased exponentially over the years. During economic downturns, however, those numbers quickly go south. In 1985 ABC and CBS paid $72 million for the rights to college football. That number decreased to $48 million in 1987 for ABC, CBS, and ESPN (Wendel, 1988).

PLANNING FOR A RECESSION

Michael Zanca, USTA, Billie Jean King National Tennis Center

My name is Michael Zanca. I have worked in the sport and events business for the last 10 years. During that time, I have been fortunate to learn and become strategically proficient in all areas of sport management, including hospitality, merchandise, facility operations, sponsorship, and on-site logistics.

Currently, I oversee special projects for the USTA–Billie Jean King National Tennis Center. The U.S. Open, held at the USTA–Billie Jean King National Tennis Center, is the best-attended annual sporting event in the world and one of the premier sports and entertainment spectacles. The U.S. Open draws over 700,000 fans per year. Currently, the U.S. Open is conducted annually in August and September over two and one half weeks, including an initial 4-day qualifying period, Arthur Ashe Kids Day (weather permitting), a full practice day, and a 14-day period for the tournament itself. The complete tournament schedule (including practice days) encompasses three weekends, including the Labor Day national holiday.

As with any business, sports notwithstanding, a recession is not something that an organization or event can ever truly prepare itself for on a year-to-year basis. Leagues like the NFL, MLB, and the NBA pull in many millions of dollars in areas such as sponsorship and broadcast revenues, which leagues have come to expect as vital revenue streams. Replacing those dollars takes a significant effort, and leagues and teams must reduce spending to survive.

Recognizing when you are in a recession and knowing how to adapt to one is crucial for financial success. Take, for example, the New York Yankees and their new billion-dollar ballpark. The stadium was designed before the collapse of the U.S. economy in 2007, at a time when the New York business community was still willing to spend a premium for the best sports and entertainment the region had to offer. The result was unsold seats and a drop in sales in most of the premium locations.

From the bleachers to the boardroom, being able to withstand a recession and hard economic times can come only from proper advanced planning and preparation. I put this to use every day during the U.S. Open and leave you with a few helpful hints that will help you plan for any situation.

- Understand your competition. What are they doing that you're not?
- Embrace change and cultivate it.
- Seize opportunities when they present themselves.
- Plan. Plan. Plan.

This chapter will focus primarily on the recession of 2007-2008. The extent of carnage seen by this recession may be felt for years to come. Some have analyzed the situation and believe that the economy, and more specifically the sport industry, will not bounce back until 2015, which would make this one of the longest lasting financial implosion in centuries. The magnitude of this recession was magnified by the global scope of pain. In the past, wars were often the most common cause of financial disasters that expanded beyond a country's borders. Largely because of the creation of the European Union and the rise of China as an international power, the financial trouble of one country has resulted in financial problems across the globe. But the financial troubles affected more than just one country. Several major countries such as Greece, Spain, Portugal, and Ireland were facing financial trouble. The financial trouble occurred because those countries borrowed too much money and were not able to repay the lenders. It is one thing when a small business fails to pay bills; it is another when countries fail to pay their bills. The cost for borrowing to keep those countries afloat and pay their bills requires significant additional interest payments and often requires lenders to restructure existing debt obligations. Financial aftershocks continued from 2007 through the writing of this text. These aftershocks spooked many investors. Whenever a news story broke highlighting a change in unemployment, increased or decreased consumer spending, or financial problems in Europe, the stock market in the United States responded.

FORESHADOWING OF PROBLEMS

College football season-ticket sales are seeing some strange dips and jumps this year, and ticket managers say the No. 1 culprit is the economy.

As Frank Cegledy Jr. of the Rayen School in Youngstown, Ohio, says, "It's crunch time." The school district there (five high schools in all) is looking at a $9 million deficit next year, which will mean the closing of one school immediately and perhaps one or two more soon after, plus the possibility of adding user fees.

Although these quotes appear to demonstrate that our current economic conditions are really hurting sports, they are from 1992 and 1993 (Alexander, 1992; Cohen, 1993).

Several years earlier the Dallas Cowboys had completed a major stadium project, yet many of their luxury suites remained empty. People could blame the lack of interest on the bad economy. The construction was undertaken when the signs of trouble were obvious, but everyone ignored the signals. This financial emergency helped usher in the sale of the Cowboys to Arkansas oil man Jerry Jones for $140 million because the previous owner had lost hundreds of millions of dollars in the Texas oil bust (Wendel, 1989).

Every economic downturn is different, and the signs can be either highly visible or extremely subtle. Signs can range from difficulty in obtaining credit to a large decline in the stock market. Other signs include increased job losses and sustained unemployment, declining corporate profits, borrowers defaulting on loans, people using credit cards to make ends meet, savings being used to pay day-to-day expenses, downsizing companies not rehiring, and rising prices for essentials. Although these occurrences reflect some of the financial concerns that can foreshadow an economic downturn, there is no one certain sign. Normally, a combination of signs might slowly evolve over a number of years and then suddenly boil up. A major financial calamity can also trigger financial problems. A stock market collapse, closure of a large company, a government defaulting on bonds, and a real estate bubble that bursts are all large triggers that can start an economic avalanche.

FINANCIAL PROBLEMS THAT EMERGED IN THE RECESSION OF 2007

Sports have survived various ups and downs over the years. The recession of 2007-2008, however, has been particularly challenging. While many sport management students were able to find paid internships before 2007, few of these internships were available after the recession started. The availability of paid internships is just one of a number of signs that some problems might be developing. Ticket sales decreased at many facilities. Those decreases came from both casual ticket buyers and season ticket buyers. Numerous tickets were making it onto the secondary market, and the lack of demand drove down prices on those markets. Sponsors and past supporters faced their own issues. When sponsors asked for a discount, teams and facilities started taking notice.

The increased pressure on government agencies because of decreased tax revenue created a ripple effect. The ripple effect was felt in park and recreation departments faced with shutdowns. The effect was felt in high school programs where salaries and funding were reduced across the board. The same concern was raised at numerous state-owned colleges whose budgets were slashed. Schools trimmed budgets, and battles raged across campuses to reduce funding for intercollegiate athletics in light of increased tuition requirements and reduced government subsidies.

The number of companies sold in 2009 declined significantly from the sales numbers in 2007. According to research by the Business Valuation Resources, the number of business sales dropped from 1,538 transactions to just 1,006 (Dahl, 2010). Sales for some businesses with positive cash flow were strong, and some sellers were eager to cash out to avoid possible capital gains taxes, which were expected to change and which could affect tax bills. Another trend is the increase in companies being sold to address the rash of people expected to retire. One estimate is that 70% of privately held businesses will be sold in the next 10 years as baby boomers start retiring.

No single smoking gun highlights financial trouble. Normally, multiple signs appear that can add up to potential trouble. Some of the keys that can be examined with a broader perspective include the following:

♦ Vendors demand immediate payment.
♦ Accounts receivable are being paid later or not at all (i.e., a cash flow issue).
♦ Unemployment numbers jump as companies start trimming their payrolls.
♦ More defaults on borrowing occur.
♦ Companies do not fill vacant or open positions.
♦ More consumers rely on credit cards to purchase life essentials.

The following brief recap highlights the state of the sport industry because of the first two years of the recession. Although the recession might end at any time, the ramifications might last for years to come.

Recreational Sport

Golf might be the game of kings, but the recession has hit the game hard. Although the Tiger Woods scandal hurt a number of professional events, the biggest concern arose at the recreational level. Private golf clubs, for example, have had a mem-

bership rate drop of 15% from 2009-2010. Golf rounds played over that period were down 3%. Approximately 15% of the roughly 4,400 private golf clubs in the United States were reporting serious financial challenges. In 2010, 140 of the nation's 16,000 golf courses closed while only 50 new courses opened. In Phoenix, Arizona, 8 golf courses went through foreclosure or bankruptcy after the recession started (Swartz, 2010).

The recreation golf industry in Connecticut is a $1.1 billion industry that employs 11,500 people. During the recession the number of rounds played dropped 12.2% to 8,299 rounds in 2011 compared with 2010. Likewise the average revenue per round dropped 7.2% in 2011 (Kane, 2011).

Although golf has suffered, so have special events. Forty states once held state games throughout the United States, but because of budget-related concerns and management issues, the number declined to 29 in 2010. The Empire State Games in New York, which was started in 1978 as the first state games, was a casualty of the recession. In 2009 the summer and winter games were canceled because of financial problems. To host the games in 2010, the state needed to raise over $1.25 million. Only through local sponsorship efforts in Buffalo was private industry able to raise the money needed to host the games. The games held in Buffalo in July 2010 attracted 6,000 athletes (Ruibal, 2010).

Solutions

Sometimes the key to changing attitudes is research. State parks were under assault because of decimated state budgets. Washington State closed 13 parks, Illinois temporarily closed 11, Arizona was considering closing 8, and Florida considered closing 19 parks in 2009. California was thinking about closing 220 of 279 parks. The California parks cost the state $4.32 billion to run, but they also generated 74.9 million visitors ("With parks on chopping block, study shows their value," 2009). Faculty and students in California surveyed 9,700 visitors at 27 parks, and the results showed that 11.95% were not Californians and that their average spending while visiting parks was $184.91. This level of spending represented significant economic activity that benefited the entire state. Thus, while cutting budgets and closing parks saved money in a budget, the results could reverberate throughout an economy. Tourism could significantly decrease, those working in the parks would be without jobs, and a state could be considered unfriendly to business.

The economy looked as if it would change in 2011, but the prospect of a double-dip recession loomed when the economy again started to falter. In one industry survey in 2011, recreation departments (including private, public, nonprofit, and colleges) indicated that they expected more financial stability in 2011. Previous surveys showed that 24.6% in 2008-2009 and 23.5% in 2009-2010 expected lower revenue. The numbers bounced back in 2011-2012 when only 11% of programs anticipated reduced revenue (Tipping, 2011). In response to the lower expected revenue, many programs started slashing costs. Average expenditures for all survey participants (over 2,000 respondents with accuracy at the 95% confidence level) declined from $1.9 million in expenditures in 2009 to $1.4 million in 2010, and that number was expected to creep up to an average of just below $1.5 million by 2012 (Tipping, 2011). The most common strategies used to reduce expenditures (90.3% of respondents undertook some form of action to reduce expenditures) are highlighted in table 17.1.

Health Clubs

Economic recessions have affected the health club industry in the past. During the 2001 recession, health clubs took a beating. Many people think that health clubs are a necessity, but the membership statistics clearly indicate that the public views club membership as a luxury (Scudder, 2001). As with all luxury items, people are willing to sacrifice a luxury item when times are tough and they feel justified in not renewing a health club membership. During down economic times, obtaining capital for expansion and leasing new equipment becomes more difficult and costs (such as salaries) rise. At the same time the amount that can be charged for memberships declines, and consumers do not spend as much (Scudder, 2001). Signs that a club will not do as well include a decrease in new membership sales in the first three months of the year, a decrease in general membership inquiries, decreases in net income, declines in attendance by current members, and continuing rises in expenses (Scudder, 2001).

Solutions

To reduce the likelihood that a recession will affect a club, the owners can take several actions:

♦ Focus more on monthly dues-paying memberships rather than cash-only memberships. The renewal rate for cash-only membership is only around 30%, whereas monthly dues-paying memberships (EFTs) have a 60% renewal rate.

♦ Eliminate or consolidate low-attendance classes to reduce costs. Monitor hours to see whether the facility could be closed during hours of low attendance.

♦ Require sales people to work the front desk as well.

♦ Review all contracts for external providers from cleaners to payroll processors. Although a contract may be expensive, bringing that function inside may end up costing more.

♦ Refrain from offering too many discounts, which can put in the prospective member's mind that the club is desperate to sell memberships.

♦ Create incentive programs to help sell more memberships and try to upsell current members with additional services (Scudder, 2001).

High School Finances

Two of the biggest concerns associated with high school sports are revenue and expenses. Of course, these are the basic financial concerns that drive all organizations. Thus, when revenues are squeezed and expenses increase, programs suffer a double whammy. Revenues are falling from lower allocations from government coffers, reduced sponsorship levels, and declining gate receipts. Expenses are being amplified by higher fuel costs, higher transportation costs, and greater costs for personnel.

To address revenue concerns, more high schools are adopting pay-to-play requirements. California and Massachusetts adopted pay-to-play requirements in the 1970s. The trend spread across the

Table 17.1 Expense Reduction Strategies Pursued by Managers

Action or strategy	Percent attempting
Improving energy efficiency	58.6
Reducing staffing levels	49.8
Increasing fees	43.1
Put capital projects on hold	39.5
Cut programming/services	29.9
Reducing hours or days of operation	28.0
Shortening seasons	12.8

Data from Tipping 2011.

Midwest and now is found in almost every state (if not every state) (Pfahler, 2010). Lower-income households are hit the hardest by such fees. Thus, many school districts allow exemptions for low-income students. The trend will probably continue for the foreseeable future because a school with 800 students participating in athletics would be hard pressed to decline receiving up to $80,000 extra per year if students are charged $100 to participate.

Solutions

School districts in general, and high school sports programs in particular, have felt the brunt of the recession. Several specific steps have been undertaken to try to save money:

- Reducing the number of sports being sponsored (eliminating sports or converting sports from competitive sports to student clubs or recreational sports)
- Terminating coaches including assistant coaches or only using existing faculty members as coaches
- Mandating that schools cut 20% of their regular season games, as Florida did in 2009, to save money
- Reducing the number of scheduled games to reduce travel expenses and related game-day costs (such as officials)
- Realigning conferences based more on geographic proximity than school size to reduce travel costs
- Scheduling multiple games in different sports on the same day so that only one bus is needed to take multiple teams
- Sharing busses with other schools who might be going to an invitational meet or event
- Eliminating athletic directors or others whose work can be reassigned to others
- Eliminating feeder teams such as junior varsity or freshman teams (King, 2010)
- Charging students more, even as much as $1,000, to participate in sports, which in the past was required only for the most expensive sports such as ice hockey (King, 2010)

Intercollegiate Athletics

Similar to high schools, colleges are facing the same concerns. Nationally, colleges have had annual subsidies of $826 million. The largest increase over the past several years has come from schools

in major conferences, including the Atlantic Coast Conference. Auburn, for example, received over $980,000 in 2004-2005 from student fees, but by 2006-2007 the number skyrocketed to $4.9 million (Upton, Gillum, & Berkowitz, 2010). Such an increase might be acceptable during good economic times, but many find such subsidies unacceptable during hard economic times. When students are deciding whether they can go to school or pay rent, charging several hundred extra dollars per year has fueled student protests.

Faculty members are also protesting the rise in collegiate expenditures, especially the large jump in coaching salaries that has occurred in the past 10 years. Many coaches earn several million dollars per year, while academic and student services programs are being cut because of insufficient funds.

Solutions

High schools were not the only entities attempting to reduce costs. The University of Maryland cut $301,000 from its football budget in part by taking buses rather than flying to all games. The change from airplanes to buses for just one game against Duke (a 270-mile [430 km] trip) saved $80,000. Many other schools cut their budgets or eliminated sports as a way to save money. Some of these changes were suggested by universities and colleges interested in reducing their costs. State colleges, however, faced the prospect of government intervention.

Cost-cutting recommendations were made in Mississippi after the governor suggested downgrading or eliminating community college athletics. These proposals included starting the football season one week later (saving housing and meal expenses), reducing the number of games by 10% except in football and soccer, eliminating all pre- and postseason scrimmages and games, consolidating buying power for insurance, and instituting one standard spring break during which all athletics would be suspended (Steinbach, 2010).

The financial crisis has improved efficiencies in certain areas. To help reduce costs and conserve the environment, some athletic departments have stopped printing media guides and only offer electronic versions. The saved printing costs can be in the five-figure range for many athletic departments. Other cost-cutting steps undertaken include

- reducing funding for coaching professional development,
- reducing funds for recruiting,

♦ traveling more frequently by bus,

♦ reducing travel budgets and the quality of travel accommodations,

♦ not holding championships in exotic locations,

♦ reducing the number of teams qualifying for playoffs,

♦ reducing the number of coaches used on various teams,

♦ not giving expensive mementos for conference champions, and

♦ reducing the time spent when teams travel to tournaments.

A number of schools have cut sports teams altogether. When cutting teams, however, colleges and universities need to be careful that they do not violate NCAA or Title IX requirements, cut sports with growth potential, alienate donors, or fail to examine the regional factors that affect sports (Sanders, 2010). After all this analysis, sometimes the only option is to close shop. If expenses cannot be controlled in any other manner, an organization may need to close for the better of its principles or the larger organization. One such example involves the Minneapolis Community and Technical College's athletic department. The college's basketball team was one of the best at its level in 2008-2009. The next year the men's and women's teams were asked to raise $118,000 to keep playing. When they failed to reach that amount, the college dropped athletics. The North Iowa Area Community College tried to fix an $800,000 budget shortfall by canceling football and saving $250,000 (Steinbach, 2010).

Although many colleges have tried to trim expenses, other programs have received significant public disdain for raising salaries for top-level coaches and for perceived excessive spending on sports. This mentality could represent detachment from the serious financial situation or possibly greed. For example, the Sugar Bowl has received $11 million in government subsidies yearly since 2000. The Sugar Bowl took this money even though its cash reserve was estimated at $23.5 million. Similarly, the Fiesta Bowl has a contract with the city of Tempe, Arizona, to pay the bowl $2.6 million per year from 2011 through 2013. At the same time the city has cut its budget for all other services by $36.2 million ("The score," 2011). Such excess can fly in the face of any attempts to save small change in other areas, discredit any cost-cutting initiatives, and appear hypocritical.

One potential solution to financial problems is spending more. This counterintuitive approach might seem out of place, but to grow, all businesses need to invest, and sometimes the best time to invest is during tough economic times. Adams State College decided during the recession to add five new sports over two years. The college decided to increase sports to help grow enrollment across the college, which had been declining. By offering a greater number of partial scholarships for minor sports, the college believed that it could increase enrollments, boost student retention, and increase graduation rates (Ulrich, 2009).

Another example of investing during tough times involves buying an existing facility. The University of Massachusetts Lowell was able to help the city with a major financial obstacle. The city was having problems paying for its Tsongas Arena, so they sold it to the university for $1. The university planned to refurbish the 6,500-seat arena at a cost of $5 million. The win–win deal allowed the city to eliminate its obligations for taking care of the facility and allowed the university to expand its presence into the downtown ("Stretching a dollar," 2010).

Professional Sports

Attendance has decreased in most professional sports in America, although new teams in new facilities have done well. New Major League Soccer (MLS) teams have been successful in drawing large crowds even in tough economic times. Another strong market has been championship events or leagues that have limited seasons such as the NFL, in which the small number of home games makes every game important for teams that may be playoff bound. But even the new Yankees Stadium saw empty seats at high price points. When a family of four might need to spend over $600 to go to a game, fans are going to start rethinking such expenditure. Families might change their purchasing patterns and decide to go to only one game per season rather than three or four. Corporations were also rethinking how much they wanted to invest in luxury suites. Corporations were signing shorter leases (3 to 5 years rather than 10 years) or were not willing to spend as much to obtain luxury suites. Other companies were willing to sign leases but were able to use the poor economic conditions to demand lower prices and then lock in the lower prices for a longer period.

Besides being unable to attract fans to some events, some teams faced even greater concerns. Several well-known sport bankruptcies affected the professional landscape in the past couple of years. Some of the major bankruptcies included the Arena Football League, the Arizona Coyotes, and the Texas Rangers. The Texas Rangers were once part of Tom Hicks' sports empire, but after taking on significant debt with the Rangers, the Dallas Stars, and the Liverpool Football Club, Hicks' sports holding company defaulted on $525 million in debt (Helyar & Keehner, 2010). Lastly, the entire AVP men's and women's pro beach volleyball tour canceled the 2010 season because of lack of financial support.

The entire professional sport industry was suffering, and the result has included numerous layoffs. Some layoffs were associated with strikes or lockouts, but some employers were shedding jobs to reduce costs. The NBA laid off 80 staffers (9% of its domestic staff) just weeks after the Charlotte Bobcats laid off 35 nonbasketball operations employees (Saraceno, 2008).

The bloodshed throughout professional sports has not been confined to American teams. Malcolm Glazer, an American, purchased Manchester United soccer team through a leveraged buyout in 2005 for $1.4 billion. The team is now in debt to the tune of $1.6 billion, and the owner's family debts are $570 million greater than previously disclosed ("Report says Man U owners deep in debt," 2010).

Solutions

Being cost sensitive is one of the best solutions to attracting price sensitive customers. The Washington Nationals allowed customers to bring some of their own food to help make the trip to the ballpark more affordable. To attract more patrons to games, the Toronto Blue Jays now offer regular game-day tickets in the upper tier for $1. Other teams have launched dollar menus to attract families. Creative pricing is forcing professional sports to be more entrepreneurial, but with significant fixed costs most teams have little room to be flexible without assuming more debt.

Teams were spending more time and money crunching numbers to determine why fans engaged in certain conduct. Although anecdotal information is valuable, crunching numbers through fan loyalty programs and other data capture points has produced solid results. Teams have developed customized programs targeted to specific fans that induce them to spend more money. Thus, instead of reducing prices, teams were engaged in finding ways to get fans to spend more, thus generating more revenue. To be successful in this process, teams need to know why fans might or might not want to attend a game. In chapter 2 we discuss the economic issue of elasticity of demand and

the likelihood that fans will change their behavior if ticket prices increase. Fans may have multiple reasons for going to an event, such as family commitments, start time, weather, quality of the game, significance of the game, economic factors, work demands, the quality of the purchased or available seats, and the presence of a major star. In response to such variables, teams try to make the game experience as meaningful as possible to keep garnering ticket revenue. Teams are packaging tickets to premium games with lesser-quality games to drive sales. New all-you-can-eat seating sections are helping to attract new fans and families trying to save money. Because teams cannot control many of the attendance variables, they have to examine other revenue sources that might be less volatile. The search for more stable (and diverse) revenue sources generates a greater preference today than ever before for income sources like sponsorship contracts and broadcasting rights. The most expensive tickets, such as the $1,250 to $2,500 single-game tickets for New York Yankees games, need to be reduced in price to sell ticket inventory. But the Yankees have not had to reduce broadcast rights fees in response to the slow economy.

Sponsorship

Nike, the world's largest sports apparel company, spends a lot of money on endorsement and sponsorship obligations; in 2002 the company spent around $1 billion on these types of obligations. By 2006 that number had grown to around $1.6 billion. The number shot up in 2008 and leveled off at $4.2 billion in 2009, fueled by spending on the 2008 Olympics, the costs of which were recorded in the fiscal year ending May 31, 2009. In 2010 Nike pulled some of its sponsorship deals and reduced expenditures by $400 million to $3.8 billion. This decline occurred even though Nike spent a significant sum of marketing and sponsorship money on Olympic and World Cup events (Kaplan, 2010). Nike was not alone in reducing its sponsorship expenditures.

Of the top 50 sports advertising spenders in 2009, 20 reduced their spending compared with what they spent in 2008. Some of the biggest drops came from car manufacturers, who reduced their spending from 20% to 50% (Rishe, 2010). Many advertisers stopped buying ads on broadcasts, reducing the ad dollars spent on sports. Broadcasters were willing to accept such behavior because they hoped that when the economy turned around, those advertisers would be back and would remember those who worked with them during tough times.

Advertisers represent only one of the sponsorship areas that faced a decline. Event sponsorship, on events such as tennis and golf tournaments, was not immune from the 2007 recession. Pacific Life ended its seven-year title sponsorship at the tournament in Indian Wells, California. Other sponsors who failed to renew their title sponsorship role included AIG, Countrywide, and Mercedes-Benz (Robson, 2008). Other sponsors bowed out of sponsoring events for a variety of reasons. Some sponsors dropped out because they were facing financial hardship, whereas others dropped out because of the unfavorable publicity that they would get from sponsoring sports events when they were receiving government assistance at the same time. For example, car manufacturers, financial institutions, and others scarred by the recession shied away from extravagancies to avoid consumer and political wrath. Sponsors such as Citibank, Bank of America, and auto manufacturers who received financial bailouts were especially wary of sponsorship deals or were not advertising in some sporting events. After spending $77.1 million on Super Bowl advertising from 1993 to 2008, General Motors pulled its advertising for the 2009 game (Epstein, 2008).

One of the industry sectors that did well during the recession was alcohol. Although fans might reduce the number of beers that they purchased for $10 at the ballpark, these same fans might buy more beer at the local store. Sales increased for cheaper beer, whereas more expensive beers saw decreased sales. The sales of inexpensive beer rose 7.3% in 2009-2010, while the sales of imported beer declined 3.8%. Similarly, expensive liquors and wine sales declined, while inexpensive varieties showed increased sales (Kalwarski, 2010).

One of the concerns associated with sponsorship is determining the value of the sponsorship investment. Another concern is the cost for putting on events. Even in a weak economy, the cost for hosting major games and events continues to increase. The 2010 Vancouver Olympic Games were estimated to cost $1.3 billion, and the final audited numbers highlighted a cost of $1.84 billion. Although this figure might seem in line with projections, the question is always about what items are classified as costs for hosting the Olympics. The amount referenced included only the operating budget but not the $900 million for security, almost $2 billion for constructing the Sea-to-Sky Highway expansion, almost $2 billion for Canada Line construction, over $1 billion for construction of the Athlete's Village, and almost $900 million for the Vancouver Convention Centre expansion.

In total the direct and indirect costs for the Games were over $9 billion.

The province of British Columbia released the total expenses of trying to win and host the Games. The initial budget was projected at $740 million but topped out at $895 million. These costs include not only the costs incurred by the Olympic Organizing Committee but also the expenditures for pavilions at the 2006 Turin and 2008 Beijing Olympics to help market Vancouver and its Games ("Cost of Vancouver Games released," 2010). Future bids need to consider whether the investment will be appropriate. The 2012 Olympics in London were won during bidding when the country was in strong financial shape. When the economy started collapsing, however, many people wished that London had not won the bid because of the huge cost to prepare for the Games.

Solutions

The key for sponsoring events in a poor economy has been to determine and prove the value of sponsorship. Companies are always going to market their products to induce consumers to make purchases. Thus, when good deals are available, companies will jump on those deals. Events then need to be able to prove that they can draw a large live or television audience to justify the sponsorship expenditure. Although such proof is important when selling sponsorship opportunities, in a slow economy the proof needs to be stronger and accurate.

During tough economic times one of the easiest ways to get involved in sponsorship entails trade outs. With a trade out a company gives goods or services instead of cash. If an event is searching for sponsorship in the $10,000 range, the event might accept a trade out valued at $15,000 instead of cash. A road-running event, for example, might ask for $1,000 to be a named sponsor but might let a T-shirt printing company cosponsor the race by donating a T-shirt to every runner.

Entertainment Industry

The recession carnage was being felt in other entertainment sectors beyond the sports world. Concert promoter and ticket seller Live Nation Entertainment Inc. was also hurting at the turnstiles after a weaker than expected concert season. The company had some major shows postponed, and others such as the Eagles, Simon and Garfunkel, and the Jonas Brothers have canceled or postponed tour dates because of poor ticket sales.

Live Nation's net loss in the three months to June 30, 2010, grew to $34.6 million, or 20 cents per share, from a loss of $27.2 million, or 33 cents per share, a year earlier. Revenue fell 10% to $1.27 billion, which includes Ticketmaster's results before its merger with Live Nation earlier in 2010.

Total concert attendance for Live Nation fell 6% to 12.4 million in the second quarter, and revenue per attendee dropped 1% to $69.47, compared with a year earlier (Nakashima, 2010).

Solutions

One of the easiest solutions to lower attendance numbers entails hosting fewer events and making sure that only the top talent was touring. Some well-known events, including American Idol, reduced the number of tour dates and canceled their tours because of low initial response. In contrast, some of the top tours in 2010, such as AC/DC, Paul McCartney, and Lady Gaga, drew significant crowds. The top tour in 2010 was Bon Jovi, which in 80 total dates grossed over $200 million.

CONCLUSION

The current tough economic times have shown that sports are not recession proof. Consumers will bounce back given time, but some sport properties might reach a point of no return. During the past two decades, consumers were willing to assume more debt, and municipalities, schools, colleges, and teams were willing to borrow money. Now that

the piper has called and debts need to be repaid, many can no longer afford to make payments or borrow more. Yet player salaries are still increasing, and teams are still raising prices for concession items and seats.

No easily followed path leads out of a recession, but spending more does not help. Thus, sport organizations need to reduce their debt and reinvent themselves to lure back fans and their wallets. With numerous entertainment options, sport organizations need to be careful that they do not completely alienate fans. For example, fans can go to the movies for $10 and to a minor league baseball game for $5. In a tough economy many hesitate to pay $100 to go to a game that they could see for free on television.

The key to surviving a recession is to develop short- and long-term plans. These plans need to carefully examine current financial realities within an organization, economic conditions, the competition, and any "white space" for future growth. Through critically analyzing these variables an organization can identify what actions should be taken and when. Similar to all planning, there is no guarantee that any given plan will work. Through testing and implementing decisions on a small scale, decisions can be made which hopefully will not result in major financial losses or gains, but rather incremental gains or losses which can be enlarged or reduced depending on the results. This is similar to someone testing out a swimming pool by slowly entering the pool to gauge how cold it is rather than jumping in all at once and freezing.

Class Discussion Topics

1. How did the economic recession of 2008-09 affect you personally?
2. When do you think the recession will end? What are the signs for such a turnaround in the sport industry?
3. How can a sport organization prepare for a future financial downturn?
4. What cost-cutting strategies, other than what has been discussed in this chapter, could you suggest to a high school or college athletic director?

chapter 18

Sport Finance Trends Across Four Sectors: A Current Analysis

Chapter Objectives

After studying this chapter, you should be able to do the following:

- Appreciate the dynamics of how quickly financial trends change within the sport industry.
- Understand the scope of the current financial problems facing sport today.
- Develop appropriate responses and solutions after a financial problem is identified.

The purpose of this chapter is to examine several key sport finance developments within the sport industry. Because focusing on every aspect of the sport industry in one chapter would be nearly impossible, we instead focus on the financial trends associated with high school, collegiate, professional, and international sports. Given the tumultuous economy, the sport landscape was not immune to the same challenges facing other industries. For example, Humphreys (2010) examined the effect of the global financial crisis on sport in North America beginning in 2007 through 2010 and reported two key findings. First, although attendance and franchise values declined, overall the sport industry appeared moderately insulated from the negative financial effects that influenced most businesses. Also, the increased reliance on future revenue streams in the form of ticket sales, premium seating, and sponsorships would be jeopardized if the disposable income for people consuming these products were negatively affected because of the global crisis. Only time will indicate what the long-term fallout of the global financial crisis will be and how sport and sport organizations were affected financially.

We now examine several financial trends affecting interscholastic sports including pay-for-play and sponsorship.

TRENDS IN HIGH SCHOOL SPORTS

Although several factors have contributed to the financial challenges facing high school athletic programs, three primary reasons serve as a starting point of discussion for this section. First, high schools nationwide have seen their athletic budgets significantly reduced over the previous decade. Furthermore, considering that funding from local school districts represents the primary revenue source for these athletic programs, reductions in this allocation severely hamper the fiscal solvency of athletic departments. Among the reasons for the decreases in local allocations were tax reductions, reductions in property values, and the economic recession. In addition, as expenses for high school athletics continue to increase, many school districts are struggling to create new revenue streams. Besides dealing with reduced budgets, schools receiving allocations from the federal government must comply with Title IX of the 1972 Educational Amendment, which essentially requires schools to provide equitable opportunities for female and male student-athletes. Although the positive social benefits associated with participating in high school sports are well documented, the dramatic increase in the number of females playing high school sports has come with a price tag. Finally, the emphasis to win and expectations from local communities have created a culture of competition in which coaches are far more accountable for their teams' performance and are consequently fired for poor records or, in some cases, for not winning a state championship. For example, despite leading his team to two consecutive state final appearances and amassing a 36-4 record, Glades Central High School fired football coach and former NFL player Jessie Hester following the 2010 season. High school football in Florida is highly competitive, and although Glades Central has won six state titles, the longest tenured coach in the previous 25 years lasted only 6 seasons, which included two state championships (Greer, 2010).

Next, we will examine the controversial topics of pay-for-play and sponsorship within high school athletics.

Pay-for-Play

Because the pay-for-play model is relatively new within high school sports, there is little consensus on how this should be structured. For example, in some school districts, participation fees are charged as a flat rate per athlete per sport or a flat fee for the entire calendar year. These fees can have various pricing tiers for families that have multiple participating children or for sports that have different equipment and transportation needs. High schools in at least 43 states charged students choosing to play sports a participation fee in 2010. Costs typically ranged from $100 to $150 per sport. Most schools offered discounts to those playing multiple sports, and others set a family cap. With tax rolls shrinking and school budgets bleeding, many of the nation's harder hit districts have given athletic administrators a choice: Find innovative ways to fund your program or watch it disappear (King, 2010).

As the director of athletics for the 72 high schools in the Los Angeles Unified School District, Barbara Fiege learned that she had to cut $1.4 million from her budget. Her calculations determined that she would have to cut about 700 coaches from 600 teams. Fiege shared the information with a reporter for the *Los Angeles Times*, whose story ignited support from the sports community in Southern California. The next day, she heard from Anita DeFrantz, president of the LA84 Foundation, a nonprofit dedicated to serving youth sports. Although DeFrantz indicated that the foundation typically did not work with school districts, she would do so in this case, providing a grant of $252,600 and encouraging others to assist the schools (King, 2010).

Through additional contributions from the Dodgers, Chivas USA, Nike, Easton, and others, the Los Angeles school district was able to avert coaching cuts and keep all sports alive for its 35,000 student-athletes. But the district slashed $650,000 in funding for athletic transportation, coming on top of $335,000 in cuts to that area in 2009. Thus, even with a full complement of coaches, Los Angeles schools faced another dilemma. They no longer had the money to bus teams to their events. Consequently, the district asked parents to contribute $24 per child for the year—a voluntary donation, not a fee—to cover the cost of ferrying teams to games. Unfortunately, many schools in tightly pinched districts face this dilemma. Although they have been able to save coaches and teams within some schools, the cost of transportation, typically about $300 per event in Los Angeles, has been problematic. The most common approach toward cuts has been a logical one: Play less often and stay closer to home (King, 2010).

Schools have shortened schedules and teams are sharing buses. Some state associations have changed rules so that schools reduce travel to play district or conference games. Even after those cuts, many districts have found that the only way to continue to offer sports has been to charge a participation fee. Opponents against charging participation fees, such as Up2Us, argue that these fees inhibit participation, pointing to an expected drop of 10% for every $100 charged. However, tracking by the National Federation of State High School Associations indicated participation has remained steady nationally, even as fees have become more common (King, 2010).

One state that is meticulously monitoring the effect of pay-to-play is Michigan. Specifically, the state high school athletic association has been surveying athletic directors about participation fees since 2003. Michigan first circulated an often-regurgitated prediction that athletic participation would drop as fees were implemented. In its most recent survey, the Michigan High School State Athletic Association (MHSAA) found 221 of 475 schools responding (47%) charged participation fees in 2009-2010, a slight increase over the 43% reporting charging fees two years earlier. Furthermore, 32% of those not charging fees said that they were considering adopting them that year. Only 14% of those charging fees reported a drop

in participation as a result. High school athletic administrators suggested a significant reason why the shift toward pay-to-play has not scared off athletes: Most schools and districts that charge participation fees offer waivers for students based on need. Thus, those students qualifying for free or reduced-price lunch pay no fee or a reduced fee for athletics (King, 2010).

Because many parents are accustomed to paying for their children's athletic endeavors from the time that they put on their first soccer, tee-ball, or basketball uniform, the concept of paying for the privilege at school does not seem foreign, especially because the cost is far less for many participants. Stakeholders supporting the pay-for-play model suggest that the overarching message is grounded in fundamental economics because the nation will pay more to cut school sports than to fund them. Specifically, cutting or charging for school sports will ultimately lead to higher dropout rates, increased teen pregnancies, and more teen violence, leading to higher societal costs (King, 2010).

Although pay-for-play appears to be relatively new, the idea originated in California and Massachusetts in the 1970s (Pfahler, 2010). Furthermore, a 2009 survey revealed that 33 high schools in Connecticut, or almost 20% of the those responding, had pay-for-play fees, although a couple of schools had integrated pay-for-play in 1990 (Yantz, 2009).

High schools are now capitalizing on the ability to generate additional dollars through a new program offered by the National Federation of State High School Associations and run by the Licensing Resource Group (LRG), which markets team merchandise nationally. At the end of 2010, more than 7,000 schools had registered for the program, and projections indicated that as many as 15,000 schools, more than half of the 27,000 high schools nationwide, would follow in the next few years (Halley, 2010).

During the first month of the 2011 high school football season in Alabama, ESPN had already broadcasted three Birmingham games live to a national audience. Hoover and South Panola played on ESPN on a Saturday when little competition was on television, as evidenced by the fact that the game was seen by 878,000 households. Although a preseason NFL game between Detroit and New England on the same day had 5.6 million viewers, the fact that a high school game could garner an audience a sixth as high as an NFL game indicates the appeal of high school football. Furthermore, the NFL Television package costs billions, but no such financial arrangement is established for high school coverage. Although many of these broadcasts have games between two teams from the same state or region, producers are aware of their national appeal, particularly when one or both of the participating teams have several players considered national recruits. Although the majority of high-profile televised high school games are broadcast nationally by ESPN, Time Warner Cable recently agreed with the California Interscholastic Federation on a 15-year deal worth $1.5 million per year for media rights to statewide playoff events on cable, Internet, and mobile devices (Ourand, 2011). This deal suggests that other state high school associations will be monitoring and potentially exploring innovative ways to generate more funds by selling broadcasting or media rights.

Sponsorship

Because of severe budget cuts for interscholastic sports nationwide, high school administrators have now turned to sponsorships to help balance their budgets or at least keep their athletic departments operational. Furthermore, high school athletic programs may view obtaining sponsorships as a viable alternative to implementing mandatory pay-for-play models. Despite these challenging financial times, in 2010-2011 the National Federation of State High School Associations reported increases in participation rates for the 21st consecutive year (National Federation of State High School Associations, 2011). Collectively, most of the work addressing high school sports and sponsorship is anecdotal in nature, consisting of media reports and trade publications with little empirical study. Forsythe (2001) reported that the top reason why small and large companies continue to sponsor high school athletic departments was to demonstrate their willingness to support local schools.

Pierce and Bussell (2011) surveyed high school athletic directors nationwide to assess the role of sponsorship within their respective athletic programs. Within the 360 responses, 89.4% of the schools were public and 10.6% were private. The median enrollment was 885 students, and median number of participating athletes was 325. Schools offered an average of 16 sports. In terms of using corporate sponsorship, 57.1% of the athletic directors used sponsorship and 42.9% did not. Just over a third (34%) indicated using participation fees to help cover their costs. Fund-raising was a primary tool used to generate additional dollars; 87% reported seeking financial support from individual donors. On a positive note, although 35% of the athletic directors reported receiving less funding compared with the previous year, only 3.6% indi-

cated that they were forced to eliminate any varsity sport in the previous two years.

With regard to using sponsorship, athletic directors reported that the top three reasons for seeking corporate sponsorship were to pay for equipment and supplies (76%), facility maintenance or renovation (56%), and uniforms (53%). The most common sponsor benefits were advertising in the game program (85%) and signage at the facility (81%). Naming rights and sponsorship on uniforms were rarely used, accounting for only 8% and 3.7% respectively. Although more than half (57.1%) of the respondents used sponsorship, 63% of the athletic directors reported that sponsorship dollars accounted for less than 5% of their overall budgets.

Sponsorship dollars for high school sports has undergone significant growth, particularly with media rights. For example, in New York City, city hall has negotiated a deal with the MSG Varsity Network to broadcast PSAL sporting events, in effect giving the city's high school athletes their own sports network. Under the proposal, MSG would pay $500,000 over two years for the right to televise and market sporting events. Student-athletes competing for college scholarships in baseball, basketball, football, soccer, track and field, and other sports figure to benefit, as do alumni looking to support their old schools and parents unable to attend their kids' games (Campanile, 2011). The benefit to MSG is that they can attract loyal viewers at an early stage and have them develop into lifelong fans.

Although sponsorships have been associated with professional and college sports, only recently has sponsorship filtered into the ranks of high school sports. Perhaps no state has witnessed this growth more than Texas, specifically in high school football. In Allen, Texas, an affluent suburb north of Dallas, local residents approved a $119 million bond issuance in 2009 by a 63% vote; over half the money was dedicated to the construction of a $60 million stadium for Allen High School (Bishop, 2011). Allen High School has over 5,000 students, and its band, with more than 600 members, is the largest high school band in the country. As impressive as this new 18,000-seat stadium was when it opened in August 2012, at least four other high schools in Texas have larger stadiums (Bishop, 2011).

TRENDS IN COLLEGE SPORTS

Over the previous decade, athletic expenses have outpaced athletic revenues in all National Collegiate Athletic Association (NCAA) Divisions. Consequently, collegiate athletic programs are facing unprecedented financial challenges. Although a myriad of factors are contributing to these challenges at all NCAA institutions, at the Division I level, coaching salaries, facility construction, and tuition increases appear to be the major items affecting collegiate budgets.

Among those institutions competing at the highest level, however, the financial gap may be widening. As noted by Fulks (2011), in the Football Bowl Subdivision (FBS) category the median revenue increased by 9.5% compared with the previous year and expenses increased only 1.7%. Furthermore, the median operating deficit (calculated by subtracting net expenses from net revenues) dropped 7.6% from $10,164,000 in 2009 to $9,446,000 in 2010 (Fulks, 2011).

Along with booster contributions, ticket sales continue to produce the largest revenue within athletic departments, and universities are continually revising how they can maximize ticket revenue. For example, Penn State University implemented a tier-pricing ticket system at the beginning of the 2011 season. Previously, fans contributed $100 annually through the Nittany Lion Club for the right to buy a season ticket anywhere in Beaver Stadium. In 2011 the price for that right increased to $600 for tickets between the 40-yard lines and to $300 to $400 for seats between the 40s and the goal lines. Therefore, a person paying $55 per game for a season ticket on the 50 for Penn State's eight home games in 2010 paid $540. In 2011 the cost jumped to $1,040 (Cook, 2009).

Although several major collegiate football programs (Nebraska, Oklahoma, Florida) have capitalized on passionate fan support to drive demand for regular season tickets, several universities have been less fortunate when it comes to demand for bowl game tickets. For example, after finishing their most successful regular season in school history in 2010, the Big East champion University of Connecticut was awarded a spot to play in the Fiesta Bowl opposite the University of Oklahoma as part of the prestigious Bowl Championship Series (BCS). The Big East paid their BCS representative $2 million to go to the game and granted a travel allowance of about $300,000. But the league does not share in ticket losses. Unfortunately for the Connecticut Huskies, the school sold only 4,600 tickets out of its allotment of 17,500 tickets for the January 1, 2011, Tostitos Fiesta Bowl. As a point of clarification, the bowl committee considers those 17,500 tickets sold, because the school was under contractual obligation to buy them, regardless of whether they were resold. Although Connecticut sold its entire inventory of $111 tickets, the university still held thousands of tickets priced at

$155, $235, and $255, collectively valued at more than $2 million. Compounding the issue was the fact that tickets could be found at stubhub.com for less than $25 in the weeks leading up to the game (Steinbach, 2011).

Similarly, Virginia Tech, which lost $1.77 million because of unsold Orange Bowl tickets in 2009, fared worst of all, failing to sell 11,000 tickets from its allotment of 17,500 for the 2011 Orange Bowl. Mercifully, the Atlantic Coast Conference (ACC) does not leave its members entirely on the hook. Although individual schools are responsible for paying for the first 6,000 tickets and partially responsible for the next 2,000, the conference covers any unsold tickets beyond that. Other conferences, including the Pac-12 and Big 12, absorb the cost of every unsold bowl ticket (Steinbach, 2011).

Paying Student-Athletes

Although certainly not a new concept, over the last several years advocates for paying student-athletes have collectively voiced support for such action. Although current NCAA president Mark Emmert publicly acknowledged that paying stipends to student-athletes would not happen under his leadership, he also strongly opined that something needs to be done sooner rather than later. Specifically, Emmert agreed that discussions should occur about how the NCAA's revenues could be distributed to the actual workforce, but his reservation about creating an employee–employer relationship should be carefully considered (Weiberg, 2011).

In an attempt to provide several perspectives regarding the compensation levels for those directly involved with the production of revenue in major collegiate sports, essentially the student-athletes and coaches, Huma and Staurowsky (2011) analyzed financial metrics including room and board, coaching salaries, and revenues produced by each team. Following four analyses, they released a report titled "The Price of Poverty in Big Time College Sport." Among their findings were the following:

► College athletes on full scholarship do not receive a "free ride." For the 2009-2010 academic year, the average annual scholarship shortfall (out-of-pocket expenses) for Football Bowl Series (FBS) "full" scholarship athletes was $3,222.

► The compensation that FBS athletes on "full scholarship" receive for living expenses (room and board, other expenses) positions the vast majority at or below the poverty level.

► If allowed access to the fair market system similar to that enjoyed by professional athletes, the average FBS football and basketball player would be worth approximately $121,048 and $265,027, respectively (not counting individual commercial endorsement deals).

▶ Football players with the top 10 highest estimated fair market values were worth between $345, 000 and $514,000 in 2009-2010. The top spot was held by University of Texas football players. Although 100% of those players received scholarships, leaving them living below the federal poverty line and with an average scholarship shortfall of $2,841 in 2010-2011, their coaches were paid an average of over $3.5 million each in 2010, excluding bonuses.

▶ Basketball players with the top 10 highest estimated fair market values were worth between $620,000 and $1 million in 2009-2010. The top spot was held by Duke basketball players. Although 80% of those players received scholarships, leaving them living below the federal poverty line and with an average scholarship shortfall of $3,098 in 2010-2011, their coaches were paid an average of over $2.5 million in 2010, excluding bonuses.

Based on these findings, Huma and Staurowsky (2011) proposed several recommendations:

▶ Support legislation allowing universities to fund their athletes' educational opportunities with scholarships that cover the full cost of attendance. The average $3,222 increase per player would be enough to free many from poverty and reduce their vulnerability to breaking NCAA rules. This initiative could be funded with the new TV revenue streams permeating throughout NCAA sports.

▶ A $3,222 scholarship increase would cost approximately $32.8 million for 85 scholarship players from each of the 120 FBS football teams, and $14.2 million would be required to do the same for 13 scholarship players on each of the 338 Division I basketball teams that offer scholarships. The total would be about $47 million annually. Should Title IX compliance require that provisions be made for female athletes to receive a similar benefit, that amount could be doubled for a total of $94 million annually.

▶ Colleges should be free to provide multiple-year scholarships in all sports if they so choose. The NCAA's one-year cap on the duration of a scholarship undermines its purported educational mission and puts in jeopardy the educational opportunities for every college athlete. High school recruits deserve to know which colleges are willing to prioritize their education so that they can make an informed decision.

Brown (2011) estimated that the rents generated by the top college football players significantly exceeded the costs associated with athletic scholarships. A top college football player, defined as one drafted into the National Football League (NFL), produced marginal revenues exceeding $1 million in 2005, representing a 30% increase from estimates 16 years earlier.

Broadcasting Deals

In 2011 the University of Texas (UT) reached an agreement with ESPN to launch the Longhorn Network, a channel devoted exclusively to broadcasting and promoting both the university's athletic department and the university. As part of the agreement, UT will receive payments totaling over $300 million dollars distributed over 20 years. This money is in addition to the share of Big 12 revenues that the university already receives as a conference member. Although the University of Texas will certainly reap the financial benefit of having their own dedicated network, the biggest advantage for Texas may not be the financial payoff, because half of the money will initially go to academics, but rather the constant presence on television and other platforms. Potential high school recruits will see the Longhorn Network in their homes and on their iPads and smart phones. Potentially, the Longhorn Network could become the nation's first regional college sports network focusing on one school with a limited high-profile inventory.

Despite the increased media attention brought to a host institution, televising collegiate sporting events are not always profitable for everyone. For example, in 2010 the University of Pittsburgh hosted a four-team subregional in the NCAA women's basketball tournament. But Pittsburgh failed to qualify and was not among the participants. Four teams without a local draw were selected, and only 2,000 tickets were sold after the participating teams were announced. Although the amount of money that Pittsburgh lost was not made public, an Associated Press report in 2009 stated that 11 of the 16 first- and second-round host sites lost money (Zeise, 2010).

Conference Realignment

Although the start of the 2010 college football season was overshadowed by off-field controversies involving high-profile coaches and player-related incidents, the 2011 season was equally compelling away from the gridiron in the form of conference realignment. Several marquee universities including the University of Nebraska (Big Ten) and Colorado (Pac-12) competed in new conferences, and the number of institutions changing conferences or contemplating a change in membership snowballed as the season began. Just a month into the 2011 football season, the Atlantic Coast Conference welcomed Syracuse University and the University of Pittsburgh to their conference, bringing their membership to 14 institutions. Other schools were also being considered, potentially creating a 16-team league (Dinch, 2011). Although stakeholders of college athletics continue to talk about conference membership being influenced by geography and academic reputations, realistically these changes are driven by financial opportunities, specifically the revenue-sharing models of each conference. Furthermore, if conferences all shared revenues equally, the number of schools seeking new conference membership would likely diminish significantly. For example, after the Big 12 conference lost members Colorado and Nebraska respectively to other conferences in 2011, the conference was criticized for its disproportionate television revenue distribution. Only after losing teams and seeing the potential exodus of several other institutions did the Big 12 conference administration agree to modify their existing revenue-sharing policy to distribute money equally among conference members.

Before this change, the Big 12 operated differently. For example, although half of the television revenue was equally shared, the remaining half was distributed proportionately to the number of television appearances for football and men's basketball. Consequently, high-profile institutions with a consistent television presence received more money than other conference members did. This revenue distribution disparity was closely aligned with the model used by several professional sport leagues. Specifically, although Major League Baseball (MLB) teams equally share revenue from national broadcast deals, local television revenues are negotiated independently and vary significantly across teams. The bidding wars among conferences to secure the most lucrative television deals will undoubtedly be an important criteria as universities become engaged in conference realignment discussions. When the Pac-12 conference negotiated a $3 billion, 12-year broadcast deal in 2011 with ESPN and Fox Sports respectively, the deal became the top financial deal in college sports (Miller, 2011). Given the dynamic state of college sports, particularly football conference affiliation, this deal will undoubtedly be surpassed in the near future.

TRENDS IN PROFESSIONAL SPORTS

Although not exhaustive, this section focuses on various issues related to professional sports including stadium subsidies, publicly owned franchises, labor issues, franchise values, international sports, and broadcasting issues.

Stadium Subsidies

Between 1990 and 2010, the total luxury-suite inventory in the four major sports leagues in the United States (MLB, NFL, NBA, and NHL) grew 147% to more than 10,000 luxury suites. Similarly, club-seat inventory experienced explosive growth, increasing by a whopping 624% to reach an estimated 450,000 club seats (Rhoda, Wrigley, & Habermas, 2010).

Although some stadiums are financed entirely by private or public dollars, a recent trend consists of using some combination of public and private funds. One of the unique aspects of stadium subsides is the type of taxes used to finance projects. Historically, these taxes have been of various types, including sales, hotel, property, and ticket taxes. When the publicly owned Green Bay Packers pursued a naming-rights deal for historic Lambeau Field, the Packer fan base united and organized a Save Lambeau campaign by collecting donations from passionate fans to prevent the local district from selling the naming rights to the stadium (Frey, 2011).

Historically, individuals, corporations, or a combination of the two owned professional sport franchises, and therefore these organizations are not considered public entities. But the 2010 Super Bowl Champion Green Bay Packers have been publicly held since 1922 and remain the only National Football League franchise to have shareholders. Although the NFL has a league policy prohibiting public ownership, the Packers were grandfathered in as a public entity and therefore remain the only publicly owned NFL franchise.

Teams competing in professional sport leagues must adhere to the various revenue-sharing policies specific to the league. In 2000 the Green Bay Packers realized that to maintain a competitive level, Lambeau Field needed a significant renovation. Although the NFL's revenue-sharing agreement designates that gate receipts be split 60% for the home team and 40% for the visiting team, additional revenue generated from club seats, luxury suites, and personal seat licenses (PSLs) are kept exclusively by the home team (Wilmoth, 2012). Therefore, a renovated Lambeau Field would provide additional revenue streams to the Packers organization. But professional sports franchises face several significant challenges when attempting to obtain a stadium subsidy. Among these is the opportunity cost of the project. Specifically, what good or service is being sacrificed for the stadium to be constructed? In addition, political issues are often present, including getting voter approval through a public referendum. As mentioned earlier in the text, in 2011 The Islanders were unsuccessful in convincing voters to approve a new arena which might mean the team will leave when its lease expires in 2015. The vote will probably encourage the team to move to Barclays Center in Brooklyn or move out of state if a new facility is not approved or built by 2015.

Aside from the controversies involved with referendums, people who oppose stadium subsidies have recently found new ways to voice their displeasure even after the financing plan for the new stadium has been approved—lawsuits. Taxpayers argue that the use of public funding benefits the team owner while simultaneously increasing the tax burden on both the municipality and the state (Frey, 2011). Many of the legal challenges have argued that the use of public funds should not benefit a private organization, in this instance, the professional sports team. Although such lawsuits have generally been unsuccessful, other lawsuits have been filed with the intent to delay a project and increase construction costs, which might eventually cause the development to be canceled (Frey, 2011).

Labor Issues

In July 2011 both the National Football League (NFL) and National Basketball Association (NBA) were embroiled in labor disputes that resulted in both leagues locking out their players over disagreements on how league revenues should be divided among owners and players. Two additional issues compounding the NFL labor strike centered on a rookie wage scale and free agency for veteran players. In addition, team owners have been unsuccessfully trying to limit the enormous guaranteed signing bonuses paid to unproven rookie players. For example, when quarterback Sam Bradford was selected as the top overall pick in the 2010 draft, he signed a $78 million dollar contract including a record $50 million guaranteed bonus. With the NBA, players have the leverage to explore the opportunity to take their talents overseas and play in international leagues. League revenue sharing and interpretation of how the league salary cap is structured were two fundamental issues leading to the lockout. Similar to NFL franchises that refuse to disclose their financials, NBA franchises remain steadfast in their claim that the majority of their franchises are losing money. Because NBA organizations operate as private entities, they are not required to share their financial statements. Philosophically, team owners would face added resistance to raising ticket prices and asking for public arena subsidies if their finances were made public and showed that the majority of NBA teams are profitable.

On July 25, 2011, the NFL ended the longest labor lockout in the history of the league (136 days). Despite the length of the lockout, many of the policies in the new collective bargaining agreement remain unchanged with a few exceptions. Specifically, team owners can point to victories, such as gaining a higher percentage of all revenue, one of the central issues. They get 53%, players 47%; the old deal was closer to 50-50. In addition, a new system will rein in spending on contracts for first-round draft picks.

In response to an ongoing labor dispute that had extended past 100 days, the NBA canceled the first two weeks of the 2011-2012 regular season on October 11, 2011. The cancellations imposed on the NBA lockout represented just the second work stoppage in league history to affect the regular season, essentially guaranteeing the loss of a full 82-game season. Unsuccessful negotiations found NBA owners and players disagreeing on key items such as luxury-tax specifics, contract lengths, and annual raises (Stein, 2011). NBA commissioner David Stern and Players Association executive director Billy Hunter were in a similar position in 1998, when a 204-day lockout resulted in a 50-game regular season.

Franchise Values

One universal practice is for owners of professional sports teams to claim that they lose money operating their franchises. Consequently, they can justify raising tickets prices, charging premiums for concessions, and persuading the public to subsidize new stadiums. Because team owners are not required to disclose their financial statements publicly, the general population has to rely on anecdotal information about the financial solvency of professional teams. Yet despite the lack of publicly available financial information, one fact is not disputed—the value of these franchises increase, often at rates far exceeding those of other business entities. In other words, although owners may not make significant money running an organization, they do so when they sell them. In 2011 *Forbes* compiled a list of the 50 most valuable sports organizations. For the seventh consecutive year Manchester United topped the list with an estimated value of $1.86 billion. Although Man U and two other soccer clubs, Real Madrid at number 5 and Arsenal at number 7, were in the top 10, every one of the 32 NFL franchises was included in the top 50 most valuable franchises. One example illustrating the explosive growth over the previous 25 years of the NFL is the fact that TV revenue jumped 700%. Specifically, the league's 32 teams now divide $3.8 billion annually under the current round of broadcast deals, which expire after the 2013 season. Consequently, teams selling for $70 million in the mid-1980s are now worth an average of $1 billion (Badenhausen, 2011).

The success that Manchester United has enjoyed on the pitch, demonstrated by their winning a record 19th English Premier League championship, is consistent with their lucrative sponsorship deals. The 2011 season marked the first year of its new shirt sponsorship with Aon, worth $32 million annually over four years and representing a 50% bump from its prior deal with AIG. Similarly, the team is reportedly in line to get an increase for its merchandise deal with Nike, which already pays United nearly $40 million per year. With the current 13-year contract set to expire in 2015, a new deal was expected to be done by 2012, potentially worth as much as $70 million annually (Badenhausen, 2011).

TRENDS IN INTERNATIONAL SPORTS

Hosting mega sporting events periodically has become increasingly important for both developing and established cities and countries to strengthen their global image and positioning. Currently, the competition is more heated than ever from emerging cities and countries who believe that hosting major sporting and entertainment events offer a fast track to global recognition and influence. Competition for the Summer Olympic Games and the FIFA World Cup is particularly fierce; cities and countries worldwide vie for the rights to host the events. Competition for the Winter Olympics

is less severe, largely because winter sports are less prevalent than their summer counterparts and because fewer locations have the mountainous terrain and cold climate necessary to host such an event. Yet among the relatively small number of qualified bidders, the level of competition remains intense (Pellegrino & Hancock, 2010).

Ticket Sales

One of the more salient issues with the 2012 Summer Olympic Games involved the sale and allocation of tickets. With 17,000 world-class athletes competing across 26 sports in 38 different disciplines, the Olympic Games remain the ultimate sporting contest, but for London's Games in 2012 the toughest competition was distributing tickets. Games organizers were pressured to reveal how many tickets for the Olympics were available and how much they cost amid concerns that the ticketing strategy will leave Londoners at the back of the line for the 9.2 million seats on sale. The economic development committee for the London Assembly, part of city government, submitted a list of questions to London 2012 officials requesting details on how they plan to fill seats at the Games. The submission calls for details about price, ticket availability, the existence of any priority access, and purchasing arrangements. The committee has asked for publication of a draft ticket strategy that can be scrutinized before anything is formally established.

Despite contributing £625 million ($946 million) to the £9.6 billion total cost of hosting the Games through council-tax payments, overarching concerns remain about whether many of the United Kingdom capital's residents would be able to attend the Olympics. In 2011 London 2012 organizers revealed that European Union competition law requires that tickets for London 2012 be made simultaneously available to the entire EU when they go on sale to Britons. Previously, the London Organizing Committee of the Olympic Games (Locog) confirmed that it had agreed to sell around 130,000 of the most highly sought after tickets to the 2012 Games to two corporate hospitality companies for potential resale at top-end prices. Another issue is the huge allocation reserved for the Olympic family. Under International Olympic Committee rules, the organizers must reserve a large number of seats for IOC representatives, athletes, the 205 National Olympic Committees (NOCs), the government, and media. In addition, an unknown number of seats would be reserved for official partners and sponsors. Although Locog did not publicly disclose how many tickets would be reserved for the Olympic family, during the 1996 Olympics in Atlanta, about 4 million of the 10 million seats were in this allocation (Clegg & Espinoza, 2010).

In 2000 the Sydney Organizing Committee was criticized for being secretive about its ticketing policy—particularly in relation to the allocation of tickets to sponsors and corporate hospitality companies—while in 2008 empty seats were a frequent sight at the Beijing Games. In 2012, London started filling empty seats with free tickets for school children and soldiers. The submission also called on Locog to adhere to previous commitments on the affordability of tickets and give details about how many tickets would be available at less than £10, £20, and £30 and how they would be distributed among the events. Although officials initially promised a range of tickets at less than £30, reports in the U.K. media have questioned whether that price barrier is too low to meet a £441 million ticketing revenue target (Clegg & Espinoza, 2010).

In February 2011 a soccer match between Manchester United and Manchester City of the English Premier League, otherwise known as the Manchester Derby, would not be just another regularly scheduled match on the British soccer calendar. Given the two clubs involved, the match was the richest competition played in any sport in history. According to analysts' estimates, team statements, and media reports, the players on the field and on the two benches in the Manchester Derby cost their teams roughly $850 million to acquire, or about as much as NASA spent to refurbish the Hubble Telescope (Futterman, 2011).

Those numbers should prove comforting to baseball fans who are worried about the profligacy of the New York Yankees and Boston Red Sox. When those teams meet, the player investment on display comes to only about $380 million. In the NFL, the record belongs to the free-spending Dallas Cowboys and Washington Redskins, who met twice in 2010 and had player salaries amounting to about $350 million. Even Spain's two notoriously extravagant teams, Real Madrid and Barcelona—which are the two biggest soccer clubs in the world by revenues—fall short in this arena when they play one another. Although Madrid's player investments are similar to those of the top English clubs, it is not scheduled to play any of them this season. Barcelona still draws many of its players from its youth development program, greatly reducing the amount of money that the club needs to assemble

a team. The reign of the Manchester Derby at the top of the money pile did not last long. In 2011 a match between Manchester City and Chelsea established a new combined record of about $900 million. By the time Manchester United and Chelsea (combined player investment of over $800 million) squared off in two matches in the 2011 season, the Derby fell to fourth place on the all-time list. These records reflect a wave of spending by English clubs in 2011 during the period known as the transfer window, when teams in the EPL can juggle their rosters. Unlike teams in North American sports, soccer clubs can't just acquire players for the cost of their salaries. They're also expected to pay the player's current club an additional "transfer fee." These payments, which are usually many multiples above what the player will earn, have increased dramatically at the high end in recent years. For instance, Chelsea spent $80 million during the January 2011 transfer window for Spanish striker Fernando Torres (Futterman, 2011).

These financial records may not be broken any time soon. Beginning in 2011-2012, the first effects of European soccer's new rules on spending, known as the Financial Fair Play regulations, rippled through the free-spending front offices of the world's best-known clubs. The rules will largely prohibit clubs from spending more than they earn in revenue. Although the regulations will not be enforced until the 2013-2014 season, the accounting process has begun, and the likely result is that the clubs that leapfrogged to the fore by shelling out hundreds of millions of dollars to acquire star players will be forced to curb spending. Although these three Premier League teams (obviously) rank near the top among all international club teams in spending, they may not be able to generate enough revenue to sustain those levels under the new rules (Futterman, 2011). Among all international clubs, Manchester United ranks 3rd by revenues, Chelsea is 6th, and Manchester City is 11th according the to the 2011 Deloitte Football Money League report. Manchester City cracked the top 20 for the first time in 2010. Chelsea's owner, Roman Abramovich, and Manchester City's Sheikh Mansour bin Zayed al-Nahyan have used their personal fortunes to invest in improving their teams (Futterman, 2011).

Broadcasting

One of the recent developments in the sports broadcasting industry encompasses the world of new media. For example, YouTube recently broke new ground by streaming live sports events, but television, in either high definition, 3D, free-to-air, or by subscription, remains the king. Currently, as is often the case in the months leading up to an event of global significance, the governing bodies of rugby union and athletics concluded agreements for the world athletics championships in Daegu and Rugby World Cup New Zealand respectively in a variety of outstanding territories. The Union of European Football Associations (UEFA), European soccer's governing body, has been busy selling rights packages to its two major club competitions for the 2012-2015 period, as well as broadcast rights around the world to the 2012 European Championships. By the start of September 2011, UEFA concluded broadcast deals for its top-tier Champions League rights in Germany, Spain, Italy, and the United Kingdom, where ITV and Sky will continue to split the rights at a cost of over US$650 million (Cushnan, 2011).

Domestic soccer rights in several markets have also yielded significant financial injections for rights sellers worldwide. For example, the Russian Premier League secured a new domestic television contract with pay-TV broadcaster NTV Plus, believed to be worth in the region of US$60 million. Similarly, Canal Plus and Al Jazeera agreed on a US$725 million per season deal (US$2.9 billion overall) to broadcast Ligue 1 in France between 2012 and 2016. This deal was historic because it will mark the first time that Qatar-based Al Jazeera has broadcast matches in France. Furthermore, the Ligue 1 television agreement provided evidence of a revitalized French sports rights market. Also in 2011 Canal Plus signed a US$228 million five-year deal to broadcast top-tier French rugby in the country—the precise final rights fee to be determined by viewership and subscriber numbers—and public service broadcaster France Télévisions renewed its comprehensive broadcast rights agreement with Amaury Sport Organization (ASO) for a variety of events, including full live domestic coverage of the Tour de France in 2014 and 2015 (Cushnan, 2011).

Other sport deals throughout Europe have also created headlines. For example, German public broadcasters ARD and ZDF signed an agreement with the German Football Association (DFB) worth US$245 million to show German national matches for the next four years. In the United Kingdom at the end of July 2011, the BBC and Sky announced that they will share the U.K. TV rights to Formula 1 from 2012 until 2018. The deal came in the midst of the BBC's need to make cuts in its sports budget, meaning that it was no longer able to shoulder the reported £40 million a year contract to broadcast

the sport exclusively. This sharing of broadcasts rights between a free-to-air broadcaster and a pay television service is a growing trend in the United Kingdom; rights to the UEFA Champions League and Masters golf tournament were sold on a similar basis (Cushnan, 2011).

Across the world in Australia, the Australian Football League (AFL) signed the biggest rights deal in its history, a five-year agreement with three domestic media companies—Channel 7, Foxtel, and Telstra—worth US$1.36 billion in total. But even that agreement paled in comparison with the deal struck by the International Olympic Committee in June 2011 with U.S. network NBC for the rights to the 2014, 2016, 2018, and 2020 Olympic Games. Under new management, following the departure weeks earlier of its legendary executive Dick Ebersol, NBC fended off bids from the combined might of ESPN, ABC, and Disney, plus Rupert Murdoch's Fox, with a US$4.3 billion sealed bid.

From NBC's perspective, continuing as the U.S. Olympic broadcaster, a role that it has held at every Games since Sydney 2000, has been just one highlight of a remarkable year of rights acquisitions. Major rights deals with the National Hockey League (NHL), Major League Soccer, and the Professional Golf Association (PGA) Tour more than tempered the loss of the U.S. rights to the Wimbledon tennis championships after 43 years to ESPN for more than US$400 million over the next 12 years (Cushnan, 2011). The network also agreed to a decade-long deal with the NHL purported to be worth as much as US$187 million over that period—the NHL's largest contract to date. A broadcasting agreement with Major League Soccer in a US$10 million per season three-year deal represents the first time that MLS has secured a network broadcast partner. These broadcasts deals further illustrate the significance to broadcasters of having sports property rights.

Technology has also helped shape the broadcasting landscape in unprecedented ways including the ability to broadcast sports in 3D. Although movies have been successfully broadcast in 3D for years, this change has only recently been implemented with sports. For example, in late 2011 the IOC and its Olympic Broadcasting Services production offshoot announced a partnership with Panasonic enabling the London 2012 Olympic Games to be broadcast in 3D. The lineup includes the Opening and Closing Ceremonies, various athletic events, gymnastics, and diving and swimming, produced and delivered to Olympics rights holders around the world—in all, more than 2,000 hours of 3D coverage.

CONCLUSION

Although anticipating future financial trends for high school, college, professional, and international sports will be difficult given their dynamic properties, it will be interesting to see how the issues discussed in this chapter evolve over the next decade. Clearly, several developments will affect the financial operations of sport, individual sport organizations, and overall league policies. For example, will the public continue to subsidize stadiums and arenas in times of scarce resources? Will college athletics continue to move closer to professional models in terms of compensating their labor force? Will high school athletic programs continue to be reduced or eliminated altogether in some circumstances?

Class Discussion Topics

1. What are the two advantages and disadvantages of publicly owned sport franchises?

2. Provide three specific examples of how stadium subsides can positively influence a local community.

3. What will the key labor issues be for professional sports leagues in the near future?

4. What variables will continue to drive up the market value of sports franchises?

5. Will all major sports events move to cable or satellite platforms in the next five years?

6. What are the primary benefits for a country to invest resources to host international sporting competitions?

chapter 19

Applied Sport Finance

Chapter Objectives

After studying this chapter, you should be able to do the following:

- ♦ Read a case and feel comfortable understanding how the facts relate to one another.
- ♦ Appreciate the revenue and expenses seen in a typical college athletic program.
- ♦ Understand how mission and vision affect financial decision making.
- ♦ Appreciate how diverse and extensive personnel costs are for an athletic department.
- ♦ Answer questions associated with the case study and each chapter in the text.

After writing two previous editions of this textbook, we were continually asked whether we could synthesize the various financial topics and theories in the book in a manner to which the average student could relate. After careful consideration, we decided to include a case study. Most business schools use the case study approach to learn about business actions and reactions and the way in which the theories covered in class can be applied and found in the real world. Case studies are frequently found for sport educators in Europe, but until recently cases about sport in the United States were hard to find. Even more difficult was locating cases associated with sport finance.

A case study requires reading the case as you would a story. The story unfolds with critical facts that need to be analyzed. Instead of conveying a happy ending as many stories do, the case study ends with a number of questions. The case study is read to help answer those questions. In some situations the material in the case will overlap what has been covered in prior chapters. At other times, a reader will come across financial material and will have to determine how it fits into the financial landscape. Readers might have a number of questions after reviewing the case. They can discuss the case with others and their instructor to try to solve any problems or answer any questions. In the business world, textbooks and theories do not cover every contingency, so professionals sometimes need to make an educated guess or work under various assumptions.

Although we have used real data in previous chapters for several large publicly traded companies, we decided to focus the case study on a small NCAA Division II program. Because of the confidentiality concerns associated with many programs, we decided to concoct a fictitious Division II athletic department and use real world numbers. Thus, all the numbers are as accurate as possible and can give the reader a good sense of the revenue and expenses for a program, which can help answer the questions at the end.

Division II Athletics

According to *Revenue and Expenses, 2004-2009, NCAA Division II Intercollegiate Athletic Programs Report*, (www.ncaapublications.com/productdownloads/2008DIIRevExp.pdf), in 2010 the National Collegiate Athletic Association (NCAA) Division II comprised 290 active (and 5 provisional) members. This group included 141 private universities and 154 publicly owned universities. The Division II schools with men's football teams had on average 247 male athletes and 142 female athletes. Thus, the average program was hosting around 380 athletes and spending on average $11,900 on each athlete. The average grant for students at private universities in 2009 was $31,600 per student-athlete. These athletes are distributed on average between seven men's and eight women's teams. Most Division II programs sponsored 14 sports.

Total revenue in 2009 for Division II programs offering football was an average of $4,593,000, and the average expense was $4,522,000. The net generated revenue in 2009 averaged $541,000, which when compared with the average expense produced a loss of $3,907,000. The average expense for Division II programs not offering football was $3,102,000. Revenues and expenses in 2009 are broken down in table 19.1.

Median Division II revenues in 2009 are shown in table 19.2.

Table 19.1 Average Division II 2009 Revenue and Expenses on a Percentage Basis

Revenue (%)	Expense (%)
Allocated revenue (87)	Athletic aid (29)
Generated revenue (12)	Coaches compensation (21)
Student fees (0.9)	Administrative staff (11)
Contributions (0.4)	Travel (0.8)
	Medical (0.2)
	Other (25)

Table 19.2 Median Division II 2009 Revenue

Category	Revenue (percentage of generated revenue created by athletic programs)
Total ticket sales	$30,100 (9.76%)
NCAA and conference distributions	12,700 (4.1)
Guarantees and options	11,500 (3.7)
Cash contributions from alumni	108,000 (35.1)
Concession, programs, novelties	6,300 (2.0)
Sponsorship and advertising	500 (0.16)
Sports camps	6,000 (1.9)
Miscellaneous (endowment, investment income, third-party support, etc.)	175,100 (56.7)
Total generated revenue	308,400
Allocated revenue:	
Direct institutional support	3,912,900
Indirect institutional support	276,400
Student fees	0
Total allocated revenue	4,217,300
Total all revenues	4,591,300

Total expenses are divided based on the gender of sport covered and gender-neutral expenses. Thus, the median expenditure on men's sports in 2009 was $2,292,900 (46.7% of expenditures), women's sports cost $1,358,700 (27.6%), and administrative (gender-neutral expenditures) were at $923,700 (18.8%), totaling a median expenditure of $4,910,900. Based on revenue of $4,591,300 the median Division II program lost $319,600 in 2009. These expenditures are broken down further in table 19.3.

Table 19.3 Median Division II 2009 Expenses

Expense category	Men	Women	Admin	Total
Grants-in-aid	$1,274,400	$719,700	0	$2,019,500
Salaries and benefits	593,100	276,000	$345,100	1,236,700
Team travel	180,600	121,200	0	319,800
Recruiting	28,900	15,100	0	45,100
Equipment, uniforms	98,400	45,700	1,600	156,600
Fund-raising	0	0	2,600	16,700
Game expense	42,100	26,400	0	84,500
Medical	0	0	70,000	75,000
Membership dues	1,200	700	20,000	25,000
Spirit group	0	0	2,200	6,400
Other	24,200	8,700	207,900	390,900
Totals	2,242,900	1,213,500	649,400	4,376,200

Other expenses can include compliance, human resources, utilities, insurance, maintenance, ticket office, information technology, purchasing and receiving, TV and radio coverage, and operational expenditures.

The median generated revenue (revenue produced by the athletic department) and expenses for selected sports are highlighted in table 19.4.

Table 19.4 Median Generated Revenue and Expenses

Sport (men/women)	Generated revenue	Expenses	Scholarships	Athletes
Baseball (M)	$28,100	$231,200	9	27
Basketball (M)	35,000	381,800	10	14
Basketball (W)	20,500	332,200	10	12
Field hockey (W)	9,600	190,900	6.3	16
Football (M)	89,600	993,100	36	82
Golf (M)	4,700	67,100	3.6	11
Golf (W)	3,300	62,700	5.4	10
Gymnastics (W)	30,800	145,200	6	12
Lacrosse (M)	11,600	209,500	10.8	15
Lacrosse (W)	14,700	146,400	9.9	19
Soccer (M)	N/A	N/A	9	23
Soccer (W)	13,400	191,200	9.9	23
Softball (W)	17,700	147,700	7.2	22
Tennis (M)	4,500	127,300	4.5	6
Tennis (W)	3,800	137,200	6	12
Track and field (M)	10,700	50,900	12.69	30
Track and field (W)	13,600	199,700	12.69	28
Volleyball (W)	6,700	139,200	4.5	26
Wrestling (M)	24,000	95,800	8	12

The salary and benefit amounts for head coaches (and all assistant coaches) in a median Division II athletic program are shown in table 19.5.

Table 19.5 Median Division II Athletic Salaries and Benefits for Coaches

Sport (men/women)	Head	All assistants	Total
Baseball (M)	$46,800	$12,800	$61,600
Basketball (M)	80,100	39,900	119,700
Basketball (W)	67,900	34,800	102,800
Field hockey (W)	44,300	5,200	52,000
Football (M)	89,900	212,600	305,200
Golf (M)	9,800	N/A	10,400
Golf (W)	9,500	6,400	9,900
Gymnastics (W)	71,100	6,400	77,400
Lacrosse (M)	40,100	4,500	44,000
Lacrosse (W)	47,600	3,900	53,700
Soccer (M)	33,900	6,200	42,800
Soccer (W)	40,300	6,200	50,100
Softball (W)	40,200	7,000	48,900
Tennis (M)	12,500	N/A	13,600
Tennis (W)	13,000	N/A	13,200
Track and field (M)	22,200	3,900	29,300
Track and field (W)	22,800	5,700	31,800
Volleyball (W)	45,800	10,200	61,100
Wrestling (M)	49,400	13,100	65,900

The median amount spent on coaching salaries in 2009 was $593,000 for men's teams and $276,000 for women's teams. The median administrative salary for Division II athletic programs in 2009 was $345,100.

History of the Program

The University of Never Land (UNL), located in Fairy Tale, California, is a comprehensive university that offers both bachelors and masters degrees. It has a world-renowned graphic arts program, as well as a cinema school. The university has a rural campus that includes a number of athletic fields, a gym, and athletic offices. The gym where the basketball and volleyball teams play can hold 1,500 people. It has an equipment room, laundry area, athletic trainer's room, and a small concession stand. A separate student recreation center serves the approximately 2,600 students on campus. Only 100 graduate students are enrolled, and they pay fees that amount to $1,000 a year. Tuition at the university is $25,000 per year. Room and board ranges from $9,000 to $12,000 per year. Every student is charged $1,500 a year for fees, but none of the fees go expressly to support athletics on campus. The university has been generous in supporting athletics from its general funds, which can come from tuition, fees, and other sources because the university uses a centralized budget and all money goes into the same revenue pool.

The university was founded in 1930. Some of its famous supporters were among the top executives in the movie industry. Mr. Walt Disney himself is rumored to have given the initial money to start the institution. Athletics at the university started in 1949. UNL is a Division II member of the NCAA and a member of the Fighting Eight Conference. All the schools in the conference are located in California to hold down travel costs. The university has produced a number of star athletes. The most famous is "Slammin" Sammy Davis Jr., who went on to NBA fame in the 1970s. The athletic director for the last 15 years has been Rocky Balboa, who attended UNL in the 1970s and is passionate about the program. He is proud of the strong academic reputation of the Tinkerbells, or Bells for short. His program provides athletic competition for 296 students, many of whom would not have come to the university were it not for the athletic program. There are 81.19 full scholarships available for men's sports and 57.69 for women's sports, totaling 138.88 full scholarships, which would equate to $4.86 million in grants-in-aid (covering tuition plus room and board) in 2012. Based on 296 student-athletes and 138.88 full scholarships, the university had 157.12 student-athletes paying the entire tuition (not including any aid based on financial need or merit scholarships). Many of the student-athletes had partial scholarships, so the aid was pretty well dispersed in 2012. Based on 157.12 nonscholarship equivalent athletes, the athletic department would generate around $5.5 million in tuition and room and board. In total, the athletic department generated $10.36 million in tuition revenue in 2012. Thus, athletics helps the university survive and is a strong revenue producer for the university. Athletics also serves as a strong alumni retention tool, and the homecoming game is a major event for big donors.

UNIVERSITY of NEVER LAND

Sports Offered

The sports currently offered by the athletic department and the number of athletes participating in each are shown in table 19.6. There are 185 male athletes and 111 female athletes, resulting in a total of 296 athletes.

Table 19.6 Sports Offered (Number of Athletes) at the University of Never Land

Men's sports	Women's sports
Baseball (24)	Softball (21)
Basketball (12)	Basketball (11)
Football (84)	Lacrosse (19)
Volleyball (23)	Volleyball (13)
Soccer (23)	Soccer (22)
Track and field (30)	Track and field (25)

Mission Statement and Goals

The following was the mission statement of the athletic department for many years. A consultant who was brought in liked the mission statement but wanted to change the goals to be more concrete and measurable. The new goals suggested by the consultant are listed after the existing goals.

Mission Statement

The Athletic Department supports and endorses the goals and objectives of the university and serves to

1. meet the competitive and educational needs of the student-athlete;
2. unify the extended university community of students, faculty, staff, alumni, and townspeople;
3. generate a positive image of the university; and
4. promote student health and wellness for life.

Goals

1. Provide the necessary resources to field competitive teams in all sports within the Fighting Eight Conference and the NCAA Division II.
2. Provide the resources to help our student-athletes maintain high academic standards and become better students and citizens of the campus and the community.

3. Bridge the gap between athletics and the campus community by fostering a communicative and inclusive relationship between faculty, staff, coaches, and administrators.

4. Foster dialogue with the general student population to rekindle pride in Tinkerbell Athletics and support for their fellow students, the athletes.

5. Generate community pride and support for Tinkerbell Athletics, thus creating a positive image of the university through athletics.

Proposed Goals

1. Generate at least one sold-out basketball and football game each year.

2. Comply with Title IX to the best of the university's ability through financial or numerical equivalency by either reducing the number of men's sports or adding a new women's sport.

3. Have at least four of the teams break even by covering their expenses.

4. Reduce the athletic department's reliance on direct institutional support by 5% per year over the next three years.

5. Reduce coaching and administrative expenses by 10% over the next three years.

Revenue and Expenses

Revenue

Table 19.7 displays the revenue for the University of Never Land in 2012.

Table 19.7 University of Never Land 2012 Revenue

Category	Revenue
Total ticket sales	$27,750 (see below)
NCAA and conference distributions	12,500
Guarantees and options	12,000
Cash contributions from alumni	300,000 (see below)
Concession, programs, novelties	8,300 (see below)
Sponsorship and advertising	2,500
Sports camps	8,000
Golf tournament	60,000
Field and gym rental	11,300
Miscellaneous (endowment, investment Income, third party support, etc.)	105,100
Total generated revenue	547,450
Allocated revenue:	
Direct institutional support	4,182,000 (see below)
Indirect institutional support	250,800
Student fees	0
Total allocated revenue	4,432,800
Total all revenues	4,980,250

Ticket Sales

> 5 home football games—300 tickets average at $5.00 a ticket = $7,500
>
> 15 men's basketball games—150 tickets average at $3.00 a ticket = $6,750
>
> 15 women's basketball games—100 tickets average at $3.00 a ticket = $4,500
>
> 20 soccer games (men's and women's)—100 tickets average at $3.00 a ticket = $6,000
>
> 25 baseball games—40 tickets average at $3.00 a ticket = $3,000.
>
> Total ticket sales average $27,750 a year.

Cash Contribution from Alumni

The athletic department currently generates $300,000 a year in donations earmarked for athletics. These donations come from 450 alumni, but one alumnus gave a gift of $100,000. The $100,000 gift is an annual gift. Thus, the additional $200,000 needs to be raised every year. Mr. Balboa and the university's president, Sally "Babe" Didrikson, want to launch an aggressive capital campaign for athletics to endow four

coaching positions. The school would need to raise $1,000,000 for each position. The endowed coaching positions would use the interest from the escrowed money to pay the coach's salaries. The money would not be used for any purpose other than salaries and benefits.

On top of the annual campaign, Balboa and Didrikson want to refurbish the athletic field because the bleachers are in need of repair and the turf field does not drain as well as it used to. Thus, the total capital campaign for 2012-2014 will be for $8 to $10 million. If that amount cannot be raised, the university may need to borrow money to make the needed repairs. The university believes that it has a 50% chance of raising the required amount, but it does not want to solicit from its annual donors for fear that they might not continue to make such donations if they make a capital contribution.

Concessions

The university can generate more novelty sales than most Division II programs because of its endearing cartoon characters, and each game program has the original work of one of its students on the cover, which helps drive sales.

Direct Institutional Support

The university has committed at least $4 million per year in institutional support as long as the total number of athletes is at least 290 a year. At that rate, the university believes that it can keep attracting a nice percentage of students to round out its student body, and with the combined tuition and room and board, it will break even (i.e., its institutional support will be offset by incoming additional tuition and other revenue).

Expenses

Expenses in 2012 for the University of Never Land are shown in table 19.8.

Table 19.8 University of Never Land 2012 Expenses

Expense category	Men	Women	Admin	Total
Grants-in-aid	$2,840,400	$2,020,000	$0	$4,860,000
Salaries and benefits	613,000	378,000	472,000	1,463,000 (see below)
Team travel	170,000	111,000	0	281,000
Recruiting	31,000	17,500	0	48,500
Equipment, uniforms	98,900	47,800	1,600	148,300
Fund-raising	0	0	14,500	14,500
Game expense	44,000	28,000	23,000	95,000
Medical	0	0	115,000	115,000 (see below)
Membership dues	1,200	700	20,000	21,900
Spirit group	0	0	7,200	7,200
Sports camp	0	0	7,500	7,500
Golf tournament	0	0	20,000	20,000
Other	24,200	8,700	207,900	390,900 (see below)
Totals	3,822,700	2,611,700	888,700	7,472,800

Administrative and Coaching Staff

The athletic department staff is composed of the following people (total compensation in salary and benefits is shown in parentheses):

Athletic director ($110,000)

Associate AD ($85,000)

Assistant AD ($60,000)

Administrative assistant ($40,000)

Director of sports medicine ($60,000)

Two athletic trainers (part-time) ($25,000 each)

Sports information director ($48,000)

Equipment manager ($40,000)

Strength and conditioning coach (part-time) ($29,000)

Baseball head coach and two assistant coaches ($64,000 total)

Softball head coach and two assistant coaches ($53,000 total)

Basketball head coach and two assistant coaches, men's ($129,000 total)

Basketball head coach and two assistant coaches, women's ($110,000 total)

Football head coach and eight assistant coaches ($317,000)

Lacrosse head coach and one assistant coach ($62,000)

Volleyball women's head coach and one assistant coach ($63,000)

Volleyball men's head coach ($23,000)

Soccer women's head coach and one assistant coach ($60,000)

Soccer men's head coach and one assistant coach ($50,000)

Track and field head coach and two assistant coaches ($60,000)

UNIVERSITY
of
NEVER LAND

Medical Expenses

Medical expenses include the salary and benefit for the director of sports medicine and two part-time athletic trainers. Also included is a medical operating budget of around $5,000 broken down as shown in table 19.9.

Table 19.9   2012 Medical Expenses

Item	Cost
Tape: white tape, stretch tape, pre-wrap, Quick Dry, skin lube, etc.	$3,545.45
Band-Aids: strips and knuckle dressings	74.65
Disinfectant products: hand and surface	101.78
Emergency care: splints, slings, crutches, etc.	130.65
Equipment: disposable cups	104.95
Instruments: scissors, clippers, blades, tape cutters, etc.	48.25
Modalities: hot and cold packs, classic wraps, ice bags, etc.	440.40
First aid products: alcohol wipes, Betadine, gauze, steri-strip, Second Skin, tongue depressors, Bio-Bags, etc.	329.25
Felt and foam (mole skin, adhesive felt)	195.15
Total	$4,967.53

Other

Some expenses are covered by the general university such as human resource, information technology, facility maintenance, and utilities. Purchasing and receiving, ticketing, and TV and radio operations are paid for by the athletic department.

Facilities

The facilities are over 35 years old, so they need repair, similar to any facility of such age. The athletic department operates several facilities:

Dumbo Arena

The Dumbo Arena is the home of UNL's basketball and volleyball programs. The arena seats 1,500 spectators for athletic events but can be configured for everything from concerts and speeches to dinners, meetings, and graduation. The facility has four restrooms, batting cages, athletic trainer's room, equipment room, laundry facilities, offices, and storage. The total are of the arena (including all ancillary activity areas) is 29,000 square feet (2,700 sq m).

Pluto Athletic Complex

The Pluto Athletic Complex accommodates facilities for all UNL outdoor sports. The 3,000-seat Goofy Field is home to UNL's football program, women's lacrosse, and men's and women's track and field teams. The natural grass field was resodded 10 years ago and has excellent drainage.

UNL's softball and baseball teams play on two of the nicest fields in the state. The fields are named after Steamboat Willie and have a steam horn that blows when players hit home runs. The softball field features a crushed red-brick infield and an agrilime warning track in the outfield. The baseball field has a crushed red-brick and natural turf infield and an outfield fence lined with beautiful trees.

Gumby Soccer Complex

The Gumby Soccer Complex seats 1,800 fans in its bleachers. The five-year-old Astroturf field allows the men's and women's soccer teams to play and host conference tournaments on a yearly basis. UNL often rents the fields for local soccer tournaments whenever the school is not using the fields. The field is a lighted, unlike the Pluto Athletic Complex, so it can be used at night for both athletics and intramurals.

Administrative Resources

Many of the resources used by the athletic department come from across the university. For example, heat during the winter comes from the power-generating plant that services the entire university. UNL pays all the electrical expenses for lights, equipment, and ventilation. The university also pays for janitorial care of the arena and landscaping care for the fields and surrounding areas. The athletic department does not need to pay for janitorial supplies, cleaning supplies, paper goods, water for watering lawns, care of landscaping equipment, and all fertilizer and related lawn care chemicals. The value of such services is estimated at over $500,000. All other expenses come from the athletic department's budget.

ASSIGNMENTS

The following questions can be researched by the reader to help provide a broader perspective and real-world application of the material.

▶ Chapter 1. Compare what is going on at UNL compared with other Division II NCAA schools. What do you think is the future of similar Division II programs? Do you think that UNL's expenditures, revenues, or sport offerings are out of line?

▶ Chapter 2. Identify 10 additional revenue sources that UNL could pursue. How much could they reasonably expect to make from such new activities (estimated revenue minus estimated costs), and how would you go about trying to generate this additional revenue?

Do you think that UNL expenses are reasonable? What is and what is not reasonable about such expenses? How would you go about reducing expenses if you have to reduce expenses by 10% next year?

▶ Chapter 3. If you were to advise the athletic department on financial planning for the future, what information would you need and where would you obtain it? Using such information, develop your ideal pro forma budget for the athletic department based on your plan for the future. If they were to drop one men's sport and add another women's sport, what do you recommend they undertake, based strictly on a financial analysis?

▶ Chapter 4. What environmental systems or conditions (government grants for students, downturn in the economy, donors not giving, and so on) could affect the future financial success of the athletic department? How can UNL prepare for such possibilities?

▶ Chapter 5. Because UNL is a nonprofit, what are some of the legal concerns (for example, paying for lobbying, unrelated business income tax) that could affect their financial status?

Do you think that the athletic department could go bankrupt? What is bankruptcy? Can UNL use it to avoid paying some of the bills associated with the athletic department?

▶ Chapter 6. What type of financial analysis could be beneficial for analyzing UNL's athletic budget? What benchmarks or comparative financials could be used to help determine whether the athletic department is doing well compared with similarly situated athletic departments?

If you were conducting a break-even analysis for the athletic department, what revenues and expenses would you use and how could you attempt to break even?

▶ Chapter 7. A wealthy local person loves the Bells and is willing to give the university $1,000,000 to name the basketball court Darth Vader. She is willing to give $1,000,000 today for that right or, if the school can wait two years, she is willing to give $1,100,000. Based on currently prevailing interest rates, how would you advise Mr. Balboa to act, and what issues should he consider when making this decision?

▶ Chapter 8. If you were Mr. Balboa and wanted to raise funds for the athletic department, what would you do? You can be creative, but you have to be realistic. There is little hope of winning the lottery or finding numerous donors with millions of dollars. Thus, assume that most traditional funding sources for a school have been tapped and that you have to look at other options. Walk through all the steps you that would take and estimate the chances of succeeding.

▶ Chapter 9. Because the university is a nonprofit organization, it cannot issue stock as a traditional corporation can. But the university's president wants to explore all possible funding options, so she wants you to write a research paper about whether nonprofits can sell shares in anything to raise money. For example, some lighthouses have sold shares in the lighthouse and have given a beautiful lithographed print to the purchaser as a memento. Likewise, the Green Bay Packers and Boise State have made stock offerings. The memo should highlight what others have done, what success they have had, and how much money you believe could be generated by such a campaign.

▶ Chapter 10. UNL is thinking about joining with a local parks and recreation department to expand its playing fields and then to share such fields and their upkeep with the local government agency. The fields are already adjoining. UNL owns 50 acres (20 ha) and the city owns the adjoining 50 acres. If such an effort is undertaken, where can the two parties go to find additional funding to support this project? Explain your choice and the cost of raising such funds.

▶ Chapter 11. If UNL can borrow $1,000,000 from the bank at prevailing interest rates, payable in 15 years, how much debt service would they have on a yearly basis? What could happen if the loan was secured by the arena and the university defaulted on the loan? How would you advise the university, and how would you advise the bank?

▶ Chapter 12. The associate AD is in charge of finance. He seems to do a good job, but he has trouble with accounts payable and accounts receivable. Bills for tickets and the summer camp are often sent a month or two after services are provided. Invoices received for service bought by the athletic department often go unpaid for several months. These delays might be caused by confusion, but some of the suppliers are alumni and late payments have caused some negative reactions. Develop a policy and procedures statement about how account payables and receivables should be handled in the future. What should the policy be for late payment and aging of accounts?

▶ Chapter 13. The concession stand suffers from food going stale and snacking students. The amount of lost merchandise is costing the university around $1,000 a year. Develop an inventory management system that will help increase sales and reduce losses. How will this new system be implemented?

► Chapter 14. If the athletic department had revenue in excess of expenses in any given year (because UNL is a nonprofit it cannot "earn" a profit), how would you use that money? Provide a specific plan for an excess of $500,000 for a given year.

► Chapter 15. The associate AD has had trouble balancing the books, but he keeps great records. Checks come in to the administrative assistant who does not record them but immediately delivers them to one of the graduate assistants. The checks are processed by a GA and then the same GA takes them to the bank. Deposit slips are then given to the associate AD. He seems to think that there should be more money but does not know what is going on. What specific steps would you recommend that he undertake to investigate his concerns? Develop a process to avoid such concerns in the future.

► Chapter 16. If UNL wants to rebuild its arena, it will have to clear out the facility before demolition and then rebuild on the same spot. If they were to clear out the facility, how could the university make money from such actions? How much do you think that they could get based on items that are likely housed in the arena (from training tables and whirlpools for therapy to toilets, video monitors, time clocks, and even the center-hung scoreboard)? Think broadly and from a fund-raising perspective.

► Chapter 17. If you have a feeling that a recession is coming that could affect the entire sport industry, how would you advise the AD? What specific suggestions would you offer to help weather the storm? How have other schools responded to similar situations?

► Chapter 18. Based on all the information that you have reviewed to date about UNL, what is your five-year projection for the athletic department? What steps would you take to correct any perceived problems or maintain growth? Assume that expenses will grow at 5% on average and that revenue will grow at 3%. Also, assume that you want to follow the goals set forth by the consultant and that you might have to change revenues and expenses accordingly. Thus, you will need to develop a budget for five years down the road.

CONCLUSION

The questions raised in each chapter as applied to this case study highlight how financial issues discussed throughout the text can occur in every sport organization, whether public or private. Every organization has issues. The sport manager who has a good grasp of how financial decision making affects all facets of an organization will know how to respond to them.

Appendix A

Time Value of Money

The tables presented in appendix A illustrate the time value of money. Table A.1 shows the future value of $1 at the end of t periods. Table A.2 shows the present value of $1 received at the end of t periods. And table A.3 shows the present value of $1 per period for t periods.

Table A.1 Future Value of $1 at the End of t Periods

Period	1%	2%	3%	4%	5%	6%	7%	8%	9%	10%	11%	
						INTEREST RATE						
1	1.0100	1.0200	1.0300	1.0400	1.0500	1.0600	1.0700	1.0800	1.0900	1.1000	1.1100	
2	1.0201	1.0404	1.0609	1.0816	1.1025	1.1236	1.1449	1.1664	1.1881	1.2100	1.2321	
3	1.0303	1.0612	1.0927	1.1249	1.1576	1.1910	1.2250	1.2597	1.2950	1.3310	1.3676	
4	1.0406	1.0824	1.1255	1.1699	1.2155	1.2625	1.3108	1.3605	1.4116	1.4641	1.5181	
5	1.0510	1.1041	1.1593	1.2167	1.2763	1.3382	1.4026	1.4693	1.5386	1.6105	1.6851	
6	1.0615	1.1262	1.1941	1.2653	1.3401	1.4185	1.5007	1.5869	1.6771	1.7716	1.8704	
7	1.0721	1.1487	1.2299	1.3159	1.4071	1.5036	1.6058	1.7138	1.8280	1.9487	2.0762	
8	1.0829	1.1717	1.2668	1.3686	1.4775	1.5938	1.7182	1.8509	1.9926	2.1436	2.3045	
9	1.0937	1.1951	1.3048	1.4233	1.5513	1.6895	1.8385	1.9990	2.1719	2.3579	2.5580	
10	1.1046	1.2190	1.3439	1.4802	1.6289	1.7908	1.9672	2.1589	2.3674	2.5937	2.8394	
11	1.1157	1.2434	1.3842	1.5395	1.7103	1.8983	2.1049	2.3316	2.5804	2.8531	3.1518	
12	1.1268	1.2682	1.4258	1.6010	1.7959	2.0122	2.2522	2.5182	2.8127	3.1384	3.4985	
13	1.1381	1.2936	1.4685	1.6651	1.8856	2.1329	2.4098	2.7196	3.0658	3.4523	3.8833	
14	1.1495	1.3195	1.5126	1.7317	1.9799	2.2609	2.5785	2.9372	3.3417	3.7975	4.3104	
15	1.1610	1.3459	1.5580	1.8009	2.0789	2.3966	2.7590	3.1722	3.6425	4.1772	4.7846	
16	1.1726	1.3728	1.6047	1.8730	2.1829	2.5404	2.9522	3.4259	3.9703	4.5950	5.3109	
17	1.1843	1.4002	1.6528	1.9479	2.2920	2.6928	3.1588	3.7000	4.3276	5.0545	5.8951	
18	1.1961	1.4282	1.7024	2.0258	2.4066	2.8543	3.3799	3.9960	4.7171	5.5599	6.5436	
19	1.2081	1.4568	1.7535	2.1068	2.5270	3.0256	3.6165	4.3157	5.1417	6.1159	7.2633	
20	1.2202	1.4859	1.8061	2.1911	2.6533	3.2071	3.8697	4.6610	5.6044	6.7275	8.0623	
21	1.2324	1.5157	1.8603	2.2788	2.7860	3.3996	4.1406	5.0338	6.1088	7.4002	8.9492	
22	1.2447	1.5460	1.9161	2.3699	2.9253	3.6035	4.4304	5.4365	6.6586	8.1403	9.9336	
23	1.2572	1.5769	1.9736	2.4647	3.0715	3.8197	4.7405	5.8715	7.2579	8.9543	11.0263	
24	1.2697	1.6084	2.0328	2.5633	3.2251	4.0489	5.0724	6.3412	7.9111	9.8497	12.2392	
25	1.2824	1.6406	2.0938	2.6658	3.3864	4.2919	5.4274	6.8485	8.6231	10.8347	13.5855	
30	1.3478	1.8114	2.4273	3.2434	4.3219	5.7435	7.6123	10.0627	13.2677	17.4494	22.8923	
40	1.4889	2.2080	3.2620	4.8010	7.0400	10.2857	14.9745	21.7245	31.4094	45.2593	65.0009	
50	1.6446	2.6916	4.3839	7.1067	11.4674	18.4202	29.4570	46.9016	74.3575	117.3909	184.5648	
60	1.8167	3.2810	5.8916	10.5196	18.6792	32.9877	57.9464	101.2571	176.0313	304.4816	524.0572	

*Future value interest factor exceeds 99,999.

				INTEREST RATE					
12%	14%	15%	16%	18%	20%	24%	28%	32%	36%
1.1200	1.1400	1.1500	1.1600	1.1800	1.2000	1.2400	1.2800	1.3200	1.3600
1.2544	1.2996	1.3225	1.3456	1.3924	1.4400	1.5376	1.6384	1.7424	1.8496
1.4049	1.4815	1.5209	1.5609	1.6430	1.7280	1.9066	2.0972	2.3000	2.5155
1.5735	1.6890	1.7490	1.8106	1.9388	2.0736	2.3642	2.6844	3.0360	3.4210
1.7623	1.9254	2.0114	2.1003	2.2878	2.4883	2.9316	3.4360	4.0075	4.6526
1.9738	2.1950	2.3131	2.4364	2.6996	2.9860	3.6352	4.3980	5.2899	6.3275
2.2107	2.5023	2.6600	2.8262	3.1855	3.5832	4.5077	5.6295	6.9826	8.6054
2.4760	2.8526	3.0590	3.2784	3.7589	4.2998	5.5895	7.2058	9.2170	11.7034
2.7731	3.2519	3.5179	3.8030	4.4355	5.1598	6.9310	9.2234	12.1665	15.9166
3.1058	3.7072	4.0456	4.4114	5.2338	6.1917	8.5944	11.8059	16.0598	21.6466
3.4785	4.2262	4.6524	5.1173	6.1759	7.4301	10.6571	15.1116	21.1989	29.4393
3.8960	4.8179	5.3503	5.9360	7.2876	8.9161	13.2148	19.3428	27.9825	40.0375
4.3635	5.4924	6.1528	6.8858	8.5994	10.6993	16.3863	24.7588	36.9370	54.4510
4.8871	6.2613	7.0757	7.9875	10.1472	12.8392	20.3191	31.6913	48.7568	74.0534
5.4736	7.1379	8.1371	9.2655	11.9737	15.4070	25.1956	40.5648	64.3590	100.7126
6.1304	8.1372	9.3576	10.7480	14.1290	18.4884	31.2426	51.9230	84.9538	136.9691
6.8660	9.2765	10.7613	12.4677	16.6722	22.1861	38.7408	66.4614	112.1390	186.2779
7.6900	10.5752	12.3755	14.4625	19.6733	26.6233	48.0386	85.0706	148.0235	253.3380
8.6128	12.0557	14.2318	16.7765	23.2144	31.9480	59.5679	108.8904	195.3911	344.5397
9.6463	13.7435	16.3665	19.4608	27.3930	38.3376	73.8641	139.3797	257.9162	468.5740
10.8038	15.6676	18.8215	22.5745	32.3238	46.0051	91.5915	178.4060	340.4494	637.2606
12.1003	17.8610	21.6447	26.1864	38.1421	55.2061	113.5735	228.3596	449.3932	866.6744
13.5523	20.3616	24.8915	30.3762	45.0076	66.2474	140.8312	292.3003	593.1990	1,178.6772
15.1786	23.2122	28.6252	35.2364	53.1090	79.4968	174.6306	374.1444	783.0227	1,603.0010
17.0001	26.4619	32.9190	40.8742	62.6686	95.3962	216.5420	478.9049	1,033.5900	2,180.0814
29.9599	50.9502	66.2118	85.8499	143.3706	237.3763	634.8199	1,645.5046	4,142.0748	10,143.0193
93.0510	188.8835	267.8635	378.7212	750.3783	1,469.7716	5,455.9126	19,426.6889	66,520.7670	*
289.0022	700.2330	1,083.6574	1,670.7038	3,927.3569	9,100.4382	46,890.4346	229,349.8616	*	*
897.5969	2,595.9187	4,383.9987	7,370.2014	20,555.1400	56,347.5144	*	*	*	*

Table A.2 Present Value of $1 Received at the End of t Periods

Period	INTEREST RATE										
	1%	2%	3%	4%	5%	6%	7%	8%	9%	10%	11%
1	0.9901	0.9804	0.9709	0.9615	0.9524	0.9434	0.9346	0.9259	0.9174	0.9091	0.9009
2	0.9803	0.9612	0.9426	0.9246	0.9070	0.8900	0.8734	0.8573	0.8417	0.8264	0.8116
3	0.9706	0.9423	0.9151	0.8890	0.8638	0.8396	0.8163	0.7938	0.7722	0.7513	0.7312
4	0.9610	0.9238	0.8885	0.8548	0.8227	0.7921	0.7629	0.7350	0.7084	0.6830	0.6587
5	0.9515	0.9057	0.8626	0.8219	0.7835	0.7473	0.7130	0.6806	0.6499	0.6209	0.5935
6	0.9420	0.8880	0.8375	0.7903	0.7462	0.7050	0.6663	0.6302	0.5963	0.5645	0.5346
7	0.9327	0.8706	0.8131	0.7599	0.7107	0.6651	0.6227	0.5835	0.5470	0.5132	0.4817
8	0.9235	0.8535	0.7894	0.7307	0.6768	0.6274	0.5820	0.5403	0.5019	0.4665	0.4339
9	0.9143	0.8368	0.7664	0.7026	0.6446	0.5919	0.5439	0.5002	0.4604	0.4241	0.3909
10	0.9053	0.8203	0.7441	0.6756	0.6139	0.5584	0.5083	0.4632	0.4224	0.3855	0.3522
11	0.8963	0.8043	0.7224	0.6496	0.5847	0.5268	0.4751	0.4289	0.3875	0.3505	0.3173
12	0.8874	0.7885	0.7014	0.6246	0.5568	0.4970	0.4440	0.3971	0.3555	0.3186	0.2858
13	0.8787	0.7730	0.6810	0.6006	0.5303	0.4688	0.4150	0.3677	0.3262	0.2897	0.2575
14	0.8700	0.7579	0.6611	0.5775	0.5051	0.4423	0.3878	0.3405	0.2992	0.2633	0.2320
15	0.8613	0.7430	0.6419	0.5553	0.4810	0.4173	0.3624	0.3152	0.2745	0.2394	0.2090
16	0.8528	0.7284	0.6232	0.5339	0.4581	0.3936	0.3387	0.2919	0.2519	0.2176	0.1883
17	0.8444	0.7142	0.6050	0.5134	0.4363	0.3714	0.3166	0.2703	0.2311	0.1978	0.1696
18	0.8360	0.7002	0.5874	0.4936	0.4155	0.3503	0.2959	0.2502	0.2120	0.1799	0.1528
19	0.8277	0.6864	0.5703	0.4746	0.3957	0.3305	0.2765	0.2317	0.1945	0.1635	0.1377
20	0.8195	0.6730	0.5537	0.4564	0.3769	0.3118	0.2584	0.2145	0.1784	0.1486	0.1240
21	0.8114	0.6598	0.5375	0.4388	0.3589	0.2942	0.2415	0.1987	0.1637	0.1351	0.1117
22	0.8034	0.6468	0.5219	0.4220	0.3418	0.2775	0.2257	0.1839	0.1502	0.1228	0.1007
23	0.7954	0.6342	0.5067	0.4057	0.3256	0.2618	0.2109	0.1703	0.1378	0.1117	0.0907
24	0.7876	0.6217	0.4919	0.3901	0.3101	0.2470	0.1971	0.1577	0.1264	0.1015	0.0817
25	0.7798	0.6095	0.4776	0.3751	0.2953	0.2330	0.1842	0.1460	0.1160	0.0923	0.0736
30	0.7419	0.5521	0.4120	0.3083	0.2314	0.1741	0.1314	0.0994	0.0754	0.0573	0.0437
40	0.6717	0.4529	0.3066	0.2083	0.1420	0.0972	0.0668	0.0460	0.0318	0.0221	0.0154
50	0.6080	0.3715	0.2281	0.1407	0.0872	0.0543	0.0339	0.0213	0.0134	0.0085	0.0054
60	0.5504	0.3048	0.1697	0.0951	0.0535	0.0303	0.0173	0.0099	0.0057	0.0033	0.0019

*The present value factor is zero rounded to four decimal places.

	12%	14%	15%	16%	18%	20%	24%	28%	32%	36%
					INTEREST RATE					
	0.8929	0.8772	0.8696	0.8621	0.8475	0.8333	0.8065	0.7813	0.7576	0.7353
	0.7972	0.7695	0.7561	0.7432	0.7182	0.6944	0.6504	0.6104	0.5739	0.5407
	0.7118	0.6750	0.6575	0.6407	0.6086	0.5787	0.5245	0.4768	0.4348	0.3975
	0.6355	0.5921	0.5718	0.5523	0.5158	0.4823	0.4230	0.3725	0.3294	0.2923
	0.5674	0.5194	0.4972	0.4761	0.4371	0.4019	0.3411	0.2910	0.2495	0.2149
	0.5066	0.4556	0.4323	0.4104	0.3704	0.3349	0.2751	0.2274	0.1890	0.1580
	0.4523	0.3996	0.3759	0.3538	0.3139	0.2791	0.2218	0.1776	0.1432	0.1162
	0.4039	0.3506	0.3269	0.3050	0.2660	0.2326	0.1789	0.1388	0.1085	0.0854
	0.3606	0.3075	0.2843	0.2630	0.2255	0.1938	0.1443	0.1084	0.0822	0.0628
	0.3220	0.2697	0.2472	0.2267	0.1911	0.1615	0.1164	0.0847	0.0623	0.0462
	0.2875	0.2366	0.2149	0.1954	0.1619	0.1346	0.0938	0.0662	0.0472	0.0340
	0.2567	0.2076	0.1869	0.1685	0.1372	0.1122	0.0757	0.0517	0.0357	0.0250
	0.2292	0.1821	0.1625	0.1452	0.1163	0.0935	0.0610	0.0404	0.0271	0.0184
	0.2046	0.1597	0.1413	0.1252	0.0985	0.0779	0.0492	0.0316	0.0205	0.0135
	0.1827	0.1401	0.1229	0.1079	0.0835	0.0649	0.0397	0.0247	0.0155	0.0099
	0.1631	0.1229	0.1069	0.0930	0.0708	0.0541	0.0320	0.0193	0.0118	0.0073
	0.1456	0.1078	0.0929	0.0802	0.0600	0.0451	0.0258	0.0150	0.0089	0.0054
	0.1300	0.0946	0.0808	0.0691	0.0508	0.0376	0.0208	0.0118	0.0068	0.0039
	0.1161	0.0829	0.0703	0.0596	0.0431	0.0313	0.0168	0.0092	0.0051	0.0029
	0.1037	0.0728	0.0611	0.0514	0.0365	0.0261	0.0135	0.0072	0.0039	0.0021
	0.0926	0.0638	0.0531	0.0443	0.0309	0.0217	0.0109	0.0056	0.0029	0.0016
	0.0826	0.0560	0.0462	0.0382	0.0262	0.0181	0.0088	0.0044	0.0022	0.0012
	0.0738	0.0491	0.0402	0.0329	0.0222	0.0151	0.0071	0.0034	0.0017	0.0008
	0.0659	0.0431	0.0349	0.0284	0.0188	0.0126	0.0057	0.0027	0.0013	0.0006
	0.0588	0.0378	0.0304	0.0245	0.0160	0.0105	0.0046	0.0021	0.0010	0.0005
	0.0334	0.0196	0.0151	0.0116	0.0070	0.0042	0.0016	0.0006	0.0002	0.0001
	0.0107	0.0053	0.0037	0.0026	0.0013	0.0007	0.0002	0.0001	*	*
	0.0035	0.0014	0.0009	0.0006	0.0003	*	*	*	*	*
	0.0011	0.0004	0.0002	0.0001	*	*	*	*	*	*

Table A.3 Present Value of $1 per Period for t Periods

Period	1%	2%	3%	4%	5%	6%	7%	8%	9%	10%	11%
1	0.9901	0.9804	0.9709	0.9615	0.9524	0.9434	0.9346	0.9259	0.9174	0.9091	0.9009
2	1.9704	1.9416	1.9135	1.8861	1.8594	1.8334	1.8080	1.7833	1.7591	1.7355	1.7125
3	2.9410	2.8839	2.8286	2.7751	2.7232	2.6730	2.6243	2.5771	2.5313	2.4869	2.4437
4	3.9020	3.8077	3.7171	3.6299	3.5460	3.4651	3.3872	3.3121	3.2397	3.1699	3.1024
5	4.8534	4.7135	4.5797	4.4518	4.3295	4.2124	4.1002	3.9927	3.8897	3.7908	3.6959
6	5.7955	5.6014	5.4172	5.2421	5.0757	4.9173	4.7665	4.6229	4.4859	4.3553	4.2305
7	6.7282	6.4720	6.2303	6.0021	5.7864	5.5824	5.3893	5.2064	5.0330	4.8684	4.7122
8	7.6517	7.3255	7.0197	6.7327	6.4632	6.2098	5.9713	5.7466	5.5348	5.3349	5.1461
9	8.5660	8.1622	7.7861	7.4353	7.1078	6.8017	6.5152	6.2469	5.9952	5.7590	5.5370
10	9.4713	8.9826	8.5302	8.1109	7.7217	7.3601	7.0236	6.7101	6.4177	6.1446	5.8892
11	10.3676	9.7868	9.2526	8.7605	8.3064	7.8869	7.4987	7.1390	6.8052	6.4951	6.2065
12	11.2551	10.5753	9.9540	9.3851	8.8633	8.3838	7.9427	7.5361	7.1607	6.8137	6.4924
13	12.1337	11.3484	10.6350	9.9856	9.3936	8.8527	8.3577	7.9038	7.4869	7.1034	6.7499
14	13.0037	12.1062	11.2961	10.5631	9.8986	9.2950	8.7455	8.2442	7.7862	7.3667	6.9819
15	13.8651	12.8493	11.9379	11.1184	10.3797	9.7122	9.1079	8.5595	8.0607	7.6061	7.1909
16	14.7179	13.5777	12.5611	11.6523	10.8378	10.1059	9.4466	8.8514	8.3126	7.8237	7.3792
17	15.5623	14.2919	13.1661	12.1657	11.2741	10.4773	9.7632	9.1216	8.5436	8.0216	7.5488
18	16.3983	14.9920	13.7535	12.6593	11.6896	10.8276	10.0591	9.3719	8.7556	8.2014	7.7016
19	17.2260	15.6785	14.3238	13.1339	12.0853	11.1581	10.3356	9.6036	8.9501	8.3649	7.8393
20	18.0456	16.3514	14.8775	13.5903	12.4622	11.4699	10.5940	9.8181	9.1285	8.5136	7.9633
21	18.8570	17.0112	15.4150	14.0292	12.8212	11.7641	10.8355	10.0168	9.2922	8.6487	8.0751
22	19.6604	17.6580	15.9369	14.4511	13.1630	12.0416	11.0612	10.2007	9.4424	8.7715	8.1757
23	20.4558	18.2922	16.4436	14.8568	13.4886	12.3034	11.2722	10.3711	9.5802	8.8832	8.2664
24	21.2434	18.9139	16.9355	15.2470	13.7986	12.5504	11.4693	10.5288	9.7066	8.9847	8.3481
25	22.0232	19.5235	17.4131	15.6221	14.0939	12.7834	11.6536	10.6748	9.8226	9.0770	8.4217
30	25.8077	22.3965	19.6004	17.2920	15.3725	13.7648	12.4090	11.2578	10.2737	9.4269	8.6938
40	32.8347	27.3555	23.1148	19.7928	17.1591	15.0463	13.3317	11.9246	10.7574	9.7791	8.9511
50	39.1961	31.4236	25.7298	21.4822	18.2559	15.7619	13.8007	12.2335	10.9617	9.9148	9.0417
60	44.9550	34.7609	27.6756	22.6235	18.9293	16.1614	14.0392	12.3766	11.0480	9.9672	9.0736

	12%	14%	15%	16%	18%	20%	24%	28%	32%	36%
	0.8929	0.8772	0.8696	0.8621	0.8475	0.8333	0.8065	0.7813	0.7576	0.7353
	1.6901	1.6467	1.6257	1.6052	1.5656	1.5278	1.4568	1.3916	1.3315	1.2760
	2.4018	2.3216	2.2832	2.2459	2.1743	2.1065	1.9813	1.8684	1.7663	1.6735
	3.0373	2.9137	2.8550	2.7982	2.6901	2.5887	2.4043	2.2410	2.0957	1.9658
	3.6048	3.4331	3.3522	3.2743	3.1272	2.9906	2.7454	2.5320	2.3452	2.1807
	4.1114	3.8887	3.7845	3.6847	3.4976	3.3255	3.0205	2.7594	2.5342	2.3388
	4.5638	4.2883	4.1604	4.0386	3.8115	3.6046	3.2423	2.9370	2.6775	2.4550
	4.9676	4.6389	4.4873	4.3436	4.0776	3.8372	3.4212	3.0758	2.7860	2.5404
	5.3282	4.9464	4.7716	4.6065	4.3030	4.0310	3.5655	3.1842	2.8681	2.6033
	5.6502	5.2161	5.0188	4.8332	4.4941	4.1925	3.6819	3.2689	2.9304	2.6495
	5.9377	5.4527	5.2337	5.0286	4.6560	4.3271	3.7757	3.3351	2.9776	2.6834
	6.1944	5.6603	5.4206	5.1971	4.7932	4.4392	3.8514	3.3868	3.0133	2.7084
	6.4235	5.8424	5.5831	5.3423	4.9095	4.5327	3.9124	3.4272	3.0404	2.7268
	6.6282	6.0021	5.7245	5.4675	5.0081	4.6106	3.9616	3.4587	3.0609	2.7403
	6.8109	6.1422	5.8474	5.5755	5.0916	4.6755	4.0013	3.4834	3.0764	2.7502
	6.9740	6.2651	5.9542	5.6685	5.1624	4.7296	4.0333	3.5026	3.0882	2.7575
	7.1196	6.3729	6.0472	5.7487	5.2223	4.7746	4.0591	3.5177	3.0971	2.7629
	7.2497	6.4674	6.1280	5.8178	5.2732	4.8122	4.0799	3.5294	3.1039	2.7668
	7.3658	6.5504	6.1982	5.8775	5.3162	4.8435	4.0967	3.5386	3.1090	2.7697
	7.4694	6.6231	6.2593	5.9288	5.3527	4.8696	4.1103	3.5458	3.1129	2.7718
	7.5620	6.6870	6.3125	5.9731	5.3837	4.8913	4.1212	3.5514	3.1158	2.7734
	7.6446	6.7429	6.3587	6.0113	5.4099	4.9094	4.1300	3.5558	3.1180	2.7746
	7.7184	6.7921	6.3988	6.0442	5.4321	4.9245	4.1371	3.5592	3.1197	2.7754
	7.7843	6.8351	6.4338	6.0726	5.4509	4.9371	4.1428	3.5619	3.1210	2.7760
	7.8431	6.8729	6.4641	6.0971	5.4669	4.9476	4.1474	3.5640	3.1220	2.7765
	8.0552	7.0027	6.5660	6.1772	5.5168	4.9789	4.1601	3.5693	3.1242	2.7775
	8.2438	7.1050	6.6418	6.2335	5.5482	4.9966	4.1659	3.5712	3.1250	2.7778
	8.3045	7.1327	6.6605	6.2463	5.5541	4.9995	4.1666	3.5714	3.1250	2.7778
	8.3240	7.1401	6.6651	6.2492	5.5553	4.9999	4.1667	3.5714	3.1250	2.7778

Appendix B

Formulas

The following balance sheet and income statement are interpreted through the financial analysis formulas and industry ratios in this appendix. Most of these formulas and ratios are discussed in chapter 6.

Additional facts include a fictitious Sport Manufacturing Company's (SMC) having one million outstanding shares currently selling for $10 a share. The stock was selling for $8 per share at the start of the year. SMC also has $10 million in outstanding bonds. The bonds are $1,000 face-value bonds redeemable in 20 years, paying 10% interest and currently selling for $1,100 each.

Balance Sheet

Assets	($000)	Liabilities and net worth	($000)
Cash	100	Note payable	0
Accounts receivable	60	Accounts payable	150
Inventory	300	Taxes payable	40
Total current assets	**460**	Other accruals	30
Plant and equipment	500	**Total current liabilities**	**220**
Less depreciation	100	Mortgage payable	150
Net	400	Common stock	250
Total assets	**860**	Retained earnings	240
		Total liabilities and net worth	**860**

Income Statement

	($000)
Sales	500
Less: Material and labor	300
Manufacturing costs	30
Cost of goods sold	**330**
Gross profit	**170**
Depreciation	20
Selling expense	20
Profit before interest and taxes	**130**
Interest payments	10
Taxes	40
Profit after taxes	**80**
Dividends	40
Retained earnings	**40**

Profit

profit margin = profit after taxes / sales (i.e., $80,000 / $500,000 = 0.16, or 16%)

corporate earnings = sales − costs (i.e., $500,000 − $330,000 = $170,000)

earnings per share = earnings / total shares (i.e., $170,000 / 1,000,000 = $0.17)

PE ratio = price per share / earnings per share (i.e., $10.00 / $0.17 = 59 times earnings)

Liquidity

acid test ratio = liquid assets / current liabilities from cash and accounts receivable (i.e., $160,000 / $220,000 = 0.73)

current ratio = current assets / current liabilities (i.e., $460,000 / $220,000 = 2.09)

solvency ratio = net worth / total assets (i.e., $490,000 / $860,000 = 0.57)

working capital = current assets − current liabilities (i.e., $460,000 − $220,000 = $240,000)

Company Value

book value = total assets − total liabilities from total current liabilities plus mortgage payable (i.e., $860,000 − $370,000 = $490,000)

owners' equity = common stock + retained earnings (i.e., $250,000 + $240,000 = $490,000)

book value per share = owners' equity / outstanding shares (i.e., $490,000 / 1,000,000 = $0.49)

dividend payout ratio = dividend per share / earnings per share (i.e., $0.04 / $0.17 = 0.235, or 23.5%)

net worth = common stock + retained earnings (i.e., $250,000 + $240,000 = $490,000)

turnover = sales / assets (i.e., $500,000 / $860,000 = 0.58)

Indebtedness

debt–equity ratio = total liabilities / shareholders' equity (i.e., $370,000 / $490,000 = 0.76)

interest coverage (IC) = (pretax income + interest expense) / interest expense (i.e., [$130,000 + $10,000] / $10,000 = 14 times)

Return on Investment

return on assets (ROA) = net income / total assets (i.e., $80,000 / $860,000 = 0.09, or 9%)

return on equity (ROE) = net income / owners' equity (i.e., $80,000 / $490,000 = 0.16, or 16%)

return on investment capital (ROIV) = net income / long-term debt + owners' equity (i.e., $80,000 / [$150,000 + $490,000] = 0.125, or 12.5%)

bond yield = 10%

Investor Information

annual return (per share) = increase or decrease in value + any dividend (i.e., $2.00 + $0.04 = $2.04 per share).

On a percentage basis, the annual return would be divided by the initial investment (i.e., $2.04 / $8.00 = 0.255, or 25.5%).

current yield = annual interest payment / current market value (i.e., $100* / $1,100 = 0.0909, or 9.09%)

Annual interest payment = bond face value × bond interest rate (i.e., $1,000 × 10%).

dividend per share = dividends / outstanding shares (i.e., $40,000 / 1,000,000 = $0.04 a share)

holding period return (HPR) = (current income + capital gains) / purchase price (i.e., $0.04 + $2.00) / $8.00 = 0.255, or 25.5%)

simple rate of return (SRR) = investment's annual income / initial investment (i.e., $0.04 / $8.00 = 0.005, or 0.5%)

Glossary

ability to pay—The ability to pay refers to a business' or customer's ability to make payment to a vendor. Thus, if you are trying to sell someone concession items, you should examine that individual's ability to purchase the items with either cash or credit.

acceleration clause—Such a clause is often included in a contract to force one party to pay the entire amount owed if another party misses a payment.

account—Accounts represent a record of a relationship between parties. A typical example is a line of credit with a bank or a simple checking account.

account balance—An account balance represents the current account status at the end of a given time period. Thus, at the end of each month a bank might send customers a checking account balance to help them identify how much money they have available for future purchases.

accounting—Accounting is the art of tabulating financial numbers to determine how much money someone earned and spent during a given period.

account reconciliation—If you have ever balanced your own checkbook, you have performed account reconciliation. Account reconciliation entails adjusting the difference between various accounts to ensure that all totals agree.

accounts payable (A/P)—Accounts payable represent outstanding obligations that are owed by a business to vendors, lenders, or anyone else from whom credit was received and goods were purchased on such credit.

accounts receivable (A/R)—Accounts receivable represent moneys that are owed to a business from customers who purchased merchandise or services on credit. Many customers do not have sufficient funds to make cash purchases and thus need credit in order to purchase necessary products or supplies. A/R are not bad; they represent significant sales and can be used as collateral to borrow money. However, A/R can become a burden if they are not repaid in a timely manner.

accrual—Accrual is an accounting term that defines anticipated future expenses and revenues. For example, in some accounting systems (accrual accounting), expenditures and revenues are recorded at the time of the transaction, regardless of when the money is actually disbursed or received. In contrast, in the **cash basis budgeting** (or accounting) system, expenditures and revenues are recorded at the time they are actually disbursed or received.

accrued dividend—Sometimes a company decides to pay a dividend to shareholders, but the company's board of directors does not make a formal declaration. Without a formal declaration, an accrued dividend does not represent a legal obligation, but it is still an obligation that should be paid to shareholders barring any unforeseen needs for such funds.

accrued interest—Similar to accrued dividends (dividends that have been earned but not yet paid), accrued interest is interest that is owed but not yet paid.

acid test ratio (quick ratio)—The acid test is an analysis of the ability of a company to liquidate current assets (excluding harder-to-sell items such as inventory) to pay off current liabilities. Cash is added to marketable securities and accounts receivable, and these liquid assets are divided by current liabilities. If the resulting number is less than 1, then the company does not have enough liquid assets to pay current liabilities. If the ratio is greater than 1, then the company has more than enough liquid assets to pay off current liabilities. If a company has $100 in cash, no marketable securities, $200 in accounts receivable, and $400 in current liabilities, the acid test ratio is ($100 + $200) / $400 = 0.75. Since the ratio is lower than 1, the company cannot cover all its current liabilities.

acquisition—Acquiring control of a corporation through stock purchase or exchange.

activity—Activity refers to the number of transactions occurring in a given account during a given accounting time period.

actual value—Actual value refers to the **book value** of an asset. To determine book value, take an item's original purchase cost and subtract all accumulated depreciation. If you bought a computer with a five-year life for $5,000 and used straight-line depreciation, after one year the actual, or book, value would be $5,000 minus $1,000 (one year's worth of depreciation) = $4,000.

actuaries—Actuaries are expert mathematicians who analyze the risks and premiums for insurance coverage based on probability estimates. Probability estimates help determine the risk that a given event will occur and the potential loss that could be incurred from such an event.

adjustable basis—This term is typically used to describe a tax situation in which the value of an asset is increased through capital expenditures or reduced by depreciation. The adjustable basis for your house changes when you incur such capital expenditures as installing a new roof. Any increase in the house's value when you try to resell the house needs to be adjusted by the cost of the new roof; this reduces your tax liability for any profits from the sale.

adjustable rate mortgage (ARM)—ARMs, also referred to as variable- or flexible-rate mortgages, are a type of mortgage for which the interest rate can change over the loan's lifetime. It is common for ARMs to be low cost for the first several years of the loan and for the interest rate to increase over time. In contrast, the interest rate for fixed-rate mortgages remains stable throughout the loan's lifetime.

adjusted balance method (ABM)—The ABM is one of several financing techniques (see also **average daily balance method** and **past-due balance method**) used to determine interest owed. As an example of how ABM is calculated, if you have a credit card that has an 18% annual interest rate, you will be paying 1.5% interest a month on your adjusted balance. If you used your credit card to buy sporting goods worth $400 in February and paid only $300 in March, you would owe 1.5% interest multiplied by the adjusted $100 balance ($400 – $300). If you made no more purchases in March, you would owe $101.50, representing the $100 balance and $1.50 in interest (Siegel, Shim, & Hartman, 1992).

adjusted gross income (AGI)—AGI is a tax term representing your total gross income minus allowed adjustments for such items as health care costs or mortgage interest.

ad valorem tax—An ad valorem tax is a levy imposed on business property (both real and possibly personal), based primarily on a percentage of the property's value.

after-tax cash flow (ATCF)—ATCF represents all income minus any taxes paid.

aggregate amount—An aggregate amount is the total, or gross, amount of a given item. For example, the aggregate income of the nation is the gross national product.

allowance—In finance terms, an allowance is a credit that a creditor allows a debtor to take for any of a number of reasons. For example, assume you bought 1,000 foam #1 fingers to sell, and 200 of them are defective. Instead of your owing $1,000 for the lot, the seller might give you a $200 allowance or reduce the amount owed to compensate you for the defective products.

amortization—Amortization refers to repaying a loan in installments. As such payments are made, typically on a property mortgage, the debtor's equity in the property increases because each installment comprises both interest and principal. Goodwill can also be amortized over several years instead of just the first year after a business has been purchased.

annual percentage rate (APR)—APR is the ratio of the finance charge to the average amount of credit in use during the lifetime of a loan (Siegel, Shim, & Hartman, 1992). Under the Truth in Lending Act, banks must disclose the APR (in percentage form) and the actual finance charge in dollars.

annual report—At the end of their fiscal years, companies produce an annual report to inform shareholders about the company's financial position. Annual reports are carefully scrutinized by more than just shareholders; potential investors, creditors, lenders, and other interested parties rely on the audited information to help make investment decisions.

annual return—The annual return is the return from a given investment over the course of a year. Assume you purchased a stock on January 1 for $1,000 and sold the stock on the following December 31 for $1,500. During the year, the stock paid a dividend of $50. Your total annual return is calculated as follows:

increased value ($1,500 – $1,000) = $500
dividend income + 50
total return $550

The percentage annual return calculation is:

percentage annual return = total annual return / initial investment

= $550 / $1,000

= 55%

Thus, the annual return on this investment is $550, or 55%. However, not all investments are this successful. If the stock decreased to $800, the annual return would be calculated as follows:

$1,000 decreased to $800 = –$200

+$50 dividend

= –$150 total revenue

percentage annual return = total return / initial investment

= –$150 / $1,000

= –15%

annuity—An annuity is typically a savings account or a retirement account with an insurance company or other investment placement company into which the investor can deposit a lump sum or scheduled deposits. When a particular event occurs, such as retirement, the investor receives regular repayments such as monthly distributions until the entire invested amount is repaid.

Annuities have several significant benefits: The government does not tax the interest earned until the funds are distributed; compounding interest quickly increases the investment value; and unlike pensions and individual retirement accounts, annuities normally do not have any limitations on the amount an investor can contribute. One drawback, among several, is that investors normally cannot recover their funds until they reach the age of 59 1/2 without incurring significant penalties (Siegel, Shim, & Hartman, 1992).

appreciation—Appreciation is the increase in an item's value. If you bought 100 shares of a stock for $1,000 and sell them for $2,000, the investment has appreciated $1,000.

appropriation—An appropriation is an amount of money set aside in a budget to cover a particular expense such as inventory or expected wages.

arrears—Being in arrears means being in default of an obligation. You are in arrears if you owe someone $10 to be paid on Friday but do not pay on Friday. Arrearage also refers to the situation in which cumulative preferred stock dividends have been declared but not paid.

ask price—The ask price is the price a seller would like to receive for the item he wishes to sell.

assessed valuation—Government entities require landowners to pay property taxes based on the assessed value of the property. The assessed value is not always the market value; it is often a percentage of the market value of the home and land.

asset—An asset is any resource or goods that might offer future benefits to a business and have value. Examples of assets are buildings, machinery, land, inventory, business goodwill, and related resources. "Hard assets" include such items as inventory and equipment that are tangible (can be touched). Intangible assets such as a company's goodwill, which has value but is hard to quantify, are called "soft assets."

assignment—Assignment refers to the transfer of property (real or personal) from one party to another. By assigning the property, the assignor gives the property to another (the assignee) with the assurance that there are no claims against the property and that the assignor has the right to transfer the property.

assumption—If you cannot pay your bills, someone can assume your debt and then become responsible for repaying the debt.

audit—An audit is an inspection by an independent external entity of all a company's accounting records and business operations. The primary purpose of a company audit by a certified public accountant (CPA) is to validate all financial statements for accuracy so that the government, lenders, shareholders, and others can obtain an accurate view of the company.

average collection period—The average collection period is the average amount of time it takes a business to collect outstanding accounts receivable. The longer the average, the more money is lost because of the inability to use such outstanding funds for investment or other growth opportunities. Furthermore, if the average is long, that means there is a greater likelihood that some accounts receivables might be difficult to collect.

average daily balance method (ADBM)—The ADBM is a method used by banks and credit card companies to calculate interest earned or owed. Using this method, a bank examines your average daily balance throughout the month and divides that amount by the number of days in the month. Assume that on the first day of the month you had $500 in the bank and on the 15th had only $100 in the bank. Also assume that your account earns 10% interest annually, or 0.83% a month. Your average daily balance is calculated as follows:

Number of days		Balance		Weighted balance
15	×	$500	=	$7,500
15	×	$100	=	$1,500
			Total	$9,000

The $9,000 weighted balance is divided by 30 days, equaling an average daily balance of $300, which if multiplied by the monthly interest rate produces an interest payment of $2.49.

backup withholding—Sometimes banks, investment companies, or other businesses cannot determine the Social Security number of someone to whom they are required to pay dividends, interest, or other payments. Instead of paying the full amount and possibly depriving the IRS of potential taxes, the entity withholds 20% of the payment and sends it to the IRS.

balance—For strict accounting purposes, balance is calculated by totaling all credits and subtracting all debt. However, in the context of **balance sheets**, balance refers to equality between all assets on the one hand and all liabilities plus owners' equity on the other hand, as shown in the equation assets = liabilities + owners' equity.

balance sheet—A balance sheet is a statement of financial condition prepared at the end of a set time period that lists a company's assets, liabilities, and owners' equity. The balance sheet is balanced when assets equal all liabilities plus the owners' equity. See the following balance sheet for the year ending October 31, 2010.

Balance Sheet

Assets		Liabilities and net worth	
	($000)		($000)
Cash	100	Note payable	0
Accounts receivable	60	Accounts payable	150
Inventory	300	Taxes payable	40
Total current assets	460	Other accruals	30
Plant and equipment	500	**Total current liabilities**	**220**
Less depreciation	100	Mortgage payable	150
Net	400	Common stock	250
Total assets	**860**	Retained earnings	240
		Total liabilities and net worth	**860**

balloon payment—Some term loans (called balloon loans) require that only interest payments are made until the loan is due; then the entire principal and remaining interest are paid in a balloon payment.

bankruptcy—A business can face bankruptcy when its debt exceeds its assets' fair market value. If a company owes $1 million and its assets are worth only $500,000, the company can voluntarily pursue bankruptcy protection from creditors or can be forced by courts into bankruptcy to help protect any remaining value that the creditors might try to salvage. Three categories of bankruptcy are available: Chapters 7, 11, and 13. Chapter 7 allows an individual's or business' property to be sold and the proceeds to be divided among creditors. Some specifically excluded items, such as a primary home and one auto, are not sold so that the debtor can still survive. Any debts that are not covered by the sale proceeds are discharged. More than one million Chapter 7 bankruptcies were filed in 1997 (Cheeseman, 2001). Chapter 11 allows a company to reorganize and maintain control over its assets and operations while it attempts to resolve repayment schedules and amounts with debtors. Once the courts confirm a reorganization plan, all debts not included in the plan are discharged (Cheeseman, 2001). Chapter 13, which is sometimes called the wage-earner plan, allows a debtor to repay debts over a three-year period. Debts are consolidated based on a court-coordinated and approved schedule that allows for installment payments (Cheeseman, 2001).

bear and **bear market**—A bear is an individual who believes the stock market will drop (typically more than 20%), and so he sells stocks, "goes **short**," or buys a **put**. A bear market is a prolonged period during which stock prices continue to decline. Bear markets can be caused by poor economic conditions, political collapses, rising interest rates, or a host of other factors that foster pessimism among investors. See **bull** and **bull market**.

bearer bonds—Bearer bonds, or coupon bonds, do not require owners to register their names with the issuing company or government unit. The person who bears the bond can clip a coupon when it becomes due and cash it in.

benchmarking—Benchmarking is the process of analyzing statistical data to compare companies against one another or against industry standards.

Best's ratings—A.M. Best performs an annual audit of insurance companies to determine their financial stability, which is a valuable tool for those seeking to buy insurance from a solid company or those interested in investing in insurance company stocks. The highest rating is A+.

bid price—A bid price is the highest price a buyer is willing to pay for a security. The asking price is the price proposed by the seller of the security.

bill—There are several different types of bills, but in general, a bill is a written statement describing the terms and conditions of a particular sales transaction.

billing cycle—Companies traditionally bill their clients on a regular basis, typically monthly, bimonthly, quarterly, semiannually, or annually. These billing periods are referred to as billing cycles (they cycle through on a regular basis).

bill of sale—A bill of sale is formal documentation that represents the transfer of title to goods.

bills payable—Bills payable are bills or promissory notes that a company owes, representing a debt. See also **accounts payable**.

bills receivable—Bills receivable refers to notes, checks, drafts, or other contractually obligated instruments representing money or obligations owed to a person or entity. See also **accounts receivable**.

binder—A binder is a temporary payment representing a good-faith deposit between contracting parties to go forward with a contract. The binder binds the parties to the agreement but can be returned if the contract is not finalized. This distinguishes a binder from a deposit, which is normally not returned if the contract is not finalized.

blank endorsement—If you receive a check and sign the back, then you or anyone else who comes into possession of the check can cash it. To prevent others from cashing the check without your permission, you should sign the check and also write "For deposit only to the account of Jane Doe," or a similar phrase, on the check. The check no longer has a blank endorsement but now has a specified endorsement.

blind pool—Investors can join together as limited partners and each contribute a specific amount toward an investment. The combined money can then be invested by a general partner in investments such as stocks, bonds, or real estate. The pool is called a blind pool because the limited partners contribute without knowing exactly where the general partner might invest the money.

blind trust—In the traditional blind trust, one person or several individuals give their assets to a third party who will manage the funds in total independence. For example, President Bush owned part of the Texas Rangers before becoming the governor of Texas, and to avoid any potential conflict of interest, he transferred his ownership interest to a blind trust ("Bush Admits," 2000).

blue-chip stocks—Blue-chip stocks are stocks issued by the strongest companies—those that have a strong reputation for success, offer quality products or services, and are financially secure. Some blue-chip companies are McDonald's, General Electric, IBM, Shell, AT&T, and Bank of America.

bond—A bond is a legal instrument through which a company or government entity promises to repay the bond purchaser both the principal and a specified interest rate; in return the bondholder receives a pledge of assets or can rely on the **full faith and credit** of the issuer. Thus, if IBM wants to expand and issues $50 million in bonds, some investors may rely on IBM's past history of not defaulting on bonds and purchase the bond backed by their faith in the company. The full faith and credit of a company can back bonds not backed by assets. If the company collapses, there will be no collateral from which to repay the investment.

bond discount—Sometimes after a bond is issued the interest rate changes, making the bond less desirable than it was previously. A company's instability can also reduce the value of a bond. A bond is at a discount when the bond's **face value**, or **par value** (what the bond is worth when it is issued), is greater than the **market value**. Market value is what the bond would be worth if sold on a bond market. If the market value exceeds the face value, then the bond is being traded at a premium.

bondholder—A bondholder is anyone who holds legal title to a bond.

bond rating—Two companies, Moody's and Standard & Poor's, issue bond ratings that range from C or D to Aaa or AAA, respectively. An AAA- or Aaa-rated bond is the highest-quality bond, while ratings at the other extreme (C or D) indicate a lower chance that bondholders will be able to recover their investment. Blue-chip companies or strong government entities (financially strong cities, municipalities, or states) typically have AAA or similar ratings.

bond valuation—Bond valuation is the complex mathematical process used to determine how much an investor should pay for a bond. The equation includes such criteria as present value, interest rate, investor-required rate of return, the bond's maturity date, and the degree of risk.

bond yield—The yield obtained from a bond represents its effective rate of return. One means to measure the yield is the current yield method, which is calculated by dividing the annual interest payment by the bond's current market value. Thus, if you have a bond with a 10% coupon rate and a $1,000 par value that is selling for $975, the **current yield** is (10% × $1,000) / $975 = 10.26%. This method shows that you are earning a little more than the stated interest rate, but it does not take into consideration the bond's maturity date, which can affect the attractiveness of the investment. Two other more complex formulas, **yield to call** and **yield to maturity**, can help provide a more detailed analysis if the bond is held for a set time period or held until it matures.

book value—Book value is calculated by subtracting total liabilities from total assets. See also **actual value**.

book value per share (BVPS)—BVPS represents the value of each share of stock based on its cost when the stock was originally issued. We can calculate BVPS by dividing total stockholders' equity by the number of outstanding shares. If a company's total shareholders' equity is $40 million and there are one million outstanding shares, then the BVPS is $40.

break-even point—The break-even point is the level of revenue generation at which total revenue exactly matches total costs. The break-even analysis is used to help determine when profit could be made on a given product. Assume that you manufacture baseballs and that the variable costs (string, rubber, hourly wages, and so on) are $0.50 per ball. Assume also that fixed costs such as rent are $10,000 per month. If you manufactured and sold 5,000 balls per month, your total costs would be $2,500 (variable) + $10,000 (fixed) = $12,500. To break even you would need to sell all 5,000 balls at an average price of $2.50 each. If you made 10,000 balls in a given month and kept the price of $2.50 per ball, then you would have $15,000 in costs and $25,000 in sales, which would generate a $10,000 profit.

break point—Sellers often indicate that if you buy 1 to 100 of an item, the price will be $1 each, for example. If you buy 101 to 500, the price will be reduced to $0.75 each. The break point for the discount is 101 units. A seller might have multiple break points at which the price continues to decline as the order quantity increases.

bridge loan—Sometimes a company needs a short-term loan while it is negotiating a long-term loan. A bridge loan is the solution, but it might cost more than traditional bank loans. A bridge loan might be needed by a buyer who wants to put a deposit down on some property before closing and securing a long-term mortgage.

budget—A budget is a road map or plan expressed in monetary terms that highlights all anticipated assets, debt, expenses, revenue, and net worth.

bull and **bull market**—A bull is an investor who has a favorable outlook on the economy and is willing to invest in stock, bonds, and other securities. A bull market is when there are prolonged market advances over a significant time period. See also **bear** and **bear market**.

business cycle—All businesses go through cyclical conditions in which they may have significant growth and then at a later time experience contraction. The entire economy can also go through cycles that include recovery and recession.

buying power—Buying power can be equated to liquid assets, which represent cash and marketable securities that could be quickly sold to make various purchases. If you do not have liquid assets, you do not have any buying power.

buy order—If you call your stockbroker and indicate that you want to purchase certain securities, you have just placed a buy order.

buyout—In a buyout, one investor, multiple investors, or a business can acquire a controlling interest in a company through buying a majority of

that company's stock. Various professional sports teams have gone public and issued stock, and some of these teams were subsequently bought out by an individual investor or investment group and became privately owned teams.

call provision—Companies that issue bonds or preferred stock can pay an investor an amount over the face value of the security and redeem the security before it reaches maturity. A company might undertake this strategy if it wants to reduce amounts owed to bondholders or reduce the number of outstanding stock shares.

capital—Capital is wealth used to produce additional wealth.

capital asset pricing model (CAPM)—The CAPM is a method of measuring the cost of common stock.

capital assets—The term *capital assets* commonly refers to fixed assets such as buildings, fields, stadiums, equipment, and other assets that can be depreciated.

capital gains and **capital losses**—Capital gains are the total gains in value of an investment, excluding dividends. However, dividends can be included in the capital gains if the dividends are reinvested in additional shares of the same stock. Capital losses are all realized losses from an investment. There are both long-term and short-term capital gains and losses. Long-term capital gains or losses are investments that have matured for more than one year and result in capital gains or losses that must be reported to the IRS. Short-term capital gains or losses apply to investments held for less than one year.

capitalization rate (cap rate)—The cap rate is used to determine the rate of return received from a real estate investment. To determine the cap rate, we divide the net operating income (NOI) from the investment's first year by the total investment cost. The higher the cap rate, the lower the perceived value of the investment. If you obtain $10,000 in NOI from a property and the property cost $200,000, then the cap rate is $10,000 / $200,000 = 5%. If banks are paying 8% interest, then the return on the real estate investment would be poor unless the real estate markedly increased in value.

capital markets—There are a number of capital markets in which long-term debt and securities are bought and sold. The most famous capital market is the New York Stock Exchange. Additional markets include the American Stock Exchange, the over-the-counter market (NASDAQ), and numerous regional and foreign exchanges.

capital outlay—A capital outlay is any expenditure for property or equipment for permanent use.

capital spending—Capital spending is the net spending on fixed assets.

cash—There are many terms for cash, including legal tender and numerous slang terms. In the business world, cash includes money, coins, checks, bearer bonds, bank accounts, negotiable instruments, and related liquid assets.

cash basis budgeting—This budgeting process recognizes income and expenses when cash is actually received or paid and does not recognize accounts receivable or accounts payable.

cash discount—Manufacturers or wholesalers often offer discounts for those who purchase items with cash. A cash discount may be expressed by the formula 2/10/30. This formula means that the buyer has 30 days to pay the net amount. However, a buyer who pays the bill within 10 days will receive a 2% discount. Sellers can use multiple discounts in addition to cash discounts, such as seasonal or volume discounts, to offer even greater savings.

cash flow—Cash flow refers to the difference between what a company brings in and what it pays out. Companies can keep track of cash payments and receipts with a cash flow statement.

cash system of accounting—The cash system of accounting calculates expenditures and income only when cash is actually paid or received. This system does not consider accounts receivable or accounts payable.

cats and dogs—A derogatory term referring to stocks that represent a poor investment choice because of their highly speculative nature.

certificate of deposit (CD)—CDs are a type of savings account that pays more than traditional passbook or other savings accounts. They earn higher interest because the depositor has to keep the money in the CD for a longer maturity period than for other types of accounts.

clear title—When real or personal property is sold, the buyer normally wants the property to have a clear title, which means that no liens or other claims exist against the property. If the property is subject to a court-ordered lien, it can still be resold, but with a clouded title.

collateral—Collateral is either real or personal property pledged as security for repaying a loan.

commercial paper (CP)—Large, stable corporations issue commercial paper, or unsecured promissory notes from the corporation for amounts exceeding $25,000. Commercial paper typically carries a higher interest rate than bank accounts or CDs and typically matures in 30, 60, or 90 days.

common stock—Common stocks are shares in either privately held or public companies, representing an equity interest in those companies.

Although common stock shareholders own an equity share in the company, if a company goes bankrupt, they are paid only after bondholders and preferred stock shareholders are paid. Stockholders have specific rights, including the right to elect the board of directors and the right of preemption, which entitles them to buy any new stocks from the company before other investors can. Preemption helps the stockholder maintain a proportional share in the company.

compensating balance—Some banks allow a depositor to borrow money but demand that the borrower maintain a specified balance in the bank. Thus, the bank might loan you $10,000 but insist that you maintain a 10% compensating balance to help hedge against the possibility of your defaulting on the loan. The borrower normally does not earn interest on the compensating balance, which effectively increases the interest on the loan. For example, assume that the $10,000 loan has a required interest payment of 8%. Since the $1,000 compensating balance does not earn interest, the true interest rate for the loan is $800 / ($10,000 – $1,000), which equals 8.89%.

compounding—Compounding entails retaining an investment's return from subsequent years after the initial investment, which results in accruing more revenue than if the investment's return was withdrawn immediately upon receipt. Thus, compounding can significantly increase an investment's total return.

compound interest—With many loans, interest is added to the principal loaned amount over the loan's life. If you borrowed $100 at 10% interest compounded annually, you would owe $110 after the first year, $121 for the second year ($110 × 110%), $133 for the third year ($121 × 110%), and so on throughout the life of the loan.

conglomerate merger—This form of merger occurs when companies in unrelated lines of business come together.

consumer credit—Consumer credit includes all nonbusiness debt (personal debt) excluding mortgages. Credit card debt represents part of the overall consumer credit.

Consumer Credit Protection Act (CCPA), also called the **Truth in Lending Act**—The CCPA requires a lender to clearly disclose the loan terms, interest rate, total payments, and total interest amount.

consumer finance companies—Sometimes a consumer has a poor credit history, and banks are unwilling to loan the individual any money. A consumer finance company can also loan the consumer money, through either a secured or an unsecured loan, for a short term and at a higher interest rate. The interest rate is higher because the loan is riskier.

consumer price index (CPI)—The Bureau of Labor Statistics publishes a monthly CPI number, which represents an average of the prices of various goods and services that consumers typically purchase in various urban areas. The CPI provides insight into the purchasing power of the U.S. dollar.

contingency fund—A contingency fund is a reserve account that an individual or entity has put money into to help pay unforeseen bills or cover emergency monetary needs.

controller—A controller is someone who controls or organizes the finances of a company or organization.

conventional mortgage—Typically, mortgages are obtained after a buyer has provided a sizable down payment on real property and offers fixed monthly payments at a set interest rate over a 15- or 30-year term.

convertibles—Convertibles is the term used to describe bonds, debentures, or preferred stocks that can be converted to common stock or other securities. An investor might convert the bonds or preferred stock to obtain an ownership interest or to benefit from dividends or continued growth. Convertible preferred stock can be converted according to a preset conversion price formula at a specified date. Debentures can also be converted to stocks if they are convertible debentures.

corporate bond—A company can issue a debt security (bond) with semiannual interest payments that is traded on the major exchanges. These bonds typically have a $1,000 face value. Bonds are backed by either collateral or the full faith and credit of the corporation.

corporate earnings—Corporate earnings are calculated by subtracting costs from sales. If earnings increase, stock prices should increase; and if earnings decrease, stock prices should decrease. This happened in late 1998, when corporate earnings slid, causing the Dow Jones Industrial Average to drop almost 2,000 points.

cosign—Lending institutions may be reluctant to loan an individual or company money because of a poor credit history. However, if a cosigner agrees to repay the loan if it goes into default, the lending institution will be much more likely to make the loan. The cosigner becomes liable for the entire loan if the borrower defaults.

coupon—When interest is due on a bond, the bondholder can clip the coupon from the bond and present it to a designated institution such as a bank to obtain payment.

creative financing—Sometimes a borrower cannot obtain a mortgage and may pursue creative financing to obtain money from a third party. Creative financing could entail a balloon payment, assumption of a prior mortgage on a property, or an adjustable rate mortgage.

credit—Credit refers to any purchase made on account, which means it is paid at a later date. In accounting terms, a credit represents an increase in funds and is usually listed on the right side in the T-account system. See also **debit**.

creditor—Anyone who is owed money is a creditor.

credit rating—Lenders use credit ratings to determine the risks associated with any given loan or extension of credit. Factors such as job history, housing, income, assets, and credit history help determine an individual's credit rating. Credit rating is a process that tracks an individual's or company's ability to repay borrowed money. Lenders use credit ratings to determine if any new moneys might be advanced.

current assets— Assets that are expected to be converted to cash in one year or less. Examples of current assets that appear on balance sheets are cash and short-term financial assets.

current ratio (CR)—Current ratio expresses a company's ability to cover current liabilities with current assets. To calculate CR, we divide current assets by current liabilities. If a company has $400 million in current assets and $100 million in current liabilities, the CR is four to one, which means the current assets can cover current liabilities four times over.

current yield—The current yield is an investment's return in relation to its current value. For a bond, the annual interest payments are divided by the bond's current market value. If you have a $1,000 bond paying 10% interest, and the bond has a par value of $950, then your current yield is $100 / $950 = 10.5%.

custodial account—A parent or guardian can establish a custodial account for a minor. The account belongs to the minor, but the minor is allowed to make transactions only with the custodian's approval.

days sales outstanding (DSO)—DSO is also referred to as the average collection period (ACP), which represents the length of time it is taking customers to repay debt owed to the company. A high DSO means that a company is not effectively collecting its accounts receivable or that credit is being extended to inappropriate customers.

debenture—Debentures are long-term bonds that are not secured by any collateral. Because these bonds are backed by a company's good name and credit history, companies need good credit ratings to issue debentures.

debit—A debit represents any decrease in revenue or net worth. It is documented by being listed on the left side of a T-account. See also **credit**.

debt—Debt is any money, goods, or services owed to someone else on the basis of a prior contractual agreement.

debt–equity ratio—The debt-equity ratio is one of the ratios obtained from analysis of financial statements and is used to determine how much protection creditors have. To calculate the ratio, divide total liabilities by total shareholders' equity. If a company has long-term debt of $200 million and shareholders' equity of $400 million, the debt–equity ratio is 0.5 to 1. If the debt-equity ratio is higher than 1, the company is not as good an investment as others because the company is paying significant interest costs relative to its assets. If a company is highly leveraged, it is not as good a credit risk compared with companies with low debt–equity ratios.

debtor—A debtor is anyone who has a legal or moral obligation to pay a debt to a creditor.

debt securities—A debt security is any security such as a bond, note, or contract that proves the existence of a debt obligation. Stocks are not a debt security but rather an **equity** security.

debt service—Debt service refers to the repayment of an obligation. The debt service on some new stadiums will be about $20 million per year for approximately 30 years.

deduction—The IRS allows specific deductions such as state and local taxes, employee expenses, and charitable contributions to reduce a taxpayer's **adjusted gross income (AGI)**.

deep-discount bond—Bonds can fall out of favor with investors for various reasons (e.g., when the coupon rate is lower than current yield rates available from newer bonds). When a bond declines more than 25% below its face value, it is called a deep-discount bond.

deferred annuity—A deferred annuity is an **annuity** that begins paying out after a specified period of time. The payout could begin either on a specific date or on the date of a particular event, such as a person's retirement.

deferred profit-sharing plan—If a company has a good year, it can share a portion of the profit through an employee trust to give employees a percentage of their salary as a bonus. The primary benefit of such plans for the company is that they are deductible as a business expense if they meet IRS requirements.

deflation—Deflation, which is the opposite of inflation, refers to conditions in which prices decline over a given period. The reduced prices are normally the result of fewer dollars in the economy.

delisting—If a company fails to follow specified stock exchange rules or regulations such as maintaining a minimum net worth, the company can be delisted from its exchange. Delisting can also occur when a company closes or merges with another company, in which case shareholders with stock in the company are issued different stocks.

demand deposit account—A checking account is an example of a demand deposit account. Funds can be withdrawn on demand through the writing or cashing of a check.

deposit insurance—Federal agencies such as the Federal Deposit Insurance Corporation can insure bank accounts to foster a sense of safety on the part of depositors.

depreciation—Every item deteriorates over time, and a business must replace items as they deteriorate. A business can better afford to purchase new equipment if it takes a charge against earnings (reduces earnings) to write off the costs of a depreciating asset based on a specified formula. The formula is derived from the depreciation base. Assume you buy a computer for $6,000 that has an estimated life of five years. After five years you could sell the computer for its salvage value of $1,000. The depreciation base is the initial cost minus the salvage value, or $5,000 in this case. The depreciation base is divided by the asset's life (five years) to produce a yearly depreciation of $1,000.

direct costs—Direct costs are directly associated with a given program. The direct costs for team promotion might include all costs associated with advertising and personnel.

discharge—The completion of the debt process through repayment of a financial obligation is called discharging the debt. A discharge in bankruptcy is a final court order whereby the debtor is relieved of all further debt obligations.

disclaimer—Accountants or auditors who have not had enough time or received enough information to make a conclusive decision about a company's financial statement can prepare a report with a disclaimer. The disclaimer can indicate that some uncertainties exist (e.g., a pending IRS audit or a lawsuit that can significantly jeopardize the company's financial position).

disclosure—All financial statements, including a company's annual report, must fully disclose all relevant facts such as contractual terms, debt issues, and equity adjustments. Under **Securities and Exchange Commission** regulations, a publicly traded company has to fully disclose to stockholders any disastrous event that could affect the company's financial condition, such as the death of a key executive or major research and development failures.

discount bond—A discount bond is sold in the marketplace below its **face value**.

discount broker—A discount broker is a stockbroker who does not give investment advice but performs trades for clients at a reduced price.

discounted net cash flow—This is a means to determine an investment's value by examining after-tax cash flows and return on an investment. By examining income streams and reducing them to represent the present value of money, an investor can critically examine how much should be paid for a given investment in order to generate a given rate of return.

discounted payback rule—This rule analyzes how long it will take a business to get its money back after investing in a capital project while also factoring in the opportunity cost of capital by discounting the future cash flows.

discount factor, or **present value factor**—The discount factor is an arithmetic calculation that is used to help calculate the **present value** of a given investment.

discounting—Discounting is the formula used to determine the present value of a sum of money to be received in the future. Comprehensive tables allow individuals to easily determine the **present value** of given sums assuming various interest rates.

discount rate—The discount rate is the interest rate or percent return that can be earned from an investment. The discount rate is used when determining the **present value** of an investment option.

discretionary funds—Discretionary funds are moneys set aside for incidental expenses. Typically an executive is given significant latitude in spending discretionary funds.

disposable income—Disposable income is the amount of money available to individuals after they have had taxes, contributions to benefits, union dues, and related deductions taken from their paychecks.

diversification—To reduce investment-related risks, investors often diversify their investments so that if one fails, the overall loss will not be as significant as it would with a single investment. Mutual funds are a classic example of diversification in that the funds traditionally purchase numerous stocks, which helps reduce investor risks.

dividend—A company's board of directors can set aside a portion of the company's net income to benefit the shareholders. Cash dividends can be given, but once received by the shareholder they are taxable. This double taxation (company pays taxes on income, then taxpayers get taxed on their dividends) is one of the key drawbacks of the corporation structure of business. **Stock dividends** consisting of additional shares of stock can also be allocated by the board of directors and are not taxed upon receipt by the shareholder. When additional stocks are given as a dividend, the stockholder pays taxes only when selling them.

dividend payout ratio—Dividend payments can be expressed as a percentage of net earnings: Dividends per share are divided by earnings per share. Assume that a company has $1 million in earnings and that the board has approved a $50,000 dividend payout to the company's 25,000 outstanding shares. The **dividend per share** is $50,000 / 25,000 shares, or $2. The **earnings per share** are $1,000,000 / 25,000, or $40. The dividend payout ratio is $2 / $40, or 5%.

dividend per share (DPS)—If a $1 million dividend is declared and there are one million shares outstanding, the DPS is $1.

dividend reinvestment plan—Stockholders use a dividend reinvestment plan to plow their dividend payments back into purchasing more shares. This approach saves money because the stockholder does not need to pay any stockbroker commissions.

dividend yield—This ratio helps determine what the percentage return is for a stock that pays a dividend. To calculate the dividend yield ratio, divide the dividends per share by the stock's market price per share. A stock that is selling for $10 per share and receiving a $0.50 dividend per share has a 5% dividend yield ($0.50 / $10).

dollar-cost averaging—An investor can reduce the risks associated with stock volatility by investing a given amount of money in a stock on a regular basis no matter what the stock price is. Using this technique, an individual could put aside $100 a month to invest in a given company. Whether the price is $10 or $75 per share, the same $100 is always invested, and over the long haul the investor using this approach is normally very successful.

double entry bookkeeping—Double entry booking is a technique in which all transactions are recorded both as a credit and a debit. This results in a balanced ledger account for both debits and credits. See also **T-system**.

Dow Jones Industrial Average (Dow)—This average tracks the price of 30 blue-chip stocks actively traded on the New York Stock Exchange to serve as a guide to how the stock market is performing. The price-weighted average takes the stocks' closing prices and adjusts the prices to reflect stock splits and dividends.

downside risk analysis—The downside risk analysis approach is a worst-case scenario process in which an investor examines the total potential loss from an investment to help determine whether to enter into an investment or whether to sell an investment.

dowry—A dowry is the total value of property, money, and other assets a prospective wife brings to a marriage.

draft—A draft is a note, such as a check, indicating the transfer of funds from one party to another. The person to whom the check is written is called the payee. The person writing the check is the drawer, and the institution being instructed to pay the payee is the drawee. See also **demand deposit account**.

early-withdrawal penalty—Investors who have money deposited in certain investments such as individual retirement accounts or CDs may have to pay a penalty if they withdraw the investment before the investment's actual maturity date. Thus, you would have to pay a penalty if you had a six-month CD and cashed it in after only four months.

earned income—Earned income is any income obtained through performing labor. Earned income contrasts with passive income, which is income generated from sources, such as stocks or bonds, that do not require any labor.

earnest money—Earnest money is the sum of money given by a buyer to a seller for the purpose of holding a contract open to the buyer for a certain time period. Thus, if you wanted to buy a used car but wanted to check the car out for a day, you could put down an earnest-money deposit. If the car proved acceptable, you would complete the contractual process with the seller. The earnest-money deposit can serve as an earnest-money credit toward the purchase price.

earnings before interest and taxes (EBIT)—EBIT represent a company's earned income, not taking into consideration any owed interest or taxes.

earnings per share (EPS)—Earnings per share helps highlight how much each share of stock is earning in dollar terms and represents one of the most important tools to measure a company's success. To calculate EPS, the company's net income is divided by the total number of outstanding shares. If the company's income is $1 million and there are one million outstanding shares, the EPS is $1.

earnings yield—Earnings yield is the opposite of the price–earnings ratio. This ratio measures the yield obtained from a stock. The higher the yield, the better. For example, if a company's earnings per share is $5 and the market price is $20, then the earnings yield is 25%.

economic indicators—The government, investors, and businesses analyze various economic indicators to help determine market conditions. Examples of leading economic indicators include the **gross national product**, the **consumer price index**, money supply indicators, and the **Dow Jones Industrial Average**.

economics—Economics blends art and science to help explain and chart the most effective and efficient use of scarce resources. Microeconomics analyzes individual markets such as baseball, football, or basketball. Macroeconomics analyzes the big picture, such as the national economy or global economy.

economies of scale—A reduction in cost per unit resulting from increased production, realized through operational efficiencies.

effective annual rate (EAR)—The EAR represents the real annual rate of return for an investment.

effective interest rate—The effective interest rate represents the real rate of interest paid on a loan. To calculate the effective interest rate, the nominal interest rate is divided by the loan amount.

elasticity of demand—Elasticity measures the degree to which a change in pricing affects the unit sales of a product. If a change in price does not impact demand, then the demand is inelastic while an elastic demand changes significantly when prices change.

employee stock ownership plan (ESOP)—An ESOP is a plan designed to give employees an ownership interest in the company through distributing company stocks to employees. ESOPs typically vest (allow for collection) when an employee leaves or retires. This allows the stocks to increase in value without the employees having to pay taxes until they are at a lower income level, thus reducing their final tax obligations.

Equal Credit Opportunity Act (ECOA)—The ECOA is a federal law that makes it illegal to discriminate against a loan applicant based on race, age, religion, or gender. The law requires all lenders to respond within 30 days to any applicant and to identify the specific reason an applicant was denied.

equity—Equity refers to an individual's net worth or a company's stock ownership value.

equity investment—An equity investment is an investment in a company through the purchase of company stock.

estate—All real and personal property owned by an individual at the time of the person's death belongs to that person's estate. If a person dies with a will, the will specifies how the estate should be distributed. The U.S. federal government charges an estate tax based on the estate's value; the first $600,000 (scheduled to increase to $1.2 million in 2007) is tax free.

even lot—Even lots are standard blocks of stocks. An even-lot block on the New York Stock Exchange contains 100 shares.

excise taxes—Numerous taxes exist for various consumed goods. These taxes are generally lumped under the designation excise taxes and are sometimes added to the purchase price of such items as gas, alcohol, and tobacco.

ex-dividend (XD)—Before the date on which a company records a stock dividend is a four-day freeze that allows the stock to trade, but without the right to obtain the dividend. The waiting period is based on the fact that stock transactions typically take five days to settle. Stocks subject to the XD provision normally trade at a reduced price that reflects the market price minus the expected dividend payment.

exempt income—Exempt income is income that is exempt from taxation, such as income from tax-exempt municipal bonds used to finance some stadiums or arenas.

expendable outlays—Expendable outlays are payments for items that are relatively low in cost and are frequently purchased, such as office supplies.

expenditure—An expenditure is any payment made to satisfy a financial obligation or to purchase assets.

expenses—Expenses are any payments, any reduction in value (such as depreciation), or any new legal obligations (such as entering into a binding contract).

experience rating—Insurance companies use a statistical method to determine insurance premiums based on past claims and projections for future claims. Experience ratings allow an insurance company to properly determine the potential payout for a given policy, which helps set the premium price for the policy.

external constraints—External constraints involve any obstacle outside of a business or organization that might limit a given strategy or action such as government regulations, actions of competitors, or investor actions (i.e., market volatility).

F—The letter *F*, as used in financial calculations, represents a company's fixed operating costs or expected rate of return from a risk-free investment.

face value—The face value, or face amount, is the stated value for a bond or other security. Most bonds, for example, have a $1,000 face value but can be sold for an amount higher or lower than the indicated value. In addition to a face value, a security has a face interest rate, which is the interest rate guaranteed for the security when the security was issued.

Fair Credit Billing Act (FCBA)—The FCBA is a U.S. federal law that is designed to correct problems in credit billing and complaints and that establishes time limits under which bills need to be sent and complaints filed. A similar law, the Fair Credit Reporting Act, establishes specific requirements for the use of and access to personal credit information.

Federal Deposit Insurance Corporation (FDIC)—The FDIC is a U.S. federal agency that insures bank accounts up to $100,000 per each depositor at the bank. All national banks and most commercial banks obtain FDIC insurance to reduce the risk for potential depositors. Before the savings and loan fallout in the 1980s, the federal government ran the Federal Savings and Loan Insurance Corporation, whose duties were assumed by the FDIC after the savings and loan disaster.

Federal Reserve System (Fed)—The Fed was established by Congress in 1913 and comprises 12 Federal Reserve district banks, branches, and all national and state banks (more than 5,800). The system operates to manage the nation's money supply by raising or lowering the reserve amount that banks need to keep on hand, by changing the discount rate charged to commercial banks for borrowing money, and by purchasing and selling government securities (Siegel, Shim, & Hartman, 1992). The system operates similarly to a bank in that member banks can deposit funds in and borrow funds from the Fed in order to run more effectively.

finance—Finance is the study of how investors and entities allocate their assets over time under conditions of certainty and uncertainty. The focus is on how to strategically deal with financial certainty and uncertainty.

finance charge—Nothing is free, and finance charges are a vehicle that assists in the transfer of money. The two types of finance charges are interest rates and points. Points can be charged when individuals apply for or are given a loan; each point charged represents 1% of the loan amount. Thus, if you were to refinance your home mortgage with a lower interest rate, the lending institution might charge you 1 or 2 points to process the loan, which for a $50,000 loan could be $500 or $1,000, just to obtain the loan.

financial assets—Financial assets are items of value that are intangible but that represent the ownership interest in a business or the investments that are funding the business. Financial assets include bonds, common stock, preferred stock, **money market certificates**, Treasury bills, and related instruments.

financial exigency—A financial exigency is an urgent financial situation (e.g., an athletic department loses a Title IX suit and has to add several new women's teams when it is already losing money).

Financial Industry Regulatory Authority (FINRA)—A subsidiary of the NASD, using electronic networking to facilitate buying and selling (trading) of the **over-the-counter** market's 5,000 most active stocks.

financial leverage—Financial leverage represents the portion of a company's assets that are financed with debt rather than equity. It is normally beneficial to reinvest your own money (equity) rather than borrow funds; but if you can reinvest borrowed funds and obtain a rate of return greater than your interest and principal payments on the borrowed funds, then leveraging is a potential strong option for growth.

financial leverage ratios—These are various ratios that help identify how a company is financed and whether it has undertaken too much debt to grow. These ratios include the acid test ratio, current ratio, debt ratio, and debt–equity ratio.

financial statements—Corporations report their financial condition in annual, semiannual, and quarterly reports that contain numerous financial statements such as balance sheets, income statements, and cash flow statements.

first in, first out (FIFO)—FIFO has different meanings in banking and inventory management. Using the FIFO method, a bank withdraws any debt from the earliest deposits in an account. Under this method, depositors lose interest—because earlier deposits are reduced by withdrawals—and this makes saving less beneficial. For example, if you deposited $1,000 in June and $1,000 in July but wrote a check for $500 in July, you would earn interest on only $500 in June ($1,000 – $500) but would earn interest on $1,000 for July. The same principle applies to inventory management application of FIFO.

fiscal year—A company's fiscal year is a one-year period used as a basis for analyzing the company's financial performance and creating new budgets for the coming year. Many companies have August 31 as the first date of the fiscal year and the following August 30 as the last day of the fiscal year.

five Cs—Lenders often use five Cs when reviewing a loan application. The five Cs are (1) the *character* of the loan applicant (is the loan applicant a reliable person or company?), (2) the *capacity* of the applicant to earn enough to cover all expenses including the loan costs, (3) the **collateral** that will be used to secure the loan, (4) the **capital** available to the loan applicant (does the applicant have a positive net worth?), and (5) current economic *conditions*. After analyzing the five Cs, a lender normally assigns a loan applicant a **credit rating** that will help determine the default risk for the applicant.

fixed assets—Fixed assets are permanent assets such as buildings or equipment required to run a business. Ice rinks, locker rooms, rental counters, spectator seating, and a Zamboni are all examples of fixed assets.

fixed costs—Fixed costs, or fixed charges, are regular expenses that are incurred regardless of activity, inactivity, or level of activity. Rent is a fixed cost because the same amount is owed regardless of potential business activity. Other examples are taxes, insurance premiums, and fixed salaries.

fixed income—Fixed income does not change over time; a fixed pension plan for former professional athletes, for example, might pay an athlete $2,000 a month for life.

fixed interest rate—A fixed interest rate does not change over time; in contrast, interest on a variable-rate loan, such as on some credit cards that are tied to various federally adjusted interest rates, changes over time.

flat rate—Items that are purchased on a flat rate basis cost the same no matter what quantity is purchased. When the rate can change based on quantity purchased, the price is considered a variable rate.

float—A float exists for money held by a bank or savings institution for checks that have not yet been cashed or deposits that have yet to be credited to a depositor's account.

flow—Flow refers to expenditure or receipt of money between two points in time.

Form 10-Q and **Form 10-K**—The Securities and Exchange Commission requires publicly traded companies to file specific quarterly (10-Q) and annual (10-K) reports featuring comprehensive financial statements.

formula budgeting—Formula budgeting involves establishing predetermined amounts that will be spent on various costs. Thus, if a team earns $1 per hot dog sold, the expenses and revenue can be calculated in the budget by estimating the total number of hot dogs that will be sold by both the purchase and potential sales price.

full faith and credit—See **bond**.

future value (FV)—Future value refers to the value that a given investment or security might have at a given time in the future. An investment's future value can be determined through various means, including the use of a future value table. FV_n is the future value at a specific (n) period. The opposite of future value is **present value**.

garnishment—An individual may lose in a legal proceeding or be required by law to make certain restitutions. Through garnishment, the person's wages, assets, or property can be attached, and any recovery can be used to pay the outstanding obligation. Attachment is the process where a court official or sheriff officially starts the collection process. For example, the sheriff could serve the employer with the court order requiring wage garnishment.

generally accepted accounting principles (GAAP)—The GAAP are industry rules developed to ensure uniformity by accountants. If an accountant follows the GAAP, others will know that there are standards behind how the numbers were calculated and that other accountants would come up with the same results using the same numbers.

general mortgage bonds—These bonds are collateralized by a blanket coverage over all company assets. However, these bonds are subordinate to (have lesser significance than) any bond collateralized by specific property. Thus, a general mortgage bond might cover all office equipment as collateral and be subordinate to another bond or obligation collateralized by photocopier machines.

general obligation bonds (GOBs)—GOBs are municipal bonds issued for such projects as stadiums or arenas, with the interest and principal payments backed by the **full faith and credit** of the municipality that issues the bonds. This means the bonds are backed by all the taxes collected by the municipality even if such taxes are not used for the facility. Under such a bond, a stadium could be constructed from a bond backed by a ticket surcharge. If the host team moves and there are no other tenants, no ticket surcharges would be collected to pay back the bondholders. The bondholders could then proceed against property tax collections or any other taxes for repayment.

golden handcuff—To prevent key employees from leaving, a company can give these employees significant stock options and a pension plan that are designed to penalize them if they leave the company before a given date. Under such a plan, an employee might have 5,000 stock options available after two years, 10,000 after four years, and 25,000 after six years.

golden parachute—Golden parachutes are given to top-level executives, offering these individuals significant money, benefits, or both if the company is purchased and the executives are subsequently terminated. Such an agreement is often created to make a company less attractive for a hostile suitor to purchase.

goodwill—Goodwill is the difference between a company's book value and its market value. The difference is based on the fact that the company has value that is not reflected in its books, or if goodwill is on the books, it is an additional value based on various valuation techniques. The name Coca-Cola, for example, represents a tremendous asset (a name recognized worldwide) that is hard to place a value on. However, some have placed the value on the goodwill of the name at more than $2 billion since that is possibly how much it would cost to develop a similar brand name with worldwide recognition.

gross national product (GNP)—The GNP is a calculation of the total value of products manufactured and services provided in the United States in a given year.

gross national product deflator—The U.S. Department of Commerce publishes a quarterly weighted average of the gross national product to more accurately reflect the price changes for goods and services purchased by consumers, businesses, and the government.

gross profit margin—The gross profit margin is the income of a company before operating expenses, interest, and taxes are paid.

guaranteed dividend—Some stocks pay a regular dividend that is assured by a third party such as the government.

hard asset—A hard asset is any item that has significant value but can be easily bought and sold, such as gold and silver. There are existing markets, so it is easy to sell such assets and convert them to cash or other liquid assets.

hedging—Investors understand that investments by their very nature involve various risks. Thus, investors try to hedge potential losses by undertaking risk-reduction strategies such as diversifying their holdings or purchasing insurance.

high-grade security—Stocks or bonds categorized as high grade have the best investment quality ratings, such as AAA. Independent companies establish the rating after reviewing a company's assets, liabilities, earnings, dividends, management, and related factors.

holder of record—The holder of record is the person whose name is recorded as the purchaser or owner of a given security. Proper recording of ownership is critical for determining who will receive dividends because only the holder of record receives dividends.

holding period return (HPR)—This calculation determines the total return earned when an investment is held for a given period. HPR = (current income + capital gains) / purchase price. If you purchased a stock for $10 and sold it one year later for $12, and during the year received a $1 dividend, then the HPR would be ($1 + $12 – $10) / $10 = 3 / 10, or 30%.

horizontal merger—This type of merger occurs when two companies in the same line of business are joined.

hostile takeover—A hostile takeover occurs against the desires of the target company's management and board of directors.

illiquid—A company is illiquid when it does not have sufficient liquid assets such as stocks and marketable securities to cover short-term debt.

implicit costs—Also called **opportunity costs**, implicit costs represent the cost of the next best alternative forgone. If you build a stadium, you will receive a certain return. However, you also face certain lost income because with the same money you could have built a convention center that might have had a greater impact on a given community.

incentive stock option (ISO)—An ISO is another option for transferring stocks to employees and is considered a benefit such as profit sharing. Compared with other stock-option plans, an ISO receives more favorable tax treatment.

income—Any money received during a given time period by either an individual or a company is considered income. Income can be derived from such sources as salaries, investment returns, asset sales, and many others.

income statement—An income statement tracks a company's revenue and expenses over any given time period. The following is a sample income statement.

Income Statement

	($000)
Sales	500
Less: material and labor	300
Manufacturing costs	30
Cost of goods sold	**330**
Gross profit	**170**
Depreciation	20
Selling expense	20
Profit before interest and taxes	**130**
Interest payments	10
Taxes	40
Profit after taxes	**80**
Dividends	40
Retained earnings	**40**

income tax—Income tax is a levy imposed by the government on an individual's taxable income. The taxable income is calculated by deducting all allowable deductions (such as unreimbursed business expenses) from the gross income.

independent audit—These audits involve an external review of the finances by individuals who are not directly involved with the documents that are being reviewed.

index of leading economic indicators—This index consists of several key economic indicators that help shed light on the economy's future direction. The index, published on a monthly basis by the U.S. Department of Commerce, analyzes such data as unemployment claims; stock prices; money supply; new building permits; changes in inventories; new orders for consumer and manufactured goods; vendor delivery delays; and the prices for oil, steel, and other essential materials.

indirect costs—Indirect costs are costs not associated with a specific activity. Administrative overhead and secretarial support are typical indirect costs; these obligations arise even if a given activity does not appear to need such assistance.

industrial development bond (IDB)—Municipalities can issue tax-exempt bonds to fund the building of factories or facilities that are then leased to private industries. Such bonds are usually issued to help attract new businesses to a region.

inflation—Inflation is an increase in the price level of products that could be due to increased demand. The increased demand for products can force prices to increase, which leads to a chain reaction of increasing wages and material costs.

initial public offering (IPO)—An IPO represents a company's first attempt at issuing and hopefully selling stocks to the public.

insider and **insider trading**—An insider is someone who has access to privileged information about a company that can affect the company's stock price. If the insider uses this information to make money on the stock or provides the information to anyone else to help that person make money, then everyone who has relied on such information has engaged in insider trading. Insider trading is a criminal offense if the trading is based on inside information. Insider trading is not always illegal if a company insider decides to purchase or sell company stocks and reports any such trades to the **Securities and Exchange Commission** within a specified time period.

interest (i)—Interest is the amount a lender charges for loaning money to a borrower. **Interest rates** are normally expressed in relation to an annual period. Interest can also mean an equity ownership position with a company. Thus, a professional sports team could own a 10% interest in a broadcasting station, which means it owns 10% of the station.

interest coverage (IC)—IC represents a company's ability to repay a loan by making required interest payments. Interest coverage is calculated by adding pretax income and interest expense and then dividing that sum by the interest expense. Thus, if a company had $90 million in pretax income and $10 million in interest expense, the IC would be ($90 + $10) / $10 = 10 times.

interest rate—The interest rate is the cost of borrowing money expressed in percentage terms over the course of a year. A bank might loan a business a certain sum at an interest rate of 10% a year.

interim financing—Businesses often need some money for a short period between deals or to help finance a quick deal; this borrowing is called interim financing.

internal constraints—Internal constraints involve any obstacles within a business or organization that might limit a given strategy or action such as governing documents, stockholder demands, directives from the Board of Directors, or union constraints.

internal rate of return (IRR)—This calculation is designed to provide an investor with the effective annual return from a given investment. The initial cash investment is analyzed in comparison with the present value of cash returns.

intrinsic value—Intrinsic value refers to the true value of any property or investment. The true value of a company can be determined through financial analysis, and this value may be different from the company's book value. Such a difference may be attributable to intangible assets, such as a health club's goodwill associated with many years of quality client service.

inventory—An inventory represents goods in stock that have not yet been sold or manufactured.

inventory turnover ratio (ITR)—The ITR shows how frequently a business is able to process and sell inventory. The higher the ITR, the more frequently the business buys inventory and sells finished goods. A high number is usually a good sign; however, if the business is a specialty manufacturer, such as handmade items, the ITR might be very low.

investment club—Single investors may not have the resources to make certain investments. However, people can create investment clubs in which multiple investors combine their money to acquire better investments through greater buying power.

jumbo certificate of deposit—A jumbo certificate of deposit is a CD with a minimum denomination of $100,000. Although jumbos carry a higher interest rate than CDs with lower values, they are not covered by the Federal Deposit Insurance Corporation.

junk bond—A high-yield bond with a low credit rating is called a junk bond. Smaller or new companies without a significant financial track record of sales or earnings often issue these bonds.

last in, first out (LIFO)—The LIFO method is used to calculate both bank interest payments and inventory values. This method does not penalize investors as much as the FIFO method, but it still hurts investors compared with those who receive interest on the actual amount in a given bank account. When we use LIFO to analyze inventories, we calculate ending inventory levels by subtracting the cost of the most recently purchased inventory from the total inventory before we subtract earlier inventories. This formula takes into account the realities of repurchasing subsequent inventories at a higher price.

layering—To garner necessary protection, a baseball team can purchase a $100,000 property liability insurance policy from one broker, a similar policy for $50,000 from another insurer, and an umbrella policy for $1 million. This results in a layering of insurance policies and may be required if certain insurers are not willing to underwrite the entire protection amount required.

lease option—If the owners of a health club wish to rent a warehouse, they might not want to sign a long-term lease that could bind them for significant payments even if the venture was not successful. Instead, with a lease option, they can lease for a specific time period and then have the option of renewing the lease for additional specified periods. The benefit for the tenant is the ability to reduce long-term debt concerns if things go wrong. The landlord benefits in that such a lease option typically results in a higher rent, and the rent normally increases each time the option is exercised.

lender—A lender is any individual or entity that lends money to a borrower for a given interest rate for repayment within a specified time.

letter of credit (LC)—If you own a sporting goods store, you could approach a bank for a letter of credit to help buy more inventory. An LC from the bank to the seller guarantees your credit for a given time period up to a certain amount. Thus, depending on its assessment of your financial strength, the bank could provide a $100,000 LC to be used to help buy inventory. The LC is like a loan from the bank that can be used at any time.

letter of intent—A letter of intent is a document among parties expressing intent to take or to refrain from taking certain actions. Two sporting goods stores could enter into a letter of intent to merge at a future date. Letters of intent are often a precursor to entering a formal contractual agreement, which often takes months; a letter of intent can provide very rough terms and can be completed in several hours.

leveraged buyout (LBO)—You can buy a professional sports franchise using borrowed funds in what is often called a leveraged buyout. The LBO is often completed using the assets of the purchased company as collateral to secure the borrowed funds, and the income or cash flow of the business is used to repay the loan.

leveraging—Leveraging is using borrowed money to make a greater return on investment than what could have been earned if no additional funds were available. Leverage is used only when the expected return on the investment will more than cover the expense of borrowing the funds.

liabilities—The term *liabilities* refers to any legal or financial obligation. Typical examples are long-term debt, retained earnings, shareholders' equity, and taxes owed. Liabilities are the opposite of **assets**.

life cycle costs—These are costs that are generated from the inception through termination of a product. If you own a fitness equipment manufacturing company, your product life cycle costs would include all research, development, prototype, market research, test marketing, full sales, and product withdrawal or cancellation costs. Traditionally, costs are greatest when a product is initially developed.

limited partner—Unlike traditional partners who are wholly liable for a partnership's losses, limited partners can be liable only for their own investment into a partnership. Limited partnerships are attractive in that the investor can maintain an ownership interest while reducing liability exposure. A general partner in a limited partnership invests capital, helps manage the business, and is personally liable for partnership debts.

line-item budget—A line-item budget lists every expense and revenue source on a separate line to help administrators identify every single source of revenue or expenses.

line of credit—A line of credit represents the maximum preapproved amount a company or individual can borrow without having to go to a different lending source.

liquid—Being liquid is a condition in which an individual or company has enough cash or liquid assets that can be sold quickly (CDs, Treasury bonds, high-quality corporate bonds, stocks) to meet current debt obligations. Inventories are traditionally not considered liquid because it can take time to sell inventory. Accounts receivable (A/R) are similar in that it can take time to collect them. Factoring, which entails selling inventories or A/R, is rapidly changing the nature of liquid assets because inventories and A/R can now be sold in a relatively short amount of time.

liquid asset—A liquid asset is a type of asset that can be quickly converted to cash such as stocks and bonds owned by a company.

liquidity—Liquidity can represent the number of stock shares available for investors to trade. Strong liquidity means there is a good supply of stocks available for purchase or trade.

loan—A loan is a transaction between a lender and a borrower in which the borrower contractually agrees to repay the principal amount and interest. By repaying the loan in a systematic manner, the borrower engages in loan **amortization**.

loan origination fee—In addition to principal, interest, and points, a lender can also impose additional fees on the borrower, including fees for credit checks, auditing of checks, appraisals, title searches, and related expenses required to protect the lender.

loan-to-value ratio (LTV)—The LTV is the ratio of the principal amount borrowed to the collateral's actual value or fair market value (amount borrowed divided by actual value). If you buy a house for $100,000 and take out a mortgage for $60,000, then the LTV is 60%.

loss prevention—Risk management techniques can be used to reduce the chances of being sued. One strategy for reducing financial risk involves purchasing liability, property, casualty, or other insurance policies.

low grade—Investments such as bonds that do not have strong industry ratings are considered low-grade investments and are riskier than high-grade investments.

lump sum distribution—Instead of borrowing money and making monthly payments to satisfy the loan, you could agree to make a lump sum payment at the loan's due date. A retirement pension or other obligation can also be repaid in a lump sum.

managerial accounting—Managerial accounting focuses on the analysis and evaluation of accounting information as part of the managerial process of planning, decision making, and controlling.

margin—If you do not have enough money to purchase stock with cash, you can purchase stock on credit, with the remainder being advanced by the stockbroker. The stocks are kept by the broker as collateral. If you want to buy $10,000 worth of stock, you might need to put down an initial margin requirement of $6,000 while borrowing the remaining $4,000 from the broker. The stock purchaser in essence is borrowing money from the broker and has to pay the broker a given interest rate for using the money. If the price of the security declines and reduces the broker's equity, the broker can issue a margin call that requires the investor to put up more funds to protect the broker. The Federal Reserve Board sets limits on the amount of margins allowed. *Also see* margin (profit).

margin (profit)—A profit margin (sometimes referred to as a net profit margin) represents profits after taxes divided by sales. This calculation shows whether a company made an acceptable percentage of profit based on total sales. A sport manufacturing company with millions in sales and minimal profits is possibly wasting money. In contrast, a company such as a sport services firm may have a lower income level but a higher profit margin. If Sport Manufacturing Company had an after-tax profit of $2 million based on $5 million in sales, then the profit margin would be 40% ($2 million / $5 million). *Also see* margin.

marginal cost—The marginal cost is the change in costs associated with the volume produced. If it costs $1 to produce each of 1,000 baseballs and $0.80 each to produce any additional balls, then the marginal cost of producing additional balls is $0.80.

marginal cost of capital (MCC)—When you are taking out a loan, MCC represents how much more you would need to pay to borrow an additional dollar. If the interest rate declines as the amount of a loan gets larger, the MCC will be lower for each additional dollar. If a bank offers a $1 million loan for 6% and a loan over $1 million for 5.75%, then the cost for borrowing each additional dollar over $1 million is 0.25% less.

marginal tax—The marginal tax is the tax paid on the last dollar earned. Thus, it can be unwise to earn more money after a certain point because the higher earning level results in a higher tax liability.

market—A market is any public location where products or services are bought and sold. There are a number of recognized financial markets, including the New York Stock Exchange, the American Stock Exchange, and the Chicago Mercantile Exchange.

marketable title—A marketable title, one that is free of any problems including financial obligations (called encumbrances), is the most easily transferable property; it is marketable to anyone.

market analysis—A market analysis is any comprehensive analysis of current financial conditions concerning a given company, industry, or the economy.

market indexes, or **market averages**—Various market gauges exist to help investors appreciate market trends. The most famous index is the Dow Jones Industrial Average (Dow), compiled by the *Wall Street Journal* and composed of 30 blue-chip stocks (high-quality stocks) that combined represent approximately 20% of the New York Stock Exchange's total value. In the early 1980s, the Dow was around 1,000, but by 1998 it had reached more than 8,000. Other indexes include Barron's 50-Stock Average, Standard & Poor's 400 Industrials, and the Value Line Average.

market-to-book (M/B) ratio—The M/B ratio represents the difference between what a security is listed for on the books and its real market value.

market value—The market value is the true price in a competitive marketplace of a product, service, or investment vehicle. Supply and demand significantly affect the market value, which is why a ticket for the Super Bowl with a face value of $150 may be sold on the street for $2,000. The $2,000 price is the market value.

materiality—This concept refers to the levels of misstatement that are allowable in financial information. Since no financial system is perfect, misstatements do occur. The auditor must determine the level of misstatement that will affect the fairness of the information.

maturity—Maturity is the time when a loan, bond, or other obligation becomes due and payable. Maturity value is the amount owed once the maturity date is reached.

merger—The combining of two or more businesses into one. Mergers are accomplished through a purchase, an acquisition, or a pooling of interests.

money—Any legal tender currency, whether in the form of coins, paper bills, or in some situations other valuable items, is considered money. During Napoleon's reign, soldiers were paid in salt, which was considered a form of money at that time.

money market certificate—Money market certificates are similar to certificates of deposit issued by banks, savings and loans, or credit unions; they usually mature in six months.

money market mutual fund—A money market mutual fund pools investors' money and purchases short-term debt securities such as government securities and commercial paper that will mature in less than one year.

mortgage—A mortgage is a long-term loan (typically 15 or 30 years) secured by real property. If the mortgage loan value is less than the property's market value, the property owner may be able to take out another loan called a second mortgage. Thus, if you buy a house for $100,000 but need a mortgage loan for only $60,000, you might be able to take out a second mortgage loan for around $35,000 to raise money to start a business. A mortgage banker is the individual or company that originates the mortgage loan and can collect payments from the borrower.

multipayment loans—Such loans are often referred to as add-on loans because the interest payments are added on to the principal. Under the actuarial method, interest is computed on unpaid principal at a fixed rate, with each initial payment being applied first to interest and the remainder to principal. The actuarial method is the simplest and most common method used for such consumer loans as mortgages, with the payment amounts often calculated through computer programs.

multiple of gross income rule—Lenders use a rule of thumb called the multiple of gross income rule to determine whether a borrower can afford a given loan. The formula multiplies the person's income by 2.5 to determine the maximum housing price the individual can afford. Thus, if you earn $50,000 per year, you should be approved for a mortgage loan (if there are no other credit problems) for a $125,000 home.

municipal bond insurance—Government-issued municipal bonds are traditionally very secure. However, to help attract investors and increase their security (and reduce the amount of interest that needs to be paid), municipalities can purchase insurance to guarantee repayment of the bond.

municipal bonds—Municipal bonds are issued by government entities and have significant benefits such as the security of a government entity to repay the loan and tax deductibility of income from the bond. However, the interest rates are typically lower than for corporate-issued bonds. Municipal bonds are nicknamed "munis."

mutual funds—Mutual funds provide an opportunity for investors to pool their money and buy a diverse collection of investment securities. These funds are very attractive to investors since they do not require a significant investment, and the risk of loss is lower because the fund invests in numerous companies. Professional managers make the buy and sell decisions.

National Association of Securities Dealers Automated Quotations (NASDAQ)—A subsidiary of the NASD, the NASDAQ uses electronic networking to facilitate buying and selling (trading) of the **over-the-counter** market's 5,000 most active stocks.

negative amortization—Negative amortization occurs when someone fails to make outstanding loan payments in a high enough amount to cover the interest owed. The low payment then leads to an increase in the balance owed on the loan.

negative cash flow—Negative cash flow occurs when a business spends more than it makes in a given time period.

negotiable instrument—A negotiable instrument is any document that can easily be converted to cash. A bank draft (check written by a bank) represents a negotiable instrument; any bank will accept and cash such an instrument.

net—Net is the amount left after all expenses or deductions are subtracted.

net asset value (NAV)—NAV refers to a mutual fund's total asset value less any debt, divided by the number of shares outstanding.

net current assets (NCA)—NCA (also called net working capital) refers to the total value of current assets minus current liabilities.

net earnings—Net earnings refers to an individual's take-home pay, which consists of the person's salary minus all tax, insurance, and related deductions.

net income—Net income is calculated by subtracting expenses from revenue.

net present value (NPV)—The NPV is the difference between the **present value** of the future income and the required investment.

net profit margin—The net profit margin is the net income of a company after interest and taxes are paid.

net working capital—Net working capital is the amount of money available to pay bills. It is calculated by subtracting current liabilities from current assets.

net worth—Net worth is the difference between a company's total assets and total liabilities. The resulting number is the owners' or shareholders' equity in the company.

New York Stock Exchange (NYSE)—The NYSE is the largest and most respected securities exchange. Often called the "big board," the NYSE requires that new companies wishing to be listed have, among other characteristics, more than 3,000 shareholders and a market value higher than $18 million. The NYSE had been privately owned, but after merging with Archipelago it became a publicly traded company in 2006. The NYSE works as an auction floor, where members who own seats can trade shares of listed companies on behalf of their clients. Current traders do not use actual seats, but the term has survived over the years. A seat can cost around $2 million and gives the owner the privilege of being able to buy and sell NYSE-listed stocks (Ceron, 2000).

no-load mutual fund—A no-load mutual fund is attractive for many investors in that no commission is charged for buying or selling shares.

nominal interest rate—The nominal interest rate is the stated interest rate on a loan or debt. If you have a $10,000 bond with a nominal interest rate of 5%, you will receive $500 in annual interest income.

note (promissory)—A note is a legally transferable debt instrument wherein the borrower agrees to pay a stated amount at a certain date, and the obligation is good no matter who eventually owns the note. Thus, after you borrow money and sign a note to purchase a car, the note can be sold to several subsequent companies without affecting your obligation to repay.

not-sufficient-funds check (NSF)—If you buy something at a store and your check bounces, the store will receive an NSF notification from your bank.

novation—A novation is a new contract that can be entered into by various parties who take the place of a former party to a legal obligation. If you borrowed money from a bank to help buy a car but want to sell the car, you can have the car's new buyer sign a novation with the bank to assume your original obligation.

obligation—Any indebtedness, such as a student loan or a mortgage loan, that is owed to anyone else is an obligation.

odd lot—Stocks are traditionally sold in blocks, such as 100 shares. An odd lot is any number of shares other than a standard block. An odd lot could consist of one share of stock or even a fraction of one share.

off-board trade—Any purchase of a stock on the over-the-counter exchange or any non-national stock exchange is considered an off-board trade.

offer price—The offer price is the initial price a seller asks for a given item or property. If a professional team owner mentions that he would sell a team for $200 million, then the $200 million price tag becomes the offer price.

open-end credit—A credit card is an example of open-end credit. The cardholder is given a credit limit when the account is opened, but no debt is incurred until the card is used.

opportunity cost—Also called **implicit cost**, opportunity cost is the cost of the next best alternative forgone. If a city invests in a football stadium, then the city will need to forgo building a new convention center that would have been built but for the stadium. This is an additional cost associated with building the stadium, over and beyond the actual construction cost.

option—An option is a contractual right to buy or sell something at a later date. If you wanted to buy a sports team for $1 million but needed to secure necessary financial backing, you could pay the team seller $1,000 for a one-month option. This option would give you the opportunity to try to raise necessary funds during that month. If you do not raise the funds, the team goes back on the market. If you do raise the funds, you can buy the team for $1 million. An option is not a deposit, which is why it does not reduce the purchase price.

overdraft—An overdraft occurs when you write a check without sufficient funds in your account, which can result in a not-sufficient-funds notice to the person cashing the check.

overextended—If you are approaching your credit limit, you might contact your credit card company to ask for an increase in the limit. If the card company increases your limit, even though you do not show the ability to afford the higher limit, the card company has overextended your credit.

over-the-counter (OTC) exchange—Unlike the New York Stock Exchange, which is a formal trading environment, the OTC is not one building or trading floor but a means to trade unlisted securities. Dealers use electronics and telecommunication through the NASDAQ network to make trades. The New York Stock Exchange requires companies to have significant capitalization, but the OTC does not have the same requirements. There are some major companies, such as Microsoft, whose shares are traded over the counter.

owners' equity—Owners' equity is the value remaining after liabilities are subtracted from assets. Stock and accumulated earnings are added together, then dividends are subtracted to calculate total owners' equity.

P—The letter P has multiple meanings as a symbol, including the price of a stock on a per share basis, the price of a unit of output, and the probability that a given circumstance will occur.

paper profit—Paper profits or losses are unrealized increases or decreases in a security, which are not real profits or losses until the security is sold. This explains how people can lose millions one day and make millions the next without actually doing anything. Such gains and losses are only hypothetical, and real gains or losses occur only when the individual sells.

par value—So that shares can be valued and sold when they are issued, an arbitrary par value is assigned.

passed dividends—A company may have customary dividends, such as biannual dividends, but the board of directors may elect not to pay a dividend. A passed dividend is not a legal obligation owed to shareholders, but it still needs to be paid to individuals who own cumulative preferred stocks.

past-due balance method—If you buy a product on credit and fail to make the necessary payment on time, you owe interest on the amount that is past due. If you pay during the specified time period, then there will be no past-due amount.

payback period—The payback period is the amount of time necessary to recover an initial investment. The payback period can be calculated by dividing the initial investment by the annual cash flow. If you invest $1,000 in a bond that will pay back $100 a year over 20 years, then the payback period is $1,000 / $100, or 10 years.

payment in kind—Payment in kind can be compared to bartering, which involves trading valuable items or services rather than paying money.

payoff—Payoff occurs when a debt is completely satisfied.

penny stocks—Penny stocks is the term used to describe inexpensive, highly speculative stocks traded on the **over-the-counter** market.

pension fund—Pension funds incorporate deposits from employers, with or without employee contributions, into various investment vehicles to develop long-term growth capable of providing employees with money after they retire, quit, or get fired.

percent of monthly gross income rule—The percent of monthly gross income rule is a rule of thumb used by mortgage companies. It states that a person should not purchase a house if the monthly mortgage, insurance, and property taxes exceed 25% of the person's monthly gross income.

percent of sales method—The percent of sales method is a technique that ties variable costs to sales to help calculate expenditures.

performance stock—A performance stock is a stable, solid, growth-oriented stock that has a better investment potential compared with other stocks.

perpetuity—A perpetuity is a single cash flow that lasts forever. If you win a lifetime lottery that pays you $1 million a year for life, that is a perpetuity.

personal property—Personal property includes items such as cars, clothes, and sporting goods that are not attached to the ground.

petty cash—Petty cash is a small amount of funds set aside to cover small purchases that do not meet the requirements for a formal purchase order. The purchase order is a formal document requesting the release of funds to cover an approved expenditure.

point(s)—Mortgage companies add to their loans a processing charge that is expressed in points. A point represents 1% of the face value of a loan. Thus, an $80,000 mortgage with 2 points would result in a processing fee of $1,600.

portfolio—To increase an investor's diversity, the investor might create a portfolio that contains stocks, bonds, CDs, Treasury notes, stamps, Beanie Babies, or any other item that could be considered an investment. Portfolios are created to protect the investor; any one investment vehicle might decline, but such a decline in a well-balanced portfolio would not hurt the investor as much as it would in a concentrated portfolio with few investments.

preemptive right (or preemption)—Allows a shareholder to purchase a percentage of any future shares issued by the company that matches the percentage of shares he currently owns. This allows an investor to maintain the same percentage control of a business before shares are sold to the general public, which can dilute his ownership interest.

preferred stock—A preferred stock has some features similar to those of a stock and some similar to those of a bond. Preferred stocks represent ownership equity and can generate dividend income, but they also have a guaranteed dividend and a superior claim right over other stocks. The superior claim rights allow preferred stock shareholders to sell assets or seize earnings if the company folds.

prepayment fee—Some mortgages or other loans have a provision imposing a prepayment fee or penalty if the note is completely paid before it matures.

present value (PV)—Present value is the current value of a future amount of money. If you win the lottery, you might be able to take several million dollars now or 10 times that amount over a number of years. Such payouts are based on the fact that if you invest a certain sum now, it will be worth more in the future. Individuals can use a present value table to analyze the value of future income streams.

pretax earnings—Pretax earnings are a company's net income before paying taxes.

price–earnings growth (PEG) ratio—While the PEG ratio and traditional price–earnings (PE) ratio have similarities, they also conceptually have one fundamental difference. Specifically, the PEG ratio estimates what the future quarterly earnings will be along with using the previous three trailing estimates.

price–earnings (PE) ratio—The PE ratio is a comparison between a stock's market value and the strength of a company's earnings. The PE ratio can help determine a stock's market price. To calculate this, multiply the estimated earnings per share by the estimated PE ratio. Assume that a sporting goods company expects to have an after-tax profit of $500,000 and has one million outstanding shares. The estimated earnings per share is $0.50. If the estimated PE ratio is 8, then the estimated market price is $0.50 × 8, or $4.00 per share.

price indexes—Various economic indicators (price indexes) help track inflation, the cost of living, and other economic measuring tools. Typical price indexes include the **consumer price index (CPI)**, which measures 400 typical consumer goods and services, and the producer price index (PPI), which tracks the costs of wholesale goods.

primary market—The primary market is the market in which new securities are traded for the first time. The secondary market is the market in which securities are traded after they are initially sold.

prime interest rate—The prime rate is the interest rate that banks charge for loans to their most financially secure customers.

principal—Principal is the amount invested in any given security.

private offering—A private offering is a first-time offering of a given security by a company, traditionally made to current shareholders, executives, institutional buyers, or larger investment institutions before the security is offered to the general public.

private placement—Some securities are initially offered privately rather than in larger financial markets open to the public. A company may issue a bond that is placed solely with current shareholders or larger institutional investors, such as pension funds or insurance companies.

profit—Profit is another term to describe revenue in excess of expenses. See also **margin (profit)**.

program trading—Program trading involves computer-based decision making in which securities are bought and sold according to set parameters. Program trading creates a phenomenon called the triple witching hour, which occurs at 4:15 p.m. EST on the third Friday of March, June, September, and December when numerous securities expire all at once. The triple witching hour at times has produced significant market shifts. However, these shifts are normally corrected the following trading day.

prospectus—A prospectus from a company highlights key financial data about the company and the proposed security but does not discuss when the security will be issued or the exact price.

proxy—A shareholder has a right to vote on company-related business issues. Shareholders who do not attend a shareholders' meeting can sign a proxy allowing a designated person to vote on their behalf.

public debt—A public debt is any debt incurred by a government institution. When a city builds a stadium or arena, it may issue bonds that represent public debt.

public offering—After filing the necessary registration with the **Securities and Exchange Commission**, a company is allowed to offer stock to the general public.

public syndicate—If two businesses wish to join together to buy a professional team, they might create a public syndicate to combine their money and make the purchase. The public syndicate allows the two companies to share costs and expenses on a predetermined basis.

purchasing power—After inflation has been adjusted for, a dollar has less purchasing power than it had in the past. Thus, employees are frequently given raises to maintain their purchasing power or standard of living. Purchasing power also refers to the credit available to someone who wishes to make a large purchase such as a car.

pure-play stock—The stock of a company that has only one line of business (i.e., only the bowling industry) is a pure-play stock. An investor may want to play (invest in) one industry, and the company's exclusive position in that industry makes it a good investment prospect for that investor. Several mutual funds were started in the 1990s to invest in specific sport categories such as auto racing or companies that own or sponsor professional sports teams.

put—A put is an option to sell a commodity or shares of a security at a specified price during a specified time period. This risky investment alternative works as follows. You might pay $100 for an option to sell 100 shares of a given stock. Each put costs you $1 per share and represents an option to sell the 100 shares at $10 each, which is the stock's price when you purchase the put. If after three months (the time specified in the put) the stock decreases to $5 per share, you realize a $500 profit ($5 per share) minus the $100 spent on the put. If the stock increased to $15 per share, you would lose $500 plus the $100 for purchasing the put.

Q—The letter Q in a financial equation represents unit sales for a given product.

quoted price—The quoted price is the last price at which a security was bought and sold.

R—The uppercase letter R is used to represent the appropriate discount factor or interest rate in financial equations.

r—The lowercase letter r represents a correlation coefficient denoting the degree of correlation between given financial variables.

rally—A rally is a sharp upturn in stock prices and trading.

real assets—Real assets are tangible assets such as real estate, gold, and other items you can touch. Real property consists of land and any buildings or equipment on the land.

real estate investment trust (REIT)—A real estate investment trust provides short-term loans for some construction projects and long-term loans (mortgage REITs) for major projects such as stadiums and arenas.

realized profit or **loss**—After an investment is sold, the investor realizes a profit, a loss, or a **wash**, which means neither losing nor making any money.

realized yield—The realized yield measures the return available if a bond is sold before reaching its maturity. This measure is also called **yield to call**. The calculation involves estimating the potential future value of a bond versus the current value to develop an estimated percentage rate of return on the investment.

receivables turnover ratio (RTR)—The RTR represents how quickly a company is obtaining repayments of accounts receivables. If a company takes too long to collect owed money, it would have a high RTR.

recession—A recession is a downturn in the business cycle in which various economic indicators such as the gross national product, employment rate, consumer spending, and other indicators decline.

red herring—The initial information about a proposed new security is sometimes called a red herring.

refinance—Refinancing involves consolidating or reworking any and possibly all outstanding debts to make repayment easier or to avoid financial hardship such as bankruptcy.

registered security—Some securities such as registered bonds are registered in the owner's name and recorded by the issuing company and the registrar. The registrar is the trustee of a new security's records and is often a bank or similar institution that tracks the registration number of both old and new securities.

reinvestment—Using the dividends, interest, or profits from an investment to buy more of that investment rather than receiving a cash payout.

replacement cost—Replacement costs are the costs you would incur if you needed to replace property. Capital equipment in sport, such as a new Zamboni or a new air-conditioning system, can be very expensive. Thus, companies have to plan for replacement costs either by setting aside money over a long period of time or by ensuring the potential to issue new securities or borrow necessary funds.

retained earnings—Earnings not paid out as dividends but instead reinvested in the core business or used to pay off debt.

return on assets (ROA)—ROA refers to the calculated investment return obtained from assets purchased by a company. Any new assets purchased should be able to generate increased return over and beyond what could have been earned if the money was invested in a CD or other liquid investment option. To calculate ROA, net income is divided by total assets.

return on equity (ROE)—Similar to ROA, ROE relates to whether or not an investment in an ownership position (equity) within a company produced a rate of return greater than what could have been earned if the money had been invested elsewhere. ROE is calculated by dividing net income by shareholders' equity.

return on investment capital (ROIV)—ROIV shows whether or not an investment in a company produced a rate of return greater than what could have been earned if the money had been invested elsewhere. ROIV is calculated by dividing net income by the sum of long-term debt and shareholders' equity.

revenue—Revenue is money coming into a business.

revenue bond—Revenue bonds are government-issued bonds whose interest and principal payments are repaid from specified revenue sources. A baseball stadium could be built using revenue bonds secured by hotel and rental-car tax revenues.

reverse stock split—A company's board of directors can decide to reduce the number of shares outstanding. A reverse stock split reduces the number of shares every investor has but does not reduce the owners' equity percentage. Thus, the number of stock shares outstanding decreases, but the remaining shares increase in value. The opposite of a reverse stock split is a **stock split**, in which the total number of shares is increased and the share values are decreased.

revolving credit—Revolving credit accounts allow a purchaser to obtain a new line of credit as soon as old loans are paid.

risk-free return—A risk-free return is an investment that provides a low return because the investment's risk is so low. To obtain a greater return, an investor needs to invest in a riskier investment. A T-bill or CD is an example of an almost risk-free investment.

risk premium (RP)—RP refers to the fact that if a security is considered risky because of poor repayment history, the security has to pay a premium over other securities to garner investor interest. Thus, an RP could increase the interest on a bond from 4% to 6% on the basis of various risk factors.

roll-up—In a roll-up, an aggressive investment company buys numerous companies in similar industries. For example, a well-funded company could start buying multiple health clubs in a region to gain market dominance.

round lot—A round lot, also called an even lot, is a block of 100 stock shares or a bond with a $1,000 face value.

rule of 69—The rule of 69 helps calculate how long it will take for an investment to double when a certain amount of money is being invested at a certain rate of return expressed as a percentage. The formula is 69 / r(%) + 0.35 periods. If you buy a security with a return of 25%, you will double your money in (69 / 25) + 0.35 = 2.76 + 0.35 = 3.11 years.

rule of 72—The rule of 72 determines how many years it takes to double an investment. The formula is 72 / the fixed rate of return (r%). Thus, if you buy land with a fixed rate of return of 25%, it will take you 2.88 years to double your money (72 / 25 = 2.88).

S—The uppercase letter *S* can represent either a dollar sales volume or the total market value of a company's equity.

s—The lowercase letter *s* is used to represent the standard deviation.

scheduled payment—Scheduled payments are fixed payments owed on loans or bonds or pursuant to a contract or security.

schedule of estimated income—A schedule of estimated income lists expected revenue sources over a given time period. Such a schedule helps highlight what revenue can be expected so a budget can be developed.

secured bond—A secured bond is a bond secured by a specific item, or collateral, that can be sold if the bond is not repaid.

secured loan—Similar to a secured bond, a secured loan is guaranteed by specified collateral.

securities—Securities are any financial instruments that provide an ownership interest in the issuing company. Typical examples include stocks and bonds.

Securities and Exchange Commission (SEC)—The U.S. federal government established the SEC in the 1930s as an independent regulatory agency to regulate securities markets. To protect investors, the SEC requires full financial disclosure for all securities and regulates issues such as insider trading.

securities exchanges—The Securities and Exchange Commission regulates several privately owned securities exchanges, the most famous of these being the New York Stock Exchange, the American Stock Exchange, and the over-the-counter exchange. Several regional exchanges also exist around the United States and in major foreign cities.

security interest, or **collateral interest**—A security interest gives a lender with a secured loan the right to go to court and take possession of the collateral if the borrower defaults on the loan.

seller's market—A seller's market is a market in which the seller has the advantage because numerous buyers are interested in purchasing the item being sold. This phenomenon is based on supply and demand, when the supply is low and the demand is high. A seller's market exists for professional sports teams because many people would like to buy a team, but only a handful of teams are available in any given year.

sell order—When investors wish to sell a security, they can give their brokers a sell order authorizing the sale. The sell order can be either oral or in writing.

senior debt—A senior debt is a superior obligation (loan) that a borrower has to repay before repaying any other obligations. If a company folds, senior debt would need to be paid before any shareholders could receive money, if any remains. A senior debt obligation can be secured by any, or all, corporate assets.

serial bond—A serial bond matures over regularly scheduled dates, in contrast to a bond that matures on only one given date.

Series E bonds—Series E bonds were issued by the U.S. government from 1941 through 1979, when they were replaced by Series EE and Series HH bonds. These bonds are purchased at 50% of the face amount, and the interest accumulates until the bonds reach their maturity date. These bonds can be redeemed before they mature, but the holder will have to pay a penalty.

shakeout—A shakeout occurs when securities prices tumble with significant trading.

share—A share represents one unit of ownership interest in either a company or a financial vehicle (e.g., a mutual fund).

shareholder—An individual who owns a share in a company.

shareholders' report—Companies that issue stocks report to their owners on a regular basis. These reports highlight a company's current financial condition and other relevant facts. Shareholders' reports are often released annually and provide audited reviews of a company's financial statements by an independent accounting firm to substantiate the claims made by the company.

short—An investor can take a short position by borrowing a security from a broker and then selling the security on the open market. The idea is that the investor is hoping the stock price will decline, at which point the investor will buy the stock at a lower price and will have made a profit. For example, an investor can sell 100 short shares borrowed from the broker for $10 each. Ten days later the stock might have dropped to $5 per share, and at this point the investor buys the stock from the broker and makes a $500 profit. Buying short is very risky—if the stock price increases, you can lose a substantial amount of money because you have to buy the stock at its higher price.

short-term debt—Short-term debts are current liabilities that need to be repaid within one year, such as utility bills, payments for inventory, taxes owed, employee wages owed, and related liabilities.

signature loan—A signature loan is any personal loan secured only by the borrower's signature. No collateral is pledged.

simple interest—Simple interest is computed only on the original loan amount, whereas compound interest is applied to the original principal and all accumulated interest. The simple interest on a $1,000 loan at 10% interest is $100.

simple rate of return (SRR)—The simple rate of return is a method used to calculate the return that can be obtained on a given investment. To calculate SRR, we divide the investment's annual income by the initial investment. If you invest $1,000 and receive an annual return of $75, the SRR is 75 / $1,000 = 7.5%.

simple yield—To calculate the simple yield of a bond, the bond's interest is divided by the face value. If you buy a $1,000 bond paying 5% interest for only $950, then the simple yield is (5% × 1,000) / 950 = 50 / 950 = 5.26%.

single-payment loans—Single-payment loans are paid in full on a given date, with the debtor repaying both the principal and required interest. There are two techniques for determining the appropriate annual percentage rate. Under the **simple interest** method, the amount repaid is computed by adding the original amount and interest, with the interest calculated by means of the following formula: interest = principal × interest rate × time period. Assume you borrow $1,000 for one year at a simple interest rate of 15%. In this situation, you would repay the lender $1,150 at the end of the year. The second method is the discount method; here the initial loan is discounted by the interest that will be owed. Using the same example, instead of receiving $1,000 and paying $1,150, you would borrow $1,000 at 15% but receive only $850, which represents the loan minus your prepayment of the interest you would owe. Unlike the 15% annual percentage rate (APR) under the simple interest method, the APR using the discount method would be 17.64%. The calculation is $150 (interest) / $850 (amount actually received). Thus, the discount method allows a lower payment upon maturity ($850 versus $1,150), but the simple interest method produces a lower APR.

sinking fund—A company can use a sinking fund to set aside money to invest in income-producing securities that are later cashed in to pay off a financial obligation. Without setting aside money in anticipation of repaying a loan, a company may be forced to issue additional securities to raise the necessary cash or may need to borrow the money.

skip-payment privilege—A lender might allow a borrower to skip a payment if the lender is notified in advance that the borrower will miss a payment.

special tax bond—A special tax bond is a municipal bond paid for with revenue from excise taxes levied on such items as alcohol or tobacco sales.

Such "sin taxes" have been used to fund stadium projects such as Jacobs Field in Cleveland.

speculative bond—A speculative bond is a low-rated bond that might be close to default. An investor might purchase such a bond at a deep discount with the hope that the company can turn around and pay off the bond.

stagflation—Stagflation represents an increase in prices that occurs when businesses are facing a slowdown.

statement of cash flows—A statement of cash flows is an accounting of where revenue is coming from and where it is being spent. These statements must be included in shareholders' annual reports.

stock—Stock refers to wealth people might have, such as cash or other investments.

stock dividend—If a company does not have enough cash to pay a dividend, the company can issue additional stock to shareholders. If a stock dividend is issued, the shares outstanding for the company are increased, and this reduces the per share value of all shares.

stock market, or **stock exchange**—A stock market or exchange is a marketplace where stock and other securities are traded.

stock split—A corporation's board of directors may authorize a stock split if the stock price is too high. Thus, for a share that sells for $200, after a 2-for-1 stock split the investor will have two shares, each worth $100. A stock split can take place for a variety of reasons and according to various formulas (e.g., 3 for 2; 2.3 for 2).

stock symbol—Each company that issues stock on a given stock exchange is given a stock symbol (also called a ticker symbol) that is used to identify the stock.

stock types—Companies can issue various stocks such as common, preferred, and class A or class B stocks. The latter two types of stock give the stockholders different voting rights.

subordinate debenture—A subordinate debenture is an unsecured bond that would be paid only after senior bonds are paid.

subordinate debt—A subordinate debt is a loan secured by just a general claim on a company's assets that would be paid after a secured debt is paid.

sunk costs—Sunk costs are past costs incurred that might affect a subsequent decision. If you bought a gym for $1 million 10 years ago, that cost is a sunk cost. The cost is irrelevant for many decisions, but it would be relevant if you wished to sell and would sell only for a specified rate of return higher than the initial purchase price.

T—The uppercase letter T represents a company's or individual's marginal tax rate on interest payments.

t—The lowercase letter t in a financial formula stands for the time frame for a given investment.

taxable income—Taxable income equals **adjusted gross income (AGI)** minus any allowed deductions or exemptions such as business expenses, capital losses, or charitable giving.

tax basis—The tax basis for an investment is the sum total of all expenses incurred for making a purchase, such as the security's cost, brokerage fee, registration fees, and any others.

tax credit—A tax credit can be created to reduce the total dollars owed to the government and can be associated with specific legislation; such legislation may call for a tax credit for starting a new business in a given neighborhood, for example.

tax-equivalent yield—A formula measures the yield of a tax-free municipal bond against other investments that might require tax payments. The formula is as follows: tax-equivalent yield = tax-exempt yield / (1 – tax rate). If a business has a 28% tax rate and a tax-exempt municipal bond pays 5% interest, the necessary return on a taxable investment would be 5% / (1 – 0.28) = 6.94%. Thus, to maximize your investment return, you should invest in the tax-exempt municipal bond unless you can find another investment that has a return greater than 6.94%.

tax-exempt bonds—Tax-exempt bonds allow investors the opportunity to receive interest income without having to pay taxes on that income. Tax-exempt bonds were essential during the sports facility construction boom in the 1990s; investors were able to buy bonds backed by facility revenue but did not need to pay taxes on the interest income.

tax incremental financing (TIF)—TIF represents tax breaks given to a project with the hope that other businesses will move to the area and increase the property value. The increased property value and resulting greater tax base is supposed to help offset the tax break given to the company that received the TIF.

tax shield—A tax shield refers to any deduction that can ultimately reduce your tax burden. For example if you spend $3,000 a year on mortgage interest and pay tax at the 28% tax rate, you could have a tax shield of ($3,000 × 0.28) = $840.

term loan—A term loan calls for regular periodic payments, usually for three years or more.

time value of money—Money decreases in value over time, and time value of money represents this concept. Because one dollar today is worth more than one dollar next year, investment decisions need to be made with a critical eye toward the future value of a dollar.

tombstone—A tombstone is a formal advertisement by a company or investment bank stating the financial terms of a pending security offering.

total asset turnover ratio—The total asset turnover ratio shows how quickly a company uses its assets to make money. A low ratio means that assets are not being turned over quickly enough to generate additional revenue.

trade—To trade is to exchange or sell a security on either a formal or an informal securities exchange. Those who buy and sell stocks for their own benefit are called traders.

treasurer—A treasurer deals with banks, stockholders, institutional investors, bondholders, and other stakeholders or potential stakeholders to educate them about how a company is doing and what it might need for future growth.

Treasury bill (T-bill)—A T-bill is a short-term government obligation issued in a minimum denomination of $10,000 and scheduled to mature in three months, six months, or a year. T-bills are the safest investment vehicle because they are 100% backed by the U.S. government.

Treasury bond—The U.S. federal government issues bonds in a minimum denomination of $1,000 that mature over 10 years and have semiannual payments of a fixed interest rate.

Treasury notes—Treasury notes are similar to T-bills and Treasury bonds, with similar security and interest rates.

treasury stocks—Treasury stocks are stocks that were once issued by a company and then subsequently repurchased by the company. Such repurchased stocks can be canceled or reissued, but while they are in the company's possession they pay no dividends and have no voting rights. In a similar vein, companies can also have treasury bonds (i.e., bonds repurchased by the issuing company).

trust—A trust is a special account established to benefit a specified individual such as a minor.

T-system—The T-system is used in accounting to post money coming in and going out in an easy-to-read manner.

turnover—Turnover is a means of determining how inventory is managed. A high turnover ratio means a company is quickly replenishing inventory as old inventory is quickly sold. A low turnover ratio reflects that a company has inventory sitting around and is not maximizing its investment. To calculate turnover, sales are divided by assets. Turnover is also calculated for assets to determine how they are being managed.

usury—Usury refers to charging an excessive amount of interest on a loan. Loan sharks often represent a last resort for those who cannot obtain funds from any other source (i.e., their credit rating is bad or they have nothing to borrow against at a pawnshop). However, charging an excessively high interest rate is illegal.

v— The value of dividend payments when calculating the cost of preferred stock.

value (V)—Value is the monetary worth of an item. Value can be expressed as what you could obtain on the market if you had to sell an item. Thus, baseball card price guides might list a card as worth $100, but if you can only find people willing to pay $20 for the card, then the card's value is only $20.

variable costs—Variable costs vary with each unit produced and include items such as raw materials. Semivariable costs vary somewhat with production such as machine maintenance. If a machine is not used maintenance will decrease while if it is used extensively maintenance costs would increase.

variance—Variances represent the difference between the amount budgeted for a given expense and the actual expense incurred.

vertical merger—A buyer expands operations forward toward the final consumer or backward in the direction of the source of raw materials.

voluntary liquidation—As a consequence of severe financial concerns, shareholders may vote to liquidate a company by selling all company assets.

voting rights—Certain stocks carry with them a voting right that allows each shareholder to vote in person or by proxy on such issues as major expenditures, changing board members, or voluntary liquidation.

Wall Street—Wall Street is a street in New York City in the heart of the financial district where the New York Stock Exchange and the American Stock Exchange are located.

warrant—A warrant is an agreement that enables the holder to buy stock at a future date at an advantageous price.

warranty deed—A warranty deed guarantees that a given investment or property has clear title and is free from any encumbrances.

wash—A wash represents no gain or loss when a given investment is sold.

watered stock—A company can exchange capital stock for assets valued at less than the stock's par value. This transaction artificially inflates the value of the exchanged assets.

weighted average cost of capital (WACC)—An average representing the expected return on all of a company's sources of capital. Each source of capital, such as stocks, bonds, and other debt, is weighted in the calculation according to its importance in the company's capital structure.

wholesale banking—Wholesale banking refers to a significant volume of transactions with major corporations or financial institutions.

working capital—Working capital is the amount of money available to pay bills. To calculate working capital, current liabilities are subtracted from current assets. The term *working capital* sometimes refers to current assets only.

year-end dividend—If a company is profitable or if the company's stock requires dividend payments, then the company can pay a dividend at the end of its fiscal year.

year to date (YTD)—The YTD notation on financial statements indicates financial activity from the start of the company's fiscal year to the date specified on the financial statement.

yield (rate of return)—The yield represents the income earned by a given investment.

yield to call (YTC)—YTC represents the yield obtained up to the point that a bond is called by the issuer.

yield to maturity (YTM)—YTM represents the annual yield that holders of a bond would receive if they held on to the bond until it matured. To calculate YTM, we analyze the bond's face value, coupon rate, and market price, taking into consideration the time remaining on the bond until it matures.

zero-based budgeting (ZBB)—The zero-based budget is founded on the concept that organizations and their programs need to justify their existence. The resulting budget would distribute money to the programs that produce the greatest benefits, and the components that produce lower benefits would either be eliminated from the budget or receive fewer funds.

zero coupon bond—A zero coupon bond does not pay interest on a semiannual or annual basis; rather the semiannual interest payments are added to the principal, with the principal and interest being paid at maturity. These bonds are called zero coupon because the bondholder does not need to clip and redeem coupons in order to obtain the interest payments.

z score—The z score is a formula used to measure the probability that a company will go bankrupt; it analyzes a host of financial measures, from retained earnings to total assets.

References

1988 baseball salaries. (1988, June). *Sport*, 24.

1997 stadium & arena managers' annual report. (1997). Tampa, FL: Price Waterhouse Sports Group.

2010-11 high school athletics participation survey. Retrieved from www.nfhs.org/content.aspx?id=3282

About Schwinn. (2007). Retrieved from www.schwinnbike.com/heritage

About the SEC. (2011). Retrieved from www.sec.gov/about/whatwedo.shtml

Alexander, R. (1992, August 14). Season-ticket sales get taken down by recession. *USA Today*, p. 14c.

Allen v. Commissioner, 50 T.C. 466. (1968).

Ambrosini, D. (2002, February 10). Bankrolled by an 'Angel.' *Connecticut Post*, p. F1.

Andelman, B. (1993). *Stadium for rent: Tampa Bay's quest for major league baseball*. Jefferson, NC: McFarland.

Antonen, M. (2010, February 15). Greener spring pastures beckon Reds, Orioles. *USA Today*, 5C.

Appenzeller, H. (2011). *Ethical behavior in sport*. Durham, NC: Carolina Academic Press.

Aramark acquires Ogden Entertainment. (2000, May-June). *Facility Manager*, 7.

Arango, T., & Stelter, B. (2011, January 19). Comcast receives approval for NBC Universal merger. *New York Times*. Retrieved from www.nytimes.com/2011/01/19/business/media/19comcast.html

Arens, A.A., & Loebbecke, J.K. (2006). *Auditing: An integrated approach* (11th ed.). Upper Saddle River, NJ: Prentice Hall.

Athlete's tax fails to meet expectations in Pittsburgh. (2000). Retrieved from www.sportslawnews.com/archive/articles/athletetax.htm

Attorney general to check into Red Sox bidding process. (2001, December 23). *Connecticut Post*, p. D3.

Average salary tops $2 million. (2001, December 13). *Connecticut Post*, p. C5.

Baade, R.A. (1994, April 4). *Stadiums, professional sports, and economic development: Assessing the reality*. Heartland Policy Study No. 62. Chicago: Heartland Institute.

Badenhausen, K. (2011, July 12). The world's 50 most valuable sports teams. *Forbes*. Retrieved from www.forbes.com

Badenhausen, K. (2005, October 4). Wie tees off. *Forbes* [Online]. Retrieved from www.forbes.com/business/2005/10/04/golf-wie-endorse-cz_kb_1005wie.html?partner=yahootix

Baim, D. (1994). *The sports stadium as a municipal investment*. Westport, CT: Greenwood Press.

Bally Total Fitness and Crunch to merge. (2001, December). *Fitness Management*, 14.

Bankruptcy filings decline in FY2006. (2006, December 5). Administrative Office of the U.S. Courts. Retrieved from www.uscourts.gov/Press_Releases/bankruptcyfilings120506.html

Bankruptcy filings down in fiscal year 2011. (2011, November 7). Retrieved from www.uscourts.gov/News/NewsView/11-11-07/Bankruptcy_Filings_Down_in_Fiscal_Year_2011.aspx

Bankruptcy judge OKs Lemieux's plan to save Penguins. (1999, June 25). *Houston Chronicle*, p. 15B.

Barrett, W. (2007, November 12). Stock with a kick. *Forbes*, p. 30.

Baseball-almanac.com (2004). Retrieved from www.baseball-almanac.com/teams/rangatte.shtml

Baseball-almanac.com (n.d.). *Colorado Rockies attendance data*. Retrieved from www.baseball-almanac.com/teams/rockattn.shtml

Battersby, M. (1999, July). Finance options. *Fitness Management*, 36-37.

Battersby, M. (2003, August). How much is your health club worth? *Fitness Management*, 19(7), 38-41.

Baumol, W. (1952, November). Transactions demand for cash: An inventory theoretic approach. *Quarterly Journal of Economics*, 66, 545-556.

Baxter, K. (2009, April 12). The taxing of life of a pro athlete. *Los Angeles Times*. Retrieved from http://articles.latimes.com/2009/apr/12/sports/sp-jock-tax12

Bedell, D. (1997, October 8). Dallas businessman pleads guilty to fraud in failed NHL deal. *Dallas Morning News*, p. 1.

Bennett, R. (2011, May 23-29). Full frontal sponsorship. *Bloomberg Businessweek*, 93.

Beltrame, J. (2000, January 24). Canada backs out of pledge to aid hockey teams. *Wall Street Journal*, p. B10.

Berkowitz, S. & Upton, J. (2011, June 28). Fees, funds help foot bill at Rutgers. *USA Today*, p. C1.

Berkowitz, S., Upton, J., McCarthy, M., & Gillum, J. (2010, September 22). How student fees quietly boost college sports. *USA Today*, pp. 1A, 6C.

Bernstein, L. (1993). *Financial statement analysis*. Irwin, Homewood, IL.

Beutler, B. (2011. August 5). *S&P downgrades U.S. bond rating from AAA to AA+, outlook negative*. Talking Points

Memo. Retrieved from http://tpmdc.talkingpoints-memo.com/2011/08/sp-downgrades-us-aaa-bond-rating-to-aa-outlook-negative.php

Bing Group capsule. (n.d.). Retrieved from www.hoovers.com/uk/co/capsule/3/0,2163,42033,00.html

Bishop, G. (2011, January 29). A $60 million palace for Texas High School Football. *New York Times.* Retrieved from www.nytimes.com

Black, L.S. (2007). *Why corporations choose Delaware.* Delaware Department of State, Division of Corporations. Retrieved from http://corp.delaware.gov/whycorporations_web.pdf

Blair, R.D., & Kaserman, D.L. (1985). *Antitrust economics.* Homewood, IL: Irwin.

Bloomberg Businessweek (2012, July 30–August 5). *In the NFL, moving always wins.*

Blue Jays sign Thomas for two years, $18.12 million. (2006, November 18). Retrieved from http://sports.espn.go.com/mlb/news/story?id=2665836

Blum, D. (1993, September 22). Booster groups brace for law requiring charities to tell donors how much of a gift is tax-deductible. *Chronicle of Higher Education,* p. A36.

Blum, R. (2006, December 20). *Average baseball salaries rise 9 percent.* Retrieved from www.boston.com/sports/baseball/articles/2006/12/20/average_baseball_salary_rises_9_percent/?rss_id=Boston.com+--+Red+Sox+News

Bogen, J. (1966). *Corporation finance.* New York: Alexander Hamilton Institute.

Bohn, P. (2011, July 25). Coaches caught in scheme. *Athletic Management.* Retrieved from www.athletic-management.com/2011/07/25/am_blog_for_patrick/index.php

Boise State sells stock to improve facilities. (2009, November 12). *USA Today,* p. 5C.

Boudette, N. (2001, January 21). Muppet meltdown. *Wall Street Journal,* p. 1A.

Bowl no bonanza for UConn. (2011, March). *Business New Haven,* p. 7

Brealey, R.A., Myers, S.C., & Marcus, A.J. (2009). *Fundamentals of corporate finance* (6th ed.). Boston: McGraw Hill-Irwin.

Brennan, T. (2001). *Schwinn/GT bidding race begins.* Retrieved from www.thedeal.com/cgibin/gx.cg.../View&c=TDDArticle&cid=TDDLYIKOXPC&live=tru Breyer, R. (1998, June 26). Wetlands "bankers" sell credits in land preserves to developers. *Austin American-Statesman,* p. C1.

Bridges, F., & Roquemore, L. (1996). *Management for athletic/sport administration: Theory and practice* (2nd ed.). Decatur, GA: ESM Books.

Briefly. (1998, January 8). *Detroit News,* p. F3.

Briefly. (2000, March 15). *Connecticut Post,* p. D4.

Brigham, E.F. & Ehrhardt, M.C. (2011). *Financial management: Theory and practice* (13th ed.). New York: Dryden Press.

Brigham, E.F., & Ehrhardt, M.C. (2005). *Financial management: Theory and practice* (11th ed.). New York: Dryden Press.

Brigham, E., & Gapenski, L. (1994). *Financial management: Theory and practice* (7th ed.). Fort Worth, TX: Thomson-South-Western Press.

Brigham, E.F. & Houston, J.F. (2009). *Fundamentals of financial management* (6th ed.). Mason, OH: South-Western.

Brigham, E.F., & Houston, J.F. (2013). *Fundamentals of financial management,* (13th ed.). Mason, OH: South-Western.

Broni, P. (1999, December). Take my loan . . . please. *Inc. Magazine,* 163.

Broome, T., Jr. (2001, September). A loan at last: Special small business loan programs. *Chiropractic Economics.* Retrieved from www.chiroeco.com/article/2001/Sept/Fin2.php

Brown, M. (2010, April 8). Inside the 2010 *Forbes* MLB franchise valuations. *Forbes.* Retrieved from http://bizofbaseball.com/index.php?option=com_content&view=article&id=4274:inside-the-2010-forbes-mlb-franchise-valuations&catid=26:editorials&Itemid=39

Brown, R. (2011). Research note: Estimates of college football player rents. *Journal of Sports Economics, 12*(2), 200-212.

Brown family eludes IRS tackle. (1997, April 30). *Cincinnati Enquirer,* p. A5.

Browning, E.S. (2000, April 13). Industrials' skid masks strength in old economy. *Wall Street Journal,* p. C1.

Building information & history. (2001). Retrieved from www.united-center.com/history/index.html

Burke, D., Hendrickson, B., & Roberts, D. (2011, March 14). The gross football product. *Sports Illustrated, 114*(11), p. 16.

Bush admits mistake. (2000, January 9). *Connecticut Post,* p. D11.

Business briefcase. (1997, December 17). *Boston Herald,* p. 41.

Business bulletin. (2000, February 10). *Wall Street Journal,* p. A1.

Byrd, A. (1999, May 10-16). Easton adding wooden bats to lineup with Stix purchase. *Street & Smith's SportsBusiness Journal, 2,* 11.

Calian, S., & Latour, A. (2000, May 15). Stockholm, once a David, is a high-tech Goliath. *Wall Street Journal,* p. C1.

Campanile, C. (2011). Air ball! MSG to televise city high-school sports. *Athletic Business* Retrieved from http://athleticbusiness.com/articles/lexisnexis. aspx?lnarticleid=1453550

Canada eyes pro team subsidies. (1998, October 10). *Seattle Times*, p. C2.

Carey, John. (2006, May 25). Under Armour. A Brawny tee house? No sweat. *Bloomberg Businessweek*, Retrieved from www.businessweek.com/smallbiz/content/may2006/sb20060525_601534.htm

Caro, R. (2000, January). A financial look at the next millennium. *Fitness Management*, 56.

Cary, M.K. (2010, April 21). *How confusing is the tax code? Even the IRS chief gets help*. Retrieved from www.usnews.com/opinion/blogs/mary-kate-cary/2010/04/21/how-confusing-is-the-tax-code-even-the-irs-chief-gets-help

CBA ceases operations. (2001, February 10). *Connecticut Post*, p. D3.

CBS Sports.com. (2009, September 8). *Predators part-owner Del Biaggio sentenced to eight years in prison*. Retrieved from www.cbssports.com/nhl/story/12175616

Ceron, G. (2000, March 13). Prices for a seat on the NYSE fall amid changes. *Wall Street Journal*, p. B19.

Certificate of participation (COP). (n.d.). Retrieved from http://investopedia.com/terms/c/cop.asp

Changing game of sports finance [Pamphlet]. (1999, April 28). New York: Fitch IBCA.

Charlton standard catalogue of Canadian coins (44th ed.). (1990). Toronto, ON: Charlton Press.

Chase, B. (1998, January 12). Hockey team buyer seen admitting $80 million fraud. *American Banker*, p. 1.

Chass, M. (1998, March 18). Turner's plan: Stop Murdoch. *New York Times*, p. C1.

Cheeseman, H. (2010). *Business law* (7th ed.). Upper Saddle River, NJ: Prentice Hall.

Chi, V. (1992, September 30). Coping with the cash crunch. *San Jose Mercury News*, p. 1D.

Chiang, H., & Wilson, Y. (1998, December 24). Appeals court throws out stadium vote challenge. *San Francisco Chronicle*, p. A15.

Churchill Downs to buy troubled track. (2004, September 2). *USA Today*, p. 17C.

Clegg, J., & Espinoza, J. (2010, March 18). Cold reality of hot tickets. *Wall Street Journal*. Retrieved from www.WSJ.com

Club hopping: Bally Total Fitness off credit watch. (2004, December 13). Retrieved from www.FitnessBusinessPro.com

Club Industry staff. (2011, October 7). Cybex fights to remain listed on NASDAQ. *Club Industry*. Retrieved from http://clubindustry.com/inside_manufacturers/cybex-fights-remain-listed-nasdaq-20111007

Cohen, A. (1993, May). School daze. *Athletic Business, 17*(5), 24-32.

Cohen, A. (1999, July). Fit financing. *Athletic Business, 11*.

Cohen, L., & Holmes, S. (2005, May 30). Can Glazer put this ball in the net? *Business Week*, p. 40.

Coke signs new 4-year NFL deal. (1998, May 23). *Houston Chronicle*, p. 2C.

Colbert, J.L., & Bolton, D.L. (1998, November-December). Accounting: Recommendations for preventing and detecting fraud in a small business. *Forensic Examiner*, 29-31.

Collinson, P. (2011, August 5). Time to tackle tax avoidance and raise corporate taxes. *The Guardian*. Retrieved from www.guardian.co.uk/money/blog/2011/aug/05/tackle-corporate-tax-avoidance

Colorado Rockies attendance records. (2007). Available: www.baseball-almanac.com/teams/rockattn.shtml. Retrieved January 12, 2007.

Company. (2002). Available: http://sandiego.padres.mlb.com/sd/team/exec_bios/moores.jsp. Retrieved August 6, 2012.

Conrad, M. (2000). *Court rules MLS a "single entity" barring antitrust claim*. Retrieved from www.sportslawnews.com/archive/Articles%202000/MLSantitrustruling.htm

Cook, R. (2009, November 18). Penn State making a good business decision. *Pittsburgh Post-Gazette*. Retrieved from www.post-gazette.com

Copeland, D. (2004, January 5). Patriots teach lesson about stadium financing. *Pittsburgh Tribune-Review*. Retrieved from www.pittsburghlive.com/x/pittsburghtrib/s_173094.html#ixzz1b0BjGnye

Corporate debt may get more play in purchases of sports teams. (2000, March 2). *Wall Street Journal*, p. A1.

Cost of Vancouver Games released. (2010, July 12). *USA Today*, p. 9C.

Crouse, K. (2006, January 18). Jets break silence for voice of Mangini. *New York Times*, p. C1.

Crow, B., Phillips, D., & Gillentine, M. (Winter, 2000). Corporate partnerships in sports. *International Sports Journal, 4*(1), 27.

Cushnan, D. (2011, September 6). The broadcast forecast. *Forbes*. Retrieved from www.sportspromedia.com

Cutler, M. (2011, August 8). Auditor report hits out at "deeply flawed" Delhi Games preparations. *Sport Business*. Retrieved from www.sportbusiness.com/news/184112/auditor-report-hits-out-at-deeply-flawed-delhi-games-preparations

Cutler, M. (2011, September 19). Real Madrid hits revenue record to slash debt. *Sports Business*. Retrieved from www.sportbusiness.com/news/184339/real-madrid-hits-revenue-record-to-slash-debts

Dahl, D. (2010, November). A tough sell. *Inc.*, pp. 108-113.

Delaware InterCorp. (2000, June 27). Retrieved from www.delawareintercorp.com/why.htm

De La Merced, M.J., & Cain, J. (2011, January 3). Confident deal makers pull out checkbooks in 2010.

DealBook. Retrieved from http://dealbook.nytimes. com/2011/01/03/confident-deal-makers-pulled-out-checkbooks-in-2010

deMause, N. (2005, June 29). NYC stadium subsidies hit $1.2 billion and rising. *Field of Schemes*. Retrieved from www.fieldofschemes.com/news/archives/001268. html

deMause, N. (2009, March 24). Marlins win final stadium approval (kinda). *Field of Schemes*. Retrieved from www.fieldofschemes.com/news/archives/2009/03/3602_marlins_win_fin.html

Detroit Empowerment Zone Transition Office. (n.d.). *Empowerment Zone projects* [Brochure]. Detroit, MI: City of Detroit.

Dinch, H. (2011). *ACC adding Big East's Syracuse and Pitt*. Retrieved from http://espn.go.com/college-sports/story/_/id/6988468/acc-accepts-pittsburgh-panthers-syracuse-orange-14-team-league

Dodgers file for bankruptcy protection. (2011, June 28). Espn. com. Retrieved from http://sports.espn.go.com/los-angeles/mlb/news/story?id=6708046

Dosh, K. (2011, June 1). How profitable is Ohio State University Athletics Department? *Business of College Sports*. Retrieved from http://businessofcollegesports. com/2011/06/01/how-profitable-is-ohio-state-university-athletics-department/

Doubleday: Baseball manufactures losses. (2002, August 7). *Connecticut Post*, p. D3.

Double play for New York. (2001, December 27). *Connecticut Post*, p. C6.

Dow Jones continues its losing streak. (2002, January 15). *Connecticut Post*, p. C3.

Dow Jones Newswire. (2007, June 1). *Bally's Total Fitness to enter bankruptcy; clubs to remain open*. Retrieved from www.azcentral.com/business/articles/0601biz-bally01-ON.html

Dreazen, Y. (2000, March 7). Bankruptcy bills may proceed despite new data. *Wall Street Journal*, p. A4.

Dunphy, S.H. (1998, June 29). Understand the stock market—now. *Houston Chronicle*, pp. 1D, 4D.

Durand, J. (2011, January 10-16). $2B? To experts, it sounds reasonable. *Street and Smith's Sportsbusiness Journal*, 13(36), 1, 40.

Elkins, L. (1996, June). Tips for preparing a business plan. *Nation's Business*, 58.

Elstein, A. (2011, August 22). Wanna see your stock drop? Put your name on a stadium. *Crain's New York Business*, 27(34), p. 4.

Eltman, F. (2011, August 2). *L.I. voters reject $400 million arena plan*. Retrieved from http://news.findlaw.com/ap_stories/s/2080/08-02-2011/20110802005000_13. html?DCMP=NWL-cons_sportslaw&&&

Eminent domain. (2002). Retrieved from www.sport-slawnews.com/archive/jargon/LJEminent.html

Epstein, D. (2008, October 13). Money changes everything. *Sports Illustrated*, *109*(14), 18-19.

Ernest, W. (2002, May). Seeing green. *Club Industry*, 41-42.

ESPN to start mobile service. (2005, September 27). Retrieved from http://mobiledia.com/news/37041.html

Euchner, C.C. (1993). *Playing the field: Why sports teams move and cities fight to keep them*. Baltimore: Johns Hopkins University Press.

Evanson, D.R. (1998, January). Easier avenues to equity capital. *Nation's Business*, pp. 44–46.

Fagan, P. (1999, September). Charitable tax planning. *Jewish Action*, p. 89.

Farrell, G. (2002, March 15). Indictment could shred Andersen. *USA Today*. Retrieved from www.usatoday. com/money/energy/enron/2002-03-15-indicted.htm

Farrell, G. (2005, July 22). NYSE submits Archipelago merger filing. *USA Today*, p. 2B.

Fatsis, S. (1998, May 14). In the NBA, shoe money is no longer a slam-dunk. *Wall Street Journal*, p. B1.

FDIC. (2002). *Deposit insurance*. Retrieved from www. fdic.gov/deposit/deposits/insure/index.html

Federal Reserve System (2006). The Federal Reserve Board. Retrieved from www.federalreserve.gov/otherfrb.htm. Retrieved February 20, 2006. *Federal tax brackets*. (2011). Retrieved from www.moneychimp. com/features/tax_brackets.htm

Feiner, R. (1977). *Operational financial analysis: A practical handbook with forms*. Englewood Cliffs, NJ: Prentice Hall.

Financial Industry Regulatory Authority. (n.d.). *About the Financial Industry Regulatory Authority*. Retrieved from www.finra.org/AboutFINRA

Fiscally friendly football. (1996, July-August). *Sidelines* (College Football Association), 2.

Fitch affirms NFL 'A+' rating despite increased allowable club debt levels. (2005, August 17). Retrieved from www. findarticles.com/p/articles/mi_m0EIN/is_2005_August_17/ai_n14928167

Flamm, M. (2010, June 21-27). LeBron-Onomics. *Crain's New York Business*, 26(25), p. 1.

Football strike? Who cares? (2001, March 26). *Business Week*, 34.

Footstar completes acquisition. (2000, March 8). *Wall Street Journal*, p. A4.

Foust, D. (2008, May 26). The perils of going public. *Business Week/Golf Digest*, pp. 64-65.

Form 10-Q. (2006, December 6). Retrieved from http:// corporate.wwe.com/documents/2qt200610-q.pdf

For the record. (1998, September 21-27). *Street & Smith's SportsBusiness Journal*, 1, 34.

For the record. (1999, May 10-16). *Street & Smith's Sports-Business Journal*, 2, 38.

Forsythe, E. (2001). *The sponsorship connection: A practical guide for high school athletic directors and coaches.* Fayetteville, AR: Athletic World Advertising.

Fraser, L., & Ormiston, A. (2009). *Understanding financial statements* (9th ed.). Upper Saddle River, NJ: Prentice Hall.

Freeman, R.J., Shoulders, C.D., & Lynn, E.S. (1988). *Governmental and nonprofit accounting* (3rd ed.). Englewood Cliffs, NJ: Prentice Hall.

Frey, L. (2011). How the smallest market in professional sports had the easiest financial journey: The renovation of Lambeau Field, *Sports Lawyers Journal, 18*(1), 259-282.

Fried, G. (2010). *Managing sport facilities.* Champaign, IL: Human Kinetics.

Fried, G., & Miller, L. (1998). *Employment law.* Greensboro, NC: Carolina Academic Press.

From $50 in 1922 to a half-billion today. (1999, December 26). *Connecticut Post*, p. D3.

From coins to credit cards. (1999, December 19). *Connecticut Post*, p. F4.

Frost, G. (2002). *Longtime fans buy Boston Celtics for $360 million.* FindLaw [Online serial]. Retrieved from http://news.findlaw.com/sports/s/20020927/nbabostoncelticsdc.html

Fulks, D. (2011). *Revenues and expenses: 2004-2010 NCAA Division I intercollegiate athletic programs report.* Indianapolis, IN: National Collegiate Athletic Association.

Futterman, M. (2011, February 10). *Wall Street Journal.* Manchester Derby will be the most expensive game in history. Retrieved from www.online.wsj.com

Gandley, W., & Stanley, D. (1978). *Canada/B.N.A. postage stamp catalogue* (9th ed.). Paris, ON: Canadian Wholesale Supply.

German soccer team scores unusual goal: Approval to go public. (1999, November 29). *Wall Street Journal,* p. B28.

Gibeaut, J. (1999, March). The money chase. *ABA Journal,* 58.

Gilpin, F. (1998, December 30). Officials cleared in arena probe. *Tampa Tribune,* p. 1.

Glier, R. (1997, July 20). With expectations unfulfilled, Atlantans still searching for legacy from games. *Houston Chronicle,* p. 18B.

Go figure. (1999, October 25). *Sports Illustrated* p. 33.

Golden Bear Golf, Inc. (n.d.). Retrieved from http://hoovers.com/print/printh.html

Golden Bear Golf, Inc. announces settlement. (1999, December 23). Retrieved from www.businesswire.com

Goldhirsh, J. (1996, November). There's nothing passive about rental income. *Nation's Business,* 71.

Goldman, S. (2011, November 18). *LA Fitness acquires 171 Bally Total Fitness clubs.* Retrieved from http://clubindustry.com/forprofits/lafitness-acquires-bally-total-fitness-20111118/

Goldstein, P., & Alden, B. (2011, April/May). Pie vs. pie. *Athletic Management, 23*(3), 39-43.

Goo, S.K. (2000, January 26). Green Mountain: Loyalty helps VT ski co-op thrive. *Wall Street Journal,* p. NE1.

Grant, E.A. (2007, December). Your cold calling? *Inc. Magazine,* p. 34.

Grant, L. (2005, March 23). Gnarly: Quicksilver buys ski company. *USA Today,* p. 5B.

Greenberg, M., & Gray, J. (1996). *The stadium game.* Milwaukee, WI: National Sports Law Institute of Marquette University Law School.

Greer, J. (2010, December 17). *Glades Central High fires football coach Jessie Hester.* Retrieved from www.pbgametime.com/news/glades-central-high-fires-football-coach-jessie-hester/111192/

Griffin, M.P. (1991). *Intermediate finance for nonfinancial managers.* Toronto, ON: Amacom.

Grover, R., & Lowry, T. (2001, September 3). Those smackdowns are taking their toll. *Business Week,* 40.

Grover, R., & Lowry, T. (2002, April 15). A cable clan on thin ice. *Business Week,* 48.

Grover, R., & Lowry, T. (2004, November 22). Rumble in regional sports. *Business Week,* 156-157.

Halley, J. (2010, December 7). High schools get in logo game. *USA Today,* p. 1C.

Harper, T. (1999, March 6). He shouts! He scares! *Toronto Star,* p. B1.

Haynie, W.H. (1998, July). Equipment financing. *Fitness Management,* 36-37.

Helyar, J., & Keehner, J. (2010, May 31-June 6). Tom Hicks says goodbye to sports. *Bloomberg Businessweek,* 42-43.

Henderson, J. (1996, September 4). Voters say yes to sales tax. *Tampa Tribune,* p. 1.

Hennepin County approves sales tax for new stadium. (2006, September 8). Retrieved from www.payden.com/pubs/muniBonds/MBCE090806.pdf

Hiestand, M. (1992, October). Illinois could eliminate funds for college teams. *USA Today,* p. 10C.

Hiestand, M. (2004, November 9). NFL again hits TV pay dirt. *USA Today,* p. C1.

High-tech injection. (1999, October 27). *Connecticut Post,* p. C1.

Hipes, P. (2011, April 19). *NBC, Versus seal NHL broadcasting rights.* Retrieved from www.deadline.com/2011/04/nbcuniversal-nets-keeping-broadcast-rights-to-nhl/

Hodges, S. (1997, February). SBA microloans fuel big ideas. *Nation's Business,* 34-35.

Hoffman, D. (1998, November). Penguins file for bankruptcy. *Stadium & Arena Financing News, 2*(21), 1.

Holmes, A.W., & Burns, D.C. (1979). *Auditing: Standards and procedures* (9th ed.). Homewood, IL: Irwin.

Horine, L. (1999). *Administration of physical education and sport programs* (4th ed.). Boston: McGraw-Hill.

Hovey, J. (1997, September). A source of funds in search of work. *Nation's Business*, 37-38.

Hovey, J. (1998, March). A little-known pathway to growth. *Nation's Business*, 40-42.

Hovey, J. (1998, July). Cheap funding through bonds. *Nation's Business*, 50-51.

Hovey, J. (1998, November). Using inventory for collateral. *Nation's Business*, 42-43.

Howard, D.R., & Crompton, J.L. (2004). *Financing sport* (2nd ed.). Morgantown, WV: Fitness Information Technology.

Howard, T. (2005, October 14). Investors can capitalize when companies score sport sponsorship. *USA Today*, p. 5B.

H.R. 4736. (1992). *Taxpayer's Right to View Act of 1992*. 102d Congress, Energy and Commerce Committee.

Hube, K. (2000, January 26). Tax rule crimps small-business deals. *Wall Street Journal*, p. C1.

Huma, R., & Staurowsky, E. (2011). *The price of poverty in big time college sport*. National College Players Association.

Humphreys, B. (2010). The impact of the global financial crisis on sport in North America.

In Butenko, S., Gil-Lafuente, J., & Pardalos, P. (Eds.), *Optimal strategies in sports economics and management* (pp. 39-57). Heidelberg, Germany: Springer.

Hundley v. Commissioner, 48 T.C. 339. (1967).

Immoo, L., Lochhead, S., Ritter, R., & Zhao, Q. (1996). The costs of raising capital. *Journal of Financial Research*, 19, 59-74.

Introduction. (1992). Washington, DC: National Association of Securities Dealers.

Inventory analyst—Easton Sports. (2000, March 3). Retrieved from www.sportlink.com/employment/jobs/jobs2000-016.html

Investopedia staff. (2010, January 2). *Knowing your rights as a shareholder*. Retrieved from www.investopedia.com/articles/01/050201.asp#axzz1eDub4QaU

Ip, G. (2000, March 10). NASDAQ pumps up to 5000. *Wall Street Journal*, p. C1.

Ip, G. (2000, March 15). Archipelago to set up new stock market. *Wall Street Journal*, p. C1.

IPO basics: A road map. (1999). Retrieved from www.inc.com/articles/details/0,6378,AGD2_ART15744_CNY56_SUB14,00.html

Internal Revenue Service. (2010). *IRS publication 535, business expenses*. Retrieved from www.irs.gov/pub/irs-pdf/p535.pdf

Isidore, C. (2002, January 31). *Superdome name goes unsold*. Retrieved from http://money.cnn.com/2002/01/31/superbowl/superbowl_noname/

Isidore, C. (2004, April 1). *AT&T, Kodak, IP out of Dow*. Retrieved from www.money.cnn.com/2004/04/04/markets/dow

Janda, J. (2001, December). Mad Dogg, Schwinn partnership ends. *Club Industry*, 24.

Jean, S. (2005, January 2). What's your money type? *Hartford Courant*, p. C1.

Joyner, J. (2010, August 27). *College athletics losing money*. Outside the Beltway. Retrieved from www.outsidethebeltway.com/college-athletics-losing-money/

Just For Feet sets deal with creditors to seek bankruptcy. (1999, November 3). *Wall Street Journal*, p. B10.

Kadet, A. (2011, June 12). Charity "cashathons": High-cost fund raising. *Wall Street Journal Sunday, Hartford Courant*, p. D4.

Kalwarski, T. (2008, August 11). The Beijing Olympics: Follow the gold. *Business Week*. 15.

Kalwarski, T. (2010, April 19). No recession hangover for the booze business. *Bloomberg Businessweek*, 17.

Kane, B. (2011, August 8). CT golf courses struggle to recover from sour start. *Hartford Business Journal*, 19(41), p. 1.

Kaplan, D. (1998, November 9-15). Slugger's bond plan striking out. *Street & Smith's SportsBusiness Journal*, 1, 3.

Kaplan, D. (1999, August 16-22). Lehman gives USTA fasttrack refinance. *Street & Smith's SportsBusiness Journal*, 2, 16.

Kaplan, D. (2001, March 12-18). Securitization era opens for athletes. *Street & Smith's SportsBusiness Journal*, 3, 1, 43.

Kaplan, D. (2009, October 26). NFL pares ownership rule. *Sports Business Journal/Daily*. Retrieved from www.sportsbusinessdaily.com/Journal/Issues/2009/10/20091026/This-Weeks-News/NFL-Pares-Ownership-Rule.aspx

Kaplan, D. (2010, August 2-8). Nike endorsement tab swooshes down. *Street & Smith's Sportsbusiness Journal*, 13(15).

Kaspriske, R. (2003, November). *Buyer's market: A sluggish economy has left many private golf clubs desperate for new members—special report*. Retrieved from www.findarticles.com/p/articles/mi_m0HFI/is_11_54/ai_109467586

Kastner & Partners, an advertising agency. (n.d.). *Red Bull. A success story*. Retrieved from www.mintinnovation.com/links/docs/Marketing/Red%20Bull%20Success%20story.pdf

King, B., & Brockington, L. (1998, December 14-20). Forces push both sides in Yanks' deal. *Street & Smith's SportsBusiness Journal*, 1, 1, 46.

King, B. (2010, August 2-8). High school sports running on empty. *Street & Smith's SportsBusiness Journal*, 13(15).

Klise, E. (1972). *Money and banking* (5th ed.). Cincinnati, OH: South-Western.

Koller, T., Goedhart, M., & Wessels, D. (2005). *Valuation: Measuring and managing the value of companies* (4th ed.). Hoboken, NJ: Wiley.

Kowall, S. (2001). *The weekly tirade*. Retrieved from www.comedyzine.com/tirade154.shtml

Kraker, D. (1998). *The economics of pro sports: The fans, the owners, and the rules*. Retrieved from www.ilsr.org/pubs/pubsrules.html

Kupetz, D.S. (1998, July). Resolving business financial crises. *California Lawyer*, 66-68.

Kurdziel, K. (2000, April 27). Dolan has one goal for the Tribe: Win the World Series. *Sun News*, p. C1.

Lamiell, P. (1999, May 4). Dow index passes 11,000 in record time. *Houston Chronicle*, p. 1C.

Largest naming rights deals. (2011, September 19-25). *Street & Smith's SportsBusiness Journal*. 14(21), 22-23.

Lascari, S. (1998, October-November). Sports facility issues, part two. Stock of sports franchises: A sound investment or scam? *For the Record* (Marquette University Law School), 9(5), 3.

Leahy, S. (2010, September 1). Stadium vs. home: Can the NFL make being there match what's on TV. *USA Today*, p. 1A.

Lederman, D. (1991, December 11). IRS rules that 2 bowls must pay taxes on money they received from corporate sponsors. *Chronicle of Higher Education*, p. A33.

Lee, C. (1999, July). Managing the process. *ABA Journal*, 62.

Lee, C.W., & Aiken, D. (2011). Changing brand associations in Taiwan: Nike's sponsorship of High-school basketball. *Journal of Sponsorship,3*(3), 249-259.

Left for dead, CBA breathes new life. (2001). *La Crosse Tribune*. Retrieved from http://lacrossetribune.com/stories/sports/left-for-dead-cba-breathing-new-life/article_f9974b80-1992-58ca-a078-5944d7dcbabe.html

Leukhardt, B. (2009, January 1). Stealing from the boss. *Hartford Courant*, p. 1A.

Lewis, A. (1999, June 8). Suits seek to halt Ascent sale: Prospective buyers wait as shareholders say $400 million bid by Lauries is too low. *Denver Rocky Mountain News*, p. 1B.

Lewis, J. (1936, February 29). Basehits, incorporated. *Liberty*, 48-49.

Liberation Investments delivers letter to Bally Total Fitness Holding Corp. (2005, July 19). Retrieved from http://home.businesswire.com/portal/site/google/index.jsp?ndmViewId=news_views&news

Lipin, S. (2000, February 28). Firms incorporated in Delaware are valued more by investors. *Wall Street Journal*, p. C21.

Liverpool sale awaits judge's ruling. (2010, October 13). *USA Today*, p. 11C.

Livingston, A. (1998, July). Avoiding pitfalls when selling a business. *Nation's Business*, 25-26.

Livingstone, J.L. (Ed.). (1997). *The portable MBA in finance and accounting* (2nd ed.). New York: Wiley.

Louisiana forks over $12.4M to Saints. (2005, July 16). *USA Today*, p. 15C.

Low, C. (2009, August 29). *Tide's Saban commits through 2017*. Espn.com. Retrieved from http://sports.espn.go.com/ncf/news/story?id=4431228

Lowenstein, R. (2011, June 13-19). The $145 million fastball. *Bloomberg Businessweek*, 86-87.

Lowry, T., & Grover, R. (2004, November 22). Football's fear factor. *Business Week*, 157.

Lyster, Stephanie. (2006). *The history of Under Armour—A mastermind for performance apparel*. Retrieved from http://ezinearticles.com/?The-History-of-Under-Armour---A-Mastermind-for-Performance-Apparel&id=127493

MacIntosh, J., & Whitehouse, K. (2011, September 29). Madoff trustee says ruling means $6B less for victims. *New York Post*. Retrieved from www.nypost.com/p/news/business/irv_decries_wolf_IIVhXsf1BtrY8WyEeGZUgO#ixzz1gfofBi6Q

Mahony, E. (2009, August 22). Official embezzled over $1.4. *Hartford Courant*, p. A5.

Managers rethinking "just-in-time" inventory management. (2001, December 28). [Trucking Technology Alert]. Retrieved from www.ttnews.com/members/topNews/0008327.html

Manchester United posts higher earnings ahead of IPO. (2011, September 1). *Singapore News*. Retrieved from www.channelnewsasia.com/stories/singaporebusinessnews/view/1150542/1/.html

Man steals $142,000 from Metropolitan Washington YMCA. (2009, September 17). *Club Industry*. Retrieved from http://clubindustry.com/nonprofits/1001-man-stealing-from-ymca

Markets consider merger. (2000, March 4). *Connecticut Post*, p. B1.

Marrocco, S. (2010, February 23). *Stratus Media Group assumes control of ProElite Inc., plans to relaunch MMA promotion*. MMAJunkie.com. Retrieved from http://mmajunkie.com/news/18063/stratus-media-group-assumes-control-of-proelite-inc-plans-to-relaunch-mma-promotion.mma

Martzke, R., & Cherner, R. (2004, August 17). Channeling how to view sports. *USA Today*, pp. 1C-2C.

Marullo, G.G. (1998, March). Rewards and risks in lending to your child. *Nation's Business*, 27-28.

Marullo, G.G. (1998, August). Selling your business: A preview of the process. *Nation's Business*, 25-26.

Massey, D. (2011, August 15). Jets goal to go: displace Giants. *Crain's New York Business, 27*(3), p. 3.

Mayer, C. (1998, July 26). Business model hikes Amazon's value. *Houston Chronicle*, p. 5D.

McAllister, P. (1998). Contributions & premiums. *Grantsmanship Center Magazine*, 9.

McCarthy, M. (2011, May 31). Labor fight could blunt NBA's boom. *USA Today*, p. 1C.

McCoy, K., & Chu, K. (2011, December 27). Disappointment in a shell. *USA Today*, p. B1.

McDonald, Duff. (2011, May 23). The mastermind of adrenaline marketing. *Bloomberg Businessweek*, 62-70.

McGraw, D. (1998, July 13). Big league troubles. *U.S. News and World Report*, pp. 40-46.

Mclean, B. (2000, February). Chase's venture capital elite. *Fortune*, 47.

McMorris, F., Smith, R., & Schroeder, M. (2000, March 15). Insider case involves attempt at two brokers and web ring. *Wall Street Journal*, p. C1.

Mehta, N., Thomasson, L., & Barrett, P. (2010, May 24-May 30). The machine that ate the market. *Bloomberg Business Week*, pp. 48-55.

Meigs, W.B., Whittington, O.R., & Meigs, R.F. (1982). *Principles of auditing*. Homewood, IL: Irwin.

Mercer, J. (1996, October 11). In dollars and cents, colleges measure what they contribute to their communities. *Chronicle of Higher Education*, p. A47.

Mickle, T. (2009, July 27-August 2). Buying into boots. *Street & Smith's SportsBusiness Journal, 12*(14), p. 1.

Miller, T. (2011). *Pac-12 says no (mostly) to expansion*. Retrieved from http://espn.go.com/blog/pac12/post/_/id/26160/pac-12-says-no-mostly-to-expansion

Miller, W.S. (1998, August-September). Sport facility issues, part one. The boom in stadium construction & financing new facilities. *For the Record* (Marquette University Law School), 9(4), 7.

Moffeit, M. (1999, March 28). Off to a fast start. *Houston Chronicle*, p. 8D.

Morgan, M. (2010, October 2). It's a new financial ballgame for Memphis Redbirds. *Commercial Appeal*. Retrieved from www.commercialappeal.com/news/2010/oct/02/its-a-new-financial-ballgame-for-birds/

Most big-time schools winning the profit game. (2011, June 16). *USA Today*, p. 6C.

Moulson, G. (2007, April 11). Sporting goods maker Puma a takeover target. *Hartford Courant*, p. E4.

Much, P. (1996, June 7). *Publicly traded sports team* [Marketing letter]. Chicago: Houlihan Lokey Howard & Zukin.

Much, P. (1997, September 9). *Estate planning for professional sports team owners* [Marketing letter]. Chicago: Houlihan Lokey Howard & Zukin.

Much, P. (1997, December 1). *Sports teams, IPOs, and some baseball nostalgia* [Marketing letter]. Chicago: Houlihan Lokey Howard & Zukin.

Much, P., & Phillips, J. (1999). *Sports teams and the stock market* [Marketing letter]. Chicago: Houlihan Lokey Howard & Zukin.

Mullen, L. (1998, November 30-December 6). Golden Bear Golf hit $14.3 million trap. *Street & Smith's SportsBusiness Journal*, 3.

Munroe, T. (1997, September 5). Fleet shuffles sports group lineup. *Boston Herald*, p. 34.

Muret, D. (2011, January 10-16). Firms work hard to find something to build. *Street and Smith's SportsBusiness Journal, 13*(36), 19.

Nakashima, R. (2010, August 5). *Live Nation posts 2Q loss on weak concert season*. Yahoo Finance. Retrieved from http://finance.yahoo.com/news/Live-Nation-posts-2Q-loss-on-apf-4236591976.html?x=0&sec=topStories&pos=1&asset=&ccode=

NASD. (2006). *Overview*. Retrieved from www.nasd.com

National Association for Sport and Physical Education and North American Society for Sport Management. (2000). *Sport management program standards and review protocol*. Reston, VA: Author.

National Federation of State High School Associations. (2011). *Participation data*. Retrieved from www.nfhs.org/content.aspx?id=3282

NBA going global with sale of Nets. (2009, September 24). *Hartford Courant*, p. B2.

Nelton, S. (1998, June). Seeking funding? Get organized. *Nation's Business*, 40-42.

Nelton, S. (1998, November). Sizing up the megabanks. *Nation's Business*, 14-21.

Nelson, S.L. (2011). *S corporations kits and more*. Retrieved from www.scorporationsexplained.com/scorporation-advantage-disadvantage.htm

Nemeth-Johannes, C. (2003). *Researching your business on the net*. Retrieved from www.abcsmallbiz.com/bizbasics/gettingstarted/research_biz.html

New ballpark for Missouri. (2007, January 9). Retrieved from http://cardinals.mlb.com/NASApp/mlb/stl/ballpark/stl_ballpark_newpark_factsheet.jsp

Newberry, J. (2001, August). Free with purchase. *ABA Journal*, 78.

New study pegs Adams State economic impact at $70 million. (2005, May 18). Retrieved from www2.adams.edu/news/may0513/may0513.php

NFL looking at reducing minimum ownership stake for partners. (2000, June 1). *Sports Business Daily*, p. 8.

NFL stadium financing landscape. (2001). Retrieved from www.vikings.com/Stadium/Stadiumlandscape.htm

NHL Press. (2005, September 12). *XM Satellite and NHL announce long-term agreement.* Retrieved from www.nhl.com/news/2005/09/234310.html

Nicholas, T. (1990). *Cash: How to get it into and out of your corporation.* Wilmington, DE: Enterprise.

Nicklaus company's stock doesn't make NASDAQ cut. (1998, August 14). *Houston Chronicle*, p. 3C.

Nicklin, J. (1997, November 21). Universities seek to cut costs by "outsourcing" more operations. *Chronicle of Higher Education*, p. A35.

Nightengale, B. (2011, April 21). MLB ousts McCourt, takes over Dodgers. *USA Today*, p. 1C.

Nightengale, B., & McCarthy; M. (2009). Empty spring seats spawn creative regular-season deals. *USA Today.* Retrieved from http://www.usatoday.com/sports/baseball/2009-03-08-Ticket_deals_N.htm

Nike. (2011). *Annual report.* Retrieved from http://investors.nikeinc.com/Investors/OVERVIEW/default.aspx

Noll, R., & Zimbalist, A. (1998). *Are new stadiums worth the cost?* Retrieved from www.breadnotcircuses.org/brooking.html

NYSE rules. (2011). Retrieved from http://usequities.nyx.com/regulation/nyse-rules-and-interpretations/rules

Olson, Elizabeth. (2011, August 8). Under Armour applies its muscle to shoes. *New York Times.* Retrieved from www.nytimes.com/2011/08/09/business/media/for-under-armour-a-focus-on-shoes-advertising.html?_r=1&pagewanted=all

Ourand, J. (2011). Time Warner signs long-term deal to produce high school sports in California. *Sports Business Daily.* Retrieved from www.sportsbusinessdaily.com/Daily/Issues/2011/09/16/Media/TWC.asp

Overview of preliminary arena development process. (1995). Denton, TX: Denton County.

Owner. (2002). Retrieved from www.nba.com/nuggets/news/kroenke_bio.html

Packers say player costs cut into profits. (2010, July 15). *USA Today*, p. 11C.

Packers sell 185,000 stock shares in first 2 days. (2011, December 8). Yahoo Sports. Retrieved from http://sports.yahoo.com/nfl/news?slug=ap-packers-stocksale.

Palazzo, A. (1999, October 4). Goal of minor league soccer team, the San Diego Flash, is to go public. *Wall Street Journal*, p. B13

Panthers' new ownership group receives NHL approval. (2002). Retrieved from www.flpanthers.com/pressbox/news/ownersapproval.shtml

Parrish, A., & Maloney, L. (1999, July). Documenting good intentions. *ABA Journal*, 63.

Parry, T. (2004, April 6). *PepsiCo extends NFL sponsorship in $560 million deal.* Retrieved from http://promomagazine.com/news/marketing_pepsico_extends_nfl_2/index.html

Pasquarelli, A. (2011, March 7). David Barton Gym to get spotting help from Chapter 11. *Crain's New York Business*, 27(10), p. 4

Patsuris, P. (2003, October 7). NASCAR pulls into prime time. *Forbes.* Retrieved from www.forbes.com/2003/10/07/cx_pp_1007nascar_print.html

Paul Allen. (2002). Retrieved from www.thestandard.com/people/profile/0,1923,1302,00.html

Pay-Rod: Rangers raise ticket prices for fifth season in row. (2001, January 8). *Sports Illustrated.* Retrieved from http://sportsillustrated.cnn.com/baseball/mlb/news/2001/01/08/rangers_tickets_ap

Pellegrino, G., & Hancock, H. (2010). *A lasting legacy: How major sporting events can drive positive change for host communities and economies.* United Kingdom: Deloitte.

Pells, E. (2006, May 26). Enterprising brothers converted NBA buyout of ABA team into multimillion-dollar windfall. http://www.seattlepi.com/news/article/Enterprising-brothers-converted-NBA-buyout-of-ABA-1204630.php.

Penguins file for bankruptcy. (1998, November 2). *Stadium and Arena Financing News*, p. 1.

Pereira, J. (2001, January 23). Converse files for bankruptcy protection, plans to shutter North American plants. *Wall Street Journal*, p. B8.

Perez-Pina, R. (2011, May 11). Sports-gear firm accused of bilking schools. *New York Times.* Retrieved from www.nytimes.com/2011/05/12/nyregion/circle-systems-group-accused-of-defrauding-many-schools.html?_r=1&partner=rss%26emc=rss

Peterson, L., & Brooks, C. (2010, October 15). *Venture capital investment declines in Q3 2010 despite stability of first-time financings.* PriceWaterhoueCoopers. Retrieved from www.pwc.com/us/en/press-releases/2010/venture-capital-investment-declines-in-Q3-2010-despite-stability-of-first-time-financings.jhtml

Pfahler, L. (2010, July 25). *Pay to play is the new norm in high school sports.* TCPalm.com. Retrieved from www.tcpalm.com/news/2010/jul/25/pay-to-play/?print=1

Phelps, M. (2011, June 20). NCAA revenue report review. *Athletic Management.* Retrieved from www.athleticmanagement.com/2011/06/20/revenue_report/index.php

Pierce, D., & Bussell, L. (2011). National Survey of Interscholastic Sport Sponsorship in the United States. *Sport Management International Journal*, (7)1, 43-62.

Planning for success. (2000, November-December). *CampBusiness*, 8-11.

Polansky, R. (2009, July 9). First stadium bonds cost taxpayers more than $2.4 billion. *Miami Today News.* Retrieved from www.miamitodaynews.com/news/090709/story2.shtml

Popke, M. (2008, March). Checks and balances. *Athletic Business*, pp. 96-98.

Portions of New Orleans Saints purchase price is allocable to Superdome lease. (1998, Spring/Summer). *Business of Sports*, 2-4.

Potkewitz, H. (2011, March 14). Yankee Stadium garage striking out. *Crain's New York Business, 27*(11), p.7.

Pounds, M. (1997, October 27). Finding the money to start up a business and how to write a business plan. *Houston Chronicle*, pp. 1D-2D.

Pratt, P., & Niculita, A. (2007). *Valuing a business* (5th ed.). New York: McGraw Hill.

Pratt, S., Reilly, R., & Schweihs, R. (2000). *Valuing a business: The analysis and appraisal of closely held companies* (4th ed.). New York: McGraw-Hill.

Predators part-owner Del Biaggio sentenced to eight years in prison. (2009, September 8). Retrieved from www.cbssports.com/nhl/story/12175616

Pristen, T. (1987, August 22). Ex-Dodger worker gets prison for grand theft. *Los Angeles Times*. Retrieved from http://articles.latimes.com/1987-08-22/local/me-1089_1_grand-theft

Pro Football Hall of Fame. (2007). *Art Rooney*. Retrieved from www.profootballhof.com/hof/member.jsp?player_id=183

Profiles of success. (2001). Boston: International Health, Racquet & Sportsclub Association.

Provision could boost teams' values. (2004, August 3). *USA Today*, p. 11C.

Pryde, J. (1998, February). A lending niche helps small firms. *Nation's Business*, 52-53.

Ranalli, R. (1997, October 8). Islanders' buyer to plead guilty to fraud charges. *Boston Globe*, p. 35.

Rangers owner Hicks agrees to sell team to Nolan Ryan group. (2010, January 23). CBS Sports. Retrieved from www.cbssports.com/mlb/story/12828467/rangers-owner-hicks-agrees-to-sell-team-to-nolan-ryan-group

Ready to wrestle the bulls. (1999, August 4). *Houston Chronicle*, p. 1C.

Report says Man U owners deep in debt. (2010, June 8). *USA Today*, p. 9C.

Reports: Thomas agrees to sell CBA, owes $750,000. Retrieved from www.canoe.ca/BasketballCBA/jun28_tho.html

Revenue Ruling 58-145, 1955-2 C.B., 25. (1958).

Revenue Ruling 88-76. (1988).

Reynes, R. (1997, November). Venturing out for rapid growth. *Nation's Business*, 54-55.

Reynes, R. (1998, October). Low-profile money sources. *Nation's Business*, 32-33.

Rhoda, B., Wrigley, B., & Habermas, E. (2010, November 1). *SportsBusiness Journal*. How to increase revenue as industry evolves. Retrieved from www.sportsbusinessjournal.com

Ripley, J., & Mabe, L.D. (2003, October 24). Changing courses: Foul weather on the fairways, plus a subpar business climate, mean that a dwindling number of golfers are being courted with discounts and coupons. *St. Petersburg Times*. Retrieved from www.sptimes.com/2003/10/24/Northoftampa/Changing_courses.shtml

Rishe, P. (2010, July 5). The recession's lasting impact on sports sponsorships. *Forbes*.

Roberts, D. (2011, October 17). Big energy woos the Big Ten. *Fortune, 164*(6), 30.

Robinson v. Commissioner, 44 T.C. 20. (1965).

Robson, D. (2008, November 18). Staying upbeat amid downturn. *USA Today*, p. 8C.

Rodgers, R. (1966). *Banking*. New York: Alexander Hamilton Institute.

Rodriguez's riches: A-Rod concerned about baseball, not business. (2001, January 9). *Sports Illustrated*. Retrieved from http://sportsillustrated.cnn.com/baseball/mlb/news/2001/01/09/arods_riches_ap

Rogus, D. (1997, June-July). America's sports stadiums: How much do they really cost you? *Your Money*, pp. 70–79.

Rosenblatt, B. (1989, February 20). Have I got a deal for you, kid. . . . *Sportsinc*, 24.

Rosenberg, J.M. (2010). *The concise encyclopedia of the great recession, 2007-2010*. Lanham, MD: Scarecrow Press.

Rosenbuh, S. (2004, December 27). Mergers: A bit of mania for 2005. *BusinessWeek Online*. Retrieved from www.businessweek.com/bwdaily/dnflash/dec2004/nf20041227_6504_db035.htm

Ross, S.A., Westerfield, R.W., & Jaffe, J. (2008). *Corporate finance* (8th ed.). Boston, MA: McGraw-Hill Irwin.

Ross, S.A., Westerfield, R.W., & Jordan, B.D. (2008). *Fundamentals of corporate finance* (8th ed.). Boston, MA: McGraw Hill.

Ruibal, S. (2010, July 22). Privately funded, Empire State Games rise again. *USA Today*, p. 10C.

Rumblings. (1997, August 25). *Crain's Detroit Business*, p. 34.

Ruxin, R. (1989). *An athlete's guide to agents*. New York: Penguin Books.

Sanders, C.T. (2010, February). To the bone. *Athletic Management, 22*(2), 43-47.

Sapsford, J. (2000, March 14). Fed to make banks boost capital to cover venture-investing risk. *Wall Street Journal*, p. A4.

Saraceno, J. (2008, October 14). Tough times force layoffs in staffing. *USA Today*, p. 2C.

SBA. (2002). Retrieved from http://www.sbaonline.sba.gov.

SBA loans top $239 million for the year. (2006, November 13). Retrieved from www.businessnewhaven.com/article_page.lasso?id=40431

Scherriek, S. (2000, December 16). What the earnings reports don't tell you. *Business Week,* 201.

Schlueb, M., & Damron, D. (2010, April 3). Orlando risks default on Magic arena bonds, analysts warn. *Orland Sentinel.* Retrieved from http://articles.orlandosentinel.com/2010-04-03/news/os-magic-arena-junk-bonds-20100403_1_arena-bonds-default-fitch-ratings

Schmidgall, R., Singh, A.J., & Johnson, A. (2007, November/December). Current sales: Forecasting practices in the U.S. club industry. *Club Management,* 26-9, 46-7.

Schreiner, J., & Damsell, K. (1998, November 11). Canucks blame record losses on dollar and taxes. *National Post,* p. C01.

Schroeder, M., & Schiller, Z. (1992, August 24). A scandal waiting to happen. *Business Week,* 32.

Scott, M. (2010, March 22 and 29). Can Man U kick its debt habit? *Bloomberg Businessweek,* 28.

Scudder, M. (2001, March). Survival strategies to win in an economic slowdown. *Fitness Management,* 17(4), 36-39.

Seay, G. (2011, October 5). SBA: CT Inc.'s borrowing soared in fiscal 2011. *Hartford Business Journal Online.* Retrieved from www.hartfordbusiness.com/article.php?RF_ITEM%5B%5D=Article$0@20808;Article

Securities and Exchange Commission. (2009, December 17). *SEC charges Ernst & Young and Six partners for roles in accounting violations at Bally Total Fitness.* 2009-271 Press Release. Retrieved from www.sec.gov/news/press/2009/2009-271.htm

Securities regulation in the United States (1994). Gaithersburg, MD: National Association of Securities Dealers.

Securitizing sports. (1998, November 16). *Stadium and Arena Financing News,* p. 8.

Shank, A. (2005, March 9). National hockey group proposes fan-owned team. *USA Today,* p. 3C.

Shapiro, S. (1999, Winter). Valuation of law practices. *Law Firm Governance,* 4(2), 26-33.

Sharecast. (2005, June 15). *Manchester United.* Retrieved from www.sharecast.com/cgi-bin/sharecast/security.cgi?csi=10245

Shaver, J. (2007, September 19). South Dakota Y bookkeeper charged with theft and forgery. *Club Industry.* Retrieved from http://fitnessbusinesspro.com/news/south-dakota-bookkepper-theft/

Shell, A. (2005, August 19). Eight more charged in Reebok case. *USA Today,* p. 5B.

Shell, A. (2008, February 12). Dow Jones 30 gets fine-tuned for finance, energy. *USA Today,* 5B.

Sherman Antitrust Act. (2012). The free dictionary. Retrieved at http://encyclopedia2.thefreedictionary.com/Sherman+Anti-Trust+Act+of+1890. July 19, 2012.

Shinn faces suit over arena profits. (1998, October 24). *Herald Rock Hill,* p. 5B.

Sichelman, L. (1998, August 24). Trumping the credit bureau. *Houston Chronicle,* p. 1D.

Siegal, A. (2000). *Practical business statistics* (4th ed.). New York: McGraw-Hill.

Siegel, J., Shim, J., & Hartman, S. (1992). *Dictionary of personal finance.* New York: Macmillan.

Simmons, C. (2000). *Business valuation bluebook: How entrepreneurs buy, sell and trade.* Prairie Village, KS: Corinth Press.

Simon, E., & Yao, D. (2007, February 3). Aramark CEO reaps rich reward in buyout. *Hartford Courant,* p. E1.

Singer, T. (1998, May). Baseball's bargains and bandits. *Sport,* 35.

"Sinners" as saints? Seems so in Cleveland. (2005, August 29). *USA Today,* p. 1C.

Sky Media. (2005). Retrieved from http://phx.corporate-ie.net/phoenix.zhtml?c=104016&p=irol-mediaprofile

Smith, B. (2001, Fall). If you build it, will they come? *Georgetown Public Policy Review,* 7(1), 45-60.

Smith, M. & Muret, D. (2010, August 2). Merger has IMG poised to compete. *Street & Smith's SportsBusiness Journal.* Retrieved from www.sportsbusinessdaily.com/Journal/Issues/2010/08/20100802/This-Weeks-News/Merger-Has-IMG-Poised-To-Compete.aspx

Smith, T. (2005, June 15). *Yankees reveal new stadium plans.* Retrieved from http://mlb.com/NASApp/mlb/content/printer_friendly/mlb/y2005/m06/d15/c1090587.jsp

Soccer quotes. (2002). Retrieved from www.soccerinvestor.com

SODA (Sportsplex Operators and Developers Association). (1993). *Sportspark construction costs.* Racine, WI: Author.

Speedway Motorsports. (2006). *10-Q report.* Retrieved from http://phx.corporate-ir.net/phoenix.zhtml?c=99758&p=irol-sec

Speedway Motorsports. (2006). *2005 annual report.* Retrieved from http://phx.corporate-ir.net/phoenix.zhtml?c=99758&p=irol-reports

Speedway Motorsports. (2011). *2010 annual report.* Retrieved from http://phx.corporate-ir.net/phoenix.zhtml?c=99758&p=irol-sec

Spiro, H. (1996). *Finance for the nonfinancial manager.* New York: Wiley.

SportsBusiness Journal Research. (2011. September 19-25). Largest naming-rights deals. *Street & Smith's SportsBusiness Journal,* 14(21), 22-23.

Sportsfund. (1996). Fields of opportunity [Promotional brochure]. Portland, ME: Author.

Sports in brief. (2001, January 8). *Seattle Union Record*, p. 1D.

Sports stadiums as "wise investments": An evaluation. (1990, November 26). *Heartland Institute, Executive Summary, No. 32.*

Standard & Poor's corporate description plus news. (1999). New York: McGraw-Hill.

Stehle, V. (1997, November 27). Rich but not so different. *Chronicle of Philanthropy*, p. 11.

Stellino, V. (1995, November 6). Lease deal for Browns is 30 years. *Baltimore Sun*, p. 1A.

Stein, M. (2011). *NBA cancels first 2 weeks of season.* Retrieved from: http://espn.go.com/nba/story/_/id/7085089/nba%20labor-david-stern-cancels-first-two-weeks-nba-season

Steinbach, P. (2010, September). Two-year forecast. *Athletic Business, 34*(9), pp. 56-57.

Steinbach, P. (2011). Schools have struggled to sell bowl tickets. *Athletic Business*. Retrieved from http://athleticbusiness.com/

Steps for improving your firm's cash flow. (1998, November). *Nation's Business*, 12.

Stevenson, W. (1982). *Production/operations management.* Homewood, IL: Irwin.

Stock quote. Retrieved from http://finance.yahoo.com/q?s=sds.pk. Retrieved June 12, 2002.Strachan, M. (2011, May 5). Total number of U.S. millionaire households will nearly double this decade, report says. *Huffington Post*. Retrieved from www.huffingtonpost.com/2011/05/04/global-millionaires-wealth-us-double-households-decade_n_857545.html

Stretching a dollar. (2010, Aug/Sept). *Athletic Management, 22*(5), 8.

Study: No taxes for stadiums. (2004, March 25). *USA Today*, p. 10C.

Swartz, J. (2010, August 3). Recession and golf don't mix. *USA Today*, p. 1B.

Tan, K. (2000, January 31). Interactive technology boosts sports business. *Wall Street Journal*, p. B9.

Tanner, R.T. (2011, September 23). *Has the estate tax question been answered yet?* Retrieved from www.tjscpa.com/index.php/2011/has-the-estate-tax-question-been-answered-yet/

Tax numbers to know. (2000, January 30). *Connecticut Post*, p. F1.

Texas, ESPN announce new network. (2011, October 17). Retrieved from www.sports.espn.go.com

Texas man sentenced for embezzlement. (2009, December 16). *Club Industry*. Retrieved from http://clubindustry.com/forprofits/lubbock-laundering-sentence-20091226/

The new bankruptcy law. (2005). Retrieved from http://bankruptcy.findlaw.com/new-bankruptcy-law/new-bankruptcy-law-basics/big-changes.html.

The score. (2011, December). *Athletic Business, 35*(12), 13.

Thomas secures his future. (1998, July 13). *Sports Illustrated, 89*(2), 32.

Thompson, Jr., Arthur, Strickland III, A.J., & Gamble, John. (2008). *Crafting and executing strategy: The quest for competitive advantage* (16th ed.). Boston: McGraw-Hill Irwin.

Thornton, E. (2002, January 12). It sure is getting hostile. *Business Week*, 28-30.

Thornton, G. (2005). *Golf course restructuring: A business and legal perspective.* Retrieved from www.grantthornton.ca/mgt_papers/MIP_template.asp?MIPID=41

Tipping, E. (2011, June). 2011 state of the managed recreation industry. *Recreation Management, 12*(6).

Tkach, J. (2011, August 1). Last-ditch effort to save the Islanders. *USA Today*, p. 7C.

Tkach, J. (2011, November 22). University of Maryland cuts eight sports. *USA Today*, p. 11C.

Toobin, J. (2011, May 30). Madoff's curveball. *New Yorker*. Retrieved from www.newyorker.com/reporting/2011/05/30/110530fa_fact_toobin?currentPage=1

Top holders of stadium bonds. (1997, September 22). *Stadium and Arena Financing News*, p. 10.

Torre, P. (2009, March 23). How athletes go broke. *Sports Illustrated, 110*(12), pp. 90-101.

Tozzi, J. (2011, November 21-27). Don't call it an IPO. *Bloomberg Business Week*, p. 66.

Trip to Super Bowl priceless (and pricey). (2001, January 16). *New Haven Register*, p. A4.

Truex, A. (1999, February 14). Going for broke. *Houston Chronicle*, p. 1B.

Turley, B. (1998, Fall). From tee to green: A primer on golf course development and financing. *Entertainment and Sports Lawyer, 16*(3), 3-5, 35.

Two Denver franchises sold. (1999, April 27). *Houston Chronicle*, p. 11B.

Two firms make bid to buy entire NHL. (2005, March 4). *Virginian-Pilot*, p. C3.

Ulrich, L. (2009, April/May). Looking to cut. *Athletic Management, 21*(3), 28-35.

Under Armour. (2011). *Annual report.* Retrieved from http://investor.underarmour.com/results.cfm

University of New Haven. (1998). *Undergraduate catalog, 1998-2000.* West Haven, CT: University of New Haven.

Univision, ABC/ESPN pays $425 million for World Cup. (2005, November 2). Retrieved from http://sports.yahoo.com/sow/news?slug=reu-dc&prov=reuters&typ=lgns

Up, up and away. (1999, December 30). *Connecticut Post*, p. 1C.

Upton, J., Gillum, J., & Berkowitz, S. (2010, January 14). Big-time sports: Worth the big-time cost? *USA Today*, p. 5C.

U.S. Department of Commerce, Bureau of the Census. (2011). *Quarterly report for manufacturing mining, trade, and selected service industries: 2011: Quarter 2.* Retrieved from www.census.gov/econ/qfr/

USA Today salaries databases. (2007). Retrieved from http://asp.usatoday.com/sports/baseball/salaries/totalpayroll.aspx?year=2006 Retrieved January 13, 2007.

USA Today salaries databases. (n.d.). Retrieved from http://content.usatoday.com/sportsdata/baseball/mlb/salaries/team

U.S. Securities and Exchange Commission. (2008, February 28). *Bally Total Fitness settles financial fraud charges with SEC.* Litigation Release #20470. Retrieved from www.sec.gov/litigation/litreleases/2008/lr20470.htm

Vennochi, J. (1997, July 30). Does the puck stop here? *Boston Globe*, p. E1.

Wachter, P. (2010, October 11-17). Why ballers go bust. *Bloomberg Businessweek*, pp. 89-91.

Waggoner, J. (2011, February 15). How rationale is stock market? *USA Today*, p. 1B.

Walker, D. (2004, August 27). Shoe companies go toe-to-toe at Olympics. *Milwaukee Journal Sentinel*. Retrieved from http://findarticles.com/p/articles/mi_qn4196/is_20040827/ai_n10981599

Walker, S. (1999, November 5). Attorney set to buy Cleveland Indians in transaction totaling $320 million. *Wall Street Journal*, p. B2.

Wal-Mart heir buying Denver teams, arena. (2000, April 25). *Connecticut Post*, p. D4.

Wanniski, J. (1991, October 9). *Trial by press: James B. Stewart vs. Michael Milken.* Retrieved from www.polyeconomics.com/searchbase/10-09-91.html

Web billionaire to buy controlling interest in Dallas Mavericks. (2000, January 5). *Wall Street Journal*, p. B16.

Weiberg, S. (2011, March 29). NCAA president: Time to discuss players getting silver of revenue pie. *USA Today*. Retrieved from www.usatoday.com/sports/

Weise, K. (2011, June 27-July 3). Hut, hut, strike! *Bloomberg Busienssweek*.

Wendel, T. (1989, March, 6). Lean times. *Sports Inc.*, *2*(10), pp. 14-26.

Wendel, T. (1988, August 1). The new endangered species. *Sports Inc.*, *1*(28), pp. 14-16.

Weygandt, J., Kieso, D., & Kimmel, P. (2005) *Managerial Accounting: Tools for Business Decision Making* (3rd ed.). Hoboken, NJ: John Wiley & Sons, Inc.

Where your tax dollar goes. (2000, January 30). *Connecticut Post*, p. F1.

Whiteside, K. (2008, October 17). College game to feel effects of economy? *USA Today*, p. 8C.

Whittington, O.R., & Pany, K. (2006). *Principles of auditing* (15th ed.). Boston: McGraw-Hill.

Who is the FDIC? (2006). Retrieved from www.fdic.gov/about/learn/symbol/index.html

Why Delaware Intercorp, Inc? (2000, June 27). Retrieved from www.delawareintercorp.com/why.htm

Wikipedia. (n.d.).John Moores. Retrieved from http://en.wikipedia.org/wiki/John_Moores_(baseball)

Wilmoth, C. (2012, April 25). *NFL lockout agreement proposal includes salary cap, revenue sharing details.* Retrieved from www.sbnation.com/2011/7/22/2288047/nfl-lockout-agreement-proposal-salary-cap-revenue-sharing-demaurice-smith

Wieberg, S. (2010, January 4). For Alabama, Saban has been worth every penny. *USA Today*, p. 1C.

Williams, C.A., Jr., Smith, M., & Young, P. (1998). *Risk management and insurance* (8th ed.). New York: McGraw-Hill.

Williams, J. (1998, August 14). Stadium financing plan is completed. *Houston Chronicle*, p. 40A.

With parks on chopping block, study shows their value. (2009, July). *Recreation Management*, p. 7.

Witner, K. (2011, March). How the home team wins. *Athletic Management*. Retrieved from www.athleticmanagement.com/2011/03/01/how_the_home_team_wins/index.php

Woodworth, R.L., & Sher, S.A. (2005). I need to report that?!?: Hart-Scott-Rodino notification requirements for individuals. *M&A Lawyer*, *9*(5). Retrieved from www.wsgr.com/PDFSearch/sher_woodworth1005.pdf

World Championship Sports Network. (2005). Retrieved from www.wcsn.com/help/about.jsp

WWF fires COO, 39 employees to aid profits. (2001, November 10). *Connecticut Post*, p. B1.

Wynter, L., & Thomas, P. (2000, February 2). New definition of "minority business" splits blacks. *Wall Street Journal*, p. B1.

Wyshynski, G. (2011, May 28). *Blue Jackets backing "sin tax" to ease arena burden.* Yahoo Sports. Retrieved from http://sports.yahoo.com/nhl/blog/puck_daddy/post/Blue-Jackets-backing-sin-tax-to-ease-arena-bur?urn=nhl-166618

XFL's hefty losses slam WWF profits. (2001, June 29). *Connecticut Post*, p. B14.

Yahoo! Finance—BOS. (2002). Retrieved from http:// ?finance.yahoo.com/q?d=t&s-BOS+

Yahoo! Finance—WWF. (2002). Retrieved from http:// ?finance.yahoo.com/q?d=t&s-WWF+

Yahoo! Finance—YHOO. (2002). Retrieved from http:// ?finance.yahoo.com/q?d=t&s-YHOO+

Yantz, T. (2009, November 23). *Prep footballers pay $500 to play as schools tighten budgets*. Retrieved from http://articles.courant.com/2009-11-23/sports/hc-paytoplay1123.artnov23_1_pay-to-play-ellington-school-board-tony-littizzio

Yip, P. (1999, March 30). Changes paved way to 10K. *Houston Chronicle*, p. 1C.

Zeise, P. (2010, March 24). Women's NCAA tournament: Pitt loses money hosting subregional. *Pittsburgh Post-Gazette*. Retrieved from www.post-gazette.com/

Zikmund, W., & d'Amico, M. (1996). *Basic marketing*. St. Paul, MN: West.

Suggested Resources

Stocks

New York Stock Exchange
www.nyse.com

North American Securities Administrators Association
www.nasaa.org.

NASDAQ Stock Market
www.nasdaq.com

U.S. Securities and Exchange Commission
www.sec.gov

U.S. Securities and Exchange Commission EDGAR Database of Filings by Public Companies
www.10kwizard.com

Business and Government Organizations and Associations

Business Consortium Fun
www.bcfcapital.com/

Certified Development Company
www.nadco.org

Federal Reserve Board
www.federalreserve.gov

National Association of Investment Companies
www.naicvc.com

National Association of Small Business Investment Companies
www.nasbic.org

National Association of Women Business Owners (NAWBO)
www.nawbo.org

National Minority Business Council
www.nmbc.org

National Minority Supplier Development Council (NMSDC)
www.nmsdc.org

Service Corps of Retired Executives (SCORE) Association
www.score.org

United States Small Business Administration
www.sbaonline.sba.gov

Women's Growth Capital Fund of Washington, DC
www.womensgrowthcapital.com

Internet Resources

American Institute of Certified Public Accountants
www.360financialliteracy.org/

Dakota State University- Finance Resources
www.courses.dsu.edu/finance/www/resource.htm

Finance Journal
http://financejournal.com/

Financial Literacy & Education Commission
www.mymoney.gov/

International Journal of Sport Finance Blog
http://ijsf.wordpress.com/

Practical Money Skills for Life
www.practicalmoneyskills.com/games/

Professor Ian Giddy's Finance Resources on the Web
http://pages.stern.nyu.edu/~igiddy/

Yahoo Finance
http://finance.yahoo.com/

Print Resources

Athletic Business: www.athleticbusiness.com
Athletic Management: www.momentummedia.com
Barron's: www.barrons.com
Business Week: www.businessweek.com
Dun & Bradstreet: www.dnb.com
Fitness Management: www.fitnessmanagement.com
Forbes: www.forbes.com
NCAA News: www.ncaa.org
Sports Business Daily: www.sportsbusinessdaily.com
Street & Smith's SportsBusiness Journal: www.sportsbusinessjournal.com
Wall Street Journal: www.wsj.com

Index

Note: Page numbers followed by an italicized f or t refer to the figure or table on that page, respectively.

About the Authors

Gil Fried, JD, is professor and chair of the management and sport management department in the College of Business at the University of New Haven. He worked as a financial analyst with Paul Kagan Associates and analyzed numerous sport broadcasting contracts. He has written numerous books and articles, taught graduate and undergraduate courses in sport finance, and lectured on finance topics to various audiences. Besides teaching, Fried coordinates the management of sports industries graduate program at the University of New Haven.

Fried enjoys playing badminton and softball and being involved in his community. Photo courtesy of Gil Fried.

Tim DeSchriver, EdD, is an associate professor in the department of business administration of Lerner College of Business and Economics at the University of Delaware. DeSchriver has worked as a field economist for the U.S. Department of Labor and has taught undergraduate and graduate instruction in sport finance and sport economics since 1998. He has authored and contributed to several books and sport finance–related publications in refereed journals.

DeSchriver enjoys road cycling, mountain biking, and hiking in his spare time. Photo courtesy of Tim DeSchriver.

Michael Mondello, PhD, is an associate professor in the department of management at the University of South Florida. Mondello teaches classes in the sport and entertainment MBA program. His research interests include finance and economics of sport organizations, and his work has been published in the *International Journal of Sport Finance, Economic Development Quarterly, Sport Marketing Quarterly, International Journal of Sport Management, Journal of Sports Economics,* and *Journal of Sport Management*. Before his appointment at USF, he was a faculty member at both the University of Florida and Florida State. Photo courtesy of Michael Mondello.